The Supreme Awakening

Throughout history, great men and women have described exalted experiences, moments of extraordinary wakefulness, freedom, and bliss — as different from our ordinary waking experience as waking is from dreaming.

Laozi, Plato, Rūmī, St. Teresa of Avila, Emerson, Emily Dickinson, Black Elk, Einstein — people of all times and places have described experiences that rank among the most inspiring in all of literature.

The Supreme Awakening:

- brings together a rich and diverse collection of these experiences
- explains these experiences in terms of a new, expanded framework of human development — the model of higher states of consciousness developed by Maharishi Mahesh Yogi, the renowned Vedic sage and scientist of consciousness
- shows how anyone can systematically cultivate these experiences through the Transcendental Meditation technique — simply, naturally, and effortlessly
- describes the wide-ranging benefits of cultivating enlightenment by means of the TM technique — inner peace and happiness, improved health, increased creativity and intelligence, improved productivity, and much more — with benefits for education, business, health care, the military, rehabilitation, and society as a whole
- shows that the sublime experiences reported by great people across time are real, universal, understandable in terms of modern science — and now available to anyone.

"The basis of a breakthrough in creating a better world."

— Robert Stowe, PhD, Executive Director, Harvard Environmental Economics Program, Harvard Kennedy School

The Supreme Awakening

Experiences of Enlightenment Throughout Time —
And How You Can Cultivate Them

CRAIG PEARSON, PhD

SECOND EDITION
Copyright © 2016 by Craig Pearson

All rights reserved. No part of this publication may be reproduced, distributed, or transmitted in any form or by any means, or stored in a database or retrieval system, without prior written permission of the author.

Transcendental Meditation®, TM®, TM-Sidhi®, Maharishi Vedic Science℠, and Maharishi University of Management® are trademarks used under license by Maharishi University of Management and the Maharishi Foundation, Ltd., a non-profit educational organization.

Maharishi University of Management Press
Fairfield, Iowa 52557 USA
Visit our website at mumpress.com

Because this page cannot accommodate all copyright notices, copyright notices appear at the end of the book.

Library of Congress Cataloging-in-Publication Data

Pearson, Craig, 1950-
  The supreme awakening : experiences of enlightenment throughout time--and how you can cultivate them / Craig Pearson. -- Second edition.
    pages cm
  Includes bibliographical references and index.
  ISBN 978-0-923569-68-6 (alk. paper)
  1. Religious awakening. 2. Spiritual life. 3. Altered states of consciousness. 4. Transcendental Meditation. I. Title.
  BL624.P426 2015
  158.1'25--dc23
                    2015024315

Jacket design by Shepley Hansen
Interior design by Craig Pearson

Printed in the United States

"Enlightenment is the supreme awakening to the true nature of life."
— Maharishi Mahesh Yogi

Also by Craig Pearson
The Complete Book of Yogic Flying

New in this second edition

- Henri Frédéric Amiel – Chapter 4 (Transcendental Consciousness) and Chapter 7 (Unity Consciousness)

- Mary Austin – Chapter 7 (Unity Consciousness)

- Ray Stannard Baker – Chapter 6 (God Consciousness)

- Bernard Berenson – Chapter 6 (God Consciousness) and Chapter 7 (Unity Consciousness)

- Dag Hammarskjöld – Chapter 4 (Transcendental Consciousness) and Chapter 5 (Cosmic Consciousness)

- Sophia von Klingnau – Chapter 6 (God Consciousness)

- Rosamond Lehmann – Chapter 6 (God Consciousness)

- Antonio Machado – Chapter 5 (Cosmic Consciousness)

- Margaret Prescott Montague – Chapter 6 (God Consciousness)

- Eckhart Tolle – Chapter 5 (Cosmic Consciousness)

- Morihei Ueshiba – Chapter 4 (Transcendental Consciousness), Chapter 5 (Cosmic Consciousness), and Chapter 7 (Unity Consciousness)

- David Yeadon – Chapter 7 (Unity Consciousness)

Personal interview – "Just a Blink of an Eye Away," page 497.

COMMENTS ON
The Supreme Awakening

"Shows the supreme value of the Transcendent for all human beings"

Dr. Craig Pearson has done it! In the clearest, most perfect way, he shows the supreme value of the Transcendent for all human beings. No matter what your religion is — no matter what nationality — no matter what walk of life — if you are a human being, get this book — read it — get inspired by it — and act upon it — right away!

— David Lynch, award-winning filmmaker, television director, artist, and author of *Catching the Big Fish*

"Delineates practical means for progressing on this journey"

A gold mine of riveting accounts and penetrating analyses of key landmarks in spiritual development. Craig Pearson not only elucidates the often-fleeting glimpses of heightened consciousness experienced by many individuals through the ages as precursors to enduring plateaus of growth, he also delineates practical means for progressing on this journey. The world has waited over a century for the sequel to William James' *The Varieties of Religious Experience*; with the appearance of *The Supreme Awakening*, the wait is now over.

— Ed Sarath, Professor of Music, Chair of the Department of Jazz and Improvisation Studies, and Director of the Program in Creativity and Consciousness Studies, University of Michigan

HEALTH AND MEDICINE

"Highlights the importance of higher states of consciousness for enhancing mental and physical well-being"

In *The Supreme Awakening*, Craig Pearson offers us an unequaled resource that reviews transcendental experiences reported by great writers and thinkers of both the West and the East for more than two thousand years. Scholars and general readers alike will turn to *The Supreme Awakening* — as I have — for its wealth of wisdom and insight. Pearson's book, however, goes beyond a literary review. By documenting the central importance of transcendence throughout the ages and in different cultures, together with the scientific research on this experience, he highlights the importance of higher states of consciousness for enhancing mental and physical well-being, not just for great writers and thinkers but for all of us.

— Norman E. Rosenthal, MD, psychiatrist, researcher, and author of *Transcendence: Healing and Transformation through Transcendental Meditation*

"Transcending is good for your health"

As a medical doctor, I have witnessed first-hand a very real, objective, and powerful transformation in the health of thousands of my patients who have learned transcending through the Transcendental Meditation technique. I've seen its benefits in a wide variety of chronic conditions, many of which eluded cure from any number of other therapies.

Hundreds of peer-reviewed studies verify that transcending (as evidenced in Transcendental Meditation) is good for our health. And, unlike most medicine, it actually makes you feel good! Transcending creates a deliciously nourishing, peaceful wholeness within — a unity of mind, body, and spirit that may well be the source of health itself.

If you already meditate, read this book to appreciate what you have and to deepen your experience. If you have yet to learn, read it now and open yourself to your inner healing power — you are your own best medicine!

— Nancy Lonsdorf, MD, integrative physician and author of *The Ageless Woman* and *Natural Health and Beauty After Forty with Maharishi Ayurveda*, and coauthor of *A Woman's Best Medicine: Health, Happiness and Long Life through Maharishi Ayurveda*. www.drnancylonsdorf.com

"Enlightenment can no longer be considered mystical or impractical"

We have been waiting for this book for a long time. It is filled with authentic and universal wisdom of life from every great tradition of humanity, overflowing with remarkable personal experiences from sages, saints, poets, scientists, and people from many different walks of life.

Dr. Pearson beautifully presents the profound knowledge of Maharishi Mahesh Yogi and reveals how all of these experiences are based upon the progressive refinement of our nervous system. Enlightenment can no longer be considered mystical or impractical. Rather it is a powerful and blissful state of awareness that anyone from any background or culture can achieve. As a scientist, I thank Dr. Pearson for this inspiring and profound research into the field of higher states of consciousness.

— Robert Keith Wallace, PhD, author of *The Physiology of Consciousness* and *The Neurophysiology of Enlightenment*

"Characterizing the experience of enlightenment in simple, scientific terms"

We are so fortunate to live in an age in which science in general, and neuroscience in particular, have advanced our knowledge of how the function of the brain underlies our conscious experience. Finally, the experience of enlightenment, beautifully recorded throughout the ages, can be analyzed and verified as reflecting changes in the style of functioning of human neurophysiology.

Dr. Pearson has done us all a great service, uplifting us by presenting the words of the enlightened from different times and cultures, and characterizing the experience of enlightenment in simple, scientific terms. To the reader's delight, he goes one step further, and describes both a practical means to experience the field of pure consciousness at the basis of our physiology, and an easy way to culture the nervous system so that our experience of enlightenment grows from fleeting moments of transcendence to a permanent reality of our everyday existence.

— Gary P. Kaplan, MD, PhD, Associate Professor of Neurology, Hofstra University School of Medicine

"A source of practical wisdom and inspiration for the parents and teachers of children and teenagers"

As a pediatric neuropsychologist, I find this beautifully written book to be profoundly encouraging. Dr. Pearson presents a remarkably broad range of experiences of transcendence, unity, and timelessness that have been reported by people around the world, showing that human potential goes far beyond what is generally imagined.

This book also provides a very clear exposition of Maharishi Mahesh Yogi's description of higher states of consciousness and the meditation technique that can promote the development of these higher states in people of all ages. It presents a simple and practical means for young people across the socioeconomic spectrum to experience a source of peace, happiness, and intelligence within themselves, which provides an extremely powerful antidote to the high stress, media-saturated environments in which they are growing up.

I believe that Dr. Pearson's book will be a source of practical wisdom and inspiration for the parents and teachers of children and teenagers, so many of whom care deeply about the health of our society and our planet but feel helpless about changing their world. Dr. Pearson shows how, by experiencing these higher states of consciousness, young people can, in the words of Gandhi, become the change in the world they wish to see.

— William Stixrud, PhD, Assistant Professor of Psychiatry, Behavioral Sciences, and Pediatrics, George Washington University School of Medicine and Health Sciences

"Helping create a new definition of mental health"

For centuries physicians have been focused on disease and relieving the suffering of illness. In recent decades there has increasingly been a shift of focus toward understanding and promoting health and wellness. As a psychiatrist, I appreciate how Pearson's description of those who have realized "higher states of consciousness" and his clear description of Maharishi's model of the seven states of consciousness is helping create a new definition of mental health.

And the really good news for psychiatrists is that Pearson has shown with historical review as well as modern science that mental techniques such as Transcendental Meditation can be "prescribed" to anyone we work with to help them experience and develop their own "supreme awakening" of growing mental health.

— James Krag, MD, Distinguished Fellow of the American Psychiatric Association | Former Assistant Professor, University of Virginia, Department of Psychiatry and Neurobehavioral Sciences | Past president of the Psychiatric Society of Virginia

EDUCATION

"Especially useful for educators at all levels"

We all know that the consciousness of an eight-year-old is different from that of an eighteen-year-old — but Craig Pearson has written a masterpiece describing how there are states of consciousness beyond the waking adult world that so preoccupies us.

These higher states of consciousness are not new. This book explores each state and shows how they have been described and experienced throughout history. More importantly, we are given tools to access these higher states today, and they offer hope for all humanity.

This book is a rich resource for anyone interested in maximizing their own potential and benefiting society at the same time. It is especially useful for educators at all levels to understand that developing students' consciousness is as important as developing their intellects, and that cultivating higher states of consciousness belongs at the foundation of education.

— Ralph A. Wolff, JD, President, Accrediting Commission for Senior Colleges and Universities, Western Association of Schools and Colleges | Past professor, University of Dayton Law School | Cofounder, Antioch School of Law | Past Dean, Antioch Graduate School of Education

BUSINESS AND LEADERSHIP

"An indispensable resource"

The day is rapidly coming when the goal of business and management will be the enlightenment of their customers and employees. As that day approaches, this remarkable book, combining the most profound theoretical and scientific analysis with the inspirational stories of great figures from all walks of life and all times and places, is an indispensable resource — a blueprint to help each of us realize our birthright as human beings.

— Rashi Glazer, PhD, Professor Emeritus, Haas School of Business, University of California at Berkeley

"For anyone who desires to lead the way every day in their organization"

Craig Pearson has captured the foundation of effective leadership in his wonderful new book, *The Supreme Awakening*. To lead, initiate direction, and influence others to be motivated followers requires more "wakefulness," more expanded awareness and enlightened consciousness. Dr. Pearson's definition of "awakening" clarifies this process.

In my over 30 years' experience providing leadership consulting and training with organizations throughout the world, I continually notice that the basis for breakthroughs to exploit opportunities always has its starting point in amplified awareness. Similarly, the capacity to overcome obstacles always originates in an expansive cognizance of what must be done differently. This is true in organizations large and small, public and private.

Dr. Pearson's description of how to be more wakeful through the Transcendental Meditation program, based on the knowledge and techniques put forward by Maharishi Mahesh Yogi, offers a practical approach that anyone can use. I recommend *The Supreme Awakening* as a manual for anyone who desires to lead the way every day in their organization.

— Warren Blank, PhD, President of The Leadership Group | Author of *The 108 Skills of Natural Born Leaders, Leadership for Smart People, The Leadership Event,* and *The Nine Natural Laws of Leadership*

"The key to success in all fields of life"

The search for the ultimate in human resource development in business has come to an end.

In the US alone we spend $48 billion a year on leadership development. According to surveys, only 12-15% of this is considered money well spent. That means $40 billion is wasted. Corporate education simply has not known how to develop the capacity of the human brain — how to promote growth from the inside.

Dr. Craig Pearson presents the model of higher states of consciousness put forward by Maharishi Mahesh Yogi. He chronicles exalted experiences of these states by renowned men and women in every culture. He describes the effortless, scientifically-validated technique by which anyone can develop these higher states. And he summarizes the unprecedented practical benefits that result.

Nothing can be more fundamental than developing consciousness, developing the brain's total potential — this is the key to success in all fields of life. The systematic program presented here is evidence-based, complements current leadership training, is culture-independent, can save organizations money, and above all produces unprecedented results.

Dr. Pearson's brilliant description of this important re-discovery is an absolute requirement for corporate leaders.

— Jim Bagnola, President of The Leadership Group International | Author of *Becoming a Professional Human Being: How to Enjoy Stress-Free Work and Personal Happiness Using the Mind/Body/Work Connection*

"The basis of a breakthrough in creating a better world"

We collectively face many seemingly intractable problems; the wisest and best-intentioned among us have not been able to solve most of these.

This book suggests that solutions may lie in a place we have neglected to look: in cultivating enlightenment — the highest expression of our full potential — on a widespread basis. *The Supreme Awakening* suggests that individual experience of higher states of consciousness — on a much larger scale than has been possible in the past — is the basis of a breakthrough in creating a better world.

Drawing widely from world literature, Pearson offers examples of individuals who have experienced higher states of consciousness and, fortunately, recorded these experiences. This collection is a magnificent accomplishment in itself. We have read some of these passages before, and they have delighted us — but also left us asking how, if at all, we might cultivate these experiences.

The book's greater accomplishment is to provide an answer. Drawing on the work of Maharishi Mahesh Yogi, Pearson explains convincingly that higher states of consciousness are natural — indeed, should be the norm, not the exception. We too can enjoy the experience of "the universal and sublime" (Underhill), the "great nature in which we rest" (Emerson), through the simple, systematic, and reliable approach Maharishi has put forward.

And these experiences, in turn, can change the world from within. Let's give it a try.

— Robert Stowe, PhD, Executive Director, Harvard Environmental Economics Program, Harvard Kennedy School

LITERATURE

"Of special interest to students of literature"

The Supreme Awakening will be of special interest to students of literature for the clarity and depth of its examination of sublime experiences in world literature. It begins with a detailed presentation of principles grounded in the latest scientific research on advanced cognitive states. It goes on to provide close readings of some of the most profound expressions of human thought and feeling, ranging from ancient Eastern and Western texts to the writings of Renaissance Neo-Platonists, English Romantics, American Transcendentalists, and others. It makes literary works such as Wordsworth's "Tintern Abbey" — generally thought of as "mystical" and obscure — transparent and immediate.

Dr. Pearson notably gives valuable insight into techniques now readily available that will raise anyone to the same level of exalted experiences of a Wordsworth or a Whitman and which engender the heights of creativity. Reading the book is an elevating experience in itself and is bound to be a source of inspiration for writers of any genre. One feels one is getting to the deep core of what it is possible to experience, to know, and to express.

— James J. Balakier, PhD, Professor Emeritus, English Department, University of South Dakota | Author of *Thomas Traherne and the Felicities of the Mind*

RELIGION

"Our generation stands on the threshold of an electrifying possibility"

In his book *The Supreme Awakening*, Dr. Pearson has collated recorded evidence of the heights of human awareness, gathered from every corner of the world, and across a very broad expanse of many different civilizations. Were this its only accomplishment, *The Supreme Awakening* already would be a very significant achievement. However, Dr. Pearson also describes how, thanks to the work of Maharishi Mahesh Yogi, our generation stands on the threshold of an electrifying possibility: that higher states of consciousness will become the legitimate property of millions of people around the world.

I have no doubt that when the experience of enlightenment becomes a mass phenomenon, the highest dreams of the Biblical prophets for peace on earth and good will among human beings will become a reality. As the prophet Isaiah foresaw so many centuries ago (11:9), "They shall not hurt, nor shall they destroy in all of my holy mountain. For the earth shall be filled with the knowledge of God, as the waters cover the sea."

— Rabbi Alan Green, Senior Rabbi, Congregation Shaarey Zedek, Winnipeg, Manitoba, Canada

"Guiding us through the variegated history of human awakening"

We should be deeply grateful to Craig Pearson for guiding us through the variegated history of human awakening, spanning East and West, from ancient times to today. He describes clearly how so many deep souls have discovered profound states of higher consciousness. But more importantly, he stimulates us to follow in their path and to experience bliss in our own lives.

— Daniel Matt, former Professor of Jewish Mysticism, Graduate Theological Union, Berkeley | Author of *The Essential Kabbalah*, *God and the Big Bang*, and the multi-volume annotated translation *The Zohar: Pritzker Edition*

"An invitation to 'dive deep'"

The Supreme Awakening illustrates the potential for unity in the experience of transcendence. It shows how people from many cultures and time periods have described this powerful human experience — and how people of various faiths and philosophies can discover and embrace it — the foundation that leads to enlightenment.

As a person of faith, my teacher, Jesus Christ, teaches me to find the Spirit at work within me, to cultivate that Spirit, and to listen to its voice — in the stillness and in the quiet. I find that place through prayer and meditation. Surrendering to "that of God within each of us" leads to authentic and transparent living — removing all extraneous distractions, aligning ourselves with the Divine, and opening the vastness of possibilities inherent in human potential.

The practice of Transcendental Meditation leads us to the quiet place where enlightenment might be encountered and where our full potential might begin to reveal itself.

Readers will find comfort and encouragement in what this book has gathered from the various faith traditions, schools of thought, world philosophies, and of course from Maharishi. It shows the path from transcendence to enlightenment. I am grateful for this effort and insight.

The Supreme Awakening is an invitation to "dive deep" through meditation, find the unity that can hold us all together, unlock our full potential, and bring about the harmony of minds for which we all hope.

— Rev. Jonathan D. Hutchison, Senior Pastor, First United Methodist Church, De Kalb, Illinois

"An inspirational resource for years to come"

For over fifty years, Maharishi Mahesh Yogi's magisterial teachings on the seven states of consciousness have provided the indispensable map for millions of meditators throughout the world in their quest for higher consciousness. In this richly developed presentation, Craig Pearson carefully elucidates the cognitive structure, physiological correlates, and essential features of each of these states, and details their enormous implications for human health and spiritual growth.

To illustrate the perennial character of these states this book also provides a fascinating compendium of reports of expanded awareness from philosophers and saints, athletes and artists, scientists and poets — together testifying to the transformative impact of these experiences throughout human history. For seekers of every background this book will provide an inspirational resource for years to come.

— Alan D. Hodder, PhD, Professor of Comparative Religion, Hampshire College | Author of *Thoreau's Ecstatic Witness* and *Emerson's Rhetoric of Revelation*

PHILOSOPHY

"Fulfills the seeking that drives philosophy as well as poetry, religion, science, and human search for the ultimate"

Craig Pearson's book, *The Supreme Awakening*, gives strong support that what is commonly called "mysticism" is fully compatible with science and is an essential part of human mental and physiological nature. Drawing on the work of Maharishi Mahesh Yogi, he clearly explains the meaning and significance of enlightenment and higher states of consciousness.

One of the book's highlights is the anthology of great writers describing their personal experiences of enlightenment. We read their accounts in a manner that goes well beyond their words to the meaning they were capturing in these words — and then past the words and meaning to the gates that open to a world of light, silence, and wisdom. Pearson brings us an abundance of profound descriptions, helping us understand this material and even awaken our consciousness to the point that we ourselves can become capable of experiencing higher states of consciousness.

Complete knowledge requires both intellectual understanding and direct experience. The wonderful thing about Pearson's book is that he gives us knowledge and then takes us to the techniques that show us how to gain the corresponding experience and make this complete knowledge a living part of who we are. Pearson gives an excellent presentation of the Transcendental Meditation and TM-Sidhi programs, Maharishi Mahesh Yogi's technologies for developing higher states of consciousness. He shows how these meditation techniques have a solid foundation in strong scientific research and how higher states of consciousness are measurable and attainable by anyone.

A book on these topics needs the most refined language to express them adequately. Craig Pearson uses language at this level, language that comes so close to silence that it is about to transcend words themselves and take us beyond ordinary life and experience to the most inner and personal worlds.

Here is a book that fulfills the seeking that drives philosophy as well as poetry, religion, science, and the human search for the ultimate. It offers much. It leads far.

Having read *The Supreme Awakening*, you will be ready to gain the full benefits of the Transcendental Meditation program and its advanced techniques. Then simply continue moving forward and inward and enjoy living in enlightenment.

— John H. Flodstrom, PhD, Professor Emeritus, Department of Philosophy, University of Louisville, Kentucky

The Supreme Awakening

CONTENTS

CHAPTER 1
Moments of Awakening 19

CHAPTER 2
Reviving an Ancient Tradition of Human Development 25

CHAPTER 3
The Seven States of Consciousness 38

CHAPTER 4
The Fourth State — Transcendental Consciousness:
Pure Consciousness Awake to Its Own Unbounded Nature 44
    ■ Glimpses of Transcendental Consciousness 56

CHAPTER 5
The Fifth State — Cosmic Consciousness:
Unbounded Awareness as a Permanent Reality 178
    ■ Glimpses of Cosmic Consciousness 196

CHAPTER 6
The Sixth State — God Consciousness:
Perceiving Nature's Celestial Glories 273
    ■ Glimpses of God Consciousness 290

CHAPTER 7
The Seventh State — Unity Consciousness:
All Experience in Terms of the Unbounded Self 347
    ■ Glimpses of Unity Consciousness 360

CHAPTER 8
A Technique for Transcending —
Systematically Cultivating Higher States of Consciousness 432

CHAPTER 9
Meditation in the Laboratory: Modern Science Measures
the Growth of Enlightenment 440

CHAPTER 10
Is Pure Consciousness the Unified Field? 472

CHAPTER 11
The Future of the World Is Bright 490

PERSONAL INTERVIEW
"Just a Blink of an Eye Away" 497

Notes 516

References 520

Acknowledgments 563

For more information 573

Index 574

About the author 583

CHAPTER 1

꒰

Moments of Awakening

"To be awake is to be alive."
— Henry David Thoreau

"Compared with what we ought to be,
we are only half awake."
— William James

ON A FRESH MORNING IN EARLY JULY, a 28-year-old man sets out on foot from his home on the southwest coast of England. A writer, he loves walking, traversing the countryside for days at a time. On this excursion, he and his sister are heading up the scenic Wye River Valley, just across the border in Wales, with its many low, forest-blanketed hills.

When they enter the valley, they climb the banks of the river. A few miles below, beside the river, they can see the ruins of Tintern Abbey, built five centuries earlier, now a stone latticework open to wind and sky. As his sister walks ahead, he sits down on the grass among the trees and closes his eyes.

Then the experience comes. He has had it before — and it's the experience he lives for. Had his sister seen him, she might have thought he was just resting. Deep within, however, he feels something changing. He settles into a state of inner quietness, beyond thought, beyond feeling — simple, natural, yet profound. In a few minutes, it's over. He opens his eyes, stands up, and walks back down the hill, resuming his tour.

As he crosses the river, words begin taking shape in his mind. The words keep coming until he returns home several days later. There he finally has a chance to set the words down on paper — a poem, nearly 160 lines. He does not change a single one. "No poem of mine," he comments later, "was composed under circumstances more pleasant for me to remember than this."[1] In the poem he describes:

> That blessed mood,
> In which the burthen of the mystery,
> In which the heavy and the weary weight
> Of all this unintelligible world,
> Is lightened: — that serene and blessed mood,
> In which the affections gently lead us on —
> Until, the breath of this corporeal frame
> And even the motion of our human blood
> Almost suspended, we are laid asleep
> In body, and become a living soul;
> While with an eye made quiet by the power
> Of harmony, and the deep power of joy,
> We see into the life of things.[2]

The young man is William Wordsworth. The year is 1798. His poem, "Lines Composed a Few Miles Above Tintern Abbey," was published later that same year in *Lyrical Ballads*, which also included several poems by his friend Samuel Taylor Coleridge — and which launched the English Romantic movement in literature, altering the course of English literature and poetry.

Wordsworth's experience lasted only a few minutes, but his words have been admired for two centuries. What was he experiencing?

His description is remarkable for its exactness. He settles into a state of increasing tranquility. The "weary weight" of the "unintelligible world" grows lighter and eventually fades away. Describing the unique condition of his body, he tells us he feels deeply rested. His breath and even his blood flow seem "almost suspended," and he feels as if "laid asleep in body."

But is he asleep? On the contrary, he seems more awake than ever. He feels he has "become a living soul" — as though in his prior state he had not been fully alive. From this deep level he is able to "see into the life of things."

Clearly this is more than a moment of relaxation — it is a unique mode of knowledge. From deep within, he experiences "harmony, and the deep power of joy." In all, he feels "blessed."

Wordsworth was known to be of good health and sound mind, not given to far-out fancy. By every indication, he is trying to describe a concrete experience as precisely as he can. His body is deeply relaxed, his mind profoundly settled and awake within itself.

This was not an isolated experience for Wordsworth. He had many such moments. They affected him powerfully. He found them physically and mentally revitalizing and believed they helped make him the great poet he was. And he celebrates them everywhere in his poetry, to the extent that the term *Wordsworthian experience* is sometimes used to refer to experiences of this type.

Yet Wordsworth speaks of *we*, *us*, and *our*, implying this is a universal experience, one for all humanity. Indeed, he offers us an excellent description of a whole category of experience that people have reported throughout history and around the world. Wordsworth seems to have experienced a state of consciousness that is simple and natural yet uniquely different from the familiar states of waking, dreaming, and sleeping.

And though he may not have been aware of it, this state forms the portal to still higher states of consciousness — higher modes of knowledge, power, and fulfillment. Wordsworth describes for us the gateway into those higher worlds.

"Tintern Abbey" has appeared in countless anthologies. It has been required reading in college classes decade after decade. These lines in particular have been singled out in numberless essays. Yet few readers have suspected what Wordsworth is really describing.

What is this experience like?

We can locate first-hand descriptions of this experience in the writings of people through history. Here are some of the qualities they ascribe to these moments:

Inner expansion, clarity, and wakefulness

These experiences involve expansion of awareness and extraordinary inner lucidity. More than 2,500 years ago, Laozi wrote that in this state, one's mind "becomes as vast and immeasurable as the night sky."[3]

Henry David Thoreau describes moments when "we become like a still lake of purest crystal," moments of "serene and unquestionable wisdom." Alfred, Lord Tennyson describes experiencing a "state of transcendent wonder, associated with absolute clearness of mind." During the past century, Thomas Merton, the American writer and Trappist monk, describes moments during which "our soul suddenly awakens us to a new level of awareness," making the ordinary waking state seem "like sleep" in comparison. French playwright Eugene Ionesco describes similar experiences, concluding, "It is as if we lived in a profound lethargy. We wake up for a few moments from time to time, then we sink into empty sleep again."

Happiness and bliss

This experience brings an infusion of happiness, joy, and bliss. Angela of Foligno, the 13th-century Italian author, writes, "My soul was in unutterable joy." The Canadian novelist Lucy Maud Montgomery describes feeling "so happy that her happiness seemed to irradiate the world with its own splendor." Clare Booth Luce, the American writer, Congresswoman, and ambassador, describes how "joy abounded in all of me. Or rather, I abounded in joy." Czech Republic president Vaclav Havel's experiences brought him "supreme bliss" and "infinite joy."

Experience of underlying reality

Along with this joy often comes a sense of profound knowledge, of direct perception of underlying reality, ordinarily inaccessible. Writes Laozi, "One finds the anchor of the universe within himself." The novelist Arthur Koestler writes, "Its primary mark is the sensation that this state is more real than any other one has experienced before — that for the first time the veil has fallen and one is in touch with 'real reality,' the hidden order of things."

The experience of the divine

A number of writers describe this underlying reality as divine. When one experiences this reality, writes the Chinese sage Zhuangzi, "His life is the working of Heaven" and he "mingles with the Heavenly Order." Plato writes that in this state "the soul is in the very likeness of the divine, and immortal," adding, "This state of the soul is called wisdom." Ralph Waldo Emerson describes these moments as "an influx of the Divine mind into our mind." Walt Whitman declares that we "reach the divine levels, and commune with the unutterable."

A feeling of naturalness and familiarity

Extraordinary though these experiences are, at the same time they are utterly natural. One feels one has "come home." Thomas Merton writes,

> We enter a region which we had never even suspected, and yet it is this new world which seems familiar and obvious. . . . You seem to be the same person and you are the same person that you have always been: in fact you are more yourself than you have ever been before. You have only just begun to exist. You feel as if you were at last fully born.[4]

Eugene Ionesco expresses it like this: "I suddenly entered the heart of a reality so blindingly obvious, so total, so enlightening, so luminous, that I wondered how I had never before realized how easy this reality was to find and how easily I found myself in it." The English writer Rita Carter says, "All my experience up until now had been in some sense unreal," adding, "It all felt entirely natural."

The moment of a lifetime

Those fortunate enough to have such an experience reverence it as the supreme moment of their lives, the touchstone by which all other experience is evaluated. The English writer Edward Carpenter observes, "The fact of its having come even once to a man has completely revolutionized his subsequent life and outlook on the world."

More than this, many people declare that only such experience deserves to be called life. "For the first time, *we exist*," writes Ralph Waldo Emerson. Tennyson regarded this experience as "the only true life." American writer Franklin Merrell-Wolff says, "It gives a feeling of being alive, beside which the ordinary feeling of life is no more than a mere shadow."

We find descriptions of these experiences in the writings of scientists and artists, writers and composers, monks and explorers, philosophers and athletes — in autobiographies and journals, poems and letters, lectures and novels. These moments are described in strikingly similar terms by people from different times, different cultures, different religions. As Edward Carpenter puts it:

> Of the existence of this [type of experience] there is evidence all down History; and witnesses, far removed from each other in time and space and race and language, and perfectly unaware of each other's utterances, agree so remarkably in their testimony, that there is left no doubt that the experience is as much a matter of fact as any other human experience.[5]

Where is the button?

On one hand, we have a class of experiences that appears universal. It has been described by people throughout history, throughout the world. The people who have had these experiences, moreover, hold them in the highest regard. Ionesco, sensing the enormous potential of these moments, writes:

> The interior mechanism that can set off this state of supernormal wakefulness that could set the world ablaze, that could transfigure it, illuminate it, is able to function in the simplest, most natural way. All one need do is press a button. Only it is not easy to find this button; we fumble about for it in the shadows.[6]

On the other hand, these experiences appear by most reports to be rare, fleeting, and unpredictable. Evidently few who describe such experiences could deliberately induce them. If the experience is so simple, natural, and valuable, why can't we have it at will? Is there some way to elicit it — where is the button? And what is its larger significance?

CHAPTER 2

ॐ

Reviving an Ancient Tradition of Human Development

Many thousands of years ago in the Himalayas of India, a remarkable research program took place. It did not involve study of the outer world. These were inner explorers. Their laboratory was their own consciousness. Their apparatus was their own nervous systems, purified and refined to the utmost. Their aim was to discover and develop, entirely from within, the total potential of human consciousness.

These were the Vedic *rishis*, or seers. Fathoming the depths of their own awareness, they discovered that the human mind has the capacity to settle into a state of perfect stillness, beyond all perceptions, thoughts, and feelings, while remaining perfectly alert and awake. Here, at the source of thought, the mind opens into an ocean of pure consciousness, a limitless sea of pure wakefulness.

They discovered something extraordinary about this transcendental field. It lies beyond the boundaries not only of perception and thought but beyond individuality, time, and space. In the innermost depth of the mind lies the fundamental reality of nature itself, the all-pervading field of unity from which the infinite diversity of the universe is born. Everything in nature, from the flowers on the mountainsides to galaxies without end, arises from within this ocean of crystal clear consciousness.[1]

Vedic literature is the record of their experience. The word *Veda* means *knowledge*. It derives from the Sanskrit root *vid*, meaning *to know*, which has numerous linguistic cousins in English — *wit, wise, wisdom, vision, vista, advise, evidence, idea, ideal.*

Vedic wisdom flowed out from India in almost all directions, influencing language, literature, philosophy, law, and religion throughout Asia and, according to some scholars, throughout the world. Greek tradition holds that Pythagoras, Thales, Empedocles, Democritus, and others journeyed to India to study philosophy and that Indian sages visited Athens to share their knowledge. Out of the Vedic tradition of knowledge arose three of the world's largest spiritual traditions — Hinduism, Buddhism, and Sikhism. Christian mystics of the first several centuries CE may have been influenced by Vedic knowledge.[2]

The vast Vedic literature was preserved down through the millennia as an oral tradition before being set down in books. But over centuries of foreign occupation and general neglect in India, Vedic literature became scattered, some elements of it all but forgotten.

The ancient Vedic rishis developed techniques for refining and purifying the human physiology so that it becomes capable of supporting the inner experience of transcendence. These techniques were handed down orally through innumerable generations, from teacher to student. But these too became distorted, the original procedures all but lost.

An American awakening

Books from Vedic literature began to reach Europe in the late 1700s, where they influenced such European philosophers as Schopenhauer, Schelling, Hegel, and Fichte. Reaching England, they touched Wordsworth, Coleridge, Blake, and others. By the early 1800s English translations of certain books were arriving in America.

When these works came into the hands of Ralph Waldo Emerson, they sparked a literary and philosophical movement that marked a new phase in American intellectual life and has influenced the entire nation ever since. For

Emerson, as well as for Henry David Thoreau and other prominent figures, the discovery of Vedic literature was as significant as Europe's rediscovery, five centuries earlier, of the literature and culture of Greece and Rome — which gave birth to the Renaissance and marked the transition from the medieval world to the modern.

Emerson encountered Vedic literature at 17, and his interest expanded from there. The *Bhagavad-Gita* exerted the greatest influence on him. He wrote:

> It was the first of books; it was as if an empire spake to us, nothing small or unworthy but large, serene, consistent, the voice of an old intelligence which in another age & climate had pondered & thus disposed of the same questions which exercise us. Let us . . . cherish the venerable oracle.[3]

Emerson introduced these books to Thoreau, who plunged in deeply. "[T]he idea of man is quite illimitable and sublime," he wrote. "There is nowhere a loftier conception of his destiny."[4] Of the *Bhagavad-Gita*, also his favorite work, he wrote: "The reader is nowhere raised into and sustained in a higher, purer, or rarer region of thought."[5]

Thoreau's celebrated experiment at Walden Pond, which reverberates in the world to this day, was inspired by these readings. He went to Walden Pond, *Bhagavad-Gita* in hand, to commune not so much with nature as with himself — to gain enlightenment, such as he understood it from his reading.

The movement launched by Emerson and his compatriots came to be called American Transcendentalism. Vedic literature formed its life-breath. Emerson and company shared the books they owned and eagerly awaited newly translated works arriving by boat. Emerson's godson William James, the pioneering psychologist and philosopher, cited the Vedic tradition in his own writings about transcendental experience.

Under the rubric of Indian philosophy, interest in Vedic literature has spread worldwide. But as Emerson, Thoreau, and others appreciated, the Vedic wisdom has less to do with philosophy than with *experience*. What they found illuminated in Vedic literature was a higher level of human development, a more exalted mode of being. They yearned to enter that world, to breathe that air, to live that reality — and as their writings indicate, they had momentary experiences of it. As Thoreau wrote to a friend, "To some extent, and at rare intervals, even I am a yogi."[6]

Vedic knowledge continued to flow westward. For example, in 1893, Swami Vivekananda became famous for the speech he delivered at the Parliament of the World's Religions in Chicago, where he emphasized the universal truth at the core of all religions. In the middle of the 20th century the teachings of Ramana Maharishi became popular through Somerset Maugham's 1944 novel *The Razor's Edge* and the subsequent movie. In 1946, the publication of Paramahansa Yogananda's *Autobiography of a Yogi* inspired people throughout the world with a vision of higher human development and meditation as a path to achieve it.

A simple, effortless technique

In the second half of the 20th century, the most well-known teacher of Vedic knowledge was Maharishi Mahesh Yogi, the renowned scholar of the Vedic tradition and scientist of consciousness. From this ancient tradition he brought to light the core meditation technique, a simple, natural, effortless procedure to which he gave the modern name Transcendental Meditation. This technique became the most widely practiced and extensively validated technique for personal development.

From the mid-1950s forward, as people started learning this technique, they began having experiences like Wordsworth's in increasing numbers. They were not poets or playwrights, not philosophers or monks. They were ordinary men and women from a wide diversity of backgrounds and cultures — in the United States, Europe, and around the world. Yet they were reporting experiences very much like those celebrated in the writings of Wordsworth, Plato, Thoreau, and many other figures across history.

Here is how one person describes the experience:

> I distinctly recall the day of instruction [in the Transcendental Meditation technique], my first clear experience of transcending. Following the instructions of the teacher, without knowing what to expect, I began to drift down into deeper and deeper levels of relaxation, as if I

were sinking into my chair. Then for some time, perhaps a minute or a few minutes, I experienced a silent, inner state of no thoughts, just pure awareness and nothing else; then again I became aware of my surroundings. It left me with a deep sense of ease, inner renewal and happiness.[7]

Maharishi devoted his life to bringing the knowledge of the Vedic tradition to light in its original purity and completeness and to formulating it in terms consistent with the standards of modern science. After earning a university degree in physics, Maharishi spent 13 years studying and working with the great master of Vedic wisdom, Brahmananda Saraswati, who occupied the chief seat of Vedic learning in India and was widely revered as one of India's foremost spiritual figures.

Maharishi began teaching the Transcendental Meditation technique in India in 1955. In 1959 he traveled to the United States. Circling the world ten times over the next decade, he instructed tens of thousands of people, establishing teaching centers worldwide and training teachers of the technique. More than six million people have learned this simple meditation procedure, including two million in the US — people of all ages, nationalities, and economic, cultural, and religious backgrounds. Several tens of thousands have received extensive training as teachers of the technique.

Deep within everyone, Maharishi taught, is an ocean of pure consciousness, pure intelligence, pure bliss — the field of unity from which the diversity of the universe arises. Everyone has access to this inner reality of life. The key to raising life to its infinite potential is to experience and awaken this inner field. This, he asserted, is every human being's birthright — and everyone's essential need at this time of rapid change and rising stress.

The Transcendental Meditation technique differs from most other procedures in that it involves no concentration or control. It is easy to learn and effortless to practice — so easy even 10-year-old children can do it. It is practiced for 20 minutes twice a day while sitting comfortably with eyes closed. It is neither a philosophy nor a belief system; one need not even believe it will work.

This technique enables mental activity to settle inward, spontaneously and naturally. Maharishi called this process *transcending*, meaning to *go beyond*. It culminates in a state of deep inner silence and peace, beyond thought — a state of *pure* consciousness, consciousness aware only of its own unbounded nature. At the same time, the body settles into a state of deep rest, enabling the body to dissolve accumulated stress and fatigue and to revitalize and rebalance itself.

This unique, restfully alert state, Maharishi contended, represents a fourth major state of consciousness, distinct from the familiar states of waking, dreaming, and deep sleep. In Vedic literature this experience is often termed *samadhi*. Maharishi called it *Transcendental Consciousness* and defined it as the first stage of *enlightenment*.

Scientific research

Experiences of exalted consciousness have been a topic of literary, philosophical, and religious interest throughout the centuries, as we have seen — but enlightenment had previously never been considered a subject of serious scientific inquiry. The term had a vague and perhaps mysterious connotation of some higher mode of being. Few scientists had considered an exotic, seemingly religious experience such as *samadhi* to be a proper subject of scientific study.

But Maharishi vigorously encouraged scientific research on the Transcendental Meditation technique, even offering predictions as to what scientists might find. The first studies, conducted at UCLA in the late 1960s, found a surprisingly wide constellation of changes spontaneously occurring throughout the body during the practice — in breath and heart rate, in brain functioning, in blood biochemistry, all indicating a physiologic state of exceptionally deep rest. But unlike during sleep, the subjects remained fully awake.

This combination of deep physiological rest coupled with full wakefulness, apparently a natural human capacity, had not been seen before in the laboratory. *We are laid asleep in body, and become a living soul*, as Wordsworth lyrically expressed it. The scientists announced the discovery of a fourth state of consciousness.

The changes in brain functioning were particularly interesting. At the start of Transcendental Meditation practice, scientists discovered, the brain switches almost immediately from an essentially random style of functioning to an integrated state, reflected in coherent EEG patterns. This unique brainwave pattern indicates the various parts of the brain are now operating synchronously, reflecting enhanced communication throughout the brain.

These holistic changes are not to be confused with biofeedback, in which one intentionally attempts to modify some aspect of physiological functioning. The broad and integrated spectrum of changes observed during Transcendental Meditation practice occur spontaneously, the byproduct of transcending.

The initial studies yielded such interesting results that scientists around the world were attracted to studying the Transcendental Meditation technique and the phenomenon of transcending. Because the technique is taught in the same, systematic way worldwide, scientists had no shortage of subjects. In ever-increasing detail, their research studies have revealed the changes that take place throughout the body during meditation practice.

A second category of studies has detailed the cumulative effects of Transcendental Meditation practice. Regular transcending triggers a remarkable — and previously unsuspected — growth process, encompassing every area of life. The benefits, including increased intelligence and creativity, improved health, balanced personality development, and improved relationships, are often unprecedented. For example, intelligence (IQ) grows during childhood, then typically levels off in adolescence, around the same time physical growth plateaus, with a slow decline beginning around age 26. With regular experience of transcending, intelligence resumes growing, regardless of age, indicating that the "freezing" of growth in adolescence can be "unfrozen" and that human development need not stop.

The same is true of moral maturity, field independence,

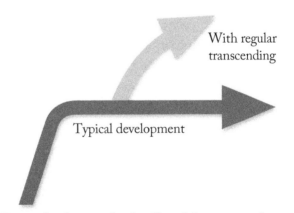

Unfreezing human development

Human development levels off in adolescence, as shown in measures of intelligence, field independence, moral maturity, and ego development. Regular transcending through the Transcendental Meditation program expands consciousness, integrates brain functioning, and promotes human development even after it has plateaued.[8]

and ego development, all of them profound measures of personal growth — all level off in adolescence, all resume their growth with regular Transcendental Meditation practice.[9]

This large and growing body of research, encompassing every area of individual life, documents in ever-increasing detail the emergence of a fifth major state of consciousness, which Maharishi calls Cosmic Consciousness — the state in which the experience of infinite pure consciousness experienced during meditation becomes a permanently lived reality.

Of equal interest, Maharishi predicted early on that when a small percentage of a population, as little as 1%, practices the Transcendental Meditation technique, the quality of life for the whole population will improve. A body of research has focused on this prediction and repeatedly confirmed it. With just 1% of a population experiencing Transcendental Consciousness through this technique, the benefits extend to the whole society, reflected in reduced crime, accidents, and violence. Such is the power of developing human consciousness and integrated brain functioning.

More than 380 peer-reviewed studies on the Transcendental Meditation technique have been published in medical and scientific journals. Studies have been conducted at 260 universities and research institutes in 33 countries. The researchers have represented a wide range of specialties, including physiology, biochemistry, neuroscience, psychology, medicine, sociology, and criminology. The results have been published in 150 leading scientific and scholarly journals.

The US National Institutes of Health has invested more than $25 million in research on the Transcendental Meditation program, particularly on such beneficial effects for cardiovascular health as reducing high blood pressure. The technique is widely prescribed by doctors and is also used in a growing number of schools across the US and worldwide to reduce stress, promote learning ability, and develop students' full creative potential.

The Transcendental Meditation technique is widely appreciated as an effective means of reducing stress. But what we are seeing here goes far beyond relaxation and stress release. We are looking at a fundamental activation of human growth, especially of our higher human capacities. A technique with the ability to produce such a broad diversity of beneficial changes — in brain and body, mind and personality, in personal relationships and society as a whole — must operate at a very foundational level. Maharishi compared regular experience of transcending to watering the root of a tree. Just as watering the root nourishes all parts of the tree in a single stroke, regular experience of Transcendental Consciousness nourishes all branches of life. The experience of transcending must activate some fundamental mechanism in mind and body that had previously been unknown in neuroscience, physiology, and psychology.

Early on, scientists realized that what they were studying was more than a meditation technique in itself. They were investigating a new possibility for human growth, involving previously unimagined improvements in mental, physiological, and emotional functioning.

Yet Transcendental Consciousness is a natural state. Everyone has the ability to experience it — every human brain is hard-wired with the potential to function coherently. Human beings are born not to suffer but to enjoy, Maharishi said — they need only develop their unbounded potential. The experience of transcending is the missing catalyst. And the Transcendental Meditation technique gives that experience effortlessly.

A universal knowledge

The core tenets of Vedic wisdom reverberate within all the world's religious and wisdom traditions, particularly their mystical branches. These core principles have been referred to as the *philosophia perennis*, or *perennial philosophy*, and the *primordial tradition*. These are its tenets:

■ At the basis of the extraordinary diversity of the universe is a field of unity, sometimes termed *the ground of being* or *the divine ground*, in which everything has its being and apart from which nothing could exist.

■ Human beings are capable of experiencing this underlying transcendental reality directly, deep within themselves.

■ The purpose of life is to discover and experience this divine ground, to reconnect with the underlying essence of life. To do so is to realize one's true nature, the eternal Self, and to transform and fulfill one's life.[10]*

This inner field is described everywhere in the world's great philosophi-

---

* For more on this topic, see Note 1, page 516.

Across traditions, the summons to go within

Hence the inscrutable God is called silent by the divine ones, and is said to consent with Mind, and to be known to human souls through the power of the mind alone.
— ZOROASTRIANISM | Zoroaster | 11th–10th century BCE | Iran

One who knows others is intelligent.
One who knows himself is enlightened.
— TAOISM | Laozi, Tao Te Ching | c. 600 BCE | China

Know thyself.
— Temple of Apollo at Delphi in Greece | c. 500 BCE

Be a lamp unto your own feet;
do not seek outside yourself.
— BUDDHISM | Gautama Buddha
c. 6th–4th century BCE | Nepal and India

What the superior man seeks, is in himself;
what the ordinary man seeks, is in others.
— CONFUCIANISM | Confucius | 551–479 BCE | China

Behold, the kingdom of God is within you.
— CHRISTIANITY | Jesus Christ | c. 5 BCE–30 CE

Look within. Within is the fountain of good,
and it will ever bubble up, if thou wilt ever dig.
— STOICISM | Marcus Aurelius | 121–180 | Roman emperor

This region of truth is not to be investigated
as a thing external to us. . . . It is within us.
— NEOPLATONISM | Plotinus | 205–270 | Egypt and Italy

cal and religious traditions. In the ancient Vedic literature it is called *Atma*. In Daoism it is referred to as the *Tao*, in Buddhism as *Adibuddha*, in Christianity as *the kingdom of Heaven within*, in Judaism as *Ein Sof*. In ancient Greece, six centuries BCE, the pre-Socratic philosopher Anaximander named it *apeiron* — meaning the *Boundless*, the *Unlimited*. Two centuries later Plato referred to it as *the Good*, *the One*, and *the Beautiful*, while his student Aristotle called it *Being*. In the third century, the Egyptian-Roman philosopher Plotinus, like Plato, described it as *the One*, also *the Infinite*. In 12th-century France, St. Bernard of Clairvaux termed it *the Word*. In 19th-century Germany, the philosopher Georg Wilhelm Friedrich Hegel called it *the Absolute*. In 19th-century America, Ralph Waldo Emerson called it *the Oversoul*. The 20th-century Swiss psychologist Carl Jung popularized the Latin term *unus mundus (one world)* to describe this underlying unity. For tribes in southern Africa it is *Hunhu/Ubuntu*, for the Aborigines of Australia the *Dreamtime*.[11] Today modern theoretical physics similarly describes a field of unity underlying nature's diversity, called the *unified field* or the *superstring field*.

The terms vary, but they all refer to the same concept — the underlying field of unity from which creation springs. As the Rik Veda declares, "Truth is one; the wise call it by different names."[12]

And at the core of many great spiritual traditions, we find the summons to look within and experience this field directly. The Indian poet Rabindranath Tagore expressed it in this way:

> This is the ultimate end of man; to find the One which is in him, which is his truth, which is his soul; the key with which he opens the gate of the spiritual life, the heavenly kingdom.[13]

Since time beyond memory, countless men and women have devoted themselves to the single-minded pursuit of transcendence. Often they have walked away from homes and families and possessions, some withdrawing into monasteries or convents or ashrams, some electing to live in solitude — in the deserts of Egypt and the Middle East, the Himalayan mountains of India and Tibet, the forests and mountains of China — stripping away everything nonessential. An enormous variety of practices, often strenuous, arose around this quest, from study of scriptural and philosophical texts to countless mental and

Across traditions, the summons to go within

Call yourself back then to yourself, O soul,
and seek in yourself all that you ought to get knowledge of.
— Hermetic Writings | 2nd–3rd centuries | Egypt

Go not outside, but return within thyself;
in the inward man dwelleth the truth.
— CHRISTIANITY | St. Augustine | 354–430 | Algeria

The greatest wisdom is to know thyself.
— JUDAISM | The Talmud | 200–500 | Israel

The heavens are still: no sound.
Where then shall God be found? . . .
Do not search in distant skies;
In man's own heart He lies.
— CONFUCIANISM | Shao Yung, Confucian philosopher | 1011–1077 | China

---

Why do you go to the forest in search of God?
He lives in all and is yet ever distinct;
He abides with you, too,
As fragrance dwells in a flower,
And reflection in a mirror;
So does God dwell inside everything;
Seek Him, therefore, in your heart.
— SIKHISM | *Guru Granth Sahib* | 15th–17th centuries | India

---

The human mind, partaking of divinity,
is an abode of the Deity, which is the spiritual essence.
There exists no highest deity outside the human mind.
— SHINTOISM | Hayashi-Razan, Shinto and Confucian philosopher | 1583–1657 | Japan

physical disciplines. As difficult as this reclusive path of life may be to comprehend in the modern world, such has been the attraction of spiritual development over millennia. Yet those who walked this path had no patent on the experience, as we will see in the chapters to come.

The birthright of everyone

Maharishi's great work was to bring meditation and the concept of enlightenment into the mainstream as well as into the arena of scientific research, vastly expanding the scope of scientific inquiry and the scientific understanding of human potential.

In the wake of the Transcendental Meditation program's widespread success, many other procedures of meditation and personal development were put forward, some from Eastern traditions, some homegrown. As research began to be conducted on some of these as well, it became clear that different procedures produce different effects, notably in the resulting style of brain functioning. But the Transcendental Meditation technique is unique in a variety of respects — in its effortlessness, in the systematic experience of transcending it facilitates, in the integrated brain functioning and range of physiological changes that occur during the practice, and in the holistic growth that results.

The reality of transcendence and practices for transcending can be found at the inception of every religious tradition, Maharishi has pointed out, but they often became lost or obscured. Yet human beings are designed for enlightenment; it is everyone's birthright. With the simple technique for transcending Maharishi brought to light, anyone and everyone can grow to enlightenment.

CHAPTER 3

The Seven States of Consciousness

As increasing numbers of people began experiencing Transcendental Consciousness through their Transcendental Meditation practice, they began describing exalted experiences outside of meditation as well. In response to these experiences, Maharishi brought to light a clear, complete, and systematic understanding of human development.

For most psychologists, the "endpoint" of mental growth, the highest level of cognitive development adults can reach, occurs in adolescence, when we gain the ability to think logically and abstractly — although as many as 60% of adults have not reached this stage.[1] We may continue to change after adolescence, refining or extending capacities we have already developed, but no major growth beyond this final stage is commonly acknowledged.

But in the Vedic understanding of human potential that Maharishi brought to light, this common "adult" level of growth is only the starting point. Complete human development involves growth through a series of higher states of consciousness. Maharishi's model comprises seven states of consciousness altogether, of which waking, dreaming, and deep sleep are but the first three.

The fourth state, Transcendental Consciousness, forms the gateway to higher states. With regular experience of the fourth state, the three higher states develop naturally. To the fifth, sixth, and seventh states of consciousness Maharishi gave the names Cosmic Consciousness, God Consciousness, and Unity Consciousness. Each is a progressive stage of awakening, of enlightenment. Each opens a distinctive new world of experience and knowledge, as different from the waking state as waking is from dreaming. And each has a corresponding style of physiological functioning, a unique physiological signature.

If the idea of higher states of consciousness seems abstract, the benefits are concrete and immensely practical. The Transcendental Meditation program has been applied from schools to universities, from boardrooms to factory floors, from substance abuse clinics to prisons, from homes for the elderly to veterans returning with post-traumatic stress disorder. Where little if anything else has succeeded, the simple experience of daily transcending has produced breakthrough results. But these results are merely byproducts of the technique's ultimate purpose, to cultivate higher states of consciousness — enlightenment.

Maharishi put forward two basic principles of states of consciousness:

■ *Knowledge is different in different states of consciousness.* As we shift from one state of consciousness to another, we move from one world to another. Each state involves a unique mode of knowledge and experience, of ourselves and the surrounding world. The world of the waking state, for example, differs radically from the illusory dream world. Both differ radically from the world of deep sleep. Similarly, each higher state of consciousness is a world in itself.

■ *Each state of consciousness has a unique mode of physiological functioning.* A physiologist can tell whether you are awake, dreaming, or asleep by measuring your breath rate, brainwaves, and so on. When you shift from one state to another, your physiology switches to a different style of functioning. Accordingly, higher states of consciousness develop when the physiology reaches specific thresholds of integration and purification. *Growth of higher states thus has nothing to do with adopting new ideas, attitudes, or moods.* It depends instead on cultivating coherent brain functioning and on refining and purifying the nervous system, culminating in optimal integration and balance. Without these refinements, higher states cannot develop.[2]

The Seven States of Consciousness

Deep sleep state

Sleep is a physical and mental state of rest during which we become inactive and unaware of our surroundings. We spend 75–80% of our sleeping time in non-REM (rapid eye movement) sleep. Most physiological functions slow down. Body temperature, blood pressure, and breathing rate all drop. Sensory and motor activity become suspended, voluntary muscles become inactive, and we become totally or partially unconscious. The brain, however, remains active throughout sleep — as active, according to some studies, as during waking.

Dreaming state

At various periods during sleep, we enter the dream state, the illusory, unpredictable world where familiar laws of nature release their hold and anything can happen — improbable shifts in time and place, unfamiliar combinations of people and events. Most dreaming takes place in REM sleep, comprising about 25% of our sleep time. Brainwave activity during REM sleep resembles that of the waking state except that the brain inhibits signals to the muscles so we cannot act out our dreams.

Sleeping and dreaming are critical for our physical and emotional health. Each stage of sleep furnishes important benefits, whether regenerating neurons, generating new synaptic connections in the cerebral cortex, processing memories, or integrating what we learned during the day. The brain's activity during sleep may also support creativity and assist problem-solving.

Waking state

The waking state is the familiar, ever-changing world of concrete sensory experience, of people and places, things and events. From the outer world we perceive through our senses to the inner world of thoughts and feelings, our waking state experience is in constant flux, while physiological functioning is more active. Our perception of reality may vary enormously through the day, depending on whether we are rested or tired, calm or agitated, attentive or bored, happy or depressed, healthy or ill.

Transcendental Consciousness — the fourth state of consciousness

In this state, attention has settled inward, beyond perceptions, thoughts, and feelings. What remains is the experience of consciousness in its pure form, awake to itself alone — unbounded pure awareness, our innermost Self. Simultaneously the body becomes deeply restful while brain functioning becomes integrated, suggesting the total brain is awake.

Cosmic Consciousness — the fifth state of consciousness

With regular experience of Transcendental Consciousness, the mind and body become accustomed to this style of functioning — one maintains unbounded awareness, the fully expanded state of mind, at all times, along with waking, dreaming, and sleeping. The physiology is now free of stress and brain functioning remains integrated throughout the day. With consciousness fully expanded and open to the unified field, one lives in accord with natural law — one's actions are spontaneously life-nourishing and one fulfills desires without strain.

God Consciousness — the sixth state of consciousness

The next phase of growth involves refinement of perceptual abilities. One gains the ability to perceive finer, subtler strata of creation. In time one perceives the very finest material structure, indescribably radiant, glorious, celestial. Maharishi calls this state *God Consciousness,* because it brings direct perception of the full range of God's creation. Fully matured, this state brings the direct experience of the Creator.

Unity Consciousness — the seventh state of consciousness

Human development culminates in the ability to experience all things in terms of their innermost essence, the underlying oneness from which all creation emerges. This is the same oneness we experience deep within when we transcend — pure consciousness, the unbounded Self. In Unity Consciousness, the pinnacle of human evolution, one experiences everything in terms of one's Self, all activity in the universe as simply the Self moving within itself. One lives a totally awakened and totally integrated life, with the ability to know anything, do anything, and achieve anything.[3]

Our global heritage

We find the vision of enlightenment, exalted states of experience, and life raised to fulfillment and perfection at the core of our global heritage.*

▪ Central to *Indian philosophy* and religion is *Yoga*. In the West, Yoga is commonly understood as a form of exercise. But Yoga properly refers to Transcendental Consciousness — the union of the individual self with the cosmic Self in the experience of pure consciousness (the word *Yoga* is related to the English word *yoke*, the wooden crosspiece that joins two animals pulling a plow or cart). The ultimate Yoga occurs in Unity Consciousness, in which everything is experienced within the unity of the Self. Indian philosophy also gives us the concept of *Moksha* (or *Mukti*), the experience that one's fundamental nature is identical with Brahman, the ground of being, the totality. Moksha — sometimes understood as transcending thought (Transcendental Consciousness), sometimes as union with God (God Consciousness), sometimes as union with creation itself (Unity Consciousness) — is regarded as conferring liberation from the cycle of death and rebirth.

▪ *Daoist* literature refers to states known as *High Pure, Most Pure,* and *Jade Pure*, corresponding, respectively, to rising Cosmic Consciousness, fully developed Cosmic Consciousness, and Unity Consciousness.[4]

▪ In *Judaism* the term *Chayah* refers to the experience of transcending, as does *Devekut*, in certain usages.

▪ The vast *Buddhist* literature offers a variety of models of spiritual growth, with various categories of experiences and stages of development, depending on the school. The term *Nirvana* (*Nibbana*) generally parallels Transcendental Consciousness. Buddhism and Zen also use the terms *Satori, Shunyata,* and *Kensho* to describe this state. Nirvana also describes a more advanced state wherein the mind remains perfectly at peace, free of anger, craving, and suffering, no longer fluctuating and identifying with sensory perceptions — Cosmic Consciousness. To attain Nirvana is to attain what the Buddha calls "the highest happiness" — Buddhahood, enlightenment. *Bodhi* is another Buddhist term for this state.

---

* For more on this topic, see Note 1, page 516.

■ In *Japanese Zen Buddhism*, the term *Kensho* (sometimes called *Shogo*) describes the first, temporary experiences of one's Buddha nature, the unbounded Self, comparable to Transcendental Consciousness. In *Satori* (also called *Daigo*), this experience becomes permanent — Cosmic Consciousness.

■ In *Sufism*, the inner, mystical branch of Islam, higher stages of human development are called *the four journeys*. The first is *Fana*, which literally means *extinction* or *annihilation* — transcendence of all mental activity, corresponding with Transcendental Consciousness. Beyond Fana lies *Baqa*, in which one's experience becomes stabilized and one becomes the *Perfect Man*. Baqa is defined in various ways that compare with Cosmic Consciousness, God Consciousness, and Unity Consciousness. The final two journeys have to do with degrees of spiritual leadership.[5] The term *Qutub* has been applied to the highest, unitive stage as well as to the highest teachership.

A systematic model

With his model of seven states of consciousness, Maharishi has put forward a systematic, comprehensive, detailed understanding of human development and placed it in the arena of empirical science. He has described the transformations in knowledge, experience, and physiological functioning that come with each higher state. He has offered these descriptions as *scientific hypotheses* amenable to both objective and subjective verification. And he has provided simple, natural techniques for cultivating higher states of consciousness. Maharishi's model of seven states of consciousness represents a unique contribution to our understanding of human potential and how it develops.

With this description of human development, we can turn to the literature of the past with clear criteria for evaluating what we find. And what we find is extraordinary: orders of experience altogether beyond the ordinary waking state yet entirely natural, experiences that may have been ignored or misunderstood until now — glimpses of higher states of consciousness.

Maharishi speaks of *the seven worlds* of the seven states of consciousness, each higher state of consciousness a world of knowledge and experience in itself. We will be spending some time in each of these worlds, starting with the experience of transcendence, Transcendental Consciousness.

CHAPTER 4

ॐ

THE FOURTH STATE

Transcendental Consciousness

Pure Consciousness Awake
to Its Own Unbounded Nature

Our minds are continuously stirred by perceptions, thoughts, and feelings, much as the ocean is swept into waves by winds and currents. But like an ocean the mind can settle down. It can become calm, quiet, silent, while remaining awake. This is Transcendental Consciousness.

In his modern reinterpretation of the ancient Vedic tradition, Maharishi describes Transcendental Consciousness as *the simplest form of human awareness*. It is the most intimate, most personal experience possible. There is nothing more simple or more natural. Your body is deeply relaxed. Your mind is awake but silent and serene. You are literally at one with yourself.

What are you experiencing in this state? Your consciousness is free of content, awake but without perceptions, thoughts, and feelings. The sea of consciousness is aware only of itself, unmixed with anything else. Maharishi calls this a state of *pure consciousness*, pure awareness, pure wakefulness.

THE FOURTH STATE • TRANSCENDENTAL CONSCIOUSNESS

Picture yourself in a movie theater. Ordinarily we are aware only of the ever-changing images before us. Imagine these images becoming fainter and fainter, eventually fading away, leaving only the pure, bright screen. This is analogous to mental activity settling inward through finer values of thought, then transcending thought altogether. What remains? Only pure consciousness — only the pure screen on which we experience all thoughts and feelings. Here Maharishi describes this state:

> The Transcendental Meditation technique is an effortless procedure for allowing the excitations of the mind gradually to settle down until the least excited state of mind is reached. This is a state of inner wakefulness with no object of thought or perception, just pure consciousness aware of its own unbounded nature. It is wholeness, aware of itself, devoid of differences, beyond the division of subject and object — Transcendental Consciousness.[1]

Unbounded awareness

The continuous flux of perceptions, thoughts, and feelings in the mind clouds the true nature of consciousness, creating "boundaries" that confine our awareness. But as the mind settles inward and moves beyond these boundaries of thought and perception, consciousness expands. Transcending thinking altogether, consciousness expands to the maximum. Unlike the ordinary waking state, in which the mind is awake only at its surface, the mind now is awake to its depth. One experiences consciousness in its pure state, infinite and unbounded. In Maharishi's words:

> On the path to experiencing Being [pure consciousness], the conscious capacity of the mind is enlarged, and the whole ocean of the mind becomes capable of being conscious. The full mental potential is thus unfolded, and the conscious capacity of the mind is increased to the maximum limit.[2]

Maharishi has described Transcendental Consciousness as the *total potential* and the *total reality* of consciousness.[3] One transcends individuality and gains universality. No experience fills the mind with greater happiness.

Self-knowledge

The inner, transcendental field of pure consciousness is the ultimate value of the self. Obviously it is quite different from the self we ordinarily experience, which is concerned with experiencing, thinking, and decision-making.

In ordinary waking consciousness, we can never know our self directly, only our feelings, thoughts, and perceptions *about* our self. Any insight we gain about our self becomes just another thought, another object of experience, another wave on the ocean — it is not the self itself. Some philosophers conclude true self-knowledge is impossible. The philosopher David Hume writes:

> For my part, when I enter most intimately into what I call myself, I always stumble on some particular perception or other, of heat or cold, light or shade, love or hatred, pain or pleasure. I never can catch myself at any time without a perception, and can never observe any thing but the perception.[4]

Hume was unable to transcend his mind's activity. Had he done so, he would have experienced his consciousness in its pure state — his true self. But if this is the true nature of the self, how can we fail to experience it? Our perceptions and thoughts "overshadow" the experience of the inner field of pure consciousness, as Maharishi has explained:

> When a flower is seen, then only the flower remains in the mind, as if the mind had been completely annihilated, void of its own real glory, and the glory of the flower had overtaken it — as if the flower had overshadowed the glory of the mind itself. The experiencer is missing, only the sight remains and the object. . . . This is called objective life, material life. Matter remains dominant. . . . Anything that we experience, that alone remains in the mind. The value of the experiencer is missing. Pure bliss consciousness, that bliss consciousness of absolute nature, has been overshadowed by the impression of the object.[5]

In Transcendental Consciousness, we experience pure, unbounded bliss consciousness. This is our true self, our self in its pure state, uncolored by waves of feeling, thought, and perception. So distinct is this from the self we ordinarily experience that Maharishi distinguishes it as the "higher Self," with a capital "S."[6]

Self-referral consciousness

Every human experience, Maharishi observes, has three fundamental components: a knower, a known, and a process of knowing linking the two — an experiencer, an object of experience, and a process of experiencing. As you read these words, for example, there is a knower (you), a known (the information you gain), and a process of knowing (the act of reading and understanding).

This threefold structure undergirds all human experience. In ordinary waking consciousness these three components remain separate. In Transcendental Consciousness, they become identical — consciousness becomes its own object of experience. No perceptions, thoughts, or feelings intervene between knower and known. There is nothing to bridge because there is no longer any distinction between subject and object — the subject *is* the object.

Thus Maharishi describes the fourth state as *self-referral consciousness* — consciousness refers only to itself. The ordinary waking state, in contrast, is *object-referral*, focused on objects, which includes thoughts and feelings.[7]

Pure knowledge

Ordinary waking consciousness brings us knowledge of specific things — perceptions, thoughts, memories, feelings — pieces of information, fragments of knowledge. Transcendental Consciousness brings the experience of what Maharishi calls *pure knowledge* — the knowledge gained when consciousness knows itself, by itself, in its pure unbounded state. If waking state thoughts and perceptions are waves on the ocean, then pure knowledge is the silent ocean knowing itself. This is the "absolute state of knowledge," a state of knowing*ness*.[8]

The source of thought

Every thought we experience emerges from deep within the mind, Maharishi observes, much like bubbles emerging from the sand at the bottom of a pool. Ordinarily we experience thoughts only after they have developed and reached the mind's surface, the conscious thinking level. The Transcendental Meditation technique enables the mind to move in the reverse direction, settling effortlessly to subtler, more refined levels of thought until one experiences the source of thought, pure consciousness.[9]

Infinite reservoir of creativity and intelligence

Pure consciousness – source of thought

Every thought we think is an impulse of energy and intelligence, Maharishi points out. Due to energy thoughts move. Due to intelligence they take a specific direction. Given the countless thoughts we have every day, the source of thought must be an infinite reservoir of energy and intelligence.[10] Maharishi has called it an ocean of *pure knowledge, power, and bliss.*

In Transcendental Consciousness, the mind opens to its unbounded inner potential, the limitless creativity and intelligence at its source. Like a sponge dipped into water, the mind becomes infused with these qualities and brings them into daily activity after meditation.

The source of creation — pure Being

Pure consciousness, Maharishi asserts, is vastly more than the simplest form of human awareness, the source of thought. It is the source of nature's intelligence, the unmanifest, nonchanging field of unity underlying the infinitely diverse, ever-changing world of forms and phenomena. Like our thoughts, all phenomena in the universe are waves on the ocean of pure consciousness. Maharishi thus describes pure consciousness as a field of pure existence, pure Being — as *the Absolute*, the silent, eternal, nonchanging field that underlies *the relative*, the ever-changing world of space and time.[11]

The unified field of natural law

Early in his teaching, in the 1950s, Maharishi predicted that modern science, through its ever-deeper investigations into the structure of natural law, would eventually arrive at the field of pure consciousness, pure Being.

Indeed, the more deeply scientists have penetrated into nature, the simpler and more unified nature is revealed to be. By the 1970s and 1980s, physicists had shown that all change in the universe may be traced back to four fundamental forces or fields. By the early 1990s, they were beginning to show mathematically that these fundamental fields emerge from a single field, an abstract, all-pervading field of infinite energy. This field, known as the unified field, is the common source from which everything in the ever-expanding universe emerges, the total potential of nature's intelligence.

The modern scientific description of nature accords with the ancient Vedic description. Both describe nature as completely unified at its source. Both describe this source as an unmanifest, all-pervading field, a continuum of concentrated energy and intelligence, beyond time and space. Both hold that everything in the universe emerges as the result of this transcendental field interacting with itself.

Pure consciousness is identical with the unified field, Maharishi repeatedly emphasizes. The human mind is a cosmic mind. The Self of everyone is the center of total natural law.[12]

Maharishi compares pure consciousness to the colorless sap in a rose. Looking at the rose from the outside, we see soft yellow petals, flat green leaves, a long green stem, spiky thorns — countless specific qualities. But all these qualities have been created out of colorless sap. Every particle of the rose, in fact, is *nothing other* than colorless sap. In this metaphor, the colorless sap displays no qualities itself, yet contains all qualities within it.[13]

Pure consciousness is like the colorless sap of the universe. It remains unchanging within itself but gives rise to everything in creation. This is the field into which the mind settles when it transcends — the unified field of natural law, the field of nature's infinite intelligence. Because of the importance of this principle, we will explore it more thoroughly in Chapter 10.

Transcendental Consciousness is the most simple and natural experience a person can have — the experience of awareness in its most quiet state. The simple act of transcending is the most vital experience in human life, the key to developing life's infinite potential. Without this experience, Maharishi has said, "Life is like a building without a foundation."[14]

Waking consciousness	Transcendental Consciousness
One's eyes are generally open.	The eyes are generally closed.
One's attention is directed outward.	Attention has settled inward.
Consciousness is object-referral, absorbed in perceptions, thoughts, or feelings.	Consciousness is self-referral, absorbed in itself, aware of itself alone, its own object of perception.
The mind is active, excited, constantly moving, its contents ever changing.	Consciousness is still, silent, an ocean of pure wakefulness, with no content other than its own nonchanging, unbounded nature.
Consciousness is localized, bound by objects it perceives.	Consciousness is unbounded, universal.
Consciousness is fragmented. The three values of knower, process of knowing, and known are separated.	Consciousness is unified. Pure consciousness is the knower of itself. Knower, knowing, and known are unified.
Only the surface of the mind is awake.	The mind is awake at its source.
The mind is using only a fraction of its potential creativity and intelligence.	The mind is open to its total potential, an unlimited reservoir of creativity and intelligence.
One is aware only of one's localized, individual self.	One's universal, unbounded cosmic Self is now awake within itself.
The mind has access only to partial values of natural law.	The mind is open to the total potential of natural law, the unified field.
Brainwave activity is random and shifting, indicating only localized communication.	Brain functioning is coherent and integrated, indicating long-range communication among all brain regions.
The body is engaged in some degree of activity.	The body is deeply restful and is dissolving fatigue and stress.

Experiences of Transcendental Consciousness

For each higher state of consciousness we consider, we will look at a few experiences from people who practice the Transcendental Meditation technique and then at a sampling of historical experiences.

People who learn the Transcendental Meditation technique are, according to psychological profiles, no different from people uninterested in meditation. They do not have higher levels of self-development, nor do they tend to have these kinds of experiences before learning to meditate.[15] Their experiences arise from adding the Transcendental Meditation program to their daily routine.

Experiences during meditation, Maharishi explains, will vary from person to person and from day to day, depending on the condition of the nervous system, whether fresh or fatigued, relaxed or stressed. When one first learns to meditate, one may experience Transcendental Consciousness only for brief moments, at the deepest points of meditation. The experience is so natural that one may be hardly aware of it. In time, with regular practice, one maintains the experience for longer periods, first during meditation, then outside as well.

Many of these reports were gathered as part of scholarly research studies in which names were kept anonymous.

"Just pure awareness and nothing else"

I will never forget the first experience I had of the Transcendental Meditation technique. I closed my eyes, began practicing this simple, natural technique, and spontaneously began to laugh. The movement of my awareness from the active level . . . to the field of silence within myself . . . was like diving into a pond of pure joy. I felt so much happiness; the laughter just bubbled up automatically. And after this first meditation, driving home that night, I remember thinking, "So this is me! This is the reality of who I am." I felt a quality of contentment and peace that I had never known before.[16]

"Experiencing awareness as an unbounded unity"

I have had the experience of transcending all activity and experiencing awareness as an unbounded unity. There is no longer any sense of "me" and "not me," no longer any thought or feelings or even a body — just the Self, and that is all there is, and that is all I am.[17]

"I am that infinity"

During the practice of the Transcendental Meditation technique I sometimes reach a state of complete silence which has come about very innocently. The experience is one of evenness and expansion, of infinity, and I am that infinity.[18]

"An unbounded ocean of awareness"

During the Transcendental Meditation technique my mind settles down, thoughts become less and then suddenly all thought activity ceases and I slip into an unbounded ocean of awareness which is pure, quiet, unexcited and infinitely extended beyond space and time. In this state, I am not aware of any thought or any thing; I am just aware of awareness, you could say, wide awake inside but not thinking. Simultaneously my body settles down, breathing becomes less, and I feel relaxed.[19]

"The experience is very nourishing"

When I sit to meditate and my awareness sinks into the transcendent, the concerns and worries that may have been gripping my mind fall away, and become supplanted with bliss (sometimes quiet, sometimes bubbly) and peace. The experience is very nourishing. . . . The transcendent is a completeness.[20]

"I have never been so clearly and entirely and fully awake"

Meditation begins as most do. I feel as if I am a small stone sinking into an ocean of filtered light. The light seems to be coming from all directions. I slow, almost pause, at certain levels before my specific gravity increases again, and I sink deeper into this ocean of consciousness — no real experience of having entered this ocean — just being there and going deeper and deeper. It is beyond peaceful, beyond serene.

Then something quite extraordinary happens. The ocean disappears. I mean it is just gone, and I am in an indescribable place. I am alone with my Self, and I have never been so clearly and entirely and fully awake. There is nothing but That — no ocean, no me, no anything, but totality. And I am fully awake to it.

I could say the individual "I" had become the Cosmic "I." But that is not quite it. Rather it's as if there never was anything but the Cosmic I. The individual "I" never existed to begin with. The wave was never anything but the ocean. It felt as if I were floating in Brahman [totality]. But that expression suggests two things: Brahman and me. Yet there is only one thing.

I have had other experiences that seemed more divine in nature — light filled with love and bliss so intense it was astonishing. This was different — it was somehow *more*. It would seem to be impossible to have more. But this was more.[21]

On the historical accounts to come

Experiences of higher states of consciousness turn up in every kind of literature — poetry, autobiography, journals, novels. How is it possible to glimpse higher states? In certain circumstances, Maharishi explains, the nervous system may shift to a style of functioning that allows such an experience. But if the nervous system has not been sufficiently refined to maintain this style of functioning, it reverts to its ordinary waking-state mode and the moment passes.

A glimpse of a state is a momentary or partial view, not the state itself. Thoreau describes experiences reminiscent of Cosmic Consciousness in his journal, but we cannot say he was in Cosmic Consciousness. When one reaches a higher state of consciousness, it can never be diminished or lost. Nor does any single historical experience in this book describe all the features of a fully matured higher state. Some writers offer clearer and more complete descriptions, others less so, perhaps reflecting varying clarity in their experience. Finally, these experiences appear to be exceedingly rare in the world's literature, and few people seemed able to cultivate the experience. As St. Bernard of Clairvaux puts it, "It is as rare as it is delightful, and as short-lived as rare."[22]

Nevertheless, we find people from a variety of cultures and historical epochs describing the same kinds of experiences. These descriptions, furthermore, accord with what we know about higher states of consciousness from Maharishi, from the scientific research on the Transcendental Meditation program, and from the experiences of people who practice this program. Thus we conclude these are universal human experiences.

These experiences, from both historical figures and people practicing the Transcendental Meditation technique, are simply individual experiences. Each person's experiences will be unique, depending on the ever-changing condition of their individual nervous system. Maharishi emphasizes the importance of remaining innocent. Thus readers should not look for these exact experiences in their own meditation practice.

Describing the indescribable

Suppose you live in a world where everyone is born color blind. Everyone experiences the world as black and white and shades of gray. There are no words for color. No one even dreams of it. One day, for a few moments, you somehow gain the capacity to perceive color. It's the same world, but a new dimension opens, rich and beautiful.

Then the experience fades. The colors evaporate. You are returned to your black-and-white world. Where did the moment come from? How can you get it back? It becomes the touchstone for everything else you experience.

You want to tell others about it — but how do you describe color to someone who has never experienced it? You strive to find words to convey this priceless information about human potential, about reality itself — only to find that few understand you.

And yet, somehow, we do. We have cherished Wordsworth's "Lines Composed a Few Miles Above Tintern Abbey" for more than 200 years because it speaks to something deep within us all. So too with the writings of Laozi, Plato, Plotinus, and many others.

As those who have had such experiences almost unanimously declare, they are fundamentally ineffable, indescribable, beyond language — they can be known and understood only through the experience itself. Says Edward Carpenter, "I do not feel that I can tell you anything without falsifying and obscuring the matter." For Walt Whitman such experiences are "beyond statement," for Tennyson "utterly beyond words." "Words," writes Eugene Ionesco, "can only disfigure" the experience. Franklin Merrill-Wolff says, "It is utterly baffling to language as such."

Utterly beyond words — yet they strove to describe it nonetheless. They may declare they failed, but they succeeded in fashioning beautifully-wrought signposts to exalted stages of human development. Now more than ever, their words take on the significance they intended.

Now let's look at some examples of how Transcendental Consciousness has been described or experienced across time and across the world.

VEDIC LITERATURE
INDIA

Now is the teaching on Yoga. Yoga is the complete settling of the activity of the mind. Then the seer is established in the Self....

When mental activity decreases, then knower, knowing and known become absorbed one into another, like a transparent crystal which assumes the appearance of that upon which it rests.

In the clear experience of *nirvicara samadhi* dawns the splendor of the Self. There resides the intellect that knows only the truth....

In the settling of that state also, all is calmed, and what remains is unbounded wakefulness.[1]   — *Yoga Sutras of Patanjali*

These, the opening sutras (verses) of the primary Vedic text on Yoga, make clear that Yoga, properly understood, is a state of transcendence, the experience of the Self, unbounded pure consciousness.

ॐ

This whole creation is ultimately *brahman*,
  And the Self,
    this also is *brahman*.

This pure Self has four quarters:

The first is the waking state,
  experience of the reality common to everyone,
The attention faces outwards, enjoying the world in all its variety.

The second is experience of subjective worlds, such as in dreaming.
Here the attention dwells within, charmed by the mind's subtler
  creations.

The third is deep sleep,
> the mind rests, with awareness suspended.

This state beyond duality
> — from which the waves of thinking emerge,
> is enjoyed by the enlightened as an ocean of silence and bliss.

The fourth, say the wise, is the pure Self alone.
Dwelling in the heart of all,
> it is the lord of all,
> the seer of all,
> the source and goal of all.

It is not outer awareness,
It is not inner awareness,
Nor is it a suspension of awareness.
It is not knowing,
It is not unknowing,
Nor is it knowingness itself.
It can neither be seen nor understood.
It cannot be given boundaries.
It is ineffable and beyond thought.
It is indefinable.
It is known only through becoming it.
It is the end of all activity,
> silent and unchanging,
> the supreme good,
> one without a second.

It is the real Self.
It, above all, should be known.[2] — *Mandukya Upanishad*

This passage describes a distinct fourth state of consciousness, silent, unbounded, transcendental, the experience of the supreme good, the source and goal of everything, the pure Self.

Beyond all conception,
the one light shines forth.
It is the Great.
It is smaller than the smallest,
    farther than the farthest,
    nearer than the nearest.
The wise know It resting deep within.

The eyes cannot see It,
Speech cannot describe It,
Nor any sense perceive It.
It is not attained by effort,
Nor through austerities.
Only when meditation has purified the mind can you know the One
    beyond all divisions.

The mind is kept ever active by the senses.
When they have withdrawn
    and the mind becomes still,
Then the subtle Self shines forth.

When the mind rests steady and pure,
    then whatever you desire
        those desires are fulfilled,
    and whatever you think of
        those thoughts materialize.

He who knows the Self
    knows the supreme abode of Brahman,
    in which the universe lies resplendent.
The wise,
    free from all desire,

devoted to this cosmic spirit,
    cast off all attachment.

Whilst you remain attached to action
    you are bound by your desires
    and must be reborn continually
        — both during life and after death.
But when you find the Self
    the goal of all desiring
    you leave both birth and death behind.

This Self cannot be realized by studying the scriptures,
    nor through the use of reason,
    nor from the words of others
        — no matter what they say.
By the grace of the Self is the Self known,
The Self reveals Itself.

. . . .

Having realized the Self,
    the wise find satisfaction.
Their evolution complete,
    at peace, and free from longing,
    they are at one with everything.[3]   — *Mundaka Upanishad*

This passage, with its serene and expansive language, begins by describing the transcendental field, the Self. Though it lies beyond the reach of the senses, it can be experienced deep within when the mind becomes still. Experiencing the Self brings "the goal of all desiring" and the completion of evolution — peace, freedom, and oneness with everything.

▪ *Also see Vedic literature in Chapter 5 (Cosmic Consciousness), Chapter 6 (God Consciousness), and Chapter 7 (Unity Consciousness).*

LAOZI
6TH CENTURY BCE • CHINA

Laozi is regarded as the founder of Daoism. His name (also spelled Lao Tzu) means Venerable Master. *According to Chinese tradition, he lived in the 6th century* BCE. *Little is known of his life; many scholars believe he may be a composite of a number of historical individuals. Popular biographies say he worked as the keeper of the archives at the royal court, and though he never established a formal school, he attracted many students and disciples. Observing the city's moral decay and the kingdom's decline, Laozi supposedly traveled west to spend the remainder of his life in solitude in the frontier. When he reached the kingdom's western gate, the guard recognized him and asked him to set down a written record of his wisdom. Thus was born the* Tao Te Ching (Daodejing), *the most widely translated work in Chinese literature and a world classic. Several other important Daoist works are attributed to Laozi.*

Become totally empty
Quiet the restlessness of the mind
Only then will you witness everything
    unfolding from emptiness
See all things flourish and dance
    in endless variation
And once again merge back into perfect emptiness —
    Their true repose
    Their true nature
Emerging, flourishing, dissolving back again
    This is the eternal process of return

To know this process brings enlightenment

To miss this process brings disaster

Be still
Stillness reveals the secrets of eternity
Eternity embraces the all-possible
The all-possible leads to a vision of oneness
A vision of oneness brings about universal love
Universal love supports the great truth of Nature
The great truth of Nature is Tao

Whoever knows this truth lives forever
The body may perish, deeds may be forgotten
But he who has Tao has all eternity[1]   — *Tao Te Ching*

Laozi calls on us to "quiet the restlessness of the mind" and "become totally empty." Then we experience the transcendental field he calls Tao. Everything good follows from this, he says: enlightenment, a "vision of oneness," universal love, and immortality. Missing this leads to disaster.

༃

A mind free of thought,
merged within itself,
   Beholds the essence of the Tao
A mind filled with thought,
   identified with its own perceptions,
   beholds the mere forms of this world[2]   — *Tao Te Ching*

We experience the transcendental field, Laozi states, only by moving beyond thought. His description of the mind "merged within itself" suggests the self-referral nature of this state, consciousness aware of itself alone.

༃

> Where there is silence
> one finds peace
> When there is silence
> one finds the anchor of the universe within himself[3]
>
> — *Tao Te Ching*

In this silent consciousness, we experience not merely inner peace but "the anchor of the universe," an expressive term for the unified field of natural law.

☙

> To obtain Tao, reduce daily
> Reduce and reduce again
> until all action is reduced to non-action
> Then no one is left
> Nothing is done
> yet nothing is left undone[4]
>
> — *Tao Te Ching*

Transcending involves a reduction of mental and physiological activity, until we are left in pure consciousness, the simplest form of awareness, from where, Maharishi has said, one does nothing and accomplishes everything.

☙

Laozi describes the experience of unbounded awareness this brings:

> The superior person settles her mind as the universe settles the stars in the sky.
> By connecting her mind with the subtle origin, she calms it.
> Once calmed, it naturally expands, and ultimately her mind becomes
> as vast and immeasurable as the night sky.[5]
>
> — *Hua Hu Ching*

■ *Also see Laozi in Chapter 5 (Cosmic Consciousness) and Chapter 7 (Unity Consciousness).*

THE BUDDHA
c. 563–c. 483 BCE • NEPAL & INDIA

▪ *We know about the Buddha's life chiefly through legends, written down several centuries after he lived. Born Siddartha Gautama in present-day Nepal, he was a prince who lived an opulent life, shielded by his father, King Suddhodana, from the world's travails. At 29 he traveled out from the palace and, encountering an old man, was informed that all people, himself included, would eventually grow old. He left the palace, renouncing wealth and family, and became a wandering monk, seeking a path to end suffering. Eventually he realized the so-called* Middle Way — *seeking moderation and avoiding the extremes of self-mortification and self-indulgence. At 35, meditating beneath a bodhi tree, he awoke to the true nature of reality, Nirvana. He became known as the Buddha, the "one who has awakened." Collections of teachings attributed to him were passed down orally and first committed to writing about 400 years later.*

"Kappa," said the Master, "for the sake of those people stuck in the middle of the river of being, overwhelmed by death and decay, I will tell you where to find solid ground.

"There is an island, an island which you cannot go beyond. It is a place of nothingness, a place of non-possession and of non-attachment. It is the total end of death and decay, and this is why I call it Nibbana [the extinguished, the cool].

"There are people who . . . have realized this and are completely cooled here and now. They do not become slaves working for Mara, for Death; they cannot fall into his power."[1]   — *Sutta-Nipata*

The *Sutta-Nipata* is one of the earliest Buddhist scriptures. Here the Buddha describes a transcendental field, beyond diversity and change. Those who experience this move beyond death and are "completely cooled." The Buddha often uses the images of heat and fire to signify dissatisfaction, stress, and suffering, and images of shade and coolness to signify pure transcendence.

༄

But it is only when all outward appearances are gone that there is left that one principle of life which exists independently of all external phenomena. It is the fire that burns in the eternal light, when the fuel is expended and the flame is extinguished; for that fire is neither in the flame nor in the fuel, nor yet inside either of the two, but above, beneath, and everywhere.[2]
— *Mahaparinirvana (Supreme Nirvana) Sutra*

In this passage, also from one of the earliest texts, the Buddha explains that when one transcends all relative values, one experiences the essential value of life, eternal and all-pervading.

༄

If you realize the self in your inmost consciousness, it will appear in its purity. This is the womb of wonder, which is not the realm of those who live only by reason.

Pure in its own nature and free from the categories of finite and infinite, Universal Mind is the undefiled wonder, which is wrongly apprehended by many.[3] — *Lankavatara Sutra*

Deep within us, the Buddha tells us, we find consciousness in its pure state, unbounded, universal, untouched by anything.

The Buddhist literature has given this "inmost consciousness" a rich variety of names: *the harbor of refuge, the cool cave, the island amidst the floods, the place of bliss, emancipation, liberation, safety, the supreme, the transcendent, the uncreated, the tranquil, the home of peace, the calm, the end of suffering, the medicine for all evil, the unshaken, the ambrosia, the immaterial, the imperishable, the abiding, the farther shore, the unending, the supreme joy, the ineffable, the detachment, the holy city,* and others.⁴

And the Buddhist literature furnishes many descriptions of how, when the mind becomes still, this inner field opens to one's experience:

> The one who has entered a solitary place,
> Whose mind is calm and who sees the way,
> To that one comes insight and truth
> And rapturous joy transcending any other.⁵   — *Dhammapada*

❦

> A questioner asked the Buddha: "I would like to know about the state of peace, the state of solitude and of quiet detachment. How does a person become calm, independent, and not wanting to grasp at anything?" . . .
>
> [The Buddha replied]: "The person should look for peace within and not depend on it in any other place. For when a person is quiet within, the self cannot be found. There are no waves in the depths of the ocean, it is still and unbroken."⁶   — *Sutta Nipata*

We find peace within, the Buddha says, when we transcend and the mind becomes still and achieves the status of unbounded wholeness.

❦

> There is a sphere where there is neither earth nor water nor heat nor air, for it is beyond the field of matter; nor is it the sphere of infinite space, or consciousness, for it is beyond the field of mind. There is not the condition of nothingness, neither is there the state of this world or another world, nor sun nor moon. This is the uncreated.
>
> This condition I call neither arising nor passing away, neither dying nor being born. It is without form and without change. It is the eternal, which never originates and never passes away. To find it is the end of sorrow.⁷   — *Udanna Sutta*

Here again we are told about a field beyond all relative values, uncreated and eternal — the transcendental field. The final sentence, eight short words, tells us that we can experience it directly and derive infinite benefit.

In the *Mahaparinirvana Sutra* the Buddha proclaims, "Every being has Buddha-Nature. This is the Self."[8]

■ *Also see the Buddha in Chapter 5 (Cosmic Consciousness), Chapter 6 (God Consciousness), and Chapter 7 (Unity Consciousness).*

PLATO
428–348 BCE • GREECE

■ *Plato, the father of Western philosophy, has influenced every era in the 2,300 years since he lived. He has been praised as "the substance of Western thought," "one of the supreme poets of the world," and "the paragon of excellence emulated by high-minded men for over two thousand years."[1] The student of Socrates and teacher of Aristotle, he founded in 387 BCE what some regard as the first university. His Academy was devoted to systematic philosophical and scientific research in natural history, biology, botany, mathematics, and law and government, and it lasted as an institution for 900 years. Though he considered this his most important work, his greatness in history has rested on his philosophical writings. Together with Socrates and Aristotle, he laid the philosophical foundations of Western culture.* IMAGE: *Sculpture by Silanion, installed at Plato's Academy in 348 BCE.*

But when returning into herself . . . [the soul] passes into the other world, the region of purity, and eternity, and immortality, and unchangeableness, which are her kindred, and with them she ever lives, when she is by herself and is not let or hindered; then she ceases from her erring ways, and being in communion with the unchanging is unchanging. And this state of the soul is called wisdom....

The soul is in the very likeness of the divine, and immortal, and intellectual, and uniform, and indissoluble, and unchangeable.[2]

— *Phaedo*

Plato describes a concrete human experience, not a mere philosophical concept. But this experience does not take place in the outer world of sense perception. "Returning into herself" suggests the settling of awareness that leads to Transcendental Consciousness. Pure consciousness, the innermost level of the mind, is pure, eternal, immortal, and unchangeable, precisely as Plato describes.

Plato calls this state *wisdom*, suggestive of Maharishi's term *pure knowledge*. Plato elsewhere refers to this level as *the Good* and as *the Beautiful*. Direct experience of the Good, he says, is the key to wisdom and virtue in life.

༃

Plato describes this experience in other dialogues. Here is the famous speech given by Socrates's teacher, Diotima of Mantinea:

And turning his eyes toward the open sea of beauty, he will find in such contemplation the seed of the most fruitful discourse and the loftiest thought, and reap a golden harvest of philosophy, until, confirmed and strengthened, he will come upon one single form of knowledge, the knowledge of the beauty I am about to speak of.

And here, she said, you must follow me as closely as you can.

Whoever has been initiated so far in the mysteries of Love and has viewed all these aspects of the beautiful in due succession, is at last drawing near the final revelation. And now, Socrates, there bursts upon him that wondrous vision which is the very soul of the beauty he has toiled so long for. It is an everlasting loveliness which neither comes nor goes, which neither flowers nor fades, for such beauty is the same on every hand, the same then as now, here as there, this way as that way, the same to every worshipper as it is to every other.

Nor will his vision of the beautiful take the form of a face, or of hands, or of anything that is of the flesh. It will be neither words, nor knowledge, nor a something that exists in something else, such as a living creature, or the earth, or the heavens, or anything that is — but subsisting of itself and by itself in an eternal oneness, while every lovely thing partakes of it in such sort that, however much the parts may wax and wane, it will be neither more nor less, but still the same inviolable whole....

And if, my dear Socrates, Diotima went on, man's life is ever worth the living, it is when he has attained this vision of the very soul of beauty....

But if it were given to man to gaze on beauty's very self — unsullied, unalloyed, and freed from the mortal taint that haunts the frailer loveliness of flesh and blood — if, I say, it were given to man to see the heavenly beauty face to face, would you call his, she asked me, an unenviable life, whose eyes had been opened to the vision, and who had gazed upon it in true contemplation until it had become his own forever?

And remember, she said, that it is when he looks upon beauty's visible presentment, and only then, that a man will be quickened with the true, and not the seeming, virtue — for it is virtue's self that quickens him, not virtue's semblance. And when he has brought forth and reared this perfect virtue, he shall be called the friend of god, and if ever it is given to man to put on immortality, it shall be given to him.[3]
— *Symposium*

Again Plato describes a concrete, personal experience involving an inward direction of awareness. What does this "inward sight" see? "An everlasting loveliness," transcendental, beyond time, space, and change. Plato describes it as "subsisting of itself and by itself in an eternal oneness" (suggesting self-referral consciousness), "while every lovely thing partakes of it" (suggesting the unified field, the source of all creation). Point by point, Plato's description applies to Transcendental Consciousness.

ZHUANGZI
369–286 BCE • CHINA

Zhuangzi (Chuang Tzu) is esteemed alongside Laozi as a founder of Daoism. He often refers to the "sages of old," suggesting the source of his knowledge is even more ancient than he is. Almost nothing is known of his personal life. But his writings (known as the Zhuangzi*) show him to be a brilliant, original thinker. He is concerned with how to live in a world of suffering and absurdity. But where other schools proposed political changes to improve individual and social life, Zhuangzi proposed a different solution: bring yourself into harmony with the Tao, the Way, nature's intelligence, and the world will change automatically. After more than 2,000 years, his writings remain remarkably contemporary — in the issues he confronts, the solutions he proposes, and the humor he employs.*

Why don't you try wandering with me to the Palace of Not-Even-Anything — identity and concord will be the basis of our discussions and they will never come to an end, never reach exhaustion. Why not join with me in inaction, in tranquil quietude, in hushed purity, in harmony and leisure? Already my will is vacant and blank. I go nowhere and don't know how far I've gotten. I go and come and don't know where to stop. I've already been there and back, and I don't know when the journey is done. I ramble and relax in unbordered vastness; Great Knowledge enters in, and I don't know where it will ever end.[1] — *Zhuangzi*

Zhuangzi's "Palace of Not-Even-Anything" is pure consciousness, silent and unbounded. His "Great Knowledge" is pure knowledge, pure knowingness, the product of consciousness knowing itself alone.

The repose of the Sage is not what the world calls repose. His repose is the result of his mental attitude. All creation could not disturb his equilibrium: hence his repose. When water is still, it is like a mirror, reflecting the beard and the eyebrows. It gives the accuracy of the water-level, and the philosopher makes it his model. And if water thus derives lucidity from stillness, how much more the faculties of the mind! The mind of the Sage, being in repose, becomes the mirror of the universe, the speculum [reflector] of all creation.[2]

Zhuangzi describes a state of perfect mental quietude and clarity. Then the mind reflects the whole creation, he says, suggesting the equivalence between pure consciousness and the unified field of natural law.

Also see Zhuangzi in Chapter 5 (Cosmic Consciousness).

JESUS CHRIST
7–2 BCE – 30–36 CE • ISRAEL

Jesus of Nazareth was born in Roman Judaea, north of Jerusalem in present-day Israel. The traditional story of his life is familiar to the two billion Christians worldwide: He was born of a virgin, was baptized by John the Baptist, performed a variety of miracles, was crucified in Jerusalem by order of the Roman governor Pontius Pilate, died sacrificially to atone for humanity's sins, rose from the dead, and ascended into heaven. After his death he came to be known as Jesus Christ (a title meaning the anointed one). Jesus is regarded by most Christians as the Son of God, the physical incarnation of God, and the savior of humanity, and his life is considered the model of virtue. Jesus is also considered a major prophet of God in Islam. IMAGE: *Detail from Deësis mosaic, Hagia Sophia, Istanbul (1271)*

Throughout his ministry Jesus emphasizes *the kingdom* — the *kingdom of heaven*, as he usually calls it in the gospel of Matthew, the *kingdom of God* in Mark and Luke. Through a series of parables, he compares the kingdom of heaven to a treasure hidden in a field, where the person who discovers the treasure sells everything he has to purchase the field; to a costly pearl for which a merchant likewise sells everything to purchase; to a net cast into the sea that gathers every kind of fish; to a mustard seed, the smallest of seeds, which grows into a large tree that attracts the "birds of the air"; to a seed planted in fertile soil; to a small amount of yeast that permeates and leavens the entire loaf.

The message is unmistakable: The kingdom of heaven is not something that awaits us only after death — it involves an experience that can transform life here and now, a thoroughgoing spiritual awakening, vastly more valuable than anything else in life.

Where is the kingdom located? Jesus is unequivocal:

One day the Pharisees asked Jesus, "When will the Kingdom of God begin?" Jesus replied, "The Kingdom of God isn't ushered in with visible signs. You won't be able to say, 'It has begun here in this place or there in that part of the country.' *For the Kingdom of God is within you."*[1*] — Luke 17:20–21

Experiencing the kingdom of God, Jesus asserts, should be our highest priority:

But seek ye first the kingdom of God, and his righteousness; and all these things shall be added unto you. — Matthew 6:33

Through this inner experience, in other words, our daily needs will be met and our desires supported.

How is this experience achieved? Jesus gives clues in his Sermon on the Mount, which we can understand afresh with our knowledge of transcending:

■ *Blessed are the poor in spirit: for theirs is the kingdom of heaven* (Matthew 5:3) — Become "poor," let go of everything, transcend all things external, allow the mind to become still, and the kingdom of heaven will open to you.

■ *Blessed are the pure in heart: for they shall see* God (Matthew 5:8) — Purify mind and body of the stress that blocks the expression of your full potential, and the experience of the divine naturally results.

In the decades following Jesus's life, dozens of gospels were in circulation, collections of his sayings and stories of his life. Many were lost or destroyed, and as what was to become the New Testament took shape over subsequent centuries, only four, known as the canonical gospels, were incorporated.

One of the major gospels not included, sometimes known as "the fifth gospel," is the *Gospel of Thomas*. This book was among twelve leather-bound papyrus manuscripts found buried in a sealed jar by a local peasant in 1945 in upper Egypt near the town of Nag Hammadi. The *Gospel of Thomas*, compiled at about the same time the Gospel of John was written, comprises 114 sayings attributed to Jesus, about half of which are found in the canonical

---

* For a discussion of alternate translations of this verse, see Note 2, page 517.

gospels, the rest previously unknown. Writes Bart Ehrman, the historian of early Christianity, "The Gospel of Thomas may well be the most outstanding discovery of Christian antiquity in modern times."[2] It may have been assembled before any of the four traditional canonical gospels and may have provided source material for the author of the Gospel of Mark, the first of the canonical gospels to be written.[3] The Gospel of Thomas emphasizes and elaborates on the theme of Luke 17:21, that the kingdom of God is within you.

The book opens with these words: "These are the hidden sayings that the living Jesus spoke and Judas Thomas the Twin recorded." (Judas Thomas was regarded in some early groups to be Jesus's twin brother.)

> Jesus said, "If your leaders say to you, 'Look, the kingdom is in heaven,' then the birds of heaven will precede you. If they say to you, 'It is in the sea,' then the fish will precede you. Rather, the kingdom is inside you and it is outside you.
>
> "When you know yourselves, then you will be known, and you will understand that you are children of the living father. But if you do not know yourselves, then you dwell in poverty, and you are poverty."[4]
>
> — *The Gospel of Thomas*

To experience the kingdom of heaven inside you, Jesus says, "know yourselves" (the transcendental Self). Then you will realize you are "children of the living father" — that is, an expression of this all-pervading field of transcendental intelligence out of which the universe is born.

༃

> [He said to them], "There is light within a person of light, and it shines on the whole world. If it does not shine, it is dark."[5]
>
> — *The Gospel of Thomas*

> Jesus said, "If you bring forth what is within you, what you bring forth will save you. If you do not bring forth what is within you, what you do not bring forth will destroy you."[6]
>
> — *The Gospel of Thomas*

About the first verse, Princeton Biblical scholar Elaine Pagels writes, "In other words, one either discovers the light within that illuminates 'the whole universe,' or lives in darkness, within and without."⁷ The second echoes the first.

⁂

"So while you are walking with me, though you do lack understanding, already you have obtained knowledge and you will be called one who knows oneself. For those who have not known themselves have known nothing, but those who have known themselves already have acquired knowledge about the depth of the universe."⁸

— *The Book of Thomas*

This passage, from another collection of Jesus's sayings found at Nag Hammadi, says that knowing the Self brings "knowledge about the depth of the universe," suggesting the equivalence of pure consciousness and the unified field.

⁂

In *The Gospel of Philip*, another Nag Hammadi text, Jesus says this:

[The master] said, "Go into your room, shut the door behind you, and pray to your father who is in secret" — that is, the one who is innermost. What is innermost is the fullness, and there is nothing further within. And this is what they call uppermost.⁹

— *The Gospel of Philip*

Again Jesus highlights the value of experiencing the innermost realm of consciousness, which he calls "the fullness" and the "uppermost."

A long tradition of Christian saints and writers, stretching across the last two millennia, has subsequently left us descriptions of the fourth state as well as higher states of consciousness.

▪ *Also see Jesus Christ in Chapter 5 (Cosmic Consciousness), Chapter 6 (God Consciousness), and Chapter 7 (Unity Consciousness). For other experiences of Transcendental Consciousness from the Christian tradition, see St. Augustine, Meister Eckhart, Angela of Foligno, St. Teresa of Ávila, St. John of the Cross, Howard Thurman, and Thomas Merton, in this chapter.*

MARCUS AURELIUS
121–180 • ITALY

■ *He was the noblest of all Roman emperors. Ruling for nearly 20 years, he symbolizes the Golden Age of the Roman Empire, when an ethical philosopher-king beloved by the people guided a thoroughly organized world nation. His reign, marked by justice and moderation, was Rome's most prosperous. Though an outstanding military leader, he deeply desired peace. He was magnanimous towards enemies, strove to eliminate corruption, and freed slaves at every opportunity. Today he is more famous as a philosopher than a ruler. He kept a daily diary that expresses his Stoic philosophy. Known as* The Meditations, *it is one of the great books of all time. John Stuart Mill, the British philosopher and economist, praised its "infinite tenderness."*

Men seek retreats for themselves in country places, on beaches and mountains, and you yourself are wont to long for such retreats, but that is altogether unenlightened when it is possible at any hour you please to find a retreat within yourself. For nowhere can a man withdraw to a more untroubled quietude than in his own soul, especially a man who has within him things of which the contemplation will at once put him perfectly at ease, and by ease I mean nothing other than orderly conduct. Grant yourself this withdrawal continually, and refresh yourself.[1]   — *The Meditations*

"Retreat within yourself," Marcus advises, and find quietude, ease, and refreshment. Time and again he emphasizes diving within for this experience:

Dig down within yourself, where the source of goodness is ever ready to gush forth, if you always dig deeply.[2]

THE HERMETIC WRITINGS
2ND & 3RD CENTURIES • EGYPT

■ *The authors of the Hermetic writings, or* Hermetica, *are unknown. Gathering a few students around them over the course of perhaps two centuries, they occasionally wrote down the gist of a talk, or a student did this for them. The writing would then be shared with others in the group or with other groups, and what survived is known as the* Hermetica. *The authors recognized no scripture, had no rituals or sacraments, and remained uninfluenced by Jewish, Christian, and earlier Egyptian thought. They started fresh, from their own experience. In the* Hermetica *we come closer to the Upanishads than perhaps any writings in the West.*

For it is a property of the Good that it becomes known to him who is able to see it. . . . It shines forth much or little, according as he who gazes on it is able to receive the inflow of the incorporeal radiance. . . . It is full of immortal life.

Then only will you see it, when you cannot speak of it; for the knowledge of it is deep silence, and suppression of all the senses. He who has apprehended the beauty of the Good can apprehend nothing else; he who has seen it can see nothing else; he cannot hear speech about aught else; he cannot move his body at all; he forgets all bodily sensations and all bodily movements, and is still. But the beauty of the Good bathes his mind in light, and takes all his soul up to itself, and draws it forth from the body, and changes the whole man into eternal substance.[1]

The *Hermetica* authors, like Plato before and Plotinus after, were concerned with "the Good," not merely as an intellectual ideal but a reality open to experience. One experiences the Good in "deep silence," beyond sensory perception, in a state of pure inner wakefulness where "the beauty of the Good bathes his mind in light." The *Hermetica* authors describe the Good as follows:

> For we can never reach the farther boundary of the Good; it is limitless, and without end; and in itself, it is without beginning, though to us it seems to begin when we get knowledge of it. . . . The Good cannot be seen by things manifest; for it has no form or shape.[2]

> The divine mind is wholly of like nature with eternity. It is motionless in itself, but though stable, is self-moving; it is holy, and incorruptible, and everlasting, and has all attributes yet higher, if higher there be, that can be assigned to the eternal life of the supreme god, that life which stands fast in absolute reality. It is wholly filled with all things imperceptible to sense, and with all-embracing knowledge; it is, so to speak, consubstantial with God.[3]

The Good, or divine mind, is unbounded, eternal, a field of "absolute reality" and "all-embracing knowledge" — and open to experience:

> If any man then has an incorporeal eye, let him go forth from the body to behold the Beautiful, let him fly up and float aloft, not seeking to see shape or color, but rather that by which these things are made, that which is quiet and calm, stable and changeless, . . . that which is one, that which issues from itself and is contained in itself, that which is like nothing but itself.[4]   — *Hermetica*

"Fly up and float aloft" — transcend ordinary waking state experience and unite with the Beautiful, the silent, nonchanging source of everything. Where do we find it? The Hermetic writings tell us: "Call yourself back then to yourself, O soul, and seek in yourself all that you ought to get knowledge of."[5]

▪ *Also see the Hermetic Writings in Chapter 6 (God Consciousness) and Chapter 7 (Unity Consciousness).*

PLOTINUS
205–270 • EGYPT & ITALY

Born to Greek-speaking parents in Alexandria, Egypt, Plotinus longed for more than book learning — he wanted experiential knowledge of the "Good." Thinking this knowledge lay in India, he joined Gordian's expedition against Persia, in 242, hoping to reach India and find someone who could guide him further. When they were attacked in Turkey, he returned with the Roman legions to Rome, where he spent the remainder of his life. Renowned for his wisdom, he became counselor to the emperor and the emperor's wife, and he acted as guardian to orphaned children. Plotinus is described as "the one great genius in an age singularly barren of greatness."[1]

The wise man recognizes the idea of the Good within him. This he develops by withdrawal into the Holy Place of his own soul. He who does not understand how the soul contains the Beautiful within itself, seeks to realize beauty without, by laborious production. His aim should rather be to concentrate and simplify, and so to expand his being; instead of going out into the Manifold, to forsake it for the One, and so to float upwards towards the divine fount of being whose stream flows within him.

You ask, how can we know the Infinite? I answer, not by reason.... You can only apprehend the Infinite ... by entering into a state in which you are your finite self no longer, in which the divine essence is communicated to you. This is Ecstasy. It is the liberation of your mind from its finite consciousness. Like only can apprehend like; when you thus cease to be finite, you become one with the Infinite. In the reduction of your soul to its simplest self, its divine essence, you realize this Union — this Identity.

But this sublime condition is not of permanent duration. It is only now and then that we can enjoy this elevation. . . . I myself have realized it but three times as yet, and Porphyry hitherto not once. All that tends to purify and elevate the mind will assist you in this attainment, and facilitate the approach and the recurrence of these happy intervals. . . . [At these times] we stand in the immediate presence of the Infinite, who shines out as from the deeps of the soul.[2]

— Letter to Flaccus

"Withdrawal into the Holy Place of his own soul" beautifully describes transcending. There, in our "simplest self," Plotinus says, we experience ecstasy and liberation from "finite consciousness." "Like only can apprehend like," he says — you can experience this inner, infinite field only by becoming one with it.

༃

This is not a journey for the feet; the feet bring us only from land to land; nor need you think of coach or ship to carry you away; all this order of things you must set aside and refuse to see: you must close the eyes and call instead upon another vision which is to be waked within you, a vision, the birthright of all, which few turn to use. . . .

Withdraw into yourself and look. . . . When you know that you have become this perfect work, when you are self-gathered in the purity of your being, nothing now remaining that can shatter that inner unity, nothing from without clinging to the authentic man, when you find yourself wholly true to your essential nature, wholly that only veritable Light which is not measured by space, not narrowed to any circumscribed form . . . but ever unmeasurable as something greater than all measure and more than all quantity — when you perceive that you have grown to this, you are now become very vision . . . you need a guide no longer. . . .

Therefore let each become godlike and each beautiful who cares to see God and Beauty.³   — *Enneads*

Plotinus describes turning within and experiencing one's "essential nature," an inner unity that is pure, infinite, and unbounded, the authentic self.

■ *Also see the Plotinus in Chapter 5 (Cosmic Consciousness) and Chapter 7 (Unity Consciousness).*

ST. AUGUSTINE
354–430 • ALGERIA

■ *St. Augustine is one of history's towering intellectual geniuses. Though he lived a hedonistic life for a while as a teen, he went on to a successful career as a teacher of rhetoric, first in his hometown of Thagaste, then in Carthage, then in Rome. Rising in prominence, he was invited to speak before the emperor. At 33 he converted to Christianity, then became a priest and later bishop of Hippo (now the Algerian city of Annaba). He was a spellbinding preacher; more than 350 of his sermons have been preserved. He was also a prolific author, writing about philosophy, theology, psychology, history, and political theory. His books greatly influenced the development of Western Christianity, philosophy, and education. Thousands of studies of his life and thought have been published. His* Confessions *has remained a popular and influential work for 1,600 years.*

And being admonished by these books to return into myself, I entered into my inward soul, guided by thee. . . . And I entered, and with the eye of my soul — such as it was — saw above the same eye of my soul and above my mind the Immutable Light. It was not the common light, which all flesh can see; nor was it simply a greater one of the same sort, as if the light of day were to grow brighter and brighter, and flood all space. It was not like that light, but different, yea, very different from all earthly light whatever. Nor was it above my mind in the same way as oil is above water, or heaven above earth, but it was higher, because it made me, and I was below it, because I was made by it. He who knows the Truth knows that Light, and he who knows it knows eternity. Love knows it, O Eternal Truth and True Love and Beloved Eternity![1] — *Confessions*

In this famous passage, Augustine tells us he experienced the innermost part of himself, transcendental to ordinary waking consciousness, "higher than I." Like so many others in this chapter, he holds this to be the realm of "eternal truth and true love and beloved eternity."

SHANKARA

700? – 750? • INDIA

Born in present-day Kerala, on the southwestern coast of India, Shankara ("bestower of happiness" in Sanskrit) is said to have mastered the four major Vedic texts by the age of eight — at which point he left home to become a sanyasi *(recluse)*, traveling northward in quest of a guru. He soon began to attract disciples himself. He traveled throughout India and as far as Kashmir, entering into discussions with noted philosophers and scholars wherever he went. He wrote commentaries on the ten major Upanishads, the Brahma Sutras, *and the* Bhagavad-Gita. *He established four* mathas, or seats, of Vedic learning, in the north, east, south, and west areas of India and placed one of his four chief disciples at the head of each one. To this day the heads of these four mathas hold the title of Shankaracharya ("the learned Shankara"). IMAGE: *Shankara with his four main disciples.*

Now I will relate to you the nature of the Supreme Self, knowing which a person is freed from boundaries and attains *Kaivalya*, Unity.

There is something eternal within, upon which the notion of "I" depends. It is the witness of the three (states of consciousness)....

It knows everything that transpires within waking, dreaming, and deep sleep, regardless of whether there are fluctuations of mind. This is the "I."...

It pervades the entire universe but nothing pervades it. It is effulgent by nature, and its splendor illumines everything....

This is the inner Self, the silent witness, the ancient, the experience of eternal, infinite bliss, ever a state of unity, pure knowledge, on whose command speech and the *pranas** fulfill their functions.

Here in the purity within oneself, in the secret place of the intellect — in the unmanifest pure consciousness — the Self, of beauteous splendor, shines like the sun on high, illumining the entire universe through its own effulgence.

It is the knower of the fluctuations of the mind and ego, and of the activities of the body, senses, and *pranas* — it does not act nor modify itself in any way, permeating them as fire permeates a heated iron.

Eternal, it is neither born nor does it die, nor does it grow nor diminish nor modify itself. It is self-sufficient and does not dissolve when the body dies, just like the space within a pot (when it is broken).

The supreme Self — whose nature is pure knowingness, separate from Nature and its expressions — indiscriminately illumines

---

* *Prana* is usually defined as *breath*, but Maharishi offers a deeper level of understanding, defining it as "the nature of Being, the motivating force of creation; it is the basic force of the mind" — in other words, as the basic force of life responsible for all activity throughout the universe.[1]

every aspect of the universe, whether positive or negative. It is the witness of the intellect, and expresses itself as the "I" within waking, dreaming, and sleep.

With the mind established in that state of total orderliness, know directly, from the purified intellect, that this Self within you is "I." Established in the Self, with *Brahm* as your own nature, cross the boundless ocean of mundane, unenlightened existence, whose waves are birth and death, and fulfill the goal of life.[2]

— *Crest Jewel of Discrimination (Vivekachudamani)*

Shankara describes the "Supreme Self" as a field deep within, unmanifest, eternal, unbounded, a field of unity and bliss, the ground not only of individual life but of the entire universe. He makes clear at the end that the mind can experience and become established in this transcendental reality, thereby gaining enlightenment and fulfilling the purpose of life.

Shankara uses the term *Brahm* to refer to the underlying, all-pervading transcendental field, as we saw at the end of the above passage. He returns to this term in this next passage:

That which is far beyond family, morality, race, and lineage; devoid of name, form, quality, or fault; transcendental to place, time, and objects of the senses — you are that *Brahm*. Awaken it within yourself.

That transcendental reality beyond the range of all speech, whose realm is open to the vision of pure knowingness, the element that is nothing but pure consciousness existing from eternity — you are that *Brahm*. Awaken it within yourself.

That which is untouched by the six afflictions of human life (hunger and thirst, decay and death, grief and illusion); which dwells within the heart of the Yogis; which cannot be appreciated through the sense organs; which is faultless and unknowable through the intellect — you are that *Brahm*. Awaken it within yourself.

That which is the self-sufficient foundation of the entire illusory world; which is beyond truth and falsehood, without parts, without form, incomparable — you are that *Brahm*. Awaken it within yourself.

That which is imperishable; which is free from birth, growth, transformation, decay, sickness, and destruction; which is the cause of the creation and destruction of the universe — you are that *Brahm*. Awaken it within yourself.

That which is without differences, unchanging, silent like an ocean without waves, eternally free, a state of Unity — you are that *Brahm*. Awaken it within yourself.

Though a state of Unity, it is the cause of diversity, the cause that sets aside all other causes. It is self-sufficient, beyond cause and effect. You are that *Brahm*. Awaken it within yourself.

That which is unchanging, infinite, imperishable, and yet beyond the distinction between what is perishable and imperishable; which is eternal, unchanging bliss, pure — you are that *Brahm*. Awaken it within yourself.

Appearing diversely due to delusion, taking on names and forms, qualities and transformations, it is self-sufficient, ever-unchanging like gold. You are that *Brahm*. Awaken it within yourself.

That which shines alone, greater than the greatest, whose joy is only within, the Self. It is existence, consciousness, bliss — eternal and imperishable. You are that *Brahm*. Awaken it within yourself.[3]

— *Crest Jewel of Discrimination (Vivekachudamani)*

Building force with recurring cadences, Shankara exhorts us to awaken within ourselves the field which, he declares, is our essential reality — an ocean of pure consciousness, pure knowingness, infinite, eternal, the unchanging source of all change, pure bliss.

In this next passage Shankara explicitly describes Transcendental Consciousness, which he terms *Samadhi* — the experience of pure consciousness.

In *Samadhi*, the wise man realizes *Brahm* in his heart. It is eternal wakefulness, absolute bliss, without equal, beyond all boundaries, eternally free, silent, unbounded like the sky, without parts, changeless.

In *Samadhi*, the wise man realizes *Brahm* in his heart. It is beyond nature and its modifications, transcendental to thought, the essence of all alike, incomparable, far from any connection with mental conception, revealed through the sounds of Veda, eternal, renowned.

In *Samadhi*, the wise man realizes *Brahm* in his heart. It is without age, immortal, the beginning and end of all realities, resembling the silent ocean, beyond name, in which qualities and transformations have come to rest, eternal, peaceful, a state of Unity. . . .

Awaken the Self that abides within you. It is free of all attributes, a state of Unity, existence, consciousness, and bliss. Then partake of the path no more. . . .

The saint of established wisdom is he who comes to eternal bliss, absorbed in *Brahm* alone, beyond change, beyond activity.

Wisdom is regarded as absorption in the purity of the oneness of *Atma* and *Brahm*. It is beyond transformation and its nature is entirely consciousness. He who rests in that is said to be of established wisdom.[4]

— *The Crest Jewel of Discrimination (Vivekachudamani)*

▪ *Also see Shankara in Chapter 7 (Unity Consciousness).*

MILAREPA

1052–1135 • TIBET

■ *Born to a wealthy noble family, Jetsun Milarepa set out at an early age to find a master and gain enlightenment. The teacher he finally found tested his worthiness: he commanded Milarepa to build one house after another on an isolated mountain, then tear them down again. Milarepa was at last accepted and given the instruction he desired. He spent 12 years meditating in seclusion in a remote cave, finally attaining enlightenment (Vajradhara). Thereafter he traveled and taught. Renowned for his beautiful singing voice, he would often switch from speaking to singing spontaneously composed songs. His fame spread throughout Tibet and Nepal, and he is regarded today as Tibet's greatest poet, yogi, and Buddhist saint. His collected works, the* Mila Grubum, *or* The Hundred Thousand Songs of Milarepa, *is widely considered the outstanding masterpiece of Tibetan literature.*

When I practice Mahamudra,
I rest myself in the intrinsic state,
Relaxingly without distraction or effort,
In the realm of Voidness,
I rest myself with Illumination.
In the realm of Blissfulness,
I rest myself in Awareness.
In the realm of Non-thought,
I rest myself with a naked mind.
In manifestations and activities,
I rest myself in Samadhi,
Meditating on the Mind-Essence in such a manner

Numerous understandings and convictions arise.
By Self-illumination all is accomplished without effort.
Looking no more for Enlightenment,
I am extremely happy.
Free from both hope and fear,
I feel very joyful.
Oh, what a pleasure it is to enjoy
Confusion when as Wisdom it appears![1]

Milarepa effortlessly experiences a state of pure consciousness, "the realm of Voidness," as he calls it, blissful pure awareness beyond thought — the classic state of *samadhi*.

༈

Now examine yourself closely:
You yourself have no color or form.
If sent you won't go. If restrained you don't stay.
If looked for you can't be seen.
If grasped for you can't be caught.
. . . .
Return to your natural state without effort or distraction.
Know the way of such relaxation, fortunate ones.[2]

Milarepa describes the nature of the true Self — transcendental, beyond perception, yet open to experience.

SUN BU-ER

1119–1182 • CHINA

> Sun Bu-er, who lived in eastern China, was said to be beautiful, intelligent, and wealthy. She married and had three children, and then around age 50 began to devote herself to Daoist practice. She and her husband became students of Wang Zhe, a founder of modern Daoism. Becoming a priestess and teacher herself, she founded her own school, the Purity and Tranquility School, and set down her teachings in verse. According to legend, she not only "attained the Dao" (reached enlightenment) but achieved immortality, rising to heaven in her physical body in broad daylight. She was named one of the "Seven Immortals" of Daoism and is a beloved figure in Chinese folklore.

All things finished,
You sit still in a little niche.
The light body rides on violet energy,
The tranquil nature washes in a pure pond.
Original energy is unified, yin and yang are one;
The spirit is the same as the universe.
When the word is done, you pay court to the Jade Palace;
A long whistle gusts a misty gale.[1]

This poem describes the mind settling to a state of tranquility, where opposites are unified. The Jade Palace symbolizes pure awareness. When she says, "The spirit is the same as the universe," she indicates that pure consciousness is the essence of creation, the unified field.

The original reality is not something with form:
It is neither existent nor nonexistent.
If people can penetrate this principle,
Then they'll understand the pearl that unifies sense experience.²

Sun Bu-er describes the experience of the "original reality" and, in the last line, suggests the possibility of perceiving this reality in everything — foreshadowing Unity Consciousness.

ATTAR OF NISHAPUR
1145–1221 • IRAN

*He was little known during his lifetime and we know little of his life — yet the Persian poet Farid ud-Din Attar is today regarded as one of the greatest Muslim mystical writers and thinkers. Born in Nishapur, the son of a prosperous pharmacist, he became a pharmacist himself (*Attar *means the perfumer). It is said that his customers confided their difficulties to him and that, deeply touched, he eventually left his pharmacy to travel, journeying to Iraq, Syria, Saudi Arabia, Turkestan, and India, seeking out Sufi scholars and masters and then finally returning to his native town. A prolific writer, he wrote six major works of poetry as well as a prose work — a collection of biographies of famous Sufi saints. Not lacking in self-esteem, he regarded himself as the greatest poet Persia would ever have. Legend has it that toward the end of his life, he met Rūmī when Rūmī was still a boy and gave him a copy of his book* Asrar Nameh (The Book of Secrets).

Joy! joy! I triumph! now no more I know
Myself as simply me, I burn with love
Unto myself, and bury me in love.
The Center is within me and its wonder

Lies as a circle everywhere about me.
Joy! joy! no mortal thought can fathom me.
I am the merchant and the pearl at once.
Lo, Time and Space lie crouching at my feet.
Joy! joy! when I would revel in a rapture,
I plunge into myself and all things know.[1]

— "The Triumph of the Soul," from *Jawhar Al Dhat*

Attar describes an experience that profoundly inspires him. "I plunge into myself," he says — and there he finds his "Center," blissful, unbounded, beyond thought, time, and space. When he says he is "the merchant and the pearl at once," he metaphorically suggests that knower and known are unified, that consciousness is knower of itself.

■ *Also see Attar in Chapter 7 (Unity Consciousness).*

MUKTABAI
13TH CENTURY • INDIA

■ *Muktabai's parents died when she was four, and she and her three brothers survived by begging. Theirs was a life of great hardship, yet they all became renowned for their holiness, and Muktabai became one of India's greatest poets, known for her spiritual depth. At the age of 14, she became a disciple of Changdev, said to have been 1,400 years old at the time due to his Yogic powers — yet even he learned from her. She was one of the first poets of the Marathi language, spoken in Western India, and is considered a saint in the Hindu tradition.*

Where darkness is gone I live,
where I am happy.

I am not troubled by coming and going,
I am beyond all vision,
above all spheres.
His spirit lives in my soul.

Mukta says: He is my heart's only home.[1]

Muktabai sketches an experience "beyond all vision / above all sphere," where "darkness is gone" and she is happy.

ॐ

Though he has no form
my eyes saw him,

his glory is fire in my mind
that knows

his secret inner form
invented by the soul.

What is
beyond the mind

has no boundary.
In it our senses end.

Mukta says: Words cannot hold him
yet in him all words are.[2]

Muktabai expands on the features of pure consciousness: it is without form, without boundaries, beyond mind and senses — yet can be experienced.

RŪMĪ
1207–1273 • PERSIA & TURKEY

He has been described as "the most popular poet in America"—a Muslim teacher and scholar who lived 800 years ago. Jalāl al-Dīn Muhammad Rūmī is the greatest poet in the Persian language and one of the greatest in world literature. He was born in present-day Afghanistan, or possibly Tajikistan. Because the whole area was then Persia, most of which is present-day Iran, Iran celebrates Rūmī as its most illustrious poet. To escape the Mongol invasion into Central Asia, his father, a renowned scholar, moved the family westward into Turkey. Rūmī was a highly regarded teacher, the head of a university, a scholar, jurist, and theologian. He believed music, poetry, and sacred dance formed a path for knowing God. By his early thirties his disciples numbered in the thousands, including the king. They organized themselves as the Mevlevi order, the Whirling Dervishes. His poetry, over 70,000 verses, has shaped Muslim thought and literature and has been translated worldwide.

At times my state resembles sleep: a misguided person may think it is sleep.

Know that my eyes are asleep, (but) my heart is awake: know that my (seemingly) inactive form is (really) in action.

The Prophet said, "My eyes sleep, (but) my heart is not asleep to the Lord of created beings."

Your eyes are awake, and your heart is sunk in slumber; my eyes are asleep, (but) my heart is in (contemplation of) the opening of the door (of Divine grace).

My heart hath five senses other (than the physical): both the worlds (external and spiritual) are the stage (theatre) for the senses of the heart.

> Do not regard me from (the standpoint of) your infirmity: to you 'tis night, to me that same night is morningtide.
>
> To you 'tis prison, to me that prison is like a garden: to me the most absolute state of occupation (with the world) has become (a state of spiritual) freedom.
>
> Your feet are in the mud; to me the mud has become roses. You have mourning; I have feasting and drums.
>
> (Whilst) I am dwelling with you in some place on the earth, I am coursing over the seventh sphere (of Heaven). . . .
>
> 'Tis not that I am seated beside you, 'tis my shadow: my rank is higher than (the reach of) thoughts,
>
> Because I have passed beyond (all) thoughts, and have become a swift traveler outside (the region of) thought.
>
> I am the ruler of thought, not ruled (by it), because the builder is ruler over the building. . . .
>
> In the view of him that has not experienced (it) this is (mere) pretension; in the view of the inhabitants of the (spiritual) horizon, this is the reality.[1] — *The Mathnawi*

Rūmī describes the combination of heightened inner wakefulness and deep physical rest that distinguishes Transcendental Consciousness as a fourth major state of consciousness. Ordinary waking experience is like sleep in comparison: your eyes might be awake, but "your heart is sunk in slumber." For those who have experienced it, he says, this inner field is the self-evident reality, transforming life from a prison to a garden, from mud to roses.

In this next poem, Rūmī calls on us to turn within, to experience "the root of the root of your own soul."

> For ages you have come and gone
>   courting this delusion.
> For ages you have run from the pain
>   and forfeited the ecstasy.

So come, return to the root of the root
    of your own soul.

Although you appear in earthly form
Your essence is pure Consciousness.
You are the fearless guardian
    of Divine Light.
So come, return to the root of the root
    of your own soul.

When you lose all sense of self
    the bonds of a thousand chains will vanish.
Lose yourself completely,
Return to the root of the root
    of your own soul.

You descended from Adam, by the pure Word of God,
    but you turned your sight
    to the empty show of this world.
Alas, how can you be satisfied with so little?
So come, return to the root of the root
    of your own soul.

Why are you so enchanted by this world
when a mine of gold lies within you?
Open your eyes and come —
Return to the root of the root
    of your own soul.

You were born from the rays of God's Majesty
    when the stars were in their perfect place.
How long will you suffer from the blows

of a nonexistent hand?
So come, return to the root of the root
    of your own soul.

You are a ruby encased in granite.
How long will you deceive Us with this outer show?
O friend, We can see the truth in your eyes!
So come, return to the root of the root
    of your own soul.

After one moment with that glorious Friend
    you became loving, radiant, and ecstatic.
Your eyes were sweet and full of fire.
Come, return to the root of the root
    of your own soul.

Shams-e Tabriz, the King of the Tavern*
has handed you an eternal cup,
And God in all His glory is pouring the wine.
So come! Drink!
Return to the root of the root
    of your own soul.

Soul of all souls, life of all life — you are That.
Seen and unseen, moving and unmoving — you are That.
The road that leads to the City is endless;
Go without head and feet
    and you'll already be there.
What else could you be? — you are That.[2]

Also see Rūmī in Chapter 7 (Unity Consciousness).

---

* Refers to Rūmī's teacher and master, Shams-e Tabriz.

HADEWIJCH

c. 1220 – c. 1260 • BELGIUM

■ *Of Hadewijch's life we know only what she reveals in writings, which is very little. Even the years of her birth and death are uncertain. She read widely in literature, philosophy, and theology in several languages, indicating she was from a wealthy family, for that kind of education was rare even among men. She was probably a member of the Beguines, the Roman Catholic lay sisterhoods that formed in and around the Netherlands in the 13th and 14th centuries and cared for the poor, and she may have led such a group. Some apparently criticized her views and she may have been asked to leave — but she continued communicating with the community in letters and poems. Though she knew French and Latin, she wrote in her vernacular language, Middle Dutch. Today she is considered one of the outstanding Dutch poets, and her collected prose writing is one of only two existing prose works in Middle Dutch.*

All things are
too small for me:
I am so wide.
I have reached
for the uncreated
in eternal time.

I have experienced it.
It has opened me
wider than wide.
All else is too small for me;
you who are also there,
know this.[1]

Hadewijch describes the experience of unbounded awareness, pure consciousness, which she finds to be uncreated and eternal.

❧

In the immense eternity
Boundless in all dimensions
The soul is separated.
Dilated, saved,
Engulfed in the One.

Her thought,
In its silent chase,
Which makes it boundless,
All in all,
Will find again
The uncircumscribed Whole.[2]

As consciousness transcends all diversity, it experiences its own pure, unbounded nature as the "One," the "Whole" — Transcendental Consciousness.

❧

And in this Unity into which I was taken and in which I was enlightened, I understood this Essence and knew it more clearly than, by speech, reason, or sight, one can know anything that is knowable on this earth.

This seems truly wonderful but, although I say this, I am sure it does not astonish you. For divine words are something this world cannot understand. Enough words in Dutch can be found for all things on earth but, for what I want to express, there are words neither in Dutch nor in any other language.[3]

Hadewijch describes her transcendental experiences in exquisite language — but like many others concludes that her words fail.

ANGELA OF FOLIGNO

c. 1248–1309 • ITALY

■ *Born to a wealthy family in central Italy, a few miles from Assisi, Angela married at age 20 and lived a worldly life. She was described as "rich, proud, and beautiful."[1] At age 40, tragedy struck: she lost her mother, husband, and children. She redirected her life, giving away her possessions and joining a Franciscan order. She began to experience an inner transformation. As word of her saintliness spread, other Franciscan lay women gathered around her, and she established a new religious order, a community of women devoted to spiritual living and acts of charity. Her experiences of transformation, recounted to her confessor, were published as a book that became highly influential in Renaissance Italy. Angela is known as the "Mistress of Theologians."*

[O]f a sudden my soul is raised ... and I take in the whole world; and it seems to me that I am not on earth, but that I stand in heaven in God. And this most excellent state, in which I now am, is far above all the other states which I have experienced as yet; for it is of such fullness, and of such clearness, and certainty, and ennoblement, and enlargement, that I feel no other state approaches it. And this manifestation of God I have had more than a thousand times, and each time in a new and other and different manner from the time before.[2] — *The Book of Visions and Instructions*

Angela describes a state of highly expanded awareness, so exalted she feels she is in heaven. She describes this kind of experience further in this passage:

And this leaves in my soul a peace, a quiet, and a solidness, the like of which I remember not to have ever had so fully; and in this I abide continually; ... I was raised up higher still. ... I saw something stable, so indescribable for me that I can tell nothing about it, save that it was All Good. And my soul was in unutterable joy; and I saw not love therein, but that something which is unutterable. And I had gone out from that former state, and was placed in this highest unutterable state, but whether I was in the body or out of the body I cannot tell.... Thus then I am left in great peace.... [A]nd never shall I forget its memory or its joy.... But oh, what depth is here!"[3]   — *The Book of Visions and Instructions*

Here are hallmarks of Transcendental Consciousness — profound peace, quietness, the sense of "All Good" and "unutterable joy." Elsewhere she says she even feels physically rejuvenated: "I was more agile in body, and renewed, than I had ever been before." She adds, "But this I cannot make known in any words whatsoever; for it is wholly above nature."[4]

■ *Also see Angela of Foligno in Chapter 5 (Cosmic Consciousness).*

MEISTER ECKHART
1260–c. 1327 • GERMANY

■ *Meister Eckhart was the most learned scholar of his time and one of the most beloved preachers — people flocked to hear his bold, fresh sermons. As the Dominican provincial superior for Saxony, he administered a territory stretching from Holland across northern Germany to the current Czech Republic. He traveled constantly through this area — and travel at that time was on foot, often alone. Eckhart was born in the mountain village of Tambach, at the center of Germany, perhaps to a noble family. At 15 he entered a Dominican priory in nearby Erfurt for a nine-year course of study*

leading to the priesthood. Later he studied in Paris, earning the title Meister (Master) of Theology. Returning to Erfurt, he was given widening administrative responsibilities. As a spiritual master, he also guided groups of monks and nuns. Late in life, ironically, Eckhart was tried as a heretic, perhaps due to jealousy of his fame. But his reputation and teachings have echoed down the centuries, with resurgent interest today. Meister Eckhart has been called "one of the greatest masters of Western spirituality."[1]

There is something that transcends the created being of the soul, not in contact with created things, which are nothing.... It is akin to the nature of deity, it is one in itself, and has naught in common with anything. It is a stumbling-block to many a learned cleric. It is a strange and desert place, and is rather nameless than possessed of a name, and is more unknown than it is known. If you could naught yourself for an instant, indeed I say less than an instant, you would possess all that this is in itself. But as long as you mind yourself or any thing at all, you know no more of God than my mouth knows of color or my eye of taste: so little do you know or discern what God is.[2]
— Sermon 144

Deep within the human soul, Eckhart says, beyond anything relative or created, lies something unified and divine. "If you could naught yourself" — if you could transcend the small self — you would experience this in its totality.

Eckhart uses many terms to refer to the inner field of pure consciousness — the *inmost recess of the spirit*, the *ground of the soul*, the *spark of the soul*, the *inmost man*, the *silent middle*, our *being* and *essence*, the *highest in the soul*, the *inward spirit*. He does not shy from calling it by the most exalted term at his disposal — *God*. But he defines God in a special way: *Esse est Deus* — God is pure Being,[3] which accords with our understanding of pure consciousness.

Therefore I say, if a man turns away from self and from all created things, then — to the extent that you do this — you will attain to oneness and blessedness in your soul's spark, which time and place never touched.... [I]t wants to get into its simple ground, into the silent desert into which no distinction ever peeped, of Father, Son or Holy Ghost. In the inmost part, where none is at home, there that light finds satisfaction, and there it is more than it is in itself: for this ground is an impartible stillness, motionless in itself, and all those receive life that live of themselves, being endowed with reason.[4] — Sermon 60

Dive within, Eckhart says, and you pass beyond time and space to the ground of the soul, silent, unified, the source of all life. And he says again:

[T]he soul flows with this richness and this sweetness into herself and beyond all things, by grace and with power, without means back into her primal source.[5] — Sermon 6

The soul in which God is to be born must drop away from time and time from her, she must soar aloft and stand gazing into this richness of God's: there there is breadth without breadth, expanseless expanse, and there the soul knows all things, and knows them perfectly.... [This] is wider than the expanse of heaven.... In this expanse and in this richness of God's the soul is aware, there she misses nothing and expects nothing.[6] — Sermon 29

In the fourth state of consciousness, consciousness becomes unbounded, enjoying a state of pure inner wakefulness.

ॐ

[I]t is in the purest thing that the soul is capable of, in the noblest part, the ground — indeed, in the very essence of the soul which is the soul's most secret part. There is the silent "middle," for no creature ever entered there and no image, nor has the soul there either activity or understanding, therefore she is not aware *there* of any image, whether of herself or of any other creature....

[I]n the soul's essence there is no activity, for the powers she works with emanate from the ground of being. Yet in that ground is the silent "middle": here is nothing but rest and celebration. . . .[7]

☙

[T]here is a power in the soul which touches neither time nor flesh, flowing from the spirit, remaining in the spirit, altogether spiritual. In this power, God is ever verdant and flowering in all the joy and all the glory that He is in Himself. There is such heartfelt delight, such inconceivably deep joy as none can fully tell of, for in this power the eternal Father is ever begetting His eternal Son without pause. . . .[8] — Sermon 8

The field of pure consciousness, Eckhart indicates, is an ocean of pure creative intelligence and pure bliss.

■ *Also see Meister Eckhart in Chapter 5 (Cosmic Consciousness) and Chapter 7 (Unity Consciousness).*

DANTE ALIGHIERI
c. 1265–1321 • ITALY

■ *Dante's chief work, the* Divine Comedy (Divina Commedia), *is widely regarded as the outstanding literary work of the Italian language and one of the supreme achievements of world literature. In Italy Dante is called the "Father of the Italian Language" and the "Supreme Poet." Born to a prominent family in Florence, he held various political positions in that city at a time of great turmoil and violence. To his sorrow, he was eventually exiled and moved to Verona, then Ravenna. Dante composed the* Divine Comedy *in a new language he named* Italian, *based on the dialect of his region, Tuscany. Before*

Dante, all serious literary and scholarly works were composed in Latin. Dante's epic work broke this barrier, establishing the Italian language as appropriate for serious artistic and philosophical expression. After Dante, an increasing number of works were published in the common language, reaching a broader audience and promoting literacy throughout the Italian peninsula.

> A divine light is directed on me,
> penetrating this glow in which I am contained,
> whose virtue, combined with my vision,
>   lifts me so far above myself that I see
>   the Supreme Essence from which it is derived.
> Thence comes the joy with which I shine,
> because I match the clarity of my flame
> to the clearness of my vision.[1]   — *Divine Comedy*

The *Divine Comedy* contains many allusions to Transcendental Consciousness. The above lines describe an experience that elevates him "so far above myself" that he sees "the Supreme Essence" and is filled with joy.

※

> [S]o my mind, in this feast of the spirit,
> becoming greater, transcended itself,
>   and what it became I cannot recall.[2]   — *Divine Comedy*

His consciousness expands and he transcends, beyond thought and memory.

※

The final part of the *Divine Comedy* is called the *Paradiso*, Italian for *paradise* or *heaven*. The last section of the *Paradiso*, entitled "The Beatific Vision," offers Dante's most detailed and beautiful description of transcendence. T.S. Eliot praised this section as "the highest point that poetry has ever reached or ever can reach."[3] These lines are among Dante's most famous:

> O abundant grace through which I presumed
> to fix my eyes on the Eternal Light
> so long that I consumed my vision on it!
> In its depths I saw contained, bound with love
> in one volume, what is scattered
> on leaves throughout the world —
> substances and accidents and their modes
> as if fused together in such a way
> that what I speak of is a single light.
> The universal form of this unity
> I believe I saw, because more abundantly
> in saying this I feel that I rejoice.[4]
>
> — *Divine Comedy*

Experiencing the inner "Eternal Light," he apprehends the unity underlying diversity. He finds all the multiplicity of life, normally "scattered / on leaves throughout the world," now unified, "fused together" into a "single light."

༄

> Thus my mind with rapt attention
> gazed fixedly, motionless and attentive,
> continually enflamed by its very gazing.
> In that light we become such
> that we can never consent
> to turn from it for another sight,
> inasmuch as the good which is the object
> of the will is all in it, and outside of it
> whatever is perfect there is defective.[5]
>
> — *Divine Comedy*

His mind is restfully alert, "motionless and attentive," immersed in "the good," an experience supremely fulfilling. Everything outside this perfection, in comparison, is "defective."

༄

O Eternal Light, abiding in Thyself alone,
Thou alone understanding Thyself, and Thou
understood only by Thee, Thou dost love and smile!⁶

— *Divine Comedy*

In this state, Dante tells us, the light of pure consciousness is aware only of itself — it is simultaneously the knower, process of knowing, and known. By the end of this great work, Dante feels in harmony with the source of creation:

Already my desire and will [in harmony]
were turning like a wheel moved evenly
by the Love which turns the sun and the other stars.⁷

— *Divine Comedy*

KABIR

1440-1518 • INDIA

Born to a Hindu family of weavers near Varanasi (Benares), Kabir was later adopted by a childless Muslim couple, also weavers. Kabir became a weaver. Though now a Muslim, he persuaded the Hindu saint Ramananda to accept him as a disciple. But he considered himself neither Hindu nor Muslim — he rejected established religion in favor of a universal approach to spiritual development. His songs, composed in everyday language and addressed to the people, have a remarkably modern flavor after 600 years and have inspired people of all religions. He is esteemed as one of the world's greatest poets. IMAGE: *1825 painting of Kabir weaving, with a disciple.*

There is an endless world, O my brother! and there is the Nameless Being, of whom nought can be said.

Only he knows it who has reached that region: it is other than all
    that is heard and said.
No form, no body, no length, no breadth is seen there: how can I tell
    you that which it is?
He comes to the Path of the Infinite on whom the grace of the Lord
    descends: he is freed from births and deaths who attains to Him.
Kabir says: "It cannot be told by the words of the mouth, it cannot
    be written on paper:
It is like a dumb person who tastes a sweet thing — how shall it be
    explained?"[1]

Kabir tells of an "endless world" beyond anything we can perceive or describe — "the Infinite." Yet we can experience it and enjoy ultimate freedom.

■ *Also see Kabir in Chapter 6 (God Consciousness).*

ST. TERESA OF ÁVILA
1515–1582 • SPAIN

■ *Born in Ávila, in west-central Spain, St. Teresa was one of the greatest women of the Roman Catholic Church. She wrote a number of influential books, including* The Interior Castle *and her autobiography, now considered masterpieces of spiritual literature. St. Teresa initiated the Carmelite Reform, which restored to the Carmelite order its original contemplative character, and which inspired St. John of the Cross to undertake a similar reform for men. In 1970 St. Teresa was named a Doctor of the Church, one of only 33 individuals — and one of the first two women — to be thus honored by the Roman Catholic Church.*

> [M]y soul at once becomes recollected and I enter the state of quiet or that of rapture, so that I can use none of my faculties and senses. . . .
>
> [E]verything is stilled, and the soul is left in a state of great quiet and deep satisfaction. . . .[1] — *Spiritual Relations*

St. Teresa describes an experience in which the mind turns inward ("becomes recollected") and becomes still while remaining awake. Later she describes this experience as one of inner peace, happiness, and utter fulfillment:

> These interior things of the spirit are so hard to describe, and still more so in such a way as to be understood, especially as they are so quickly gone. . . .
>
> There sometimes springs an interior peace and quietude which is full of happiness, for the soul is in such a state that it thinks there is nothing that it lacks. Even speaking — by which I mean vocal prayer and meditation — wearies it: it would like to do nothing but love. This condition lasts for some time, and may even last for long periods.[2] — *Spiritual Relations*

St. Teresa describes the experience of inner quietude in exalted terms:

> In the orison [prayer] of union, the soul is fully awake as regards God, but wholly asleep as regards things of this world and in respect of herself. During the short time the union lasts, she is as it were deprived of every feeling, and even if she would, she could not think of any single thing. Thus she needs to employ no artifice in order to arrest the use of her understanding: it remains so stricken with inactivity that she neither knows what she loves, nor in what manner she loves, nor what she wills. In short, she is utterly dead to the things of the world and lives solely in God. . . . I do not even know whether in this state she has enough life left to breathe. It seems to me she has

not; or at least that if she does breathe, she is unaware of it. Her intellect would fain understand something of what is going on within her, but it has so little force now that it can act in no way whatsoever. . . .

Thus does God, when he raises a soul to union with himself, suspend the natural action of all her faculties. She neither sees, hears, nor understands, so long as she is united with God. But this time is always short, and it seems even shorter than it is. God establishes himself in the interior of this soul in such a way, that when she returns to herself, it is wholly impossible for her to doubt that she has been in God, and God in her. This truth remains so strongly impressed on her that, even though many years should pass without the condition returning, she can neither forget the favor she received, nor doubt of its reality. If you, nevertheless, ask how it is possible that the soul can see and understand that she has been in God, since during the union she has neither sight nor understanding, I reply that she does not see it then, but that she sees it clearly later, after she has returned to herself, not by any vision, but by a certitude which abides with her and which God alone can give her.[3]   — *The Interior Castle*

Maharishi describes pure consciousness as an ocean of pure knowledge, power, and bliss. In the deepest moments of Transcendental Consciousness, one experiences infinite expansion of awareness, unbounded bliss. It's not surprising that some people would identify this inner, infinite field of consciousness with God, as St. Teresa does here.

But what's happening is clear. Her mind turns inward and transcends all thought and feeling while remaining awake. She even describes a key physiological component of the fourth state of consciousness: her breathing becomes quiescent, even suspended (more on this in Chapter 9). As with so many others in this book, the experience for St. Teresa is so powerful and clear as to be self-validating and incontrovertible.

▪ *Also see St. Teresa of Ávila in Chapter 5 (Cosmic Consciousness). See Chapter 6 for more on the relation between pure consciousness and God.*

ST. JOHN OF THE CROSS
1542–1591 • SPAIN

St. John of the Cross is one of the greatest figures in the Catholic Church and one of Spain's greatest poets. Born near Ávila, Juan de Yepes Álvarez entered the Carmelite order at 21, studied philosophy and theology at the university in Salamanca, and at 25 was ordained a priest. Around this time he met St. Teresa of Ávila, who inspired him with her work in restoring the Carmelite order's original contemplative intent. St. John worked with her for ten years, establishing and administering monasteries around Spain. Then a group of his superiors, trying to counter their efforts, jailed him. Though his work had been approved by a higher authority, he was imprisoned and treated harshly. Yet out of his tiny dungeon cell came his most famous work, The Spiritual Canticle. After nine months he escaped and continued his work. He was made a saint in 1726 and a Doctor of the Church in 1926.

So little of this is describable that we would never succeed in fully explaining what takes place in the soul that has reached this happy state. If she attains the peace of God which, as the Church says, surpasses all understanding, all understanding will be inadequate and mute when it comes to explaining this peace. . . .

[This] song is so charming it enraptures and enamors its hearers and makes them forget all things as though they were in a transport. Similarly the delight of this union absorbs the soul within herself and gives her such refreshment. . . .[1] — *The Spiritual Canticle*

St. John of the Cross describes a state of profound inner peace, restorative bliss, in which the soul (consciousness) is unified with itself. He compares it to waking up from ordinary waking experience:

> [T]he soul] is moved and awakened from the sleep of natural vision to supernatural vision. Hence it very adequately uses the term "awakening."[2]
> — *The Living Flame of Love*

> [W]hen a person has finished purifying and voiding himself of all forms and apprehensible images, he will abide in this pure and simple light, and be perfectly transformed into it. . . . [H]is soul in its simplicity and purity will then be immediately transformed into simple and pure Wisdom, the son of God.[3]
> — *The Ascent of Mount Carmel*

Here St. John calls to mind Transcendental Consciousness as the simplest form of human awareness, a self-referral state of *pure* knowledge.

> This knowledge savors of the divine essence and of eternal life. . . .
>
> Some of these divine touches produced in the substance of the soul are so enriching that one of them would be sufficient not only to remove definitively all the imperfections which the soul would have been unable to eradicate through its entire life, but also to fill it with virtues and blessings from God.[4]
> — *The Ascent of Mount Carmel*

This experience, he says, purifies and sets one on the path to perfection.

> This supernatural, general knowledge and light shines so purely and simply in the intellect and is so divested and freed of all intelligible forms (the objects of the intellect) that it is imperceptible to the soul. . . .
>
> The purity and simplicity of the knowledge is the cause of this oblivion. While occupying a man's soul, it renders it simple, pure, and clear of all the apprehensions and forms through which the

senses and memory were acting when conscious of time. And thus it leaves the soul in oblivion and unaware of time.

Although, as we asserted, this prayer lasts a long while, it seems of brief duration to the individual, since he has been united with pure knowledge which is independent of time. This is the short prayer which, it is said, pierces the heavens. [Ecclesiasticus 35:21] It is short because it is not subject to time, and it penetrates the heavens because the soul is united with heavenly knowledge. When the individual returns to himself he observes the effects this knowledge produced in him without his having been aware of this. These effects are: an elevation of mind to heavenly knowledge, and a withdrawal and abstraction from all objects, forms, and figures as well as from the remembrance of them.

David declares that such was his experience upon returning to himself after this oblivion: *Vigilavi, et factus sum sicut passer solitarius in tecto* (I became conscious and discovered that I was like the solitary sparrow on the housetop). [Psalms 101:8] By solitary he refers to the withdrawal and abstraction from all things; by the housetop, to the mind elevated on high. . . .

As we mentioned, it seems to a person when occupied with this knowledge that he is idle because he is not at work with his senses or faculties. Nevertheless he must believe that he is not wasting time, for even though the harmonious interaction of his sensory and spiritual faculties ceases, his soul is occupied with knowledge in the way we explained.[5]   — *The Ascent of Mount Carmel*

With clinical precision, St. John describes how the mind moves beyond all mental content to experience a state of utter simplicity and purity. One becomes united with what he calls *pure knowledge*. This inner field is independent of time, he says — so when one experiences it, hours can seem like a moment.

*I entered into unknowing,
And there I remained unknowing
Transcending all knowledge.*

I entered into unknowing,
Yet when I saw myself there
Without knowing where I was
I understood great things;
I shall not say what I felt
For I remained in unknowing
Transcending all knowledge.

That perfect knowledge
Was of peace and holiness
Held at no remove
In profound solitude;
It was something so secret
That I was left stammering,
Transcending all knowledge.

I was so whelmed [submerged],
So absorbed and withdrawn,
That my senses were left
Deprived of all their sensing,
And my spirit was given
An understanding while not understanding,
Transcending all knowledge.

He who truly arrives there
Cuts free from himself;
All that he knew before
Now seems worthless,

And his knowledge so soars
That he is left in unknowing
Transcending all knowledge.

. . . .

This knowledge in unknowing
Is so overwhelming
That wise men disputing
Can never overthrow it,
For their knowledge does not reach
To the understanding of not understanding,
Transcending all knowledge.

And this supreme knowledge
Is so exalted
That no power of man or learning
Can grasp it;
He who masters himself
Will, with knowledge in unknowing,
Always be transcending.

And if you should want to hear:
This highest knowledge lies
In the loftiest sense
Of the essence of God;
This is a work of His mercy,
To leave one without understanding,
Transcending all knowledge.[6] — "Stanzas Concerning an Ecstasy
Experienced in High Contemplation"

"Transcending all knowledge" indicates going beyond thought, leaving consciousness "in profound solitude," awake within itself, in a state of "perfect knowledge," of "peace and holiness." St. John reminds us of Transcendental Consciousness as a state of pure knowledge, pure knowingness, the mind having transcended all relative values of knowledge.

THOMAS TRAHERNE
1637–1674 • ENGLAND

The son of a shoemaker, Thomas Traherne studied at Oxford, earned a master's degree in arts and divinity, and was ordained an Anglican priest. He was little known during his lifetime. For ten years he served a parish in a village in southwest England, then in London. His enduring fame rests on his poetry and his prose work Centuries of Meditations. *These works remained unknown for over 200 years after his death. Manuscripts were discovered in a London street bookstall in 1896–97 and quickly recognized as masterpieces. Other discoveries followed, most recently in 1996–97. One of the most frequently-occurring words in Traherne's work is "felicity" — intense happiness.* IMAGE: *St. Mary's Church in Credenhill, Hereford, Herefordshire, where Traherne served as the parish priest from 1657 to 1666. It was built in the 12th century, the tower added in the 14th century, and remains in operation today.*

[T]he Mind of Man lifting it self above it self, goeth easily from it self to the Divine Nature from whence it came.[1]

— "Seeds of Eternity"

In this simple sentence Traherne describes the process of transcending, which culminates in the experience of pure consciousness. Traherne speaks glowingly of his early experience of this inner dimension of the mind:

This Endless Comprehension of my Immortal Soul when I first saw it, so wholly Ravished and Transported my spirit, that for a fortnight after I could Scarcely Think or speak or write of any other thing. But Like a man Doting with Delight and Ecstasy, Talk of it Night and Day as if all the Joy of Heaven and Earth were Shut up in it. For in very Deed there I saw the Divine Image Relucent and shining. There I saw the foundation of man's Excellency, and that which made him a Son of God. Nor ever shall I be able to forget its Glory.... The Heaven of Heavens are not able to contain me. For my Soul Exceedeth all Limitations.[2]   — *Select Meditations*

Traherne experiences his innermost nature as unbounded, divine, a source of bliss and light. In one of his poems Traherne elaborates on this experience:

Then was my soul my only all to me,
   A living endless eye,
     Far wider than the Sky.
Whose power, whose act, whose essence, was to see:
   I was an inward Sphere of Light,
Or an interminable Orb of Sight,
   An endless and a living day,
A vital Sun that round about did ray
     All life, all sense,
A naked simple pure Intelligence.
. . . .
   A meditating inward eye
Gazing at quiet did within me lie,
     And every thing
Delighted me that was their heavenly King.
. . . .
   'Tis not the Object, but the Light
That maketh Heaven; 'Tis a purer Sight.
      Felicity
Appears to none but them that purely see.

A disentangled and a naked sense,
    A mind that's unpossest,
    A disengaged breast
An empty and a quick intelligence
    Acquainted with the golden mean,
An even spirit pure and serene,
    Is that where beauty, excellence,
And pleasure keep their Court of Residence.
    My soul retire,
Get free, and thou shalt even all admire.[3]   — "The Preparative"

Traherne seems to be describing the experience of consciousness aware of itself alone, "disentangled" from all sense perception and mental activity — pure, unbounded, serene, blissful, and free, the experience of pure intelligence.

This, for Traherne, is the mind's simplest and most natural state:

> Few will believe the soul to be infinite: yet Infinite [infinity] is the first thing which is naturally known. Bounds and limits are discovered only in a secondary manner.... That things are finite therefore we learn by our senses. But infinity we know and feel by our souls, and feel it so naturally as if it were the very essence and being of the soul.[4]   — *Centuries*

> Were nothing made but a Naked Soul, it would see nothing out of itself. For Infinite Space would be seen within it. And being all sight it would feel it self as it were running Parallel with it. And that truly in an Endless manner, because it could not be conscious of any Limits: nor feel itself Present in one Center more than another. This is an Infinite Sweet Mystery: to them that have Tasted it.[5]   — *Select Meditations*

THE FOURTH STATE • GLIMPSES OF TRANSCENDENTAL CONSCIOUSNESS

When consciousness becomes a "Naked Soul" — comes to its pure essence — we experience our essential nature as infinite and unbounded.

■ *Also see Traherne in Chapter 6 (God Consciousness) and Chapter 7 (Unity Consciousness).*

HAKUIN ZENJI
1685–1769 • JAPAN

■ *Hakuin Zenji, also known as Hakuin Ekaku, is a founder of modern Zen. As a boy he persuaded his parents to let him leave home and enter a temple. He was ordained at 14, but his spiritual quest led him from one temple and priest to another. Finally he found one who gave him the knowledge and experience of enlightenment he sought. Hakuin spent the remainder of his life helping others find it. He traveled throughout the country, his virtue and wisdom welcomed everywhere. He was sought out by nobility, students, peasants. He would speak to peasants in the rice fields where they worked. He taught that the experience of life's inner reality is not limited to the cloister but is the birthright of everyone. His writings, collected in eight volumes, are known for their clear and polished style. He is the author of the celebrated Zen koan "What is the sound of one hand clapping?" At 60 he took up painting and is regarded today as one of Japan's foremost Zen painters as well as one of its greatest saints.* IMAGE: *Self-portrait, 1764, Eisei Bunko Museum, Tokyo.*

In the twinkling of an eye, he turns towards that place where no busy world affairs can trouble him.... And then he may, almost without knowing it, cross the borders of life and death, transcend the limits of perception and illusion and achieve that state which is called the unbreakable, hard real body of the Diamond World. Is not this indeed, the discovery of the divine elixir of never growing old and of never dying? Is it not the very recollection of one's own birth into this world of humanity? Is it not the dignity attaching to the shaven priesthood? Is it not the spiritual experience of the mystery of the Way of the Buddha?[1]   — *The Embossed Tea Kettle*

Though flavored with Eastern images, this passage clearly describes an *experience* that transcends perception, time, and change and reaches underlying reality. It involves a state of "super-consciousness," he says later.[2] "Without raising thoughts in one's mind," he says, "one illuminates the whole universe."[3]

He elaborates on this experience in a later passage:

> Before long you will find that the mind-nature has become settled in you — like a great rock, immovable and peaceful. . . . But do not then leave off. . . . Then what one often hears about will take place. . . . All your usual, everyday consciousness will cease, and it will be as though you have entered the Diamond Circle, as though you were seated upon the Emerald Throne. . . . [Then] the one, pure, un-confused truth, all, as it were, in one whole, will rise up before your very eyes, and you will instantly attain to the true dignified beauty of the Lotus Blossom. Then the Tathagata, the primeval and eternal reality, will appear before you, and nothing will be able to make him depart from you — even if you try to push him away! This is when you enter what is called, in the Tendai sect, "The Calm of the Absolute, and the Treasure House of Calm and Perpetual Light." This is when you will be lightened by what the Shingon sect calls "The Sun Light of the Non-Origin of the Adhi Buddha." This is when you accomplish what the Jodo (Pure Land) sect calls "The Fundamental Purpose of Immediate Heart Birth in the Pure Land." . . . Now your eyes will be opened to see the truth that this universe and the absolute are identical. . . . So, what is there in this world of men or in the land of the gods which can be compared with this?[4]   — *The Embossed Tea Kettle*

When the mind settles inward, Hakuin tells us, it passes beyond "everyday consciousness" and enters the realm of pure truth, of eternal reality. Different sects describe this state with different names, he observes, but all refer to the same experience. "This universe and the absolute are identical," he declares — this inner absolute field of life is the essential nature of the universe itself.

※

Everyone can experience the transcendental, infinite value of life, Hakuin asserts here — it is everyone's birthright, and no experience is more valuable:

> In this matter there is no difference between man and woman, priest and layman, poor and rich, good or bad looking people. For this is that uttermost and final way.... Suddenly one will find that he has pierced through to the truth, and he will realize that there is no "ten-direction space," nor any single inch of the great earth. Everything, the coarse and the fine, the outer and the inner, will be merged in the infinite....
>
> For even if a man were to obtain all the wealth and honor of ten thousand feudal estates, that would be, in comparison with the supreme good, nothing but the emptiness of a half-forgotten dream.[5]
>
> *— The Embossed Tea Kettle*

※

> So, everybody, wake up!... Find out what your mind really is and open your eyes in true wakefulness.[6]   *—The Embossed Tea Kettle*

Also see Hakuin Zenji in Chapter 5 (Cosmic Consciousness).

DOV BER OF MEZERITCH
c. 1710–1772 • UKRAINE

As a young man Rabbi Dov Ber adopted an ascetic lifestyle, which weakened his health. Then he met the great Rabbi Baal Shem Tov, who taught that the body is not to be mortified but regarded as a vessel for holiness. Dov Ber became his disciple, then his successor. The Baal Shem Tov founded Hasidic Judaism in eastern Europe in the 1700s, counterbalancing the emphasis on formal Talmud Torah study that preceded it. Reaching out to common people, it emphasized that the divine presence lies within and placed devotional prayer at the foundation of spiritual life. Dov Ber formalized and popularized the Hasidic teachings. He became known as the Maggid, *or preacher. Under his leadership, Hasidism spread quickly. Although Dov Ber left no writings, his teachings were recorded by his students and collected in anthologies.*

You must forget yourself in prayer.
Think of yourself as nothing
   and pray only for the sake of God.
In such a prayer you may come to transcend time,
   entering the highest realms
   of the World of Thought.
There all things are as one;
Distinctions between "life" and "death,"
   "land" and "sea,"
   have lost their meaning.
But none of this can happen
   as long as you remain attached
   to the reality of the material world.
Here you are bound to the distinctions
   between good and evil
   that emerge only in the lower realms of God.
How can one who remains attached to his own self
   go beyond time to the world where all is One?[1]

Dov Ber describes a type of prayer different from what most people understand (i.e., speaking with God). He instructs us to transcend everything relative — the material world, time, even the self. Only then can we enter the realm "where all is One." The term "World of Thought" (line six) comes from the Kabbalah, the ancient tradition of Jewish mysticism, and refers to the highest of ten levels of reality, where individual awareness unites with the divine.

༄

The human body is always finite;
It is the spirit that is boundless.
Before he begins to pray,
    a person should cast aside that which limits him
    and enter the endless world of Nothing.
In prayer he should turn to God alone
    and have no thoughts of himself at all.
Nothing but God exists for him;
    he himself has ceased to be.
The true redemption of man's soul can only happen
    as he steps outside the body's limits.[2]

Dov Ber equates God with "the endless world of Nothing," beyond thought, beyond time and space — suggesting pure, unbounded consciousness. This experience comes only by transcending speech and thought:

As long as you can still say the words
"Blessed art Thou"
    by your own will,
        know that you have not yet reached
the deeper levels of prayer.
Be so stripped of selfhood that you have
    neither the awareness
    nor the power
        to say a single word on your own.[3]

JOHANN WOLFGANG VON GOETHE

1749–1832 • GERMANY

■ *Poet, playwright, novelist, philosopher, and scientist, Goethe is Germany's greatest literary figure and one of the most significant personalities in Western culture. So wide-ranging were his interests and his styles of writing that he simply cannot be categorized. His most famous work, the drama* Faust, *is considered one of the great creations in world literature. But his scientific interests were as vital to him as his writing. He did important scientific work in botany, anatomy, optics, and geology. He has been described as "one of the few manifestations in literary history of transcendental genius." Active and creative to the end of his life, he was regarded in his later years as "the wise old man of Europe."*

How yearns the solitary soul
To melt into the boundless whole,
And find itself again in peace!
The blind desire, the impatient will,
The restless thoughts and plans are still;
We yield ourselves — and wake in bliss.¹   — "One and All"

"Goethe's Nirvana" — that is how one scholar describes the poem with this stanza.² Goethe describes transcendence, the union of individual self with boundless Self, pure consciousness, and the resulting experience of peace and bliss.

> No thing on earth to nought can fall,
> The Eternal onward moves in all;
> Rejoice, by being be sustained.
> Being is deathless: living wealth,
> With which the All adorns itself,
> By laws abides and is maintained.
> . . . .
> Now turn yourself about, within:
> Your center you will find therein,
> No noble soul can this gainsay.
> No principle within you'll miss
> For independent conscience is
> The sun that rules your moral day.[3]   — "Testament"

Everything on earth, Goethe observes, is an expression of an underlying field he calls "the Eternal," "Being," "the All." And this field can be directly experienced by turning within. Here he comments on how he values this:

> My greatest wealth is the deep stillness in which I strive and grow and win what the world cannot take from me with fire or sword.[4]

RALPH WALDO EMERSON
1803–1882 • UNITED STATES

In 1836, an essay entitled Nature *was published anonymously. It created a great stir, especially among college students, who formed clubs to discuss it. The book marked the beginning of a movement that came to be called American Transcendentalism and influenced the entire nation. Its founder, Ralph Waldo Emerson, was 33 when his book* Nature *was published. Emerson, who came from a long line of clergymen, entered Harvard at 14 and became a minister at 26. Though a popular sermonizer, he left the ministry to lecture and write. He was considered one of America's foremost orators, and his journals form one of the world's great documents of spiritual growth. His primary source of inspiration was Vedic literature, which gave expression to his own experience.*

Yet there is a depth in those brief moments which constrains us to ascribe more reality to them than to all other experiences. . . .

[T]hat great nature in which we rest, as the earth lies in the soft arms of the atmosphere [is] that Unity, that Over-Soul, within which every man's particular being is contained and made one with all other. . . . We live in succession, in division, in parts, in particles. Meantime within man is the soul of the whole; the wise silence; the universal beauty, to which every part and particle is equally related; the eternal ONE. And this deep power in which we exist, and whose beatitude is all accessible to us, is not only self-sufficing and perfect in every hour, but the act of seeing and the thing seen, the seer and the spectacle, the subject and the object, are one. We see the world piece by piece, as the sun, the moon, the animal, the tree; but the whole, of which these are the shining parts, is the soul. . . .

All goes to show that the soul in man is . . . the background of our being, in which they lie, — an immensity not possessed and that cannot be possessed. From within or from behind, a light shines through us upon things, and makes us aware that we are nothing, but the light is all. A man is the facade of a temple wherein all wisdom and all good abide. . . . When it breathes through his intellect, it is genius; when it breathes through his will, it is virtue; when it flows through his affection, it is love. . . .

Of this pure nature every man is at some time sensible. Language cannot paint it with his colors. It is too subtle. It is undefinable, unmeasurable, but we know that it pervades and contains us. We know that all spiritual being is in man. . . . We lie open on one side to the deeps of spiritual nature, to the attributes of God.[1]

— "The Over-Soul"

Emerson wrote often of experiencing consciousness in its unified state and consistently identified this as the source of natural law. Here he describes moments containing "more reality" than anything else, when he experiences what is ordinarily hidden: the source of his being, of life, the "Over-Soul" — "the eternal ONE." When we experience this unity, "the act of seeing and the thing seen, the seer and the spectacle, the subject and the object, are one." In Transcendental Consciousness, awareness becomes its own object — knower, known, and process of knowing become unified in one wholeness of experience.

☙

For, the sense of being which in calm hours rises, we know not how, in the soul, is not diverse from things, from space, from light, from time, from man, but one with them and proceeds obviously from the same source whence their life and being also proceed. We first share the life by which things exist and afterwards see them as appearances in nature and forget that we have shared their cause.

Here is the fountain of action and of thought. Here are the lungs of that inspiration which giveth man wisdom. . . . We lie in the lap of immense intelligence. . . .² — "Self-Reliance"

Emerson again describes his experience of "being," the source of thought and the source of creation, "the life by which all things exist." He captures as clearly as anyone the identity between human consciousness and nature's infinite intelligence, the unified field.

▪ *Also see Emerson in Chapter 5 (Cosmic Consciousness) and Chapter 7 (Unity Consciousness).*

ALFRED, LORD TENNYSON
1809–1892 • ENGLAND

▪ *Tennyson, descended from King Edward III, began writing and publishing poetry in his teens. In 1850, when he was 41, he succeeded Wordsworth as Poet Laureate of England, and held this position until the end of his life, more than 40 years — a longer term by far than any other laureate. He was a huge and powerful figure. The Scottish historian and philosopher Thomas Carlyle described Tennyson as "one of the finest-looking men in the world," with "bright, laughing hazel eyes" and a "most massive yet most delicate" face. Later in his life, a photographer called him "the most beautiful old man on earth." His resonant, booming voice riveted listeners when he read his poetry. A highly popular poet in his own lifetime, Tennyson continued writing into his 80s and earned considerable money from his works. He was revered as a poet who reflected the collective mind, "the Poet of the People."*

A kind of waking trance — this for lack of a better word — I have frequently had, quite up from boyhood, when I have been all alone.... All at once, as it were out of the intensity of the consciousness of individuality, the individuality itself seemed to dissolve and fade away into boundless being, and this not a confused state but the clearest, the surest of the surest... utterly beyond words — where death was an almost laughable impossibility, the loss of personality (if so it were) seeming no extinction, but the only true life....

I am ashamed of my feeble description. Have I not said the state is utterly beyond words? ...[1]

There is no delusion in the matter! It is no nebulous ecstasy, but a state of transcendent wonder, associated with absolute clearness of mind.[2] — *Alfred, Lord Tennyson: A Memoir by His Son*

"Individuality itself seemed to dissolve and fade away into boundless being" — a perfect description of transcendence, the expansion of consciousness from the self to the Self. He describes his experiences in verse as well. On a number of occasions while sitting alone, he says,

> The mortal limit of the Self was loosed,
> And passed into the Nameless, as a cloud
> Melts into Heaven. I touch'd my limbs, the limbs
> Were strange, not mine — and yet no shade of doubt,
> But utter clearness, and thro' loss of Self
> The gain of such large life as match'd with ours
> Were Sun to spark — unshadowable in words,
> Themselves but shadows of a shadow-world.[3]
> — "The Ancient Sage"

Compared to this experience of "utter clearness," he says, normal waking consciousness is like a spark compared to the sun. When he was 60, he wrote:

> [Y]ou never, never can convince me that the I is not an eternal Reality, and that the Spiritual is not the true and real part of me.[4]

HENRY DAVID THOREAU
1817–1862 • UNITED STATES

■ *After graduating from Harvard, Thoreau met Ralph Waldo Emerson, who employed him in his house, mentored him, and encouraged him to write. At 28 Thoreau went to Walden Pond, seeking spiritual regeneration through harmony with nature. He built a cabin on a piece of land owned by Emerson and lived there for two years, reading, writing, and studying the woodland life. He published his experiences and reflections in his book* Walden. *Though neglected during Thoreau's life,* Walden *has become a world classic. Even without* Walden, *Thoreau would have become renowned for his journals, published posthumously in 1906 from 29 handwritten notebooks. In his reading of Vedic literature, Thoreau found a conception of human life and human potential that became his ideal, and it was this he sought to develop at Walden Pond. As he wrote to a friend, "To some extent, and at rare intervals, even I am a yogi."*[1]

If with closed ears and eyes I consult consciousness for a moment, immediately are all walls and barriers dissipated, earth rolls from under me, and I float ... in the midst of an unknown and infinite sea, or else heave and swell like a vast ocean of thought, without rock or headland, where are all riddles solved, all straight lines making there their two ends to meet, eternity and space gambolling familiarly through my depths. I am from the beginning, knowing no end, no aim. No sun illumines me, for I dissolve all lesser lights in my own intenser and steadier light. I am a restful kernel in the magazine of the universe....

Men are constantly dinging in my ears their fair theories and plausible solutions of the universe, but ever there is no help, and I return again to my shoreless, islandless ocean.[2] — *Journal*

When he closes his ears and eyes and turns his attention within, beyond sensory experience, Thoreau says, all boundaries are dissolved and consciousness becomes an "infinite sea," an ocean without islands or shores. As so many others report, this experience brings a pure wisdom wherein all riddles are solved.

༄

In my better hours I am conscious of the influx of a serene and unquestionable wisdom. . . . What is that other kind of life to which I am thus continually allured? which alone I love? . . . Are our serene moments . . . simply a transient realization of what might be the whole tenor of our lives?

To be calm, to be serene! There is the calmness of the lake when there is not a breath of wind. . . . So it is with us. Sometimes we are clarified and calmed healthily, as we never were before in our lives, not by an opiate, but by some unconscious obedience to the all-just laws, so that we become like a still lake of purest crystal and without an effort our depths are revealed to ourselves. All the world goes by us and is reflected in our deeps. Such clarity![3]   — *Journal*

Thoreau could hardly emphasize the silent state of awareness more eloquently. The experience brings "serene and unquestionable wisdom," suggesting pure consciousness as pure knowledge, and aligns one with "the all-just laws," suggesting pure consciousness as the unified field of natural law.

Thoreau suspects these transient moments have the potential to become "the whole tenor of our lives" — that we might live this "other kind of life" permanently. In any case, he asserts, the experience is available to everyone:

Silence is the communion of a conscious soul with itself. If the soul attend for a moment to its own infinity, then and there is silence. She is audible to all men, at all times, in all places.[4]   — *Journal*

▪ *Also see Thoreau in Chapter 5 (Cosmic Consciousness) and Chapter 6 (God Consciousness).*

EMILY BRONTË
1818–1848 • ENGLAND

Emily Brontë was the second of the three famous Brontë sisters (the others were Charlotte and Anne) and the fifth of six children. They grew up in an isolated Yorkshire village with no real schooling, their only pastimes walking, reading, and writing. The three sisters published a book of poems using pseudonyms to avoid the bias against women writers. Emily published her one novel, Wuthering Heights, *at 29. Despite uneven reviews, it became a classic and established Emily as a major figure in English literature.* IMAGE: *Part of a painting of the sisters by their brother, Branwell.*

A messenger of Hope comes every night to me,
And offers, for short life, eternal liberty.

. . . .

But first a hush of peace, a soundless calm descends;
The struggle of distress and fierce impatience ends;
Mute music soothes my breast — unuttered harmony
That I could never dream till earth was lost to me.
Then dawns the Invisible, the Unseen its truth reveals;
My outward sense is gone, my inward essence feels —
Its wings are almost free, its home, its harbour found;
Measuring the gulf it stoops and dares the final bound![1]

— "Julian M. and A.G. Rochelle"

Brontë describes her awareness settling to her "inward essence," to the silence and freedom of the transcendent, where truth is revealed.

WALT WHITMAN
1819–1892 • UNITED STATES

■ *Walt Whitman left school at 11 and worked at a variety of trades — he was a printer, a teacher, a newspaper writer and editor, a stationer, and a real estate speculator. In 1855, he self-published his collection of poems,* Leaves of Grass. *Ralph Waldo Emerson immediately wrote to him, calling the book "the most extraordinary piece of wit and wisdom that America has yet contributed," adding, "I find incomparable things said incomparably well."*[1] *The poems seemed so radical in form and content that Whitman became a revolutionary figure in American literature. In fact, he was initially acclaimed more as a prophet of democracy and the "common man" in the West than as a poet. His aim, he states in the preface, is to "wellnigh express the inexpressible." At the beginning of "Song of Myself" he sings, "I celebrate myself" — a self, he makes clear, beyond the one we usually experience.* IMAGE: *Steel engraving of Walt Whitman published in the 1855 edition of* Leaves of Grass.

There is, in sanest hours, a consciousness, a thought that rises, independent, lifted out from all else, calm, like the stars, shining eternal. This is the thought of identity — yours for you, whoever you are, as mine for me. Miracle of miracles, beyond statement, most spiritual and vaguest of earth's dreams, yet hardest basic fact, and only entrance to all facts. In such devout hours, in the midst of the significant wonders of heaven and earth, (significant only because of the Me in the centre,) creeds, conventions, fall away and become of no account before this simple idea. Under the luminousness of real vision, it alone takes possession, takes value. Like the shadowy dwarf in the fable, once liberated and look'd upon, it expands over the whole earth, and spreads to the roof of heaven.[2]   — "Democratic Vistas"

Whitman describes a state of consciousness that stands beyond everything else, beyond boundaries. Though abstract it is the ultimate reality, the "hardest basic fact, and only entrance to all facts." He continues:

> Only in the perfect uncontamination and solitariness of individuality. . . . Only here, and on such terms, the meditation, the devout ecstasy, the soaring flight. Only here, communion with the mysteries. . . . The soul emerges, and all statements, churches, sermons, melt away like vapors. Alone, and silent thought and awe, and aspiration — and then the interior consciousness, like a hitherto unseen inscription, in magic ink, beams out its wondrous lines to the sense. Bibles may convey, and priests expound, but it is exclusively for the noiseless operation of one's isolated self, to enter the pure ether of veneration, reach the divine levels, and commune with the unutterable.[3]   — "Democratic Vistas"

The mind is awake but without thoughts, Whitman indicates — the Self stands alone in "perfect uncontamination." No experience surpasses this "interior consciousness," from where all intellectual beliefs "melt away like vapors." Only in the silence deep within can we "reach the divine."

※

O Thou transcendent,
Nameless, the fibre and the breath,
Light of the light, shedding forth universes, thou center of them,
Thou mightier center of the true, the good, the loving,
Thou moral, spiritual fountain — affection's source — thou reservoir,
(O pensive soul of me — O thirst unsatisfied — waitest not there?

Waitest not haply for us somewhere there the Comrade perfect?)

Thou pulse — thou motive of the stars, suns, systems,
That, circling, move in order, safe, harmonious,
Athwart the shapeless vastnesses of space,
How should I think, how breathe a single breath, how speak, if,
    out of myself,
I could not launch, to those, superior universes?[4] — "Passage to India"

Whitman speaks directly to the transcendent, the source and center of universes, of truth, goodness, and love — and declares at the end that everything he does, everything he is, depends on his ability to transcend, to move "out of myself" to that superior state.

༃

There is that in me — I do not know what it is — but I know it is in me.

Wrench'd and sweaty — calm and cool then my body becomes,
I sleep — I sleep long.

I do not know it — it is without name — it is a word unsaid,
It is not in any dictionary, utterance, symbol.

Something it swings on more than the earth I swing on,
To it the creation is the friend whose embracing awakes me.

Perhaps I might tell more. Outlines! I plead for my brothers and
    sisters.

Do you see O my brothers and sisters?
It is not chaos or death — it is form, union, plan — it is eternal life
    — it is Happiness.[5]   — *Song of Myself*

▪ *Also see Whitman in Chapter 5 (Cosmic Consciousness) and Chapter 6 (God Consciousness).*

HENRI FRÉDÉRIC
1821–1881 • SWITZERLAND

■ *A philosopher, poet, critic, and professor of aesthetics and philosophy at the academy at Geneva, Amiel published seven volumes of poetry and several philosophical works. But he is known today primarily for his* Journal Intime, *or* Private Journal, *which he began in his 20s and continued until the end of his life. Published posthumously, it became famous throughout Europe. Numbering more than 17,000 manuscript pages, it is considered a masterpiece of self-reflection and has been translated into many languages.*

A sense of rest, of deep quiet even. Silence within and without. A quietly-burning fire. A sense of comfort. . . . Whatever may be the charm of emotion, I do not know whether it equals the sweetness of those hours of silent meditation, in which we have a glimpse and foretaste of the contemplative joys of paradise. Desire and fear, sadness and care, are done away. Existence is reduced to the simplest form, the most ethereal mode of being, that is, to pure self-consciousness. It is a state of harmony, without tension and without disturbance. . . . It is difficult to find words in which to express this moral situation, for our languages can only render the particular and localized vibrations of life; they are incapable of expressing this motionless concentration, this divine quietude, this state of the resting ocean, which reflects the sky, and is master of its own profundities. . . . [T]he soul is only soul, and is no longer conscious of itself in its individuality and separateness. It is something which feels the universal life, a sensible atom of the Divine, of God. It no longer appropriates anything to itself, it is conscious of no void. Only the Yogis and Sufis perhaps have known in its profundity this humble and yet voluptuous state, which combines the joys of being and of non-being, which is neither reflection nor will, which is above both the moral existence and the intellectual existence, which is the return to unity....[1] — *Amiel's Journal*

Amiel describes the experience of pure consciousness with exceptional clarity — its qualities of silence, unboundedness, universality, unity, and bliss. Here, deeper than what we usually mean by "consciousness," lies the essence of our life:

> The center of life is neither in thought nor in feeling, nor in will, nor even in consciousness, so far as it thinks, feels, or wishes.... Deeper even than consciousness there is our being itself, our very substance, our nature.[2]

This level of consciousness, he declares, alone is real:

> In these moments of *tête-à-tête* with the infinite, how different life looks! How all that usually occupies and excites us becomes suddenly puerile, frivolous and vain. . . . At such moments, how everything becomes transformed, how everything changes! . . . Consciousness alone is immortal, positive, perfectly real. The world is but a firework, a sublime phantasmagoria, destined to cheer and form the soul. Consciousness is a universe, and its sun is love....[3]

The human mind and the universe share the same infinite source, Amiel tells us, and this source is open to direct personal experience:

> [T]he mind may experience the infinite in itself;...in the human individual there arises sometimes the divine spark which reveals to him the existence of the original, fundamental, principal Being, within which all is contained like a series within its generating formula. The universe is but a radiation of mind....[4] — *Amiel's Journal*

Also see Amiel in Chapter 7 (Unity Consciousness).

EMILY DICKINSON
1830–1886 • UNITED STATES

Her grandfather founded Amherst College. Her father was a multi-term state legislator and US Congressman. But Emily Dickinson lived a rather less worldly life. Born in Amherst, Massachusetts, she traveled outside her home village only a few times, outside of Massachusetts but once. After the age of 42, she rarely left her house and yard. She never married. She deliberately chose a life of Thoreau-like simplicity — her vocation was poetry. Of the 1,775 poems she wrote, fewer than a dozen were published during her lifetime, all anonymously and usually reworked by editors to conform to contemporary standards. Only in 1955 was a complete and unmodified collection of her poems published. Dickinson forged a brilliantly original style, full of power, and is acclaimed today as one of America's greatest poets.

The Soul's Superior instants
Occur to Her — alone —
When friend — and Earth's occasion
Have infinite withdrawn —
Or She — Herself — ascended
To too remote a Height
For lower Recognition
Than Her Omnipotent —
. . . .
Eternity's disclosure
To favorites — a few —
Of the Colossal substance
Of Immortality[1]   — "306"

Dickinson's language is telegraphic as always, but her meaning seems clear. Her most exalted inner experiences, "the Soul's Superior instants," occur when the soul is alone and all ordinary experience is "infinite withdrawn." She feels her soul ascend beyond the reach of sense perception. To try to describe this inner reality she uses the words *omnipotent, eternity, colossal,* and *immortality*. This experience, she tells us, is bestowed only to a fortunate few.

※

There is a solitude of space
   A solitude of sea
A solitude of death, but these
Society shall be
Compared with that profounder site
That polar privacy
A soul admitted to itself —
Finite infinity.[2]   — "1695"

There are many forms of solitude, Dickinson observes in the first three lines. But these are all "society" next to the far more profound solitude one gains when the soul is "admitted to itself" — when consciousness turns within to become aware of itself alone. This is a state of "finite infinity" — the experience of unboundedness within the boundaries of individual existence.

EDWARD CARPENTER

1844–1929 • ENGLAND

■ *Writer, poet, and educator, Edward Carpenter was a man of many talents. He also wrote and published his own musical compositions, mathematical discoveries, and articles on topics of all sorts. He became a traveling lecturer for the newly-established extension of Cambridge University, which aimed to serve people unable to attend universities. Although known today as a social reformer — he wrote pamphlets criticizing the industrialization of society — Carpenter devoted his major books to his experiences of higher states of consciousness. During his lifetime, his works were translated into languages worldwide, from Bulgarian to Russian to Japanese.*

There comes a time however, and at last, when — the real self emerging into consciousness, abysmal, adamantine, founded deep below and beyond all worlds — the Brain ceases from its terrified and insatiate quest. . . .

The brain is stilled. It does not cease from its natural and joyful activities. But it ceases from that terrified and joyless quest which was inevitable to it as long as its own existence, its own foundation, its own affiliation to the everlasting Being was in question and in doubt. The Man at last lets Thought go; he glides below it into the quiet feeling, the quiet sense of his own identity with the self of other things — of the universe. He glides past the feeling into the very identity itself, where a glorious all-consciousness leaves no room for separate self-thoughts or emotions. He leans back in silence on that inner being, and bars off for a time every thought, every movement of the mind, every impulse to action, or whatever in the faintest degree may stand between him and That; and so there comes to him a sense of absolute repose, a consciousness of immense and universal power, such as completely transforms the world for him. All life is changed; he becomes master of his fate; he perceives that all things are hurrying to perform his will; and whatever in that region of inner Life he may condescend to desire, that already is shaping itself to utterance and expression in the outer world around him. . . .

For the ceaseless endeavor to realize this identity with the great Self, there is no substitute. No teaching, no theorizing, no philosophizing, no rules of conduct or life will take the place of actual experience. . . . What is learnt by this actual experience is so much more, and so much more important, than anything that can be learnt by teaching or philosophy, that at any rate *without* it the latter can hardly be accounted of much value. . . .

This true Ego — this Self above and beyond the separate Me — to know it one must, as I say, become identified with it; and that is ultimately the only way of knowing it. . . .[1]

Hidden or clouded though it may be, yet it is recognizable to some degree in all men — nay, I believe that it is the very foundation of our individual life.[2] — *The Art of Creation*

Carpenter describes "the real self" awakening deep within, "beyond all worlds." His mind settles into a silent, "glorious all-consciousness" of "universal power." Here he experiences "the self of other things — of the universe."

I say, this heart and kernel of a great and immortal self, this consciousness of a powerful and continuing life within, is there — however deeply it may be buried — within each person; and its discovery is open to everyone who will truly and persistently seek it. And I say that I regard the discovery of this experience — with its accompanying sense of rest, content, expansion, power, joy, and even omniscience and immensity — as the most fundamental and important fact hitherto of human knowledge and scientific enquiry, and one verified and corroborated by thousands and even millions of human kind....

Whatever physical death may bring... there still remains that indefeasible fact, the certainty of the survival of the deepest, most universal portion of our natures.... I think it evident that this is the state of affairs which we ought to put before ourselves as the goal of our endeavor.... And it suggests to us that our persistent and unremitted effort during ordinary life should be to realize and lay hold of this immortal Thing, to conquer and make our own this very Heart of the universe.³ — *The Drama of Love and Death*

■ *Also see Carpenter in Chapter 5 (Cosmic Consciousness) and Chapter 7 (Unity Consciousness).*

BLACK ELK (HEHAKA SAPA)
1863–1950 • UNITED STATES

■ *Black Elk was a medicine man, or holy man, of the Oglala Lakota Sioux tribe. In 1876, at about 12, he fought in the Battle of Little Big Horn in Montana, led by his second cousin Crazy Horse. In 1887, at 24, he joined Buffalo Bill's Wild West Show and traveled to England, an experience he did not enjoy. In 1890, he was present at the Wounded Knee Massacre in South Dakota. He became widely known through the 1932 publication of* Black Elk Speaks, *narrating his life story to poet and writer John Neihardt (see Chapter 6). In* The Sacred Pipe, *he tells the story of Sioux beliefs and rituals, to preserve them for his people and the good of the world.*

> I am blind and do not see the things of this world; but when the Light comes from Above, it enlightens my Heart and I can see, for the Eye of my Heart sees everything; and through this vision I can help my people. The heart is a sanctuary at the Center of which there is a little space, wherein *Wakan-Tanka* dwells, and this is the Eye. This is the Eye of *Wakan-Tanka* by which He sees all things, and through which we see Him. If the heart is not pure, *Wakan-Tanka* cannot be seen. . . . In order to know the Center of the Heart in which is the Mind of *Wakan-Tanka*, you must be pure and good, and live in the manner that *Wakan-Tanka* has taught us. The man who is thus pure contains the Universe within the Pocket of his Heart.[1]
> — *The Spiritual Legacy of the American Indian*

Wakan-Tanka, often translated as *the Great Spirit*, is the Sioux term for the unmanifest, all-pervading field of intelligence, sacred and divine, that created the universe and is embodied in the universe. *Wakan-Tanka* is identified as one's real Self.[2] Black Elk tells us that he experiences *Wakan-Tanka* deep within, in the center or eye of his heart. He associates this experience with universal knowledge.

> [O]f all the created things or beings of the universe, it is the two-legged men alone who, if they purify and humiliate themselves, may become one with — or may know — Wakan-Tanka.[3]
> — *The Sacred Pipe*

Black Elk emphasizes that *Wakan-Tanka* is open to human experience, through a process of purification and simplification. Living in accord with *Wakan-Tanka* enables one to "know all things," to realize the ultimate oneness of the universe, and to fulfill one's desires with ease.[4]

■ *Also see Black Elk in Chapter 7 (Unity Consciousness).*

RABBI ABRAHAM ISAAC KOOK
1865–1935 • LATVIA & PALESTINE

■ *Abraham Isaac Kook was one of the greatest figures in 20th century Judaism. Considered a prodigy as a child, Kook (pronounced* cook*) became a rabbi at the age of 23, serving first in small communities in Latvia and Lithuania. In 1904, at 39, he moved to Palestine and established a Jewish academy (yeshiva) in the seaport town of Jaffa. During World War I, while visiting Germany, he was taken prisoner as an alien, but he escaped to England. There he became rabbi of a congregation in London, where he helped win popular support for establishing a home for the Jewish people in Palestine. In 1921 he was elected Palestine's first chief rabbi, a position he held the rest of his life. He was a renowned Torah scholar, an expert in Jewish law, and a student of the Kabbalah, dedicated to traditional Jewish values but open to new ideas. His expansive personality embraced and unified divergent political and religious viewpoints. He did not belong to any political party; he insisted that all Jews needed to work together. In his philosophy of "repentance," human separation from God results from our losing our connection with this divine source, which lies within.*

The greater you are, the more you need to search for your self. Your deep soul hides itself from consciousness. So you need to increase aloneness, elevation of thinking, penetration of thought, liberation of mind — until finally your soul reveals itself to you, spangling a few sparkles of her lights.

Then you find bliss, transcending all humiliations or anything that happens, by attaining equanimity, by becoming one with everything that happens, by reducing yourself so extremely that you nullify your individual, imaginary form, that you nullify existence in the depth of your self. "What are we?" Then you know every spark of truth, every bolt of integrity flashing anywhere.

Then you gather everything, without hatred, jealousy, or rivalry. The light of peace and a fierce boldness manifest in you. The desire to act and work, the passion to create and to restore yourself, the yearning for silence and for the inner shout of joy — these all band together in your spirit, and you become holy.[1]

Rabbi Kook repeatedly emphasizes the value of reconnecting with what he calls the "deep soul." Normally hidden, it is a realm of bliss, peace, truth, and liberation. It lies beyond all activity, even beyond our sense of individual self. When we experience it, he says, we discover who we really are — and when we emerge, our thoughts and actions are bold and joyful.

༄

The most significant talent is the ability to penetrate to the depths of our own being. But to effect this penetration it is important to know that it is an easy endeavor, that labor and exertion only impairs this august domain, that it is necessary to heed the claim for the delight of inner tranquility. Thus will be enhanced the substantive significance in the fruits of creation, and the sparks of holy light will begin to flash on all life and its spiritual concerns. . . .

And eternal truths will be released to us from the fountain of life, the source of the soul, which knows no falsehood or deceptive speech. It is hewn from the torch of truth. What flows from its light is only truth and justice which will abide forever.[2]

It should be easy to experience the "depths of our being," Rabbi Kook says, because this field of inner tranquility is a source of delight. In fact, he adds, making an effort is counterproductive. This is the principle underlying the Transcendental Meditation technique — the mind is drawn spontaneously inward because this inner field of bliss is inherently charming to the mind.

It turns out that the unity achieved in our souls serves to unite the world as a whole. And all those noble effects of the riches of the soul which everyone who is wise of heart, of a sensitive and holy spirit, can feel within himself through his own ascent because of the manifestation of the mystical discovery of inner unity — these spread and release light and vitality and become a source of blessing and an ornament of peace to the world and its fullness.³

For Rabbi Kook, the experience of transcending benefits not only the individual but the entire world. The unity we experience within us radiates outward, bringing nourishment and peace to everyone around us. This is now a scientifically validated effect, which we will explore in Chapters 9 and 10.

PAUL VALÉRY
1871–1945 • FRANCE

Poet, playwright, essayist, and philosopher, Valéry was one of the most honored intellectual and cultural figures of his era. He wrote about a remarkable variety of topics — literature, art, music, history, and current affairs. He was a popular public speaker throughout Europe. In 1931 he founded the Collège International de Cannes, a private college specializing in French language and civilization. Each morning he would rise at dawn for several hours' contemplation of the arts, the sciences, mathematics, language, and consciousness. His reflections were later published as the famous Cahiers *(Notebooks), an immense intellectual achievement. Though he wrote fewer than 100 poems, he was considered France's preeminent poet. His poems are known for their subtlety and breadth and the sensitivity of their language. Yet he always asserted that poetry, like mathematics and the sciences, was useful to him only as a reflection of the functioning of his own mind.*

Is there purer expectation, more detached from the world, emancipated from the self — and at the same time a completer self-possession — than I find at the day's threshold, in that first moment of proposal, of unity of my powers, when the sole desire of the mind (desire preceding all thought) is to steal a march on thought and be the love in what loves?

The soul rejoices in its uncluttered light. Its silence is the sum of all its speech: the sum of all its powers is its repose. It feels withdrawn from names and forms alike. As yet no figuration alters or constrains it. The least act of judgment would spot its perfection.

My body being at rest, I know of nothing except the *potential*. My waiting is a self-sufficient delight: it infers, while it defers, all possible conception.

How marvelous that a universal instant should erect itself in the frame of a man, and that the life of an individual should breathe forth its little puff of eternity!

Is it not in such unmoored states that men have invented the most mysterious and audacious words of their language?

O moment, Time's diamond . . . I am all trifles and wretched cares outside your gate.

On the summit of being I breathe an indefinable force like the force latent in the air before a storm. I sense the impending. . . . I do not know what is to follow: but I know what is happening: *to see what exists as purely possible; to reduce what is seen to the purely visible — this is the deepest work.*

Ah, consciousness, forever and forever demanding events! No sooner you are, than you are to be filled. . . .

Irresistibly also you divide yourself, and cling to one of your parts. . . . Why? — Farewell.[1] — "Meditation Before Thought"

Even the title, "Meditation Before Thought," suggests Valéry's experience — consciousness silent and awake within itself before rising into waves of thought. His mind quiet, his body at rest, he experiences "a universal instant," "eternity." But it does not last. As he moves into ordinary waking awareness, he observes his mind becoming active, localized, divided — "You divide yourself, and cling to one of your parts." Consciousness is essentially unified, he understands, but he cannot maintain that experience.

MARTIN BUBER
1878–1965 • AUSTRIA

A philosopher, educator, writer, and translator, Buber was one of the 20th century's leading intellectuals. Born in Vienna, he took an early interest in the Zionist movement, but soon became interested in Jewish Hasidism, the mystical movement which, in contrast to a rigid academic approach, emphasized experience and living one's religion in daily life. In 1916 he founded Der Jude, a central forum for Jewish intellectuals. In 1938, as Nazi power rose, Buber left Germany for Jerusalem and became a professor at Hebrew University. He translated Hasidic lore and the Hebrew Bible into German. He collected experiences of higher states of consciousness from around the world and published them in his book Ecstatic Confessions. *An early advocate of a binational Jewish-Arab state, he believed Jews and Arabs would someday live together peacefully in a single nation.*

Now from my own unforgettable experience I know well that there is a state in which the bonds of the personal nature of life seem to have fallen away from us and we experience an undivided unity. . . . Responsibly — that is, as a man holding his ground before reality — I can elicit from those experiences only that in them I reached an undifferentiable unity of myself without form or content. I may call this an original pre-biographical unity and suppose that it is hidden unchanged beneath all biographical change, all development and complication of the soul. Nevertheless, in the honest and sober account of the responsible understanding this unity is nothing but the unity of this soul of mine, whose "ground" I have reached, so much so, beneath all formations and contents, that my spirit has no choice but to understand it as the groundless. But the basic unity of my own soul is certainly beyond the reach of all the multiplicity it has hitherto received from life. . . .[1]

— *Between Man and Man*

Buber describes a state in which boundaries fall away and he experiences "an undivided unity," without content, beyond multiplicity and change, a ground state of consciousness.

Buber refers to this type of experience as *ecstasy* and elaborates on it here:

[T]here is an experience which grows in the soul out of the soul itself, without contact and without restraint, in naked oneness. It comes into being and completes itself beyond the commotion, free of the other, inaccessible to the other. It needs no nourishment, and no poison can touch it. The soul which stands in it stands in itself, has itself, experiences itself — boundlessly. It experiences itself as a unity . . . because it has submerged itself entirely in itself, has plunged down to the very ground of itself, is kernel and husk, sun and eye . . . at once. This most inward of all experiences is what the Greeks call *ek-stasis*, a stepping out. . . .

The human being who trudges along day by day in the functions of bodiliness and unfreedom receives in ecstasy a revelation of freedom. One who knows only differentiated experience — the experience of meaning, of thought, of will . . . comes to know an undifferentiated experience: the experience of the I. One who always feels and knows only particulars about himself suddenly finds himself under the storm cloud of a force, a superabundance, an infinity. . . .

Of all the experiences which are said, in order to mark their incomparability, to be incommunicable, only ecstasy is by its very nature the ineffable. It is such because the human being who experiences it has become a unity into which no more dualities extend. . . .

Now all powers have vibrated together into one force, all sparks have blazed together into one flame. Now one is removed from the commotion, removed into the most silent, speechless heavenly kingdom — removed even from language. . . .

Being lifted so completely above the multiplicity of the I, above the play of the senses and of thought, the ecstatic is also separated from language, which cannot follow him. . . .

One's unity is not relative, not limited by the other; it is limitless, for it is the unity of I and world. One's unity is solitude, absolute solitude: the solitude of that which is without limits. . . .

The unbounded ones do not speak even to themselves, in themselves, because there are no boundaries within them either: no multiplicity, no duality, no more Thou in the I.[2]

— *Ecstatic Confessions*

The classic state of ecstasy, as Buber defines it, seems identical with Transcendental Consciousness. He elucidates its key characteristics: it is silent, unbounded, self-referral, unified. It is beyond sensory experience, beyond language and thought, beyond any duality. Ecstasy brings the experience of "the I" — the Self, the transcendental field. This he defines as "a superabundance, an infinity" and as "the most silent, speechless heavenly kingdom."

■ *Also see Buber in Chapter 7 (Unity Consciousness).*

ALBERT EINSTEIN
1879–1955 • SWITZERLAND & UNITED STATES

Albert Einstein is widely regarded as the greatest scientist who ever lived. By age 12 he had decided to dedicate his life to solving the riddle of "the huge world." His work converges into one supreme goal: to understand the unity underlying nature's diversity. His theory of special relativity (1905) showed the underlying unity of matter and energy and of light and time. His theory of general relativity (1916) showed the unity of gravity and acceleration, of space and time, and of matter and space. Einstein profoundly altered the way we think of ourselves and the universe. He spent the last half of his life trying to develop a unified field theory, a description of the single field which, he felt certain, underlies all of nature. He persisted despite criticism, and though he never succeeded, the theory of unity he felt intuitively and sought mathematically nears completion today. Famed also for his pacifism, he came to be seen as a world citizen, devoting his last years to bringing harmony to the world.

Where did Einstein's conviction of nature's underlying unity come from? What impelled his life's work? Einstein himself gives us a clue in a letter he wrote to Queen Elizabeth of Belgium (1876-1965) that contains this passage:

> Still there are moments when one feels free from one's own identification with human limitations and inadequacies. At such moments, one imagines that one stands on some spot of a small planet, gazing in amazement at the cold yet profoundly moving beauty of the eternal, the unfathomable: life and death flow into one, and there is neither evolution nor destiny; only being.[1]

Einstein describes moments of apparently unbounded awareness, an underlying unity beyond life and death, evolution and destiny. All that remains is the experience of "the eternal, the unfathomable" — "only being."

Maharishi emphasized that when we transcend, we experience not merely the source of thought but the ocean of intelligence from which the whole universe is born and sustained. Einstein alluded to this in a letter he wrote:

> A human being is a part of the whole, called by us "Universe," a part limited in time and space. He experiences himself, his thoughts and feelings as something separate from the rest — a kind of optical delusion of his consciousness. This delusion is a kind of prison for us, restricting us to our personal desires and to affection for a few persons nearest to us. Our task must be to free ourselves from this prison by widening our circle of compassion to embrace all living creatures and the whole of nature in its beauty.[2]

Einstein's quest for unity, it appears, was no mere intellectual exercise. He sought to understand, through the methodology of modern science, what he experienced deep within. This experience, for Einstein, was all-important.

> The finest emotion of which we are capable is the mystic emotion. Herein lies the germ of all art and all true science. Anyone to whom this feeling is alien, who is no longer capable of wonderment and lives in a state of fear is a dead man. To know that what is impenetrable for us really exists and manifests itself as the highest wisdom and the most radiant beauty, whose gross forms alone are intelligible to our poor faculties — this knowledge, this feeling . . . that is the core of the true religious sentiment. In this sense, and in this sense alone, I rank myself among profoundly religious men.[3]

The "mystic emotion" Einstein refers to does not imply mysterious or incomprehensible. The word *mystic* stems from a Greek word meaning *to close*, i.e., the eyes and ears, presumably to dive within and experience "the germ of all art and all true science," as Einstein worded it — indeed, the source of all creation. This, for Einstein, was the goal of human life:

The true value of a human being is determined primarily by the measure and the sense in which he has attained to liberation from the self.[4]

Liberation from the self, in Maharishi's understanding, means transcending the individual self — the self related to our mind and ego — and experiencing the universal Self, unbounded pure consciousness. Glimpses of this sublime experience seemed to propel Einstein's quest to understand the ultimate unity of life.

HELEN KELLER
1880–1968 • UNITED STATES

Though blind and deaf from age two, Helen Keller graduated with honors from Radcliffe College — the first blind and deaf person to earn a college degree. She devoted her life, through lecturing and writing, to social reform. The play and film The Miracle Worker *tells the story of how her teacher, Anne Sulllivan, helped her emerge from her world of dark silence to become celebrated as one of the greatest women of her time. Keller published a dozen books and visited 40 countries, gaining international fame as she campaigned for peace and for rights for women, workers, and the disabled. She helped found the American Civil Liberties Union in 1920. Her friends included Alexander Graham Bell, Mark Twain, and Charlie Chaplin. She was awarded the Presidential Medal of Freedom and honors from around the world.*

I sense a holy passion pouring down from the springs of Infinity.
... Bound to suns and planets by invisible cords, I feel the flame of eternity in my soul. Here, in the midst of the every-day air, I sense

the rush of ethereal rains. I am conscious of the splendor that binds all things of earth to all things of heaven — immured by silence and darkness, I possess the light which shall give me vision a thousandfold when death sets me free.[1] — *My Religion*

Keller describes the experience of a deep level of mind she associates with infinity and eternity. In this deep inward place, she experiences "the splendor that binds all things of earth to all things of heaven." Though blind and deaf, she nonetheless experiences the same inner light that illuminates each of us from within.

☙

There is in the blind as in the seeing an Absolute which gives truth to what we know to be true, order to what is orderly, beauty to the beautiful, touchableness to what is tangible.... Reality, of which visible things are the symbol, shines before my mind. While I walk about my chamber with unsteady steps, my spirit sweeps skyward on eagle wings and looks out with unquenchable vision upon the world of eternal beauty.[2] — *The World I Live In*

Helen Keller recognizes this deep inner field as "Absolute," the source of truth, order, and beauty. Like so many others, she apprehends it as "Reality," from where all visible things emerge — the realm of "eternal beauty."

MORIHEI UESHIBA
1883–1969 • JAPAN

The founder of the martial art Aikido, Morihei Ueshiba — whose name means "abundant peace" — is regarded by many as the greatest martial artist of all time. Born to a wealthy landowner, and frail and sickly as a child, he studied various forms of martial arts growing up. He served in the Japanese army and pursued several careers, including agriculture, while continuing to study and teach martial arts. Little more than five feet tall, he possessed the documented ability to disarm any attacker, throw a dozen men simultaneously to the ground, bring an opponent down and hold him there with a single finger, and even pin opponents without touching them. Yet Ueshiba's life was a spiritual quest. He developed Aikido as a spiritual path. The word Aikido can be translated as "the art of peace." Its ultimate goals are enlightenment and peace. In his later years Ueshiba was lavished with honors, in Japan and internationally.

When Ueshiba was 42, a naval officer and kendo expert visited the town where he lived. Knowing of Ueshiba's renown, he challenged him to a kendo match (Japanese fencing with bamboo swords). Remaining unarmed, Ueshiba easily avoided the man's thrusts and cuts, and the man conceded defeat. Afterward Ueshiba went outside to his garden to wash himself at the well and to rest.

Suddenly the earth trembled. Golden vapor welled up from the ground and engulfed me. I felt transformed into a golden image, and my body seemed as light as a feather. I could understand the speech of the birds. All at once I understood the nature of creation: the Way of a Warrior is to manifest divine love, a spirit that embraces and nurtures all things. Tears of gratitude and joy streamed down my cheeks. I saw the entire earth as my home, and the sun, moon, and stars as my intimate friends. All attachment to material things vanished.[1]

At that moment he realized: *I am the universe.* He saw that the true purpose of *budo* (Japanese martial arts) is *love* — love that cherishes and nourishes all things. After this experience, Ueshiba seemed to become invincible as a martial artist — easily defeating opponents who had previously defeated him, leaping amazing distances, vaulting over attackers, moving boulders, and other feats.

All the fighting techniques he had learned, he realized, were actually instruments for cultivating life, knowledge, and virtue, not throwing people to the ground. The true task of the samurai is not to destroy but to protect all life and cultivate peace.

Thus Ueshiba developed Aikido, whose supreme goal is to lead the practitioner to enlightenment and cultivate world peace. He said, "Aikido is the principle and the path that join humanity with the Universal Consciousness,"[2] and "Its function is to join with the heart of the universe and give love."[3]

Ueshiba taught that the source of power in the universe lies within us:

> The Divine is not something high above us. It is right in our very center; it is our freedom.[4]

> The heart of a human being is no different from the soul of heaven and earth.[5]

> If you have life in you, you have access to the secrets of the ages, for the truth of the universe resides in each and every human being.[6]

And he taught that we can directly experience this inner source of divine power through a process of transcending. He repeatedly urged people to experience the transcendental field:

> You cannot see or touch the Divine with your gross senses. The Divine is within you, not somewhere else. Unite yourself to the Divine. . . .[7]

> Create each day anew by clothing yourself with heaven and earth, bathing yourself with wisdom and love, and placing yourself in the heart of Mother Nature. Your body and mind will be

gladdened, depression and heartache will dissipate, and you will be filled with gratitude.[8]

To practice properly the Art of Peace, you must: Calm the spirit and return to the source.[9]

Each one of us must strive to . . . experience the heart of the universe which brings about the harmony of perfect balance.[10]

Cast off limiting thoughts and return to true emptiness. Stand in the midst of the Great Void. This is the secret of the Way of a Warrior.[11]

If you do not blend
with the emptiness of
the Pure Void
you will never know
the path of aiki (peace)[12]

༃

Ueshiba lyrically describes his own experience of transcendence:

Crystal clear, sharp and bright,
my mind has no opening for evil to roost.
The morning sun shines in,
My mind, too, is clear and bright;
from the window, I let myself
soar to the highest heaven,
bathed in divine light.[13]

▪ *Also see Ueshiba in Chapter 5 (Cosmic Consciousness) and Chapter 7 (Unity Consciousness).*

D.H. LAWRENCE
1885–1930 • ENGLAND

▪ *Lawrence began his working life as a teacher while also writing poems, short stories, and a novel. He was soon able to devote himself full-time to writing. He spent much of his life traveling — to Italy and Sicily, Australia, Sri Lanka, the United States, Mexico, France — writing novels while gaining fame as a travel writer. He wrote 13 novels, over 400 poems, four travel books, an acclaimed study of American literature, other literary criticism, and translations of Russian and Italian authors. His letters are published in eight volumes. He was also an avid oil painter. Through all of his work, he was concerned with the dehumanizing influence of modern industrialized society. The English novelist E.M. Forster called Lawrence "the greatest imaginative novelist of our generation."*[1]

In the following passage, from Lawrence's novel *The Rainbow*, the main character is caring for a small child and is seeking shelter from a storm.

He opened the doors, upper and lower, and they entered into the high, dry barn, that smelled warm even if it were not warm. He hung the lantern on the nail and shut the door. They were in another world now. The light shed softly on the timbered barn, on the white-washed walls, and the great heap of hay; instruments cast their shadows largely, a ladder rose to the dark arch of a loft. Outside there was the driving rain, inside, the softly illuminated stillness and calmness of the barn.

Holding the child on one arm, he set about preparing the food for the cows, filling a pan with chopped hay and brewer's grains and a little meal. The child, all wonder, watched what he did.... She was silent, quite still.

In a sort of dream, his heart sunk to the bottom, leaving the surface of him still, quite still. . . .

The two sat very quiet. His mind, in a sort of trance, seemed to become more and more vague. He held the child close to him. . . . Gradually she relaxed, the eyelids began to sink over her dark, watchful eyes. As she sank to sleep, his mind became blank.

When he came to, as if from sleep, he seemed to be sitting in a timeless stillness.[2] — *The Rainbow*

Even the setting suggests transcending. Coming in from the driving rain outside, the man experiences the barn as "another world," a world of illuminated silence. After he enters the barn, his mind settles inward, moving beyond thought. When thoughts return, he feels he remains in a "timeless stillness," as if retaining something of pure consciousness.

In one of his essays Lawrence asks, "What is the real thing in life? What is it that makes you *feel* right, makes life really feel good?" He answers:

> It is the great question. And the answers are the old answers. But every generation must frame the answer in its own way. What makes life good to me is the sense that, even if I am sick and ill, I am alive, alive to the depths of my soul, and in touch, somewhere in touch with the vivid life of the cosmos. Somehow my life draws strength from the depth of the universe, from the depth among the stars, from the great "World." Out of the great World comes my strength, and my reassurance. One could say "God," but the word "God" is somehow tainted. But there is a flame or a Life Everlasting wreathing through the cosmos forever and giving us our renewal, once we can get in touch with it.[3] "The Real Thing"

For Lawrence, in other words, the real thing is transcendence.

FRANKLIN MERRELL-WOLFF
1887–1985 • UNITED STATES

■ *Born and raised in California, the son of a Methodist minister and pioneer in the California citrus growing business, Merrell-Wolff studied mathematics, philosophy, and psychology at Stanford. He did a year of graduate study in philosophy at Harvard, where he took a seminar from Rabindranath Tagore, by whom he was profoundly impressed. He then returned to Stanford to teach mathematics for a time. But he determined that academia would not satisfy his thirst for knowledge. Supporting himself and his family by maintaining a 45-acre orange grove on land his father had sold him and later by prospecting for gold in the California mountains, he pursued a path that took him through the Theosophical, Sufi, and Indian traditions, with Shankara a major influence. When he was 49, he began to have experiences of higher states of consciousness. Thereafter he devoted himself to writing and lecturing about the importance of developing consciousness. The author of three books and nearly 250 audio essays, he lived to be 98 years old.*

I found myself at once identical with the Voidness, Darkness, and Silence, but realized them as utter, though ineffable, Fullness. . . . The deepening of consciousness that followed at once is simply inconceivable and quite beyond the possibility of adequate representation. . . .

    The first discernible effect in consciousness was something that I may call a *shift in the base of consciousness*. From the relative point of view, the final step may be likened to a leap into Nothing. At once, that Nothing was resolved into utter Fullness, which in turn gave the relative world a dreamlike quality of unreality. I felt and knew myself to have arrived, at last, at the Real. I was not dissipated in a sort of spatial emptiness, but on the contrary was spread out in a Fullness beyond measure. . . .

It is as though the "I" became the whole of space. The Self is no longer a pole or focal point, but it sweeps outward, everywhere, in a sort of unpolarized consciousness, which is at once self-identity and the objective content of consciousness. It is an unequivocal transcendence of the subject-object relationship. Herein lies the rationale of the inevitable ineffability of mystical insight. All language is grounded in the subject-object relationship, and so, at best, can only misrepresent transcendent consciousness. . . .

I knew myself to be beyond space, time, and causality. As the substantial, spatial, and transcendent "I," I knew that I sustained the whole phenomenal universe, and that time, space, and law are simply the Self-imposed forms whereby I am enabled to apprehend in the relative sense. I, thus, am not dependent upon the space-time manifold, but, on the contrary, that manifold is dependent upon the Self with which I am identical.

Closely associated with the foregoing realization there is a feeling of *complete freedom*. . . .

Through the Recognition, I attained a state wherein I could be at rest and contented in the most profound sense. For me, individually, it was not necessary to seek further, to achieve further, nor to express further in order to know full enjoyment.

There is a decided increase in the realization of the affective qualities of *calmness* and *serenity*. . . .

In the transcendent state I felt myself to be grounded in the Real, in a sense of the utmost intimacy. . . .

The most marked affective quality precipitated within the relative consciousness is that of *felicity*. Joy is realized as a very definite experience. It is of a quality more intense and satisfying than that afforded by any of the experiences or achievements that I have known within the world-field. It is not easy to describe this state of felicity....

One feels that there is nothing more right or more righteous, for that matter, than to be so harmonized in one's consciousness as to feel the Joy at all times. It is a dynamic sort of Joy that seems to dissolve such pain as may be in the vicinity of the one who realizes it. This Joy enriches rather than impoverishes others.

I doubt that anyone could possibly appreciate the tremendous value of this felicity without directly experiencing it....

It induces a sense of physiological, as well as emotional and intellectual, well-being....

Clearly there are detectable physiological effects. Nervous tensions are reduced.... In fact, one does have a curious sense of feeling nourished....

It gives a feeling of being alive, beside which the ordinary feeling of life is no more than a mere shadow. And just as the shadow life is obviously mortal, the higher Life is as clearly deathless.[1]

— *The Philosophy of Consciousness Without an Object*

Merrell-Wolff's description matches Maharishi's description of Transcendental Consciousness point by point. He describes unbounded awareness in several places, most vividly when he says he felt "the 'I' became the whole of space." He feels he has transcended all relative facets of life, even "the subject-object relationship," and experiences consciousness aware of itself alone. This brings him serenity, physiological well-being, and surpassing joy. No words adequately capture this, he says — one must experience it directly.

In this next passage, Merrell-Wolff describes an experience he had while sitting on the swing on his front porch in the mountains of California:

> Presently I felt the Ambrosia-quality in the breath with the purifying benediction that it casts over the whole personality, even including the physical body. I found myself above the universe, not in the sense of leaving the physical body and being taken out in space, but in the sense of being above space, time, and causality. My karma seemed to drop away from me as an individual responsibility. I felt intangibly, yet wonderfully, free. I sustained this universe and was not bound by it. Desires and ambitions grew perceptibly more and more shadowy. All worldly honors were without power to exalt me....
>
> I found but one interest: the desire that other souls should also realize this that I had realized, for in it lay the one effective key for the solving of their problems. The little tragedies of men left me indifferent. I saw one great Tragedy, the cause of all the rest, the failure of man to realize his own Divinity. I saw but one solution, the Realization of this Divinity.[2]   — *Pathways through to Space*

Merrell-Wolff again describes a dimension of consciousness beyond space, time, and causation. He feels complete freedom, beyond boundaries. This experience, he asserts — "the Realization of this Divinity" within — is the key to solving humanity's problems.

■ *Also see Merrell-Wolff in Chapter 5 (Cosmic Consciousness) and Chapter 7 (Unity Consciousness).*

HOWARD THURMAN

1899–1981 • UNITED STATES

■ *Minister, author, philosopher, theologian, educator, civil rights leader, and one of the most important figures in African American history, Howard Thurman was born in Florida and grew up in a world of segregation. He went to Morehouse College, a classmate and friend of Martin Luther King, Sr., and graduated first in his class. He next went to divinity school and at 26 was ordained a Baptist minister. After pastoring a church in Ohio, he became the dean of chapel and a faculty member in the School of Divinity at Howard University. Traveling to India, he was able to meet two people he revered, Mahatma Gandhi and Rabindranath Tagore. He helped establish the Church for the Fellowship of All Peoples in San Francisco, the first racially and culturally integrated church in the US. He went to Boston University, where he taught in the School of Theology and served as dean of chapel, the first black to hold a deanship at a predominantly white university. He mentored Dr. Martin Luther King, Jr., who was doing his doctoral studies there, introducing King to Gandhi's philosophy of nonviolent resistance. Thurman authored 20 books, beautifully written, deeply felt reflections on life and living.*

There is no clear distinction between mind and spirit; but there is a quality of mind that is more than thought and the process of thought: this quality involves feelings and the wholeness in which the life of man has its being. . . . What is being considered is what a man means totally when he says, "I am." This "self" shares profoundly in the rhythm that holds and releases but never lets go. There is the rest of detachment and withdrawal when the spirit moves into the depths of the region of the Great Silence, where world weariness is washed away and blurred vision is once again prepared for the focus of the long view where seeking and finding are so united that failure and frustration, real though they are, are no longer felt to be ultimately real. Here the Presence of God is sensed as an all-pervasive aliveness which materializes into concreteness of communion: the reality of prayer. Here God speaks without words and the self listens without ears. Here at last, glimpses of the meaning of all things and the meaning of one's own life are seen with all their strivings. To accept this is one meaning of the good line, "Rest in the Lord — O, rest in the Lord."[1]

— "The Need for Periodic Rest," in *The Inward Journey*

Thurman experiences a region deep within that he calls "the Great Silence." Transcending sense perception, he feels withdrawn from everything, while deep rest refreshes the body and clears the mind. "Seeking and finding" become united in the experience of the divine and the meaning of all things.

Elsewhere Thurman refers to this as "the Time of Quiet," in which he experiences the "Light, the Truth, that is within," in "the stillness of our own spirits."[2] At these times he feels "invaded by the Eternal."[3]

※

There is a sense of wholeness at the core of man
That must abound in all he does;
That marks with reverence his ev'ry step;
That has its sway when all else fails;
That wearies out all evil things;
That warms the depth of frozen fears
Making friend of foe,
Making love of hate,
And lasts beyond the living and the dead,
Beyond the goals of peace, the ends of war!
This man seeks through all his years:
To be complete and of one piece, within, without.[4]

— "Knowledge . . . Shall Vanish Away," in *The Inward Journey*

When we experience the "wholeness at the core" of life, Thurman says, we find evil transformed to goodness, enemies to friends, hate to love. This experience, he says, transcends time and is the ultimate goal of human seeking.

■ *Also see Howard Thurman in Chapter 5 (Cosmic Consciousness), Chapter 6 (God Consciousness), and Chapter 7 (Unity Consciousness).*

DAG HAMMARSKJÖLD
1905–1961 • SWEDEN

■ *Diplomat, economist, and author, Dag Hammarskjöld became Secretary-General of the United Nations in 1953, the second person to hold that post and, at 47, the youngest ever. He was born into a distinguished Swedish family with a long record of public service. With a PhD in economics from Stokholm University, he became chairman of Sweden's central bank, then served in government. Virtually unknown when he became Secretary-General, he gained worldwide admiration for his vision, integrity, courage, eloquence, and problem-solving brilliance. Described as "a world-class peacemaker who proved effective in the most potentially explosive conflicts in the Cold War,"[1] Hammarskjöld was deeply committed to equal rights for all human beings. He invented shuttle diplomacy and established the UN peacekeeping forces. En route to the Congo to negotiate a ceasefire in the Katanga conflict, his DC-6 airliner crashed mysteriously. He was awarded the Nobel Peace Prize posthumously. Profoundly spiritual, he considered Meister Eckhart his teacher and steeped himself in Indian and Chinese spiritual classics. US President John F. Kennedy called him "the greatest statesman of our century."*

After Dag Hammarskjöld's death, a diary was found in his New York house, a mix of short personal reflections and haiku poetry that he had kept since he was 25. It was published two years later as *Markings* and was immediately recognized as a classic of spiritual literature. These passages are from that book.

Clad in this "self," the creation of irresponsible and ignorant persons, meaningless honors and catalogued acts — strapped into the strait jacket of the immediate.

To step out of all this, and stand naked on the precipice of dawn — acceptable, invulnerable, free: in the Light, with the Light, of the Light. *Whole*, real in the Whole. Out of myself as a stumbling block, into myself as fulfillment.[2]   — *Markings*

Hammarskjöld describes the experience of transcending — moving from the "small" self inward to freedom, light, wholeness, and fulfillment.

༄

Now. When I have overcome my fears — of others, of myself, of the underlying darkness:

at the frontier of the unheard-of.

Here ends the known. But, from a source beyond it, something fills my being with its possibilities.

Here desire is purified into openness: each action a preparation, each choice a yes to the unknown.

Prevented by the duties of life on the surface from looking down into the depths, yet all the while being slowly trained by them to descend as a shaping agent into the chaos, whence the fragrance of white wintergreen bears the promise of a new belonging.

At the frontier — [3]   — *Markings*

Hammarskjöld again seeks to capture the experience of transcending, the mind's move from the outer world of boundaries and fear to the inner world of freedom and all possibilities. He uses the word *chaos* in the original Greek sense, meaning the primordial void, that which exists prior to anything else — in other words, pure consciousness.

You wake from dreams of doom and — for a moment — you *know*: beyond all the noise and gestures, the only real thing, love's calm unwavering flame in the half light of an early dawn.[4]

— *Markings*

In the gap between sleeping and waking one can experience stillness, transcendence — love.

※

Only in man has the evolution of the creation reached the point where reality encounters itself in judgment and choice. Outside of man, the creation is neither good nor evil.

Only when you descend into yourself and encounter the Other, do you then experience goodness as the ultimate reality — united and living — in Him and through you.[5]   — *Markings*

Turning within, one experiences "the Other" — the transcendental field, beyond the constrictions of time and space, the field of purity and good.

※

In a dream I walked with God through the deep places of creation; past walls that receded and gates that opened, through hall after hall of silence, darkness and refreshment — the dwelling place of souls acquainted with light and warmth — until, around me, was an infinity into which we all flowed together and lived anew, like the rings made by raindrops falling upon wide expanses of calm dark waters.[6]   — *Markings*

With lyrical language Hammarskjöld describes the experience of silence, unboundedness, and unity — the experience of transcendence.

If you tour the UN headquarters in New York City, you will be shown the Meditation Room — planned and overseen in detail by Dag Hammarskjöld as a space devoted to inner silence, where anyone, regardless of religion, can turn within. This room, he felt, should be the UN's heart. You can take home a leaflet with the message he wrote for its inauguration, which reads in part:

We all have within us a center of stillness surrounded by silence.

This house, dedicated to work and debate in the service of peace, should have one room dedicated to silence in the outward sense and stillness in the inner sense.

It has been the aim to create in this small room a place where the doors may be open to the infinite lands of thought and prayer. . . .

There is an ancient saying that the sense of a vessel is not in its shell but in the void. So it is with this room. It is for those who come here to fill the void with what they find in their center of stillness.[7]

■ *Also see Hammarskjöld in Chapter 5 (Cosmic Consciousness).*

ARTHUR KOESTLER
1905–1983 • HUNGARY & ENGLAND

■ *Journalist, novelist, essayist, and author, Arthur Koestler was born in Budapest and studied science and psychology at the University of Vienna. He lived in Israel for three years, then turned to journalism. As the science editor for a Berlin newspaper, he was part of a 1931 Zeppelin expedition to the North Pole. He traveled throughout the Soviet Union. As a correspondent for a British newspaper, he covered the Spanish Civil War, where he was captured and sentenced to death — but was later returned to Great Britain in a prisoner exchange. During World War II he served in the French Foreign Legion and the British Army, then spent the remainder of his life writing and lecturing. He spoke and wrote in Hungarian, German, French,*

Hebrew, and English (most of his later work was in English). In addition to autobiographical works, he wrote books about science, the creative process, Indian and Japanese mysticism, synchronicity, and scientific research on paranormal phenomena. In the 1970s he was made a Commander of the Order of the British Empire.

In his book *The Invisible Writing*, Koestler describes his experience as a prisoner of war in Spain. "I was standing at the recessed window of cell No. 40," he writes, "and, with a piece of iron-spring that I had extracted from the wire mattress, was scratching mathematical formulae on the wall." He went on to recall Euclid's proof that the number of primes is infinite, remembering the deep, aesthetic satisfaction this proof always gave him — and now, in his prison cell, feeling the same enchantment, he realized its source: "The scribbled symbols on the wall represented one of the rare cases where a meaningful and comprehensive statement about the infinite is arrived at by precise and finite means." This insight led immediately to the following experience:

> Then I was floating on my back in a river of peace, under bridges of silence. It came from nowhere and flowed nowhere. Then there was no river and no I. The I had ceased to exist.
>
> It is extremely embarrassing to write down a phrase like that when one has read *The Meaning of Meaning* and nibbled at logical positivism and aims at verbal precision and dislikes nebulous gushings. Yet, "mystical" experiences, as we dubiously call them, are not nebulous, vague or maudlin — they only become so when we debase them by verbalization. However, to communicate what is incommunicable by its nature, one must somehow put it into words, and so one moves in a vicious circle. When I say "the I had ceased to exist," I refer to a concrete experience that is verbally as incommunicable as the feeling aroused by a piano concerto, yet just as real — only much more real. In fact, its primary mark is the sensation that this state is more real than any other one has experienced before — that for the first time the veil has fallen and one is in touch with "real reality," the hidden order of things, the X-ray texture of the world,

normally obscured by layers of irrelevancy.

What distinguishes this type of experience from the emotional entrancements of music, landscapes or love is that the former has a definitely intellectual, or rather noumenal, content. It is meaningful, though not in verbal terms. Verbal transcriptions that come nearest to it are: the unity and interlocking of everything that exists, an interdependence like that of gravitational fields or communicating vessels. The "I" ceases to exist because it has, by a kind of mental osmosis, established communication with, and been dissolved in, the universal pool. It is this process of dissolution and limitless expansion which is sensed as the "oceanic feeling," as the draining of all tension, the absolute catharsis, the peace that passeth all understanding.

The coming-back to the lower order of reality I found to be gradual, like waking up from anaesthesia. There was the equation of the parabola scratched on the dirty wall, the iron bed and the iron table and the strip of blue Andalusian sky. But there was no unpleasant hangover as from other modes of intoxication. On the contrary: There remained a sustained and invigorating, serene and fear-dispelling after-effect that lasted for hours and days. It was as if a massive dose of vitamins had been injected into the veins. Or, to change the metaphor, I resumed my travels through my cell like an old car with its batteries freshly recharged.

Whether the experience had lasted for a few minutes or an hour, I never knew. In the beginning it occurred two or even three times a week, then the intervals became longer. It could never be voluntarily induced. After my liberation it recurred at even longer intervals, perhaps once or twice in a year.[1] — *The Invisible Writing*

Koestler experienced what he called "real reality." His body is deeply relaxed. His mind is silent, unbounded, dissolved in "the universal pool." This experience, though beyond description, is actually more real than any other experience, Koestler asserts — the ordinary waking state is a "lower order of reality" that becomes meaningful only through perception of the higher order.

The experience held immense practical value for him. "It was always the 'oceanic' type of experience," he wrote, "which dictated the really important decisions of my life." They "filled me with a direct certainty that a higher order of reality existed, and that it alone invested existence with meaning."[2]

EUGENE IONESCO
1909–1994 • ROMANIA & FRANCE

Born in Romania, Ionesco grew up in France, then returned to Romania at 16, where he attended college, married, and had a daughter. At 27, he moved with his family back to France and lived there the rest of his life. He wrote literary criticism and, at 39, his first play, the one-act "antiplay," The Bald Soprano. *First performed in 1950, it made him famous. It inspired a revolution in dramatic techniques and helped launch the "theatre of the absurd." Ionesco published a number of one-act and full-length plays, popularizing many surrealistic techniques and opening new possibilities for drama. He also wrote novels, stories, poetry, and children's stories. He received many awards as well as honorary doctoral degrees from four universities.*

Once, on a May morning, just before noon, a day that seemed full of sap, in a leafy park where the light streamed down, white, blue, green: that day it all began with a senseless, inexplicable joy that I have never again felt so concretely, so carnally, so obviously a *joie de vivre* sustained by an indescribable astonishment at being alive. As a matter of fact the consciousness of being and the astonishment at being were one and the same thing. I suddenly woke up — from what sleep? — I woke to a light which dislocated the old meanings of things, of the time when my consciousness had gone to sleep. The intense astonishment that took possession of me was only the realization that I was. There was no more fear, no more anxiety, only calm, certainty, joy. Either abandoning or waking from a sleep peopled by the phantoms of everyday existence, I suddenly entered the heart of a reality so blindingly obvious, so total, so enlightening, so luminous, that I wondered how I had never before realized how easy this reality was to find and how easily I found myself in it. How can one not be anxious, how can one not feel lost and distressed, I said to myself, if one doesn't know this, if one is not at the very center of this astonishment?

So though the first step of this state of consciousness began with an emptying of the content of notions, the second, the essential step was a unified plenitude beyond definitions and limits. . . .

It began with the feeling that space was emptying itself of its material heaviness, which explains the euphoric sense of relief I felt. Notions were freed of their content. Objects became transparent, permeable; they were no longer obstacles and it seemed as if one could pass through them. It was as if my mind could move freely, as if there were no resistance to its movement.

Thus my mind could find its center again, reunited, reassembled out of the matrixes and limits within which it had been dispersed. And it was from this moment on that the feeling of plenitude took hold.[1] — *Present Past Past Present*

Ordinary waking experience is a kind of sleep from which Ionesco has somehow awakened. He experiences "a reality so blindingly obvious, so total, so enlightening, so luminous" that he wonders why he had never known it before. When he describes "consciousness of being," he suggests experience of the field of pure existence, pure awareness, pure Being, beyond mental activity.

He characterizes it as "unified plenitude beyond definitions and limits," suggesting the unified and unbounded fullness of pure consciousness. Without this experience, he declares, one cannot help feeling distressed.

▪ *Also see Ionesco in Chapter 5 (Cosmic Consciousness) and Chapter 6 (God Consciousness).*

THOMAS MERTON
1915–1969 • UNITED STATES

▪ *Born in France, Merton spent his boyhood in New York and in his teens was educated at boarding schools in France and England. He enrolled at Cambridge, then transferred to Columbia University, where he studied English and completed a master's degree. There he became interested in Catholicism and the priesthood. At 27, after teaching English for a year, he was accepted as a novice monk at the Abbey of Our Lady of Gethsemani, near Bardstown, Kentucky, and was later ordained as a priest. Encouraged by his superior, he published two volumes of poetry and then his autobiography,* The Seven Storey Mountain, *which established him as a leading spiritual writer. He published 70 books — spiritual writings, poetry, fiction, and essays — and participated in movements for social justice and peace, gaining an international reputation. He took an abiding interest in Eastern religions, particularly Zen, for the light they shed on the depth of human consciousness. From the seclusion of the monastery, he exerted a worldwide influence.*

In the following passage Merton describes the experience of *contemplation*. He uses the term not in the current sense (thinking intently about something) but in its older sense of transcending thought:

The utter simplicity and obviousness of the infused light which contemplation pours into our soul suddenly awakens us to a new level of awareness. We enter a region which we had never even suspected, and yet it is this new world which seems familiar and obvious. The old world of our senses is now the one that seems to us strange, remote and unbelievable — until the intense light of contemplation leaves us and we fall back to our own level.

Compared with the pure and peaceful comprehension of love in which the contemplative is permitted to see the truth not so much by seeing it as by being absorbed into it, ordinary ways of seeing and knowing are full of blindness and labor and uncertainty.

The sharpest of natural experiences is like sleep, compared with the awakening which is contemplation. The keenest and surest natural certitude is a dream compared to this serene comprehension. . . .

Although this light is absolutely above our nature, it now seems to us "normal" and "natural" to see, as we now see, without seeing, to possess clarity in darkness, to have pure certitude without any shred of discursive evidence, to be filled with an experience that transcends experience and to enter with serene confidence into depths that leave us utterly inarticulate. . . .

A door opens in the center of our being and we seem to fall through it into immense depths which, although they are infinite, are all accessible to us; all eternity seems to have become ours in this one placid and breathless contact. . . .

All variety, all complexity, all paradox, all multiplicity cease. Our mind swims in the air of an understanding, a reality that is dark and serene and includes in itself everything. Nothing more is desired. Nothing more is wanting. . . .

For already a supernatural instinct teaches us that the function of this abyss of freedom that has opened out within our own midst, is to draw us utterly out of our own selfhood and into its own immensity of liberty and joy.

You seem to be the same person and you are the same person that you have always been: in fact you are more yourself than you have ever been before. You have only just begun to exist. You feel as if you were at last fully born.[1] — *New Seeds of Contemplation*

Merton describes a new level of awareness, transcendental to ordinary experience, that takes us to the "center of our being," where we are awake to our infinite depth, absorbed in "the truth." He enumerates key characteristics of Transcendental Consciousness: It is unbounded, pure, peaceful, silent. It brings supreme fulfillment, freedom, and bliss. It brings the mind to the field of unity, the field of all possibilities that includes all things within it. In this experience, Merton asserts, you become "more yourself than you have ever been before." Compared with this, ordinary waking experience is like sleep.

༄

Then, in the deep silence, wisdom begins to sing her unending, sunlit, inexpressible song: the private song she sings to the solitary soul. It is his own song and hers — the unique, irreplaceable song that each soul sings for himself with the unknown Spirit, as he sits on the doorstep of his own being, the place where his existence opens out into the abyss of God. It is the song that each of us must sing, the song God has composed Himself, that He may sing it within us. It is the song which, if we do not listen to it, will never be sung. And if we do not join with God in singing this song, we will never be fully real: for it is the song of our own life welling up like a stream out of the very heart of God's creative and redemptive love. . . .[2]

Merton describes an experience he says everyone must have, in which one "sits on the doorstep of his own being," resting in the transcendental field from which all thought and all creation arises.

ANWAR EL SADAT
1918–1981 • EGYPT

Sadat served as President of Egypt from 1970 until his death. As a military officer during World War II, he plotted to free Egypt from British rule, was imprisoned by the British, and later escaped. He served as vice-president under Gamal Abdel Nasser, Egypt's second president, and succeeded him after his death. Sadat was most influential in foreign affairs. He liberated Egypt from Russian interference and was the first Arab leader to re-take territory from Israel. Then, despite strong opposition from the Arab world, he began to work for peace in the Middle East. Sadat was awarded the Nobel Peace Prize in 1978, along with Israeli Prime Minister Menachem Begin. The following year they achieved the first peace treaty between Israel and any Arab nation.

In his autobiography, *In Search of Identity*, Sadat describes his experiences in prison as a young man, a time he recognized as the turning point in his life:

In Cell 54 I could only be my own companion, day and night, and it was only natural that I should come to know that "self" of mine. I had never had such a chance before, preoccupied as I had been with work in the army and with politics, and hurried along by the constant stream of daily life.

Now in the complete solitude of Cell 54, when I had no links at all with the outside world — not even newspapers or a radio — the only way in which I could break my loneliness was, paradoxically, to seek the companionship of that inner entity I call "self." . . .

Through that feeling which came to be an indivisible part of my very being (and which, though unconsciously, remained with me all my life) I was able to transcend the confines of time and place. Spatially, I did not live in a four-walled cell but in the entire universe. Time ceased to exist once my heart was taken over by the love of the Lord of all Creation: I came to feel very close to Him wherever I was. . . .

Everything came to be a source of joy and delight. All creatures became my friends. . . . Everything in existence became an object of love. . . .

Inside Cell 54, as my material needs grew increasingly less, the ties which had bound me to the material world began to be severed, one after another. My soul, having jettisoned its earthly freight, was freed and so took off like a bird soaring into space, into the furthest regions of existence, into infinity. . . .

Once released from the narrow confines of the "self," with its mundane suffering and petty emotions, a man will have stepped into a new, undiscovered world which is vaster and richer. His soul would enjoy absolute freedom, uniting with existence in its entirety, transcending time and space. Through this process of liberation, the human will develops into a love-force, and all earthly forces (even those that might perturb a man's mind) come to contribute to the achievement of perfect inner peace, and so provide a man with absolute happiness.

This is why I regard my last eight months in prison as the happiest period in my life. . . . This could never have happened if I had not had such solitude as enabled me to recognize my real self. . . .

Now that I had discovered and actually begun to live in that "new world," things began to change. My narrow self ceased to exist and the only recognizable entity was the totality of existence, which aspired to a higher, transcendental reality. . . .

For now I felt I had stepped into a vaster and more beautiful world and my capacity for endurance redoubled. I felt I could stand the pressure, whatever the magnitude of a given problem. My paramount object was to make people happy. To see someone smile, to feel that another man's heart beat for joy, was to me a source of immeasurable happiness. I identified with people's joys. Such despicable emotions as hate and vengeance were banished as the faith that "right" ultimately triumphs came to be ineradicably implanted in my consciousness. I came to feel more deeply than ever the beauty of love....

Love helped me to know myself. When my individual entity merged into the vaster entity of all existence, my point of departure became love of home (Egypt), love of all being, love of God. And so I have proceeded from love in discharging my duty (my responsibility), whether it was during my last few months in prison ... or now that I am President of Egypt.[1]   — *In Search of Identity*

Transcending the boundaries of time and space, Sadat feels no longer confined to a prison cell but fills the entire universe. This experience brings him absolute freedom, peace, and happiness. His ordinary, localized self dissolves, leaving him awake to "the totality of existence," to "a higher, transcendental reality." He begins maintaining this experience for longer periods and his life begins changing. Entering "a vaster and more beautiful world," he discovers an inner depth that enables him to guide Egypt through a turbulent period.

༄

To preserve his entity as a human being, a man should maintain conscious communion with all existence. Without such communion he will be left with nothing beyond ephemeral success (or failure). He will be reduced to a slave to time and place, and his being becomes quite simply unreal.

It is only through such communion, I believe, that a man can really exist. His consciousness can then expand to encompass the entire universe.[2]   — *In Search of Identity*

CHAPTER 5

༈

THE FIFTH STATE

Cosmic Consciousness

Unbounded Awareness as a Permanent Reality

As one of history's greatest tennis players and one of the greatest athletes of all time, Billie Jean King would put on dazzling displays of tennis. But what was most important to her in her many victories was something no one in the stands could see.

Born in California in 1943, King elevated women's athletics to new heights. She won a record 20 Wimbledon titles and 39 Grand Slam titles altogether. In addition, she founded the Women's Tennis Association, the Women's Sports Foundation, *Women's Sports* magazine, and GreenSlam, an environmental sports initiative. In 1990 she was named one of the "100 Most Important Americans of the 20th Century" by *Life* magazine, and in 2009 she was awarded the Presidential Medal of Freedom, the nation's highest civilian honor, by President Obama in a ceremony at the White House.

But for all her achievements, most meaningful to her were her peak moments on the tennis court:

THE FIFTH STATE • COSMIC CONSCIOUSNESS

On my very best days I have this fantastic, utterly unself-conscious feeling of invincibility. . . .

I don't worry about how I'm hitting the ball, and I hardly notice my opponent at all. It's like I'm out there by myself. . . . I concentrate only on the ball in relationship to the face of my racket, which is a full-time job anyway, since no two balls ever come over the net the same way. I appreciate what my opponent is doing, but in a very detached, abstract way, like an observer in the next room. I see her moving to her left or right, but it's almost as though there weren't any real opponent, as though I didn't know — and certainly didn't care — whom I was playing against.

When I'm in that kind of state . . . I feel that tennis is an art form that's capable of moving both the players and the audience. . . . When I'm performing at my absolute best, I think that some of the euphoria that I feel must be transmitted to the audience.[1]

King is describing the rare experience athletes call *the zone*. She captures its classic features: peak performance and euphoria coupled with a sense of peaceful detachment. Having described the ideal game, King goes on to describe the ideal shot. She will use the word *perfect* seven times:

The perfect shot is another matter. They don't come along very often, but when they do, they're great. It gives me a marvelous feeling of almost perfect joy — especially if I can pull one off on the last shot of the match.

I can almost feel it coming. It usually happens on one of those days when everything is just right, when the crowd is large and enthusiastic and my concentration is so perfect it almost seems as though I'm able to transport myself beyond the turmoil on the court to some place of total peace and calm. I know where the ball is on every shot, and it always looks as big and well-defined as a basketball. Just a huge thing that I couldn't miss if I wanted to. I've got perfect control of the match, my rhythm and movements are excellent, and everything's just in total balance.

That perfect moment happens in all sports. . . .

It's a perfect combination of a violent action taking place in an atmosphere of total tranquility. My heart pounds, my eyes get damp, and my ears feel like they're wiggling, but it's also just totally peaceful. . . . And when it happens I want to stop the match and grab the microphone and shout, "That's what it's all about." Because it is. It's not the big prize I'm going to win at the end of the match or anything else. It's just having done something that's totally pure and having experienced the perfect emotion, and I'm always sad that I can't communicate that feeling right at the moment it's happening. I can only hope the people realize what's going on.[2]   — *Billie Jean*

Here again is the effortless superior performance, the inner quietude, the transcendent happiness — suggesting glimpses of the fifth state of consciousness.

This state is not reserved for elite athletes. Cosmic Consciousness resolves basic issues we face day by day: How can we most easily fulfill our desires? How can we be sure our desires are virtuous and good? How can we avoid harming anyone else? How can we be most supportive to those around us? How can we be more loving? Where do we find happiness? Freedom? Peace?

We contend with these questions every day. Normally our sole recourse is to analyze our behavior and keep trying our best. Cosmic Consciousness resolves these issues automatically and spontaneously by vastly expanding our inner potential — and enabling us to live that unbounded reality in daily life.

The growth of unbounded awareness

If the mind can become fully awake for short periods of time, as it does in Transcendental Consciousness, can it remain fully awake permanently? The answer is, it can. And with repeated transcending, it does.

When one first learns the Transcendental Meditation technique, one typically experiences the unbounded awareness of the fourth state only for brief moments, at the deepest points of meditation. But in time, with repeated, twice-daily experience, one's mind becomes so familiar with pure consciousness that one begins to maintain the experience of it for longer periods — first during meditation and then outside meditation as well.

Gradually Transcendental Consciousness becomes permanent, forming an underlying continuum that coexists with waking, dreaming, and sleeping. These three states continue to come and go as before. But the underlying continuum of pure consciousness is never broken. The experience of inner silence is never lost — the inner light of the Self is never extinguished.

This is a fifth state of consciousness, altogether different from waking, dreaming, sleeping, and Transcendental Consciousness. This fifth state Maharishi terms Cosmic Consciousness. Cosmic means *all-inclusive, all-encompassing*. In Cosmic Consciousness, the mind is fully expanded. The ocean of consciousness is awake to its depth.[3]

The experience of growing Cosmic Consciousness is natural, normal, and enjoyable. As your nervous system becomes progressively free of stress, you spontaneously express more of your inner potential. You grow in creativity and intelligence, alertness and evenness, happiness and fulfillment.

Cosmic Consciousness does not involve some new kind of thought, attitude, or mood. It's not about positive thinking. The only difference is that the silent and unbounded field of pure consciousness, once hidden by physical and mental stress, no longer remains hidden. It becomes the eternal background of all experience.[4]

Cosmic Consciousness transforms one's life, as Maharishi explains:

> It influences the life of the individual on all levels to such a degree that the whole life is transformed to a value beyond the human mind's imagination. . . .

> How can it be possible for an individual functioning with a limited degree of his mental potential to gauge the great possibilities of creative energy when he would be able to function with the whole of his potential and remain in tune with the center of creative intelligence of absolute Being?[5]

On the other hand, there are no fantastic visions, no fireworks. Developing Cosmic Consciousness means becoming normal and natural, more successful and fulfilled in daily life. Maharishi likens it to coming back home — one gains more of one's self, more of life. He writes:

> Cosmic consciousness should not be considered as something far beyond the reach of normal man. The state of cosmic consciousness should be the state of normal human consciousness. Any state below cosmic consciousness can only be taken to be subnormal human consciousness. The human mind should be a cosmically conscious mind.[6]

Refinement of mind and body

Growth to Cosmic Consciousness involves both mind and body. It develops as the mind becomes increasingly familiar with pure consciousness and the body becomes increasingly refined and free of accumulated stress, strain, and fatigue.

Maharishi defines stress as the structural and chemical abnormalities in the physiology that result from an overload of experience. Imagine a flash bulb going off in front of your eyes. The eyes have a certain degree of resiliency — but if the flash exceeds that, overloading the system, it will produce stress in optical circuitry. It does not matter whether the source of the stress is "negative" or "positive" — winning a fortune can overload the system every bit as much as losing one. These stresses, large and small, accumulated over a lifetime, obstruct the growth of our full potential and prevent us from enjoying the natural experience of pure consciousness at all times.

Thus mind and body must develop hand in hand. As the mind settles down during Transcendental Meditation practice, the body gains deep rest and the structural and chemical abnormalities created by stress and fatigue dissolve. The mind can then settle even more deeply — enabling the body to gain deeper rest and dissolve deeper stress.

Each state of consciousness has a corresponding state of physiology. In Transcendental Consciousness, the body is deeply restful while the mind is awake and alert. But initially the nervous system is neither flexible nor refined enough to sustain this state after meditation. Stress and fatigue cause the nervous system to function in a disorderly way, creating "noise" that impedes experience of consciousness in its pure state. This is why, initially, one experiences Transcendental Consciousness as separate from the waking state — one style of physiological functioning inhibits the other.

But with repeated transcending, stress dissolves and the nervous system becomes more flexible and refined. This allows deeper and clearer experiences of Transcendental Consciousness, more frequent and longer-lasting. Eventually the nervous system becomes virtually free of stress. Now it is so flexible that it can maintain two styles of physiological functioning at once — the restful alertness of Transcendental Consciousness along with the styles characteristic of waking, dreaming, or sleeping. Each style functions perfectly, neither inhibiting the other. This enables unbounded awareness to be maintained permanently. This is Cosmic Consciousness.[7]

Nor can stress accumulate. Ordinarily, our ongoing experience creates stresses that are difficult to remove. But in Cosmic Consciousness, the nervous system is so stable and flexible that any physical fatigue or wear and tear resulting from daily experience is spontaneously dissolved in the night's sleep. The permanently established state of restful alertness perpetually rejuvenates mind and body.[8]

Now the experience of pure consciousness is never lost, even in the most heated game of tennis. The mind's innermost core remains fully awake at all times. Nothing shadows the shining inner light of pure consciousness, the Self. No matter how noisy the world around you, no matter how chaotic, no matter how unsettled your circumstances, you are forever established in an inner sanctuary of infinite silence, peace, and joy. This inner center cannot be shaken, cannot be touched — it is pure, silent, transcendental bliss consciousness, and once you reach Cosmic Consciousness, it cannot be lost.

The simple formula: meditate and act

Maharishi compares the growth of Cosmic Consciousness to the old method of dyeing cloth. To make the dye colorfast, the cloth is dipped into the dye, allowing it to absorb as much color as it can, then exposed to the sun. Almost all the color fades, but a small amount remains. As you repeat this process, the color becomes stronger, more resistant to fading. Eventually the color becomes so strong that it never fades again, no matter how long it remains in sunlight.

During Transcendental Meditation practice, your mind "dips" into pure consciousness. After meditation, when you become active again, the nervous system resumes its usual style of functioning and the experience of pure awareness is all but lost. But the next meditation leaves your mind more established in unbounded awareness, the nervous system more fine-tuned and purified. Repeating this process twice a day, day after day, you reach a state in which the experience of unbounded awareness never fades and the nervous system never loses its perfect tuning, even in the most dynamic activity.[9]

Could one meditate continuously until all stress is dissolved and gain Cosmic Consciousness in a single stroke? No — no more than cloth could become colorfast in a single soaking. The nervous system must adjust, gradually and progressively, to a new style of functioning. Alternating short periods of Transcendental Consciousness with dynamic activity is the most efficient way to accomplish this. Both rest and activity are necessary for developing higher states of consciousness. Thus Maharishi's formula for gaining Cosmic Consciousness is simply *meditate and act* — experience Transcendental Consciousness, then engage in daily activities.[10]

Perspectives on Cosmic Consciousness

Self-realization

We experience objects in the outer world by means of the senses; the senses convey the impression of the object onto the screen of the mind. Prior to Cosmic Consciousness, our experiences overshadow the experience of the Self. If you look at a flower, the impression of the flower dominates your awareness, obscuring your mind's essential, unbounded nature. "The seer, or the mind, is as though lost in the sight," Maharishi writes. He continues:

> The essential nature of the subject or the experiencer within is lost in the experience of the object, just as though the object had annihilated the subject, and the subject misses the experience of its *own* essential nature while engaged in the experience of the *object*. Only the object remains in the consciousness. This is what the common experience of people is.[11]

In Transcendental Consciousness, you experience your true Self, unbounded and eternal. With Cosmic Consciousness, Self-realization becomes permanent, never lost to experience, even during deep sleep. In this state, whatever your activity, whatever your perceptions and thoughts, they no longer obscure the experience of inner unbounded silence — you see the flower but maintain the experience of your unbounded Self deep within.

Freedom and liberation

When we think of freedom, we may think of freedom of speech, freedom of the press, freedom to do as we wish. But the freedom of Cosmic Consciousness goes infinitely beyond these.

Though almost no one has any conception of it, our ordinary waking consciousness is a state of *bondage*, Maharishi explains. The mind's infinite, unbounded nature is concealed or bound by the images, thoughts, and feelings constantly rippling across its surface — as if an ocean had been squeezed into a drop. Transcendental Consciousness brings the liberation of unbounded awareness. This freedom becomes perpetual in Cosmic Consciousness, with the mind ever awake in its unbounded reality. As Maharishi has written:

> When the individual consciousness achieves the status of cosmic existence then, in spite of all the obvious limitations of individuality, a man is ever free, unbounded by any aspect of time, space or causation, ever out of bondage.[12]

The experience of witnessing

We normally live our lives in the ever-changing world of perceptions, thoughts, and feelings, the waves on the mind's surface. In Cosmic Consciousness, the mind is wide awake at its source, the transcendental field, beyond space and time. This is the platform from which experience now takes place.

As a consequence, the Self experiences itself as separate from activity, a silent, nonparticipating observer or *witness* to the world of change. One experiences the world as if across a gap. On one side is the Self, the unbounded, eternal, uninvolved witness. On the other side is everything else, everything relative and changing. Even our feelings, thoughts, and perceptions, which seem so intimately connected with what we normally consider to be our self, are now recognized as outer, beyond this gap. Even the ego becomes an object of the witnessing Self.[13]

This is not a so-called "out-of-body" experience, in which mind and body are purportedly separated. With Cosmic Consciousness, mind and body become more fully integrated than ever.

You still think and act. You still have feelings. In fact, your feelings are more blissful, your thoughts more powerful, your actions more successful. But the Self remains ever awake, silent, unbounded, and uninvolved.

The experience of witnessing brings a new dimension to sleep. Normally falling asleep means losing awareness altogether. But in Cosmic Consciousness, the mind remains awake deep within even while the surface of the mind sleeps and dreams. This experience, known as *witnessing sleep*, is not some drowsy mixture of waking and sleeping but rather pure awareness awake within itself.[14]

Initially the experience of witnessing may occur only momentarily. For example, it may begin in the deepest moments of meditation, when unbounded awareness is no longer displaced when a thought arises. With regular transcending, the experience grows more frequent. As the mind becomes increasingly grounded in the Self, the witnessing value grows until it is not displaced by even the most vigorous activity. Eventually, like the cloth becoming colorfast, unbounded awareness becomes the nonchanging, ever-awake background of all experience, an unbroken continuum underlying the cycle of waking, dreaming, and sleeping. When inner wakefulness is sustained even in the dullness of deep sleep, Maharishi indicates, Cosmic Consciousness has been established.[15]

This experience of separation or witnessing that characterizes Cosmic Consciousness has unfortunately been misunderstood to be the *means* to the end, not the end itself — the goal has been mistaken for the path. This has given rise to mental exercises that involve trying to create a sense of detachment, an experience of the self as separate from the world of change.

But the experience of the Self cannot be maintained through effort any more than it can be experienced through effort in the first place. For the experience of Cosmic Consciousness to be authentic rather than imagined, mind and body must be cultivated — the mind to be able to maintain the experience of pure awareness, the body to be able to support that experience. Otherwise, all one has through contriving is a mood or attitude, a superficial feeling of being separate, not the state of being established in the transcendental Self.

Such practices, moreover, can actually weaken the mind and blunt perceptual abilities, as Maharishi has pointed out. When you are engaged in activity and try simultaneously to maintain a certain frame of mind, you only divide the mind, drawing your attention away from the task at hand and rendering your activity less effective and successful. When you focus on something, you should be fully focused — and the regular experience of transcending, besides establishing the mind in the Self, sharpens the mind and the senses.[16]

24-hour bliss — 200% of life

Ordinarily the mind is always moving, forever searching for greater happiness, yet never finding anything so fulfilling as to hold it permanently. But pure consciousness is an ocean of pure knowledge, power, and bliss. In Cosmic Consciousness, permanently established in the transcendental field, one experiences what Maharishi calls *24-hour bliss*. He describes this as follows:

> This is the glory of the nature of the Self. Having come back home, the traveler finds peace. The intensity of happiness is beyond the superlative. The bliss of this state eliminates the possibility of any sorrow, great or small. Into the bright light of the sun no darkness can penetrate; no sorrow can enter bliss-consciousness, nor can bliss-consciousness know any gain greater than itself. This state of self-sufficiency leaves one steadfast in oneself, fulfilled in eternal contentment.[17]

You still have emotions, likes and dislikes. You still feel pain if you hit your thumb with a hammer. But none of these touch the Self, for the bliss of the Self thoroughly saturating the mind infinitely outweighs any relative happiness or unhappiness. The mind is grounded in its essential nature, the Self, an immovable ocean of bliss. In this state, you enjoy what Maharishi calls *200% of life* — 100% of the relative value of life supported by 100% of its absolute, unbounded spiritual value.

Life supported by natural law

We have all experienced a parking place appearing the moment we need it, or unexpectedly finding the person we need to speak with, or being handed the very thing we are thinking about. It's as if our surroundings want the same thing we want and help us get it. And we have all experienced the opposite — obstacles rising up to block even our simplest wish.

Everyone has desires, ambitions, goals. But in our efforts to fulfill them, we may enjoy progress and success or encounter resistance and failure. Resistance fatigues us and failure stresses us — further restricting our awareness and begetting a vicious cycle.

Regular transcending reverses this cycle. Instead of desiring from the surface level of the mind, where thought is scattered and weak, we begin to desire from deeper levels of the mind, which, like deeper levels of nature, are more powerful. As we access deeper levels of creativity and intelligence, our thoughts and actions become more powerful and effective. Maharishi calls this *skill in desiring*.

We also live in increasing accord with the progressive flow of the laws of nature. Pure consciousness is the unified field, the source of natural law, the intelligence that manages the universe in perfect harmony. Each time we dive within we stimulate this field, enliven it, awaken it. We draw increasingly on its power to support everything we do. As a consequence, the environment responds more favorably to whatever we undertake. We gain what Maharishi calls *support of nature,* enabling us to fulfill desires with greater ease.[18]

In the ordinary waking state, consciousness is not fully awake and expanded; we have access only to partial values of natural law. In such a state, Maharishi explains, we cannot avoid violating laws of nature — which is to say, we inevitably make mistakes, creating stress and suffering for ourselves and others. Maharishi traces all problems and suffering in life, whether individual or social, to violation of natural law.

But in Cosmic Consciousness, when our awareness is unbounded, the total potential of natural law is lively within it. Nature's infinite intelligence flows without restriction through every thought and action. Naturally and spontaneously, we act in perfect alignment with the progressive direction of natural law, like a skilled canoeist perfectly aligned with the river's current, letting the river do the work. Our thoughts and actions are propelled by the all-powerful force of nature itself. We achieve greatest success with least effort. Maharishi describes this as *skill in action*, the ability to *do less and accomplish more*.[19]

In Cosmic Consciousness, moreover, everything we think and do is spontaneously life supporting, nourishing everything around us. How is this possible? Not through intellectual analysis, Maharishi observes. The effects of even the simplest act are unfathomable — everything we do, every thought we think influences our surroundings, rippling outward in every direction and, for better or worse, ultimately affecting the whole of creation.

It is inconceivable that, through intellectual evaluation, we could choose a course of action perfectly nourishing on every level. But when consciousness is fully expanded, all the computing is carried out, spontaneously and automatically, by nature's infinite intelligence, now wide awake within us. We no longer violate laws of nature, no longer create problems and suffering. Maharishi calls this *spontaneous right action*.

> This training is of supreme practical value for our lives. Through it we gain alliance with the totality of natural law in a spontaneous manner. We ensure that before we think and act we are always supported by natural law, and life supported by natural law is spontaneously evolutionary and most orderly. We get ourselves out of that unfortunate situation which brings to us all kinds of difficulties, sicknesses, and suffering in life. All these negative values result from not knowing how to be spontaneously orderly and evolutionary, not knowing how to think and act according to the laws of nature.[20]

Fully developed capacity for love

Our capacity to love depends on the degree to which our potential is developed. Only a full cup can overflow, Maharishi has observed — only when our consciousness is expanded to the maximum can we fully appreciate and

Typical waking consciousness	Cosmic Consciousness
Consciousness is active, excited.	Consciousness is active and excited at its surface but remains ever awake and nonactive at its silent source.
The mind is localized, absorbed in and bound by ever-changing perceptions, thoughts, memories, feelings.	The mind maintains unbounded awareness even while aware of ongoing mental activity.
Ordinary waking consciousness is a state of bondage.	Cosmic Consciousness is a state of liberation.
Only the surface of the mind is awake.	The depth of the mind is awake and remains awake even while the mind's surface shifts among waking, dreaming, and sleeping.
Consciousness is lost during sleep.	Inner wakefulness is maintained in sleep.
The mind uses only a fraction of its potential creativity and intelligence.	The mind is fully expanded, its full creative potential ever lively and awake.
One is aware only of one's localized, individual self.	One is established in the unbounded Self — Cosmic Consciousness is a state of Self-realization.
Brainwave patterns are continuously changing.	Brainwave activity is highly coherent and integrated.
The mind has access only to partial values of natural law and one enjoys only partial support of nature in fulfilling desires.	The total potential of natural law, the unified field, is ever awake deep within, and one enjoys full support of nature in fulfilling desires.
The body is engaged in some degree of activity.	One level of physiological functioning remains restful even while another level is active.
Physiological stresses and strains inhibit the experience of the Self.	The body is virtually free of stress; any incoming stress is quickly dissolved.
Happiness is transitory, superficial; the mind moves ever in search of greater happiness.	Cosmic Consciousness is a state of supreme contentment, 24-hour bliss.

love and give significantly to others.[21] In Cosmic Consciousness we are free of stress and limitations. The heart's capacity to love is now unbounded.[22] Growth toward the sixth state, God Consciousness, entails the flow of love to its maximum value, serving to draw together — and finally unify — inner and outer.

Experiences of growing Cosmic Consciousness

Here are some experiences reported by people who practice the Transcendental Meditation technique:

"Unaffected by the change and challenges of daily life"

This person describes how he comes to identify with the mind's most silent level, pure consciousness, the Self:

> More often in activity, I am aware of a silent aspect of my Self which seems to be unaffected by the change and challenges of daily life. This part of me, when I recognize it, seems to fill me with thrills of happiness that lend a kind of non-attached perspective to my activity.[23]

"My awareness is this unbounded wholeness of my Self"

> Gradually over the years, as the experience of pure consciousness became increasingly familiar in Transcendental Meditation, I began to experience it not just as a state with no thought but rather as having no boundaries; then as unbounded, beyond the limitations of my individuality; then as the unbounded, unchanging essence of my existence. . . .
>
> Also there is less of a contrast between activity and meditation. Sometimes during the day with varying degrees of clarity, my awareness is this unbounded wholeness of my Self, quietly accompanying the thoughts and feelings in my daily life. It is not a mood or conception about myself, it is a natural state in which I am myself more fully.[24]

"I know what perfection in my life means"

The next passages illustrate how growing Cosmic Consciousness brings a growing sense of bliss, perfection, universality, and freedom:

> Sometimes when I am witnessing in activity, I know what perfection in my life means. No matter how menial the task — it could be washing fruit or drying dishes — that simple motion or activity seems to send a thrill through creation and enlivens a stir of bliss in the physiology. Then every action is just an expression of the perfection of life and the reflection of the perfection of natural law.[25]

"Fabulous inner mental and physical blissfulness"

> The experience of bliss consciousness has become more clear, intense, and stable not only during Transcendental Meditation but also during activity. Now I find that a soft but strong feeling of blissful evenness is present most of the time in both mind and body. Physically it is experienced as an extremely delightful liveliness throughout the body.
>
> This evenness is so deep and stable that it is able to maintain its status even in the face of great activity. Even when faced with great problems, this blissful evenness of mind and body continues. Every day it grows stronger and more stable. The evenness cushions one against all possible disruptions and makes all activity easy and enjoyable. Every place is heaven when you feel that evenness. One is completely self-sufficient. Nothing can prevent one from having that fabulous inner mental and physical blissfulness.[26]

"My self is primarily identified with this enormous awareness"

In the many variations of daily life, I don't get overshadowed by anything anymore. The activity doesn't damage that inner feeling of invincibility or bliss. All my activity seems to take care of itself. . . .

I am connected to the universal value of life. Things don't disturb that level of life. Not only is there a feeling of strength, invincibility, and bliss, but also the feeling of great comfort. I feel that I am taken care of, and my needs seem to be met very easily in activity.

My self is primarily identified with this enormous awareness. I am struck by the fact that I feel huge, although I am physically small. I am going through my activity and feel just absolutely enormous, being more connected or identified with this expanded awareness than with my little personal individual characteristics.[27]

These next two accounts describe the experience of inner wakefulness or transcending during sleep, known as witnessing sleep:

"The light never goes out deep within"

Something inside doesn't go to sleep. . . . My attention softly goes within. I become less and less aware of my surroundings, I become less and less aware of thoughts. At some point, all melts away. I stop experiencing everything except pure clarity. It's crystal clear alertness inside. Time doesn't exist. The light never goes out deep within.

Sometimes I'll wake up in the middle of the night or very early in the morning and realize I had been dreaming. If I didn't have dreams I might think I'd never fallen completely asleep, because the inner alertness is so strong. . . .

I wake up with the joy from witnessing.[28]

"Inside I am just aware that I am"

Often during deep sleep I am awake inside, in a very peaceful, blissful state. Dreams come and go, thoughts about the dreams come and go, but I remain in a deeply peaceful state, completely separate from the dreams and the thoughts. My body is asleep and inert, breathing goes on regularly and mechanically, and inside I am just aware that I am.[29]

"I was that pure Being, pure simple awareness"

I had invited my sister and her husband to join my husband and me for the grand finale of a television talent show. And to celebrate, I was making homemade strawberry shortcake.

As I stood at my kitchen counter slicing the warm shortbread before filling it with fresh strawberries and whipped cream, I slipped very innocently into a sweet and different state of consciousness.

There was only silence, crystal-clear pure consciousness. There was nothing else but "That" — no thoughts, no intellect, no ego, no experience of some "thing." It was just that simplest state of awareness, awake within itself. The kitchen and the shortcake were still there. The physiology was still there. But I was only experiencing the "it." I was that pure Being, pure simple awareness. That was my Self. It was my home, my abode.

It was so natural, so innocent, that I realized that "it" had always been there. But this time it was by itself, awake within itself — but being experienced in activity! It was very sweet.

At some point, I continued making the strawberry shortcake for my family, but nothing could compare to that silent state of pure Being, pure self-referral consciousness experiencing the "sweetness" of its own infinite, eternal existence.[30]

"I was the Self flowing and glowing"

I was on a short walk, and after some time a very sweet level of witnessing came about. I felt a very soft, warm glow inside that bubbled up into my awareness. It was more than just a sense of Self, it was a warm flowing bliss in my awareness. It made me feel like there was nowhere to go or anything I needed to do or any place I needed to be. This feeling became stronger as I went along on my journey.

My awareness was inside, absorbed in Being. Yet, at the same time, I felt that my movement, my senses of perception, and my physiology were all embraced by a soft flow or glow of Being that was most natural and automatic. It wasn't like I was watching myself; I was the Self flowing and glowing. This experience translated into everything around me. The boundaries of the relative were not in my awareness, just the flow, and I felt I was walking in a heaven. I felt perfect and everything around me was perfect.[31]

VEDIC LITERATURE
INDIA

Practice is the endeavor to become established in the state of yoga. Yoga becomes firmly established through regular and respectful practice for a long time. . . . The highest state of non-attachment is freedom from all change, which comes through knowledge of the Self. . . .

Through the repeated experience of settling, a continuum of calmness develops.[1] — *Yoga Sutras of Patanjali*

The *Yoga Sutras* define yoga as "the complete settling of the activity of the mind," as we saw in the last chapter. With repeated experience, we are told here, it becomes established as a continuum of experience, bringing abiding freedom and peace. These are characteristics of Cosmic Consciousness.

༃

One who is in Union with the Divine and who knows the Truth will maintain "I do not act at all." In seeing, hearing, touching, smelling, eating, walking, sleeping, breathing, speaking, letting go, seizing, and even in opening and closing the eyes, he holds simply that the senses act among the objects of sense.[2] — *Bhagavad-Gita*

"In Union with the Divine" means established in pure consciousness, the Self, silent and nonmoving, beyond the field of the senses. In Cosmic Consciousness, experience takes place from here.

༃

Established in Yoga, O winner of wealth, perform actions having abandoned attachment and having become balanced in success and failure, for balance of mind is called Yoga.[3] — *Bhagavad-Gita*

"Established in Yoga" means established in pure consciousness. One witnesses the world from the transcendental field, unattached and perfectly balanced. This next verse expresses the same state in different words:

> He whose mind is unshaken in the midst of sorrows, who amongst pleasures is free from longing, from whom attachment, fear and anger have departed, he is said to be a sage of steady intellect.[4]
> — *Bhagavad-Gita*

༄

> He is in his own Being, pure, never-changing, never-moving, unpollutable; and in peace beyond desires he watches the drama of the universe.[5]
> — *Maitri Upanishad*

Here again we have the state of being established in the peaceful silence of the Self (Being) and from here watching or witnessing the world of change.

༄

> He is awake but enjoys the calmness of deep sleep; he is unaffected in the least by pleasure and pain. He is awake in deep sleep.... His wisdom is unclouded by latent tendencies. He appears to be subject to likes, dislikes and fear; but in fact he is as free as space. He is free from egotism and volition; and his intelligence is unattached whether in action or in inaction. None is afraid of him; he is afraid of none.[6]
> — *Yoga Vasishta*

This passage describes the phenomenon of inner wakefulness maintained even during sleep, of "witnessing sleep," a key characteristic of Cosmic Consciousness. One acts in the world as others act but remains utterly free.

▪ *Also see Vedic literature in Chapter 4 (Transcendental Consciousness), Chapter 6 (God Consciousness), and Chapter 7 (Unity Consciousness).*

LAOZI

6TH CENTURY BCE • CHINA

■ *See biography on page 60.*

One who knows this secret [of the Tao]
is not moved by attachment or aversion,
> swayed by profit or loss, nor touched
> by honor or disgrace
He is far beyond the cares of men
> yet comes to hold the dearest place
> in their hearts[1]   — *Tao Te Ching*

Laozi describes a state of permanent transcendence, in which the mind, awake at its source, remains untouched by changes in the relative world.

৵

You won't have to hide away forever in spiritual retreats. You can be a gentle, contemplative hermit right here in the middle of everything, utterly unaffected, thoroughly sustained and rewarded by your integral practices.

Encouraging others, giving freely to all, awakening and purifying the world with each movement and action, you'll ascend to the divine realm in broad daylight.

The breath of the Tao speaks, and those who are in harmony with it hear quite clearly.[2]   — *Hua Hu Ching*

We don't have to retire from the world to enjoy transcendence as a permanent state, Laozi assures us — we can live it "in the middle of everything." In this state, moreover, we awaken and purify the world with everything we do. In Cosmic Consciousness, all our thoughts and actions are in harmony with natural law, spontaneously life-supporting.

> They have the same mind as heaven. . . .
> Outwardly they evolve along with things, yet inwardly they do not lose their true state.³ — *Wen-Tzu*

"The same mind as heaven" — one is forever established in pure consciousness, one's "true state." And in this permanently maintained "true state," one holds the key to success in anything:

> If one never leaves the source, what action would not be successful?⁴ — *Wen-Tzu*

> Those who attain the Way are like the axles of carriages turning in their hubs, not moving themselves yet conveying the carriages for a thousand miles, revolving endlessly in an inexhaustible source.⁵ — *Wen-Tzu*

The Way is the Tao, the source of natural law, the wellspring of nature's infinite intelligence, unchanging in itself yet the source of all change. Acting from here, Maharishi observes, one can achieve success in anything.

Also see Laozi in Chapter 4 (Transcendental Consciousness) and Chapter 7 (Unity Consciousness).

THE BUDDHA

c. 563–c. 483 BCE • NEPAL & INDIA

■ *See biography on page 63.*

His journey is over!
All sorrow is gone,
Every shackle undone,
He is completely free.
. . . .

Who can trace the path of these great
    ones?
These beings who are pure at heart,
not swayed by the senses,
living without attachment,
and accepting of whatever life gives them?

More difficult than following the flight of birds
    is it to follow these beings,
These great ones who wander through the infinite skies
    with absolute freedom.

Even the gods envy them:
Their senses controlled like a well-trained horse,
Their souls free from pride and jealousy.
These great beings welcome everyone like the earth,
Are steadfast like a stone foundation,
Pure like the waters of a lake,
And no longer bound by birth or death.
Perfect wisdom has filled them with peace:

Their every thought, word, and action
> are in perfect harmony with the universe.

Having seen the Eternal Truth
All falsehood has vanished,
All bonds have been cut,
All desires have been conquered.
They are indeed the kings among men.

Holy is the place where such great ones dwell.
They fill with delight the village and the forest,
> the valley and the hill;
They fill with delight
> every place in this world.[1] — *Dhammapada*

The *Dhammapada*, traditionally attributed to the Buddha himself, is one of the best known texts in the Theravada school, the oldest surviving school in Buddhism. This passage describes a state of utter freedom, purity, and peace. Everything one does, moreover, is in accord with all the laws of nature — "in perfect harmony with the universe."

❦

The one whose mind knows the clarity of perfect wisdom is never afraid or even anxious. Why? Because when being at one with the living power of wisdom, the mother of all the buddhas, that person has the strength to remain in a state of undivided contemplation even while ceaselessly and skillfully engaging in compassionate action.[2] — *Prajnaparamita*

This passage describes maintaining two states of consciousness simultaneously — action along with "undivided contemplation," defined here as being unified with "the living power of wisdom, the mother of all the buddhas" — pure consciousness.

> And the Saint whose peace is no more disturbed by anything whatsoever in all the world, the pure one, the sorrowless, the freed from Craving, he has swum across the ocean of Birth and Decay.
>
> He truly penetrates to the cause of sensations, enlightened is his mind. And for a disciple so delivered, in whose heart dwells peace, there is no longer any pondering over what has been done, and naught more remains for him to do. Just as a rock of one solid mass remains unshaken by the wind, even so, neither forms, nor sounds, nor odors, nor tastes, nor contacts of any kind; neither the desired nor the undesired can cause such an one to waver. Steadfast is his mind, gained is Deliverance.³
>
> *— Anguttara Nikaya*

In this state of liberation, the Buddha says, the peace in one's heart is so steadfast that it cannot be shaken any more than a solid mass of rock can be shaken by the wind. More than seventeen centuries later, in Medieval Germany, Meister Eckhart would use this same simile to describe this state in which the mind is established in the transcendent, beyond the field of change (see page 212).

> Just as a blue or red or white lotus is born in water, grows in water and stands up above the water untouched by it, so too I, who was born in the world and grew up in the world, have transcended the world, and I live untouched by the world. Remember me as one who is enlightened.⁴
>
> *— Anguttara Nikaya*

■ *Also see the Buddha in Chapter 4 (Transcendental Consciousness) and Chapter 7 (Unity Consciousness).*

ZHUANGZI

369–286 BCE · CHINA

■ *See biography on page 69.*

With the sage, his life is the working of Heaven.... He sleeps without dreaming, wakes without worry. His spirit is pure and clean, his soul never wearied. In emptiness, nonbeing, and limpidity, he joins with the Virtue of Heaven....

When the mind is without care or joy, this is the height of Virtue. When it is unified and unchanging, this is the height of stillness. When it grates against nothing, this is the height of emptiness. When it has no commerce with things, this is the height of limpidity. When it rebels against nothing, this is the height of purity....

To be pure, clean, and mixed with nothing; still, unified, and unchanging; limpid and inactive; moving with the workings of Heaven — this is the way to care for the spirit....

Its name ["pure spirit"] is called One-with-Heaven. The way to purity and whiteness is to guard the spirit, this alone; guard it and never lose it, and you will become one with spirit, one with its pure essence, which communicates and mingles with the Heavenly Order. The common saying has it, "The ordinary man prizes gain, the man of integrity prizes name, the worthy man honors ambition, the sage values spiritual essence." Whiteness means there is nothing mixed in; purity means the spirit is never impaired. He who can embody purity and whiteness may be called the True Man.[1]   — *Zhuangzi*

Zhuangzi describes a state in which the mind is perfectly even, unified, pure, with "no commerce with things." One's mind in Cosmic Consciousness is fully awake inside, anchored in pure awareness, a silent witness to the ever-changing world. In harmony with natural law, one's life becomes "the working of Heaven." As Maharishi calls Cosmic Consciousness "the state of normal human consciousness," Zhuangzi calls such a person "the True Man."

༄

He who understands Heavenly joy incurs no wrath from Heaven, no opposition from man, no entanglement from things, no blame from the spirits. So it is said, his movement is of heaven, his stillness of earth. With his single mind in repose, he is king of the world; the spirits do not afflict him; his soul knows no weariness. His single mind reposed, the ten thousand things submit — which is to say that his emptiness and stillness reach throughout Heaven and earth and penetrate the ten thousand things. This is what is called Heavenly joy. Heavenly joy is the mind of the sage, by which he shepherds the world."[2]   — *Zhuangzi*

This selection suggests awareness established in unified, silent, unbounded awareness. One's "soul knows no weariness," suggesting the permanent restful alertness of Cosmic Consciousness, in which stress and fatigue cannot accumulate. The sage in this state "shepherds the world," suggesting both the support of nature and all-nourishing thought and right action of Cosmic Consciousness.

༄

He who practices the Way does less every day, does less and goes on doing less, until he reaches the point where he does nothing, does nothing and yet there is nothing that is not done.[3]

■ *Also see Zhuangzi in Chapter 4 (Transcendental Consciousness).*

JESUS CHRIST
7–2 BCE–30–36 CE • ISRAEL

See biography on page 71.

I will show you what everyone is like who comes to me, hears my words, and acts on them. They are like a person building a house, who dug a deep hole to lay the foundation on rock. When a flood came, the floodwaters pushed against that house but couldn't shake it, because it had been founded on the rock. But the person who hears what I say but doesn't act on it is like someone who built a house on the ground without any foundation. When the floodwaters pushed against it, that house quickly collapsed, and the resulting destruction of that house was extensive.[1] — Luke 6:47–49

These verses offer a striking metaphor for Cosmic Consciousness. In the fifth state the mind is fully awake and anchored in the transcendental field, pure consciousness. This field cannot be touched by change; no sorrow, darkness, or negativity can penetrate. Established at this level, one is unshakable. Short of Cosmic Consciousness, the experience of the Self is obscured. One is subject to the thoughts and impressions that continuously flood the mind's surface, and stressful experiences can be overwhelming.

༄

Be ye therefore perfect, even as your Father which is in heaven is perfect.[2] — Matthew 5:48

> Jesus answered them, Is it not written in your law, I said, Ye are gods? — John 10:34

Life can be lived in perfection, Jesus teaches. How? "Seek ye first the kingdom of God, and his righteousness; and all these things shall be added unto you" (Matthew 6:33) — for how else would perfection be attained than through the transformation resulting from experiencing the kingdom of God. And where is the kingdom of God? Within you (Luke 17:21).

Perfection in life, Maharishi explains, dawns in Cosmic Consciousness, when the mind is established in pure consciousness, the unified field of natural law. Maharishi equates *natural law* with the *will of God* — so acting in accord with natural law means acting in accord with God's will and living a mistake-free life. This feature of Cosmic Consciousness is reflected in this verse:

> No one who abides in him sins; no one who sins has either seen him or known him. — 1 John 3:6

To sin is to think or act in a way that violates natural law, the will of God. But when one reaches the state of perfect life Jesus describes, one spontaneously lives the virtues of love and compassion he taught.

In Cosmic Consciousness, moreover, one enjoys the *support* of natural law in fulfilling one's desires without strain. The following well-known verse alludes to this state:

> Ask, and it shall be given you; seek, and ye shall find; knock, and it shall be opened unto you. — Matthew 7:7

༄

Turning to the *Gospel of Thomas* (see discussion in the previous chapter), we find several verses evocative of Cosmic Consciousness:

> Jesus said, "If they say to you, 'Where have you come from?' say to them, 'We have come from the light, from the place where the light came into being by itself, established [itself], and appeared in their image.' If they say to you, 'Is it you?', say, 'We are its children,

and we are the chosen of the living father.' If they ask you, 'What is the evidence of your father in you?' say to them, 'It is motion and rest.'"[3] — *The Gospel of Thomas*

"The light," as the larger context makes clear, is the inner field of pure consciousness; Jesus is saying we are expressions of this inner divine reality. In Cosmic Consciousness, even when in motion, one remains at rest, established in the eternal silence of pure consciousness — motion and rest exist side-by-side. Jesus characterizes himself in just this way:

> Jesus said, "I stood at rest in the midst of the world."[4]
> — *The Gospel of Thomas*

༃

> Jesus said. . . . "Blessings on one who stands at the beginning: that one will know the end and will not taste death."
>
> Jesus said, "Blessings on one who came into being before coming into being."[5] — *The Gospel of Thomas*

These otherwise cryptic statements make sense in light of our understanding of Cosmic Consciousness. To stand at the beginning is to be established in the eternal field pure consciousness, the source of thought and the source of creation. To come into being "before coming into being" is to be fully and permanently awake at this transcendental level, beyond time and change.

Also see Jesus Christ in Chapter 4 (Transcendental Consciousness), Chapter 6 (God Consciousness), and Chapter 7 (Unity Consciousness).

PLOTINUS

205–270 • EGYPT & ITALY

■ *See biography on page 78.*

[W]hile in some men it is present as a mere portion of their total being — in those, namely, that have it potentially — there is, too, the man, already in possession of true felicity, who is this perfection realized, who has passed over into actual identification with it. All else is now mere clothing about the man. . . .

To the man in this state, what is the Good?

He himself by what he has and is. And the author and principle of what he is and holds is the Supreme, which within Itself is the Good. . . .

The sign that this state has been achieved is that the man seeks nothing else.

What indeed could he be seeking? Certainly none of the less worthy things; and the Best he carries always within him.

He that has such a life as this has all he needs in life.

Once the man is a Proficient, the means of happiness, the way to good, are within, for nothing is good that lies outside him. . . . He knows himself to stand above all such things, and what he gives to the lower he so gives as to leave his true life undiminished.

Adverse fortune does not shake his felicity: the life so founded is stable ever. Suppose death strikes at his household or at his friends; he knows what death is, as the victims, if they are among the wise, know too. And if death taking from him his familiars and intimates does bring grief, it is not to him, not to the true man, but to that in him which stands apart from the Supreme, to that lower man in whose distress he takes no part. . . .

If the man that has attained felicity meets some turn of fortune that he would not have chosen, there is not the slightest lessening of his happiness for that. . . . No: a thousand mischances and disappointments may befall him and leave him still in the tranquil possession of [happiness]. . . .

There is always the radiance in the inner soul of the man, untroubled like the light in a lantern when fierce gusts beat about it in a wild turmoil of wind and tempest. . . .

The Proficient sees things very differently from the average man; neither ordinary experiences nor pains and sorrows, whether touching himself or others, pierce to the inner hold. . . .

No one rules him out of felicity in the hours of sleep; no one counts up that time and so denies that he has been happy all his life. . . .

The Proficient arrived at this state has the truer fullness of life, life not spilled out in sensation but gathered closely within itself. . . .

The Proficient would like to see all men prosperous and no evil befalling anyone; but though it prove otherwise, he is still content. . . .

All that is good is immediately present to the Proficient and the Proficient is present to himself: his pleasure, his contentment, stands, immovable.

Thus he is ever cheerful, the order of his life ever untroubled: his state is fixedly happy and nothing whatever of all that is known as evil can set it awry — given only that he is and remains a Proficient. . . .

In the Proficient there is . . . the Self-Gathered which, as long as it holds itself by main force within itself, can never be robbed of the vision of the All-Good. . . .

> Giving freely to his intimates of all he has to give, he will be the best of friends by his very union with [Divine Intelligence].[1] — *Enneads*

Plotinus writes at length about a state in which one enjoys perfection, fullness, and unbroken felicity (bliss), even during sleep. One identifies with the "Good" and the "Supreme," now fully lively within. From this platform one stands above all changing, relative values; everything else becomes "mere clothing." Whatever happens, no matter how grievous, does not affect "the true man" within — nothing can "pierce to the inner hold."

This state grows by degrees, Plotinus indicates in another passage. "Newly awakened," he says, "it is all too feeble to bear the ultimate splendor." But when you purify yourself of "all that is crooked," "all that is overcast," then "you shall see the perfect goodness surely established in the stainless shrine."[2] This accords with how Cosmic Consciousness develops — by purifying one's physiology of accumulated stress along with expanding one's consciousness.

Also see Plotinus in Chapter 4 (Transcendental Consciousness) and Chapter 7 (Unity Consciousness).

ANGELA OF FOLIGNO
c. 1248–1309 • ITALY

See biography on page 98.

Yet I have it not merely for the space of opening or shutting the eyes, but I have it for a good space of time, and very often in this way, but very efficaciously. But in another way, although not so efficaciously, I have it almost continually.

And although I can receive sorrow and joy externally in some little way, yet inwardly my soul is a chamber in which no joy nor sorrow entereth, nor delight of any virtue whatsoever, or of anything that can be named; but there entereth into it all that is good. And in this . . . is the whole Truth, and in it I understand and possess the whole truth, that is in heaven and in earth . . . together with so great a certainty that in nowise, were the whole world to say the opposite, could I believe otherwise.[1]

— *The Book of Visions and Instructions*

Angela of Foligno suggests she experiences Transcendental Consciousness not only with eyes closed (as she indicated in the last chapter) but "almost continually." The result? She continues to experience joy and sorrow but only externally and only "in some little way." Inwardly she experiences a chamber of goodness and truth that neither joy or sorrow penetrate.

Also see Angela of Foligno in Chapter 4 (Transcendental Consciousness).

MEISTER ECKHART
1260–c. 1327 • GERMANY

See biography on page 99.

[T]he mind of him who stands detached is of such nobility that whatever he sees is true, and whatever he desires he obtains, and whatever he commands must be obeyed. And this you must know for sure: when the free mind is quite detached, it constrains God to itself, and if it were able to stand formless and free of all accidentals, it would assume God's proper nature. . . . [T]he man who stands thus in utter detachment is rapt into eternity in such a way that nothing transient can move him. . . .

Now you may ask what this detachment is that is so noble in itself. You should know that true detachment is nothing else but a mind that stands unmoved by all accidents of joy or sorrow, honour, shame or disgrace, as a mountain of lead stands unmoved by a breath of wind. This immovable detachment brings a man into the greatest likeness to God. For the reason why God is God is because of His immovable detachment, and from this detachment He has His purity, His simplicity and His immutability. Therefore, if a man is to be like God, as far as a creature *can* have likeness with God, this must come from detachment. This draws a man into purity, and from purity into simplicity, and from simplicity into immutability, and these things make a likeness between God and that man. . . .

You should know that the outer man can be active while the inner man is completely free of this activity and unmoved. . . . Here is an analogy: a door swings open and shuts on its hinge. I would compare the outer woodwork of the door to the outer man, and the hinge to the inner man. When the door opens and shuts, the boards move back and forth, but the hinge stays in the same place and is never moved thereby. It is the same in this case, if you understand it rightly.

Now I ask: "What is the object of pure detachment? My answer is that the object of pure detachment is neither *this* nor *that*. It rests on absolutely nothing, and I will tell you why: pure detachment rests on the highest, and he is at his highest, in whom God can work all His will. . . . And so, if the heart is to be ready to receive the highest, it must rest on absolutely nothing, and in that lies the greatest potentiality which can exist. . . .

Again I ask: "What is the prayer of a detached heart? My answer is that detachment and purity cannot pray, for whoever prays wants God to grant him something, or else wants God to take something from him. But a detached heart desires nothing at all, nor has it anything it wants to get rid of. Therefore it is free of all prayers, or its prayer consists of nothing but being uniform with God. That is all its prayer. . . .

Therefore it is totally subject to God, and therefore it is in the highest degree of uniformity with God, and is also the most receptive to divine influence. . . .

Now take note, all who are sensible! No man is happier than he who has the greatest detachment.[1] — "On Detachment"

Meister Eckhart writes in detail about a dual state of life in which the "outer man" is active while the "inner man" remains beyond activity. The inner man is no more moved than a mountain of lead is moved by a breeze (the Buddha used this same image seventeen centuries earlier in India — see page 202). Anchored in inner purity and silence, one lives in harmony with God's will, able to fulfill desires easily and enjoying the greatest happiness.

These words characterize Cosmic Consciousness — the mind awake and stationed in inner silence, untouched by anything relative. Wide open to the inner ocean of creative intelligence, one spontaneously acts in accord with natural law (God's will), fulfilling desires with least effort.

▪ *Also see Meister Eckhart in Chapter 4 (Transcendental Consciousness) and Chapter 7 (Unity Consciousness).*

ST. TERESA OF ÁVILA
1515–1582 • SPAIN

■ *See biography on page 106.*

In this passage St. Teresa refers to herself in the third person and to pure consciousness, the transcendental field as the "Mansion."

I may tell you some of the many things which there are to be said and which God reveals to every soul that He brings into this Mansion. . . .

This may lead you to think that such a person will not remain in possession of her senses but will be so completely absorbed that she will be able to fix her mind upon nothing. But no: in all that belongs to the service of God she is more alert than before; and, when not otherwise occupied, she rests in that happy companionship. . . . This Presence is not of course always realized so fully — I mean so clearly — as it is when it first comes, or on certain other occasions when God grants the soul this consolation; if it were, it would be impossible for the soul to think of anything else, or even to live among men. But although the light which accompanies it may not be so clear, the soul is always aware that it is experiencing this companionship. . . .

It seems that the Divine Majesty, by means of this wonderful companionship, is desirous of preparing the soul for yet more. . . . The person already referred to found herself better in every way, however numerous were her trials and business worries, the essential part of her soul seemed never to move from that dwelling-place. So in a sense she felt that her soul was divided; and when she was going through great trials, shortly after God had granted her this favor, she complained of her soul, just as Martha complained of Mary. Sometimes she would say that it was doing nothing but enjoy itself in that quietness, while she herself was left with all her trials and occupations so that she could not keep it company.

You will think this absurd, daughters, but it is what actually happens. Although of course the soul is not really divided, what I have said is not fancy, but a very common experience.[1] — *Interior Castle*

St. Teresa tells her fellow nuns how, deep within, she remains anchored in the transcendental field even when she opens her eyes and comes out of the meditative state. Even during hardships she experiences the "companionship" of inner silence, standing apart from everything else.

Oh, who would be able to explain to your Excellency the quiet and calm my soul experiences! . . . [T]his soul is no longer in part subject to the miseries of the world as it used to be. For although it suffers more, this is only on the surface. The mind is like a lord in his castle, and so it doesn't lose its peace. . . . It goes about so forgetful of self that it thinks it has partly lost its being. In this state everything is directed to the honor of God, to the greater fulfillment of His will, and to His glory.[2]

The following passage comes from a letter St. Teresa wrote to the Bishop of Osma, who had been her confessor:

St. Teresa again describes the state in which, whatever happens on the mind's surface, the mind remains peaceful at its depth, "like a lord in his castle." In this state, she tells us, one lives in accord with the will of God. For Maharishi, living in accord with the will of God is synonymous with living in accord with natural law, a key characteristic of Cosmic Consciousness.

Also see St. Teresa in Chapter 4 (Transcendental Consciousness).

HAKUIN ZENJI
1685-1769 • JAPAN

■ *See biography on page 117.*

The spirit of the Way is never to be lost even for a single moment....

What is of absolute importance, is that the two states — activity and calm... must have the pure, unmixed, complete and whole truth in the forefront. It must be such, indeed, that so that even if one were surrounded by a thousand or ten thousand people one would be as if one were dwelling alone in a wide open space of thousands of miles.... Thus should it be all the time.... If, when that time comes, you do not go back, but deliberately go forward, then there will come to you such a joy as has not been seen in all the forty years of your life, nor will you have heard anything so joyous — it will be as if you had broken through a large pack of ice, or had breached a veritable fortress of stones.[1]

— *The Embossed Tea Kettle*

Hakuin describes a state in which the "spirit of the Way" is never lost, a dual state of activity and calm simultaneously. Whether active or silent, alone or with others, your mind remains unbounded, anchored in truth, full of joy. It's as if you were "dwelling alone in a wide open space of thousands of miles" — witnessing all experience from the platform of unbounded awareness.

ॐ

If... while remaining normally amongst the "six dusts" of the active life, a man clothes himself with a sort of spiritual sheen, is simple, unalloyed, complete and of one piece, that man will not err to any great degree. He may be compared to the man in the story who delivered that treasure of gold while passing through the great riots and disturbances of the world's life. He is one who boldly and successfully displays his courageous disposition and advances without delay or hesitation. And by the very fact of so doing such a man raises up the very source and origin of his own soul and mind, and brings to a final end all those roots of existence which tie us to the cycle of life and death. For such a man there is nothing but great joy, enough to dissolve the sky and shatter the iron mountains. He is to be compared with the lotus which blossoms and becomes ever more beautiful and more deliciously scented.[2]   —*The Embossed Tea Kettle*

Elaborating on this state, Hakuin explains that one rests forever in the simplest form of awareness, no longer acts in a way that creates problems and suffering, and stands beyond time and change, where "there is nothing but great joy."

Also see Hakuin Zenji in Chapter 4 (Transcendental Consciousness).

RALPH WALDO EMERSON
1803–1882 • UNITED STATES

■ *See biography on page 124.*

Crossing a bare common, in snow puddles, at twilight, under a clouded sky, without having in my thoughts any occurrence of special good fortune, I have enjoyed a perfect exhilaration. I am glad to the brink of fear. . . . Standing on the bare ground, — my head bathed by the blithe air and uplifted into infinite space, — all mean egotism vanishes. I become a transparent eyeball; I am nothing; I see all; the currents of the Universal Being circulate through me; I am part or particle of God. . . . I am the lover of uncontained and immortal beauty.[1] — *Nature*

Emerson describes moments of bliss, "perfect exhilaration." His ordinary sense of self dissolves and his consciousness seems to become unbounded. He experiences himself as a nonparticipating witness of the universe around him — "a transparent eyeball," unified with the divine.

■ *Also see Emerson in Chapter 4 (Transcendental Consciousness) and Chapter 7 (Unity Consciousness).*

HENRY DAVID THOREAU
1817–1862 • UNITED STATES

See biography on page 128.

With thinking we may be beside ourselves in a sane sense. By a conscious effort of the mind we can stand aloof from actions and their consequences; and all things, good and bad, go by us like a torrent. We are not wholly involved in Nature. I may be either the driftwood in the stream, or Indra in the sky looking down on it. I *may* be affected by a theatrical exhibition; on the other hand, I *may not* be affected by an actual event which appears to concern me more. I only know myself as a human entity; the scene, so to speak, of thoughts and affections; and am sensible of a certain doubleness by which I can stand as remote from myself as from another. However intense my experience, I am conscious of the presence of and criticism of a part of me, which, as it were, is not a part of me, but spectator, sharing no experience, but taking note of it; and that is no more I than it is you.[1] — *Walden*

Thoreau experiences a level of mind separate from and unaffected by events around him, "not a part of me, but spectator, sharing no experience, but taking note of it." Sometimes he experiences ordinary waking consciousness ("I may be either the driftwood in the stream"); but other times he seems to be witnessing the world from the platform of unbounded awareness ("or Indra in the sky looking down on it"). Thoreau describes this level as "no more I than it is you," suggesting pure consciousness as universal, the Self of everyone.

Thoreau also describes experiences "when first returning to consciousness in the night or morning":

> The mind works like a machine without friction. I am conscious of having, in my sleep, transcended the limits of the individual.... As if in sleep our individual fell into the infinite mind, and at the moment of awakening we found ourselves on the confines of the latter. On awakening we resume our enterprises, take up our bodies, and become limited mind again.[2]
> — *Early Spring in Massachusetts and Summer*

Thoreau tells us that during sleep he transcends his individual limits and falls "into the infinite mind." These words describe witnessing sleep. But when he wakes up, his mind becomes active; he loses the unbounded state and becomes "limited mind" once more.

At the end of *Walden* Thoreau delivers his famous line suggesting inner wakefulness during sleep: "We must learn to reawaken and keep ourselves awake, not by mechanical aids, but by an infinite expectation of the dawn, which does not forsake us in our soundest sleep."[3]

■ *Also see Thoreau in Chapter 4 (Transcendental Consciousness) and Chapter 6 (God Consciousness).*

WALT WHITMAN
1819–1892 • UNITED STATES

See biography on page 131.

Trippers and askers surround me,
People I meet, the effect upon me of my early life or the ward and city I live in, or the nation,
The latest dates, discoveries, inventions, societies, authors old and new,
My dinner, dress, associates, looks, compliments, dues;
. . . .

These come to me days and nights and go from me again,
But they are not the Me myself.

Apart from the pulling and hauling stands what I am,
Stands amused, complacent, compassionating, idle, unitary,
Looks down, is erect, or bends an arm on an impalpable certain rest,
Looking with sidecurved head curious what will come next,
Both in and out of the game and watching and wondering at it.

Backward I see in my own days where I sweated through fog with linguists and contenders,
I have no mockings or arguments, I witness and wait.

I believe in you, my Soul — the other I am must not abase itself to you,
And you must not be abased to the other.[1]   — *Song of Myself*

Whitman inventories various elements in his life, then announces that these are not the true "Me myself." "What I am," he declares, stands apart from all this, unified and restful. He lives "both in and out of the game," suggesting the dual experience in Cosmic Consciousness of the self as ever-changing and the Self as a never-changing, transcendental witness. In the last two lines he honors these two sides of himself: "my Soul" (his unbounded, witnessing Self) and "the other I am" (his waking state personality). Both, he indicates, have their important roles to play.

In this next passage, Whitman gives voice to the 24-hour bliss characteristic of Cosmic Consciousness:

> Hymns to the universal God from universal man — all joy!
> A reborn race appears — a perfect world, all joy!
> Women and men in wisdom innocence and health — all joy!
> . . . .
> War, sorrow, suffering gone — the rank earth purged — nothing but joy left!
> The ocean fill'd with joy — the atmosphere all joy!
> Joy! joy! in freedom, worship, love! joy in the ecstasy of life!
> Enough to merely be! enough to breathe!
> Joy! joy! all over joy!²   — "The Mystic Trumpeter"

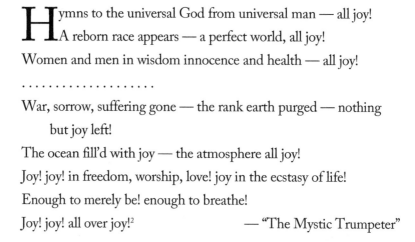 *Also see Whitman in Chapter 4 (Transcendental Consciousness) and Chapter 6 (God Consciousness).*

LEO TOLSTOY
1828–1910 • RUSSIA

Count Lev Nikolayevich Tolstoy was born into a family of old Russian nobility. After a brief stint in the army, he began writing. He quickly became regarded as one of the world's greatest living authors. His novels War and Peace and Anna Karenina are considered masterpieces. Inspired by the Sermon on the Mount, he developed a radical Christian philosophy, expressed in his book The Kingdom of God Is Within You, that emphasized striving for perfection by following the commandment to love God and one's neighbor. He also held that pacifism lies at the heart of Christianity. Mahatma Gandhi read this book as a young man and considered it one of his most important influences. Tolstoy's 1908 work, "A Letter to a Hindu," contends that the Indian people could overthrow the colonial British Empire solely through passive resistance, using the weapon of love. Gandhi asked Tolstoy's permission to reprint this letter in India and adopted this idea over his own 30-year work. The two men corresponded, and Tolstoy's last letter before he died was to Gandhi.

In the very heat of the day the mowing did not seem such hard work to him. The perspiration with which he was drenched cooled him, while the sun, that burned his back, his head, and his arms, bare to the elbow, gave a vigor and dogged energy to his labor; and more and more often now came those moments of unconsciousness, when it was possible not to think what one was doing. The scythe cut of itself. These were happy moments....

The longer Levin mowed, the oftener he felt the moments of unconsciousness in which it seemed not his hands that swung the scythe, but the scythe mowing of itself, a body full of life and

> consciousness of its own, and as though by magic, without thinking of it, the work turned out regular and well-finished of itself. These were the most blissful moments. . . .
>
> Levin did not notice how time was passing. If he had been asked how long he had been working he would have said half an hour — and it was getting on for dinner-time. . . .
>
> Levin looked about him and hardly recognized the place, everything was so changed. The immense stretch of meadow had been mown and was sparkling with a peculiar fresh brilliance. . . . [A]ll was perfectly new.[1]   *— Anna Karenina*

If Levin were an athlete, we would say he was in the zone. Despite the physical exertion, he experiences blissful periods when the work goes by itself, almost magically. Levin no longer identifies himself as the doer of the action; he even has a sense of being outside of time. Yet the work turns out "well-finished," reminding us the heightened skill in action that accompanies Cosmic Consciousness. The passage describes refined perception at the end, pointing toward God Consciousness.

Tolstoy based the character of Levin, the hero, on himself (his first name was Lev) — so he may be describing his own experience.

In the following passage, from an epilogue to *War and Peace,* Tolstoy suggests a much more expanded, transcendental experience of consciousness, calling to mind Cosmic Consciousness:

> Consciousness says: (1) I alone am, and all that exists is but me, consequently I include space. (2) I measure flowing time by the fixed moment of the present in which alone I am conscious of myself as living, consequently I am outside time. (3) I am beyond cause, for I feel myself to be the cause of every manifestation of my life.[2]

EMILY DICKINSON
1830–1886 • UNITED STATES

See biography on page 136.

The blunder is in estimate.
   Eternity is there
We say, as of a Station —
Meanwhile he is so near
He joins me in my Ramble —
Divides abode with me —
No Friend have I that so persists
As this Eternity.[1]   — "1684"

In Chapter 4, Emily Dickinson described her experience of "eternity" in a way suggestive of Transcendental Consciousness, of consciousness aware only of itself. Eternity reappears in this poem as an experience during activity. Eternity "is so near," she says, "he joins me in my Ramble."

❧

The Infinite a sudden Guest
   Has been assumed to be
But how can that stupendous come
Which never went away?[2]   — "1309"

Here Eternity becomes "the Infinite." Dickinson assumed the experience of the Infinite comes and goes like "a sudden Guest" — but wonders how something so remarkable can come if it never departs. Is she describing pure consciousness sustained in activity, the sign of rising Cosmic Consciousness?

Also see Emily Dickinson in Chapter 4 (Transcendental Consciousness).

JOHANNES BRAHMS
1833–1897 • GERMANY

Born in Hamburg, Brahms as a teenager contributed to his impoverished family's income by playing the piano in dance halls, near where the Beatles played early in their career. But Brahms's genius as a composer and piano virtuoso was recognized by his early 30s. He spent much of his life in Vienna. He wrote symphonies, concerti, chamber music, piano works, choral works, and more than 200 songs. A force of stability, Brahms preserved traditions yet he added new elements to develop a powerful, energetic, and personal Romantic style. Even his contemporaries spoke of the "three great B's" — Bach, Beethoven, and Brahms. Though financially successful, he lived a modest life; he gave money to relatives and anonymously supported aspiring young musicians. In 1889, he was visited by a representative of Thomas Edison, who asked him to make an experimental recording; despite poor quality, this was the first recording by a major composer.

To realize that we are one with the Creator, as Beethoven did, is a wonderful and awe-inspiring experience. Very few human beings ever come into that realization and this is why there are so few great composers or creative geniuses in any line of human endeavor. I always contemplate all this before commencing to compose. This is the first step. . . .

I immediately feel vibrations that thrill my whole being. . . . In this exalted state, I see clearly what is obscure in my ordinary moods; then I feel capable of drawing inspiration from above, as Beethoven did. . . .

Straightaway the ideas flow in upon me, . . . and not only do

I see distinct themes in my mind's eye, but they are clothed in the right forms, harmonies, and orchestrations. Measure by measure, the finished product is revealed to me when I am in those rare, inspired moods.... I have to be in a semi-trance condition to get such results — a condition when the conscious mind is in temporary abeyance and the subconscious is in control, for it is through the subconscious mind, which is part of Omnipotence, that the inspiration comes. I have to be careful, however, not to lose consciousness, otherwise the ideas fade away.[1]

[The term "subconscious"] is the most inappropriate name ... super-conscious could be a much better term.[2]

The real genius draws on the Infinite source of Wisdom and Power as Milton and Beethoven did. That is, in my opinion, the best definition of genius.... Great powers like Goethe, Schiller, Milton, Tennyson and Wordsworth received the Cosmic vibrations of eternal Truths because they linked themselves to the infinite energy of the Cosmos....

The themes that will endure in my compositions all come to me in this way. It has always been such a wonderful experience.... I felt that I was, for the moment, in tune with the Infinite, and there is no thrill like it.[3] — *Talks with Great Composers*

All great achievement, Brahms tells us, is the expression of a field of infinite creativity and intelligence, "the infinite energy of the cosmos." Human creativity and nature's creativity have a common source, he says, recalling Maharishi's equation of pure consciousness with the unified field. Brahms felt his most enduring music came when, even during the activity of composing, his awareness remained settled and expanded, "in tune with the Infinite." He terms this a "super-conscious" state, suggesting the heightened wakefulness of Cosmic Consciousness.

EDWARD CARPENTER

1844–1929 • ENGLAND

See biography on page 138.

I feel that the object of life at seventy is practically the same as it was at twenty. Only one thing has been added. One thing. Beneath the surface waves and storms of youth, beneath the backward and forward fluctuations, deep down, there has been added the calm of inner realization and union. I know now that these two primordial and foundational things (or perhaps they are one) are there. Our union with Nature and humanity is a fact, which — whether we recognize it or not — is at the base of our lives; slumbering, yet ready to wake in our consciousness when the due time arrives.

With this assurance one certainly discovers that life — even in old age — may be delightful. . . .

Near the surface the self is very definite and constructive in this or that direction; it is limited in its aims and operations, and so far its activity seems to be at variance with other aims and operations. At the centre it is neither this nor that, because it is All. It vanishes from sight because it has become the Whole. . . .

I find at the age of seventy that I am getting nearer to that place in the centre where nothing exists and yet all is done — and that I suppose is satisfactory.[1]

— *My Days and Dreams*

Carpenter talks about "the calm of inner realization and union" he experiences throughout all the changes in his life. At the center of his self he feels what he calls "All," "the Whole." When this experience becomes fully developed and permanently established, the result is Cosmic Consciousness.

▪ *Also see Carpenter in Chapter 4 (Transcendental Consciousness) and Chapter 7 (Unity Consciousness).*

ROMAIN ROLLAND
1866–1944 • FRANCE

▪ *After earning a doctorate in art, Rolland turned to writing. He became famous for his novels, plays, and essays and was awarded the Nobel Prize in Literature in 1915. He wrote a series of books on great people and on musical history. During World War I, he moved to Switzerland and served the International Red Cross. One of the few great literary figures to denounce the war, he found his pacifist views bitterly attacked, yet he remained unafraid — he considered himself "a citizen of the world." In the 1920s he turned to the study of India, seeking to interpret its spiritual philosophy to the West and befriending Rabindranath Tagore and Gandhi. In the 1930s, he opposed fascism and Nazism. His vast correspondence with the great men of his day, including Leo Tolstoy, Albert Schweitzer, Albert Einstein, Bertrand Russell, Sigmund Freud, and Tagore, was published in 1948. Rolland was involved in the major social, political, and spiritual events of his age, becoming as famous for his personal integrity, social conscience, high ideals, and universal love of humanity as for his literary achievements.*

I feel the Divine very strongly; which is like the central fire in the heart of all life. I have an immediate and direct certainty of this eternity (or this continuity).... I feel very clearly that the Self is independent, not only from my body, but from my thoughts. I feel the power of life and the divine force which upholds the universe. I imbibe it as much as I am able to; as much as I am able to I try to become aware of it, to enjoy it, and have those I love enjoy it.[1] — Letter

Rolland describes the experience of pure consciousness, the Self, which he understands as "the divine force which upholds the universe" — the unified field in the parlance of modern physics.

༳

Peace is in my heart, and I am overly happy about the certainty I have, — at this moment (since honestly I never engage in the future). I feel such fullness of Being! — Referring to the reality, it appears to me an admirable drama. An inner smile does not cease to enlighten all my feelings; I feel all Being in me; I am no more myself, it is all Being. This is tender and powerful and cheerful.[2] — Letter

Really only the constant feeling of Being exists. I cannot feel anything without feeling that It is. I cannot feel that It is without feeling this in an absolute manner, in itself and through itself.

I feel with certainty that Being manifests itself now under this form, now under another.... It is all self ... and in all selves, in the universe of souls. Everyone is therefore Being.... Rolland and Suarès are distinct selves of the same absolute Self.[3] — Letter

"I am no more myself," Rolland writes, alluding to his "small" self — "it is all Being," pure consciousness. He captures the peace, fullness, and unbroken bliss of this state. The second text hints at unity when he says, "It is all self."

■ *Also see Rolland in Chapter 7 (Unity Consciousness).*

PAUL VALÉRY
1871–1945 • FRANCE

See biography on page 144.

On the breast of night, in the
    night's center.
The mind's wakefulness well poised
    against the substance of the night:
Notably alone, distinct, at rest.
Apart from the night, sharply dividing
    her powers!
Then the darkness lightens it,
Silence speaking near:
Then the weightless body in the calm
Knows itself to the last promontories of foot and finger:
And all language is there,
And all remembrance is there,
And all the mind's movements and operations
Are there to be felt and seen:
. . . .
And knowledge is known, not *things*. . . .

    *

The heard.
Listen to this delicate endless susurration which is silence.
Hear what is heard when nothing is heard.

    *

All is gone under the sand of silence
. . . .

> But hear this lone far pure whistling, creating space, as if alone it existed, of itself, to its depth.
>
>   *
>
> Now nothing. But this nothing is huge in the ears.
> . . . .
> Between sleep and waking all things are possible. He can stretch to right or left. The substance of his luck is still molten; his dreams come bidden to hand.   — "Lost Verses"

Valéry describes experiencing silent, wakeful, unbounded consciousness during the night. Here he finds the source of language and memory. The phrase "knowledge is known, not *things*" implies the experience of pure knowledge, consciousness aware solely of itself. The poem continues:

> *Waking.*
> How gentle the light at waking, how lovely this living blue!
> The word "Pure" opens my lips.
> That is the name I give you.
> Here, linked to the day that never yet has been, are the perfect thoughts that never will be. Seeds, eternal seeds, the highest general plane of existence and action.
> The Universal is a seed, the Universal experienced without particulars, the Universal awaking sketchily in the gold, unblemished yet by individual affect.
> I am born everywhere, far from this Identity, in every sparkling of light upon this hem, this fold, the edge of this thread, that mass of lucent water.
> . . . .
> Why should I not delay my being I, and idle in the universal?[1]

As Valéry shifts from sleeping to waking he seems to maintain unbounded awareness. His mind remains in "the highest general plane of existence and action," the unmanifest source of the entire universe.

ANTONIO MACHADO
1875–1939 • SPAIN

Considered one of Spain's greatest poets, Antonio Machado also wrote prose, plays, and literary criticism. He earned a doctoral degree in literature in Madrid, studied at the Sorbonne, and taught French by profession. He rejected the popular modernist approach to poetry, instead composing poems flowing more from intuition than intellect — "a deep palpitation of the spirit," as he described them.[46] He also collaborated with his brother Manuel, a recognized poet in his own right, in composing verse plays. During the Spanish literary revival of 1898, Machado helped to restore his country to a position of intellectual and literary prominence.

Has my heart gone to sleep?
Beehives in my dreams,
have you stopped working? Is the waterwheel
of thought dry,
its buckets empty,
spinning and filled with shadow?

No, my heart is not asleep,
It is awake. Awake.
Not asleep or dreaming, it looks
with open bright eyes
at far signals and listens
on the shores of a great silence.[1] — Untitled, in *Solitudes*

Machado suggests the experience of inner wakefulness and witnessing during sleep, a signpost of Cosmic Consciousness. He locates his mind "On the shores of a great silence," a lovely metaphor for pure consciousness.

Machado hints playfully at this state in these two untitled koan-like poems. He appears to locate it first in the gap between ordinary states of consciousness, then in the transcendent, beyond ordinary states of consciousness:

Between living and dreaming
there is a third way.
Guess it.²

Beyond living and dreaming
is what matters more:
waking.³

MORIHEI UESHIBA
1883–1969 • JAPAN

See biography on page 153.

Always keep your mind as bright and clear as the vast sky, the highest peak, and the deepest ocean, empty of all limiting thoughts.¹

A true warrior is always armed with three things: the radiant sword of pacification; the mirror of bravery, wisdom, and friendship; and the precious jewel of enlightenment.²

Ueshiba understood that transcendence can become a permanent feature of daily life and that this constitutes enlightenment. Established in unbounded pure consciousness, the Self, we remain forever free, unattached, untouched by anything relative. He alludes to this state in many of his talks:

> Practice of the Art of Peace enables you to rise above praise or blame, and it frees you from attachment to this and that.[3]

> Forget about your little self, detach yourself from objects, and you will radiate light and warmth. Light is wisdom; warmth is compassion.[4]

In Cosmic Consciousness, anchored in the source of natural law deep within, we live in harmony with the universe, with the divine. Ueshiba urged his students to rise to this state:

> Your mind should be in harmony with the functioning of the universe; your body should be in tune with the movement of the universe; body and mind should be bound as one, unified with the activity of the universe.[5]

> Aikido is not an art to fight or to defeat an enemy. . . . The essence of Aikido is to tune oneself with the functioning of the universe, to become one with the universe. . . . Martial artists who are not in harmony with the universe are merely executing combat techniques, not Takemusu Aiki.[6]

Living in harmony with the universe, Ueshiba asserted, we gain access to the power of nature itself:

> The Art of Peace functions everywhere on earth, in realms ranging from the vastness of space down to the tiniest plants and animals. The life force is all-pervasive and its strength boundless. The Art of Peace allows us to perceive and tap into that tremendous reserve of universal energy.[7]

My energy, my power, is not controlled by me. I am empty, but through my body flows the energies of the universe. My power is not my power. This is the universal power.[8]

We can put this power to use for ourselves:

Transcend the realm of life and death, and then you will be able to make your way calmly and safely through any crisis that confronts you.[9]

And we create life-nourishing influences around us:

The totally awakened warrior can freely utilize all elements contained in heaven and earth. The true warrior learns how to correctly perceive the activity of the universe and how to transform martial techniques into vehicles of purity, goodness, and beauty. A warrior's mind and body must be permeated with enlightened wisdom and deep calm.[10]

In these passages Ueshiba clearly describes important features of Cosmic Consciousness.

■ *Also see Ueshiba in Chapter 4 (Transcendental Consciousness) and Chapter 7 (Unity Consciousness).*

EDWIN FISCHER

1886–1960 • SWITZERLAND

■ *Edwin Fischer was one of the 20th century's great pianists, piano teachers, and conductors. He specialized in Bach, Mozart, Beethoven, and Schubert. His recording of the Bach "48" remains the yardstick against which all pianists measure themselves. The great Czech pianist Alfred Brendel, a student of Fischer, wrote: "Edwin Fischer was, on the concert platform, a short, leonine, resilient figure, whose every fibre seemed to vibrate with elemental musical power.... With Fischer, one was in more immediate contact with the music: there was no curtain before his soul when he communicated with the audience.... [As a conductor] his achievement was breathtaking. His way of directing the concertos of Bach, Mozart and Beethoven from the keyboard remains inimitable.... As a teacher, Fischer was electrifying by his mere presence. The playing of timid youths... would suddenly spring to life when he grasped them by the shoulder. A few conducting gestures, an encouraging word, could have the effect of lifting the pupil above himself."*[1]

But no amount of studying, no amount of talent, no amount of industry suffices if one's whole life is not dedicated to the idea of being the mediator of great thoughts and emotions. Every deed, and indeed every thought leaves its mark on the personality. The purity of one's life should even extend to the food one eats. Thus prepared, that which cannot be taught will come, the grace of the tranquil hour in which the spirit of the composer speaks to us, that moment of the subconscious, of rapture — call it intuition, grace, or what you will — when all ties are loosened, all constraints disappear. One seems to hover. One no longer feels: I am playing. Rather, IT is playing. And lo, everything is right, as if led by the hand of God the melodies stream from your fingers. It streams through you, and you allow yourself to be carried along, humbly experiencing the greatest joy of the recreative artist, of being nothing but a medium, a mediator between the Godly, the Eternal, and human beings.[2]

Fischer's peak musical performance comes in times of tranquility, when consciousness expands and "all constraints disappear." At these moments of rapture, intuition, and grace, he tells us, one does not perform, one witnesses the performance: He no longer feels he is playing but becomes simply the vehicle delivering something divine.

FRANKLIN MERRELL-WOLFF
1887–1985 • UNITED STATES

See biography on page 158.

I had been doing a little manual work and, at the moment, was stooping and looking at some gravel that had been carried from a distant valley. While doing so I sank into a brooding state and seemed to retreat to a distance where there was a profound, palpable, and pregnant Silence.... There were no words, no ideas, nor any other form, yet, one might say, It was the very essence of Sound or Meaning. It was utterly satisfactory and filling. It was the very Power that makes all things to become clear. Again there flowed the Current of gentle Joy that penetrates through and through.

THE FIFTH STATE • GLIMPSES OF COSMIC CONSCIOUSNESS

I shall attempt an analysis of this Current of Joy as it affects the outer consciousness including the physiological man.... It penetrates all tensions with the effect of physical release. Spots that are not so well feel both rested and stronger. All over and through and through there is a quality that may well be described as physiological happiness.

Relative consciousness by its own momentum continued to function all this time, so that I never for one moment lost sight of my environment or the ceaseless train of thoughts. It was simply a discriminative abstraction of the pure subjective moment and Recognizing myself as That. At this moment, I found Myself above space, time, and causality, and actually sustaining the whole universe by the Light of Consciousness which I AM. Almost at once, there followed the Nectar-like Current and the gentle, yet so powerful Joy.

It is even possible to go to sleep and later wake up without there having been a break in the continuity of self-consciousness. In such an instance the body does go to sleep and consciousness ceases to function on the physical plane, but it remains active on other levels with the continuity of self-consciousness remaining unbroken....

Just as it is true that man can be essentially dreaming while active in the physical body — and most life here is in this state — it is likewise true that some of the states entered while the body sleeps are far more truly waking-states.... The experiencing of these states with most men is very rare, but they do occur more or less frequently with some individuals. They have certain noble earmarks. The most important of these is the effect they have on the waking life. They may enrich, deepen, or give new direction to the outer life. They tend toward an increase of genuine rationality. These are adumbrations of the Real Life.[1] — *Pathways through to Space*

Merrell-Wolff describes experiencing pure awareness along with waking activity. The silent core of the mind awakens and becomes the witness to his experience, filling him with bliss, even a "physiological happiness" and release of tension. Ordinary waking consciousness continues. The only difference is that the mind's deepest level, beyond space and time, is now awake. He recognizes this field of consciousness as "actually sustaining the whole universe."

☙

How shall I ever describe what transpired last night? It is utterly baffling to language as such.... As the Infinite is to the finite, so was that Consciousness of last night to the relative consciousness of the subject-object manifold. I penetrated a State wholly beyond the relative field....

Let us try and see what may be said. After retiring last night I lay awake for some time....

I first became aware of being enveloped in an extraordinary State of Consciousness when I found myself seemingly surrounded by, and interpenetrated through and through with, a quality for which there is no adequate word but which is most nearly represented by calling it "satisfaction." I do not simply mean that the State was satisfactory. It was Satisfaction.... He who is enveloped in this Satisfaction is in need of nothing whatsoever to satisfy him. The Satisfaction I realized is a real and substantial Existence prior to all experiencing.... There was nothing more required, so far as desire for myself was concerned, for at that time I had the full value of everything that could possibly be desired. It might be called the culminating point, the highest to which desire, individually centered, could reach. Only in one sense did I find a desire that could take me away from that State, and that was the desire to convey this new value to others....[2]

His consciousness transcends everything relative, delivering him to a state he experiences as infinite, filling him with utter satisfaction and fulfillment.

☙

Along with this was a sense of simply tremendous Authority. It was an Authority of such stupendous Majesty as to reduce the power of all Caesars relatively to the level of insects....

I am well aware that in this we have a State of Consciousness which falls quite outside the range of ordinary human imagination. Heretofore I have for my own part never been able really to imagine a state of so superior an excellence.... Yet now, deep within me, I feel that I am centered in a Level from which I look down upon all objects of all possible human desire, even the most lofty. It is a strange, almost a weird, Consciousness when viewed from the perspective of relative levels. Yet, on Its own Level, It is the one State that is really complete or adequate. What there may be still Beyond, I do not Know, but this State I do know consumes all others of which I have had any glimpse whatsoever.

The word "Indifference" is not altogether satisfactory, but I know of no other that serves as well.... The High Indifference is to be taken in the sense of an utter Fullness that is even more than a bare Infinity. To borrow a figure from mathematics, It is an Infinity of some higher order, that is, an INFINITY which comprehends lesser Infinities....

How long I continued in the state of the High Indifference I do not know. I was long awake that night — well beyond the midnight hour — and the state continued to deepen. Throughout the whole period the relative consciousness remained present as a witness. The Personality, with the physical form, seemed to shrink toward a pointlike insignificance. The "I" spread out indefinitely like space, enveloping and piercing through all form, so far as my personal consciousness took note. So far as my thought could reach, there were no limits....

I moved about in a kind of Space that was not other than Myself, and found Myself surrounded by pure Divinity, even on the physical level when I moved there.[3] — *Pathways through to Space*

From the majestic, transcendental field of unbounded awareness, he feels he is looking down upon everything in the relative field. To the experience of witnessing the boundaried world from the vantage of unbounded awareness he gives the name High Indifference.

■ *Also see Merrell-Wolff in Chapter 4 (Transcendental Consciousness) and Chapter 7 (Unity Consciousness).*

HENRY MILLER
1891–1980 • UNITED STATES

■ *After growing up in Brooklyn, Miller left college after two months and worked at various jobs while writing. He visited Paris several times, finally moving there in 1930, where he lived for ten years. Returning to the United States, he lived in Big Sur, then in Pacific Palisades, California. He produced a voluminous body of work. With exuberant and joyous prose, his books address the moral decadence of society along with his personal search for meaning and redemption. He is seen as an heir to the American transcendentalist movement inspired by Emerson, Thoreau, and Whitman a century earlier. His watercolor paintings were exhibited internationally, and he was an accomplished pianist. Miller was elected to the National Institute of Arts and Letters in 1958 and in 1961 received a special citation of the Prix International des Editeurs for his book* Tropic of Cancer.

I had gone to the theater nearby to see a vaudeville show; it was the matinee and I had a ticket for the balcony. Standing in line in the lobby, I already experienced a strange feeling of consistency. It was as though I were coagulating. . . . It was like the ultimate stage in the healing of a wound. I was at the height of normality, which is a very abnormal condition. . . . No harm could possibly come to me. . . . There was a plus integer in the blood which meant that, for a few moments at least, disease was completely routed. If one had the wisdom to take root in such a moment, one would never again be ill or unhappy or even die. . . . I was experiencing for the first time in my life the meaning of the miraculous. I was so amazed when I heard my own cogs meshing that I was willing to die then and there for the privilege of the experience.

What happened was this. . . . As I passed the doorman holding the torn stub in my hand the lights were dimmed and the curtain went up. I stood a moment slightly dazed by the sudden darkness. As the curtain slowly rose I had the feeling that throughout the ages man had always been mysteriously stilled by this brief moment which preludes the spectacle. I could feel the curtain rising in man. . . . I didn't think this thought — it was a realization, as I say, and so simple and overwhelmingly clear was it that the machine stopped dead instantly and I was standing in my own presence bathed in a luminous reality. I turned my eyes away from the stage and beheld the marble staircase which I should take to go to my seat in the balcony. I saw a man slowly mounting the steps, his hand laid across the balustrade. The man could have been myself, the old self which had been sleepwalking ever since I was born. . . . I saw only that which was alive! the rest faded out in a penumbra. And it was in order to keep the world alive that I rushed home without waiting to see the performance and sat down to describe the little patch of staircase which is imperishable.[1] — *Tropic of Capricorn*

Miller experiences a sense of heightened integration, of "my own cogs meshing," suggesting the integrated physiological functioning that comes with Transcendental Consciousness and becomes permanent in Cosmic Consciousness. He also describes a heightened state of balance and health and a sense of invincibility.

He tells us he had been "sleepwalking" his entire life. But now he finds himself "standing in my own presence bathed in a luminous reality." He seems to be experiencing the inner reality of life, pure consciousness, now awakened. Miller believed this mode of awareness could become permanent and that everyone has this potential:

> The men who are thoroughly wide-awake and completely alive are in reality, and for these reality has always been close to ecstasy, partaking of a life of fulfillment which knows no bounds. Of them only may it be said that they live in the present. Through them is it permitted us to grasp the meaning of timelessness, of eternity which is victory. It is they who are truly of this world. . . . We live on the edge of the miraculous every minute of our lives. The miracle is in us, and it blossoms forth the moment we lay ourselves open to it.[2]
>
> — *The Wisdom of the Heart*

CHARLOTTE WOLFF
1897–1986 • POLAND & ENGLAND

Charlotte Wolff studied medicine and philosophy at Königsberg, Freiberg, and Berlin universities, qualifying as a doctor. She established a medical practice in Berlin but fled Germany in 1933 for Paris. She then moved to England, where she earned a PhD in psychology and became a fellow of the British Psychological Society. Between the 1930s and 1950s, she conducted extensive research on the psychology of the human hand — the relationship between one's personality and one's hands and manner of gesturing. She published her findings in a number of scientific journals and books. She was also a poet. Her work brought her into contact with Thomas Mann, Aldous Huxley, Julian Huxley, and other literary and artistic figures.

One morning when I walked to school, on a day that seemed like any other day, something happened to me which may have been a decisive landmark in my destiny.

In a narrow street opposite the side entrance of Danzig's main

Post Office, I had to stop. I halted in obedience to an inner command close to the window of a jeweler's shop. I looked neither to the right nor to the left nor anywhere. I was seized by an overwhelming emotion.... At the same time I felt different in size, taller and larger than I really was. A wonderful sense of levitation gave me the feeling that my feet had left the ground and that I was suspended in the air. An unknown and powerful force had got hold of me, a force which was too strong for me to grasp. It gave me a feeling of omnipotence. At that moment of that day I knew the Universe, which I held and beheld inside myself. It was nothing less.... It was like a miracle.... I had undergone the birth of my creative spirit and the birth of that part of the mind which reaches out beyond the material and visible world.... Time did not exist in this eternal moment....

It altered my life. I started to write poetry and got absorbed in reading the philosophy of Plato, Kant, Nietzsche and Spinoza....

The doors opened themselves. But they shut again, and I possessed no key to enable me to re-enter the world I had glimpsed. In spite of the impossibility of repeating the experience at will, its repercussions changed my life....

Everything around me changed its significance.... My wonderful experience had shot me out of the range of my contemporaries and also, to some extent, of my teachers.[1]   — *On the Way to Myself*

Wolff vividly conveys a sense of expanded awareness along with lightness and power, feeling physically larger than she actually is. She feels she experiences the universe inside herself — and the awakening of that part of the mind that "reaches out beyond the material and visible world," beyond time itself. Here she captures the identity between pure consciousness and the unified field, from which the universe is born. Her experience, though fleeting and irretrievable, sparks "the birth of my creative spirit."

HOWARD THURMAN

1899–1981 • UNITED STATES

■ *See biography on page 162.*

A good life is what a man does with the details of living if he sees his life as an instrument, a deliberate instrument in the hands of Life, that transcends all boundaries and all horizons. It is this *beyond dimension* that saves the individual life from being swallowed by the tyranny of present needs, present hungers, and present threats. This is to put distance *within* the experience and to live the quality of the beyond even in the intensity of the present moment.[1] — *The Inward Journey*

Thurman describes experiencing two dimensions simultaneously: ordinary experience plus a "*beyond* dimension" that transcends all boundaries. Then one enjoys a sense of distance from ordinary experience and becomes "a deliberate instrument in the hands of Life." Thurman's words point toward Cosmic Consciousness, where the mind is established in the transcendent and one's thoughts and actions are in harmony with natural law, nourishing everything.

Thurman next describes how inner silence can become a permanent feature of one's experience, also suggesting Cosmic Consciousness. He refers to

[T]he great power that there is in what is here referred to as the central stillness. For it is in the quiet which invades us and which becomes a characteristic of our total respiration that we are most acutely aware of the operation of the Presence of God.[2]

— "Be Still and Cool in the Mind," in *Meditations of the Heart*

Turning to poetry, Thurman considers the hate and hurt that he sees in the world around him, the "blight, dread, and death" human beings bring upon the world. The poem concludes with these lines:

> High above the turmoil, the Voice is clear:
> "Thou art made for wholeness,
> Body, mind, spirit: one creative synthesis,
> Moving in perfect harmony within, without,
> With fellow man and nature all around
> To make Heaven where Hell is found."[3]
> — "All Mysteries and All Knowledge," in *The Inward Journey*

The purpose of human life, Thurman asserts, is to live wholeness of life, to live in harmony with oneself and with nature — qualities of life fulfilled in Cosmic Consciousness. Achieving this wholeness, Thurman maintains, will create heaven on earth.

Also see Howard Thurman in Chapter 4 (Transcendental Consciousness), Chapter 6 (God Consciousness), and Chapter 7 (Unity Consciousness).

CHARLES LINDBERGH
1902-1974 • UNITED STATES

In 1927, at 25, Lindbergh achieved international acclaim overnight when, as an unknown airmail pilot, he became the first person to complete a nonstop solo flight across the Atlantic, flying from Long Island to Paris. For this historic achievement he was awarded the Medal of Honor. He urged the United States to stay out of World War II — but once the US entered the war, he flew numerous combat missions in the Pacific as a civilian consultant. A man of wide-ranging talents, he collaborated on rocket research with Robert Goddard and medical research with Nobel Laureate Alexis Carrel. In the early 1950s he undertook a long series of study expeditions for conservation and wildlife preservation, an interest he maintained the rest of his life. He received many honors and tributes.

Lindbergh here describes his 3,600-mile solo flight across the Atlantic:

[I experienced] a state of semiconsciousness in which an awareness exists that is less acute but apparently more universal than that of the normal mind.... Over and over again on the second day of my flight, I would return to mental alertness sufficiently to realize that I had been flying while I was neither asleep nor awake. My eyes had been open. I had responded to my instruments' indications and held generally to compass course, but I had lost sense of circumstance and time. During immeasurable periods, I seemed to extend outside my plane and body, independent of worldly values, appreciative of beauty, form, and color without depending upon my eyes. It was an experience in which both the intellectual and sensate were replaced by what might be termed a matterless awareness.[1] — *Autobiography of Values*

Lindbergh describes a more universal state of awareness, beyond thought and perceptions, immensely expanded. He reminds us of Cosmic Consciousness, where the mind remains silent, unbounded, and awake deep within even while active at the surface.

☙

Lindbergh describes similar experiences of expanded awareness on other occasions — recognizing this expanded awareness as a fundamental level of nature and life:

> [M]y awareness rayed out beyond the heavy walls of knowledge, around the earth and through the sky, bending into past and future.... you knew a wisdom deeper than the mind, a reality beyond the touch of substance....
>
> Watching satellites and staring at the stars, I seemed to lose contact with my earth and body and to spread out through the cosmos by means of an awareness that permeates both space and life — as though I were expanding from a condensation of awareness previously selected and restricted to the biological matter that was myself.[2]
>
> *— Autobiography of Values*

Lindbergh experiences what he calls the core, a deep inner level of awareness characterized by simplicity, expansion, balance, and joy. "The important thing was the core," he writes. "But what was it: how much of it was physical, how much mental, how much spiritual? How could one reach one's core?"[3]

Fleeting though his experiences were, they gave Lindbergh a deep insight: "Our individuality is universality condensed in a cosmic moment," he wrote.[4] And though he lacked a technique for transcending, he sensed the inward direction he felt humanity must take: "Will we discover that only without spaceships can we reach the galaxies; that only without cyclotrons can we know the interior of atoms?"[5]

CLARE BOOTHE LUCE
1903–1987 • UNITED STATES

■ *Clare Boothe Luce began her career as an editor at* Vogue *and then* Vanity Fair, *where she started writing short satirical pieces about New York society. She then commenced a successful career as a playwright. During World War II, she became a war correspondent, traveling to Europe, China, Burma, India, and Africa. In 1939, she became one of the first women in the United States Congress, representing Connecticut, and in 1953 became ambassador to Italy. She was awarded the Presidential Medal of Freedom in 1981. Her husband was Henry Luce, the publisher of* Time, Fortune, *and* Life *magazines.*

Clare Boothe Luce recounts an experience she had when she was 16 or 17:

I no longer remember where it took place, except that it was a summer day on an American beach....

I remember that it was a cool, clean, fresh, calm, blue, radiant day, and that I stood by the shore, my feet not in the waves. And now — as then — I find it difficult to explain what did happen. I expect that the easiest thing to say is that suddenly SOMETHING WAS. My whole soul was cleft clean by it, as a silk veil slit by a shining sword. And I knew. I do not know now what I knew. I remember, I didn't know even then. That is, I didn't know with any "faculty." It was not in mind or heart or blood stream. But whatever it was I knew, it was something that made ENORMOUS SENSE. And it was final. And yet that word could not be used, for it meant end, and there was no end to this finality. Then joy abounded in all of me. Or rather, I abounded in joy. I seemed to have no nature, and yet my whole nature was adrift in this immense joy, as a speck of dust is seen to dance in a great golden shaft of sunlight.

I don't know how long this experience lasted. It was, I should think, closer to a second than an hour — though it might have been either....[1]

Luce seems to have transcended for a time and experienced the field of pure existence, pure Being. Her experience now seems to take place from this transcendental field, outside time and space. She experiences unboundedness and bliss. While the experience lasts, everything makes sense to her.

DAG HAMMARSKJÖLD
1905–1961 • SWEDEN

See biography on page 164.

Every deed and every relationship is surrounded by an atmosphere of silence.[1]   — *Markings*

To preserve the silence within — amid all the noise. To remain open and quiet, a moist humus in the fertile darkness where the rain falls and the grain ripens — no matter how many tramp across the parade ground in whirling dust under an arid sky.[2]

— *Markings*

The experience of inner silence, Hammarskjöld understood, can be maintained in the midst of dynamic daily activity. This is the fifth state of consciousness, Cosmic Consciousness.

The "mystical experience." Always here and now — in that freedom which is one with distance, in that stillness which is born of silence. But — this is a freedom in the midst of action, a stillness in the midst of other human beings. The mystery is a constant reality to him who, in this world, is free from self-concern, a reality that grows peaceful and mature before the receptive attention of assent. In our era the road to holiness often passes through the world of action.[3]
— *Markings*

Inner silence, Hammarskjöld tells us, can coexist with outer activity. In this state, whatever one's outer circumstances, inside one is ever free and at peace.

⌘

Understand — through the stillness,
Act — out of stillness,
Conquer in the stillness.
In order for the eye to perceive color, it must divest itself of all colors.[4]
— *Markings*

Hammarskjöld counsels us to let inner silence, pure inner wakefulness, undergird everything we know and do. The last line above is taken from one of Meister Eckhart's sermons.

⌘

To have humility is to experience reality, not in relation to ourselves, but in its sacred independence. It is to see, judge, and act from the point of rest in ourselves. Then, how much disappears, and all that remains falls into place.

In the point of rest at the center of our being, we encounter a world where all things are at rest in the same way. Then a tree becomes a mystery, a cloud a revelation, each man a cosmos of whose riches we can only catch glimpses. The life of simplicity is simple, but it opens to us a book in which we never get beyond the first syllable.⁵   — *Markings*

Authentic humility, Hammarskjöld observes, arises when we are established "in the point of rest at the center of our being." Then life becomes much simpler and easier, and the true nature of the world begins to reveal itself.

Hammarskjöld reiterates this in this one-sentence entry in his journal:

> You are liberated from things, but you encounter in them an experience which has the purity and clarity of revelation.⁶
>   — *Markings*

In Cosmic Consciousness, Maharishi explains, established in inner silence, one lives in accord with natural law; one becomes an instrument of divine purpose. Hammarskjöld captures this reality in another elegant sentence:

> The best and most wonderful thing that can happen to you in this life is that you should be silent and let God work and speak.⁷
>   — *Markings*

> In the One you are never alone, in the One you are always at home. . . .
> Remain at the Center, which is yours and that of all humanity.⁸
>   — *Markings*

Also see Hammarskjöld in Chapter 4 (Transcendental Consciousness).

EUGENE IONESCO
1909–1994 • ROMANIA & FRANCE

■ *See biography on page 170.*

I remember myself walking one summer day around noon in a little village in the provinces in the sunshine, beneath a deep, dense sky. It was a little street, bordered with little white houses whose immaculate walls shone so brightly....

Suddenly I felt as if I had received a blow right in the heart, in the center of my being. A stupefaction surged into being.... "Nothing is true," I said, "outside of this" — a *this* that I was, of course, unable to define, since the *this* itself was what escaped definition, because it itself was the beyond, that which went beyond definitions. Perhaps I could translate this feeling and this *this* by "a certainty of being."

A joy, something more than a joy lifted me up, carried me away. The steps I took seemed to be someone else's.... I watched myself walk, I saw myself walk from outside myself. I said to myself when I saw myself: "So I who am walking on this sidewalk am really the one that I see walking, and what a strange thing, what universe do these houses and these walls and these fences belong to, how all of this is at once the same thing and a different thing".... The sky, which was made, it seemed to me, of an intermediate substance between air and water, had descended on the city and enveloped me, enveloped all the objects, the walls, and was almost palpable, almost velvet, blue; the deeper and denser the blue of the sky became, the more it could be perceived through the sense of touch, while the whiter the houses became, the less material they became. . . .

My euphoria became enormous, inhuman. I breathed the air and it was as if I were swallowing pieces of blue sky that replaced my lungs, my heart, my liver, my bones with this celestial substance, somewhere between water and air, and this made me so light, lighter and lighter, that I could no longer feel the effort of walking. It was as if I were not walking now, but leaping, dancing. I could have flown, this depended on just a few things; with a simple concentration of will, of energy, I could have risen from the earth as in a dream or *as once upon a time*.

However, even the pleasure of flight would have been less great than the pleasure I felt at this moment. . . . And above all neither flight nor anything else could give me greater euphoria than that of becoming aware that *I was*, once and for all, and that this was an irreversible thing, an eternal miracle: the universe merely appears to be, perhaps, perhaps it is only an appearance, but *I am*, I am sure of being. That was completely obvious to me. Everything was merely evidence of this. How blind I had been! What had happened to me, what deep sleep had I been made one with, had I been plunged into? . . .

I was saved now. It was impossible for me to become the prey of the mud of shadows again, because I knew now, in a luminous sort of way, I knew and could no longer forget that I am, I myself am, everything is. The miracle of being, the miracle of being, the miracle of being. . . .

This lasted a very long time. It lasted a few seconds. A cloud hid the sun. The intensity of the light diminished only slightly but that was enough for everything to collapse in coldness and darkness. ... The miraculous evidence vanished. The sky became just any sky. The light of the sun that had seemed to envelop me drew away from me, took its astronomical distance once again. Things, the walls, took on their usual form again; the street became an ugly, vulgar, provincial street again; the dogs barked noisily. My lungs took their place in my chest again; I breathed, and became aware of how painful it was to breathe. All that was left was this world of ice, or of shadows, or of empty clarity, of gray light, of ashes. It seemed to me that there was still a corner of light within myself, which I tried to keep, to enlarge. Alas, everything around me grew dark and everything that had been a sphere or a circle became angles once again. The everyday world took its usual place again, and I went back to my usual place in the everyday world.

We are like Cinderella who lived her life expecting a transfiguration of the world, who lived her life expecting a few hours of glorious, sumptuous festivities; the rest of the time we are there in rags, in the dirty shanties of reality. It is as if we lived in a profound lethargy. We wake up for a few moments from time to time, then we sink into empty sleep again.

Nonetheless, nonetheless the interior mechanism that can set off this state of supernormal wakefulness that could set the world ablaze, that could transfigure it, illuminate it, is able to function in the simplest, most natural way. All one need do is press a button. Only it is not easy to find this button; we fumble about for it in the shadows on one of the walls of an enormous strange house.[1]

— *Present Past Past Present*

"The steps I took seemed to be someone else's," Ionesco tells us. "I watched myself walk, I saw myself walk from outside myself." He seems to describe the experience of witnessing, the feature of Cosmic Consciousness in which one observes or witnesses one's thoughts and actions from the field of unbounded pure consciousness, beyond the realm of change.

He finds the experience supremely blissful. His senses become refined, his perceptions indescribably rich. But none of this, he says, compares with his inner experience of unbounded awareness, pure knowledge, pure bliss.

He feels saved, feels he will never fall back into the old world. But the experience fades and the reality fades with it. How simple it should be, Ionesco declares, to live in this state of "supernormal wakefulness." We only need press a button, he says — but where is it?

■ *Also see Ionesco in Chapter 4 (Transcendental Consciousness) and Chapter 6 (God Consciousness).*

SIR ROGER BANNISTER
b. 1929 • ENGLAND

■ *One of the greatest accomplishments in the history of athletics occurred when Roger Bannister became the first person to run a mile in under four minutes — the sports equivalent of being the first to climb Mount Everest. A medical student at Oxford University at the time, Bannister later retired from running to pursue a career as a neurologist. He has published more than 50 papers in medical journals and since 1968 has edited an important textbook on clinical neurology. He has served as president of the International Council for Sport and Physical Recreation, an advisory body to UNESCO. He was knighted by Queen Elizabeth in 1975.*

In his book *The Four-Minute Mile*, Bannister recounts his famous race on May 6, 1954. There had been a rain shower just before the meet, followed by a gale-force wind that would slow him by a second a lap. But just before the event, the wind died down momentarily. Here he describes his experience before and during his great race, dubbed "the Mile of the Century."

In my mind I had settled this as the day when, with every ounce of strength I possessed, I would attempt to run the four-minute mile....

I had reached my peak physically and psychologically. There would never be another day like it....

There was complete silence on the ground . . . a false start. . . . The gun fired a second time. . . . Brasher went into the lead and I slipped in effortlessly behind him, feeling tremendously full of running. My legs seemed to meet no resistance at all, as if propelled by some unknown force.

We seemed to be going so slowly! . . .

I was relaxing so much that my mind seemed almost detached from my body. There was no strain....

I had a moment of mixed joy and anguish, when my mind took over. It raced well ahead of my body and drew my body compellingly forward. I felt that the moment of a lifetime had come. There was no pain, only a great unity of movement and aim. The world seemed to stand still, or did not exist....

I felt at that moment that it was my chance to do one thing supremely well....

I knew that I had done it before I even heard the time....

The stop-watches held the answer. The announcement came — "Result of one mile ... time, 3 minutes" — the rest lost in the roar of excitement....

In the wonderful joy my pain was forgotten and I wanted to prolong those precious moments of realization....

No words could be invented for such supreme happiness, eclipsing all other feelings.[1] — *The Four-Minute Mile*

Bannister experiences something like witnessing during his race: "My mind seemed almost detached from my body," he says. He feels deeply relaxed and integrated. In Cosmic Consciousness, one's awareness is grounded in transcendental silence, unshaken even in dynamic activity, and one's physiology functions in a dual mode, restful even while active, much as Bannister describes.

For experiences from other sports figures, see Billie Jean King (at the beginning of this chapter) as well as Patsy Neal and Pelé (later in this chapter).

RAY REINHARDT
b. 1930 • UNITED STATES

While serving in the Army, Ray Reinhardt got a part in the play Golden Boy *and has been an actor ever since. He studied drama in London and was a founding member of San Francisco's American Conservatory Theater repertory company, where he performed for 27 years. He has also had roles in numerous movies and television shows. Among his films are* The Hunt for Red October *and* Star Trek. *He also had roles in the* Star Trek *television series and* LA Law.

There are two stages to having the audience in your hand. The first one is the one in which you bring them along, you make them laugh through sheer skill — they laughed at that, now watch me top it with this one. But, there's a step beyond that which I experienced, but only two or three times. It is the most — how can you use words like satisfying? It's more ultimate than ultimate: I seemed to be part of a presence that stood behind myself and was able to observe, not with my eyes, but with my total being, myself and the audience. It was a wonderful thing of leaving not only the character, but also this person who calls himself Ray Reinhardt. In a way, I was no longer acting actively, although things were happening: my arms moved independently, there was no effort required; my body was loose and very light. It was the closest I've ever come in a waking state to a mystical experience.[1]   — "The World a Stage"

"I seemed to be part of a presence that stood behind myself," Reinhardt says. He observes himself and the audience not with his eyes but with his "total being." This describes what it might be like to witness the world of change from the unchanging, unbounded platform of pure consciousness. He seems to transcend the "small" self and experience the universal, transcendental Self. His performance becomes both effortless and highly skilled, an experience "more ultimate than ultimate."

VÁCLAV HAVEL
1936–2011 • CZECH REPUBLIC

One of the 20th century's great leaders, Havel began his career as a stagehand in Prague. He started writing plays and quickly became one of Europe's most esteemed writers, composing more than 20 plays as well as poetry and works of nonfiction. After the Communist invasion of Czechoslovakia, in 1968, he was imprisoned multiple times for his dissenting views, including once for five years. Yet he continued to publish, and his writings, together with his unrelenting example, inspired the Czech people to demand he be made head of state. He became the ninth and final President of Czechoslovakia (1989–1992) and the first President of the Czech Republic (1993–2003). Under his leadership his country became a multi-party democracy and a free-market economy, *and in 2004 it joined the European Union. Havel received many honors, including the US Presidential Medal of Freedom, the Philadelphia Liberty Medal, the Order of Canada, the International Gandhi Peace Prize, and many honorary doctoral degrees. Described as "a global ambassador of conscience," Havel epitomized the power of people to triumph peacefully over totalitarian rule. His famous motto: "Truth and love must prevail over lies and hatred."*

When I was still in Hermanice, something happened to me that superficially was in no way remarkable, but was nevertheless very profoundly important to me internally: I had an afternoon shift, it was wonderful summer weather, I was sitting on a pile of iron, resting, thinking over my own affairs and at the same time, gazing at the crown of a single tree some distance beyond the fence. The sky was a dark blue, cloudless, the air was hot and still, the leaves of the tree shimmered and trembled slightly. And slowly but surely, I found myself in a very strange and wonderful state of mind.... It seemed to me that all the beautiful summer days I had ever experienced and would yet experience were present in that moment.... I seemed to be experiencing, in my mind, a moment of supreme bliss, of infinite joy (all the other important joys, such as the presence of those I love, seemed latent in that moment), and though I felt physically intoxicated by it, there was far more to it than that: it was a moment of supreme self-awareness, a supremely elevating state of the soul, a total and totally harmonic merging of existence with itself and with the entire world.[1] — *Letters to Olga*

Havel tells us about a moment of surpassing bliss that involves "supreme self-awareness, a supremely elevating state of the soul." These phrases call to mind the bliss and unbounded awareness of Cosmic Consciousness. Havel's last phrase — his sense of existence merging completely with itself and with the world — foreshadows Unity Consciousness.

Later in the book Havel writes, "In the essence of the mind, there is transcendence, the effort to step beyond all horizons."[2] He then returns to the Hermanice experience, emphasizing its importance and furnishing more detail:

> All at once, I seemed to rise above all the coordinates of my momentary existence in the world into a kind of state outside time in which all the beautiful things I had ever seen and experienced existed in a total "co-present"; I felt a sense of reconciliation, indeed of an almost gentle consent to the inevitable course of things as revealed to me now, and this combined with a carefree determination to face what had to be faced. A profound amazement at the sovereignty of Being became a dizzying sensation of tumbling endlessly into the abyss of its mystery; an unbounded joy at being alive, at having been given the chance to live through all I have lived through, and at the fact that everything has a deep and obvious meaning; . . . I was flooded with a sense of ultimate happiness and harmony with the world and myself, with that moment, with all the moments I could call up, and with everything invisible that lies behind it and which has meaning. I would even say that I was somehow "struck by love," though I don't know precisely for whom or what.[3]
> — *Letters to Olga*

Havel seems to transcend ordinary existence to a state beyond time. He experiences "the sovereignty of Being" (one of Maharishi's synonyms for pure consciousness), bringing him extraordinary joy. Havel again foreshadows Unity Consciousness when he describes feeling "harmony with the world and myself" as well as "with everything invisible that lies behind it."

These experiences surely shaped Havel's views as a national and global leader. His widely-covered public speeches express ideas surprising for a politician. Addressing the US Congress as his country's new president, he declared,

> Consciousness precedes being, and not the other way around. For this reason, the salvation of this human world lies nowhere else than in the human heart.[4]

When awarded the Liberty Medal, in 1994 in Philadelphia, he said,

It logically follows that, in today's multicultural world, the truly reliable path to coexistence, to peaceful coexistence and creative cooperation, must start from what is at the root of all cultures and what lies infinitely deeper in human hearts and minds than political opinion, convictions, antipathies or sympathies: it must be rooted in self-transcendence.... Transcendence is the only real alternative to extinction.[5]

PATSY NEAL
b. 1938 • UNITED STATES

■ *In high school Patsy Neal set the Georgia state women's basketball scoring record with 64 points in one game. She became a three-time AAU All-American, helped her college basketball team win two AAU national titles as well as second and third place finishes, helped the US team capture a gold medal at the 1959 Pan American Games, captained the US team that competed in the 1964 World Basketball Tournament in Lima, Peru (finishing fourth), and played on the US All-Star team in 1965, among other sports achievements. She taught health, physical education, and recreation at the college level for 19 years. She has written eight books on sports and a volume of poetry. In 2003 she was inducted into the Women's Basketball Hall of Fame.*

In her book *Sport and Identity* Neal describes her experience in the National Free-Throw Championship at the 1957 National AAU Basketball Tournament, where she won the title by hitting 48 of 50 free throws.

I felt as though I was *floating* through the day, not just living it. That evening, when I shot my free-throws in the finals, I was probably the calmest I have ever been in my life. I didn't even see or hear the crowd. It was only me, the ball, and the basket. The number of baskets I made really had no sense of importance to me at the time. The only thing that really mattered was what I *felt*. But even so, I would have found it hard to miss even if I had wanted to. My motions were beyond my conscious control ... the ball and I *had* to react in a certain way. It was like being on skis and going down a steep mountain. I was carried along by the force of the momentum of *whatever* I was at that time. I know now what people mean when they speak of a "state of grace." I was in a state of grace, and if it were in my power to maintain what I was experiencing at that point in time, I would have given up everything in my possession in preference to that sensation. But it was beyond my will ... beyond my own understanding ... beyond *me*. Yet, I was *it*.

That evening, I hit 48 out of 50 free-throws to win the 1957 Free-Throw Championship. The only thing that surprised me was the fact that two of the shots missed. I felt in such a state of perfection that it seemed only right that my performance would have been perfect. In fact, as I recall, every shot went through cleanly except the two I missed — and they rimmed the basket before dropping out. Even now, when I think of the Free-Throw Championship, I don't think about the fact that I won it ... I think of what I *was* that evening. . . .

There have been other moments in my life where I have touched on this unlimited source of power — where things *happened* in spite of me. But never once have I been able to consciously *will* it to happen. I have been open to it because I know it's *there* ... and I want to be a part of the complete *freeness* every chance it will have me as a part of it. But the occasions are so rare — perhaps this adds to the preciousness of it. The experience at the 1957 tournament was such an intense one, such a *transcending* one. . . .

But as a result of that experience, and the few ones in other situations which were similar, I do know that spirit and bodily movements can be correlated. As they intertwine, one seems to hang between the real world and another world of miracles. One accomplishes things one never dreamed of doing. One walks beyond the usual physical powers and goes *into* the power of the universe, finding streams and sensations that seem to have no beginning or end within the self. . . .

This feeling of *being* life, rather than just an isolated *part* of life. . . . Attaining this heightened sense of being alive . . . is probably the closest thing to *real* morality man can experience.[1]

— *Sport and Identity*

Neal describes a state of "complete *freeness*" along with extraordinary mental and physical calm. She calls it a state of grace and perfection. Also "transcending" — she feels her mind has gone beyond ordinary, relative levels — beyond her will, beyond her understanding, "beyond *me*." "I was *it*," she states — she identifies with that transcendental field.

She recognizes this inner field as a source of unlimited power, "the power of the universe." Directly experiencing this field, Neal realizes, brings inner freedom and perfect coordination of mind and body. From here, she says, "one accomplishes things one never dreamed of doing."

This is the most important experience not only in sports, she concludes, but in life. She presents another eloquent description of it:

Something *unexplainable* takes over and breathes life into the known life. One stands on the threshold of miracles that one cannot create voluntarily. . . . Call it a state of grace, or an act of faith . . . or an act of God. It is there, and the impossible becomes possible, and the last becomes first. The athlete goes beyond herself; she transcends the natural. She touches a piece of heaven and becomes the recipient of power from an unknown source.

The power goes beyond that which can be defined as physical or mental. The performance almost becomes a holy place — where a spiritual awakening seems to take place. The individual becomes swept up in the action around her — she almost *floats* through the performance, drawing on forces she has never previously been aware of.[2]

▪ *For experiences from other athletes, see Billie Jean King (at the beginning of this chapter), also Sir Roger Bannister and Pelé (earlier and later in this chapter, respectively).*

PELÉ
b. 1940 • BRAZIL

▪ *Known during his career as "The King of Football," or "The King," Pelé is regarded as the greatest soccer player of all time. He scored nearly 1,300 goals, more than any other player, and is the only one to play on three world championship teams. In international games, he scored an average of one goal per game — equivalent to hitting a home run in every World Series game for 15 years. More people have watched Pelé play soccer than any other athlete in any sport. In 1967, when Pelé's team traveled to Nigeria to play an exhibition game, a 48-hour truce was called in the civil war there so both sides could watch. He has been an outspoken supporter of policies to help the poor, has met with more than a hundred heads of state, and is an honorary citizen of more countries and cities than anyone else in history. He is also an actor, poet, musician, and composer. In 1978 Pelé received the International Peace Award. In 1999 he was named Soccer Player of the Century by UNICEF, Athlete of the Century by both the International Olympic Committee and the Reuters News Agency, and one of the 100 Most Important People of the 20th Century by* Time *magazine. The Brazilian government has declared him a national treasure.*

In his autobiography, Pelé describes an experience he had during his first World Cup. He was 17 years old, playing against Sweden in the final game, and Sweden had just scored the first goal, putting Pelé's team down 1–0.

> We started off again and suddenly I felt a strange calmness I hadn't experienced in any of the other games. It was a type of euphoria; I felt I could run all day without tiring, that I could dribble through any of their team or all of them, that I could almost pass through them physically. I felt I could not be hurt. It was a very strange feeling and one I had never felt before. Perhaps it was merely confidence, but I have felt confident many times without that strange feeling of invincibility.[1]   — *My Life and the Beautiful Game*

Pelé's experience has several features that call to mind the fifth state of consciousness. He feels a remarkable calm in the midst of exceedingly dynamic activity. This is coupled with superior performance, bliss, and a sense of invincibility. Of the thousands of games he played, of all his dazzling performances, he had this special experience just once.

For experiences from other sports figures, see Billie Jean King (at the beginning of this chapter) and Sir Roger Bannister and Patsy Neal (earlier in this chapter).

ECKHART TOLLE

b. 1948 • GERMANY & CANADA

▪ *Born in northwestern Germany, Tolle had an unhappy childhood. At 13, he joined his father in Spain, schooling himself by reading books on literature, astronomy, and languages. At 19, he moved to London, where he taught German and Spanish in a language institute. At 22, he enrolled at the University of London, where he studied philosophy, psychology, and literature. He then went to Cambridge to pursue a doctorate but remained only briefly. At 29 he had a life-changing experience that dissolved his anxiety and led to his becoming a counselor and teacher. He moved to Vancouver in 1995. His books have sold more than 12 million copies and have been translated into 35 languages.*

In his first book, *The Power of Now*, Tolle describes the transformative experience he had when he was 29. For most of his life he had lived in almost continuous anxiety mixed with depression. One night he awoke in the early hours feeling "absolute dread." The thought kept recurring: "I cannot live with myself any longer."[1]

> Then suddenly I became aware of what a peculiar thought it was. "Am I one or two? If I cannot live with myself, there must be two of me: the 'I' and the 'self' that 'I' cannot live with." "Maybe," I thought, "only one of them is real."
>
> I was so stunned by this strange realization that my mind stopped. I was fully conscious, but there were no more thoughts.[2]

He felt himself being drawn into a "vortex of energy," a void within himself. "I have no recollection of what happened after that," he writes.

I was awakened by the chirping of a bird outside the window. I had never heard such a sound before. . . . I opened my eyes. The first light of dawn was filtering through the curtains. Without any thought, I felt, I knew, that there is infinitely more to light than we realize. That soft luminosity filtering through the curtains was love itself. Tears came into my eyes. I got up and walked around the room. I recognized the room, and yet I knew that I had never truly seen it before. Everything was fresh and pristine, as if it had just come into existence. I picked up things, a pencil, an empty bottle, marveling at the beauty and aliveness of it all.

That day I walked around the city in utter amazement at the miracle of life on earth, as if I had just been born into this world.

For the next five months, I lived in a state of uninterrupted deep peace and bliss. After that, it diminished somewhat in intensity, or perhaps it just seemed to because it became my natural state. I could still function in the world, although I realized that nothing I ever *did* could possibly add anything to what I already had.

I knew, of course, that something profoundly significant had happened to me, but I didn't understand it at all. It wasn't until several years later, after I had read spiritual texts and spent time with spiritual teachers, that I realized that what everybody was looking for had already happened to me. . . . [I experienced] my true nature as the ever-present *I am*: consciousness in its pure state prior to identification with form. Later I also learned to go into that inner timeless and deathless realm that I had originally perceived as a void and remain fully conscious. I dwelt in states of such indescribable bliss and sacredness that even the original experience I just described pales in comparison. . . .

But even the most beautiful experiences come and go. More fundamental, perhaps, than any experience is the undercurrent of peace that has never left me since then. Sometimes it is very strong, almost palpable, and others can feel it too. At other times, it is somewhere in the background, like a distant melody.³   — *The Power of Now*

Tolle's experience begins with spontaneous and profound transcending. When he awakens, he sees and hears a new dimension in the world around him, suggesting the refined perception of God Consciousness, the sixth state. But the enduring experience is of "the ever-present I am: consciousness in its pure state," suggesting Cosmic Consciousness.

ॐ

Those who have not found their true wealth, which is the radiant joy of Being and the deep, unshakable peace that comes with it, are beggars, even if they have great material wealth. They are looking outside for scraps of pleasure or fulfillment, for validation, security, or love, while they have a treasure within that not only includes all those things but is infinitely greater than anything the world can offer. . . .

The word *enlightenment* conjures up the idea of some superhuman accomplishment, and the ego likes to keep it that way, but it is simply your natural state of felt oneness with Being. It is a state of connectedness with something immeasurable and indestructible, something that, almost paradoxically, is essentially you and yet is much greater than you. It is finding your true nature beyond name and form.⁴   — *The Power of Now*

Tolle uses the word *Being* to refer to the field of pure consciousness that lies deep within us and forms the essence of everything. Established in that eternal field, one finds true freedom, peace, joy, and love:

Having access to that formless realm is truly liberating. It frees you from bondage to form and identification with form. It is life in its undifferentiated state prior to its fragmentation into multiplicity. We may call it the Unmanifested, the invisible Source of all things, the Being within all beings. It is a realm of deep stillness and peace, but also of joy and intense aliveness.[5]   — *The Power of Now*

※

The realm of Being, which had been obscured by the mind, then opens up. Suddenly, a great stillness arises within you, an unfathomable sense of peace. And within that peace, there is great joy. And within that joy, there is love. And at the innermost core, there is the sacred, the immeasurable, That which cannot be named.[6]
— *The Power of Now*

※

When you know who you are, there is an abiding alive sense of peace. You could call it joy because that's what joy is: vibrantly alive peace. It is the joy of knowing yourself as the very life essence before life takes on form. That is the joy of Being — of being who you truly are.[7]   — *Stillness Speaks*

In Tolle's view, all creativity and peak performance stems from greater access to this inner field. His description reminds us of the zone experience in sports:

Artistic creation, sports, dance, teaching, counseling — mastery in any field of endeavor implies that the thinking mind is either no longer involved at all or at least is taking second place. A power and intelligence greater than you and yet one with you in essence takes over. There is no decision-making process anymore; spontaneous right action happens, and "you" are not doing it. Mastery of life is the opposite of control. You become aligned with the greater consciousness. It acts, speaks, does the works.[8]
— *Stillness Speaks*

※

When Tolle uses the terms *the Now* and *the power of Now*, he is referring to pure consciousness, pure Being — the ever-present transcendental field, which lies outside the flow of time.

When one is established in this essential reality of life, as one is in Cosmic Consciousness, then the possibility of still higher states of consciousness opens. In these next two passages, Tolle hints first at the sixth state, God Consciousness, and then at the seventh state, Unity Consciousness:

> Indirectly, you are aware of the Unmanifested in and through the sensory realm. In other words, you feel the God-essence in every creature, every flower, every stone, and you realize: "All that is, is holy."[9]
> — *The Power of Now*

> Pure consciousness is Life before it comes into manifestation, and that Life looks at the world of form through "your" eyes because consciousness is who you are. When you know yourself as That, then you recognize yourself in everything. It is a state of complete clarity of perception. You are no longer an entity with a heavy past that becomes a screen of concepts through which every experience is interpreted.[10]
> — *Stillness Speaks*

CHAPTER 6

THE SIXTH STATE

God Consciousness
Perceiving Nature's Celestial Glories

RABINDRANATH TAGORE STEPPED OUT onto the veranda of his brother's house in Kolkata (Calcutta), at the eastern point of India, where he had been living — and the world revealed its celestial secret.

Born in 1861 to a very wealthy Indian family, Tagore studied law at University College in London. But he found himself powerfully drawn to writing. He wrote prolifically, publishing several dozen collections of poems, as well as novels, stories, plays, essays, travelogues, and nonfiction books. He revitalized Bengali literature and music by experimenting with new forms, such as prose-songs and dance-dramas. For his collection of poems, *Gitanjali*, he won the Nobel Prize in Literature in 1913 — the first non-European to win the prize.

He lectured all over the world, befriending some of the great people of his time: Albert Einstein, Thomas Mann, George Bernard Shaw, H.G. Wells, Romain Rolland, Robert Frost. A talented composer, Tagore wrote more than 2,000 songs, including the national anthems of both India and

Bangladesh. He was also one of India's leading painters and was an ardent proponent of Indian independence.

But on this morning, no different from any other, Tagore stood casually on his brother's porch and looked down one of the streets toward a garden. He describes what happened from there:

Where the Sadar Street ends, trees in the garden of Free School Street are visible. One morning I was standing in the veranda, looking at them. The sun was slowly rising above the screen of their leaves; and as I was watching it, suddenly, in a moment, a veil seemed to be lifted from my eyes. I found the world wrapt in an inexpressible glory with its waves of joy and beauty bursting and breaking on all sides. The thick shroud of sorrow that lay on my heart in many folds was pierced through and through by the light of the world, which was everywhere radiant.

That very day the poem known as *The Fountain Awakened from its Dream* flowed on like a fountain itself. When it was finished, still the curtain did not fall on that strange vision of beauty and joy. There was nothing and no one whom I did not love at that moment.... I stood on the veranda and watched the coolies as they tramped down the road. Their movements, their forms, their countenances seemed strangely wonderful to me, as if they were all moving like waves in the great ocean of the world. When one young man placed his hand upon the shoulder of another and passed laughingly by, it was a remarkable event to me.... I seemed to witness, in the wholeness of my vision, the movements of the body of all humanity, and to feel the beat of the music and the rhythm of a mystic dance.

> For some days I was in this ecstatic mood. My brothers had made up their minds to go to Darjeeling, and I accompanied them. I thought I might have a fuller vision of what I had witnessed in the crowded parts of the Sadar Street, if once I reached the heights of the Himalayas.
>
> But when I reached the Himalayas the vision all departed. That was my mistake. I thought I could get at truth from the outside. But however lofty and imposing the Himalayas might be, they could not put anything real into my hands. But God, the Great Giver, Himself can open the whole Universe to our gaze in the narrow space of a single lane.[1]
>
> — *Letters to a Friend*

A veil seemed to be lifted from my eyes. With this, Tagore writes, a new, previously hidden world was revealed, a world full of radiant light, "wrapt in an inexpressible glory with its waves of joy and beauty bursting and breaking on all sides." Mundane sights become a source of ecstasy. He experiences love flowing out to everything and everyone. He feels that the whole universe has somehow opened to him.

The poem he wrote during this experience, "The Fountain Awakened from its Dream," is a jubilant ode to joy. It begins:

> How is it that this morning the sun's rays enter my very heart!
> How comes it that early bird-song pierces today the cavern's gloom!
> I do not know why, but after so very long my soul is awake.
> My whole being surges and the waters break their bonds.[2]

Beyond Cosmic Consciousness

We have all had moments when the world seems to shine with a brighter luster, when we feel a little more affection and connection to people and things around us. We may realize it's not the world that has changed but our perception of it — beauty is in the eye of the beholder.

But the possibilities of perception reach far beyond this. As Tagore's story indicates, there is so much more that we do not ordinarily perceive. As Jesus remarks in the *Gospel of Thomas*, "The father's kingdom is spread out upon the earth, and people do not see it."[3] Or as the English poet William Blake famously puts it, "If the doors of perception were cleansed every thing would appear to man as it is, infinite."[4]

Cosmic Consciousness brings a transformation of life. The body is now free of stress, consciousness is unbounded, and we are ever anchored in the Self. We enjoy absolute freedom and 24-hour bliss. We live in accord with natural law, with nature supporting our every thought and action.

Yet, as Maharishi has observed, "It is as if gaining cosmic consciousness is not actually attaining the ultimate fulfillment of life, but it is merely gaining the ability for acquiring real and ultimate fulfillment."[5]

What remains to be developed? In Cosmic Consciousness, although consciousness is unbounded, our senses still experience the outer world superficially, much as in the ordinary waking state. We perceive only the cruder values of objects. The world remains a collection of things, separate from each other and separate from one's Self. If there is to be further growth, Maharishi points out, it will have to be in our relation to the world around us.

The refinement of perception

The world surrounding us offers vastly more than we ordinarily experience. Scientists extend the range of their senses with such instruments as telescopes and microscopes, enabling them to examine nature at larger and smaller distance scales. But however great the increase, there are still subtleties that lie beyond the range of their perception. Maharishi has described this as follows:

> The subtle fields of Nature are beyond our present capacity for experience. Our lives are spent in the cognition of the gross aspects of creation, and the glory of the subtle aspects eludes us because we have not the habit or ability to perceive them. Since greater power and greater beauty are to be found in the subtler fields of creation, we should derive great enjoyment and benefit from the perception of these fields — if only we could achieve it.

THE SIXTH STATE · GOD CONSCIOUSNESS

Maharishi continues:

> The subtle aspects of Nature, of all creation, are also infinitely more beautiful, more fascinating, more charming than the gross aspects can ever be. But while we confine ourselves to experiencing only the gross aspects through the senses, we are limiting our joys of life.[6]

Cosmic Consciousness provides the platform from where our perceptual machinery becomes profoundly refined. With unbounded awareness now established on the level of the conscious mind and with the physiology now virtually free of stress, the organs of perception now embark upon a remarkable and spontaneous process of refinement. We gain the ability to perceive finer and finer levels of nature, increasingly subtle strata of creation.

In time perception becomes so exquisitely refined that we can discern nature's subtlest material structure. In everything around us, we perceive what Maharishi terms the *finest relative* domain of nature — the most delicate, most refined value of matter, or "relative" existence.

This represents an altogether new state of consciousness, distinctly different from Cosmic Consciousness — unbounded awareness coupled with perception of the finest relative. Perception now embraces the entire range of relative life, from surface values to the subtlest material level — the full majesty of God's creation. Maharishi calls this state *God Consciousness*.

Human beings possess a remarkably sensitive sensory apparatus as it is. Our eyes can distinguish ten million different colors, detecting the most minute changes of vibration of light energy. The sensors in the retina can respond to a single photon of light — and a single photon makes a smaller impression on the retina than a particle of dust drifting down onto a baseball field. The nose can detect a single molecule of gas and distinguish at least a trillion odors. Our taste receptors can perceive a bitter taste in a dilution of 1/2,000,000. Human ears can detect 340,000 different tones; if they were any more sensitive, we would hear a continuous roar of air pressure fluctuations resulting from the random movement of air molecules.

But refined perception does not mean seeing molecules and atoms — these are smaller aspects of matter, not subtler. God Consciousness involves qualitatively different perception.

Recall Maharishi's comparison of pure consciousness to colorless sap. In a yellow rose, colorless sap takes the form and color of yellow petals. As perception becomes refined, one sees values that lie progressively closer to the colorless sap itself, less manifest, nearer to pure consciousness, nature's source, until eventually we perceive the very finest value of nature.

Before gaining this state, this finest value is hidden from view because we perceive only the rigid, well-defined boundaries of the object, only those qualities that distinguish the object from the rest of the environment. But when unbounded awareness becomes established on the level of the conscious mind (in Cosmic Consciousness), then our perception naturally begins to appreciate deeper, more fluid, more universal values of the object. Over time it becomes so refined that we spontaneously perceive the finest relative value.[7]

Refined perception reveals to us a previously hidden world, one of inexpressible beauty and wonder, vibrancy and life. The ordinary waking state presents only the veneer of reality, while the deeper, richer dimensions of life remain concealed. The sap was always at the surface — the depth of life is always at the surface — we just cannot perceive it. But as our perception becomes refined, nature's inner grandeur and glory comes increasingly to light, a dimension of life so beautiful, so infinitely rich, that it can only be called heavenly. Maharishi refers to this new mode of perception as *celestial perception*.[8]

What is the nature of this finest relative level of life? Maharishi describes it as *vibrant infinity, vibrant Absolute*.[9] Here is where unbounded pure consciousness has just become vibrant and ready to create, like a seed swollen with moisture and ready to sprout. This supreme relative field, now open to our direct experience, is omnipresent, forming a common, unified basis of the entire relative creation.[10]

The essential nature of this finest relative field is light. Maharishi has described it as "the self-illuminant effulgence of life."[11] When the finest material level of life opens to our perception, we see everything as alive, glowing with celestial radiance, as "bright and brilliant and full of light."[12]

Refined perception is not limited to sight. All the physical senses become refined, so that through every channel of perception — sight, sound, smell, taste, touch — we experience the subtlest, most celestial values. Every perception becomes nourishing, a wave of joy. We enjoy greater harmony, evenness, and intimacy in the quality of our vision, our emotions, the whole of our life.[13]

Nor is God Consciousness limited to waking experience. It transforms even the quality of sleep. Cosmic Consciousness brought the phenomenon of witnessing sleep — the continuum of inner wakefulness sustained even during the inertia of deep sleep. With God Consciousness comes what Maharishi has called *celestial sleep* — inner wakefulness witnessing the celestial light.[14]

Nothing in the world around us has changed — but our ability to appreciate it has now risen to its maximum value.

Further refining the physiology

Every state of consciousness has a corresponding style of physiological functioning. For higher states of consciousness to develop, physiological functioning must be progressively refined.

In Cosmic Consciousness, the nervous system is virtually free of stress; any incoming stress that may result from daily experience is dissolved during the night's rest. In God Consciousness, when every perception is a wave of nourishing joy, the chances of incurring even these negligible stresses are greatly diminished. The nervous system becomes increasingly cultured, refined, purified.[15]

Growth beyond Cosmic Consciousness also entails refinements in two basic physiological processes, Maharishi explains — breathing and digestion.

■ *Breathing* — In the deeply restful experience of Transcendental Consciousness, breath rate slows and breathing becomes softer, more refined. When the nervous system becomes purified of stress, breathing becomes increasingly refined. As this happens, Maharishi explains, breath (*prana*) is able to penetrate more thoroughly throughout the physiology, much as a highly refined oil is able to permeate all the fine parts of the machine that a cruder oil cannot reach. The result: otherwise dormant areas become enlivened, making possible more refined functioning of the whole physiology. This refined *prana* supports the maintenance of pure awareness in Cosmic Consciousness as well as celestial perception in God Consciousness.[16]

■ *Digestion* — In Cosmic Consciousness, with the nervous system free of stress and functioning normally, digestive processes become optimal,

Maharishi explains, delivering maximum nourishment to the body. Digestion also begins to produce a biochemical called *soma*. *Soma* is the most refined and valuable product of digestion. As such, it strengthens the finest, most delicate impulses of the body's inner intelligence, including those supporting sensory perception. This makes the nervous system increasingly powerful and promotes refined perceptual abilities. When eyesight, for example, has become most powerful, then refined visual perception results. So *soma* nurtures the growth of the celestial perception of God Consciousness as well as the infinite perception of Unity Consciousness.[17]

Thus, as God Consciousness develops, the *whole nervous system* becomes glorified. The physiology of God Consciousness, Maharishi explains, involves far more than just freedom from stress and strain. The nervous system becomes more powerful, more sublime and delicate — and able to produce more refined *prana* and more glorified values of *soma*. This is how Cosmic Consciousness develops into God Consciousness and God Consciousness into Unity Consciousness.[18]

Narrowing the gap: the unifying force of love

Cosmic Consciousness involves a dual style of functioning, with the restfully alert style operating side by side with waking, dreaming, and sleeping. For God Consciousness and Unity Consciousness to develop, these two independently functioning styles must become integrated.

Tagore tells us that, during his experience of refined perception, "There was nothing and no one whom I did not love at that moment." This brings us to the key dynamic in how Cosmic Consciousness rises to God Consciousness.

How does this integration take place? Through the progressive refinement of the nervous system and through what Maharishi calls *mental activity of ultimate refinement* — love and devotion.[19]

In Cosmic Consciousness, our experience is characterized by duality. On one side is the silent field of our unbounded pure awareness, the Self, ever silent, ever awake, untouched by anything in time and space. On the other side, as if across a gap, is the field of time and space, the field of change — the non-

Self. This generates the phenomenon of witnessing, with the Self remaining an ever-silent, unbounded, nonparticipating observer of all change.

But Cosmic Consciousness is characterized by something else as well. In this state, with mind and heart virtually free of stress, Maharishi explains, "Universal love then dominates the heart."[20] Love unifies. This universal love, flowing outward, closes the gap of separation between Self and surroundings, drawing us into increasing intimacy and connectedness with everything.

We know from experience that our ability to perceive grows hand in hand with our ability to love. When we're in love with someone or something, we perceive fine qualities we did not notice before. Recognizing these qualities inspires even greater love, enabling us to see and appreciate still finer qualities. Growth toward God Consciousness involves a similar process, Maharishi explains. Perceiving more glorified levels of creation elicits deeper appreciation and love — which cultures increasingly refined perception.[21]

As perception becomes refined and love flows outward, Maharishi says, the gap between Self and non-Self, silence and activity, narrows. The witnessing value diminishes. As progressively subtler values open to our perception, we see objects as increasingly familiar and intimate. Why? Because subtler values are closer to pure consciousness, closer to the Self.

When we come to perceive the *most* refined value, the gap narrows to virtually nothing, to a "junction point," like two banks of a river drawing together, Maharishi has said. Perception has virtually reached the level of infinity.[22]

As universal love flows from the heart, devotion increasingly becomes a feature of one's life. This highly refined mental activity refines physiological functioning, culturing the integration necessary to support God Consciousness (and, later, Unity Consciousness).[23] As this physiological integration grows, the sense of separation between Self and activity gradually dissolves. Because of the physiological refinement that must occur, Maharishi observes, God Consciousness requires some time to develop. But once one attains Cosmic Consciousness, God Consciousness develops spontaneously.

The love we experience in God Consciousness is not just for someone or something, it's for everyone and everything, at all times, overflowing and unbounded. Maharishi explains how every sense perception calls forth this universal love, culminating in the supreme expression of love — devotion to God:

> [U]niversal love flows and overflows in the heart; divine intelligence fills the mind, and perfect harmony in the behavior results. In such a state of integrated life, where all the planes of living are infused with divine consciousness, and when the universal love overflowing for everything becomes concentrated in devotion to God, then life finds fulfillment in the unbounded ocean of divine wisdom.
>
> The world is the active divine; everything rises as a wave on the eternal ocean of bliss consciousness. Every perception, the hearing of every word, the touch of every little particle, and the smell of whatever it may be, brings a tidal wave of the ocean of eternal bliss — in every arising of a thought, word, or action is the arising of the tide of bliss.
>
> In every static and dynamic state of life the divine glory of the unmanifested is found dancing in the manifested field of life. The Absolute dances in the relative. Eternity pervades every moment of transitory existence. The life is then ultimately fulfilled when cosmic consciousness is centered in devotion to God. Such is the condition of perfection of life where a cosmically evolved man rises to the realm of devotion.

Maharishi goes on to say:

> To live this state of concentrated universal love is the ultimate fulfillment of life. Here is the unbounded flow of love — at the sight of everything, at the hearing of everything, at the smelling of anything, at the tasting of anything, at the touch of anything. But entire life in its multifarious diversity is nothing but fullness of love, bliss, and contentment — eternal and absolute.[24]

The experience of God

When we experience the celestial radiance shining as the inner reality of everything around us, we find it evoking from within us a continuous upsurge of appreciation, love, and devotion for all of life. This brings with it the desire to know the source of this resplendent creation, just as we would desire to meet the artist whose work we admire.

The desire to know and experience God is natural to human life, Maharishi observes. But fulfilling this desire on the highest level becomes possible only when consciousness has become permanently unbounded and one has developed the ability to experience and appreciate the full range of creation, from the surface to the subtle. This ability comes with God Consciousness.

Maharishi distinguishes two aspects of God — impersonal and personal.

Impersonal aspect of God

Maharishi describes the impersonal aspect of God as "eternal and absolute Being." He continues:

> It is without attributes, qualities, or features, because all attributes, qualities, and features belong to the relative field of life, whereas the impersonal God is of an absolute nature. It is absolute, impersonal, and attributeless, but it is the source of all relative existence. It is the fountainhead of all the different forms and phenomena of creation. All the attributes of relative existence have their source in the attributeless absolute Being of impersonal nature.[25]

Maharishi points out how hydrogen and oxygen can take on different qualities, appearing as vapor, water, and ice while remaining unchanged in themselves. We can think of the impersonal God in the same way:

> Similarly, omnipresent impersonal almighty Being, while remaining as the Absolute, manifests into different qualities of forms and phenomena of creation. This is the ultimate reality of life. It is life eternal; It knows no change in its character. It is the ultimate of creation, the source, the be-all and end-all of the entire creation.[26]

Thus the impersonal aspect of God is pure Being, the unbounded Absolute — pure consciousness. This transcendental field is the ultimate essence of everything — photons, trees, people, galaxies. The unbounded Absolute is the impersonal aspect of God, but it's also the impersonal aspect of all of us, the counterpart of the unified field from a physics perspective. In Maharishi's words, "The impersonal God is that Being which dwells in the heart of everyone."[27]

Personal aspect of God

By definition, the Absolute is silent, omnipresent, formless, nonchanging. But to give rise to the phenomenal world, the Absolute must, as it were, assume the "form" of the Creator — bringing us to the personal aspect of God.

Approaching this idea from the relative field of life, Maharishi points out that creation is structured in different grades, with varying degrees of power, energy, intelligence, creativity, joy, and peace, ranging from lesser to greater.

> Ultimately, on the top level of evolution, is He whose power is unlimited, whose joyfulness is unlimited, whose intelligence and energy are unlimited. All knowing is He, all powerful is He, all blissful is He, almighty is He who dwells on the top level of evolution.*[28]

Thus the personal aspect of God is both the source or foundation of the creation as well as its culminating height. And what role does the personal God play? Maharishi explains it in this way:

> The whole field of relative existence is governed by the laws of nature automatically functioning in a perfect rhythm of life. That rhythm, that harmony of life is maintained by the almighty will of the almighty God at the highest level of creation, controlling and commanding the entire process of life.[28]

Maharishi describes God as bridging and presiding over the Absolute and relative,[29] and the Absolute and relative as "the two aspects of the nature of God."[30]

With this distinction in mind, what can we say about the experience of God? Let's start with the impersonal aspect of God. If this is identical with pure Being, pure consciousness, the transcendental field, then this is what we experience in the deepest moments of transcendence — in the self-referral experience of consciousness knowing itself, beyond thought and perception, beyond time and space.[31]

Experiencing the personal aspect of God, on the other hand, is a matter of *sensory* experience in the relative field of life.[32] Our capacities of physical

---

* Maharishi writes: "To some, the personal God is He and to others it is She. Some say it is both He and She, but certainly it is not It, because of the personal character."[33]

perception must be refined to the utmost, to the ability to perceive at the level of ultimate refinement — the "top level of evolution," as Maharishi describes it above, the supreme height of relative creation. Here resides nature's greatest intelligence and power. Here lies the relative foundation from which the whole of creation emerges — here is the domain of the Creator. When our perception arrives at this supreme level of creation, the door opens to experiencing God directly.

As with other states of consciousness, the growth is gradual. Starting from within, one experiences the diversity of nature increasingly in the unified light of God. When growth of the sixth state has fully matured, one cognizes the full reality of God's nature.

The experience comes automatically, Maharishi explains — one need not seek it. He illustrates this by analogy. Imagine that a great artist places a sculpture in a remote village. One of the villagers appreciates this sculpture with profound depth; every facet, down to the most delicate details that almost no one else discerns, fills him with joy. The artist, hearing about this person, naturally wishes to meet him, and he travels to the village to do so.[34]

The experience of God cannot come through thinking about God, Maharishi emphasizes — for the thought of God is merely another thought. Only by transcending thought can one systematically cultivate this experience:

> Therefore let the mind transcend thought and enter that realm of absolute purity which is the abode of God. Thinking about it is wasting time on the surface of life. A thought keeps the mind away from that blessed realm. A thought of bread neither gives the taste of bread nor fills the stomach. If you want bread, go to the kitchen and get it instead of sitting outside and thinking about it. We remain thinking of God, or trying to feel Him, only so long as we lack knowledge of Him, so long as we do not know how to break through the phenomenal field of experience and enter the realm of transcendental bliss, the pure kingdom of the Almighty.
>
> The records that history has brought us of the direct communion of saints and sages with God reveal their blessed lives, but the secret of the success of such lives lay in their transcending the fields of thought, emotion and experience. The secret of God-realization lies in transcending the thought of God.[35]

God Consciousness can be known only through direct experience, Maharishi says — and this experience is straightforward and available to all:

> Philosophers call this a mystical experience, but it is no more mysterious than is the working of a clock for a child. On one level of consciousness it is normal, on another it is mysterious, and again on another it is impossible. The intensity of God-realization in its personal and its impersonal aspects depends upon the level of Being, or the purity of consciousness. It is not possible to conceive of God-consciousness through any state of consciousness that is not God-consciousness itself; but it is possible for everyone, at any level of human consciousness, to rise to the realization of God-consciousness through the practice of Transcendental Meditation, which is a simple and direct way of developing pure consciousness.[36]

Bridging the languages of science and religion, Maharishi equates *natural law* with the *will of God*. Living in harmony with natural law means living in harmony with God's will, meaning one's thoughts and actions are maximally life-nourishing for oneself and the world.[37]

Does all of this place Maharishi's model of higher states of consciousness in the sphere of religious doctrine or belief? Not at all. There is no question here of faith or ideology. Maharishi's approach is experiential. He is concerned with a fact of perception, a stage in the growth of consciousness. His model of higher states of consciousness is to be understood scientifically, not as a belief but as a hypothesis to be tested and confirmed through personal experience and, ultimately, objective validation.

Watching unity becoming diversity

We have understood that the finest relative domain of life is vibrant Absolute — the ocean of pure consciousness warmed up and ready to rise into waves, ready to create — and that this finest relative field is itself unified, unbounded, and all-pervading. As God Consciousness matures to its most highly developed state, with perceptual faculties refined to their utmost and operating at this level, we gain the ability to see, first-hand, the process of unity becoming diversity. Maharishi describes it in this way, again using the terms *Absolute* and *Being* as synonyms for pure consciousness.

[O]ne recognizes the reality of how the Absolute expresses itself into the multiple relative . . . where one clearly sees the process of creation. . . . And then what one finds is that the diversity of the relative is coming to a close and is coming to that one value of the faintest relative which is just the nature of the Absolute, the vibrant nature of the Absolute. And this is that level of awareness which starts to recognize very clearly, on one side unmanifest Absolute and on the other this faint, faintest relative impulse, which is the sprouting of creation — as a seed sprouts, the Absolute is sprouting — and that sprout as a reverberation of the entirety of the Absolute into the faintest relative impulse of existence. . . . One cognizes Being, completely like a still ocean, omnipresent, without an activity, as the finest spur of action — that is, the basis of all relative diversity.[38]

This is the experience of what Maharishi calls the *mechanics of creation* and *Being becoming* — and it brings us to the very threshold of Unity Consciousness.

Experiences of growing God Consciousness

The following passage, reported by an advanced Transcendental Meditation participant, describes the experience of increasingly refined perception:

"Objects are perceived as almost transparent structures of soft, satiny light"

Generally, whenever I put my attention on an object (e.g., when looking at scenery out the window, or sitting in the kitchen), I become aware of the subtler qualities of the objects around me. For instance, when looking at a tree, I first become aware of the object as it is — a concrete form bound in space and time. But then I perceive finer aspects of the object coexisting along with its concrete expression. On this subtler level, objects are perceived as almost transparent structures of soft, satiny light (unlike harsher, normal daylight) through which the very essence of life appears to flow. This flowing field of life underlies and permeates the objects of perception. Perceiving these finer aspects of creation completely nourishes the finest aspect of my own being.[39]

This next one describes refined perception, the upsurge of universal love that nourishes all values of life, and a growing intimacy with the surrounding world.

"Everything I saw seemed to be glowing with divine radiance"

I noticed an ever-increasing evenness, balance, and concrete smoothness developing. The contrast between meditation and activity grew less and less, and my focus on difference began to recede as harmony and smoothness began to predominate. Simultaneously, a lightness of body developed, a buoyancy, a fluidity, and effortlessness of movement, as if I could walk without touching the ground. I noticed much less resistance, both on a physical level and in terms of fulfillment of desires. . . . I felt so in tune with nature that virtually every desire has been fulfilled very quickly. . . .

But, at the same time as I felt my power and inner strength increase, I also noticed a totally new feeling of softness and sweetness develop. There were days when I felt my heart melting, as if I could take everything in creation into myself and cherish it with the greatest love. Often I would have long periods of the day when everything I saw seemed to be glowing with divine radiance. Sometimes I would even be able to see the tremendous energy at the basis of every object, minute particles of energy (light?) moving very rapidly at a different rate and pattern for every object, yet unified somehow in a "unified field."

I noticed especially that along with a comfort and deep at-home feeling in activity, my alertness and perception became very, very sharp and clear, very acute. I noticed details more and also perceived connections between things more. But, at the same time, I also was not nearly as overshadowed by my environment. It is as if my receptivity were greater. . . . I also felt that at the same time my perceptions were becoming sharper and more refined; they were not making such deep impressions on my mind.[40]

"The power of the Self and the power of God are being revealed"

The Transcendental Meditation program now is like sinking into a soft, velvet cushion of pure love. . . . The silence flows like an ever-full ocean of pure love — unmanifest, undiminishable, all-pervading — existing equally everywhere.

The silent ocean of pure love draws my awareness inward and bathes my heart in a sweet nectar-like fullness that cannot be described, and yet I feel that this sweetness is unlimited in its exquisite magnitude. There is so much more to be experienced. I feel that the power of the Self and the power of God are being revealed at the same time. I am finding that love, which I have sought all my life, exists within my Self — within the very heart of creation, within the temple of the heart, at the feet of God.

This is the greatest gift . . . just to taste the nectar of life, to be finding that living water that can quench my thirst for peace, for joy, for love, in the ocean of fullness within the Self. When every fiber of my being is totally saturated with that ocean of pure love, then I am certainly invincible — because there is absolutely nothing separate from the Self.[41]

On the ground of transcending, this person describes the sense of God within "the very heart of creation" and ultimately the sense of "nothing separate from the Self."

VEDIC LITERATURE
INDIA

When consciousness rules speech, with speech we can speak all words.

When consciousness rules breath, with inbreath we can smell all perfumes.

When consciousness rules the eye, with the eye we can see all forms.

When consciousness rules the ear, with the ear we can hear all sounds.

When consciousness rules the tongue, with the tongue we can savor all tastes.

When consciousness rules the mind, with the mind we can think all thoughts.[1]

— *Kaushitaki Upanishad*

When consciousness is so fully developed that it "rules" the senses (when it is permanently unbounded, in Cosmic Consciousness), the senses become so refined that we can perceive *all* forms, sounds, etc., presumably including the most refined relative values of perception. This defines God Consciousness.

ॐ

Behold the universe in the glory of God: and all that lives and moves on earth. Leaving the transient, find joy in the Eternal.[2]

— *Isa Upanishad*

This simple passage summons us to enjoy the most refined realm of life, the light of the celestial.

■ *Also see Vedic literature in Chapter 4 (Transcendental Consciousness), Chapter 5 (Cosmic Consciousness), and Chapter 7 (Unity Consciousness).*

JESUS CHRIST
7–2 BCE – 30–36 CE • ISRAEL

See biography on page 71.

His disciples said to him, "When will the kingdom come?"

"It will not come by watching for it. It will not be said, 'Look, here it is,' or 'Look, there it is.' Rather, the father's kingdom is spread out upon the earth, and people do not see it."[1]

— *The Gospel of Thomas*

The father's kingdom, Jesus explains, is everywhere but people fail to see it. This does not mean it is incapable of being seen, for Jesus himself must be able to see this — it must involve a higher order of perception.

Also see Jesus Christ in Chapter 4 (Transcendental Consciousness), Chapter 5 (Cosmic Consciousness), and Chapter 7 (Unity Consciousness).

THE HERMETIC WRITINGS
2ND & 3RD CENTURIES • EGYPT

■ *See background information on page 76.*

For it is the height of evil not to know God; but to be capable of knowing God, and to wish and hope to know him, is the road which leads straight to the Good; and it is an easy road to travel. Everywhere God will come to meet you, and everywhere he will appear to you, at places and times at which you look not for it, in your waking hours and in your sleep, when you are journeying by water and by land, in the night-time and in the day-time, when you are speaking and when you are silent; for there is nothing which is not God. And do you say "God is invisible"? Speak not so. Who is more manifest than God? For this very purpose he has made all things, that through all things you may see him. This is God's goodness, that he manifests himself through all things.[1]   — *The Hermetica*

The subtlest, most refined level of creation, Maharishi explains, is the domain of the Creator. In God Consciousness, this field of life opens to direct perception. As this passage explains, one gains the ability to perceive God as the reality within every experience.

■ *Also see the Hermetic Writings in Chapter 4 (Transcendental Consciousness) and Chapter 7 (Unity Consciousness).*

SOPHIA VON KLINGNAU
13TH OR 14TH CENTURY • SWITZERLAND

Sophia von Klingnau entered Kloster Töss, a convent in Klingnau, a small town near the northern border of Switzerland, as a young woman. There she enjoyed what she called "a great comfort" — the experience of her soul in its purity. She shared the details of this experience only at the end of her life. Her writings appear in the Schwesterbücher, *or* Sister Books, *a compilation of the works of the nuns at Klingnau and nearby villages in the 13th and 14th centuries.* IMAGE: *Kloster Töss, which was built in the 1200s and was in use through the 1800s.*

In the following passage, Sophia is talking with a fellow nun who has asked her about her experience of the soul. Sophia responds as follows:

The soul is so entirely spiritual a thing that one cannot really compare it to any physical thing. But because you desire it so much, I will give you a parable which may help you understand a little how its form and shape was. It was a round, beautiful, and illuminating light, like the sun, and was of a gold-colored red, and this light was so immeasurably beautiful and blissful that I could not compare it with anything else. For if all the stars in the sky were as big and beautiful as the sun, all their splendor could not compare with the beauty my soul had. And it seemed to me that a splendor went out from me that illuminated the whole world, and a blissful day dawned over the whole earth. And in this light which was my soul, I saw God blissfully shining, as a beautiful light shines out of a beautiful radiant lamp, and I saw that he nestled up to my soul so lovingly and so kind that he was wholly united with it and it with him. And in this union of love my soul acquired from God the certainty that all my sins had been wholly forgiven me, and that it was as pure and clear and wholly stainless as it was when I came out of the baptismal font. And from this my soul became so blithesome and joyful that it felt as if it possessed all bliss and all joy, and if it had the power of wishing it could not and would not wish for anything more. . . .

And this grace lasted in me for eight days, and when I came to myself again and became aware that a living spirit was in me, I stood up and was the most joyful person, so it seemed to me, on the whole earth. For all the joy that all humans ever gained or may gain until the Judgment Day seemed as small to me in comparison to my joy as the tiniest claw of a gnat in comparison to the whole world. And from the abundance of the measureless joy my body had grown so light and agile and so without any infirmity that for those eight days I never felt whether I had a body, so that I was not aware of any physical illness, small or great, and I had no hunger nor thirst nor desire to sleep, and yet I went to table and to bed and to the choir and did as the others did, so that my grace would be hidden and no one would notice it. And when I had passed these eight days in such bliss, the grace was withdrawn from me, so that I no longer had the contemplation of my soul and of God in my soul, and then for the first time I felt I had a body.[1]

Sophia experiences her soul as a source of unbounded radiant beauty and bliss. "And it seemed to me," she continues, "that a splendor went out from me that illuminated the whole world, and a blissful day dawned over the whole earth," filling her with boundless joy. She even describes a physiological dimension — her body feels "so light and agile and so without infirmity" that she is unaware she even has a body.

KABIR
1440-1518 • INDIA

See biography on page 105.

O Sadhu! the simple union is the best.
Since the day when I met with
my Lord, there has been no end to
the sport of our love.
I shut not my eyes, I close not my ears,
I do not mortify my body;
I see with eyes open and smile, and
behold His beauty everywhere:
I utter His Name, and whatever I see,
it reminds me of Him; whatever I do, it becomes His worship.
The rising and the setting are one to me; all contradictions are solved.
Wherever I go, I move round Him,
All I achieve is His service:
When I lie down, I lie prostrate at His feet,
He is the only adorable one to me: I have none other.
My tongue has left off impure words, it sings His glory day and night:
Whether I rise or sit down, I can never forget Him; for the rhythm
of His music beats in my ears.
Kabir says: "My heart is frenzied, and I disclose in my soul what is
hidden. I am immersed in that one great bliss which transcends
all pleasure and pain."[1]

Kabir describes the refined perception and experience of divine beauty distinctive of God Consciousness, in which every experience becomes unified.

Also see Kabir in Chapter 4 (Transcendental Consciousness).

THOMAS TRAHERNE
1637–1674 • ENGLAND

See biography on page 114.

Traherne describes how he perceived the world as a youth:

All appeared new, and strange at first, inexpressibly rare and delightful and beautiful. I was a little stranger, which at my entrance into the world was saluted and surrounded with innumerable joys. My knowledge was Divine. ... All things were spotless and pure and glorious: yea, and infinitely mine, and joyful and precious. I knew not that there were any sins, or complaints or laws. ... Everything was at rest, free and immortal. I knew nothing of sickness or death. ... In the absence of these I was entertained like an Angel with the works of God in their splendor and glory, I saw all in the peace of Eden; Heaven and Earth did sing my Creator's praises, and could not make more melody to Adam, than to me. All Time was Eternity, and a perpetual Sabbath. Is it not strange, that an infant should be heir of the whole World, and see those mysteries which the books of the learned never unfold?

The corn was orient and immortal wheat, which never should be reaped, nor was ever sown. I thought it had stood from everlasting to everlasting. The dust and stones of the street were as precious as gold: the gates were at first the end of the world. The green trees when I saw them first through one of the gates transported and ravished me, their sweetness and unusual beauty made my heart to leap, and almost mad with ecstasy, they were such strange and wonderful things. The Men! O what venerable and reverend creatures did the aged seem! Immortal Cherubims! And young men glittering and sparkling Angels, and maids strange seraphic pieces of life and beauty! Boys and girls tumbling in the street, and playing, were moving jewels. I knew not that they were born or should die; But all things abided eternally as they were in their proper places. Eternity was manifest in the Light of the Day, and something infinite behind everything appeared, which talked with my expectation and moved my desire. The city seemed to stand in Eden, or to be built in Heaven.[1] — *Centuries of Meditations*

Traherne perceives everything as brimming with beauty, splendor, and glory, filling him with ecstasy. He sensed unboundedness permeating boundaries, eternity permeating change, the infinite behind everything. He lost this faculty as he grew older — he blamed education — but regained it as an adult.

༄

You will not believe what a world of joy this one satisfaction and pleasure brought me. Thenceforth I thought the Light of Heaven was in this world: I saw it possible, and very probable, that I was infinitely beloved of Almighty God, the delights of Paradise were round about me, Heaven and Earth were open to me, all riches were little things; this one pleasure being so great that it exceeded all the joys of Eden. So great a thing it was to me, to be satisfied in the manner of God's revealing Himself unto mankind. Many other enquiries I had concerning the manner of His revealing Himself, in all which I am infinitely satisfied.[2] — *Centuries of Meditations*

Traherne describes living in a richly beautiful world, shining with heavenly light, the self-revelation of God.

In another well-known passage, Traherne draws on his own experience to describe what human life should be. He emphasizes celestial perception, but if you read carefully you'll find allusions to all four higher states of consciousness:

Your enjoyment of the world is never right, till every morning you awake in Heaven; see yourself in your Father's Palace; and look upon the skies, the earth, and the air as Celestial Joys: having such a reverend esteem of all, as if you were among the Angels. . . .

You never enjoy the world aright, till the Sea itself floweth in your veins, till you are clothed with the heavens, and crowned with the stars: and perceive yourself to be the sole heir of the whole world, and more than so, because men are in it who are every one sole heirs as well as you. . . .

Till your spirit filleth the whole world, and the stars are your jewels; . . . till you are intimately acquainted with that shady nothing out of which the world was made: till you love men so as to desire their happiness, with a thirst equal to the zeal of your own . . . you never enjoy the world. . . .

Yet further, you never enjoy the world aright, till you so love the beauty of enjoying it, that you are covetous and earnest to persuade others to enjoy it. . . . The world is a mirror of infinite beauty, yet no man sees it. It is a Temple of Majesty, yet no man regards it. It is a region of Light and Peace, did not men disquiet it. It is the Paradise of God. . . . It is the place of Angels and the Gate of Heaven.³

— *Centuries of Meditations*

Heaven surrounds us, Traherne declares — "the World is a Mirror of infinite Beauty," "the Paradise of God," wide open to us when perceptual abilities are sufficiently refined. And he describes the transcendent love that the experience of this celestial beauty calls forth from within. Everyone, Traherne asserts, has this ability. Everyone, he wrote, should be "naturally seeing those things, to the enjoyment of which he is naturally born."⁴

■ *Also see Traherne in Chapter 4 (Transcendental Consciousness) and Chapter 7 (Unity Consciousness).*

JONATHAN EDWARDS
1703–1758 • UNITED STATES

▪ *Edwards was admitted to Yale College at 12. His goal was simple: to perfect himself. He awoke at 4:00 a.m., studied 13 hours a day, and spent part of each day walking. At 26 he became pastor of the church in Northampton, Massachusetts, succeeding his grandfather, one of New England's most influential figures. He served 24 years, tending his growing church, delivering magnificent sermons, writing books, and raising five children. Edwards was concerned with defining true religious experience and awakening it in his parishioners. His influence extended throughout the East Coast; this period was called the* Great Awakening. *Late in his life, there was a reaction against him, and he was dismissed. He was later named president of what became Princeton University. He had a lifelong fascination with science, particularly the then recent work of Isaac Newton, and he wrote on light and optics. He is esteemed as one of America's greatest intellectuals and most important philosophical theologians.*

I walked abroad alone, in a solitary place in my father's pasture, for contemplation. And as I was walking there, and looking upon the sky and clouds, there came into my mind so sweet a sense of the glorious *majesty* and *grace* of God, as I know not how to express....

After this my sense of divine things gradually increased, and became more and more lively, and had more of that inward sweetness. The appearance of everything was altered; there seemed to be, as it were, a calm, sweet cast, or appearance of divine glory, in almost everything. God's excellency, his wisdom, his purity, and love, seemed to appear in everything; in the sun, moon, and stars; in the clouds and blue sky; in the grass, flowers, trees; in the water and all nature; which used greatly to fix my mind. I often used to sit and view the moon for a long time, and in the day, spent much time in viewing the clouds and sky, to behold the sweet glory of God in these things. . . .[1] — "Personal Narrative"

During one of his walks, Edwards feels a "sweet sense of the glorious majesty and grace of God." As the experience deepens, his perception becomes progressively refined and he perceives "divine glory in almost everything."

AHMAD HATIF OF ISFAHAN
d. 1783 • IRAN

Ahmad Hatif, the great Sufi writer, was born and lived in Isfahan, the city south of Tehran that was the capital of Persia at the time. Widely educated, he studied mathematics, medicine, philosophy, literature, and foreign languages (Turkish and Arabic), and composed in Arabic as well as Persian. He wrote poems using a variety of complex structures but is most famous for his ghazals, *or odes, and for his descriptions of higher human experience. His son and daughter both became poets.*

Let the eye of your heart be opened that you may see the spirit and behold invisible things.

If you set your face towards the region where Love reigns, you will see the whole universe laid out as a rose-garden. What you see, your heart will wish to have, and what your heart seeks to possess, that you will see. If you penetrate to the midst of each mote in the sunbeams, you will find a sun within, in the midst. . . .

You will journey beyond the narrow limitations of time and place and thence you will pass into the infinite spaces of the Divine World. What ear hath not heard, that you will hear, and what no eye hath seen, you shall behold: until you shall be brought to that high Abode, where you will see One only, out of the world and all worldly creatures. To that One you shall devote the love of both heart and soul, until with the eye that knows no doubt, you will see plainly that "One is and there is nothing save Him alone: there is no God save Him."[1]

Hatif describes a distinctly refined mode of perception, capable of finding a sun within a speck of dust floating in the sun. Perception moves beyond time and space and into the divine realm of the Creator, where all perception calls forth feelings of love and devotion, and where all forms of love culminate in love of God.

∂

From the shadow of door and wall the Beloved appears, unveiled, in all His Glory; O you who are possessed of insight, you are looking for a candle, while the sun is shining aloft: the day is radiant in all its splendor, while you remain in the depths of night. If you would only pass out from your own darkness, you would see the whole universe as the place where the dawn is breaking, where light begins to shine forth. . . . Open your eyes to the Rose-garden and there you will see clear water shining within rose and thorn. From that clear water, without any color of its own, come forth a hundred thousand different hues: you have only to look at the tulip and the rose in this fair flower-garden.[2]

Hatif employs a rose garden as a metaphor for the celestial realm of life. At this level one perceives the "clear water" that creates the garden's myriad colors, recalling Maharishi's analogy of colorless sap permeating the rose much as pure consciousness permeates creation. Compared with refined perception, Hatif tells us, ordinary perception is like night. When sufficiently refined, this glorified perception extends to the whole universe.

NAZIR

1735-1830 • INDIA

▪ *Probably born in Delhi, Indian poet Nazir Akbarabadi is said to have written 200,000 short poems, of which about 6,000 — still an immense body of work — have survived. He wrote in Urdu, one of the major languages of India and Pakistan. He often wrote about everyday life, using the language of everyday speech. Through his use of telling detail, his poems bring mundane events to life. Though very popular among common people, he was mostly overlooked by the literati of the day and long neglected after his death. Today Nazir is regarded as one of India's finest poets.*

I opened my eyes and gazed on the face
Of the One I had sought;
The veils rolled away from earth and sky,
And the fourteen planes of existence stood revealed!
In an instant sorrow was past forever.
Non-duality became my friend,
Duality took wings, like quicksilver in fire,
Doubts and imaginings vanished.

Says Nazir: Since that day I have visited every place,
And found Him everywhere!
He is the object of understanding and knowledge.
Oh, I see He has always been with me!
Now the Hindu, the Moslem and the Jew
Are the same in my eyes.[1]

Nazir experiences the divine in everything. Again we have the image of a veil falling, revealing the hidden celestial reality. God Consciousness involves a kind of unity, Maharishi has said, in that everything is experienced in light of one thing — the finest, celestial reality of life. Nazir expresses this when he says, "Non-duality became my friend."

WILLIAM WORDSWORTH
1770–1850 • ENGLAND

Wordsworth was born in the beautiful Lake District, in northwest England, one of five children. His mother died when he was seven, his father when he was 13. But he had a good education, going on to Cambridge. During summer vacations, he visited France and was inspired by the ideals of the revolution. In his late 20s, he met the poet Samuel Taylor Coleridge. Together they reshaped the direction of English poetry. Departing from the formality of Neoclassical verse, they wrote about common human experiences in common language, seeking to reveal what Wordsworth called "the primary laws of our nature." He portrayed nature in a new light, exploring the interconnections between nature and the human mind, seeing nature ultimately as a symbol of God's mind. He pioneered self-exploration as a way to understand human nature. Critics assailed his work for years. When he was about 50 the tide began to turn, and in 1843, when he was 73, he became England's poet laureate. The poet Matthew Arnold revered the "healing power" of Wordsworth's poetry.

There was a time when meadow, grove, and stream,
The earth, and every common sight,
   To me did seem
Apparelled in celestial light,

> The glory and the freshness of a dream.
> It is not now as it hath been of yore; —
>> Turn wheresoe'er I may,
>>> By night or day,
> The things which I have seen I now can see no more.[1]
>
>> — "Ode: Intimations of Immortality from Recollections of Early Childhood"

Like Traherne, Wordsworth seemed able to see nature's celestial values early in life — only to find this ability fading as he aged, leaving only "shadowy recollections," as he says elsewhere in this poem. Yet even these recollections retained enormous power for him. He says they

> Are yet the fountain light of all our day,
> Are yet a master light of all our seeing;
>> Uphold us, cherish, and have power to make
> Our noisy years seem moments in the being
> Of the eternal Silence: truths that wake,
>> To perish never....[2]   — "Ode: Intimations of Immortality"

Some of Wordsworth's most famous passages reflect his attempts to capture these experiences in words. In these next lines, he describes how his experience of refined perception brought him a sense of a blissful intimacy with everything and a distinctly different mode of knowledge:

> All that I beheld
> Was dear to me, and from this cause it came,
> That now to Nature's finer influxes
> My mind lay open, to that more exact
> And intimate communion which our hearts
> Maintain with the minuter properties
> Of objects which already are belov'd,

And of those only. Many are the joys
Of youth; but oh! what happiness to live
When every hour brings palpable access
Of knowledge, when all knowledge is delight,
And sorrow is not there![3]   — *The Prelude*

❧

Such was the Boy — but for the growing Youth
What soul was his, when, from the naked top
Of some bold headland, he beheld the sun
Rise up, and bathe the world in light! He looked —
Ocean and earth, the solid frame of earth
And ocean's liquid mass, in gladness lay
Beneath him: — Far and wide the clouds were touched,
And in their silent faces could he read
Unutterable love. Sound needed none,
Nor any voice of joy; his spirit drank
The spectacle: sensation, soul, and form,
All melted into him; they swallowed up
His animal being; in them did he live,
And by them did he live; they were his life.
In such access of mind, in such high hour
Of visitation from the living God,
Thought was not; in enjoyment it expired.
No thanks he breathed, he proffered no request;
Rapt into still communion that transcends
The imperfect offices of prayer and praise,
His mind was a thanksgiving to the power
That made him; it was blessedness and love![4]   — *The Excursion*

Wordsworth experiences joy and love emanating from everything. Everything he beholds seems to melt into him, and he feels his own life pervading everything. He feels the living presence of God. The experience transcends thought, drawing him into "still communion" with nature — in which, he says a few lines later, "the least of things / seemed infinite."

☙

And I have felt
A presence that disturbs me with the joy
Of elevated thoughts, a sense sublime
Of something far more deeply interfused,
Whose dwelling is the light of setting suns,
And the round ocean, and the living air,
And the blue sky, and in the mind of man —
A motion and a spirit that impels
All thinking things, all objects of all thought,
And rolls through all things.[5]   — "Tintern Abbey"

In these celebrated lines, Wordsworth describes perceiving the essence of creation that underlies, unifies, and gives life to everything.

☙

[In childhood] I was often unable to think of external things as having external existence, and I communed with all that I saw as something not apart from, but inherent in, my own immaterial nature.[6]   — "Author's Note," *Ode: Intimations of Immortality from Recollections of Early Childhood*

Here Wordsworth takes us to the threshold of Unity Consciousness, in which nothing is external because everything is seen as the Self moving within itself. Wordsworth sees everything as part of his "own immaterial nature," suggesting his unbounded, transcendental Self.

■ *Also see Wordsworth at the beginning of Chapter 1.*

HENRY DAVID THOREAU
1817–1862 • UNITED STATES

See biography on page 128.

But now there comes unsought, unseen,
Some clear divine electuary,*
And I, who had but sensual been,
Grow sensible, and as God is, am wary.

I hearing get, who had but ears,
And sight, who had but eyes before,
I moments live, who lived but years,
And truth discern, who knew but
   learning's lore.

I hear beyond the range of sound,
I see beyond the range of sight,
New earths and skies and seas around,
And in my day the sun doth pale his light.

A clear and ancient harmony
Pierces my soul through all its din,
As through its utmost melody —
Farther behind than they, farther within.

More swift its bolt than lightning is,
Its voice than thunder is more loud,
It doth expand my privacies
To all, and leave me single in the crowd.

---

* An *electuary* is a medicine mixed with honey or another sweet substance.

It speaks with such authority,
With so serene and lofty tone,
That idle Time runs gadding by,
And leaves me with Eternity alone.¹   — "Inspiration"

Thoreau describes experiences of refined perception that reveal what is normally hidden beyond the range of sound and sight — "truth," as he calls it. From this realm seems to come a radiance that makes sunlight pale in comparison, leaving him feeling he has passed beyond time and is joined with eternity.

Also see Thoreau in Chapter 4 (Transcendental Consciousness) and Chapter 5 (Cosmic Consciousness).

WALT WHITMAN
1819–1892 • UNITED STATES

See biography on page 131.

That Thou O God my life hast lighted,
With ray of light, steady, ineffable,
   vouchsafed of Thee,
Light rare, untellable, lighting the very
   light,
Beyond all signs, descriptions,
   languages....¹
            — "Prayer of Columbus"

Whitman seems to be describing the perception of divine, transcendental light, calling to mind the experience of God Consciousness. He alludes to this experience in other poems:

> As in a swoon, one instant,
> Another sun, ineffable, full-dazzles me,
> And all the orbs I knew, with brighter, unknown orbs, then
>   thousand fold,
> One instant of the future land, Heaven's land.[2] — "As In a Swoon"

༃

> I cannot be awake, for nothing looks to me as it did before, or else I am awake for the first time, and all before has been a mean sleep.[3]

In the first of the two passages above, Whitman again describes the experience of divine light, the sense of looking into heaven. In the second he emphasizes his transformed perception, making everything else seem like sleep.

༃

> Why should I wish to see God better than this day?
>   I see something of God each hour of the twenty-four, and
>   each moment then,
> In the faces of men and women I see God and in my own face in
>   the glass,
> I see letters from God dropped in the street, and every one is signed
>   by God's name.[4]   — "Song of Myself"

Here Whitman describes a refined mode of perception that brings the sense of God's presence everywhere.

This next passage, among his most famous, describes the experience of a transcendental, divine unity pervading everything:

> Swiftly arose and spread around me the peace and knowledge that
>   pass all the argument of the earth,
> And I know that the hand of God is the promise of my own,
> And I know that the spirit of God is the brother of my own,
> And that all the men ever born are also my brothers, and the women
>   my sisters and lovers,

And that a kelson of creation is love. . . .⁵ — "Song of Myself"

In the following lines, Whitman takes us to the threshold of unity:

Strange and hard that paradox true I give,
Objects gross and the unseen soul are one.⁶

▪ *Also see Whitman in Chapter 4 (Transcendental Consciousness) and Chapter 5 (Cosmic Consciousness).*

BERNARD BERENSON
1865–1959 • LITHUANIA & UNITED STATES

▪ *Bernard Berenson, who was born in Lithuania and moved to the United States as a boy, was early recognized as a great authority on Italian art and became renowned for authenticating Italian Renaissance paintings. Many masterpieces now on display in U.S. museums were purchased on the basis of Berenson's recommendation. He wrote the most influential books on Italian Renaissance painting in the 20th century, including the monumental* Italian Painters of the Renaissance. *His Italian villa (bequeathed to Harvard), with its magnificent art collection and library, is administered as a Center for Italian Renaissance Culture.*

Then one morning as I was gazing at the leafy scrolls carved on the door jambs of S. Pietro outside Spoleto, suddenly stem, tendril, and foliage became alive and, in becoming alive, made me feel as if I had emerged into the light after long groping in the darkness of an initiation. I felt as one illumined, and beheld a world where every outline, every edge, and every surface was in a living relation to me and not, as hitherto, in a merely cognitive one. Since that morning, nothing visible has been indifferent or even dull. Everywhere I feel the ideated pulsation of vitality, I mean energy and radiance, as if it all served to enhance my own functioning. In nature nothing is dead for me. . . .

This revelation increased my enjoyment of the work of art. . . . I acquired faith in my vision and its revelation of values. This faith has never abandoned me.¹   — *Aesthetics and History*

The carving Berenson was studying was probably no more remarkable than hundreds of others he had seen in Italy. Yet now he seems to perceive the inner light of the objects he looks at and feels a keen intimacy with everything.

▪ *Also see Berenson in Chapter 7 (Unity Consciousness).*

RAY STANNARD BAKER
1870–1946 • UNITED STATES

▪ *Born in Michigan, Ray Stannard Baker studied literature and law, then worked as a journalist and magazine editor. In 1919, he served as President Woodrow Wilson's press secretary at Versailles during the World War I peace negotiations. Wilson asked Baker to edit his presidential papers, and in 1939, after 14 years of research and writing, Baker was awarded the Pulitzer Prize for his monumental eight-volume work,* Woodrow Wilson: Life and Letters. *Baker published books on many topics, including his highly successful* Following the Color Line *(1908), the first book by a prominent journalist to examine America's racial divide. Under the pseudonym David Grayson he wrote a nine-volume series of wise, congenial, best-selling books on country life.*

All that summer I had worked in a sort of animal content. Autumn had now come, late autumn, with coolness in the evening air. I was plowing in my upper field — not then mine in fact — and it was a soft afternoon with the earth turning up moist and fragrant. I had been walking the furrows all day long. I had taken note, as though my life depended upon it, of the occasional stones or roots in my field, I made sure of the adjustment of the harness, I drove with peculiar care to save the horses. With such simple details of the work in hand I had found it my joy to occupy my mind. Up to that moment the most important things in the world had seemed a straight furrow and well-turned corners — to me, then, a profound accomplishment.

I cannot well describe it, save by the analogy of an opening door somewhere within the house of my consciousness. I had been in the dark: I seemed to emerge. I had been bound down: I seemed to leap up — and with a marvellous sudden sense of freedom and joy.

I stopped there in my field and looked up. And it was as if I had never looked up before. I discovered another world. It had been there before, for long and long, but I had never seen nor felt it. All discoveries are made in that way: a man finds the new thing, not in nature but in himself.

It was as though, concerned with plow and harness and furrow, I had never known that the world had height or color or sweet sounds, or that there was *feeling* in a hillside. I forgot myself, or where I was. I stood a long time motionless. My dominant feeling, if I can at all express it, was of a strange new friendliness, a warmth, as though these hills, this field about me, the woods, had suddenly spoken to me and caressed me. It was as though I had been accepted in membership, as though I was now recognized, after long trial, as belonging here.

Across the town road which separates my farm from my nearest neighbor's, I saw a field, familiar, yet strangely new and unfamiliar, lying up to the setting sun, all red with autumn; above it the incalculable heights of the sky, blue, but not quite clear, owing to the Indian summer haze. I cannot convey the sweetness and softness of that landscape, the airiness of it, the mystery of it, as it came to me at that moment. It was as though, looking at an acquaintance long known, I should discover that I loved him. As I stood there I was conscious of the cool tang of burning leaves and brush heaps, the lazy smoke of which floated down the long valley and found me in my field, and I finally heard, as though the sounds were then made for the first time, all the vague murmurs of the countryside — a cow-bell somewhere in the distance, the creak of a wagon, the blurred evening hum of birds, insects, frogs. So much it means for a man to stop and look up from his task. So I stood, and I looked up and down with a glow and a thrill which I cannot now look back upon without some envy and a little amusement at the very grandness and seriousness of it all. And I said aloud to myself:

"I will be as broad as the earth. I will not be limited."

Thus I was born into the present world, and here I continue, not knowing what other world I may yet achieve. I do not know, but I wait in expectancy, keeping my furrows straight and my corners well turned. Since that day in the field, though my fences include no more acres, and I still plow my own fields, my real domain has expanded until I crop wide fields and take the profit of many curious pastures. . . .

Thus I have delighted, secretly, in calling myself an unlimited farmer.[1] — *Adventures in Contentment*

Baker experiences a new dimension of nature — far more intimate, sweet, and soft. He feels he has moved from darkness and bondage to light, freedom, and joy. As love wells up, he feels "a glow and a thrill" and realizes he is "unlimited." He had other such moments:

> And yet sometimes — mostly in the forenoon when I am not at all tired — I will suddenly have a sense as of the world opening around me — a sense of its beauty and its meanings — giving me a peculiar deep happiness, that is near complete content — [2]

In another David Grayson book, Baker recounts an experience, "immeasurably real," of God's presence:

> Some time after noon — for the sun was high and the day was growing much warmer — I turned from the road, climbed an inviting little hill, and chose a spot in an old meadow in the shade of an apple tree, and there I lay down on the grass and looked up into the dusky shadows of the branches above me. I could feel the soft airs on my face; I could hear the buzzing of bees in the meadow flowers, and by turning my head just a little I could see the slow fleecy clouds, high up, drifting across the perfect blue of the sky. And the scent of the fields in spring! — he who has known it, even once, may indeed die happy.
>
> Men worship God in various ways: it seemed to me that Sabbath morning, as I lay quietly there in the warm silence of midday, that I was truly worshipping God. That Sunday morning everything about me seemed somehow to be a miracle — a miracle gratefully accepted and explainable only by the presence of God. There was another strange, deep feeling which I had that morning, which I have had a few other times in my life at the rare heights of experience — I hesitate always when I try to put down the deep, deep things of the human heart — a feeling immeasurably real, that if I should turn my head quickly, I should indeed see that Immanent Presence.[3]   — *The Friendly Road*

LUCY MAUD MONTGOMERY
1874–1942 • CANADA

■ *Canadian writer Lucy Maud Montgomery was the author of the hugely popular* Anne of Green Gables *books. First published in 1908,* Anne of Green Gables *was an instant success. It has been translated into 36 languages and made into a stage play and twice into a movie. Montgomery followed this book with a series of sequels. Altogether she wrote more than 20 novels and over a thousand stories, poems, articles, and other works. Prince Edward Island, where Montgomery was born and where she set many of her stories, has become a literary landmark and much-visited historic site.*

It has always seemed to me, ever since early childhood, that, amid all the commonplaces of life, I was very near to a kingdom of ideal beauty. Between it and me hung only a thin veil. I could never draw it quite aside, but sometimes a wind fluttered it and I caught a glimpse of the enchanting realm beyond — only a glimpse — but those glimpses have always made life worthwhile.[1]

— *The Alpine Path: The Story of My Career*

Montgomery's glimpses of "ideal beauty" evoke a sense of refined perception. Watch now how she describes the same kind of experience at the beginning of her book *Emily of New Moon* — even using some of the same phrases:

The evening was bathed in a wonderful silence — and there was a sudden rift in the curdled clouds westward, and a lovely, pale, pinky-green lake of sky with a new moon in it.

Emily stood and looked at it with clasped hands and her little black head upturned. She must go home and write down a description of it in the yellow account book. . . . She must not forget how the tips of the trees on the edge of the hill came out like fine black lace across the edge of the pinky-green sky.

And then, for one glorious, supreme moment, came "the flash."

Emily called it that, although she felt that the name didn't exactly describe it. It couldn't be described — not even to Father, who always seemed a little puzzled by it. Emily never spoke of it to anyone else.

It had always seemed to Emily, ever since she could remember, that she was very, very near to a world of wonderful beauty. Between it and herself hung only a thin curtain; she could never draw the curtain aside — but sometimes, just for a moment, a wind fluttered it and then it was as if she caught a glimpse of the enchanting realm beyond — only a glimpse — and heard a note of unearthly music.

This moment came rarely — went swiftly, leaving her breathless with the inexpressible delight of it. She could never recall it — never summon it — never pretend it; but the wonder of it stayed with her for days. It never came twice with the same thing. Tonight the dark boughs against that far-off sky had given it. It had come with a high, wild note of wind in the night, with a shadow wave over a ripe field, with a greybird lighting on her window-sill in a storm, with the singing of "Holy, holy, holy" in church, with a glimpse of the kitchen fire when she had come home on a dark autumn night, with the spirit-like blue of ice palms on a twilit pane, with a felicitous new word when she was writing down a "description" of something. And always when the flash came to her Emily felt that life was a wonderful, mysterious thing of persistent beauty.

She scuttled back to the house in the hollow, through the gathering twilight, all agog to get home and write down her "description" before the memory picture of what she had seen grew a little blurred. She knew just how she would begin it — the sentence seemed to shape itself in her mind: "The hill called to me and something in me called back to it."

She found Ellen Greene waiting for her on the sunken front doorstep. Emily was so full of happiness that she loved everything at that moment, even fat things of no importance.[2]

— *Emily of New Moon*

Montgomery describes glimpsing "the enchanting realm beyond." Glorified perception seems to flow through each sense, in response to seeing almost any ordinary thing. This is no mere mood or idea — Emily can "never pretend it."

The book concludes with these evocative words:

She was so happy that her happiness seemed to irradiate the world with its own splendor. All the sweet sounds of nature around her seemed like the broken words of her own delight.[3]

— *Emily of New Moon*

MARY WEBB

1881–1927 • ENGLAND

▪ *Novelist and poet Mary Webb was born and raised in Shropshire, in central England, and spent most of her life there. Her novels, which have been compared to those of Thomas Hardy, are known for the rich picture they present of the Shropshire countryside and its people and their dialect, as well as her own deep appreciation of nature. Despite praise from noted writers, she did not achieve wide recognition during her lifetime. Only afterward did her work receive its proper estimation. Her books became bestsellers in the 1930s and were republished many times. The following passage is from her best-known novel,* Precious Bane, *which received the Prix Femina Vie Heureuse.*

The attic was close under the thatch, and there were many nests beneath the eaves, and a continual twittering of swallows.... Somewhere among the beams of the attic was a wild bees' nest, and you could hear them making a sleepy soft murmuring and morning and evening you could watch them going in a line to the mere for water. So, it being very still there,... there came to me, I cannot tell whence, a most powerful sweetness that had never come to me afore. It was not religious, like the goodness of a text heard at a preaching. It was beyond that. It was as if some creature made all of light had come on a sudden from a great way off, and nestled in my bosom. On all things there came a fair, lovely look, as if a different air stood over them. It is a look that seems ready to come sometimes on those gleamy mornings after rain, when they say, "So fair the day, the cuckoo is going to heaven."

> Only this was not of the day, but of summat* beyond it. I cared not to ask what it was. For when the nut-hatch comes into her own tree, she dunna ask who planted it, nor what name it bears to men. For the tree is all to the nut-hatch, and this was all to me. . . . There was naught in it of churches nor of folks, praying nor praising, sinning nor repenting. . . . It was a queer thing, too, that a woman who spent her days in sacking, cleaning sties and beast-housen, living hard, considering over fardens,* should come of a sudden into such a marvel as this. For though it was so quiet, it was a great miracle, and it changed my life; for when I was lost for something to turn to, I'd run to the attic, and it was a core of sweetness in much bitter. . . .
>
> One evening in October I was sitting there, with a rushlight,* practising my writing. The moon blocked the little window, as if you took a salver* and held it there. All round the walls the apples crowded, like people at a fair waiting to see a marvel. . . .
>
> I fell to thinking how all this blessedness of the attic came. . . . [If I hadn't come] into my own lonesome soul, this would never have come to me. The apples would have crowded all in vain to see a marvel, for I should never have known the glory that came from the other side of silence.
>
> Even while I was thinking this, out of nowhere suddenly came that lovely thing, and nestled in my heart, like a seed from the core of love.[1] — *Precious Bane*

Webb experiences a glorified dimension in everything around her. Inside she feels "a most powerful sweetness," an inner light she associates with heaven that bestows loveliness on all things — a miracle that changes her hard life. She sees this celestial beauty as originating "from the other side of silence."

---

* *Summat* is a British regional word meaning *something*. *Fardens* means *farthings*. A *rushlight* is a candle made by dipping the pith of a rush in tallow. A *salver* is a serving tray, usually made of silver, used for ceremonial occasions.

EVELYN UNDERHILL
1875–1941 • ENGLAND

Evelyn Underhill was the outstanding writer on mysticism and spirituality of the first half of the 20th century. Following her great work Mysticism, *she published other books on mystical experience, plus translations of Jan van Ruysbroeck, the* The Cloud of Unknowing, *and others — introducing the great but forgotten figures of medieval spirituality to a modern audience. With Rabindranath Tagore, she translated the poems of Kabir. She wrote more than 30 books. She was the first woman to address the clergy in the Church of England, the first woman to lead a spiritual retreat for clergy, and one of the first women to lecture on religion in English universities.*

I remember you told me once the first thing you "found out" was a sense of intense refinement. The first thing I found out was exalted and indescribable beauty in the most squalid places. I still remember walking down the Notting Hill main road and observing the (extremely sordid) landscape with joy and astonishment. Even the movement of the traffic had something universal and sublime in it. Of course that does not last: but the after-flavor of it does, and now and then one catches it again. When one *does* catch it, it is so real that to look upon it as wrong would be an unthinkable absurdity. At the same time, one sees the world at those moments so completely as "energized by the invisible" that there is no temptation to rest in mere enjoyment of the visible.

This is all very scrappy and unsatisfactory I know; but if there is anything I have left out that I *could* answer, do tell me.[1]

— *The Letters of Evelyn Underhill*

Underhill experiences indescribable beauty even in squalor, "something universal and sublime" even in the passing cars. She sees the world "energized by the invisible" — a fine description of refined perception. Underhill's words illustrate Maharishi's principle that "the world is as we are." The sordid landscape does not suddenly become beautiful; her momentarily refined perception allows her to see the beauty underlying even this unpromising scene.

ॐ

In this next passage, writing about mystical experience, Underhill connects the experience of refined perception with the flow of love from within — and makes clear in the final sentence that she is speaking from her own experience:

A harmony is thus set up between the mystic and Life in all its forms. Undistracted by appearance, he sees, feels, and knows it in one piercing act of loving comprehension. . . . The heart outstrips the clumsy senses, and sees — perhaps for an instant, perhaps for long periods of bliss — an undistorted and more veritable world. All things are perceived in the light of charity, and hence under the aspect of beauty: for beauty is simply Reality seen with the eyes of love. . . . For such a reverent and joyous sight the meanest accidents of life are radiant. The London streets are paths of loveliness; the very omnibuses look like colored archangels, their laps filled full of little trustful souls.[2] — *Mysticism*

MARGARET PRESCOTT MONTAGUE
1878–1955 • UNITED STATES

West Virginia-born and writing under the pseudonym Jane Steger, Margaret Prescott Montague is that state's most filmed novelist — at least five films have been made of her works, including a 1981 Walt Disney movie. In 1919 she won the O. Henry Award for the year's best short story, the first year this prize was offered; her story, regarded as an appeal for a league of nations, was admired by President Woodrow Wilson. She published a number of novels and several volumes of short stories, poetry, and other writing. She is best known for her 1916 Atlantic Monthly *article entitled "Twenty Minutes of Reality." First published anonymously, it was re-published as a book the next year and translated into many languages. In it, Montague describes an experience she had while sitting on a porch in a hospital. The article inspired many letters to* The Atlantic Monthly, *in which people from all walks of life shared similar experiences.*

It was an ordinary cloudy March day. . . . The branches were bare and colorless, and the occasional half-melted piles of snow were a forlorn gray rather than white. Colorless little city sparrows flew and chirped in the trees, while human beings, in no way remarkable, passed along the porch. . . .

Yet here, in this everyday setting, and entirely unexpectedly (for I had never dreamed of such a thing) my eyes were opened and for the first time in my life I caught a glimpse of the ecstatic beauty of reality.

I cannot now recall whether the revelation came suddenly or gradually; I only remember finding myself in the very midst of those wonderful moments, beholding life for the first time in all its young intoxication of loveliness, in its unspeakable joy, beauty, and importance. I cannot say exactly what the mysterious change was. I saw no new thing but I saw all the usual things in a miraculous new light — in what I believe is their true light. I saw how wildly beautiful and joyous, beyond any words of mine to describe, is the whole of life....

It was not that for a few keyed-up moments I imagined all existence as beautiful, but that my inner vision was cleared to the truth so that I saw the actual loveliness which is always there, but which we so rarely perceive; and I knew that every man, woman, bird, and tree, every living thing before me, was extravagantly beautiful, and extravagantly important. And, as I beheld, my heart melted out of me in a rapture of love and delight. A nurse was walking past; the wind caught a strand of her hair and blew it out in a momentary gleam of sunshine, and never in my life before had I seen how beautiful beyond all belief is a woman's hair. Nor had I ever guessed how marvelous it is for a human being to walk. As for the interns in their white suits, I had never realized before the whiteness of white linen.... A little sparrow chirped and flew to a nearby branch, and I honestly believe that only "the morning stars singing together, and the sons of God shouting for joy" can in the least express the ecstasy of a bird's flight. I cannot express it, but I have seen it.

Once out of all the gray days of my life I have looked into the heart of reality; I have witnessed the truth; I have seen life as it really is — ravishingly, ecstatically, madly beautiful, and filled to overflowing with a wild joy, and a value unspeakable. For those glorified moments I was in love with every living thing before me — the trees in the wind, the little birds flying, the nurses, the interns, the people who came and went. There was nothing that was alive that was not a miracle. Just to be alive was in itself a miracle. My very soul flowed out of me in a great joy.

No one can be as happy as I was and not have it show in some way. A stranger passing paused by my bed and said, "What are you lying there all alone looking so happy about?" I made some inadequate response as to the pleasure of being out-of-doors and of getting well. How could I explain all the beauty that I was seeing? How could I say that the gray curtain of unreality had swirled away and that I was seeing into the heart of life? It was not an experience for words. It was an emotion, a rapture of the heart.

Besides all the joy and beauty and that curious sense of importance, there was a wonderful feeling of rhythm as well, only it was somehow just beyond the grasp of my mind. I heard no music, yet there was an exquisite sense of time, as though all of life went by to a vast, unseen melody. Everything that moved wove out a little thread of rhythm in this tremendous whole. When a bird flew, it did so because somewhere a note had been struck for it to fly on; or else its flying struck the note; or else again the great Will that is Melody willed that it should fly. When people walked, somewhere they beat out a bit of rhythm that was in harmony with the whole great theme.

Then, the extraordinary importance of everything! Every living creature was intensely alive and intensely beautiful, but it was as well of a marvelous value....

For those fleeting, lovely moments I did indeed, and in truth, love my neighbor as myself. Nay, more: of myself I was hardly conscious, while with my neighbor in every form, from wind-tossed branches and little sparrows flying, up to human beings, I was madly in love. Is it likely that I could have experienced such love if there were not some such emotion at the heart of Reality? If I did not acutely see it, it was not that it was not there, but that I did not see quite far enough....

> What I saw that day was an unspeakable joy and loveliness, and a value to all life beyond anything that we have knowledge of; while in myself I knew a wilder happiness than I have ever before or since experienced.[1]
> — *Twenty Minutes of Reality*

"I saw no new thing," Montague writes, "but I saw all the usual things in a miraculous new light," leading her to conclude that she is looking "into the heart of reality." Hand in hand with this refined perception, she feels "in love with every living thing before me."

As her article progresses, Montague reflects on her experience. "Heaven," she concludes, "is here and now" — it's just a matter of perception:

> Heaven, in all its springtide of beauty, is here and now, before our very eyes, surging up to our very feet, lapping against our hearts; but we, alas, know not how to let it in![2]

> Perhaps some day I shall meet it face to face again. Again the gray veil of unreality will be swirled aside; once more I shall see into Reality. Sometimes still, when the wind is blowing through trees or flowers, I have an eerie sense that I am almost in touch with it. The veil was very thin in my garden one day last summer. The wind was blowing there, and I knew that all that beauty and wild young ecstasy at the heart of life was rioting with it through the tossing larkspurs and rose-pink canterbury bells, and bowing with the foxgloves; only I just could not see it. But it is there — it is always there — and some day I shall meet it again. The vision will clear, the inner eye open, and again all that mad joy will be upon me. Some day — not yet perhaps — but some day![3]
> — *Twenty Minutes of Reality*

JOHN NEIHARDT
1881–1973 • UNITED STATES

▪ *Neihardt is best known as an authority on the traditions of the Sioux Indians and for his writings about the American West. He grew up in Kansas and Nebraska, worked for 12 years as literary editor for the* St. Louis Post-Dispatch, *and was poet-in-residence and lecturer in English at the University of Missouri (Columbia) from 1949 to 1965. He published 32 books of poetry, fiction, and philosophy. Most prominent are* Cycle of the West *(five book-length narrative poems covering the time from the opening of the Missouri Territory through the 1890s) and* Black Elk Speaks *(an autobiographical narrative of the Sioux warrior and holy man's life).*

Fancy yourself as going forth some golden day of early spring into a windless forest. You have gone there to chop summer wood, and you are looking for a tree that will make the most satisfactory fuel. You pass the basswoods and the sycamores and even the oaks. You are scientific, and you know that, although oak makes a good fire, hickory is better. You do not fall to chopping the first hickory tree you find, for trees differ in adaptability to your purpose. You want the most wood for the least effort. At last you stand before a hickory that suits your common-sense purpose, and you gaze upward along the bole, noting the soaring taper of it. The place is very quiet.... The sap has already begun to lift; the maples are oozing; there is a stippling of leaf buds against the blue; soft white clouds go over; a few birds flute and chatter.

Then, if you are a certain sort of person — that is to say, if you are not altogether sense-bound — something wonderful may happen to you. Suddenly the tree, conceived as hickory firewood, fades away. With a timeless sense, in which the very identity of the woodchopper is lost, you may feel the ecstatic upward suck of resurrected life through bole and branch and twig, almost as though the body of the tree were your own. And there will be something very much like love in the sense and something near to happy tears — when it has become a memory. This may pass in a flash, however long the time; but all that day you are likely to be kinder than usual — even to the dogs you may chance to meet. You have felt the larger relations and lost yourself in them. . . .

And it is not only when in contact with what we ordinarily call nature that such a swift change may occur. It may happen in crowded streets at the very moment when you feel most disgusted with the brawling, wriggling mess of humanity and with yourself as a part of it. Here too the sense of love and loss of self may occur.

— *Poetic Values*

Neihardt describes an experience of transcending, of timelessness, and of sublime intimacy with the tree, "almost as though the body of the tree were your own." He describes the characteristic surge of love, the expansion of the heart for everything around him, leading him to greater kindness even after the moment passes. This kind of experience can happen anywhere, Neihardt observes, even in "crowded streets" — reminiscent of Tagore's and Underhill's experiences earlier.

HOWARD THURMAN
1899–1981 • UNITED STATES

See biography on page 162.

What is forgotten is the fact that life moves at a deeper level than the objective and the data of our senses. We are most alive when we are brought face to face with the response of the deepest thing in us to the deepest thing in life. Consider the hackneyed illustration of the beautiful sunset! We see the sunset, we recognize color, shape, the general quality of the atmosphere — to these we respond. Then when in the midst of all this something else emerges — the sunset opens a door in us and to us, to another dimension, timeless in quality, that can be described only as ineffable, awe-inspiring — then we know radical amazement.[1]

— "Radical Amazement," in *The Inward Journey*

Human beings are capable of transcending ordinary sense perception, Thurman asserts. As an example he offers his own experience of a sunset where, beyond the beauty we are accustomed to, a door opens to a timeless dimension, beautiful beyond words.

৵

There are other moments when one becomes aware of the thrust of a tingling joy that rises deep within until it bursts forth in radiating happiness that bathes all of life in its glory and its warmth. Pain, sorrow, grief, are seen as joy "becoming" and life gives a vote of confidence to itself, defining its meaning with a sureness that shatters every doubt concerning the broad free purpose of its goodness.[2]

— "The Binding Unity," in *The Inward Journey*

Here Thurman describes a subjective counterpart of refined perception — the upsurge of radiant joy from deep within, so powerful that all of life is perceived in its glorious light and even pain and sorrow are transmuted into expressions of joy.

༃

The spirit swept upon him
 Like some winged creature from above!
Light was all around:
 Every leaf shimmered and danced,
 A swirling dervish in a timeless trance.
The sky was lost in light.
He saw and felt the light.[3]

— "Not by Bread Alone," in *The Inward Journey*

With these words Thurman calls to mind the experience of the finest relative dominion of life, the celestial, resplendent with light.

■ *Also see Howard Thurman in Chapter 4 (Transcendental Consciousness), Chapter 5 (Cosmic Consciousness), and Chapter 7 (Unity Consciousness).*

ROSAMOND LEHMANN
1901–1990 • ENGLAND

■ *The daughter of a member of Parliament, Lehmann studied English and modern and medieval languages at Cambridge and went on to become one of the leading authors of her time. She published seven novels, a play, and a collection of short stories, and she translated two French novels into English. Two of her novels were made into movies, and her books were also dramatized on television and radio. Nine biographies have been written of her life, and, from the 1980s forward, her work has enjoyed a resurgence of interest. She served as the president of the British chapter of International PEN, the worldwide association of writers. In 1982 she was made a Commander of the British Empire as well as a Fellow of the Royal Society of Literature in recognition of her literary achievements.*

Lehmann was visiting some friends in the countryside. One afternoon, while they went for a walk, she decided to go back to her room to rest. She lay down on her bed, and then:

I looked at my watch and found that over an hour had passed. I sprang up, went to the window and looked out . . . and beheld a visionary world. Everything around, above, below me was shimmering and vibrating. The tree foliage, the strip of lawn, the flower-beds — all had become incandescent. I seemed to be looking through the surfaces of all things into the manifold iridescent rays which, I could now see, composed the substances of all things. Most dramatic phenomenon of all, the climbing roses round the window frame had "come alive" — the red, the white. The beauty of each one of them was fathomless — a world of love. I leaned out, they leaned towards me, as if we were exchanging love. I saw, I *saw* their intensity of meaning, feeling.

I came downstairs to join the others. I couldn't think of anything to say except: "I've had a wonderful rest." L. glanced at me and said: "You look as if you had." Later she told me that she wondered if it was a hallucination that I suddenly looked about thirty years younger.

After tea, J. took me for a drive through the midsummer countryside. What a drive! The sun shone powerfully among full-sailed somnolent cloud-galleons; but the light suffusing earth and sky was not the sun's: it was a universal, softly gold effulgence. Hills, woods, groves, clouds, cornfields, streams and meadows — all were moving and interlacing buoyantly, majestically, as if in the ineffable rhythm and pattern of a cosmic dance. I was outside, watching the animating, moulding eternal principle at work, at play, in the natural world; and at the same time I seemed to be inside it, united with and freely partaking in its creativity.

Astounded; awestruck. . . . Awestruck, astounded. What words are possible? *And yet,* the sense of recognition, recollection, was predominant. Again and again I told myself: "Yes. Yes. This is reality. I had *forgotten.*"[1]   — *The Swan in the Evening*

This passage speaks for itself. For a brief period Lehmann sees through to what she recognizes as "reality" the world shimmering with effulgent light and life, unlike anything she had seen before, drawing her into a realm of surpassing beauty and mutual love. Her experience suggests a glimpse of Unity Consciousness as well: "I was outside," she says, ". . . and at the same time I seemed to be inside it, united with and freely partaking in its creativity."

GOPI KRISHNA

1903–1984 • INDIA

■ *Neglecting to take courses that would prepare him for university study, Gopi Krishna failed his college entrance exams. He secured a low-level government job, married, and set about an ordinary life supporting a family. Early on he became the leader of a social organization dedicated to helping the underprivileged in his community, and he was a lifelong champion of women's rights and well-being, giving special attention to bettering the lives of widows in India. In his latter teens, shamed by not having had a university education and determined to improve himself and stay on a right course, he took up meditation. Each day he woke up hours before dawn to meditate. At the age of 34, he began to experience higher states of consciousness, which he recounted in a number of books. Altogether he wrote 17 books, including three books of poetry, and he traveled and lectured worldwide. Together with the German physicist and philosopher Carl Friedrich von Weizsäcker he founded a research institute to encourage empirical study of eastern knowledge.*

One sunny day, when on my way to the office, I happened to look at the front block of the Rajgarh Palace, in which the government offices were located, taking in my glance the sky as well as the roof and the upper part of the building. I looked casually at first, then, struck by something strange in their appearance, more attentively, unable to withdraw my gaze, and finally rooted to the spot I stared in amazement at the spectacle, unable to believe the testimony of my eyes....

[W]hat I saw now was so extraordinary as to render me motionless with surprise. I was looking at a scene belonging not to the earth but to some fairyland, for the ancient, weather-stained front of the building, unadorned and commonplace, and the arch of the sky above it, bathed in the clear light of the sun, were both lit with a brilliant silvery luster that lent a beauty and a glory to both and created a marvelous light-and-shade effect impossible to describe. Wonderstruck, I turned my eyes in other directions, fascinated by the silvery shine which glorified everything. Clearly I was witnessing a new phase in my development; the luster which I perceived on every side and in all objects did not emanate from them but was undoubtedly a projection of my own internal radiance. . . .

On entering my room, instead of sitting at my desk I walked out onto the veranda at the back, where it was my habit to pass some time daily for a breath of fresh air while looking at the fine view open in front. There was a row of houses before me edged by a steep woody slope leading to the bank of the Tawi River, whose wide boulder-covered bed glistened in the sun with a thin stream of water running in the middle, bordered on the other side by another hillock with a small medieval fortress on top. . . .

I was utterly amazed at the remarkable transformation. . . . I was gazing fascinatedly at an extraordinarily rich blend of color and shade, shining with a silvery luster which lent an indescribable beauty to the scene. . . .

Days and weeks passed without alteration in the lustrous new form of perception. A bright silvery sheen around every object, across the entire field of view, became a permanent feature of my vision. The azure dome of the sky, whenever I happened to glance at it, had a purity of color and a brightness impossible to describe. . . .

In the course of a few weeks, the transformation ceased to cause me wonder or excitement, and gradually I came to treat it as an inseparable part of myself, a normal characteristic of my being. Wherever I went and whatever I did, I was conscious of myself in the new form, cognizant of the radiance within and the lustrous objectivity without. I was changing. The old self was yielding place to a new personality endowed with a brighter, more refined and artistic perceptive equipment, developed from the original one by a strange process of cellular and organic transformation.[1]   — Autobiography

Here is a vivid description of a more refined mode of perception, everything appearing lustrous and shining — the byproduct, in his view, of the expansion of consciousness he had been experiencing within.

▪ *Also see Gopi Krishna in Chapter 7 (Unity Consciousness).*

KATHLEEN RAINE
1908–2003 • SCOTLAND & ENGLAND

▪ *Kathleen Raine, the distinguished British poet, literary scholar, and critic, composed twelve books of poetry, four autobiographical books, and a body of scholarly work. A professor at Cambridge University, she was noted especially for her studies of Blake and Yeats. She helped found the* Temenos Review *(which she later edited) and the Temenos Academy, to publish and promote creative work that acknowledges spirituality as one of humanity's prime needs. For her contributions to the arts she received numerous literary awards and honorary doctoral degrees from universities in the United Kingdom, France, and the United States. She was awarded the Queen's Gold Medal for Poetry in 1992, and in 2000 she was made a Commander in the Order of the British Empire and Commandeur in the French Ordre des Arts et des Lettres.*

As a student at Cambridge, Raine studied botany and zoology; the following passage reflects her gift for scientific observation.

There was also a hyacinth growing in an amethyst glass; I was sitting alone, in an evening, at my table, the Aladdin lamp lit, the fire of logs burning in the hearth. All was stilled. I was looking at the hyacinth, and as I gazed at the form of its petals and the strength of their curve as they open and curl back to reveal the mysterious flower-centres with their anthers and eye-like hearts, abruptly I found that I was no longer looking at it, but *was* it; a distinct, indescribable, but in no way vague, still less emotional, shift of consciousness into the plant itself. Or rather I and the plant were one and indistinguishable; as if the plant were a part of my consciousness. I dared scarcely to breathe, held in a kind of fine attention in which I could sense the very flow of life in the cells. I was not perceiving the flower but living it. I was aware of the life of the plant as a slow flow or circulation of a vital current of liquid light of the utmost purity. I could apprehend as a simple essence formal structure and dynamic process. This dynamic form was, as it seemed, of a spiritual not a material order; or of a finer matter, or of matter itself perceived as spirit. There was nothing emotional about this experience which was, on the contrary, an almost mathematical apprehension of a complex and organized whole, apprehended *as* whole. This whole was living; and as such inspired a sense of immaculate holiness. Living form — that is how I can best name the essence or soul of the plant. By "living" I do not mean that which distinguishes animal from plant or plant from mineral, but rather a quality possessed by all these in their different degrees. Either everything is, in this sense, living, or nothing is; this negation being the view to which materialism continually tends; for lack, as I now knew, of the immediate apprehension of life, as life. The experience lasted for some time — I have no idea how long — and I returned to dull common consciousness with a sense of diminution. I had never before experienced the like, nor have I since in the same degree; and yet it seemed at the time not strange but infinitely familiar, as if I were experiencing at last things as they are, was where I belonged, where in some sense, I had always been and would always be. That almost continuous sense of exile and incompleteness of experience which is, I suppose, the average human state, was gone like a film from sight. In these matters to know once is to know for ever. My mother when she was over eighty confided to me an experience she had had as a girl. "I have never told anyone before," she said, "but I think you will understand." It was simply that, one day, sitting among the heather near Kielder "I saw that the moor was alive." That was all. But I understood that she had seen what I had seen.[1] — *The Land Unknown*

Raine feels she discerns the plant's essence or soul, "a vital current of liquid light of the utmost purity." She finds its essential form to be spiritual rather than material, or "matter itself perceived as spirit." She seems to glimpse unity as well as God Consciousness. "I was no longer looking *at* it, but *was* it," she says — "as if the plant were a part of my consciousness."

Also see Kathleen Raine in Chapter 7 (Unity Consciousness).

EUGENE IONESCO
1909-1994 • ROMANIA & FRANCE

See biography on page 170.

When I was an adolescent, I was sometimes overwhelmed by an intense, luminous joy: it was an inexplicable, irrational happiness that mounted from the earth, from my feet, and went up to my knees to my belly, to my heart, to lay hold of all of me. It was as if a light had suddenly gone on in a dark room. Where did this welcome fire that illuminated and purified even the most secret corners of my soul come from? I felt I was in harmony with everything. Everything became beautiful, at once new and familiar. My heart beat faster and I had the impression that I was rising and getting bigger. If I tried to explain the reasons for this extravagant joy to myself, or if I said to myself with false lucidity that I had no reason to rejoice (as if euphoria could justify itself), this state of happiness vanished like a luminous fog and the world then became ashes and life dull and unlivable.

I feel very close to the essential or to being when, in the aura of a luminous morning on which everything gives the appearance of being, I open my eyes at that very moment as if for the first time, and filled with astonishment I ask myself: "What is this? Where am I?" and then: "Why this, who am I, what am I doing here?"[1]

— *Present Past Past Present*

Ionesco describes moments of "intense, luminous joy" that illuminate and transforms him. He feels harmony with everything and sees everything as beautiful, as if he is seeing things for the first time. He feels light, expanded, and "very close to the essential or to being."

■ *Also see Ionesco in Chapter 4 (Transcendental Consciousness) and Chapter 5 (Cosmic Consciousness).*

JACQUETTA HAWKES
1910–1996 • ENGLAND

■ *Jacquetta Hawkes was the daughter of the pioneering biochemist Sir Frederick Hopkins, who won a Nobel Prize in 1929 for his discovery of vitamins. She studied archeology and anthropology at Cambridge University (one of the first women to do so), then worked as an archeologist at sites in Britain, France, and Israel. She was enormously productive. She was the archaeology correspondent for London's* Sunday Times. *She published scholarly articles, detailed works on the Mediterranean and ancient Egypt, books on prehistoric Britain, histories of archeology, beautifully illustrated commemorative volumes, guidebooks, poetry, plays, a novel, and children's books. She appeared on radio and television. Through all of her work, Jacquetta Hawkes held fast to what she believed was the true purpose of archaeology — to understand what it means to be human.*

In this passage, Hawkes describes an experience she had as a young woman while working at a site in Israel.

One night when the land was still fresh from the rain, I was wandering near our camp enjoying the moonlight when an immense exaltation took possession of me. It was as though the White Goddess of the moon had thrown some bewitching power into her rays. It seemed to me that our arid satellite was itself a living presence bounding in the sky — I do not myself understand this use of the word "bounding," but it comes insistently, and I cannot but use it to express some deeply felt vitality. Indeed, the whole night was dancing about me.

It appeared that the moonlight had ceased to be a physical thing and now represented a state of illumination in my own mind. As here in the night landscape the steady white light threw every olive leaf and pebble into sharp relief, so it seemed that my thoughts and feelings had been given an extraordinary clarity and truth.

So powerfully was I moved by this sense of possession that I climbed up on to a high outcrop of rock against the mouth of the wadi and knelt down there. The moonlight swam round, and in, my head as I knelt looking across the plain to the shining silver bar of the Mediterranean.

From far behind me, still muffled in the folds of the mountain, I heard the bronze sound of camel-bells. To my sharpened but converging senses they seemed like a row of brown flowers blooming in the moonlight. In truth the sound of bells came from nothing more remarkable than a caravan, perhaps twenty camels with packs and riders, coming down the wadi on its way north to Haifa. But even now I cannot recognise that caravan in such everyday terms; my memory of it is dreamlike, yet embodies one of the most intense sensuous and emotional experiences of my life. For those minutes, and I have no notion how many they were, I had the heightened sensibility of one passionately in love and with it the power to transmute all that the senses perceived into symbols of burning significance. This surely is one of the best rewards of humanity. To be filled with comprehension of the beauty and marvelous complexity of the physical world, and for this happy excitement of the senses to lead directly into an awareness of spiritual significance. The fact that such experience comes most surely with love, with possession by the creative eros, suggests that it belongs near the root of our mystery. Certainly it grants man a state of mind in which I believe he must come more and more to live: a mood of intensely conscious individuality which serves only to strengthen an intense consciousness of unity with all being. His mind is one infinitesimal node in the mind present throughout all being, just as his body shares in the unity of matter.

The bells came nearer and another sound mingled with theirs; a low, monotonous chanting. I looked behind me for a moment and saw the dark procession swaying out from behind the last bend in the wadi. Then I turned back so that the column should pass me and enter my world of vision from behind. I found myself comprehending every physical fact of their passage as though it were a part of my own existence. I knew how the big soft feet of the camels pressed down upon and embraced the rough stones of the path; I knew the warm depth of their fur and the friction upon it of leather harness and the legs of the riders; I knew the blood flowing through the bodies of men and beasts and thought of it as echoing the life of the anemones which now showed black among the rocks around me. The sound of bells and the chanting seemed rich and glowing as the stuff of the caravan itself.

So the swaying line came from behind, went past, and moved away across the plain. It was a procession of life moving through the icy moonlight. It was coming from the mountains and going towards the sea. That was all I knew, but as the moon leapt and bounded in the sky I took full possession of a love and confidence that have not yet forsaken me.[1] — *Man on Earth*

With a sense of immense inner exaltation and illumination, Hawkes perceives the earth and even the sky as alive. Even the sound of ordinary camel bells strikes her as remarkably beautiful, "like flowers blooming in the moonlight," eliciting a profound sense of love.

Her experience melds into an "intense consciousness of unity with all being." Sensing "the mind present throughout all being," she perceives every detail of her experience as "a part of my own existence," evoking Unity Consciousness. Then she returns to her sublimely intimate and rich perception of the caravan passing by, the sounds seeming "rich and glowing."

Elsewhere in this book Hawkes writes, "We can serve by learning to experience the inner life, discovering what we can of the kingdom of heaven to which all have access."[2]

IRINA STARR
1911–2002 • UNITED STATES

A child prodigy, Irina Starr read philosophical and spiritual literature before she was five. By 18, however, she became tired of being "different," and for the next 20 years she tried to conform to the "prevailing patterns of worldliness and sophistication I saw around me."[1] In her 40s she began to experience higher states of consciousness. She wrote seven books about these experiences. Best-known is The Sound of Light, *which features her Traherne like poetry. Starr worked as a purchasing secretary, but her books say nothing about her personal life — her sole focus was her inner experience and its implications for understanding human life. She lived in the beautiful Ojai Valley north of Los Angeles.*

It was a morning late in July of the year 1955 and the beginning of four days that still remain deeply etched upon my consciousness. I awakened on that morning to a world altogether different from the one I had closed my eyes upon the night before. It was different not only from my world of the day before, but from that of any day I had ever known. I was aware of an unusual feeling of joy as I slipped into the wakened state, but I was quite unprepared for what I beheld when I became fully conscious of my surroundings.

Even before my eyes were really open I was aware of much light in the room and I recall a moment's wonder at how there could be so much light when the heavy drapes were closed. . . . The radiance which permeated my eyelids and suffused the entire room caught me unawares. Everything around me had come to life in some wondrous way and was lit from within with a moving, living, radiance. It was somewhat as it must be with one blinded, whose vision is first restored.

I was obviously seeing with vision other than the purely physical, but what I saw did not conflict with what my ordinary vision registered. . . . I saw objects in the ordinary way as well as with some extraordinary extension of the visual faculty; I saw into them with an inner vision and it was this inner sight which revealed the commonplace objects around me to be of the most breathtaking beauty. . . .

I was literally transfixed as my gaze rested upon first one thing and then another: my hand upon the bedspread, the maple table beside the bed, the dust which rested lightly upon it, the telephone, the flowers in a vase, the several books. There was the luminous quality — a light which contained color in the way that a brilliant diamond refracts color, only this color seemed an integral part of the essential substance and not a form of refracted light. The one thing which was, above all, significant was that everything was literally *alive*; the light was living, pulsating, and in some way I could not quite grasp, *intelligent*. The true substance of all I could see was this living light, beautiful beyond words. . . .

As I gazed about the room on that first morning, one of the

things which particularly fascinated me was that there was no essential difference between that which was animate and that which was inanimate — only in form and function, not in basic substance, for there was only the one Substance, that living, knowing, Light which breathed out from everything. I was aware of the outward difference of each object which drew my attention, but that superficial difference in no way concealed or conflicted with the one substance or living light which composed each alike. Ever since I could remember, I had accepted the fact of one-ness of all life and manifestation, but it was purely theoretical, an intellectually accepted condition. But here I was literally beholding the fact itself so very far beyond any concept I had ever held.

There was such beauty in all that met my eye that I could have remained for hours gazing at any one thing. . . . I recall that I was near-bursting with a tremendous, non-conceptual, understanding of life — like a balloon which is expanded to its utmost capacity — so that my mind was strained with this great, formless "knowing" and I actually prayed, Enough! . . .

I finally arose and drew back the drapes and the sunlight streamed into the already illuminated room, and I fell back upon the bed to become rapt in the jewels of light that were the motes in the broad beam of sunlight which poured down upon the rug. I gasped at the beauty of a neighbor's cat which ambled slowly across the lawn, and at the lawn itself which was a sea of shimmering jewels, an ocean of iridescent light in both sun and shade. . . .

I thought, We dwell in a fairyland of unimaginable beauty and sublimity and know nothing of it. . . .

My new-found world was an immense cathedral in which I moved, flooded with wonder, joy, and reverence. An irrepressible joy and an inward hush of reverence existed simultaneously. . . . This condition of seeing, knowing, and experiencing, seemed as delicately poised and impermanent as a hummingbird stationed in mid-air, and from moment to moment beneath my joy and reverence, there hovered the knowing that this could not last and the next moment might well see it end for me. . . .

I was amazed and my heart positively leapt with joy and gratitude as I awakened each morning and nothing had dimmed, nothing had stilled; all was there about me in the same breathtaking luminosity and holy living-ness. But, just as four days before, I had emerged into waking consciousness with an intimation of euphoria and exultation, the morning of the fifth day, as I slipped into wakefulness, a momentary panic gripped me and a flash of premonition that something was terribly wrong. The feeling of foreboding increased, until, fully conscious, I felt the darkness around me before I opened my eyes. It was close to tangible and I was almost afraid to open my eyes. . . . I opened them at last and looked about me. . . .

Colors were drab; even sunlight was in some inexplicable way muted. Mass pressed about me, and where before the life-motion within matter had been one of creation and ever-changing form, vital with the breath of God, now the apparent deadness, the terrible heaviness, spoke only of disintegration.

I looked at the same things which had, only a few short hours before, filled me with almost unbearable joy and love, and saw them sadly, dully, as things which existed with me and opposed me in a drab and colorless world.[2]   — *The Sound of Light*

Starr gives us an exceptional account of an extended experience of refined perception, the revelation that at the subtlest level of life everything is radiantly alive, celestially beautiful, and profoundly united — if only we can see it.[3]

Also see Irina Starr in Chapter 7 (Unity Consciousness).

JANE GOODALL
b. 1934 • ENGLAND

Inspired by a lifelike chimpanzee toy her mother gave her as a child, Goodall earned a PhD in ethology from Cambridge without having earned a bachelors degree — then gained world renown for her 55-year study of chimpanzee family and social behavior in Tanzania. She discovered that chimpanzees make tools — an ability thought to belong solely to humans. The only human to be accepted into chimpanzee society, she is a global leader in protecting chimpanzees and their habitats. In 1977 she established the Jane Goodall Institute, which supports research and sponsors community-centered conservation and development programs in Africa as well as a global youth program, Roots & Shoots, with more than 10,000 groups in over 100 countries. She has been showered with awards for her environmental and humanitarian work, including nine honorary doctorates. She is a Dame Commander in the Order of the British Empire and a United Nations Messenger of Peace.

Down below, the lake was still dark and angry with white flecks where the waves broke, and rain clouds remained black in the south. To the north the sky was clear with only wisps of gray clouds still lingering. The scene was breathtaking in its beauty. In the soft sunlight, the chimpanzees' black coats were shot with coppery brown, the branches on which they sat were wet and dark as ebony, the young leaves a pale but brilliant green. And behind was the dramatic backcloth of the indigo sky where lightning flickered and distant thunder growled and rumbled.

Lost in awe at the beauty around me, I must have slipped into a state of heightened awareness. It is hard — impossible, really — to put into words the moment of truth that suddenly came upon me then. Even the mystics are unable to describe their brief flashes of spiritual ecstasy. It seemed to me, as I struggled afterward to recall the experience, that self was utterly absent: I and the chimpanzees, the earth and trees and air, seemed to merge, to become one with the spirit power of life itself. The air was filled with a feathered symphony, the evensong of birds. I heard new frequencies in their music and also in the singing insects' voices — notes so high and sweet I was amazed. Never had I been so intensely aware of the shape, the color of the individual leaves, the varied patterns of the veins that made each one unique. Scents were clear as well, easily identifiable: fermenting, overripe fruit; waterlogged earth; cold, wet bark; the damp odor of chimpanzee hair, and yes, my own too. And the aromatic scent of young, crushed leaves was almost overpowering....

That afternoon, it had been as though an unseen hand had drawn back a curtain and, for the briefest moment, I had seen through such a window. In a flash of "outsight" I had known timelessness and quiet ecstasy, sensed a truth of which mainstream science is merely a small fraction. And I knew that the revelation would be with me for the rest of my life, imperfectly remembered yet always within. A source of strength on which I could draw when life seemed harsh or cruel or desperate.[1]   — *Reason for Hope: A Spiritual Journey*

Goodall describes an experience of heightened awareness she compares to mystics' spiritual ecstasy. Her senses become highly refined, enabling her to hear "new frequencies" in the music of birds and insects. She shades into an experience of unity: she and everything around her "seemed to merge, to become one with the spirit power of life itself."

CHAPTER 7

❦

THE SEVENTH STATE

Unity Consciousness

All Experience in Terms of the Unbounded Self

It was a freezing night in January, well past midnight, and a hailstorm was hammering Manchester, in northwest England. Rita Carter was driving through the suburbs searching for a place to stay when her car broke down.

Carter, the distinguished British science writer, broadcaster, and lecturer on the human brain, had been driving around England for several weeks, interviewing people for a new book. Her work has appeared in the *New York Times*, the *Washington Post*, *New Scientist*, and other prominent publications, and she has twice been awarded the Medical Journalists' Association prize for her outstanding contribution to medical journalism.

But now, tonight, all she needed was a place to sleep — and first she had to get her car fixed.

A mechanic finally answered her call and came and repaired the problem. By now it was 3:00 a.m. He suggested she stay with his aunt, who lived nearby

 and had a small spare room. The woman took her in, insisted she take a hot bath, lit a fire in the room, and took her soaking clothes to dry. Carter slipped into bed. In her book *Exploring Consciousness*, she recounts what happened next:

When I noted the fire — one of those built-in gas burners — was still on, I thought I should probably get out of bed and switch it off. But as I looked at it something very strange happened. I realized that I was not only looking at it from the perspective of where I lay, but — weird as this may sound — I was seeing it too from within the flame itself. I was the fire — absorbed into its redness and warmth, both giving and receiving its heat. At the same time (it was not a sequential realization) I became aware that I was also the bed, and the walls, and the window and the sheets. My self seemed to have bled out of its boundary and infiltrated every crevice of the room. Stranger yet, I was not just in the room, but beyond it too. Although I could not, literally, see beyond its four walls, I seemed to be outside them as well as within. Indeed, I felt that I was everywhere, and everything — embracing the most distant stars and yet also inhabiting the smallest speck of dust. All sense of space, location, boundedness and division disappeared.

As all this happened I thought — or rather, I knew — that what I was experiencing was the real state of things; that I was part of some much greater whole and that all my experience up until now had been in some sense unreal. Despite its peculiar nature I felt no anxiety, and — odder — no curiosity. It all felt entirely natural.

I have no idea how long the feeling lasted. At some stage I lay down and slept. In the morning the fire (still burning) was back in its appointed location and so was I. But, unlike a dream, the experience remained crystal clear and as real and significant as it had been while it happened.[1]

— *Exploring Consciousness*

As Carter looks at the fire, she begins to experience herself in everything around her. "I was everywhere, and everything — embracing the most distant stars and yet also inhabiting the smallest speck of dust," she says, while her sense of self expands to infinity. This, she realizes, is "the real state of things," while ordinary existence is somehow unreal. And momentous though this experience is, it feels entirely natural.

The great affliction of our age, in the view of many thinkers, is alienation, disintegration. People feel cut off — from each other, from nature, from life, from themselves. The world's great spiritual traditions attest to the underlying unity of existence. But for most people this remains an intellectual proposition.

Beyond God Consciousness

God Consciousness brings an extraordinary capacity of perception and knowledge. One now perceives the subtlest material essence of nature. Everything shines with an awe-inspiring, effulgent, divine beauty, the light of God. One experiences a profound intimacy, appreciation, and love for all things.

Yet knowledge remains incomplete. The ultimate, transcendental reality of nature remains hidden, concealed behind the thinnest of veils — the finest material level of nature itself, the first expression of matter from consciousness. The final stroke of growth carries across this last threshold.

How does this occur? Through the power of one's own unbounded awareness. As one's unbounded awareness falls on the finest relative value in everything one sees, it begins to enliven the unmanifest, transcendental field that pervades the finest relative level. Maharishi explains it in this way:

> [W]hen the unbounded awareness of the conscious mind falls on the boundaries of the finest relative, the unmanifest value which is permeating the finest relative value becomes lively, and that liveliness of the transcendental value of the object is nothing other than the liveliness of the unbounded value on the level of the conscious mind.[2]

As this happens, one experiences the infinite value of the object. This involves a new mode of experience — the cognition of infinity within the finest relative perception. Maharishi describes this as follows:

> This value of cognition has a different characteristic than that value of cognition which cognizes the finest relative. Here, in the cognition of the finest relative, is the liveliness of the absolute, infinite. On the bed of the finite, here is the liveliness of the infinite. And this is possible only when the conscious mind is vibrant in that infinite value and perception has become so refined that it spontaneously cognizes the finest relative. In this situation the finest relative perception rises to the infinite value of perception on the level of one's own awareness.[3]

Now, radiating through the finest relative value of life is the absolute, infinite value of life. In all things, wherever our attention turns, we experience the unbounded, the transcendent.

Recall Maharishi's colorless sap analogy: When we look at a pink rose, we see only its colors, shapes, and textures; the colorless sap from which everything is formed remains hidden. The sap resides throughout the flower, as much at the surface as the color, yet we fail to see it because the sap is transparent and color predominates. As God Consciousness develops, we perceive values ever closer to the sap, until we see the most refined value, the colorless sap in the process of becoming color. In Unity Consciousness, we experience the deepest reality, the colorless sap itself. We see both the color and the colorless, the manifest petal and the unmanifest sap, together on the rose's surface.

Maharishi points out that actually there is no distinction between the very finest level of material creation and pure consciousness, the Absolute:

> The level which is the highest in the relative is one with the Absolute.... Faintest pink of the petal and colorless sap are two sides of the same coin. The supreme relative doesn't have to transcend — the transcendental is along with it.[4]

This means that the transition to Unity Consciousness simply involves the recognition of this reality. In Maharishi's words, "It is only the knowledge that was hidden and is now unfolded."[5]

The Self moving within itself

In Unity Consciousness, we experience the unbounded within everything. And we realize that this unboundedness is identical with the unboundedness of our own Self — the same Self we first experienced in Transcendental Consciousness as our innermost reality. When this happens, the distinction between the Self and the non-Self dissolves. They become unified.

Now we experience the Self within everything and everything within the Self — everything as a wave on the ocean of pure consciousness. Dominating every faculty of perception — sight, hearing, touch, taste, and smell — is the experience of the Self, the unbroken wholeness of unbounded awareness.

The world of change does not somehow fall away. We do not lose the ability to distinguish one thing from another. In Unity Consciousness our senses remain open to the changing world. We see all the details of relative life we have always seen, including the celestial perception that developed with God Consciousness. Maharishi has explained the state of unity as follows:

> This does not mean that such a man fails to see a cow or is unable to distinguish it from a dog. Certainly he sees a cow as a cow and a dog as a dog, but the form of the cow and the form of the dog fail to blind him to the oneness of the Self, which is the same in both. Although he sees a cow and a dog, his Self is established in the Being of the cow and the Being of the dog, which is his own Being. . . . The enlightened man, while beholding and acting in the world of diversified creation, does not fall from his steadfast Unity of life, with which his mind is saturated and which remains indelibly infused into his vision.[6]

In the ordinary waking state and in Cosmic Consciousness, boundaries were opaque, concealing the boundless. In God Consciousness, boundaries became translucent. Now, in Unity Consciousness, though boundaries remain, they have become transparent, allowing the unbounded to shine through.

When we look out onto the ocean, we see individual waves, but what dominates our experience is the ocean as a whole. Similarly, in Unity Consciousness, we see the boundaries of relative life as always, but they no longer overshadow the unity at their basis. Boundaries and divisions move to the background of experience, unboundedness and unity to the foreground. The fullness of the ocean radiates through every wave of everyday life. We experience the Self as if moving within itself and appearing as waves of diversity.

In Unity Consciousness, even God is experienced in terms of the Self. Because there is no longer any separation or duality, the ability to sense the Creator becomes far more exalted than in God Consciousness — it is infinite.[7]

In this state, Maharishi explains, every object becomes as dear as one's own Self — for you experience that every object *is* your Self. Transcendental Consciousness fulfilled the precept *Know thyself.* Unity Consciousness fulfills the precept *Love thy neighbor as thyself* — for in this state you experience your neighbor literally in terms of your Self.

The problem of alienation that characterizes modern life is dissolved. We are no longer cut off from the universe — we *are* the universe. We do not have to find our place in it because we have found its place in us — in the Self.

Supreme knowledge and fulfillment

Prior to Unity Consciousness, our experience of life is divided in the most fundamental way — we experience an "inner" self and an "outer" world. Philosophers have argued that we can never gain direct knowledge of the world around us — we can know only our perceptions, thoughts, and feelings *about* the world, only what is filtered through our senses and processed in our minds.

This may be true in the ordinary waking state. But in Unity Consciousness, we experience the infinite reality of the Self in everything. The separation between inner and outer, between subject and object, dissolves. Inside and outside become one. The gap between the relative and absolute fields of life, which God Consciousness had virtually bridged, finally closes, leaving the unchanging, uncreated, infinite reality of pure consciousness, the Self. Wholeness of life saturates one's experience.

This is what Maharishi calls supreme knowledge, *total knowledge*. He describes this in the following way:

> [T]he experiencer and the object of experience, and the entire phenomenon of perception which is also the phenomenon of action, have been brought on the same level of infinite value. The knowledge has

bridged the gulf between the knower and the object of knowing. The object is being verified in its total reality when the infinite value of the object, which hitherto was underlying, has come up to be appreciated on the surface. Then the perception is of supreme value. The perception is of ultimate value when the perception opens the infinite value of the object to the awareness. Then the perception is total, when the perceiver, the knower, is able to know the object in its completeness.[8]

For knowledge to be complete, reliable, and true for all times, Maharishi points out, we must gain a state of consciousness that does not change. Waking, dreaming, and sleeping do not qualify — each continually gives way to the other, and the knowledge of one state is not valid in the others. Nor do Transcendental Consciousness, Cosmic Consciousness, or God Consciousness, for in each of these states a higher state and higher mode of knowledge is possible. Absent an unchanging level of consciousness, knowledge will always be changing — we see something one way today, another way tomorrow.

Only in Unity Consciousness is no further change in knowledge possible. We experience every object in its supreme, infinite, unchanging value. There can be no knowledge beyond this.

Unity Consciousness raises life to supreme fulfillment. Prior to this state one is only a partial knower, only a seeker of fulfillment. But in the seventh state of consciousness, knowledge is complete. When we cognize every object in terms of its infinite reality, then we are fulfilled in our knowledge. The unbounded knower finds the object of knowing to be of the same unbounded nature as his own Self — nothing further remains to be known.[9]

Mastery of natural law

Growth from Cosmic Consciousness through God Consciousness to Unity Consciousness brings an immense increase in power.

In Cosmic Consciousness, the mind is fully awake, stationed in unbounded pure consciousness, the unified source of nature's intelligence. The "small self" is perfectly coordinated with the "big Self," the source of natural law. Because our thoughts and desires are in tune with natural law, they are spontaneously and fully nourishing to life and supported by natural law.

But in Cosmic Consciousness, the big Self is silent and transcendental,

The process of transcending	Growth to Unity Consciousness
Starting from the waking state, as one transcends, one experiences finer and finer levels of thought.	Starting from Cosmic Consciousness, one's senses become increasingly refined; one perceives finer and finer levels of the outer material world.
Eventually the mind reaches the finest level of thought, the level from where thought first emerges from pure consciousness.	Eventually one is able to perceive the finest level of nature, the subtlest stratum of creation, from where the relative first emerges from the unified field. This perception defines God Consciousness.
Then the mind transcends even the finest level of thought and identifies with pure consciousness itself, the Self, deep within. This is Transcendental Consciousness.	As consciousness continues to develop, one moves beyond even the finest relative and experiences pure consciousness, the Self, as the reality of everything. This is Unity Consciousness.

a non-participating witness. We witness our thoughts and actions as separate from the Self, as part of the play of the ever-changing relative world.

As Unity Consciousness grows, the big Self starts to move, to become fully functional. We experience everything as the flowing wholeness of our own Self. Because every impulse of thought is now an impulse of total natural law, nature's unbounded intelligence, our thoughts become enormously powerful. This brings a natural *command* of total natural law. We are no longer single individuals acting in isolation in the world. We are the totality. When we act, it's "the entirety of cosmic life" that acts.[10]

Our intuitions and desires are fulfilled powerfully and immediately. As a consequence, Maharishi explains, our desires may come to fruition even before they become conscious desires, much as children find their mother has purchased winter coats for them even before the onset of winter, without their having asked.[11] This highest stage of enlightenment, in which we experience everything in terms of its infinite, unmanifest essence, as the flow of totality, brings the ability to know anything, do anything, and accomplish anything.[12]

Unity Consciousness arises on the ground of complete physiological refine-

Transcendental Consciousness	Unity Consciousness
In Transcendental Consciousness, the senses are turned inward and are then transcended.	In Unity Consciousness, there is no longer any distinction between inner and outer.
Transcendental Consciousness is a self-referral state in which consciousness is aware of itself alone.	Unity Consciousness is a self-referral, self-interacting state in which consciousness knows itself as the reality within everything.
In Transcendental Consciousness, one experiences pure consciousness as one's innermost Self.	In Unity Consciousness, one experiences pure consciousness as the Self of everything.
Transcendental Consciousness is a temporary state — it is lost when the mind becomes active again and the senses turn outward.	Unity Consciousness is a permanent state. Whether the mind is active or silent, one experiences the Self in all things and all things in the Self.
The experience of Transcendental Consciousness marks the beginning of growth toward higher states of consciousness.	Unity Consciousness marks the culmination of growth toward higher states of consciousness, the pinnacle of human development.

ment and integration. The integration of physiological functioning that began with God Consciousness reaches perfection in Unity Consciousness. With all experience in terms of the Self, not even the slightest stress can accumulate.

The maturing of Unity — Brahman Consciousness

In the early days of Unity Consciousness, Maharishi explains, we see only the primary focus of attention in terms of the Self; we experience background objects as before. Over time, the experience of unity expands, encompassing ever more distant objects. In its fully matured state, we experience the entire universe in terms of the Self.[13]

This fully developed state Maharishi terms *Brahman Consciousness (Brahman* is a Sanskrit term meaning *totality* — the unbounded totality of life, relative and absolute together). We experience the infinitely diverse and ever-expanding universe as one ultimate reality, one unified wholeness, eternal and infinite silence appearing as infinite dynamism. This silent wholeness is pure, unbounded, crystal clear bliss consciousness — the Self.

Maharishi describes Unity Consciousness in exalted terms — as the supreme awakening, life in wholeness, in totality, every particle of creation experienced as a blissful ripple in the ocean of the unbounded cosmic Self. Yet anyone can achieve it, he emphasizes, for it is simply the full blossoming of life to itself. When the very nature of life is infinite, then nothing can restrict life from realizing its own nature. Everyone can realize the seventh state of consciousness because everyone's very nature is just that and nothing else. Only stresses and strains inhibit the growth of this ultimate value of knowledge and experience.[14]

Unity Consciousness therefore is the normal state of awareness of a fully developed human being.[14] It is the birthright of every human being. And it all begins with transcending — with diving within and experiencing the simplest form of human awareness. The supreme awakening is supremely simple:

> The search for total knowledge starts from the Self and finds fulfillment in coming back to the Self, finding that everything is the expression of the Self — everything is the expression of my own Self.[15]

Experiences of growing Unity Consciousness

These passages, gathered during research projects from Transcendental Meditation participants, describe the progression from experiencing pure consciousness deep within to beginning to experience it within everything:

"This rich flowing nectar of bliss which is my own Self"

During meditation I experience a warmth and expansion of consciousness which glows with fullness of life, lively, vibrant and golden bliss. Sometimes I experience this flow of bliss in activity, which seems to flow through me and the environment. It is as if all things are sustained and nourished from this pure lively bliss and sometimes it seems as if all my surroundings are comprised of this rich flowing nectar of bliss which is my own Self.[16]

"Consciousness, my own consciousness, comprises all that there is"

The prevailing sense now is that I am the entire universe. I happen to see and speak from here, but that seems almost incidental, just a reference point for the sake of perception. When I look at anything, I see consciousness.... I see subjectivity which has taken a form, which has adopted an appearance of matter. I perceive the boundaries of the objective, material world, but I see them as boundaries on the surface of a more significant underlying reality — that consciousness, my own consciousness, comprises all that there is.[17]

"The deep silence of my Self seems all-pervading"

I feel an underlying continuum of quiet bliss and fullness, of infinite and universal love. Often the deep silence of my Self seems all-pervading, everywhere the same. Objects seem transparent, and I perceive unboundedness, the unmanifest, in everything I see. At such times I feel infinitely full and enveloped in softness. Perception is often very glorified and rich. I feel very self-sufficient and self-contained; activity makes no impression on the growing wholeness which I feel. At the same time, however, I feel a growing intimacy with everything. Nothing seems foreign to me; I feel at home with everything, everyone, and with any situation. I feel truly invincible, for I feel established in my own unbounded Self.[18]

"As if my Self is smiling and radiating everywhere"

A very nice change which has taken place is an unbroken intimacy between my Self and the environment. It is a sort of liveliness of Self that I experience in everything around me. The continuum of Self within myself and outside of me just seems to have a very enjoyable, lively, intimate quality — as if my Self is smiling and radiating everywhere. For the first time I feel concretely, tangibly clearer and closer to all that is meant by God, to all that He is.

I feel a very solid stability and invincible strength growing in my life. I do not ever remember feeling so uncompromisingly complete and confident about myself and the direction my life is taking. My favorite companion is the bliss and silence of my Self which is growing by leaps and bounds and spilling into the relative. I feel eternally protected and infinitely blessed.[19]

"Full of delight, full of joy, full of bliss"

Increasingly I experience everything and everyone as nothing other than my own Self. This is especially clear when walking in the woods but is also apparent in town or anywhere. It seems that Being [pure consciousness] is shining and glistening and even smiling at me from the surface of everything.

This is difficult to describe. How does one perceive Being in activity? It's as if the inner Being, the Self of everything, somehow rises to the surface and makes itself apparent. It is a truly simple experience, and truly beautiful and magnificent.

With this experience of becoming aware of my own Self in all things, love begins to flow — love without boundaries, without exceptions, without considerations of any sort. Love flows out towards all that I perceive and seems to flow back to me as well.

This is simply an augmentation of the experience of Being that became a constant feature of my own waking, dreaming, and sleeping awareness for the past two and half years — it's just that the experience of Being has become ever more insistent, ever more dense around me and in my awareness, ever more powerful.

And now it has become apparent in all things. Yet as subtle as this change is, it is also huge. This experience is utterly full of delight, full of joy, full of bliss, and, as I have said, full of love.

I feel so physically insubstantial at times that it truly seems as if when I walk my feet are not even touching the ground. It feels as if I am constantly surrounded by a dense sphere of Being, cushioning me from the world that I had known before. And that Being is my own Self as well as the Self of all things.[20]

"The finite and the infinite blended together"

When walking outside I notice the scenery filled with some new quality, some vitality, beyond description. I see both the unbounded and boundaries existing together, both the tree and the sky as one underlying wholeness, the finite and the infinite blended together in one totality. It is indescribable to be seeing the same scenery in a different way, without having done anything. I see infinity expressed everywhere, and nowhere can I find the finite only.[21]

"Everyone and everything as nothing other than my own silent Self"

The deep, and pervasive, and almost solidified quality of the inner silence continued [after meditation]. . . . I was completely fulfilled. I needed nothing beyond what I was experiencing, nothing at all. There were no concerns about the outer, phenomenal world whatsoever: no issues, no nagging worries, no list of things to accomplish or address. There was simply nothing from that realm that could in any way disturb this profound level of remarkable inner peace and silence.

At the same time, I clearly perceived everyone and everything as nothing other than my own silent Self. It was as if this silence was the basis for this perception, somehow. This grand, blissful, soothing, infinite silence was also saturated with love . . . love for everything and everyone. It was not a flashy or overwhelming thing. It was very quiet and very profound and supremely unshakable. Really, it feels as if I am in the presence of God, or even inside of God, one with God.[22]

VEDIC LITERATURE
INDIA

Far, far away the indweller of the house, the Self, is seen reverberating.[1]
— *Rik Veda*

This simple statement, from the cornerstone of Vedic literature, describes how even the farthest distances are experienced in terms of the Self.

ॐ

He who sees everything as nothing but the Self, and the Self in everything he sees,
Such a seer withdraws from nothing.
For the enlightened, all that exists is nothing but the Self,
So how could any suffering or delusion continue for those who know
    this Oneness?[2]   — *Isa Upanishad*

This short passage defines Unity Consciousness, the experience of everything in terms of the Self.

ॐ

The Self is all-knowing,
    it is all-understanding,
        and to it belongs all glory.
It is pure consciousness,
    dwelling in the heart of all,
        in the divine citadel of Brahma.
There is no space it does not fill.

Dwelling deep within,
    it manifests as mind,

silently directing the body and the senses.
The wise behold this Self,
> blissful and immortal,
> shining forth through everything.

When It is seen to be
> both the higher and the lower,
> all doubts and uncertainties dissolve.

The knot of the heart is loosed.
One is no longer bound to action or its fruits.

The golden realms of the celestial are the subtlest levels of life.
Within them lies Brahman.
Pure, indivisible, brilliant,
It is the light of lights.
They who know the Self know this.[3] — *Mundaka Upanishad*

This passage identifies the Self as pure consciousness and pure consciousness as the source of all things. The wise, we are told, perceive this blissful and immortal Self "shining forth through everything."

༃

Where one sees nothing but the One, hears nothing but the One, knows nothing but the One — there is the Infinite. Where one sees another, hears another, knows another — there is the finite. The Infinite is immortal, the finite is mortal. . . .

This Infinite is the Self. . . . I am all this. One who knows, meditates upon, and realizes the truth of the Self — such a one delights in the Self, revels in the Self, rejoices in the Self. He becomes master of himself, and master of all the worlds. Slaves are they who know not this truth. . . .

He who knows, meditates upon, and realizes this truth of the

Self, finds that everything — primal energy, ether, fire, water, and all the other elements — mind, will, speech, sacred hymns and scriptures — indeed the whole universe — issues forth from it.

It is written: *He who has realized eternal Truth does not see death, nor illness, nor pain; he sees everything as the Self, and obtains all.*[4]

— *Chandogya Upanishad*

The One is the Infinite, the Infinite is the Self, everything is an expression of this, and I am all this — here is the great teaching of the Upanishads, the teaching of the highest stage of human development, Unity Consciousness.

ॐ

He whose self is established in
Yoga, whose vision everywhere is
even, sees the Self in all beings,
and all beings in the Self.

. . . .

He who sees everything with an
even vision by comparison with the
Self, be it pleasure or pain, he
is deemed the highest yogi, O Arjuna.[5]   — *Bhagavad-Gita*

In this supreme awakening, one "is deemed the highest yogi" — *yoga* meaning *union* and the union first experienced in Transcendental Consciousness having been raised to its supreme level.

▪ *Also see Vedic literature in Chapter 4 (Transcendental Consciousness), Chapter 5 (Cosmic Consciousness), and Chapter 6 (God Consciousness).*

LAOZI

6TH CENTURY BCE · CHINA

See biography on page 60.

See the world as your self. Have faith in the way things are. Love the world as your self; then you can care for all things.[1] — *Tao Te Ching*

Laozi calls on us to rise to Unity Consciousness. He does so again in another work attributed to him.

Attain self-realization, and the whole world is found in the self.[2]

— *Wen-tzu*

⌛

This world is nothing but the glory of the Tao
   expressed through different names and forms
One who sees the things of this world
   As being real and self-existent
   has lost sight of the truth
To him, every word becomes a trap
   every thing becomes a prison

One who knows the truth
   that underlies all things
   lives in this world without danger
To him, every word reflects the universe
   every moment brings enlightenment[3]   — *Tao Te Ching*

"This world is nothing but the glory of the Tao" — nothing, finally, but pure consciousness, the Self. Miss this, Laozi says, and you miss the truth and live in a prison. If we do not experience the unbounded reality within everything, Maharishi has said, it's as if an ocean has been lost in a drop of water.

■ *Also see Laozi in Chapter 4 (Transcendental Consciousness) and Chapter 5 (Cosmic Consciousness).*

THE BUDDHA
c. 563–c. 483 BCE • NEPAL & INDIA

■ *See biography on page 63.*

When the perfect wisdom is first seen, a new perception comes into being that does not depend on any structure. The great quest of the seeker now blossoms as various vast and mysterious doors swing open at the mere touch of the new perception.

There is the door that opens to a vista of the essenceless essence, that which is the real nature of the manifested world. There is the door of liberation from a merely partial perception or muddled perspective of this real nature. And there is the door that opens directly into the authentic realization of this true nature.

There is the wonderful door that opens into an intensity of sights and sounds, color and beauty. And there is the door of balance and ease through which one looks in awe at all the limitless structures of the world as one looks at the star-studded night sky. And there is the door to the exquisite happiness that would never want to own any worldly treasures or to possess even that same happiness. Finally, there is the door of total awakening itself.[1] — *Prajnaparamita*

Prajnaparamita means "the Perfection of Wisdom" in Sanskrit. This passage takes us through all the higher states of consciousness. First comes experiencing the "essenceless essence," the "real nature" of creation — Transcendental Consciousness. Next comes "authentic realization of this true nature," suggesting the permanency of this experience in Cosmic Consciousness. This is followed by refined perception, suggesting God Consciousness. All of this culminates in "total awakening itself," which we take to be Unity Consciousness.

༃

Then Subhuti asked: "What does *enlightenment* mean?"

The Buddha replied: "Enlightenment is a way of saying that all things are seen in their intrinsic empty nature, their Suchness, their ungraspable wonder. Names or words are merely incidental, but that state which sees no division, no duality, is enlightenment."[2] — *Prajnaparamita*

Suchness in Buddhism refers to the common ground of all things. Also known as the *Buddha Mind, Emptiness,* and the *Universal Principle,* it refers to pure consciousness. When we perceive this essence in all things, division and duality dissolve. This is Unity Consciousness.

༃

All beings in the world
Are beyond the realm of words.
Their ultimate nature, pure and true,
Is like the infinity of space.[3] — *Prajnaparamita*

Unity Consciousness brings knowledge of the "ultimate nature" of things, which is infinite — unbounded pure consciousness.

ॐ

When appearances and names are put away and all discrimination ceases, that which remains is the true and essential nature of things and, as nothing can be predicated as to the nature of essence, it is called the "Suchness" of Reality. This universal, undifferentiated, inscrutable "Suchness" is the only Reality but it is variously characterized as Truth, Mind-essence, Transcendental Intelligence, Noble Wisdom, etc. This Dharma of the imagelessness of the Essence-nature of Ultimate Reality is the Dharma which has been proclaimed by all the Buddhas, and when all things are understood in full agreement with it, one is in possession of Perfect Knowledge....[4]   — *Lankavatara Sutra*

Perfect knowledge, this passage informs us, comes when we see things in their true and essential nature, universal and undifferentiated, as manifestations of consciousness itself. Then we experience ultimate reality and truth.

▪ *Also see the Buddha in Chapter 4 (Transcendental Consciousness) and Chapter 5 (Cosmic Consciousness).*

JESUS CHRIST
7–2 BCE–30–36 CE • ISRAEL

See biography on page 71.

I and my father are one.[1]
— John 10:30

Holy Father, keep through thine own name those whom thou hast given me, that they may be one, as we are. — John 17:11

I pray . . . that they all may be one; as thou, Father, art in me, and I in thee, that they also may be one in us. . . . And the glory which thou gavest me I have given them; that they may be one, even as we are one: I in them and thou in me, that they may be made perfect in one. . . . — John 17: 20–23*

Jesus taught that life is to be spiritually transformed through experiencing the kingdom of heaven within and thereby lived in perfection. His ultimate teaching, as these verses show, is of unified consciousness. *I and my father are one*: Taking "the father" as a metaphor for pure consciousness, pure Being, we recognize this verse as describing what we experience first in Transcendental Consciousness and then in Unity Consciousness as the supreme reality of life.

The final verse above reminds us of God Consciousness having risen to Unity Consciousness, with God experienced in terms of the Self. Everyone, Jesus emphasizes in the last two verses, can live this supreme state.

I in them and thou in me remarkably parallels the phrase describing Unity Consciousness from the *Bhagavad-Gita*, cited earlier: *the Self in all beings, and*

---

* For a comment on modern Biblical scholarship on John, see Note 3, page 519.

all beings in the Self. The English writer William Hale White, cited later in this chapter, quotes this Biblical passage in describing his own glimpse of unity.

> Thou shalt love thy neighbor as thyself.
> — Mark 12:31

This verse is traditionally taken to mean one should love one's neighbor as much as one loves oneself. But read literally, it means love your neighbor — appreciate, perceive, *experience* your neighbor — *as* your self. This is possible only in Unity Consciousness.

ॐ

> They said to him, "Then shall we enter the kingdom as babies?"
> Jesus said to them, "When you make the two into one, and when you make the inner like the outer and the outer like the inner, and the upper like the lower, and when you make male and female into a single one... then you will enter [the kingdom]."²
> — *The Gospel of Thomas*

This otherwise abstruse passage makes sense in light of Unity Consciousness. "When you make the two into one" — when the experience of duality recedes and unity predominates. "When you make the inner like the outer and the outer like the inner" — when the distinction between inner and outer gives way to experiencing everything in terms of the Self. "When you make male and female into a single one" — when you experience the unity within diversity.

ॐ

> Jesus said, "When you make the two into one, you will become children of humankind, and when you say, 'Mountain, move from here,' it will move."³
> — *The Gospel of Thomas*

This statement echoes Jesus's teaching in Matthew 17:20: "If ye have faith as a grain of mustard seed, ye shall say unto this mountain, Remove hence to yonder place; and it shall remove; and nothing shall be impossible unto you."

You gain this ability, Jesus says here, "when you make the two into one" — that is, in Unity Consciousness, which brings command of natural law.

☙

Jesus said, "I am the light that is over all things. I am all: From me all has come forth, and to me all has reached. Split a piece of wood; I am there. Lift up the stone, and you will find me there."[4]

— *The Gospel of Thomas*

Jesus cannot mean we will find him personally or physically inside a piece of wood or under a stone. The statement makes sense when we understand "I" and "me" as referring to the Self — the Self of all things, the all-pervading ocean of pure consciousness, the unified field. In Unity Consciousness, one experiences this unmanifest reality everywhere, in the most ordinary things.

☙

For this reason I say, if one is (whole), one will be filled with light, but if one is divided, one will be filled with darkness.[5]

— *The Gospel of Thomas*

In every state prior to Unity Consciousness, one is "divided" — there is a subject and an object, an inner and an outer. In Unity Consciousness, the unified wholeness of pure consciousness, the Self, predominates one's experience — one can be said to be "whole."

In summary, Jesus enjoins us to experience the kingdom of heaven, rise in purity, love, and perfection, and live life in full union with God. "I have come in order that you may have life, life in all its fullness" (John 10:10) — and reach, even exceed, the height of development he himself reached:

Verily, verily, I say unto you, He that believeth on me, the works that I do shall he do also; and greater works than these shall he do. . . .

—John 14:12

▪ *Also see Jesus Christ in Chapter 4 (Transcendental Consciousness), Chapter 5 (Cosmic Consciousness), and Chapter 6 (God Consciousness).*

THE GOSPEL OF TRUTH
2nd CENTURY · EGYPT & ROME

■ The Gospel of Truth *is one of the early Christian texts discovered in Nag Hammadi in Egypt in 1945, along with the* Gospel of Thomas *and other works (see page 72). Eloquent and poetic, it begins, "The gospel of truth is joy." It is widely attributed to Valentinus (c. 100–160). Born in northern Egypt and educated in Alexandria, Valentinus was said to be a student of Theudas, one of St. Paul's disciples. Valentinus said he received from Theudas the secret teaching Jesus had given privately to Paul and his closest followers. Valentinus taught in Rome between 135 and 160, where he became a candidate for bishop of Rome, the equivalent of the pope at that time. His "Valentinian" philosophy of Christianity attracted adherents throughout the Roman Empire.*

The *Gospel of Truth* outlines a progression of human development that begins with the desire for transcendence and culminates in Unity Consciousness.

> All have sought for the one from whom they have come forth. All have been within him, the illimitable, the inconceivable, who is beyond all thought.[1]

But people have grown forgetful of their source, which the *Gospel of Truth* refers to as "the father" — and so people live in error, fear, confusion, and division, "as if they were fast asleep and found themselves a prey to troubled dreams."[2] Jesus's mission was to bring knowledge — memory — of this source:

> Through him he enlightened those who were in darkness because of forgetfulness. He enlightened them and gave them a path. And that path is the truth that he taught them.[3]

Once people begin experiencing this source, they begin to grow:

> Each one will speak concerning the place from which they have come forth, and to the region from which they received their essential being they will hasten to return once again and receive from that place, the place where they stood before, and they will taste of that place, be nourished, and grow. And their own place of rest is their fullness.[4]

So far this suggests transcending and becoming established in the transcendent — Transcendental Consciousness and Cosmic Consciousness. But the *Gospel of Truth* brings us to a vision of life in unity:

> For where there is envy and strife, there is an incompleteness, but where there is unity, there is completeness. Since this incompleteness came about because they did not know the father, from the moment when they know the father, incompleteness will cease to exist. As one's ignorance disappears when one gains knowledge, and as darkness disappears when light appears, so also incompleteness is eliminated by completeness. Certainly, from that moment on, form is no longer manifest but will be dissolved in fusion with unity. Now their works lie scattered. In time unity will make the spaces complete. By means of unity each one will understand himself. By means of knowledge one will purify himself from multiplicity into unity, devouring matter within himself like fire and darkness by light, death by life.
>
> Certainly, if these things have happened to each one of us, it is fitting for us, surely, to think about all so that the house may be holy and silent for unity.[5]

With direct experience of our transcendental source, incompleteness disappears, like darkness before light. Then the *Gospel of Truth* gives us a beautiful evocation of Unity Consciousness, the experience of the material world in its ultimate reality as unified pure consciousness, of diversity in light of unity.

PLOTINUS
205–270 • EGYPT & ITALY

■ *See biography on 78.*

Rather, every spirit has all and is all and is with all because he is with it, and possesses all things, without possessing them in the usual sense (as individual objects external to himself). For he does not possess it as something different from himself. That which is possessed is not one thing and he himself another. What there is (of that which is possessed) in him is not each thing separate for itself. For each is the whole, and is wholly all. Yet still it is not mingled but is again itself separate.[1]

Plotinus seeks words to describe experiencing everything within oneself, as a unity, without losing the ability to distinguish one thing from another.

༂

A pleasant life is theirs . . . ; they have the Truth for mother, nurse, real being, and nutriment; they see all things, not the things that are born and die, but those which have real being; and they see themselves in others. For them all things are transparent, and there is nothing dark or impenetrable, but everyone is manifest to everyone internally, and all things are manifest; for light is manifest to light. For everyone has all things in himself and sees all things in another; so that all things are everywhere and all is all and each is all, and the glory is infinite.[2]

Plotinus again describes the state in which one experiences "all things in himself," a state he associates with truth and infinite glory.

⌁

He who has allowed the beauty of that world to penetrate his soul goes away no longer a mere observer. For the object perceived and the perceiving soul are no longer two things separated from one another, but the perceiving soul has [now] within itself the perceived object.[3]

In Unity Consciousness, the knower and the known are united, all things experienced in terms of the Self.

■ *Also see Plotinus in Chapter 4 (Transcendental Consciousness) and Chapter 5 (Cosmic Consciousness).*

THE HERMETIC WRITINGS
2ND & 3RD CENTURIES • EGYPT

■ *See background information on page 76.*

Here the pupil Tat asks his teacher Hermes to explain the nature of *Rebirth*.

— *Hermes.* What can I say, my son? This thing cannot be taught; and it is not possible for you to see it with your organs of sight, which are fashioned out of material elements. I can tell you nothing but this; I see that by God's mercy there has come to be in me a form which is not fashioned out of matter, and I have passed forth out of myself, and entered into an immortal body. I am not now the man I was; I have been born again in Mind, and the bodily shape which was mine before has been put away from me. I am no longer an object colored and tangible, a thing of spatial dimensions; I am now alien to all this, and to all that you perceive when you gaze with bodily eyesight. To such eyes as yours, my son, I am not now visible.

— *Tat.* Father, you have driven me to raving madness. Will you tell me that I do not at this moment see my own self?

— *Hermes.* Would that you too, my son, had passed forth out of yourself, so that you might have seen, not as men see dream-figures in their sleep, but as one who is awake.

— *Tat.* Now indeed, father, you have reduced me to speechless amazement. Why, I see you, father, with your stature unchanged, and your features the same as ever.

— *Hermes.* Even in this you are mistaken. The mortal form changes day by day; it is altered by lapse of time, and becomes larger and smaller; for it is an illusion.

— *Tat.* What then is real, thrice-greatest one?

— *Hermes.* That which is not sullied by matter, my son, nor limited by boundaries, that which has no color and no shape, that which is without integument, and is luminous, that which is apprehended by itself alone, that which is changeless and unalterable, that which is good. . . .

— *Tat.* Is it then beyond my power, father?

— *Hermes.* Heaven forbid, my son. Draw it into you, and it will come.

Tat then gains the experience himself. Now he describes the unbounded, omnipresent nature of pure consciousness back to Hermes:

— *Tat.* Father, now that I see in mind, I see myself to be the All. I am in heaven and in earth, in water and in air; I am in beasts and plants; I am a babe in the womb, and one that is not yet conceived, and one that has been born; I am present everywhere.

— *Hermes.* Now, my son, you know what the Rebirth is.[1]

— *The Hermetica, Libellus XIII*

This discussion underscores the difficulty of explaining higher states of consciousness to someone who lacks the experience. "Mind" in the first paragraph refers to pure consciousness. When Hermes says, "I am not now visible," he means he has transcended to this field, beyond perception. This alone is real, he asserts, and "is apprehended by itself alone." So far Hermes might be referring to Transcendental Consciousness. But when Tat relates his Rebirth experience, we see the discussion is about Unity Consciousness, the experience of everything in terms of the Self, "the All."

■ *Also see the Hermetic writings in Chapter 4 (Transcendental Consciousness) and Chapter 6 (God Consciousness).*

SHANKARA
700?–750? • INDIA

■ *See biography on page 81.*

This is the teaching of the Vedic literature: Individual life and the material world are nothing but *Brahm*; abiding in the indivisible alone is enlightenment; *Brahm* is without a second. The Vedic texts declare it. . . .

I do not know what is "this" or "not this," nor what or how great is this unbounded bliss.

It is not possible to express through speech, nor to conceive with the mind, the glory of the ocean of the supreme Brahm, abounding in the swelling of the immortal bliss of the Self. Having dissolved in its minutest portion, like a hailstone melting into the ocean, my mind is now satisfied with its blissful essence.

Where has the universe gone? Who took it away? Where did it dissolve? Just now I saw it, and it is no more. What a magnificent wonder!

In the ocean of *Brahm*, filled with the nectar of unending bliss, what is to be avoided? What is to be taken? What is "other"? What is different?

I do not see anything here nor do I hear or know anything. I am the Self alone, I am eternal bliss, undifferentiated. . . .

I am without attachments, without limbs, without characteristics, imperishable. I am infinite peace, without sin, eternal. . . .

I am indeed separate from the seer, the listener, the speaker, the doer. I am fully awake, unattached, limitless, beyond activity, infinite, eternal.

I am indeed that *Brahm*, beyond duality, Totality, with no inside nor outside. Though I am neither this nor that, I am the illuminator of both, the Supreme, the pure.

I am indeed that *Brahm*, beyond duality, eternal, the single essence of eternal bliss, far from notions such as "you" or "I," "this" or "that," the reality that is beginningless, incomparable. . . .

I alone am within all beings as the Self of knowledge, their inner and outer support. I myself am the experiencer and the thing experienced — whatever I perceived before as separate, as "this-ness."

For me, who am eternally one and indivisible, there is neither engagement in activity nor cessation from it. For how can there be doing for one who is Unity with no intervals or spaces, who is full like the sky?[1]   — *Crest Jewel of Discrimination (Vivekachudamani)*

Shankara tries to capture in words an experience that is beyond words — the experience of everything in terms of the Self, in terms of unified wholeness, totality, *Brahm*. Without the experience of this "nondual" state, his words will seem paradoxical. When he asks, "Where has the universe gone?", he does not mean it has disappeared, only that it is no longer something separate from the Self. When he says, "I do not see anything here nor do I hear or know anything," he does not mean he can no longer perceive or know things, only that unity has moved to the foreground of experience, diversity to the background. He resides in perpetual peace and bliss.

ॐ

The absence of the notion of inside and outside, owing to a saint's absorption in the experience of the bliss of *Brahm*, is the characteristic of the enlightened state. . . .

He who knows in his own consciousness that there is never a distinction between individual and *Brahm*, nor between the material creation and *Brahm*, is enlightened.[2]

— *Crest Jewel of Discrimination (Vivekachudamani)*

In this unified state, Shankara tells us, there is no longer a distinction between inner and outer, nor between the material world and Brahm (the Self), for everything is known in terms of the Self.

ॐ

Everything from the Creator to a clump of grass is merely a fake, an appearance. Therefore one should experience oneself as Totality, abiding in the one Self.

When discrimination is gained, something imagined through error is perceived as merely "That," and not at all distinct from "That." When the mistaken perception has disappeared, the essence . . . shines forth. . . . Thus, the universe in reality is Atma, the Self. . . .

The Self is within, the Self is without; the Self is in front, the Self is behind; the Self is in the south, the Self is in the north; likewise the Self is above and the Self is below.

As the wave, foam, whirlpool, etc., are all in reality water, so everything from the body to the ego are all consciousness. Everything is made of pure consciousness alone, the one essence....

The supreme *Brahm*, our own Self, is like the sky — pure, undifferentiated, unbounded, silent, changeless, devoid of inside and outside, alone, without a second. Is there anything else to be known?...

When mental activities are settled within the undifferentiated *Brahm*, the supreme Self, then there is no experience of diversity. Anything else is mere gossip.[3]

— *Crest Jewel of Discrimination (Vivekachudamani)*

Prior to Unity Consciousness, Shankara is saying, all things are merely an "appearance" because they conceal their ultimate inner reality — the Self, pure consciousness. Once one's experience has penetrated to this inner reality, then one recognizes that "everything is made of pure consciousness alone, the one essence." Know this, Shankara says, and there is nothing further to be known.

▪ *Also see Shankara in Chapter 4 (Transcendental Consciousness).*

ATTAR OF NISHAPUR
1145–1221 • IRAN

See biography on page 89.

For you there is an ascent of the soul towards the Divine Light, therefore shall your heart and soul in the end attain to union with that Light. With your whole heart and soul, seek to regain Reality, nay, seek for Reality within your own heart, for Reality, in truth, is hidden within you. The heart is the dwelling-place of that which is the Essence of the Universe....

Be unveiled within and behold the Essence. Form is a veil to you and your heart is a veil. When the veil vanishes, you will become all light....

If you draw aside the veils of the stars and the spheres, you will see that all is one with the Essence of your own pure soul.... When you have cast aside the veil, you will see the Essence and all things will be shown forth within the Essence. If you draw aside the veil from the Face of the Beloved, all that is hidden will be made manifest and you will become one with God, for then will you be the very Essence of the Divine.[1]

Attar invites us first to experience the inner reality, the "Essence of the Universe," then to discover that the whole cosmos is identical with that.

Also see Attar in Chapter 4 (Transcendental Consciousness).

RŪMĪ
1207–1273 • PERSIA & TURKEY

See biography on 92.

Now comes the final merging,
 Now comes everlasting beauty.
Now comes abundant grace,
 Now comes boundless purity.

The infinite treasure is shining,
The mighty ocean is roaring,
The morning of grace has come —
Morning? — No!
This is the eternal Light of God!

Who occupies this beautiful form?
Who is the ruler and the prince?
Who is the wise man? —
 Nothing but a veil.

. . . .

Your head of clay is from the earth,
Your pure awareness is from heaven.
O how vast is that treasure
 which lies beneath the clay!
 Every head you see depends on it!

Behind every atom of this world
 hides an infinite universe.

. . . .

> The Light of Truth shines from Tabriz.*
> It is beyond the beyond
> > yet it is here,
> > shining through every particle of this world.[1]

Rūmī wrote beautifully about his experiences of transcendence and refined perception, as we have seen. His poetry culminates in such verses as these, seeking in words to capture his experience of unity. Here he describes "the final merging," leading to the experience of infinity shining within everything.

ᘐ

The soul comes once,
> this body a thousand times.

I am everything,
> coming in, going out
> > How can I speak of another?

Like a wave my body is here and gone,
Look closely —
> a million waves,
> > one sea.

The soul comes once,
> this body a thousand times.

Why talk of the soul? Why mention the body
> when both are myself?

With much effort I have stayed on this path,
> and now this body
> > finds a great soul within it.

---

* Tabriz, a major city in Iran, here refers to Rūmī's spiritual instructor, Shams-i Tabrizi.

The soul comes once,
　this body a thousand times.

What can I do? —
　I talk yet no one hears me.

I see thousands of people who are myself
Yet they keep thinking they are themselves!²

　In this unified state, experiencing himself as everything, Rūmī wonders, "How can I speak of another?" Body and soul, far from being different, are merely aspects of his Self — as is everyone he sees.

With every step I take
　another attachment falls away.

I take a hundred steps,
the veils fall,
　　The Beloved appears —
　　beautiful, radiant —
I am in love!

O brother, can't you see? —
　　It is myself I have fallen in love with!³

　God, the "Beloved," opens to his experience — and is ultimately experienced as a reflection of the Self.

The marvelous sound
　That comes from the sky — I am That.
The sweet fragrance
That comes from the garden — I am That.

The great beauty that comes from the heart and soul
Until I leave . . . Wait!
I can't leave — I am That.

I am filled with splendor,
    spinning with your love.

It looks like I'm spinning around you,
    but no — I'm spinning around myself![4]

Here again is all experience in terms of "That," the Self. Rūmī's declaration "I am That" calls to mind the great statement from the Upanishads, *Aham Brahmasmi* — I am that totality (Brahman).

Also see Rūmī in Chapter 4 (Transcendental Consciousness).

MEISTER ECKHART
1260–c. 1327 • GERMANY

See biography on page 99.

Now listen to a marvel! How marvelous, to be without and within, to embrace and be embraced, to see and be the seen, to hold and be held — *that* is the goal, where the spirit is ever at rest, united in joyous eternity![1]

— Sermon 9

"To see and be the seen" — to see the Self in all things — is the hallmark of Unity Consciousness. Eckhart elaborates:

There all is one, and one all in all. There to her (the perceiving soul) all is one, and one is in all. It (i.e., the empirical world) carries contradiction in itself. What is contradiction? Love and suffering, white and black, these are contradictions, and as such these cannot remain in essential Being itself.

Herein lies the soul's purity, that it is purified from a life that is divided and that it enters into a life that is unified. All that is divided in lower things, will be unified so soon as the (perceptive) soul climbs up into a life where there is no contrast. When the soul comes into the light of reasonableness (the true insight) it knows no contrasts. Say Lord, when is a man in mere "understanding" (in discursive intellectual understanding)? I say to you: "When a man sees one thing separated from another." And when is he above mere understanding? That I can tell you: "When he sees all in all, then a man stands above mere understanding."[2]

There all is one, and one all in all — another variation of the earlier phrases "the Self in all beings, and all beings in the Self" (*Bhagavad-Gita*) and "I in them and thou in me" (Jesus Christ). Eckhart distinguishes the waking experience of diversity (which he terms "contradiction") from that of unity. In this unified state one "sees all in all" — one experiences the unified totality.

ॐ

In distinction one can find neither being, nor God, nor rest, nor bliss, nor satisfaction. Be one, that you may find God! And in truth, if you were truly one, then you would even remain one in difference, and difference would be one to you, and then nothing could hinder you.[3] — *The Nobleman*

"In distinction" means in a state of consciousness in which one sees only diversity. Eckhart then describes a state of consciousness that remains unified even in diversity and experiences diversity as unity.

The masters say that when one knows creatures in themselves, that is evening knowledge, for then one sees the creatures in images of varied distinction; but when one sees creatures in God, that is called morning knowledge, and then one sees creatures without all distinction, stripped of form and deprived of all "likeness," in the One that is God Himself.[4]   — *The Nobleman*

Eckhart contrasts two kinds of knowledge — *evening knowledge,* or ordinary perception, and *morning knowledge,* knowledge of all things in light of the underlying unity of "the One," which he associates with God.

༄

The person who has abandoned all things where they are lowest and transitory receives them again in God where they are truth. All that is dead here is life there, and everything that is coarse and material here is there spirit in God. It is just as if someone poured pure water into a clean barrel that was completely spotless and clean and let it become still; and if then a person put his face over it, he would see it on the bottom just exactly as it is as part of himself. This happens because the water is pure and clean and unmoving. This is how it is with all those people who exist in freedom and unity in themselves.[5]

In ordinary waking state perception, Eckhart indicates, the world around us is "coarse and material" and essentially dead. In contrast stands the state that reveals the innermost truth and spirit within things, the true life. In this unified state of consciousness, one sees into the interior essence of things and perceives everything "as it is" — "as part of himself."

Eckhart makes his accustomed use of the word *God*, which he equates with the "inmost recess of the spirit," the "ground of the soul" — in other words, pure consciousness, pure Being.

༄

All that a man has here externally in multiplicity is intrinsically One. Here all blades of grass, wood, and stone, all things are One. This is the deepest depth.⁶

I say that in the kingdom of heaven everything is in everything else, and that everything is one, and that everything is ours. . . . [I]t is something within me as my own, not something coming from outside myself.⁷

■ *Also see Meister Eckhart in Chapter 4 (Transcendental Consciousness) and Chapter 5 (Cosmic Consciousness).*

THOMAS TRAHERNE
1637–1674 • ENGLAND

■ *See biography on page 114.*

My naked simple Life was I;
   That Act so strongly shin'd
Upon the earth, the sea, the sky,
It was the substance of my mind;
   The sense itself was I.

. . . .

But being simple like the Deity
   In its own centre is a sphere
Not shut up here, but everywhere.
It acts not from a centre to
   Its object as remote,
But present is when it doth view,
Being with the Being it doth note
   Whatever it doth do.

....
>
> This made me present evermore
> With whatsoe'er I saw.
> An object, if it were before
> My eye, was by Dame Nature's law,
> Within my soul. Her store
> Was all at once within me; all Her treasures
> Were my immediate and internal pleasures,
> Substantial joys, which did inform my mind.
> With all she wrought
> My soul was fraught,
> And every object in my heart a thought
> Begot, or was; I could not tell,
> Whether the things did there
> Themselves appear,
> Which in my Spirit *truly* seem'd to dwell;
> Or whether my conforming mind
> Were not even all that therein shin'd.

Traherne seems to be describing experience in terms of the Self. In everything he sees he experiences "the substance of my mind." He apprehends everything as "all at once within me." The poem continues:

> But yet of this I was most sure,
> That at the utmost length,
> (So worthy was it to endure)
> My soul could best express its strength.
> It was so quick and pure,
> That all my mind was wholly everywhere,
> Whate'er it saw, 'twas ever wholly there;
> The sun ten thousand legions off, was nigh:
> The utmost star,

> Though seen from far,
> Was present in the apple of my eye.
>   There was my sight, my life, my sense,
>   My substance, and my mind;
>   My spirit shin'd
> Even there, not by a transient influence:
>   The act was immanent, yet there:
>   The thing remote, yet felt even here.
>
>   O Joy! O wonder and delight!
>   O sacred mystery!
>   My Soul a Spirit infinite!
>   An image of the Deity!
>   A pure substantial light!
> That Being greatest which doth nothing seem!
> Why, 'twas my all, I nothing did esteem
> But that alone. A strange mysterious sphere!
>   A deep abyss
>   That sees and is
> The only proper place of Heavenly Bliss.
>   To its Creator 'tis so near
>   In love and excellence,
>   In life and sense,
> In greatness, worth, and nature; and so dear,
>   In it, without hyperbole,
>   The Son and friend of God we see.

Traherne describes the experience of unbounded awareness and celestial perception — he perceives heavenly bliss everywhere. Again he seems to experience everything in terms of the Self — "my Mind," "my Substance," "my Spirit." Even distant objects are present within him. This transcendental, infinite value of life is now his dominant reality, "my all." The poem concludes:

A strange extended orb of Joy,
   Proceeding from within,
  Which did on every side, convey
   Itself, and being nigh of kin
    To God did every way
Dilate itself even in an instant, and
Like an indivisible centre stand,
At once surrounding all eternity.
  'Twas not a sphere,
   Yet did appear,
One infinite. 'Twas somewhat every where,
   And though it had a power to see
    Far more, yet still it shin'd
    And was a mind
Exerted for it saw Infinity.
  'Twas not a sphere, but 'twas a might
  Invisible, and yet gave light

    O wondrous Self! O sphere of light,
    O sphere of joy most fair;
  O act, O power infinite;
  O subtile and unbounded air!
    O living orb of sight!
Thou which within me art, yet me! Thou eye,
And temple of His whole infinity!
  O what a world art Thou! A world within!
    All things appear
    All objects are
Alive in Thee! Supersubstantial, rare,
  Above themselves, and nigh of kin

> To those pure things we find
>   In His great mind
> Who made the world! Tho' now eclipsed by sin
>   There they are useful and divine,
>   Exalted there they ought to shine.¹   — "My Spirit"

Traherne again describes experiencing unity within diversity, infinity within boundaries. And his name for this infinity? "O wondrous Self!" The infinite, radiant temple of the world, alive as never before, is entirely within him — it's all "Me." He experiences everything as the Self moving within itself.

■ *Also see Traherne in Chapter 4 (Transcendental Consciousness) and Chapter 6 (God Consciousness).*

RALPH WALDO EMERSON
1803–1882 • UNITED STATES

■ *See biography on page 124.*

Who shall define to me an Individual? I behold with awe & delight many illustrations of the One Universal Mind. I see my being imbedded in it. As a plant in the earth so I grow in God. I am only a form of him. He is the soul of Me....

A certain wandering light comes to me which I instantly perceive to be the Cause of Causes. It transcends all proving. It is itself the ground of being; and I see that it is not one & I another, but this is the life of my life.

That is one fact, then; that in certain moments I have known that I existed directly from God, and am, as it were, his organ. And in my ultimate consciousness Am He.[1]

Emerson is clearly describing experiences of heightened consciousness. Some phrases suggest Transcendental Consciousness, others God Consciousness. But he suggests Unity Consciousness when he says he beholds "many illustrations of the One Universal Mind," and adds, "I see my being imbedded in it" and declares that he is that.

■ *Also see Emerson in Chapter 4 (Transcendental Consciousness) and Chapter 5 (Cosmic Consciousness).*

HENRI FRÉDÉRIC AMIEL
1821–1881 • SWITZERLAND

■ *See biography on page 134.*

Shall I ever enjoy again those marvelous reveries of past days, as, for instance, once, when I was still quite a youth, in the early dawn, sitting among the ruins of the castle of Faucigny; another time in the mountains above Lavey, under the midday sun, lying under a tree and visited by three butterflies; and again another night on the sandy shore of the North Sea, stretched full length upon the beach, my eyes wandering over the Milky Way? Will they ever return to me, those grandiose, immortal, cosmogonic dreams, in which one seems to carry the world in one's breast, to touch the stars, to possess the infinite? Divine moments, hours of ecstasy, when thought flies from world to world, penetrates the great enigma, breathes with a respiration large, tranquil, and profound, like that of the ocean, and hovers serene and boundless like the blue heaven! Visits from the muse, Urania, who traces around the foreheads of those she loves the phosphorescent nimbus of contemplative power, and who pours into their hearts the tranquil intoxication, if not the authority of genius, moments of irresistible intuition in which a man feels himself great like the universe and calm like a god! From the celestial spheres down to the shell or the moss, the whole of creation is then submitted to our gaze, lives in our breast, and accomplishes in us its eternal work with the regularity of destiny and the passionate ardor of love. What hours, what memories! The traces which remain to us of them are enough to fill us with respect and enthusiasm, as though they had been visits of the Holy Spirit. And then, to fall back again from these heights with their boundless horizons into the muddy ruts of triviality! what a fall! . . . What a pale counterfeit is real life of the life we see in glimpses, and how these flaming lightnings of our prophetic youth make the twilight of our dull monotonous manhood more dark and dreary![1] — *Amiel's Journal*

Amiel describes times when he experienced the whole world within him, when he seemed to be able to "touch the stars, to possess the infinite" — when the whole of creation seems to be performing its eternal work within him. Compared to this, ordinary waking experience is nothing more than "muddy ruts of triviality" and "a pale counterfeit."

Amiel describes apparent glimpses of unity elsewhere in his journal:

How present and sensible to my inner sense is the unity of everything! It seems to me that I am able to pierce to the sublime motive which, in all the infinite spheres of existence, and through all the modes of space and time, every created form reproduces and sings within the bond of an eternal harmony. From the infernal shades I feel myself mounting towards the regions of light; my flight across chaos finds its rest in paradise.² — *Amiel's Journal*

Amiel wished to live this state perpetually. He recognized that to do so involved gaining alignment with natural law.

The eternal life is not the future life; it is life in harmony with the true order of things — life in God. We must learn to look upon time as a movement of eternity, as an undulation in the ocean of being. To live, so as to keep this consciousness of ours in perpetual relation with the eternal, is to be wise; to live, so as to personify and embody the eternal, is to be religious.³ — *Amiel's Journal*

Also see Amiel in Chapter 4 (Transcendental Consciousness).

GUSTAVE FLAUBERT
1821–1880 • FRANCE

Gustave Flaubert studied law for six years but left school before completing his degree. Three years later he had completed a draft of his first novel. He is known for his meticulous devotion to style and his quest for finding le mot juste, *the right word. He spent five years on his most celebrated work,* Madame Bovary, *sometimes a week on a single page, always seeking to avoid the abstract and imprecise, also any intrusion of his own sentiments.* Madame Bovary *thus introduced a new approach — the novel as a meticulous likeness of actual life. He possessed, in his own estimation, "an extraordinary faculty of perception." Flaubert is regarded as one of the greatest writers in Western literature and his best works as impeccable models of style.*

It is true, often I have felt that something bigger than myself was fusing with my being: bit by bit I went off into the greenery of the pastures and into the current of the rivers that I watched go by; and I no longer knew where my soul was, it was so diffuse, universal, spread out. . . .

Your mind itself finally lost the notion of particularity which kept it on the alert. It was like an immense harmony engulfing your soul with marvelous palpitations, and you felt in its plenitude an inexpressible comprehension of the unrevealed wholeness of things; the interval between you and the object, like an abyss closing, grew narrower and narrower, until the difference vanished, because you both were bathed in infinity; you penetrated each other equally, and a subtle current passed from you into matter while the life of the elements slowly pervaded you, rising like a sap; one degree more, and you would have become nature, or nature become you. . . .

Immortality, boundlessness, infinity, I have all that, I am that! . . .

I understand, I see, I breathe, in the midst of plenitude. . . . how calm I am![1]   — *The Temptation of Saint Anthony*

Flaubert's first sentences hint at Cosmic Consciousness — his awareness expands until it is unbounded, "diffuse, universal, spread out." The second paragraph suggests growth of God Consciousness, as the gap between subject and object, Self and non-Self, grows narrower. Then the gap disappears, leaving knower and known "bathed in infinity" — "you penetrated each other equally." Thus the passage begins with experiencing the infinity of the self and ends with experiencing infinity in everything. He feels immortal, unbounded, infinite and exclaims — echoing the *Upanishads* — "I am that!"

WILLIAM HALE WHITE
1831–1913 • ENGLAND

▪ *White studied for the ministry but grew disillusioned and worked as a journalist, then took a position in the civil service at the Admiralty. He is best known for his autobiographical novels, describing his inner development from Protestant Christianity to a Wordsworthian view of nature as divine. He wrote a number of other novels as well, all under the pen name Mark Rutherford.*

I was no longer young: in fact I was well over sixty. The winter had been dark and tedious. . . . Suddenly, with hardly any warning, spring burst upon us. Day after day we had clear, warm sunshine which deepened every contrast of color, and at intervals we were blessed with refreshing rains. I spent most of my time out of doors on the edge of a favorite wood. . . .

One morning when I was in the wood something happened which was nothing less than a transformation of myself and the world, although I "believed" nothing new. I was looking at a great, spreading, bursting oak. The first tinge from the greenish-yellow buds was just visible. It seemed to be no longer a tree away from me and apart from me. The enclosing barriers of consciousness were removed and the text came into my mind, *Thou in me and I in thee.* The distinction of self and not-self was an illusion. I could feel the rising sap; in me also sprang the fountain of life up-rushing from its roots, and the joy of its outbreak at the extremity of each twig right up to the summit was my own: that which kept me apart was nothing. I do not argue; I cannot explain; it will be easy to prove me absurd, but nothing can shake me. *Thou in me and I in thee.* Death! what is death? There is no death: *in thee* it is impossible, absurd.¹

For a few joyful moments, White sees the oak tree literally within himself and himself in the tree. There is no longer distinction between self and not-self — everything rests "in me." Reflecting on this experience, he writes,

> All my life I had been a lover of the country, and had believed, if this is the right word, that the same thought, spirit, life ... which was in everything I beheld, was also in me. But my creed had been taken over from books; it was accepted as an intellectual proposition. Most of us are satisfied with this kind of belief, and even call it religion.²

In contrast to the "intellectual proposition," White has now *experienced* unity.

EDWARD CARPENTER
1844–1929 • ENGLAND

■ *See biography on page 138.*

Of all the hard facts of Science: as that fire will burn, that water will freeze, that the earth will spin on its axis, and so forth, I know of none more solid and fundamental than the fact that if you inhibit thought (and persevere) you come at length to a region of consciousness below or behind thought, and different from ordinary thought in its nature and character — a consciousness of quasi-universal quality, and a realization of an altogether vaster self than that to which we are accustomed. And since the ordinary consciousness, with which we are concerned in ordinary life, is before all things founded on the little local self, and is in fact *self*-consciousness in the little local sense, it follows that to pass out of that is to die to the ordinary self and the ordinary world.

It is to die in the ordinary sense, but in another sense it is to wake up and find that the "I," one's real, most intimate self, pervades the universe and all other beings — that the mountains and the sea and the stars are a part of one's body and that one's soul is in touch with the souls of all creatures. Yes, far closer than before. It is to be assured of an indestructible immortal life and of a joy immense and inexpressible — "to drink of the deep well of rest and joy, and sit with all the Gods in Paradise."

So great, so splendid is this experience, that it may be said that all minor questions and doubts fall away in the face of it; and certain it is that in thousands and thousands of cases the fact of its having come even once to a man has completely revolutionized his subsequent life and outlook on the world....

To experience all this with any degree of fullness, is to know that you have passed through Death; because whatever destruction physical death may bring to your local senses and faculties, you know that it will not affect that deeper Self. [1]   — *The Drama of Love and Death*

Carpenter asserts the reality of a region of consciousness transcending thought, "an altogether vaster self" than we typically experience. It "pervades the universe and all other beings" — and it can be experienced in everything. This experience brings an indescribable joy and the assurance that one is immortal — but it remains beyond description:

> I really do not feel that I can tell you anything without falsifying and obscuring the matter.... The perception seems to be one in

which all the senses unite into one sense. In which you become the object. But this is unintelligible, mentally speaking.[2] 　— Letter

The object is suddenly seen, is *felt*, to be one with the self. . . . The knower, the knowledge, and the thing known are once more one. . . . This form of Consciousness is the only true knowledge — it is the only true existence. And it is a matter of experience; it has been testified to in all parts of the world and in all ages of history. There is a consciousness in which the subject and the object are felt, are *known,* to be united and one — in which the Self is felt to *be* the object perceived . . . or at least in which the subject and the object are felt to be parts of the same being, of the same including Self of all. And it is the only true knowledge.[3] 　— *The Art of Creation*

Carpenter recognizes this unified state, where everything is experienced in terms of the "Self of all," as "the only true knowledge" and "the only true existence." He reminds us of Maharishi's principle that knowledge is different in different states of consciousness and that only in Unity Consciousness is knowledge complete, for now no further knowledge of the object is possible.

■ *Also see Carpenter in Chapter 4 (Transcendental Consciousness) and Chapter 5 (Cosmic Consciousness).*

BLACK ELK (HEHAKA SAPA)
1863–1950 • UNITED STATES

■ *See biography on page 140.*

The first peace, which is the most important, is that which comes within the soul of men when they realize their relationship, their oneness with the universe and all its Powers, and when they realize that at the center of the universe dwells *Wakan-Tanka,* and that this center is really everywhere, it is within each of us. This is the real Peace, and the others are but reflections of this. The second peace is that which is made between two individuals, and the third is that which is made between two nations. But above all you should understand that there can never be peace between nations until there is first known that true peace which, as I have often said, is within the souls of men.[1]

— *The Sacred Pipe*

We experience our "oneness with the universe," Black Elk says, by experiencing the field of peace that is within us and "at the center of the universe." This experience underlies peace at all scales. What Black Elk describes is fulfilled first in Transcendental Consciousness and finally in Unity Consciousness.

■ *Also see Black Elk in Chapter 4 (Transcendental Consciousness).*

BERNARD BERENSON
1865–1959 • LITHUANIA & UNITED STATES

See biography on page 310.

As I look back on fully seventy years of awareness and recall the moments of greatest happiness, they were, for the most part, moments when I lost myself all but completely in some instant of perfect harmony. In consciousness this was due not to me but to the not-me, of which I was scarcely more than the subject in the grammatical sense.

In childhood and boyhood this ecstasy overtook me when I was happy out of doors. Was I five or six? Certainly not seven. It was a morning in early summer. A silver haze shimmered and trembled over the lime trees. The air was laden with their fragrance. The temperature was like a caress. I remember — I need not recall — that I climbed up a tree stump and felt suddenly immersed in Itness. I did not call it by that name. I had no need for words. It and I were one.

— *Sketch for a Self-Portrait*

Following this passage, Berenson quotes the beautiful paragraph from Thomas Traherne's *Centuries of Meditation*, which suggests it describes his own experience as well: 'The corn was orient and immortal wheat, which never should be reaped, nor was ever sown. I thought it had stood from everlasting to everlasting. The dust and stones of the street were as precious as gold. . . ." (see page 296). Berenson continues:

> A revelation, a vision, a psychological equipoise, what you will, this experience has furnished me with a touchstone. It has remained for seven decades the goal of my yearning, my longing, my desire. Not always alas! but often enough in moments when passion, or ambition, or self-righteousness would have had their way with me, the feeling of that moment at the dawn of my conscious life would present itself and like a guardian angel remind me that IT was my goal and that IT was my only real happiness.[1]
>
> — *Sketch for a Self-Portrait*

By "It," Berenson seems to be referring to an essential, all-pervasive field of life. For Berenson, arts's highest purpose is to produce such moments of unified perception in the viewer:

> In visual art the aesthetic moment is that flitting instant, so brief as to be almost timeless, when the spectator is at one with the work of art he is looking at, or with actuality of any kind that the spectator himself sees in terms of art, as form and color. He ceases to be his ordinary self, and the picture or building, statue, landscape, or aesthetic actuality is no longer outside himself. The two become one entity; time and space are abolished and the spectator is possessed by one awareness. When he recovers workaday consciousness it is as if he had been initiated into illuminating, exalting, formative mysteries. In short, the aesthetic moment is a moment of mystic vision.[2]
>
> — *Aesthetics and History*

Berenson clearly speaks from personal experience, describing the sense of unity he sometimes feels with a work of art.

Also see Berenson in Chapter 6 (God Consciousness).

ROMAIN ROLLAND
1866–1944 • FRANCE

■ *See biography on page 229.*

He cracked the very bounds of existence. He filled the sky, the universe, space. . . .

But that mystic exaltation was not the only experience he had of it: it recurred several times, but never with the intensity of the first. It came always at moments when Christophe was least expecting it. . . .

He rediscovered the world, as though he had never seen it. It was a new childhood. It was as though a magic word had been uttered. An "Open Sesame!" — Nature flamed with gladness. . . . Everything sang aloud in joy.

And that joy was his own. That strength was his own. He was no longer cut off from the rest of the world. . . .

He heard all these sounds and cries [of insects and trees] within himself. Through all these creatures from the smallest to the greatest flowed the same river of life: and in it he too swam. So, he was one of them, he was of their blood, and, brotherly, he heard the echo of their sorrows and their joys: their strength was merged in his like a river fed with thousands of streams. He sank into them. . . . Now everywhere he found infinite and unmeasured Being, now that he longed to forget himself, to find rebirth in the universe.[1]   — *Jean-Christophe*

Rolland patterned this novel's main character after himself. This passage describes the experience of unbounded awareness and refined perception, then rises to evoke Unity Consciousness. All the sounds Christophe hears seem to resound within him. He perceives "the same river of life" flowing through all creatures, himself included. He feels one with everything, finding "infinite and unmeasured Being," the universal underlying reality, in everything.

In another work he describes an experience he had near the Breithorn, a mountain in Switzerland's Matterhorn region:

There was a moment where my soul had left me to merge into the sparkling mass of the Breithorn. . . . Yes, as peculiar as this may seem, for several minutes, I *was* the Breithorn.[2]

■ *Also see Rolland in Chapter 5 (Cosmic Consciousness).*

H.G. WELLS
1866–1946 • ENGLAND

■ *H.G. Wells studied under T.H. Huxley at the Royal College of Science, then taught science until tuberculosis forced him to retire from active life for several years. When he was 25, the* Fortnightly Review *published one of his essays, launching a long and remarkably prolific career. Wells became famous at 29 when he wrote* The Time Machine, *and he maintained his renown with a long string of striking scientific fantasies. Alongside Jules Verne, Wells is regarded as the father of science fiction. His numerous books also include character studies, social criticism, history, and political and social comedy. He composed 156 works in all, and at least 20 films have been based on his books.*

It was soon after sunset. The summer holidays had just begun and he had gone for a long ramble towards Bray Island. . . .

He had watched many sunsets before, and here, he realized, was a very magnificent one indeed. He loved to watch sunsets. This had a distinctive vast simplicity. Slowly the sun burnt its way out beneath the cloud-bank, thrust it aside, turned it to red and purple, lit its ragged edges to dazzling gold and projected a fan of broadening bands of light and shade athwart the blue.

And as he watched these changes the miracle happened.

The sunset was there still, but suddenly it was transfigured. The weedy rocks below him, the flaming pools and runlets, the wide bay of the estuary shining responsive to the sky, were transfigured. The universe was transfigured — as though it smiled, as though it opened itself out to him, as though it took him into complete communion with itself. The scene was no longer a scene. It was a Being. It was as if it had become alive, quite still, but altogether living, an immense living thing englobing himself. He was at the very centre of the sphere of Being. He was one with it.

Time ceased. He felt a silence beneath all sounds; he apprehended a beauty that transcends experience.

He saw his universe clear as crystal and altogether significant and splendid. Everything was utterly lucid, and all was wonder. Wonder was in Theodore's innermost being and everywhere about him. The sunset and the sky and the visible world and Theodore and Theodore's mind, were One. . . .

If time was still passing, it passed unperceived, until Theodore found himself thinking like a faint rivulet on the melting edge of Heaven. This he realized quite clearly was the world when the veil of events and purposes was drawn aside, this was the timeless world in which everything is different and lovely and right. This was Reality.

> The sun sank into the contours of the island, softened in shape as though it were molten, broadened down to an edge of fire and was lost. The sky burned red and grew pale.
>
> Something was ebbing away from him, receding from him very rapidly, something he would, if he could, have retained for ever. The stupendous moment was passing, had passed, and he was back in the world of everyday. He was roused by the mewing of a seagull and trailing whisper of a faint breeze. . . .
>
> He turned his face homeward.
>
> He felt he had made some profound discovery. He had been initiated. He knew.
>
> But did he know? What was it he knew?
>
> He had no words for it. . . .
>
> The glow remained a living light in his mind for several days, albeit a fading glow, and then it became a memory. . . . It had seemed at first as though Heaven had revealed itself to Theodore in a personal appeal. Then later it was rather as though he had taken the universe unawares and for a few brief moments seen through it and down into it to its very heart.[1]   — *The Bulpington of Blup*

Theodore (the name means *gift from God*) experiences "complete communion" with the universe, now open and alive. He experiences everything as one. The sunset is glorious to begin with, but as his experience unfolds, he apprehends "a beauty that transcends experience," pointing to the refined perception of God Consciousness. "This was Reality," he says. "Heaven had revealed itself."

MARY AUSTIN
1868-1934 • UNITED STATES

American novelist and essayist Mary Austin wrote about American Indian culture and social issues. Born in Illinois, she moved with her family to California just after graduating from college. She spent 17 years studying Indian life in the Mojave Desert and then wrote about the detailed, first-hand knowledge she gathered. Her first book, The Land of Little Rain, *brought her immediate fame. The book describes the people, wildlife, vegetation, and spirituality of the area stretching from the High Sierra to the Mojave Desert of southern California. She wrote prolifically — novels, poems, plays, criticism. She coauthored a book with the photographer Ansel Adams. She actively defended the rights of women, Native Americans, and Spanish-Americans. A mountain in California is named after her, Mount Mary Austin, in the Sierra Nevada, nine miles from Independence, where she lived for many years. Her house in Independence is now a California Historical Landmark.*

I must have been between five and six when this experience happened to me. It was a summer morning, and the child I was had walked down through the orchard alone and come out on the brow of a sloping hill where there was grass and a wind blowing and one tall tree reaching into infinite immensities of blueness. Quite suddenly, after a moment of quietness there, earth and sky and tree and wind-blown grass and the child in the midst of them came alive together with a pulsing light of consciousness. There was a wild foxglove at the child's feet and a bee dozing about it, and to this day I can recall the swift inclusive awareness of each for the whole — I in them and they in me and all of us enclosed in a warm lucent bubble of livingness. . . .

How long this ineffable moment lasted I never knew. It broke like a bubble at the sudden singing of a bird, and the wind blew and the world was the same as ever — only never *quite* the same. The experience so initiated has been the one abiding reality of my life, unalterable except in the abounding fullness and frequency of its occurrence. I can recall, even as a child, leaving the companions of my play to bask in it, as one might abandon the shade to walk in the sun. There is scarcely any time in my adult life in which it can not be summoned; with more effort at some times than at others. It is furthest from me when I am most absorbed in the emotional reactions of personal existence, but never entirely out of reach. Often it seems to float like a bubble beside me, and in moments of abstraction and relaxation, it encloses me with ineffable warmth and light. . . . It is a force, a source of energy.

When I speak of warmth and light in this connection, these are analogies only. I see nothing with my eyes, feel nothing with my hands, hear nothing with my ears. [It] is *inside* me, a portion of my innermost deep-self functioning; as much a part of my constitution as the clapper is of the bell. . . . I am chary of using the term "subconscious" in this connection because I do not wish to confuse it with any of the operations of what we ordinarily call "mind" or "intelligence." As the brain is obviously not the seat of such experience, it can not be called mental. All that the intelligence can do is to account for and explain the experience.[1]   — *Experiences Facing Death*

"I in them and they in me and all of us enclosed in a warm lucent bubble of livingness" — a lovely evocation of Unity Consciousness. This experience, she declares, "has been the one abiding reality of my life."

MARTIN BUBER

1878–1965 • AUSTRIA, GERMANY, & ISRAEL

■ *See biography on page 146.*

On a gloomy morning I walked upon the highway, saw a piece of mica lying, lifted it up and looked at it for a long time; the day was no longer gloomy, so much light was caught in the stone. And suddenly as I raised my eyes from it, I realized that while I looked I had not been conscious of "object" and "subject"; in my looking the mica and "I" had been one; in my looking I had tasted unity. I looked at it again, the unity did not return.[1] — *Daniel: Dialogues on Realization*

Central to Buber's philosophy is the relation between self and world, *I* and *it*, *Ich* and *es*. Like Kant, he held that all objects in the world are merely thoughts in one's mind, with an implicit duality remaining between object and self. But here Buber seems to transcend that duality and experience unity. Though fleeting, the experience shows him that ultimately there is no subject and object, only the "one" underlying them both. He returns to this experience in another book:

O fragment of mica, looking on which I once learned, for the first time, that *I* is not something "in me" — with you I was nevertheless only bound up in myself; at that time the event took place only in me, not between me and you.[2] — *I and Thou*

■ *Also see Buber in Chapter 4 (Transcendental Consciousness).*

MORIHEI UESHIBA
1883–1969 • JAPAN

See biography on page 153.

Whenever I held a sword, I lost all sense of sword, opponent, time, and space; I was breathing in the universe — no, the universe was contained within me. One swing of the sword gathers up all the mysteries of the cosmos.[1]

The boundaries of ordinary life recede and are replaced by the experience of wholeness, totality, "the universe," which he experiences within him. For Ueshiba, the whole goal of Aikido is unity, oneness with the universe:

Aikido will come to completion when each individual, following his or her true path, becomes one with the universe.[2]

The secret of Aikido is to harmonize ourselves with the movement of the universe and bring ourselves into accord with the universe itself. He who has gained the secret of Aikido has the universe in himself and can say, "I am the universe."[3]

Also see Ueshiba in Chapter 4 (Transcendental Consciousness) and Chapter 5 (Cosmic Consciousness).

FRANKLIN MERRELL-WOLFF
1887–1985 • UNITED STATES

See biography on page 158.

At the time of the culminating Recognition I found myself spreading everywhere and identical with a kind of "Space" that embraced not merely the visible forms and worlds, but all modes and qualities of consciousness as well.... That totality was, and is, not other than myself, so that the study of things and qualities was resolved into simple self-examination. Yet it would be a mistake to regard the state as purely subjective. The preceding Recognition had been definitely a subjective penetration, and during the following month I found myself inwardly polarized to an exceptional degree. In contrast, the final Recognition seemed like a movement in consciousness toward objectivity, but not in the sense of a movement toward the relative world-field. The final state is, at once, as much objective as subjective, and also as much a state of action as of rest....

Speaking in the subjective sense, I am all there is, yet at the same time, objectively considered, there is nought but Divinity spreading everywhere.... The sublimated object and the sublimated self are one and the same Reality....

Yet there was no sense of being in a strange world. I have never known another state of consciousness that seemed so natural, normal, and proper. I seemed to know that this was the nature that

Reality must possess, and somehow, I had always known it. It rather seemed strange that for so many years I had been self-conscious in another form and imagined myself a stranger to this. It seemed to be the real underlying fact of all consciousness of all creatures....

I found myself so identical with all, that the last most infinitesimal element of distance was dissolved....

The full cycle of this final Recognition lasted for some hours, with the self-consciousness alert throughout the period. But the depth of the State developed progressively and at the final stage entered a peculiarly significant phase.... There finally arrived a stage wherein both that which I have called the Self and that which had the value of Divinity were dissolved in a Somewhat, still more transcendent. There now remained nought but pure Being.... No longer was "I" spreading everywhere through the whole of an illimitable and conscious Space, nor was there a Divine Presence all about me, but everywhere only Consciousness with no subjective nor objective element.[1]

— *The Philosophy of Consciousness Without an Object*

༄

Merrell-Wolff feels his consciousness expand, growing to an all-embracing totality he identifies as nothing other than himself. No matter where he looks, he finds the Self. The previous phase of the "Recognition" was inward, leading to him feeling "inwardly polarized," suggesting the witnessing experience of Cosmic Consciousness. In this "final Recognition" his consciousness overflows "toward objectivity." He finds himself identical with everything. All sense of distance dissolves, and subject and object become "one and the same Reality." No other state of consciousness seems as "natural, normal, and proper" as this.

▪ *Also see Merrell-Wolff in Chapter 4 (Transcendental Consciousness) and Chapter 5 (Cosmic Consciousness).*

VLADIMIR NABOKOV
1899–1977 • RUSSIA

Born to a wealthy, aristocratic family in St. Petersburg, Nabokov described his childhood as "perfect." His family spoke Russian, French, and English. Following the turbulence of the revolution, they moved to England, where he studied at Cambridge, then to Berlin. In 1940, to escape the war (he was Jewish), he moved to the US. Nabokov taught Russian literature at Wellesley and Cornell. He and his wife spent his last 16 years in Switzerland. He wrote his first nine novels in Russian, then became internationally famous as a master of English prose. He is regarded as one of the 20th century's most brilliant literary figures. He also had a distinguished career as an entomologist. While at Wellesley, he was curator of lepidoptery at Harvard's Museum of Comparative Zoology, and a genus of butterflies and a number of butterfly and moth species are named after him. He is also a noted composer of chess problems.

I confess I do not believe in time. I like to fold my magic carpet, after use, in such a way as to superimpose one part of the pattern upon another. Let visitors trip. And the highest enjoyment of timelessness — in a landscape selected at random — is when I stand among rare butterflies and their food plants. This is ecstasy, and behind the ecstasy is something else, which is hard to explain. It is like a momentary vacuum into which rushes all that I love. A sense of oneness with sun and stone. A thrill of gratitude to whom it may concern — to the contrapuntal genius of human fate or to tender ghosts humoring a lucky mortal.[1] — *Speak, Memory*

Nabokov describes a sense of timelessness, ecstasy, a sense of oneness with everything, and "a thrill of gratitude." Though he stops short of describing this experience in terms of the Self, his experience is a step in that direction.

HOWARD THURMAN
1899–1981 • UNITED STATES

■ *See biography on page 162.*

As a boy in Florida, I walked along the beach of the Atlantic in the quiet stillness. . . . I held my breath against the night and watched the stars etch their brightness on the face of the darkened canopy of the heavens. I had the sense that all things, the sand, the sea, the night, and I, were one lung through which all of life breathed.[1]
— *For the Inward Journey*

Even as a boy Thurman glimpsed the ultimate unity of life. This experience evidently grew as he moved through adulthood:

There is a unity that binds all living things into a single whole. This unity is sensed in many ways. Sometimes, when walking alone in the woods far from all the traffic which makes up the daily experience, the stillness settles in the mind. Nothing stirs. The imprisoned self seems to slip outside its boundaries and the ebb and flow of life is keenly felt. One becomes an indistinguishable part of a single rhythm, a single pulse. . . .

There is nothing new nor old, only the knowledge that what comes as the flooding insight of love binds all living things into a single whole. The felt reverence spreads and deepens until to live and to love are to do *one* thing. . . . To love is the act of adoration and praise shared with the Creator of life as the Be-all and the End-all of everything that is.

And yet there always remains the hard core of the self, blending and withdrawing, giving and pulling back, accepting and rejoicing, yielding and unyielding — what may this be but the pulsing of the unity that binds all living things in a single whole — the God of life extending Himself in the manifold glories of His creation?[2]

— "The Binding Unity," in *The Inward Journey*

When his mind becomes still and "the imprisoned self" expands beyond boundaries, Thurman experiences the underlying, unified wholeness of life all around him. He feels indistinguishably part of this single wholeness. Reverence and adoration expand to encompass everything. He finds his innermost self to be the divine, creative essence that pervades and unifies everything.

■ *Also see Howard Thurman in Chapter 4 (Transcendental Consciousness), Chapter 5 (Cosmic Consciousness), and Chapter 6 (God Consciousness).*

GOPI KRISHNA

1903–1984 • INDIA

■ *See biography on page 332.*

At 34, Gopi Krishna began to experience what he called "the awakening." While meditating, he says, "I felt myself expanding in all directions." This inner transformation continued until he was 49, then became a permanent dimension of his experience. Previously, he says, "I was living in this world thinking, seeing, perceiving in the same way as other people do." But at 49 he began living in "the world which is much higher, much more happy and which is totally apart from anything that we can know of the earth. It is the world of consciousness." Asked how he sees the world, Gopi Krishna responds:

> We know what all people perceive of this world. I can understand what you perceive of it, you can understand what I perceive of it. That is, this perception is uniform. Everyone has the same perception. But this other perception is different. In this other perception you do not see the world as a solid, real, objective creation. The real objective creation is consciousness. You see consciousness everywhere. You see the ocean as if it is consciousness everywhere. You see the ocean as if it is living; you see a mountain as if it is living; you see the sky as if it is living; you see the Earth as if it is living; you see life or consciousness everywhere.
>
> And this life or consciousness is not something which is really dead or which is something you can understand. It is unfathomable. It is wonder and every time you see it, you perceive it. The wonder grows deeper. I am never tired of sitting in quiet and reflecting on myself. I am never tired of looking at the sky. The sky, to me, does not appear as it appeared before my 34th year; it is so fascinating. It is such a beautiful vision that I would like to look at it for days and months on end. In other words, in the air a fountain of happiness — a new kingdom, I should say — is opened.
>
> This is probably what Christ meant when he said, "The Kingdom of Heaven is within you." This is the Nirvana of Buddha; and this is the state of Vada mentioned by the Sufi mystics. In fact, in this inactive state what we perceive is consciousness in its most magic form, in its glorious form, and not consciousness as a point looking through the eyes or hearing through the ears, but a consciousness which has its own channels and which knows that it is the master and not the slave of the material forces, which knows it is the creator. It is infinite: it is deathless.

> In this state one feels himself to be a king, he feels himself to be the master of what he sees. It is not the ego. I should say it is not the ego; it is the very condition of this consciousness. That is the reason why it is said that no mystic would change his state even for a kingdom. It is something so unique, so glorious, so elevating that I have no words to describe this state.[1]

Gopi Krishna describes experiencing everything around him as fundamentally made of consciousness. Thus he sees everything as living, as wondrous and beautiful, glorious and infinite, as if a "new kingdom" has opened.

In this next passage, Gopi Krishna gives a first-hand account of what he experienced. Sitting one evening at dinner, he becomes aware of "a marvelous phenomenon in progress in the depths of my being" that leads him into a state of "exaltation and self-expansion" similar to what he first experienced in 1937:

> The marvelous aspect of the condition, lay in the sudden realization that although linked to the body and surroundings, I had expanded in an indescribable manner into a titanic personality, conscious from within of an immediate and direct contact with an intensely conscious universe, a wonderful inexpressible immanence all around me. My body, the chair I was sitting on, the table in front of me, the room enclosed by walls, the lawn outside and the space beyond including the earth and sky appeared to be most amazingly mere phantoms in this real, interpenetrating and all-pervasive ocean of existence which, to explain the most incredible part of it as best I can, seemed to be simultaneously unbounded, stretching out immeasurably in all directions, and yet no bigger than an infinitely small point. From this marvelous point the entire existence, of which my body and its surroundings were a part, poured out like radiation, as if a reflection as vast as my conception of the cosmos were thrown out upon infinity by a projector no bigger than a pinpoint, the entire intensely active and gigantic world picture dependent on the beams

issuing from it. The shoreless ocean of consciousness in which I was now immersed appeared infinitely large and infinitely small at the same time, large when considered in relation to the world picture floating in it and small when considered in itself, measureless, without form or size, nothing and yet everything.

It was an amazing and staggering experience for which I can cite no parallel and no simile, an experience beyond all and everything belonging to this world, conceivable by the mind or perceptible to the senses. I was intensely aware internally of a marvelous being so concentratedly and massively conscious as to outluster and outstature infinitely the cosmic image present before me, not only in point of extent and brightness but in point of reality and substance as well. The phenomenal world, ceaselessly in motion characterized by creation, incessant change, and dissolution, receded into the background and assumed the appearance of an extremely thin, rapidly melting layer of foam upon a substantial rolling ocean of life, a veil of exceedingly fine vapor before an infinitely large conscious sun, constituting a complete reversal of the relationship between the world and the limited human consciousness. It showed the previously all-dominating cosmos reduced to the state of a transitory appearance and the formerly care-ridden point of awareness, circumscribed by the body, grown to the spacious dimensions of a mighty universe and the exalted stature of a majestic immanence before which the material cosmos shrank to the subordinate position of an evanescent and illusive appendage.

At the deepest moments of this experience, he explains,

[I]t assumed such an awe-inspiring, almighty, all-knowing, blissful, and at the same time absolutely motionless, intangible, and formless character that the invisible line demarcating the material world and the boundless, all-conscious Reality ceased to exist, the two fusing into one....²

Maharishi describes pure consciousness as ranging from infinity to a point, from larger than the largest to smaller than the smallest. Gopi Krishna describes the experience of that. More importantly, he perceives everything in terms of this unbounded, all-knowing, blissful consciousness.

■ *Also see Gopi Krishna in Chapter 6 (God Consciousness).*

KATHLEEN RAINE
1908–2003 • ENGLAND

■ *See biography on page 334.*

I lived in a world of flowers, minute but inexhaustible; the wild fragrance of thyme on the moor outside my grandfather's stone garden wall filled me to the brim with itself; it was the moor and the light high air and the thrilling bird-voice on the moor. In the shade of the north wall there was a bed of mint and cool pansies I was allowed to pick; and these flower-faces looked at me, each and every one greeted me in a here and now that had no beginning and no end. All were mine, whatever I saw was mine in the very act of seeing. To see was to know, to enter into total relationship with, to participate in the essential being of each *I am*.... Their beauty was, again, distinctly intelligible to me, was knowledge of essential meaning which, in living form, states itself more perfectly than any words can name it.[1] — *Farewell Happy Fields*

Later in the same work Raine describes a similar experience:

I remember the palpable stillness of that pine-plantation, the fir-cones lying where they fell on the carpet of needles muting sound in a place shunned by all life but that of the trees themselves, with their branches forever dying away below to form overhead an endlessly entangled dead thicket. In my fear of its dusk was also an exultation in the experience of the wood-in-itself, as another vista of awareness into which consciousness could flow. The circumference of consciousness was the circumference of the perceptible world; the world perceived was that consciousness, that consciousness the world: there was no distinction between seer and seen, knowledge and its object. All was mine, because myself.

Perhaps those called "nature-mystics" simply retain longer than others our normal consciousness, our birth-right, lost sooner or later, or returning only rarely; or it is we who return only rarely, and lose Eden by a turning away, a refusing to look. Our separate identity grows over us like a skin, or shroud.[2] — *Farewell Happy Fields*

Also see Kathleen Raine in Chapter 6 (God Consciousness).

PEACE PILGRIM
1908–1981 • UNITED STATES

> On January 1, 1953, a 44-year-old woman walked away from her ordinary life in California and set out on foot with the mission of calling national attention to the need for peace. Born Mildred Norman, she now called herself Peace Pilgrim. Over the next 30 years she crossed the country seven times, walking more than 25,000 miles. Everywhere she walked, she spoke about the need for inner and outer peace. She spoke to individuals, to church and college and civic groups, to radio and television audiences. Her speaking schedule became booked three years in advance, and her pilgrimage was chronicled by Swarthmore College.

I was out walking in the early morning. All of a sudden I felt very uplifted, more uplifted than I had ever been. I remember I knew *timelessness* and *spacelessness* and *lightness*. I did not seem to be walking on the earth. There were no people or even animals around, but every flower, every bush, every tree seemed to wear a halo. There was a light emanation around everything and flecks of gold fell like slanted rain through the air. . . .

The most important part of it was not the phenomena: the important part of it was the realization of the oneness of all creation. Not only all human beings — I knew before that all human beings are one. But now I knew also a oneness with the rest of creation. The creatures that walk the earth and the growing things of the earth. The air, the water, the earth itself. And, most wonderful of all, *a oneness with that which permeates and binds all together and gives life to all.* . . .

I have never felt separate since. I could return again and again to this wonderful mountaintop, and then I could stay there for longer and longer periods of time and just slip out occasionally.

The inspiration for the pilgrimage came at this time. . . .

I entered a new and wonderful world. My life was blessed with meaningful purpose.[1]

— *Peace Pilgrim: Her Life and Work in Her Own Words*

Peace Pilgrim experiences "*timelessness* and *spacelessness*," suggesting unbounded awareness and Cosmic Consciousness. She evokes the glorified perception of God Consciousness when she describes seeing halo-like light around everything. But dominating her experience is her sense of "the oneness of all creation," oneness with the all-pervading, all-nourishing transcendental field.

༃

I now know myself to be a part of the infinite cosmos, not separate from other souls. . . .

With inner peace I felt plugged into the source of universal energy, which never runs out. . . .

The feeling accompanying this experience is that of complete oneness with the Universal Whole. One merges into a euphoria of absolute unity with all life: with humanity, with all the creatures of the earth, the trees and plants, the air, the water, and even earth itself.[2]

— *Peace Pilgrim*

MARGIAD EVANS

1909–1958 • WALES

▪ *Novelist, poet, and artist Margiad Evans (originally Peggy Eileen Whistler) was born in Uxbridge, London. By the time she was 27 she had published three novels and was known for her exceptional descriptions of the natural world. One of her novels,* Country Dance, *recently rediscovered as a classic, was serialized by BBC Radio in 2006. Her Autobiography, written when she was 34, presents a fascinating picture of her life: she presents her journal entries over the course of a single year, showing us her inner life more deeply than had she narrated the facts of her life. The following passage appears in that work. Her manuscripts and papers are maintained by the National Library of Wales.*

I am twelve years old, reading on the window sill in the fruit shed. I am kneeling on a wicker hamper, and my knees are numb. The daylight is cold and cramped. Rubbing my hands I sniff the air. . . .

Suddenly I come awake with a rush of feeling. My crowded head feels suddenly clear, empty and airy as craning out of the window, I look hungrily around. This is real, I think, the colors, the brick, the ivy. It is as though something is going to be shown to me, once and forever. Things seem so *clear*, they seem to declare themselves aloud. My eyes have touch, my skin on which the air plays seems to be as glass through which I can look from every pore. Awake, awake to all, I know it is a rare moment, perhaps a beginning of a life separate from ordinary existence.

And yet what is there? The elm tree dropping leaves yellow golden all over, into the rainwater tank. They slide slowly downward on the point and settle with the faintest breath of sound on the olive surface. . . .

I lean out, sighing with the strange feeling in me. I can touch the cold sides of the tank; I feel as though I can touch with my mind the tree trunk, the hedge, the hurdle, even the farthest hill that I can see. What are all these familiar things saying so clearly? Why have I never seen them like this before? A moment ago they existed but quietly and without me. Now the leaves keep falling so queerly — queerly as though I had something to do with their falling. Something is happening which makes me able to say and know that it is true: "I shall remember this. I shall remember each vein on each leaf. I shall be able to see this whenever I want to, wherever I am!" . . .

Those are the eras, the visions, when the inner and outer meaning of the earth and sky and all that is in them, fit exactly the one over the other, when there is no slipping, no edge of obscurity, no groping. Ah, how impossible it is to keep those moments, to hold down more than a single instant that joy of being oneself contained in all one sees! Feeling with the leaves, traveling with the clouds, seeing back from the star, into one's own breast that is the very essence of perception. It is then that one can live for an instant in the million kinds of life which fumble for the sun, or in the stars which search through space for the earth to shine on, and on the earth, a spirit to enter. . . .

Sometimes I seem to know each separate thing while lost in the one, and then it is that I feel profoundly the almost palpable linking up of the universe. From life to life, from kind to kind, through the mind to the sky and out to each planet, the chain reaches. Ah, who can doubt it? . . . The air itself is felt to be woven of threads of life. Even in the darkness they are there. . . . Even in sleep it does not leave me — the least thrill in the cord recalls me, and in the morning it is there directly the day is felt on my eyelids. Yes, even before I wake, I come to it. . . . I believe in it. But I have failed to describe it, because... it is wordless and unimaginable and pictureless, an inhabitant unseen.[1] — *Autobiography*

Evans shifts to a state of heightened wakefulness with exceptional clarity of mind and senses. She feels intimately connected with everything. As the experience deepens, she feels "that joy of being oneself contained in all one sees," able "to know each separate thing while lost in the one," deeply feeling "the almost palpable linking up of the universe." She preserves this even in sleep.

IRINA STARR
1911-2002 • UNITED STATES

See biography on page 341.

[I]n some peculiar way my consciousness seemed to have expanded until it was present in a general way, far beyond even this planet. I was aware of no specific details of anywhere beyond my immediate vicinity, but I *was* a vastness somehow, that in no way contradicted or conflicted with my limited individuality. Subject and object had become one — had fused, in some way. There was the objective world around me, as six months before there had also been the "simple" vision, but now, as then, there was a vast "plus." I was both my individual self and in some greater way, "I" was also everything. Not the personal I, but the greater I AM. There were no longer two, only one, I AM....

I felt as though I had truly just been born, and I was to say many times in the days and weeks which followed, "I am finally all the way *here*!" My life previous to this time possessed a dream-like quality as I now saw it, and I could see where I had been only partly present; but now I had landed here with a magnificent thud and it was glorious beyond anything I could have imagined.

There were several phrases which kept running through my head during the next several days, each of them like a running refrain which would sound over and over. The first one was, I have lost my God, I have lost my God. . . . I had for a number of years been of an increasingly devotional turn, given to both voluntary and involuntary outpourings of adoration, as well as deep, mystical, contemplation of the Divine. There was now no longer any object of my devotion, for there was only I AM and it was not apart from me. I could not enter into an attitude of inner devotion any more than one of my eyes could turn back upon itself and view itself from outside. Not that I *was* God, personally — there was nothing of the inflation of the self in this at all — just that there was no longer any Thee and me, only I AM. In some strange way, this made me a little sad; while something immeasurable had been given, something precious had been taken in the process, and I could only hope that somehow, sometime, it would be restored at some other level. . . .

The final phrase which resounded within me was something I had read but not understood, long before, There is nothing more, nothing less, than a touch. This was of the simplest reality, for one thing was everything; the all was concentrated in the part; the ocean was in the drop. The relativity of things, the arbitrary values, dissolved in the ocean of Being, of Is-ness, and there really seemed nothing as important to say about anything as simply, it *is* — that encompassed everything that was, is, and could be. . . .

For three days I experienced the state of fusion, at-oneness, the merging of subject and object, and aside from the faint sadness at having "lost" my God, my joy was almost a living thing in itself.

Irina Starr beautifully describes the experience of unity. Notable is her initial sense that "I have lost my God" — because now "there was no longer any Thee and me, only I AM." Her experience recalls Maharishi's description of what happens as God Consciousness rises to Unity Consciousness, of how even the experience of God becomes experience in terms of the Self.

When she awakes on the fourth day, she feels that this state of awareness had begun to slip away. But something memorable happens that morning. Before leaving for work, she trips over a telephone cord and stumbles against a large, heavy ottoman, breaking one of her toes. Here is how she describes it:

> I need hardly point out how painful such an accident can be. I walked into the bathroom, leaned against the wall, and was overcome by such an ecstatic joy as defies my efforts to truly describe. I felt the intense pain in my toe and all the way up my leg — but my feeling was not of suffering. Instead, it was as though sensation itself were sheer joy of the most unimaginable kind, and there existed no real difference between what I ordinarily classified in my mind and feelings as pain and pleasure. The sensation which would have ordinarily registered as severe pain, was now neither pain nor pleasure, but a pure, spiritual, bliss. It was neutral as is electricity — the very current of life and quickening, pure, white, and intense. I laughed and exclaimed aloud in exultation — my ecstasy was nearly uncontainable, and had I been able to shout from the roof in sheer joy, it would have been scant release for the vibrant alive-ness I was experiencing. This in no way lessened my realization that here was an injury which must be cared for in an orthodox manner, even though I did not at the time realize the toe was broken, and it was not till several hours later that I went to a doctor for an X-ray.

The experience continued diminishing over the next several days.

This gradual blurring of one-ness continued until the seventh day found me back once more in the divided, relative state of consciousness. There had been three days of full fusion and three days of its gradual diminishment, and now the whole life-shaking experience was over. But I was not the same person I had been one short week before. Nor could I ever experience my world again but in a new and revelatory manner; I had emerged into a dawn-fresh and excitingly Life-filled dimension.[1] — *The Sound of Light*

▪ *Also see Irina Starr in Chapter 6 (God Consciousness).*

BERNADETTE ROBERTS
b. 1931 • UNITED STATES

▪ *Born to a devout Catholic family, Bernadette Roberts from early childhood had experiences she understood as revelations of God — of the divine within her and in the natural world around her. When she was 15 she entered the Carmelite order, where for the next ten years she lived a traditional life of seclusion and where her experiences continued growing. With her superiors' permission, she left the order, married, and raised four children, while her experiences continued developing. She began exploring other traditions to find parallels to her experience. The author of three books, she is honored as an outstanding modern-day contemplative.*

I was making a retreat with the Hermit Monks on the Big Sur. About the second day, toward late afternoon, I was standing on their windy hillside looking down over the ocean when a seagull came into view, gliding, dipping, playing with the wind. I watched it as I'd never watched anything before in my life. I almost seemed to be mesmerized; it was as if I was watching myself flying, for there was not the usual division between us. Yet, something more was there than just a lack of separateness, "something" truly beautiful and unknowable. Finally I turned my eyes to the pine-covered hills behind the monastery and still, there was no division, only something "there" that was flowing with and through every vista and particular object of vision. To see the Oneness of everything is like having special 3D glasses put before your eyes; I thought to myself: for sure, this is what they mean when they say "God IS everywhere."

I could have stood there looking for the rest of my life, but after a while, I thought it was all too good to be true; it was some hoax of the mind and when the bell rang, it would all disappear. Well, the bell finally rang, and it rang the next day and for the rest of the week, but the 3D glasses were still intact. What I had taken as a trick of the mind was to become a permanent way of seeing and knowing. . . .[1]

Reflecting on this experience, she writes:

> Though it could not be localized or found within any object of sight or mind, somewhere out-of-doors life was flowing peacefully, assuredly. On a bluff above the sea it revealed itself: life is not *in* anything; rather, all things are *in* life. The many are immersed in the One, even that which remains when there is no self, this too, is absorbed in the One. No longer a distance between self and the other, all is now known in the immediacy of this identity. Particulars dissolve into the One; individual objects give way to reveal that which is the same throughout all variety and multiplicity. To see this new dimension of life is the gift of amazing glasses through which God may be seen everywhere.[2] — *The Experience of No-Self*

Roberts recounts her experience of oneness, of utter lack of separation between herself and what she sees, of the unity underlying multiplicity, flowing, beautiful, divine. Commenting on this kind of experience, she says:

> This was the great reality. The relative mind cannot hold, grasp, convey, see, or even believe, that which has revealed itself. This

identity can never be communicated because it is the one existent that is Pure Subjectivity, and can never be objectified. This is the Eye seeing itself, and wherever it looks it sees nothing but itself.³

CAROL BURNETT
b. 1934 • UNITED STATES

Comedienne, actress, singer, dancer, and writer Carol Burnett first became successful on Broadway, then came to national attention on television in the 1950s. She went on to host a weekly variety hour, The Carol Burnett Show, which won 23 Emmy Awards and five Golden Globe Awards over its widely popular 11-year run. In 1969, she appeared on the first episode of Sesame Street, the first celebrity to do so. She has appeared in a dozen films as well as further stage work. She continues to star in films and television specials. She received Kennedy Center honors in 2003 and the Presidential Medal of Freedom in 2005. The following passage is from her memoirs.

I'm lying on the grass, looking at the sky and making up pictures with the clouds. It's hot, and I have on shorts and a sun top. I'm four. It's very still, and the clouds have stopped moving.

I don't know how long it was — it dawned on me only after it was all over — but for a time there, I was everything and everything was me. I've never felt that way since.

But it's possible.¹   — *One More Time*

Burnett may have been only four at the time, but her words here touch the highest reality of life, expressed in the *Upanishads* and other great texts, that we can experience the Self in all things and all things in the Self.

DAVID YEADON

b. 1942 • UNITED STATES

■ *One of the world's best travel writers, as well as a photographer and illustrator, David Yeadon is known for his books that explore the world's hidden corners, back roads, and unusual and exotic places. He has written more than 25 books, plus hundreds of feature articles as a regular travel correspondent for* National Geographic, National Geographic Traveler, *the* Washington Post, *the* New York Times, *and many other major American, European, and Asian travel magazines. The following passage is taken from an article Yeadon originally wrote for a Lands' End catalog, commissioned to travel to Inner Mongolia to describe the region where kashmir goats are raised and the herdsmen who raise them.*

And over the slow, easy days, we watched and became part of the steady rhythm of their lives. I sat crosslegged on the ground while the goats were combed for their precious white cashmere fleece. . . .

And in the silences my mind would fall silent and become as vast as the spaces around me. It seemed that everything I saw was actually within me, within an all-enveloping mind — an eagle, alone and soaring on spiralling air, a flash of light on quartz crystals, a wisp of wind rattling the grasses, the crack of rocks splitting in the dry, hard heat. I had never sensed the power of silence so intensely — each object seemed wholly distinct and full of individual energy and yet so totally a part of everything around me. And even my own body and spirit — for fleeting but seemingly infinite moments — became a part of the land in the vibrant wholeness of this magic place.

And so, eventually, we left — a lot more quietly and stilled in spirit than when we arrived. The herdsmen had allowed us to become part of their world for a brief period and to sense the slow, steady rhythms — the strong underpinnings of their lives.[1]

— *The Back of Beyond*

Yeadon's mind seems to become silent and unbounded, and from there he seems to experience everything as residing within him — within the Self.

CHAPTER 8

A Technique for Transcending

Systematically Cultivating Higher States of Consciousness

THE HISTORICAL GLIMPSES of higher states of consciousness we have looked at have two sides, seemingly contradictory. On one side, we find people describing how natural the experience is. It arrives simply and easily, without effort. Ionesco, for instance, writes, "I wondered how I had never before realized how easy this reality was to find and how easily I found myself in it." And it comes not only with ease but with intimate familiarity. Writes Kathleen Raine, "It seemed at the time not strange but infinitely familiar, as if I were experiencing at last things as they are, was where I belonged, where in some sense, I had always been and would always be." Franklin Merrell-Wolff puts it similarly: "There was no sense of being in a strange world. I have never known another state of consciousness that seemed so natural, normal, and proper. I seemed to know that this was the nature that Reality must possess, and somehow, I had always known it."

On the other side, such moments are exceedingly rare and, when they do come, fleeting. Lucy Maud Montgomery observes, "This moment came rarely — went swiftly." And such moments seldom come at will, she tells us: "She could never recall it — never summon it — never pretend it." Arthur Koestler makes the same point, saying, "It could never be voluntarily induced."

If this experience is so simple, natural, and beneficial, why is it so rare? Why can it not be summoned?

As we observed earlier, the mind is normally absorbed in a continuous stream of thoughts and perceptions, like a wavy ocean. Yet just as oceans can become calm, everyone's mind has the natural capacity to settle down, to transcend to the silent, wakeful state of Transcendental Consciousness. One simply needs a technique.

Many meditation and relaxation procedures are available today. While each may have value, it's important to understand that different techniques produce different effects.

Every experience we have, moment by moment, changes the brain. As you read these words, for example, your brain functions differently than if you were listening to someone reading them. Playing a piano activates and strengthens different brain circuitry than playing bridge. Studying for a degree in chemistry will promote different brain connections than studying art or history. This reflects a characteristic of the brain that neuroscientists call *neuroplasticity*.

Likewise, because different meditation techniques involve different mental procedures, they change brain functioning in different ways and consequently lead to different outcomes. Based on the changes in brain functioning, scientists have identified three basic categories of meditation (see the table opposite).

The first category of procedures, termed *focused attention*, keeps attention focused on an object and aims to cultivate a particular feeling or psychological state, such as loving-kindness and compassion or nonjudgmental awareness, and can help cultivate empathy. Practices in the second category (*open monitoring*), such as mindfulness meditation, keep attention involved in the monitoring process and aim to enhance awareness of moment-to-moment experiences. Mindfulness meditation offers a perspective for coping.

Meditation practices in both of these categories explore the nature of *waking* experiences. And they elicit exactly the types of brain functioning already known to result from these kinds of cognitive processing.

The Transcendental Meditation technique, on the other hand, doesn't

Category of meditation	Procedures involved	Source traditions	Style of brain functioning elicited
Focused attention	These procedures involve focused, sustained attention on an object or emotion — the classic concentration meditation.	Tibetan Buddhist, Zen Buddhist, and Chinese (Qigong) traditions.	Beta/gamma activity — seen during any active cognitive processing or control of the mind.
Open monitoring	These procedures involve dispassionate, non-evaluative monitoring of ongoing experience such as thoughts, breathing, or body sensations.	Buddhist (mindfulness and zazen), Chinese (Qigong), and Sahaja Yoga traditions.	Theta activity — seen when reflecting on mental concepts.
Automatic self-transcending	These procedures go beyond their own activity, enabling the mind to transcend the process of meditation and leading to the experience of pure consciousness.	The Transcendental Meditation technique. Also seen in a study of a Qigong meditator after 45 years' practice.	Frontal alpha-1 coherence — seen during transcendence, indicating the brain's executive control center is functioning in an integrated manner.

focus on a specific skill. Rather it allows one to effortlessly experience the fourth state of consciousness, Transcendental Consciousness. This brings us to the third category, *automatic self-transcending*, distinctive for its absence of focus and individual effort or control. These procedures elicit *frontal alpha-1 coherence*, meaning the frontal area of the brain, its executive control center or "CEO," is functioning in an integrated manner. This style of functioning is correlated with the experience of transcendence, pure consciousness.[1]

Maharishi similarly groups other procedures of personal development into two categories, corresponding to the first two categories just mentioned. Techniques of *contemplation* ("open monitoring") involve exploring an idea or feeling; this he likens to swimming around the surface of a lake. Techniques of *concentration* ("focused attention") involve trying to focus the mind on a thought or image or trying to clear the mind of thoughts — similar to treading water in one place. Both types of procedures involve effort and hold the mind on the conscious thinking level. But to reach the fourth state of consciousness, the mind must dive inward and transcend thought.

Because our interest here is transcendence, our focus in this and following chapters will be on the Transcendental Meditation technique, precisely because of its ability to transcend its own activity and elicit the experience of Transcendental Consciousness, the fourth state of consciousness — the regular experience of which promotes growth of still higher states of consciousness.

About the technique

The Transcendental Meditation technique is a simple, natural, and effortless procedure for transcending. It is practiced for 15 or 20 minutes twice daily while sitting comfortably with the eyes closed. Anyone can easily learn and practice it, even children, and more than six million people worldwide have done so, people of all ages, cultures, and religions. It is neither a religion nor a philosophy. It requires no change in one's beliefs, diet, or lifestyle. It prescribes no codes of behavior. Nor does it even require the belief it will work.

Where many other types of meditation involve concentrating on an idea or mental image, focusing on one's breathing, trying to still or "blank" the mind, or trying to be mindful of the present moment, the Transcendental Meditation technique differs in being effortless. It does not involve controlling the mind or trying to change one's breathing or relax the body. There is no contemplating of values or ideals, thinking positive thoughts, or examining feelings or beliefs.

How does it work? Every thought we experience, Maharishi observes, emerges from deep within the mind and undergoes a process of development before we experience it consciously. He compares this process to a bubble emerging from the sand at the bottom of a pond and rising upward.

Just as we see the bubble only after it reaches the water's surface, we

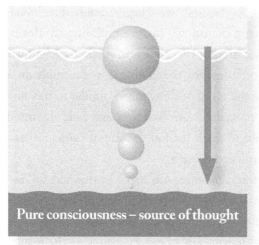

Pure consciousness – source of thought

experience thoughts only at the mind's surface, the conscious thinking level. We do not usually experience the earlier stages of thought or the source of thought.

In transcending, the mind moves in the opposite direction. The Transcendental Meditation technique allows the mind to settle inward, through less active states. Eventually one experiences the very faintest level of thought and, transcending even that, comes to rest beyond perceptions, thoughts, and feeling in the source of thought, the ocean of pure consciousness. As the mind settles down, the body also settles down and becomes deeply relaxed. This is Transcendental Consciousness, the fourth state.

How does the technique do this? It simply creates the proper initial condition. Once this condition is created, the mind settles inward by itself, spontaneously and naturally. The Transcendental Meditation technique allows the mind to follow what Maharishi calls its "natural tendency."

The natural tendency of the mind

Many people believe the mind is an unruly thing whose nature is to wander. After all, it moves from one perception, thought, or feeling to another, never seeming to rest. Anyone who has attempted to hold the mind fast (focusing on some noble thought or value) or to clear the mind of thoughts altogether knows the effort required, and any success is momentary.

Maharishi acknowledges that the mind is ever moving but observes that it moves purposefully, in a specific direction — always toward greater happiness, toward fields of what he calls "greater charm." For instance, if someone were to start playing your favorite song nearby, your mind would require no effort from you to move away from this page and toward the music. The mind remains in constant motion simply because no single thought or perception by itself offers sufficient happiness to give permanent fulfillment.

The field of pure consciousness offers in superabundance everything the mind seeks — it gives the experience of pure bliss, freedom from limitations, unbounded creativity and intelligence. The Transcendental Meditation technique simply allows the mind to remain awake and alert without being focused on a thought. Once this initial condition is created, the mind spontaneously settles inward.

Maharishi compares the process to diving — you just take the correct angle and let go, and the force of gravity does the rest. The Transcendental Meditation technique enables the mind to dive within. This is why anyone can meditate successfully, regardless of intellectual or emotional development. The procedure, using the very nature of the mind, is simple and automatic.

The natural tendency of the body

The Transcendental Meditation technique also enlists the natural tendency of the body. The body is constantly seeking to restore balance, to dissolve stress and eliminate impurities. This happens most effectively when we are resting, and the body rests most deeply when the mind is most settled. As the mind settles inward during Transcendental Meditation practice, the body enjoys exceptionally deep rest. Freed of the usual demands upon it, the body uses the opportunity to dissolve accumulated stress and fatigue.

Physiological stress impedes transcending. These imbalances and impurities create "noise" in the system. As the Transcendental Meditation technique enables the mind to transcend, in the same stroke it allows the body to dissolve the stresses that hinder transcending. The nervous system must become refined and purified, Maharishi explains, for higher states to develop.

Accelerating growth of higher states

In 1976 Maharishi introduced an advanced meditation practice, the Transcendental Meditation-Sidhi program, or TM-Sidhi program, which includes a technique called Yogic Flying. This program derives from the *Yoga Sutras*, an ancient Vedic text. *Sidhi* means *perfection* in Sanskrit. These simple, effortless techniques accelerate growth toward higher states of consciousness. More than 100,000 people worldwide have learned this program.

Whereas the Transcendental Meditation technique allows the mind to settle inward to the silent field of pure consciousness, the TM-Sidhi program trains the mind to *think and act* from this most powerful field. This makes the experience of pure consciousness increasingly stable and permanent. One's thought and action become powerful, more attuned with natural law, with increasing support of nature for success in daily life.

The Yogic Flying technique in particular has been shown to produce an upsurge in brainwave coherence. When people practice the TM-Sidhi program in groups, coherence spreads throughout the environment, neutralizing social stress and promoting social harmony and positivity. As we will see in the next chapter, this is reflected in reduced rates of crime, sickness and accidents, even reduced terrorism and warfare.[2]

The loss and revival of knowledge

The simple procedure to which Maharishi gave the modern name Transcendental Meditation was universally known and taught during the ancient Vedic civilization in India, he has explained. Gradually, however, due to the long lapse of time, this effortless and natural method of gaining enlightenment was largely lost. Vedic literature preserved descriptions of higher states of consciousness, but without a technique to develop higher states readily and widely, these descriptions became misunderstood and ignored.

Substitute procedures were invented, generally requiring effort, even austerity and renunciation. Because these procedures were more difficult and less effective, enlightenment came to be seen as impractical and difficult to achieve, at best the goal of the recluse but of no value in practical daily affairs.

But time is like a pendulum, Maharishi observes. Having swung to one extreme, it begins swinging back, and knowledge is eventually revived and re-established.[3] Maharishi has brought to light the core principles and practices of the Vedic tradition, particularly the techniques for gaining higher states of consciousness, and presented them in a modern scientific framework.

Maharishi always gave credit to his own teacher, Brahmananda Saraswati, or *Guru Dev* ("great teacher"), widely acknowledged in India as the embodiment of Vedic wisdom and enlightenment. During the last 13 years of his life, from 1941 to 1953, he held the position of Shankaracharya of Jyotir Math in the Himalayas, the chief seat of the Vedic tradition in India, a position that had been vacant for 150 years for want of an individual deemed worthy. He had gained the knowledge from his own teacher, who in turn gained it from his, and so on back through countless generations. The knowledge of enlightenment is thus never completely lost, Maharishi explains. In every generation there are a handful of people who preserve it and pass it on.

This knowledge is always given in the traditional method, through oral instruction from teacher to student, and always with utmost care to preserve its essential purity. Loss of purity means loss of effectiveness, and loss of effectiveness means loss of knowledge. When the knowledge of developing the full human potential of higher states of consciousness is lost, Maharishi explains, life falls out of accord with natural law and suffering inevitably results.

The knowledge embodied in the ancient Vedic tradition is universal, eternal, intrinsic to the nature of life itself, Maharishi explains — structured in the nature of consciousness and available to anyone who is fully awake. "The truth of Vedic wisdom," he wrote, "is by its very nature independent of time and can therefore never be lost."[4]

CHAPTER 9

༃

Meditation in the Laboratory

Modern Science Measures the Growth of Enlightenment

In the accounts of exalted experience we have reviewed, we have seen authors taking care to describe physiological and psychological changes occurring during their experience or afterward. Many describe experiencing a deep state of rest. St. Teresa, William Wordsworth, and Thomas Merton describe changes in their breathing. Wordsworth and Henry Miller sense changes in the blood. Franklin Merrell-Wolff recounts his feeling of greater youthfulness. Others describe mental and emotional changes — heightened clarity of mind, well-being, goodwill, appreciation for others.

These kinds of changes are measurable today. Physiologists can trace moment-by-moment changes in respiration, metabolism, blood chemistry, brain functioning. Psychologists can document changes in affective states. Even so, these glimpses of higher states have been so rare, random, and fleeting as to be impossible to study this way.

The Transcendental Meditation program made the fourth state of consciousness accessible to scientific study. Subjects could elicit the state at will.

Moreover, many subjects were available, they all practiced the same systematic procedure, and the procedure invariably produced measurable results.

Since the late 1960s, people who practice the Transcendental Meditation technique have been invited into laboratories at universities and research institutions all over the world. They have been asked to meditate with EEG leads attached to their scalps to monitor brain activity, with masks over their faces to monitor breath rate and oxygen consumption, with electrodes attached to their chests to gauge heart rate and function, with catheters in their arms to assess blood chemistry.

Even under such potentially distracting conditions, it was clear from the start that something remarkable happens during Transcendental Meditation practice, far different from simply resting with the eyes closed. Scientists found a wide constellation of changes, many never observed before — in brain functioning, blood flow, blood chemistry, muscle and blood cell metabolism, hormone production — and always toward rest and repair, balance and health.

The technique is effortless. It involves no attempt to control physiological functioning, as in biofeedback. Yet numerous changes take place as spontaneous byproducts of the simple, natural process of transcending, which even the person meditating scarcely notices.

Scientific research has now been conducted at 260 universities and research institutions in over 30 countries, yielding more than 380 peer-reviewed, published scientific studies and articles in more than 150 scientific and scholarly journals in a broad range of disciplines.

This must rank among the most significant research in all of science, for it documents dramatic new possibilities for human growth, giving us an increasingly clear picture of Transcendental Consciousness and Cosmic Consciousness.

We will now look at the highlights of the research on Transcendental Consciousness (changes during meditation) and then the cumulative changes in daily life, reflecting growing Cosmic Consciousness. As people's experiences of God Consciousness and Unity Consciousness become more stable and widespread, these states too will become the subject of research.

CHANGES DURING MEDITATION
Scientific research on Transcendental Consciousness, the fourth state

A transformation in brain functioning

If the brain were an orchestra, its range of sound would vary from that of the orchestra tuning up (a sleepy brain) to harmonious music (a wide-awake brain). The brain's electrical patterns are continuously changing. The degree of coordination among the parts depends on the state of consciousness.

During Transcendental Meditation practice — in fact, within the first 60 seconds of closing one's eyes — the brain switches to a dramatically more highly integrated, orderly style of functioning than is ordinarily seen even in a wide-awake brain. The various regions produce rhythmic, consistent, nonvarying electrical EEG (electroencephalographic) patterns.

This is the result of billions of underlying neurons — even those widely separated — now firing synchronously. Their independent activities, instead of canceling each other out, are now more unified, becoming visible as high amplitude activity in the alpha-theta frequency range. It's as if the different sections of the orchestra were now all exactly following the synchronous pace of the conductor. This phenomenon is called *EEG coherence*.

This elegant new mode of functioning, unique to Transcendental Consciousness, reflects functional coordination among different brain areas. The coherence between hemispheres suggests that the global, intuitive, spatial skills associated with the right hemisphere are integrated with the analytic, verbal skills of the left. The front-to-back synchrony — encompassing the regions governing higher-order thinking, and physical coordination, and perception — suggests heightened synchrony between thought and action, mind and body.

Most significant is the coherence at the front of the brain, the pre-frontal cortex. The frontal lobes comprise the brain's "CEO," its "executive control center," responsible for higher order thinking — empathy, moral reasoning, attention, problem-solving, decision-making, activities involving creativity and intelligence, and sensory-motor integration.[1]

The spreading of coherence during meditation

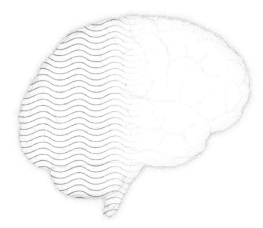

SIMPLE EYES CLOSED

When you close your eyes, the back of your brain almost immediately begins generating alpha-2 EEG waves (10.5-12 cycles/second). The rear brain processes incoming visual information (almost 60% of all sensory input). Closing your eyes shuts off this information stream, and the rear of the brain goes into an "idling" or resting state, as indicated by the alpha-2 and by a reduction of cerebral metabolic rate.

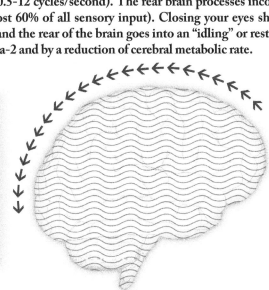

TRANSCENDENTAL MEDITATION

When you begin Transcendental Meditation practice, another highly coherent kind of alpha, called alpha-1 (7.5-10 cycles/second), begins in the frontal cortex and spreads rapidly to encompass the entire brain. Cerebral metabolic rate increases in the front of the brain.[2] This, along with the increased alpha-1, indicates restful alertness, inner wakefulness, and inner directed attention, a state distinctly different from ordinary rest. The frontal cortex is the brain's CEO or executive control center. This highly coherent alpha-1 EEG emanating from the brain's CEO to the entire brain is unique to the Transcendental Meditation technique.

This is your brain on transcendence

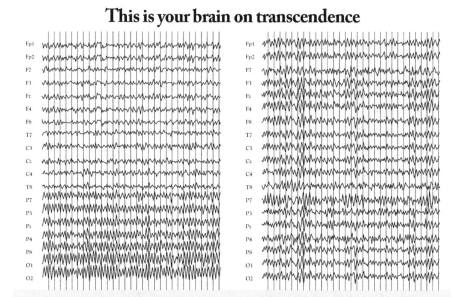

This chart shows 6 seconds of EEG during a simple eyes-closed period and during Transcendental Meditation practice. The 19 lines show the electrical activity from the front, center, and back of the brain (the top, middle, and bottom).

• EYES CLOSED — Notice the high rhythmical activity in the bottom tracings (back of the brain). This is an alpha-2 wave — seen when the eyes are closed and the brain is restful and awake, not receiving visual inputs.

• TRANSCENDENTAL MEDITATION — This tracing shows that during Transcendental Meditation practice, alpha-1 activity spreads throughout the brain — the entire brain is restfully alert. Notice also how the EEG tends to go up and down together. This is *coherence*: the different brain regions are functioning in synchrony. High alpha coherence in the frontal brain (the top right of the chart), the executive control center, typifies TM practice. Mental activity has come to rest while full alertness is maintained, indicating the total brain is awake and integrated.[3]

Other transformations in brain functioning

Elegant, highly coherent brainwaves are the signature EEG pattern of Transcendental Consciousness, the counterpart of the mind settling inward during Transcendental Meditation practice and becoming silent and unbounded. But this is only part of how brain functioning is transformed. Other changes also indicate a significant upgrading of function:

Increased blood flow to the brain

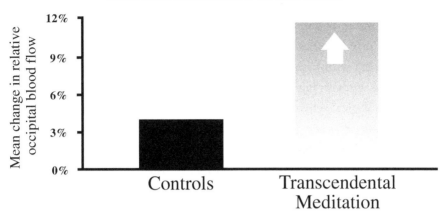

During Transcendental Meditation practice, blood flow to the brain increases significantly, indicating delivery of extra oxygen, glucose, and other vital nutrients needed for optimal function.[4]

■ *Blood flow to the brain increases significantly.* Brain blood flow is normally constant. The increased blood flow during Transcendental Meditation practice delivers extra oxygen, glucose, and other vital nutrients needed for optimal functioning, while more efficiently carrying away wastes.[4]

■ *The brain's transmission speed increases significantly.* Also normally constant, this increased speed enables faster information processing. This speed remains higher after meditation, as if the brain hardware has been upgraded.[5]

■ *Hidden brain reserves are awakened.* Research at the Moscow Brain Institute showed that when meditating subjects were given a stimulus, the brain responded in a more integrated and comprehensive manner, suggesting unused electrical pathways had opened and hidden brain reserves had been awakened.[6]

■ *The body increases its manufacture and release of serotonin,* the neurotransmitter associated with rest, repair, contentment, well-being, and health, even with leadership and success. Serotonin also helps the body adapt to change and helps regulate respiration, heart rate, blood pressure, and body temperature. Low manufacture and release of serotonin is linked with a host of health and behavior problems, from depression to overt aggression and suicide.[7]

Profoundly deep physical rest

When scientists began studying what happens during Transcendental Meditation practice, they discovered something unusual — low physiological activity coupled with high alertness. In the waking state, physiological activity and alertness are both high, while in sleep they are both low. The combination of low physiological activity and high alertness had not been seen.

Scientists described this condition as a *wakeful hypometabolic state* (*hypo*, the opposite of *hyper*, means *low*). It was on this basis that they announced the discovery of a fourth major state of consciousness, distinct from waking, dreaming, and deep sleep.[8] Maharishi gave the state a simpler but equally descriptive name — *restful alertness*.

The Transcendental Meditation technique brings exceptionally deep physiological rest. At whatever level of physiology scientists have investigated, they have found a rapid downshift to a profoundly restful state. For example:

■ *Breath rate declines*, significantly more than just sitting with eyes closed. The body may become so restful that breathing may become momentarily suspended. In some experiments, subjects were asked to press a button just after they had transcended most deeply. At these times, their breathing was also quiescent and brainwave coherence was highest. These periods occurred naturally, with no faster rate of breathing afterward, as happens after holding the breath.[9]

■ *The autonomic nervous system becomes more relaxed and stable*. This system, normally beyond conscious control, is your body's automatic pilot, keeping your heart, lungs, organs, glands, and other systems working and maintaining internal stability. Under stress, it can become overexcited, creating anxiety and tension. But during meditation it quickly settles down and, afterward, remains more relaxed and stable and recovers more quickly from stress.[10]

■ *The muscles become deeply relaxed*, far more so than during ordinary rest. But deep rest is only the beginning. Muscle tissues normally burn fat and carbohydrates to release energy, consuming oxygen and producing carbon dioxide. But during meditation a remarkable transformation occurs: muscle tissue consumes less oxygen and stops creating carbon dioxide.[11]

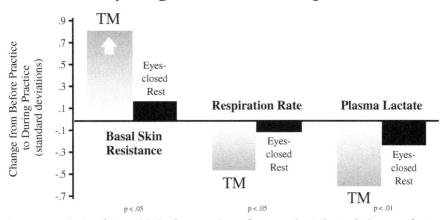

Physiological indicators of deep rest

A meta-analysis of 31 published research studies on physiological changes during Transcendental Meditation practice found evidence of profound relaxation — significant decreases in basal skin conductance, respiration rate, and plasma lactate levels — compared with control subjects who rested with eyes closed. These physiological changes occur spontaneously, as the mind effortlessly settles to the state of restful alertness, Transcendental Consciousness. Meta-analysis is the preferred scientific procedure for drawing objective conclusions from large bodies of research.[12]

■ *The stress hormone cortisol drops sharply*, more than 50% on average, while eyes-closed rest brings little or no change. Cortisol, pumped into your bloodstream by your adrenal glands, primes you for action when you are under stress. But chronic stress keeps your cortisol escalated, ratcheting up your blood pressure and promoting aging and disease. Low cortisol, in contrast, reflects reduced stress and increased relaxation.[13]

■ *Blood lactate declines sharply*, much more so than during eyes-closed rest. High levels of lactate (lactic acid), a waste byproduct of metabolism, correspond with anxiety, tension, and high blood pressure. This finding indicates the body is resting deeply and metabolizing more efficiently.[14]

■ *Even the red blood cells become deeply relaxed*. Their metabolic rate drops significantly, signaling a downshift to a state of rest and repair and a slowing of the aging process at the cellular level. This is especially notable because physiologists had thought red blood cells' metabolic rate never changed, even during sleep. But this finding posed a mystery. Unlike the heart, lungs, and muscles, where the switch to a more restful state might be explained by their being hard-wired to the brain, each red blood cell is a separate living and breathing organism floating freely through the circulatory system. What causes them to shift to a restful state? Researchers speculated that in Transcendental Consciousness the body may produce more of some as yet unidentified hormone or other circulating substance that brings rest to the entire system.[15]

LONG-TERM CHANGES
Scientific research on growing Cosmic Consciousness, the fifth state

---

What happens when you experience this deep, restfully alert, integrated state of Transcendental Consciousness twice each day? A large body of research has investigated this. Here are some of the most important findings:

Continuing transformation in brain functioning

■ *High brainwave coherence outside of meditation* — With regular transcendence, the brain becomes increasingly accustomed to the coherent, integrated style of functioning and begins to maintain this coherence even during daily activity.[16]

One study looked at two groups of people with an average age of 19. One group had been meditating a year or less, the other group about nine years on average. During meditation, both groups showed high brainwave coherence — the EEG patterns for both groups were virtually identical. The big difference was that the longer-term meditators showed this same high coherence outside of meditation as well. They also reported clearer experiences of witnessing sleep, a subjective sign of growing Cosmic Consciousness.

This study showed that when one learns the Transcendental Meditation technique, brainwave coherence during meditation is high from the start — the technique is quickly mastered and there is no "practice effect" with time. Whether you've experienced Transcendental Consciousness ten times or 10,000 times, the brainwave pattern is about the same. What does increase over time is EEG coherence throughout the day, suggesting the brain is using more of its potential and the fourth state of consciousness is becoming integrated with the waking, dreaming, and sleeping states.[17]

Frontal EEG coherence

Coherence in the brain's executive control center reaches a high level after two months of Transcendental Meditation practice. Then this coherence becomes part of the ongoing EEG signature during tasks. These computer-generated drawings illustrate alpha-range coherence. The lighter lines show coherence (communication) between the two linked brain areas of about 70%, the heavier lines coherence of 80% or higher (100% is perfect coherence). The more effectively the various brain areas communicate, the better the brain performs.[18]

Before learning to meditate

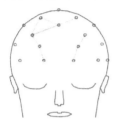
Eyes-closed rest

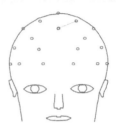
During challenging computer task

After 2 months of Transcendental Meditation practice

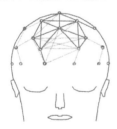
During meditation

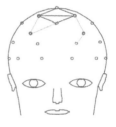
During challenging computer task

After 7 years of Transcendental Meditation practice

During meditation

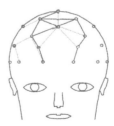
During challenging computer task

■ *Increased power of attention* — Other research, looking at changes in the brain's electrical potential at the scalp (called *contingent negative variation*), shows Transcendental Meditation participants have greater power of attention than the general population, a stronger and richer background of awareness, and greater processing power, indicating a more fully developed brain — and the longer they have been meditating, the greater these values become.[19]

■ *A more flexible and dynamic brain* — When you engage in analytic tasks, your brain's left hemisphere becomes more active, while during spatial tasks, your right hemisphere dominates. This is called *lateralization*. Transcendental Meditation participants show greater symmetry between hemispheres during meditation, indicating enhanced communication between brain areas. But afterward they show greater lateralization during analytic and spatial tasks. This means that, depending on the task, the appropriate hemisphere responds more flexibly and dynamically.[20]

■ *Unique brain functioning during sleep* — A key marker of Cosmic Consciousness is experiencing pure consciousness outside meditation. When one experiences the continuum of deep inner wakefulness during sleeping and dreaming, it is called *witnessing sleep*. Examining the EEG of long-term TM participants who reported witnessing sleep consistently, researchers found that subjects displayed a state never seen before during sleep:

- a unique dual pattern of brain functioning — the delta brainwaves typical of deep restorative sleep but also the theta/alpha brainwaves that characterize the inner wakefulness of Transcendental Consciousness
- unusually low muscle tone, indicating increased inner alertness
- a higher density of rapid-eye movements during REM periods — associated with heightened intelligence and development.[21]

This research confirms that the unique experiences associated with Cosmic Consciousness are based on refinement of physiological functioning. It also suggests that if we can experience the pure wakefulness even during the extreme nonwakefulness of deep sleep — if we can experience Transcendental Consciousness 24 hours a day — we may be able to perform at a significantly heightened level of intelligence, creativity, and happiness.

Higher brain integration and world-class performance

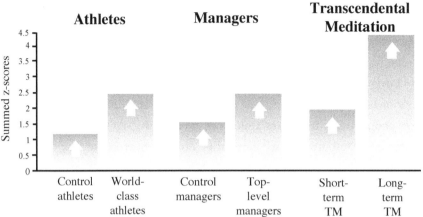

See discussion below. These studies used a brain integration scale consisting of frontal EEG coherence, alpha relative power, and brain preparatory response.[22] "Short-term TM" — subjects' average practice was 7 years; 2/3 also practiced the advanced TM-Sidhi program. "Long-term-TM" — 24 years average practice; all also practiced the TM-Sidhi program, and all reported witnessing sleep.[22]

Integrated brain functioning and superior performance

What distinguishes world-class athletes from athletes the next level down? Normally one would look for differences in experience, training, and motivation. Recent research studies in Norway looked at brain functioning.

The research compared professional athletes who placed in the top ten in the Olympics, world games, or national games for three consecutive years with control athletes who competed at the top level but did not place in the top 50% in championships. The athletes were matched for gender, age, and sport. The finding: the world-class performers displayed higher levels of brain integration.

The researchers then examined top-level managers — independently selected from private and public sectors, who had expanded their businesses multiple times or reversed the fortunes of failing businesses and who were also known for being ethically and socially responsible. The researchers also tested individuals who worked at middle and lower levels, matched for gender and type of organization. The result was the same. The top-level managers scored higher in brain integration — they displayed "world-class" brain functioning.

The top athletes and managers also showed higher levels of moral reasoning (known to be correlated with brain functioning) and reported more frequent peak experiences (moments of intense happiness and peak performance).

These athletes and business leaders did not practice the Transcendental Meditation technique. By some biological luck of the draw, their brain functioning was just more integrated than most other people's.

Long-term Transcendental Meditation participants showed far higher levels of brain integration.[22] This does not mean that long-term TM practice turns people into world-class athletes or executives, only that people will bring greater brain resources to whatever they do. We now know that whatever its level of coherence, brain functioning becomes increasingly integrated with regular experience of Transcendental Consciousness.

Unprecedented human development

As children grow, they develop such cognitive values as intelligence, creativity, moral maturity, and field independence. This development normally levels off in the mid-teens. It can be haphazard, and not everyone reaches the same level by the time this growth plateaus. And these values tend to decline in older age.

A large body of research indicates that with regular Transcendental Meditation practice these values grow significantly — the practice "unfreezes" human development. This is an unprecedented scientific finding, for despite extensive research, no previous strategies have succeeded in accomplishing this.

This growth is rapid, holistic, and cumulative. Significant gains in intelligence (IQ), creativity, and field independence have been measured within just a few months of learning the technique. All domains of cognitive development grow, and there is balanced growth within domains.

■ *Multiple forms of intelligence increase significantly* — not only IQ but creative, experiential, contextual, practical, and physiological intelligence. The longer subjects have been meditating, the greater the gain. This finding is vitally important: intelligence is at the root of all problem-solving — and, reciprocally, lack of fully-developed intelligence is at the root of all problems.[23]

■ *Moral maturity develops significantly* with Transcendental Meditation practice. Moral maturity refers to our sense of right and wrong, the degree to which we consider how our actions affect others. Young children base their actions on

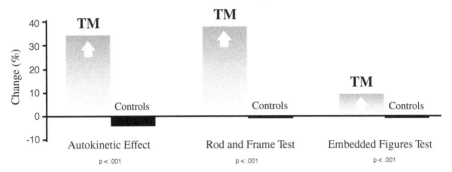

Increased field independence

Subjects were given three measures of field independence, then randomly assigned to one of two groups — a control group and a group that learned the Transcendental Meditation technique. Three months later, all subjects took the tests again. The Transcendental Meditation group displayed significantly increased field independence compared with the control group.[24]

gaining reward or avoiding punishment. As they mature, they become less self-centered, more apt to consider their effect on others. At the highest stages of moral development, one takes the whole society, even the world, into account.[24]

■ *Field independence increases significantly.* This refers to the ability to maintain broad comprehension (synthetic thinking) while focusing sharply on details (analytic thinking). People with high field independence have a stable internal frame of reference. They are more self-sufficient, less dependent on their physical and social environment or *field*. They can focus attention without being distracted by the surroundings. Highly field-independent people tend to be highly creative and intelligent and better able to think for themselves, better able to take another person's viewpoint yet less easily persuaded to do something wrong. The growth of field independence, which has been measured within a few months of Transcendental Meditation practice, indicates an awakening of deeper, more silent, more stable levels of the mind.[25]

■ *Other mental capacities improve as well* — short-term and long-term memory and learning ability, for example. Among college students, learning ability improved significantly after just two weeks of Transcendental Meditation practice, and the more difficult the material, the better they performed. Academic performance (GPA) also improves significantly.[26]

Toward optimal health — awakening the body's inner intelligence

Study after study has shown that when people experience the fourth state of consciousness regularly through the Transcendental Meditation program, they become healthier. Here are some examples from the research literature.

Balanced and finely-tuned physiology

▪ *Greater relaxation outside of meditation* — Like coherent brain functioning, the more relaxed style of physiological functioning of Transcendental Consciousness also carries over from meditation into daily life. The autonomic nervous system remains more stable, respiration and heart rates remain lower, and cortisol and blood lactate levels remain lower — all signs of better health.[27]

▪ *Healthier response to stress* — With regular meditation, studies show, one reacts to stress with greater calm and stability and recovers from stress more rapidly. One's body becomes simultaneously more stable and more adaptable, able to eliminate accumulated stress and prevent new stress from accumulating.[28]

▪ *Increasingly vibrant and responsive nervous system* — Reaction time grows faster.[29] Motor reflexes and motor neurons respond more quickly, and muscles respond faster to stimulation from neurons, even after just a few weeks of Transcendental Meditation practice.[30] Nerve cells recover more quickly from each input and can respond more quickly to the next one.[31] Perceptual abilities improve — hearing, near-point vision, perceptual organization, and more.[32] Even athletic ability improves.[33] On the whole, your nervous system enjoys a greater state of integration when it's resting — then responds to outer demands more quickly, intensively, and effectively — and then returns more quickly to its state of internal balance and rest.

Improved cardiovascular health

Cardiovascular disease claims more lives each year worldwide than any other disease — 2,200 deaths a day in the US, or one every 39 seconds, accounting for nearly 25% of all deaths. Some 82 million people in the US suffer from some form of cardiovascular disease. Modern medicine has failed to cure or curb cardiovascular disease or even identify the cause. It has succeeded only in identifying the risk factors. Alternative treatments relieve symptoms but likewise offer no cure.

Since the early 1990s, the US government's National Institutes of Health (NIH) has funded some $26 million in research studies on the Transcendental Meditation program and cardiovascular disease at universities around the US. These rigorously controlled studies, greeted by national and international publicity, show that the program can help prevent and even reverse the damaging effects of this devastating disease, without any change in diet or exercise.

▪ *Reduced high blood pressure* — In study after study, the Transcendental Meditation technique has proven as effective as hypertensive drugs in reducing hypertension — but less costly, with higher patient compliance, and without the negative side-effects of drug treatments.[34]

▪ *Reduction in other major risk factors for heart disease* — including cholesterol and lipid peroxides, metabolic syndrome, smoking, alcohol abuse, psychological stress, and socio-environmental stress.[35]

▪ *Reduction in free radicals*, the toxic, unstable waste molecules that attack other body cells, leading to many common diseases and accelerating the aging process.[36]

▪ *Reversal of damages of heart disease* — Transcendental Meditation practice has been shown to actually reverse *atherosclerosis* (clogging of the arteries), the cause of stroke and heart attacks. It has been shown to reverse *left ventricular hypertrophy*, the dangerous condition of enlarged heart muscle resulting from working harder to pump blood through clogged arteries. And it has led to improved capacity in patients with *congestive heart failure*, which claims 300,000 lives annually — a number that has risen steadily over the past decade despite medical advances.[37]

Reversal of aging, longer and better life

In addition to your chronological age you also have a *biological age*, the age of your body as determined by various physiological measures. Normally these two ages are about the same. But people in their 50s who had been meditating for five or more years had an average biological age 12 years younger than their chronological age, independent of diet and exercise — and the longer subjects

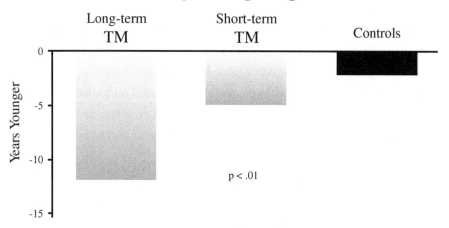

This study found that, as a group, long-term Transcendental Meditation participants (those practicing the technique more than five years) were physiologically 12 years younger than their chronological age (measured by lower blood pressure, better near-point vision, and better auditory discrimination). Short-term TM participants were physiologically five years younger than their chronological age. The study statistically controlled for the effects of diet and exercise.[38]

had been meditating, the younger their biological age. Some subjects tested were up to 27 years younger.[38]

A study conducted in a residential home for the elderly found that subjects who practiced the Transcendental Meditation technique lived 23% longer than subjects in randomly-assigned control groups who practiced either mindfulness training (designed to culture alertness) or progressive muscle relaxation (a common relaxation procedure) or who received the usual care. Besides living longer, the meditating group reported *feeling* younger, and indeed, objective measures showed they had greater mental clarity, better mental health, and lower blood pressure.[39]

An identical result came from a similarly designed comprehensive NIH-funded study of older subjects with mild high blood pressure, tracking them for up to 18 years. Those practicing the Transcendental Meditation technique lived 23% longer than others and were 30% less likely to die from cardiovascular disease and 49% less likely to die from cancer.[40]

A landmark NIH-funded study, eliciting massive publicity, showed a striking *48% reduction* in risk for mortality, heart attack, and stroke over a five-year period among people who already have coronary heart disease when they learn the Transcendental Meditation technique, compared to controls participating in a health education program. This study showed that the TM technique has long-term effects on important objective measures in patients with serious health problems, a finding that has not been demonstrated for any other meditation type.[41] Imagine the sales of a pill that produced this result.

How do we explain these findings of improved health? A major factor is reduced stress. Stress causes or contributes to more than 90% of all disease, and the uniquely deep rest elicited by the Transcendental Meditation technique allows the body to dissolve stress with unparalleled efficiency.

But dissolving stress is only part of the story. Transcending integrates brain functioning and resyncs physiological functioning. It connects mind and body to their source in pure consciousness, enlivening what Maharishi calls the body's *inner intelligence* and restoring balance. In this view, all disease has its root in imbalance — so establishing physiological balance is fundamental to treating and preventing disease. Transcending fundamentally balances mind and body.

Holistic personality growth

Scores of studies have demonstrated that regular transcending through Transcendental Meditation practice leads to rapid, balanced, holistic personality development and to a reduction in negative personality traits.

■ *Self-esteem grows significantly.* High self-esteem, many experts believe, forms the foundation of psychological health and success and fulfilling personal relationships. It has proven difficult to increase self-esteem after early childhood. But self-esteem naturally grows with regular transcendence, regular experience of the unbounded inner Self.[42]

■ *Self-actualization increases significantly.* Self-actualization is the most well-accepted measure of psychological health and development of potential. Highly self-actualized people have high self-esteem and emotional maturity, high aspirations and ideals, and high moral standards. They are more open and sensitive, more creative and successful. Living more fully in the present, they think and act more spontaneously and naturally, without anxiety and stress. With a broad, positive perspective on life, they easily form close, fulfilling relationships.

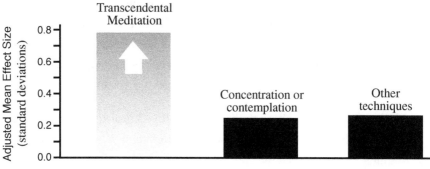

Increased self-actualization

Statistical meta-analysis of all available research (42 independent study results) indicated that Transcendental Meditation practice increased self-actualization by about three times as much as procedures of contemplation, concentration, or other techniques. The Transcendental Meditation subjects improved significantly on all 12 subscales compared with controls over an average three-month period, indicating balanced growth of all aspects of personality.[43]

The problem is, psychological maturation is usually slow and haphazard and typically ceases in the late teens. No one has discovered any reliable method of boosting self-actualization. Self-actualized people, moreover, are rare — only about two of every 100 people reach the highest levels.

Research on the TM program shows that even among adults, whose development has plateaued, self-actualization can be increased. This growth is quick (significant growth measured in as little as six weeks), comprehensive (improvements in every quality the tests measure), and cumulative (two- to four-year meditators showing almost double the growth of one- to two-year meditators and long-term meditators often scoring at the top level).[43]

Abraham Maslow, who brought the concept of self-actualization to prominence, discovered that highly self-actualized people tend to have "peak experiences." Even a single transcendental experience, he believed, could promote self-actualization and psychological health.

■ *Holistic self-development increases to unprecedented levels.* For this study, researchers used a measure called *ego development*, which assesses the maturity of the whole person — mental, emotional, social, and moral. Such development ordinarily plateaus by about age 18 and does not change thereafter; even a college education has no effect on it. As with self-actualization, only a tiny percentage, about 3%, score in the top two of the nine stages on this measure.

To further strengthen the study, the researchers added measures of moral maturity and interpersonal warmth. They then tested groups of students at four universities, including Maharishi University of Management in Iowa, where everyone practices the Transcendental Meditation technique.

At pre-test, 1% of the students at other schools scored at the highest two levels — in the range of the national norm. At Maharishi University, 9% did so; these students had been meditating an average of four years.

Ten years later, the same subjects, now out in the working world, were given the same test. Those from the other universities had not changed. But the scores from the Maharishi University graduates were astounding. An unprecedented 38% scored at the two highest levels of ego development. This group had also increased substantially in moral maturity and interpersonal warmth. Such growth had never been seen before.[44]

Transcendental Meditation practice "unfreezes" ego development and moral reasoning even in incarcerated felons, whose level of development has been halted at an immature level. These results show we now have a way to promote holistic self-development even in adulthood.[45]

■ *Anxiety declines significantly.* Anxiety is the most widespread of all mental disorders. It may stem from a specific event or may be a general condition, with no obvious cause, resulting in chronic worry, restlessness, and tension. At greatest risk are women, young people, African Americans, and those of lower socioeconomic status. Regulating anxiety is critical to health. Study after study has shown the Transcendental Meditation program's effectiveness in reducing anxiety — even in prisons and psychiatric settings and with such challenging forms of anxiety as post-traumatic stress disorder.[46]

■ *Interpersonal relationships become increasingly rich and satisfying*, measurable after just two months of Transcendental Meditation practice. People develop a more positive view of human nature and greater ability to appreciate others, along with greater sociability, greater tolerance, and fewer feelings of social inadequacy. Successful relationships depend on being strong within oneself and capable of giving — the natural result of growth of consciousness.[47]

As brain functioning becomes increasingly coherent, all these other values improve as well

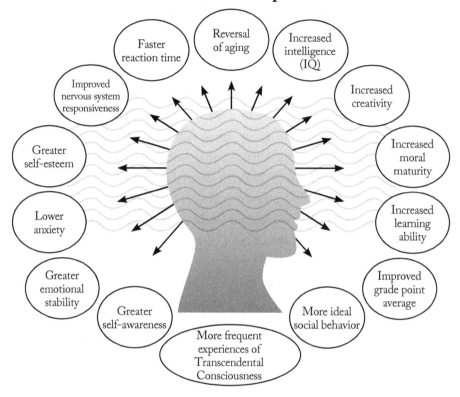

■ *Correlations with coherent brain functioning* — These findings of growth in every dimension of life are highly significant in their own right. But out of this research has come another remarkable discovery. Many of these findings have a common denominator — they are significantly correlated with brainwave coherence. Coherent brain functioning, in other words, lies at the center of this cognitive, psychological, and emotional development.

This means the higher your EEG coherence, the higher your IQ, the greater your field independence, the greater your moral maturity, etc. It also means each of these values is correlated with the others. No one had previously known that high intelligence is correlated with fast nerve cell recovery time or that moral development has its basis in coherent brain functioning. And all these values are correlated with clarity of experience of Transcendental Consciousness.[48]

This gives us insight into peak performance and genius in any area. The source of superior performance lies in expanded consciousness and integrated brain functioning. Some people are more highly developed than others in these values — but now they can be systematically cultivated in anyone.

Addressing urgent public policy challenges

Health care — improved health, reduced costs

A startling number of Americans suffer from poor health — 50 million from high blood pressure, 7 million from heart disease, 33 million from chronic disabling conditions, 18 million from alcohol-related health problems. Altogether 40% of Americans have at least one chronic disease — a disease, by definition, with no cure. Health care costs are soaring, straining the national economy. US health care expenditures surpassed $2.3 trillion in 2008, more than three times the $714 billion spent in 1990, and over eight times the $253 billion spent in 1980. No program has systematically reduced costs.

And incredibly, the fourth leading cause of death in the United States is modern medicine itself, with all its hazardous side effects.[49]

People who practice the Transcendental Meditation technique are healthier and require less health care than the general population. A study using Blue Cross health insurance statistics showed they require significantly less medical treatment in every disease category recorded. They were hospitalized less than half as often, had major surgery 76% less often, and had less than half the number of doctors' visits. The difference was greatest for people over 40, the high-risk group — meditators were hospitalized 70% less often.[50]

A series of studies using the Canadian government's insurance statistics yielded similar results. The data showed that after people learned the Transcendental Meditation technique, their health care costs dropped an average of 10% per year. Those aged 65 years and older who practiced the TM technique had a 70% drop in health care costs over five years. Those with consistently high health care costs experienced a 28% cumulative decrease in physician fees after five years of TM practice.[50]

These findings are extraordinary because no other approach has been able to reduce health care costs in the long run. They suggest a way to rescue

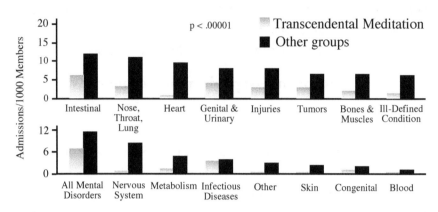

Decreased incidence of disease

This study looked at Blue Cross health insurance statistics over a 5-year period for more than 2,000 people throughout the US who practiced the Transcendental Meditation and TM-Sidhi programs — and compared them with other groups matched for age, gender, and insurance terms. The TM participants needed much less medical treatment in all 16 disease categories — including 87% less hospitalization for heart disease, 55% less for cancer, 87% less for nervous system disorders, and 73% less for nose, throat, and lung problems.[51]

Medicare and Medicaid without reducing benefits or raising taxes — simply add coverage for learning the Transcendental Meditation technique.

Education — reduced stress, improved educational performance

American education is failing. Out of every 100 9th-graders, only 28 will graduate from college. SAT scores are declining, illiteracy has reached epidemic proportions, and American students fall far behind students from other industrialized countries in mathematics and the sciences. The teaching profession is plagued by stress, low self-esteem, and burnout.

More than 50 research studies have shown the benefits of the Transcendental Meditation program for education. These include reduced stress and improved intelligence, creativity, memory, learning ability, self-concept, self-actualization, and moral maturity. ADHD symptoms decline. And academic performance improves, a result demonstrated at all levels, from elementary school to graduate school, and among low-income inner-city children.[53] The program is being adopted by schools around the US and the world.[54]

Management — reduced stress, improved health, greater productivity

Stress in the workplace costs the United States billions each year. Despite intensive efforts to reduce the effects of stress, stress and burnout plague every profession. Business and industry continue to be threatened by spiraling health care costs, lack of job satisfaction, and employee accidents, absenteeism, and crime. The turbulent economy has only exacerbated stress.

Studies in the US and Japan show that executives and employees who practice the Transcendental Meditation technique enjoy significantly increased job performance and job satisfaction and better relations with fellow workers. They become more relaxed at work and enjoy improved health, vitality, and well-being, among many other benefits. Absenteeism and sick days decline, the desire to change jobs decreases, corporate productivity and profit increase significantly, and leadership skills are enhanced.[55]

Substance abuse — significantly reduced addiction-related problems

Drug abuse is the nation's number one health problem, causing more deaths, illnesses, and disabilities than any other preventable health condition. Approximately 15% of the American population is chemically addicted to alcohol or drugs. About half of all serious crimes are committed by people under the influence of drugs or alcohol. Alcohol, nicotine, and drug abuse cost the nation $655 billion per year in medical problems, crime, lost productivity, treatment, and auto insurance. The cost in human suffering — physical, emotional, familial, and social — is beyond calculation. Yet no treatment has worked effectively.

More than two dozen research studies have shown the Transcendental Meditation program to be effective in treating addiction-related problems, from cigarette smoking to alcoholism to drug addictions. The longer and more regularly people meditate, the greater the improvement.[56]

The Transcendental Meditation program corrects the internal chemical imbalances underlying addictions. With regular experience of the fourth state of consciousness, people gain the experience they are looking for: relief from stress, enhanced well-being and happiness, a growing sense of self, and the realization that life is meaningful and they are in control of it.

Prison rehabilitation — significantly reduced recidivism

The problem is staggering. The number of Americans in prison or jail has increased sixfold since 1972. By 2010 more than 7.2 million US adults were in prison or jail or on parole or probation — almost one out of 40 Americans. The US has the highest incarceration rate in the world. Crime costs the US $1.7 trillion annually, and the criminal justice system is under enormous strain.

Yet prison "rehabilitation" has been a global failure. More than 65% of ex-prisoners are re-arrested within three years of their release. Many experts believe rehabilitation is impossible and speak instead of "warehousing" prisoners.

More than 20 studies, conducted in prisons throughout the US, including Folsom and San Quentin, have shown the Transcendental Meditation program's effectiveness in prison rehabilitation. Inmates show improved behavior, improved health, increased personal growth, and less anxiety, hostility, and aggression. Above all, they are far less likely to commit crime when released.[63] Reducing recidivism by even a small percentage would be a remarkable achievement. Taken together, these studies indicate the Transcendental Meditation program reduces recidivism by 40% over three years.[57]

Crime is a complex social phenomenon shaped by such factors as chemical and physiological imbalances, stress and anxiety, social stress, and alcohol and drug abuse. The Transcendental Meditation program addresses these elements simultaneously by dissolving stress, balancing the physiology, integrating brain functioning, and cultivating moral maturity. The fundamental antidote to criminal behavior is development of consciousness, of full creative potential.

Military — post-traumatic stress disorder

Every day, 18 veterans commit suicide, and more troops die by suicide annually than are killed in combat. This is just one consequence of post-traumatic stress disorder (PTSD). More than 500,000 US troops deployed to Afghanistan and Iraq since 2001 suffer from PTSD. PTSD can lead to alcohol and drug abuse and mental and physiological imbalance and illness. Of all homeless people, 40% are veterans. Health care costs for PTSD veterans exceed $6 billion annually. Little if anything has worked to treat it.

The Transcendental Meditation technique effectively relieves PTSD symptoms. The effects can be immediate and extremely powerful — veterans are able to sleep again, work again, live again with their families. One study found that, at post-test 12 weeks after learning to meditate, subjects reported feeling significantly more rested and peaceful, less depressed and anxious, happier and more alive, more focused and engaged in their lives, and enjoying better relationships with family, friends, and coworkers. An earlier study, on Vietnam veterans with PTSD, found similar results, while the control group assigned to psychotherapy did not improve significantly.

The effect, moreover, is independent of culture. A study among refugees in the Congo, where the Second Congo War killed 5.4 million people and displaced millions more, found that after just 30 days of Transcendental Meditation practice, those who had PTSD were symptom free and remained symptom free four months later.[58]

Different meditation techniques produce different outcomes

We have seen that different meditation techniques, because they involve differing mental activities, lead to different styles of brain functioning. Not surprisingly, they also differ in outcomes.

Over the past several decades scientists at various universities have gathered all the published research results on different meditation techniques and analyzed them using an advanced statistical procedure called *meta-analysis*, which enables precise objective comparisons of data from different studies.

The first of these, conducted at Stanford, showed the Transcendental Meditation technique was twice as effective in reducing anxiety as such other techniques as the relaxation response, progressive muscle relaxation, EMG biofeedback, etc. This is a clinically important finding — anxiety is implicated in many major mental and physical health problems. Other meta-analyses found the Transcendental Meditation technique significantly more effective than other procedures in promoting self-actualization, psychological health and maturity, and relaxed physiological functioning, as well as in reducing high blood pressure and drug abuse, alcohol abuse, and cigarette use.[59]

According to the American Heart Association (AHA), the Transcendental Meditation technique is the only meditation practice that has been shown to lower blood pressure. Their statement, released in 2013, reports:

Because of many negative studies or mixed results and a paucity of available trials, all other meditation techniques (including MBSR, or Mindfulness-Based Stress Reduction) received a "Class III, no benefit, Level of Evidence C" recommendation. Thus, other meditation techniques are not recommended in clinical practice to lower BP [blood pressure] at this time.[60]

The AHA scientific statement additionally reported that lower blood pressure through Transcendental Meditation practice is also associated with substantially reduced rates of heart attack, stroke, and death. The AHA statement concludes that alternative treatments that include the Transcendental Meditation technique are recommended for consideration in treatment plans for all individuals with high blood pressure.

The research literature also indicates that the Transcendental Meditation program is also the most effective means of elevating intelligence and ego development, reducing illness and health care costs, and rehabilitating prisoners — and the only known method of creating coherence in society.

Higher states and world peace

As early as 1960 Maharishi predicted that when even 1% of a population learned the Transcendental Meditation technique, the whole population would become peaceful, so powerful is the inner peace of Transcendental Consciousness. Coherent brain functioning in a relative handful of people, in other words, can create harmony and orderliness in a city, a nation, or the world.

Maharishi's hypothesis was confirmed in the early 1970s, when the number of people who had learned the Transcendental Meditation technique had reached 1% of the population in a number of US cities. Studies found that as soon as cities reached the 1% threshold, crime trends decreased significantly — while in matched control cities, crime continued climbing. The decline could not be attributed to other factors known to influence crime rate. Another study found drops in automobile accidents and suicides. Crime, accidents, and suicides are expressions of social disorder — and so the simultaneous drop in these values suggests an underlying effect of increased orderliness in society. Indices of economic health and growth also improved.

These were astonishing findings. In cities around the United States, a few hundred people meditating twice daily in their homes were reducing crime and improving quality of life city-wide, without even knowing it.[61] Scientists named this phenomenon the *Maharishi Effect.*

In 1976, when Maharishi introduced the advanced TM-Sidhi program, including Yogic Flying, he predicted even smaller numbers could produce this effect — the *square root* of 1% of a population practicing these programs as a group. Such tiny numbers meant coherence-creating groups could be created deliberately. This has been done again and again, in all parts of the world, east and west, in developed and developing nations alike, since the late 1970s.

Extensive research, including 50 scientific replications and 23 studies published in peer-reviewed journals, have shown that Transcendental Meditation practice, and in particular group practice of the Transcendental Meditation and TM-Sidhi programs, is a powerful and highly cost-effective approach for defusing societal stress and markedly reducing violent crime and social conflict — including war and global terrorism.

The Maharishi Effect has been demonstrated, in short-term experiments, on every scale of society, in cities, states, countries, groups of countries, and even, on several occasions when the groups have been large enough, for the whole world. The predicted effect has been seen in every case. A few examples:

Israel and Lebanon — reduced warfare and improved quality of life

A two-month assembly of Transcendental Meditation and TM-Sidhi participants convened in Jerusalem in 1983. The group was large enough, in theory, to influence Lebanon to the north, where a terrible civil war had been raging for years. A day-by-day study showed that on days when the number of participants was high, war deaths in Lebanon dropped 76% and war intensity 45%. During the two weeks when attendance was highest, war deaths plummeted from nearly 34 per day to 1.5 per day, while war intensity fell 67%. Jerusalem saw significant declines in crime rate, automobile accident rate, and fires, while crime rate fell throughout Israel. No other alternative explanations — such as the effects of holidays, temperature, and weekends — could account for this pattern of change. The odds that this happened by chance: one in 10,000.

Improved quality of life and reduced conflict in the Middle East

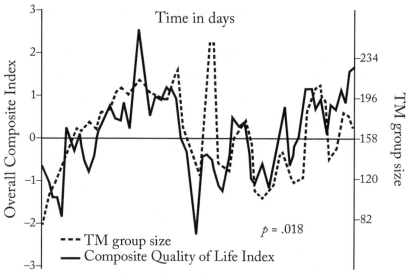

Group practice of the Transcendental Meditation and TM-Sidhi programs improved the quality of life in Israel, measured by improvement on an index consisting of reduced crime rate, reduced traffic accidents, reduced fires, reduced war deaths in Lebanon, and improvements in the national stock market and national mood. Notice the strong correspondence between the number of participants in the Jerusalem group and the composite index of all the above variables.[62]

Before the project began, the researchers described the experiment to groups of independent research scientists in the US and Israel, including the major hypotheses, the dates of the assembly, the statistics to be gathered, and the predicted results. They forwarded the daily assembly attendance numbers to these boards at the midpoint and end of the experiment.[62]

These results were subsequently replicated in seven consecutive experiments over a two-year period during the peak of the Lebanon war. The results of these interventions included:

- 71% decrease in war-related fatalities [$p<10^{-10}$]
- 68% decrease in war-related injuries [$p<10^{-6}$]
- 48% decrease in the level of conflict [$p<10^{-8}$]
- 66% increase in cooperation among antagonists [$p<10^{-6}$]

The probability that all these results were due to chance? Less than one in 10^{19} (ten million trillion) — making this the most rigorously confirmed approach for reducing social stress and conflict in the history of conflict management.[63]

Reduced international terrorism

On several occasions groups gathered that were large enough, in theory — the square root of 1% of the world's population, or close to it — to produce a *global* influence of peace. Data provided by the Rand Corporation, the nonprofit global policy think tank, revealed that during three large peace-creating assemblies of Transcendental Meditation and TM-Sidhi program participants, fatalities and injuries due to international terrorism plummeted 72%, as compared to all other weeks during a three-year period. In addition, all forms of international conflict dropped by an average of 32% compared with previous years.

These outcomes were predicted prior to each assembly. No other factors could explain these results — not trends or cycles in the data or seasonal changes or anything else happening in the world at those times. The researchers concluded, "The fact that all of these variables displayed a near-simultaneous improvement indicates that there was a worldwide and holistic influence of reduced tension" during these assemblies.[64]

Washington, DC — reduced violent crime

A highly public National Demonstration Project, conducted in Washington, DC, in June and July 1993, tested this approach to reducing crime and social stress and improving the effectiveness of government. In this carefully-controlled experiment, the results were predicted in advance, and all aspects of the project were monitored by an independent, 24-person project review board consisting of some of the nation's leading sociologists and criminologists as well as the DC Metropolitan Police Department and local government and civic leaders. This board advised on the research design, oversaw the research process, and gave critical feedback on the research report.

Some 4,000 experts in the Transcendental Meditation and TM-Sidhi programs from 50 countries traveled at their own expense to Washington for this project. They did not march, they did not speak with government leaders. They simply meditated in groups in hotels throughout the city twice each day.

The group increased in size from 800 to 4,000 over the two-month period. Although violent crime (homicide, rape, and assault) had been steadily increasing during the first five months of the year, soon after the study began, FBI crime statistics showed violent crime began decreasing and continued to drop until the end of the experiment, with a maximum decrease of 23.3%.

The likelihood that this result could be attributed to chance variation in crime levels was less than two parts per billion ($p<.000000002$). The drop in crime could not be attributed to other possible causes, including temperature, precipitation, weekends, and police and community anticrime activities.

At the same time, quality of life in Washington improved significantly, as measured by a drop in four stress-related variables: emergency psychiatric calls, complaints against the police, hospital trauma cases, and accidental deaths, including suicide. When the demonstration project ended and the participants returned home, social stress began rising once more, and with it violent crime.[65]

A peace technology

These are just a few examples. Some 50 studies on the Maharishi Effect have been conducted to date, with the results replicated repeatedly. Studies have been published in such peer-reviewed journals as the *Journal of Conflict Resolution* (edited at Yale), *Social Indicators Research*, *Journal of Mind and Behavior*, *Journal of Social Behavior and Personality*, *International Journal of Neuroscience*, *Journal of Crime and Justice*, *Journal of Offender Rehabilitation*, *Psychological Reports*, *Social Science Perspectives Journal*, and *Psychology, Crime, and Law*.

In each of these studies, the evidence consists of open, publicly gathered statistics that anyone can verify. These statistics have been analyzed using state-of-the-art statistical methods. Could anything else have caused the observed changes? Alternative explanations have been statistically controlled for. Could these effects have happened by chance? Statistical analysis shows the odds are vanishingly small. The Maharishi Effect has been confirmed to a degree of certainty unprecedented in the social and even the physical sciences.

Social science research has shown that war has its origin in rising social tension and stress. If you can reduce collective tension, you can neutralize the possibility of war. This is what the Maharishi Effect does.

Maharishi explains these results in terms of what he calls *collective con-*

sciousness. A nation's collective consciousness reflects the sum of every individual's consciousness. If the consciousness of the citizens is stressed and incoherent, the national consciousness will mirror that. Just as stress in the individual can express itself as disease, anger, or violence, stress in collective consciousness is seen in crime, governmental gridlock, destabilizing economic fluctuations, social conflict, terrorism, and war.

Peace treaties, political negotiations, military interventions — over thousands of years, nothing has given us permanent peace. We have not addressed the root of the problem. The key to solving social problems is to create coherence in collective consciousness, and this is easily accomplished. We now have a technology not only of enlightenment, but of peace.

It's not difficult to recognize the same dynamics — and the same potential for improvement — in the other global problems we face. Today's massive global poverty, for example, testifies to systemic underdevelopment of creativity and intelligence in the world. Even pollution, environmental degradation, and global warming result, finally, from stressed, narrow-minded thinking and lack of coherence in the collective consciousness.

In sum, the Transcendental Meditation and TM-Sidhi programs excel — and may be unsurpassed — not only in developing individual consciousness but in contributing to positive societal change. This large and growing body of research on these programs shows the immense practical value of developing higher states of consciousness.

CHAPTER 10

༃

Is Pure Consciousness the Unified Field?

We have seen figures throughout history testifying to potentials of consciousness far beyond what we ordinarily suppose. In their glimpses of higher states of consciousness, many sensed that human consciousness, in its pure state, is more than just the essence of the human mind — it is also, somehow, the essence of creation itself.

Laozi, in the *Tao Te Ching*, identifies the Tao as the source of everything in creation, inner and outer, and says that when one achieves inner silence, "one finds the anchor of the universe within himself." Zhuangzi expresses the identical idea: "The mind of the Sage, being in repose, becomes the mirror of the universe, the speculum [reflector] of all creation."

Jesus, in *The Book of Thomas*, says, "Those who have known themselves already have acquired knowledge about the depth of the universe." The 12th-century Chinese Daoist teacher Sun Bu-er writes that when the mind becomes tranquil, "The spirit is the same as the universe."

Emerson describes the Oversoul not only as the source of our mental life but as the source of creation. When we experience it, he says, we "share the life by which things exist," and he concludes, "The sources of nature are in [one's] own mind." Johannes Brahms says that during his transcendental moments he experienced "the infinite energy of the Cosmos" and "the power that created our earth and the whole universe, including you and me."

Romain Rolland echoes the same thought: "I feel the power of life and the divine force which upholds the universe." Writes Franklin Merrell-Wolff: "I found Myself above space, time, and causality, and actually sustaining the whole universe by the Light of Consciousness which I AM."[2]

These descriptions recall the perennial philosophy — that underlying all diversity is a field of unity, that this field of unity is identical to (or at least intimately connected to) the human soul or consciousness, that it can be experienced deep within, and that this experience brings surpassing benefit to life.

Maharishi also explicitly equates pure consciousness with what mathematical physics calls the unified field. This, he explains, is why growth of enlightenment draws life into harmony with natural law, bringing one the support of nature to fulfill desires.

Is there any reality to this? Is human consciousness, in its silent state, identical with the source of the universe? This is a critical question. If the answer is no, then a major pillar of the perennial philosophy falls to the ground. If yes, a profound new vision for human life opens before us. We need to explore this question to fully appreciate the significance of higher states of consciousness.

Human consciousness is widely regarded as the greatest frontier facing science today — yet science has made little progress in understanding it. As the Australian philosopher David John Chalmers writes:

> Consciousness poses the most baffling problems in the science of the mind. There is nothing that we know more intimately than conscious experience, but there is nothing that is harder to explain. All sorts of mental phenomena have yielded to scientific investigation in recent years, but consciousness has stubbornly resisted. Many have tried to explain it, but the explanations always seem to fall short of the target. Some have been led to suppose that the problem is intractable, and that no good explanation can be given.[1]

Modern science has confirmed an underlying unity in nature, as we will see. But is it connected with human consciousness? Is it open to experience?

Not from the standpoint of neuroscience. The prevailing scientific view defines consciousness as the continuous and ever-changing stream of thoughts and perceptions in the mind. Consciousness, from this viewpoint, is merely the byproduct of the brain's electrochemical functioning, much as the images on a television screen are byproducts of electronic circuitry — they possess no fundamental reality in themselves. Nor, in the view of most scientists, does consciousness. Neuroscientists typically regard mental states as identical with brain states. Thus consciousness or awareness equates with electrochemistry; thoughts emerge from the firing of neuron sets. The apparent duality of mind and matter does resolve to a unity, and in the prevalent "physicalist" view, that unity is matter.

Consciousness and the universe

In this view, the physical world is a closed system. This leads to some perplexing conclusions: In a closed system there is no place for independently conscious minds; there is no way conscious minds can insert intentions into this system that change it (as we do all day long); and any sense of self and free will we possess is illusory.

These conclusions raise obvious logical dilemmas. As the cosmologist Edward Harrison commented, "Those who adopt this [viewpoint] must show us where they themselves are fully portrayed in the physical universe in the act of conceiving that universe in which mind is an illusion."[3]

Even its foremost advocates concede that this model cannot explain consciousness. Nor does the physicalist view account for phenomena that suggest there is a deep relationship between consciousness and nature, mind and matter:

The intelligibility of the universe

"The eternal mystery of the world is its comprehensibility," Einstein remarked. "The fact that it is comprehensible is a miracle."[4] Einstein believed that our ability to understand nature's workings so deeply as to precisely predict physical phenomena reflects a deep connection between human intelligence and the intelligence displayed by nature. We take for granted the fact that we can understand how nature functions — but physicists have pointed out that neither the universe nor the human mind need have been fashioned in this way.

The ability of mathematics to describe nature

Mathematics is a purely mental discipline — an "independent world created out of pure intelligence," as the English physicist, astronomer, and mathematician Sir James Jeans put it.[5] Mathematical relationships mirror something of the orderly, logical structure of human consciousness itself.

Yet mathematics possesses an astonishing power to describe and predict the workings of nature. Eugene Wigner, the Nobel Prize-winning physicist and a founder of quantum mechanics, famously referred to "the unreasonable effectiveness of mathematics in the natural sciences."[6]

Sometimes mathematical formulas and properties are derived that have no known practical application at the time — and years later are discovered to precisely describe some new discovery in physics. As Einstein wrote:

> Here arises a puzzle that has disturbed scientists of all periods. How is it possible that mathematics, a product of human thought that is independent of experience, fits so excellently the objects of physical reality? Can human reason without experience discover by pure thinking the properties of real things?[7]

The observer as participant in nature

In 1927, physicist Werner Heisenberg set forth his *uncertainty principle*, which shook the foundations of physics and transforms the way we understand nature and our relationship to it. Quite simply, Heisenberg declared that observers alter whatever they observe through the sheer act of observation. This in turn implies that consciousness plays a role in the physical universe.

Physics, like all sciences, had been founded on the assumption that an objective reality exists prior to and independent of consciousness. But quantum physics has shown the interdependence of observer and observed. For example, the electron, like all subatomic particles, is not really a particle at all — it possesses the mysterious ability to behave sometimes as a particle, sometimes as a wave, depending on how one chooses to measure (observe) it. That is, electrons are merely energy potentials that become particles or waves through the act of observation. This suggests a deep interrelationship between mind and matter at the quantum level. The American physicist John Wheeler said:

The universe does not exist "out there," independent of us. We are inescapably involved in bringing about that which appears to be happening. We are not only observers; we are participators. In some strange sense, this is a participatory universe.[8]

Wheeler concludes: "Simply put: without an observer, there are no laws of physics."[9] Amherst University physicist George Greenstein concludes that "the very cosmos does not exist unless observed. And . . . only a conscious mind is capable of performing such an observation."[10]

A universe designed for consciousness

As many physicists have pointed out, the laws of nature governing the universe must contain the potential for creating observers. This notion is known as the *anthropic principle*. The term was invented in the 1970s by Brandon Carter, an astrophysicist at Cambridge, based on his observation of the numberless coincidences that had to take place for stars to form.[11] For example, if the gravitational force had varied by only one part in 10^{40} as the universe was forming, stars could never have formed, nor could life on earth. A similarly delicate balance exists in the force holding protons and neutrons together in an atom's nucleus. If this force were a shade weaker, atoms would never have formed; if stronger, it would be strong enough to draw all the protons in the universe together into a single mass. In either case, neither stars nor human life as we know it could have formed. Such "anthropic coincidences" go on in remarkable numbers.

The British-born American physicist Freeman Dyson wrote:

> I conclude from the existence of these accidents of physics and astronomy that the universe is an unexpectedly hospitable place for living creatures to make their home in. . . . I do not claim that the architecture of the universe proves the existence of God. I claim only that the architecture of the universe is consistent with the hypothesis that mind plays an essential role in its functioning.[12]

George Greenstein goes a step further: "The very cosmos itself depends for its being on the uttermost mystery of consciousness."[13]

Modern physics and the quest for unity

There is excitement today in the physics community, the result of ambitious efforts to formulate a *theory of everything* — a single, all-encompassing description of the laws of nature, of the fundamental principles upon which the cosmos is built.

According to these new theories, known collectively as *superstring theory*, there is a single, unified field at the basis of all change throughout the universe. Though there is debate over the details, there is agreement about the general features. It is unmanifest, transcendental, beyond space and time. It is a field of infinite, unmanifest energy. Interacting solely with itself — at this level there is nothing else to interact with — it gives rise to all the energy and matter in the universe. At nature's surface, we see infinite diversity, numberless things. At its essence, there is only one thing.

This discovery represents the supreme achievement of modern science, the culmination of 400 years of scientific effort. For all science is fundamentally the quest for unity. Progress in science has shown that the deeper we penetrate into nature, the simpler and more unified nature becomes.

Until the mid-1800s, for example, electricity and magnetism were regarded as two separate forces — what could a lightning bolt have in common with a compass needle? But in 1864, English scientist James Clerk Maxwell showed that they are the dual expressions of a single underlying field, the *electromagnetic field*. In 1905, in his theory of special relativity, Einstein showed the underlying unity of matter and energy. In 1916, in his theory of general relativity, he showed the unity of gravity and acceleration, space and time, and matter and space.

With each new discovery of underlying unity, scientists are encouraged to believe there is an ultimate unity to nature. And they have striven to unearth it.

In the Newtonian view of nature, scientists regarded matter as the fundamental stuff of the universe. In their quest to understand nature, they set out to discover the fundamental "building blocks" of matter, the "elementary particles" out of which everything else was constructed.

By the early decades of the 20th century, however, physicists began to realize that subatomic particles are not elementary — nor even particles. They merely express the interactions of various underlying fields. All forms of energy, matter, and motion in the universe are mere excitations of these unmanifest, abstract, all-pervading fields. The foundation upon which the material universe is erected has proven to be *nonmaterial*.

By the 1970s, all change was recognized as the activity of four fundamental forces: *gravity* (the attractive force everyone is familiar with), *electromagnetism* (responsible for virtually everything we experience, including light, sound, and touch, as well as the functioning of our bodies), the *strong force* (responsible for binding protons and neutrons together in the nucleus of the atom), and the *weak force* (responsible for radioactive decay and fusion within stars).

One by one these four remaining forces have been unified, recognized as expressions of even simpler underlying forces. And today we stand at the threshold of the ultimate unification — Einstein's lifelong dream.

Along the way, we have harnessed the fundamental forces and developed technologies to use them. We use the electromagnetic force in every device that uses electricity, from radios and televisions to computers and communications systems. We employ the strong and weak forces in nuclear technology.

But probing the unified field directly using conventional technologies would require awesome energy — by some estimates, a particle accelerator as big as our galaxy. Short of that, quantum field theorists can only describe the unified field's dynamics mathematically. Our supreme scientific achievement, the discovery of the unified field, remains an intellectual construct, known solely by inference.

Is the unified field a field of consciousness?

The ancient Vedic tradition of knowledge, which Maharishi revived, identifies a single field of unity at the basis of life — a field of abstract pure consciousness. Pure consciousness, in this tradition, underlies not only all perceptions, thoughts, and feelings but also all forms and phenomena in the universe. It comprises the ultimate stuff of creation. The first reality of creation, in this view, is an unbounded ocean of consciousness, of pure knowledge, power, and bliss. Eternally awake within itself, it is the "self" of the universe and the Self of everyone. We find this theme echoed in other traditions as well.

Thus both the most modern and most ancient understandings of nature identify a single field, unified within itself, underlying the whole of the universe. In both cases it is described as unbounded, nonmaterial, unmanifest, beyond space and time, transcendental. In both cases it is described as an infinitely dynamic field of pure intelligence that, purely by interacting with itself, gives rise to the laws of nature and to nature's wondrous diversity.

Can these be two separate orders of reality, two independent categories of existence that never touch? As early as 1963, decades before the breakthroughs in unified field theories, Maharishi predicted that modern science, through its ever-deeper exploration of nature, would discover an underlying field of unity, and that this will be the field of pure consciousness.

Despite the mechanistic, materialistic view of nature and consciousness that prevails for scientists and nonscientists alike, over the past century a number of preeminent physicists have departed from this view, asserting that human consciousness is, somehow, intimately connected with the universe.

Among the first were physicists who developed quantum mechanics, the principles underlying the fundamental description of physical systems at the atomic level. Realizing that the pure act of observation can influence the behavior of physical systems, they were compelled to include consciousness in the equations of quantum theory. As Max Planck, the first architect of quantum theory, declared,

> I regard consciousness as fundamental. I regard matter as derivative from consciousness. We cannot get behind consciousness. Everything that we talk about, everything that we regard as existing, postulates consciousness.[14]

Eugene Wigner said, "The very study of the external world led to the conclusion that the content of the consciousness is an ultimate reality."[15] James Jeans wrote:

> Today there is a wide measure of agreement, which on the physical side of science approaches almost to unanimity, that the stream of knowledge is heading toward a non-mechanical reality; the universe begins to look more like a great thought than like a great machine. Mind no longer appears as an accidental intruder into the realm of matter; we are beginning to suspect that we ought rather to hail it as the creator and governor of the realm of matter.[16]

Freeman Dyson put it this way:

> The mind, I believe, exists in some very real sense in the universe. But is it primary or an accidental consequence of something else? The prevailing view among biologists seems to be that the mind arose accidentally out of molecules of DNA or something. I find that very unlikely. It seems more reasonable to think that mind was a primary part of nature from the beginning and we are simply manifestations of it at the present stage of history. It's not so much that mind has a life of its own but that mind is inherent in the way the universe is built. . . .[17]

Sir Arthur Stanley Eddington, the English astrophysicist, phrased it concisely: "The stuff of the world is mind-stuff."[18]

A number of physicists have more recently developed this idea in further detail. Here are a few examples:

David Bohm and the implicate order

The American physicist David Bohm, one of the 20th century's most distinguished scientists, referred to by Einstein as his successor, admired quantum mechanics' unprecedented predictive abilities. But like Einstein, he could not accept that it was complete. He found it difficult to accept a fundamental principle of quantum mechanics, namely the random character of the quantum world. This level of nature's functioning is distinguished by indeterminism and chance. The motion of subatomic particles such as electrons is fundamentally ambiguous and uncertain, with no apparent underlying reason.

Bohm suspected there must be deeper causes behind the apparently haphazard nature of the subatomic world. This led him to formulate a "causal interpretation" of quantum mechanics, which posits an underlying *quantum potential*. Pervading all of space and interconnecting all quantum systems, the quantum potential furnishes the intelligence that guides motion in the quantum world, much as radar signals guide the motion of a ship.

From here Bohm developed his concepts of the *explicate* and *implicate* orders. The *explicate order* is the universe we inhabit — from galaxy clusters to our countless ecosystems on our planet to our interior world of perceptions, thoughts, and feelings. It is the world of space and time, of objects and events.

The explicate order is a projection of the *implicate order*. Corresponding to the quantum potential, the implicate order is a field of "undivided wholeness in flowing movement." The explicate order is constantly unfolding based on information enfolded in the implicate order.

Bohm grounds his thesis in a rigorous analysis of quantum mechanics. But he makes the principle clear with an analogy: Everything that takes place in the explicate order may be likened to ripples on the stream of the implicate order:

> On this stream, one may see an ever-changing pattern of vortices, ripples, waves, splashes, etc., which evidently have no independent existence as such. Rather, they are abstracted from the flowing movement, arising and vanishing in the total process of the flow. Such transitory subsistence as may be possessed by these abstracted forms implies only a relative independence or autonomy of behavior, rather than absolutely independent existence as ultimate substances.[19]

Mind and matter, Bohm holds, have a common source in the implicate order. Mental and physical processes are essentially the same; the mind acts on the body "by reaching the level of the quantum potential and of the 'dance' of the particles." Bohm continues:

> It is thus implied that in some sense a rudimentary mind-like quality is present even at the level of particle physics, and that as we go to subtler levels, this mind-like quality becomes stronger and more developed.[20]

Consciousness and life are enfolded deeply into the very nature of the implicate order — meaning that everything in the universe, even seemingly inanimate objects, is infused with consciousness and life to some degree.[21] The implicate order, in Bohm's words,

> . . . could equally well be called Idealism, Spirit, Consciousness. The separation of the two — matter and spirit — is an abstraction. The ground is always one.[22]

Bohm subsequently developed the concept of the *super-implicate order*, a completely unified field that generates the implicate and explicate orders and from where the implicate order derives the information enfolded within it.[23]

Amit Goswami and the self-aware universe

Born in India, Goswami is professor emeritus at the University of Oregon. Like Bohm and Einstein, he acknowledges the enormous explanatory and predictive power of quantum mechanics. But he points to the quantum phenomena that seem paradoxical, impossible: the ability of a quantum object such as an electron to be in two places at once; the ability of an object to disappear from one place and appear simultaneously somewhere else without, apparently, traveling through space; and more.

These results only seem absurd, he says, because of the philosophy we bring to bear on the data — the materialistic paradigm that has dominated science for centuries. This philosophy, known as *material realism*, holds that only matter is real, that everything in the universe is based on the interplay of atoms and subatomic particles. But this is an unproven assumption, Goswami contends, with no direct evidence for all things. The findings of quantum mechanics seem paradoxical because our unproven assumption is false. He adds:

> Many physicists today suspect that something is wrong with material realism but are afraid to rock the boat that has served them so well for so long. They do not realize that their boat is drifting and needs new navigation under a new worldview.[24]

Goswami flips the paradigm, arguing that consciousness, not matter, is fundamental. He calls this approach *monistic idealism*. Because consciousness is unified, nonlocal, and infinitely interconnected, an understanding of physical phenomena that has consciousness at its foundation explains the paradoxes:

> [T]he philosophy of monistic idealism provides a paradox-free interpretation of quantum physics that is logical, coherent, and satisfying. Moreover, mental phenomena — such as self-consciousness, free will, creativity, even extrasensory perception — find simple, satisfying explanations when the mind-body problem is reformulated in an overall context of monistic idealism and quantum theory. This reformulated picture of the brain-mind enables us to understand our whole self entirely in harmony with what the great spiritual traditions have maintained for millennia.[25]

John Hagelin and harnessing the power of the unified field

The starting point for the American quantum physicist John Hagelin is the mind's ability to settle to a state of silent wakefulness. Borrowing terms from physics, he describes the pure consciousness experience as the *ground state* or *state of least excitation* of consciousness. And just as the ground state of a quantum system is a state of maximum orderliness ("zero entropy"), the state of Transcendental Consciousness brings maximum order to brain functioning.

An authority on quantum field theory, Dr. Hagelin helped develop the Grand Unified Theory, known as the Flipped SU(5) model, derived from the deeper-level superstring, that to date most successfully unites nature's fundamental forces and particles. From the 1980s forward he also worked with Maharishi in identifying the correspondences between Vedic and modern descriptions of reality. He argues that pure consciousness and the unified field are one and the same. Here are his main reasons:[26]

1. Common sense

Can there be two fundamental fields of unity in life, one at the basis of mind, the other at the basis of matter? Or is there just one? Of two competing understandings, science always favors the simplest, the most "parsimonious," as being the most likely true. Given these two viewpoints on the core reality of existence, the simplest understanding is that there is a single fundamental field of unity and therefore that pure consciousness and the unified field are the same.

2. Qualitative correspondence

The unified field and pure consciousness share fundamental qualities. Both are unbounded, infinitely dynamic, self-interacting fields of pure intelligence. Moreover, just as pure consciousness is conscious of itself, the unified field, unlike other fields, also displays a self-awareness — it responds dynamically to its own presence. In this it differs from, say, the electromagnetic field, in which two rays of light can cross paths with no interaction and hence no "awareness" of the other. The unified field's property of self-interaction systematically leads to the emergence of all the diversity of the universe. Dr. Hagelin comments:

This is a powerful argument. By definition, the unified field of physics is purely self-interacting — the self-sufficient source of all created things. Similarly, pure consciousness is purely self-interacting, or "self-referral" — the self-sufficient source of all mental activity. If these two fields are both purely self-interacting, and if they interact with one another — as, for example, the subjective mind and the material body ultimately must — then they must be one and the same.

3. Quantitative correspondence

Dr. Hagelin has identified precise quantitative correspondences between pure consciousness and the unified field, based on analyzing their properties of self-interaction and the subsequent emergence of diversity from unity.

From the perspective of consciousness, Maharishi has explained that the property of self-awareness creates a reverberant quality within pure consciousness, an internal, unmanifest dynamism. This unmanifest dynamism gives rise to the appearance of all mental phenomena and ultimately to the whole universe. Viewed another way, the reverberations within consciousness are the laws of nature.

The Vedic rishis, with their highly refined nervous systems, were able to experience these internal reverberations of consciousness with such clarity that they were able to reproduce these unmanifest sounds in speech. These *primordial sounds*, as Maharishi calls them, have been preserved as an oral tradition by countless generations of Vedic pandits. Eventually these sounds were set down in books and comprise what is known today as the Veda and Vedic literature. Thus, in Maharishi's radical reinterpretation, the Veda and Vedic literature were not composed by anyone, in the sense one might compose a poem or song. Rather they are the reverberations or sounds experienced within consciousness. In the Vedic tradition they are referred to as *shruti*, or *heard*.

This literature, Maharishi recognized, reflects a precise mathematical structure, from the sequence of sounds and silence at the level of syllables up through the number of verses, *padas* (sub-sections), and *mandalas* (major sections), and eventually all forty branches of Vedic literature.

Dr. Hagelin discovered that the underlying mathematical structure of Rik Veda, the cornerstone of Vedic literature, exactly matches the mathematical formulas describing the unified field, in particular what theorists call the fundamental vibrational degrees of freedom of the superstring, beyond classical space-time. The structure of consciousness, as embodied in the Rik Veda, matches the structure of the unified field.

Modern physics, furthermore, describes emergence of the universe from the unified field in a manner parallel to Maharishi's Vedic description. Just as pure consciousness, in being aware of itself, creates a set of unmanifest reverberations, so does the self-interaction of the unified field. The analysis is quite technical on both sides of the equation, ancient Vedic and modern scientific, beyond the scope of this chapter.

But the conclusion is simple: We have two detailed understandings, one ancient and subjective, the other modern and objective, that address the age-old question of how "the one becomes many" (or, more precisely, *appears* to become many, for it never actually loses its unified reality) — and there are remarkable parallels between the two.

From the subjective viewpoint, this is no mere intellectual construct. In principle, every human being has the potential, as the ancient Vedic rishis did, to experience the unmanifest reverberations within the silence of consciousness. In the early stages of transcending, one experiences pure consciousness as silent, "flat." But as one becomes increasingly familiar with the experience of Transcendental Consciousness, one can experience, within this sea of silence, the internal, unmanifest reverberations, the inner dynamics of consciousness. To phrase it more accurately (since there is no duality at this level), *consciousness experiences itself* as infinitely silent and infinitely dynamic, both together.

4. Maharishi Effect

An additional argument for the unity of pure consciousness and the unified field is the Maharishi Effect, described in the previous chapter — the phenomenon of quality of life improving for a whole population when just 1% of the population practices the Transcendental Meditation technique or when the square root of 1% of a population practices the TM and TM-Sidhi programs, including Yogic Flying, together in one place. The documented social changes resulting from the Maharishi Effect range from reduced rates of crime, accidents, and sickness to reductions in international terrorism and even open warfare.

How can people sitting with eyes closed, practicing techniques of consciousness, decrease crime, accident, and sickness rates and improve positive trends over large areas? Some field must carry the effect. It cannot be the electromagnetic field, because electromagnetic effects diminish rapidly with distance. It cannot be the gravitational field. Each of the four fundamental force fields can, for various reasons, be ruled out. Only the unified field can mediate this effect, Dr. Hagelin asserts. This is the most compelling evidence that pure consciousness and the unified field are identical and that this field can be experienced universally by everyone.

What does this all add up to? Hagelin reasons as follows:

> The most natural conclusion to be drawn from such a detailed qualitative and quantitative correspondence is that the unified field of pure, self-interacting consciousness and the unified field of modern theoretical physics are one and the same. In other words, the deepest level of human experience, pure consciousness, constitutes the direct, subjective experience of the unified field currently being explored by modern theoretical physics.
>
> This conclusion is both parsimonious and consistent with common sense: It is difficult to conceive of two distinct unified fields of natural law — one at the basis of conscious experience, and one at the basis of everything else in the universe.
>
> Human consciousness has access to the unified level of nature's intelligence. The basis of human consciousness is identical with the unified field of all the laws of nature.
>
> The clear and electric implication of this equivalence is that human beings can experience — and harness — the concentrated source of orderliness at the unified basis of nature's functioning.

The direct experience of unity

For all the remarkable parallels between these two descriptions of underlying unity — one ancient, the other modern — there is a critically important difference. Mathematical physics allows us to understand nature's ultimate reality, but only conceptually. As Eddington expresses it:

> What we are dragging to light as the basis of all phenomena is a scheme of symbols connected by mathematical equations. That is what physical reality boils down to when probed by the methods which a physicist can apply....
>
> We have learnt that the exploration of the external world by the methods of physical science leads not to a concrete reality but to a shadow world of symbols, beneath which those methods are unadapted for penetrating.[27]

But human consciousness is "adapted for penetrating" the most fundamental level of nature. Considering the unimaginable energy required to probe the unified field conventionally, one may wonder how this is possible. Yet nothing could be more natural. In its least excited state, consciousness *is* the unified field. The unified field *is* consciousness. When the mind settles to its simplest, least active state, we experience nature's unified intelligence directly, within our own awareness. This is the marvel of the human brain. Unfathomably sophisticated, the brain possesses the sensitivity and flexibility to reflect the total potential of nature's intelligence directly in conscious experience. It is not an intellectual process, entailing some new thought or understanding. It is simply the experience of one's unbounded Self.

And this, Maharishi observes, is the only way the unified field can be known. At its own level, the unified field is all there is. We can describe it mathematically but we cannot truly know it objectively, "from the outside," because at this level of nature there is no "outside." The unified field is a unity, while the objective approach depends upon maintaining duality, a distinction between the observer and the observed. Only one thing can truly know the unified field — the unified field itself.

Mastery of natural law

In the observable sector of the universe, astronomers estimate there are 100 billion galaxies. Each galaxy comprises billions of stars, each star countless trillions of atoms, each atom a bewildering array of ghostly subatomic particles. What organizes this infinite variety and maintains harmony within and among so many scales of nature, from larger than the largest to smaller than the smallest?

The laws of nature — the abstract, unmanifest, all-pervading intelligence vibrating in the unified field. And natural law governs human life as surely as the life of plankton and planets, quarks and quasars. The laws of nature hum within every neuron in our brains, every cell of our bodies, every atom in every molecule of DNA.

Human consciousness, properly cultivated, has the marvelous capacity to experience the source of natural law, the unified field of all the laws of nature — to stimulate it, harness its limitless energy, command it. This has been the assertion of thinkers throughout the ages, revitalized and reformulated in a modern scientific framework by Maharishi. When consciousness is fully awake, in this understanding, one gains the ability to mobilize the infinite organizing power of natural law. And then there is no limit to what one can achieve — nothing is impossible. With all possibilities available, one can *know anything, do anything, and accomplish anything,* in Maharishi's words, without strain or loss of time — the mere thought achieves the desire.

In Unity Consciousness, you recognize the laws of nature as different modes of the functioning of your own unbounded awareness. You command total natural law because you *are* total natural law. Everything you do, moreover, nourishes everything and everyone, naturally and spontaneously. Every thought and action is always for good, always supportive to life. In fulfilling your own life, you fulfill the life around you.[28]

The unified field is not down deep somewhere, not out in space, not far away. It is all-pervading. Everything is made out of that. Everything is only a fluctuation of that, is nothing but that. It is the Self — the Self of the individual and the Self of the universe.

The universe unfolds within the Self. The human mind partakes of the same creative dynamics as the universe itself. This is what we experience and progressively awaken within us each time we transcend. We awaken cosmic intelligence and grow in command of total natural law. This is the gift of higher states of consciousness, and it's everyone's birthright.

A universal knowledge

None of this is new. In every culture, in every age, this knowledge has been known and expressed. That we are fundamentally related to nature forms a tradition as old as human thought. Traditions worldwide hold that at the basis of nature's diversity is a field of unity, that this *divine ground* exists at the center of the human soul and can be directly experienced, and that life is fulfilled only when one discovers and experiences this essence of life, the reality of one's Self. This is the primordial tradition, the perennial philosophy. The scientific terminology and mathematical equations may be new. But the understanding that all of life, both inner and outer, emerges from a single underlying field, and that this field is open to direct personal experience, is ancient and universal.

This knowledge is not the result of philosophical speculation. It reflects the direct experience of countless people through history — the experience of the unity of pure consciousness deep within and the ultimate reality of the universe as this same pure consciousness. The English poet Robert Browning (1812–1889) spoke for the ages when he wrote:

> Truth is within ourselves; it takes no rise
> From outward things, whate'er you may believe.
> There is an inmost centre in us all,
> Where truth abides in fullness.[29]

We now possess a detailed understanding of the underlying reality of pure consciousness, the universally revered divine ground. The technologies of consciousness Maharishi has brought to light enable any person anywhere to dive within, experience this inner treasure, nature's central reality — and rise to the exalted state of enlightenment.

CHAPTER 11

༄

The Future of the World Is Bright

The individuals featured in this book have offered eloquent testimony that there is vastly more to human life than most of us imagine. Voice after voice has testified to the reality of higher states of consciousness — even if only glimpsed — and to the incalculable benefits that flow from this experience. Boundless bliss, inner peace, pure knowledge, a sense of the ultimate meaning of life. Creativity, harmony, and goodwill. A sense of wholeness, fullness, fulfillment. Freedom from tension, doubt, uncertainty, fear, isolation — freedom even from the boundaries of time and space. Physical vitality and health. Direct perception into nature's subtlest and most radiant glories. A profound sense of oneness with the whole of creation. The realization of the entire cosmos as a divine unity, as one's own Self.

But many of our authors go even beyond this. These authors recurrently describe their experience in terms of heaven.

"His life is the working of Heaven," writes Zhuangzi; he "mingles with the Heavenly Order" and experiences "Heavenly joy." Rūmī writes: "(Whilst) I am dwelling with you in some place on the earth, I am coursing over the seventh sphere of Heaven." "It seemeth not unto me that I am on earth," writes Angela of Foligno, "but that I stand in heaven."

Thomas Traherne perceives that "the city seemed to stand in Eden, or to be built in Heaven." One may come to a state, he says, in which "every morning you awake in Heaven; see yourself in your Father's Palace; and look upon the skies, the earth, and the air as Celestial Joys" — a state in which you are "clothed with the heavens, and crowned with the stars." Until you reach this state, Traherne states, "your enjoyment of the world is never right."

Tennyson experiences his awareness expanding "as a cloud / Melts into Heaven." Whitman frames his experience similarly, describing how one's awareness "expands over the whole earth, and spreads to the roof of heaven." H.G. Wells describes moments when one's awareness seems to touch "the melting edge of Heaven." "It had seemed," he writes, "as though Heaven had revealed itself."

"The athlete goes beyond herself," writes Patsy Neal of such moments. "She transcends the natural. She touches a piece of heaven and becomes the recipient of power from an unknown source." Jacquetta Hawkes holds that each of us can "experience the inner life, discovering what we can of the kingdom of heaven to which all have access." For Howard Thurman, such experiences have the power "To make Heaven where Hell is found."

These statements call to mind the age-old belief, found in almost every world mythology, that civilization has descended from a golden age, a paradise, an age of perfection at the beginning of time — an age characterized by innocence and happiness, peace and prosperity, freedom and abundance, long and healthy life. In this idyllic world, all the blessings of life come of their own accord, and earth is a replica of heaven. Gradually, however, human life falls out of harmony with nature. The golden age deteriorates into an age of labor and hardship, sorrow and strife. Moral and physical health declines, life expectancy grows shorter, and permanent happiness is no longer possible. There is fighting even among brothers, and goodness and justice are no longer esteemed. The paradise is lost. In time, however, after each decline, there is eventually a regeneration, an ascent to the golden age — the happy time of the beginning returns. This ranks among humanity's oldest and most universal ideas.

These twin themes — transcendental experience and a golden age — are deeply intertwined. In the *Tao Te Ching*, Laozi declares that to experience "the One," the transcendental field, is to experience heaven and to create an idyllic life on earth:

> From ancient times till now
> the One has been the source of all attainments
> By realizing the One
> > Heaven becomes clear, Earth becomes still
> > spirits gain power and hearts fill up with joy
>
> By realizing the One
> > kings and lords become instruments of peace
> > and creatures live joyfully upon this earth[1]

We find this theme in traditions worldwide, that the peace of the world depends upon peace within. As Ralph Waldo Emerson expresses it: "The reason why the world lacks unity, and lies broken and in heaps, is because man is disunited with himself."[2]

Watering the root

Daily news reports make the prospect of a golden age seem highly improbable if not absurd. Stress is pandemic. We are awash in its symptoms: crime and conflict, disease and drug abuse, child abuse and divorce, accidents and suicides, ethnic and racial strife, corporate and governmental corruption, poverty and economic failure, terrorism and war, cultural conflict and environmental destruction.

Is there a way out?

Only by going to a deeper level. A gardener, faced with a withering tree, does not try to heal each of the thousands of ailing leaves and branches. Instead the gardener waters the root and thereby nourishes every part of the tree.

What is the root of the innumerable problems we face? They stem, fundamentally, from a massive disconnect with the Self. This means constricted awareness and stunted creative intelligence. It means inability to act in accord with natural law, leading inevitably to making mistakes and creating problems and suffering, for ourselves and others. The challenges we confront, in other words, are created by our constricted waking state consciousness. The way out must involve expansion of consciousness.

In the simple act of transcending, consciousness opens to the limitless creativity and intelligence at its source, the field of infinite intelligence that governs the universe. Transcending reconnects life with its foundation, realigns it with natural law. It dissolves the stress that prevents our unlimited potential from developing.

We know in increasing empirical detail what changes take place during Transcendental Meditation practice — the uniquely deep physiological rest, integrated brain functioning, increased brain blood flow, the changes in blood chemistry. We understand the transformations that regular practice sets in motion — in the brain and nervous system, in mental and psychological development, in personal relationships. The research has documented reduced stress and anxiety, growth of intelligence and creativity and wisdom, increased happiness and self-esteem, improved health, reversal of aging, development of personality — all evidence of unfolding human potential. The scientific findings are without precedent.

We also know in detail what happens to the surrounding society. The social side-benefits are equally unprecedented. Small numbers of people practicing the Transcendental Meditation technique by themselves — and even smaller numbers practicing the Transcendental Meditation and TM-Sidhi programs in groups — create a social coherence powerful enough to reverse rising crime, accident, and sickness rates, improve economies, reduce international terrorism, promote positivity and cooperation among nations and their leaders — evidence that human potential can be awakened on a broad social scale.

For both the individual and society, the effect is like watering the root of a tree, nourishing all parts of the tree simultaneously, transforming life from the core.

What if these technologies of consciousness were applied widely — in schools, business and industry, the military? Schools are leading the way. So far more than 400 schools in 54 countries, enrolling 250,000 students, have incorporated the Transcendental Meditation program, with the number rising rapidly. Students' lives are being transformed, as are schools themselves. Given the small numbers necessary to create the Maharishi Effect, we can readily envision a transformation of cities, countries, the world as a whole. It is possible, practical, and achievable.

A transition point in history

More than 50 years ago, when Maharishi first started teaching the simple technique of Transcendental Meditation, he declared his aim to bring not only enlightenment to each individual but peace to the world — and more, to create heaven on earth. The method was simple. Give people an effortless way to dive within, to experience the simplest form of awareness, the fourth state of consciousness — the vital experience long missing from human life.

We are living at a transition point in history, when ancient and modern traditions of knowledge are converging. Ancient traditions identify the unified source of creation and the value of experiencing it; from the Vedic tradition in particular Maharishi has brought to light systematic techniques for awakening this field from within. Modern science is in the process of describing this unified basis mathematically. The procedures of modern science, moreover, are being used for empirically identifying and validating the effects of these ancient techniques. Modern technologies are being employed to disseminate this knowledge worldwide and preserve it for all time. The converging of these two streams of knowledge, ancient and modern, subjective and objective, places in our hands the possibility of profoundly elevating the quality of life for everyone.

Maharishi brought the ancient Vedic knowledge into a modern scientific framework, expanding the domain and direction of scientific research and impelling modern science to recognize, utilizing its own empirical methodology, the reality of higher states of consciousness. We can only begin to imagine the long-term consequences of this discovery.

As for Maharishi's model of seven states of consciousness, the English writer Vernon Katz has this to say:

> His account of the growth of consciousness has a grandeur, a sweep, a clarity, and a depth of psychological insight that has never, to the best of my knowledge, been equaled, let alone surpassed. Others may have had insight into this or that facet of the path but where they see the part

he seems to see the whole. Not only is everything there, but it is there in the correct order, with all the mechanics laid out. Each detail fits perfectly into a design that is more than the sum of its parts. The whole scheme has a rightness, an inevitability reminiscent of a great work of art.[3]

The testimonies of history

In account after account in this book, we have seen people describing their experience as overwhelmingly positive and good. They enjoy profound happiness, well-being, peace. Through their experience many recognize the source of goodness, moral behavior, physical and psychological health. Many come away with a sense of abiding love for their fellow human beings, a conviction of the ultimate oneness of humanity, the central unity of life itself.

Many recognize that human consciousness has immeasurably greater capacities than we use or even imagine, that ordinary waking state experience is superficial and fragmented, a shadow of genuine life — that we are asleep to our higher potentials. Such moments become the apex of their lives. Even a glimpse transforms their sense of life's possibilities, leaving them yearning for another taste of the ineffable fulfillment.

They strive to describe these moments, to communicate them, to share them — yet find their language inadequate. The experience can be known, they tell us, only through the experience itself. Yet their words resonate deep within all of us, and for this reason we have preserved them, sometimes for millennia.

These accounts affirm the reality of higher states of consciousness. They express features of the higher states described by Maharishi, recorded in the ancient Vedic literature and other traditions, reported today by Transcendental Meditation participants in cultures worldwide, and verified by the scientific research on that technique. They affirm the core principles of the world's great spiritual and wisdom traditions — the *philosophia perennis:* Within every human being is a boundless ocean of pure knowledge, power, and bliss, the essence of nature itself. We can experience this field in the simplest form of our own awareness. This experience sets in motion the growth of higher states of consciousness, transforming and fulfilling human life.

"To go within is so simple"

Though experiences of enlightenment have been described intermittently across time, they have not been broadly available to the public, nor have they been an object of scientific inquiry. This has changed. The time is not far away when these experiences, rich beyond language, will not be rare and fleeting, limited to a fortunate few. The supreme awakening of human consciousness is not beyond reach. Nothing, in fact, could be more within our reach, for it is our own nature. In Maharishi's words:

> Transcendental Meditation is just the simple technique of going within, and there you are! To go within is so simple; it is so natural for every man to go to a field of greater happiness.

Maharishi elaborates:

> And how can it be simple? The question arises because constantly I am emphasizing its simplicity. All this message of the inner life and outer life is not new, the same age-old message of the Kingdom of Heaven within. "First seek ye the Kingdom of God and all else will be added unto you." It is the same age-old, centuries-old message, but the message emphasizes today that it is easy for everyone. Without exception, born as man, every man has the right, the legitimate right to enjoy all glories that belong to him, all glories of the inner world and all glories of the outside world. And here is a process every man can directly experience for himself.[4]

With a simple technique for transcending now readily available to all, Maharishi forecast a dawning era of peace and prosperity, free of suffering, lived in higher states of consciousness, in harmony with natural law — heaven on earth. He said, "The future of the world is bright, and that is my delight."[5]

PERSONAL INTERVIEW

☙

"Just a Blink of an Eye Away"

Born in Los Angeles and raised in Texas and Massachusetts, Greg P. attended the University of Massachusetts and earned a master's in education at Harvard. He has worked in higher education, K-12 education, and private business. He is married and has three grown children.

When did you learn the Transcendental Meditation technique, and why?

After some difficult time in my 20s, I suddenly realized something was missing. This was something of an epiphany. Someone suggested I go to a TM introductory lecture. Before it was half over I knew, as forcefully as I have known anything, that I would do this and would never stop. This was 1973, and I was 29. Five years later, I learned the advanced TM-Sidhi program.

What changed after you began your TM practice?

For me at least, life begins when you learn to transcend. For the first time I was pointed in the inward direction, where I discovered life in its most essential and pure nature. I remember how amazed and grateful I was. A new and richer life was somehow magically given to me. It was hugely transforming.

What happened over time?

Like most of us, I had a career to manage during all those years and a family to support. I made time for my meditation twice a day no matter what, even if it meant, as it often did, meditating in a bus, airplane, hotel lobby, train, or library. Once the only place I could find privacy was on the cement floor of a pump house. It never occurred to me to stop meditating or even miss a meditation.

Over the years, of course, I waited expectantly and patiently for Cosmic Consciousness, God Consciousness, and Unity Consciousness to arrive. Always feeling it must be just around the corner.

Yet as the decades of practice elapsed, I began to abandon the notion that I would achieve Cosmic Consciousness in this life. I never stopped believing it was a reality, or that Maharishi's TM and TM-Sidhi programs could lead one there. I just stopped imagining it was going to happen to me.

While I pretty much always enjoyed my meditations, there was never anything "flashy" going on. And as the years passed the changes I noticed in myself when I first began meditating seemed to dwindle or maybe even disappeared. I felt like I was on some plateau. Almost like I was walking in place.

My general attitude was, "I'll just keep doing it because I should go as far as I can in this life. Who knows — maybe next time around. . . ." Like that.

And then what?

In November 2008, after I finished my morning meditation, I realized that something, or rather everything, was different.

Immediately I realized what had happened. It was utterly simple and natural: The experience of pure consciousness, pure Being, had followed me out. Here I was in activity again, but now the experience of pure consciousness, which had become so intimate and familiar in meditation over the years — that soft transcendence, that feeling of unboundedness — was with me in activity.

Everything was the same . . . yet different. This new element was with me as if dogging my footsteps, this new soft sweetness, this new purity, this new feeling of lightness, this new utter clarity.

Of course my first thought was, "Well, this isn't going to last." But it did.

There are no words to describe this experience, so I'll just say, it was well worth the wait. Cosmic Consciousness had arrived, softly and unexpectedly.

What were the first weeks like?

I was both astounded and delighted. It seemed so delicate and fragile, almost shy. I really did not expect it to last. As the days and weeks went by, the experience not only endured but seemed to grow stronger. I finally came to accept that it was here to stay. And with that, I began to relax into it and just let it be what it was, without any expectations or preconceived notions.

But initially you were surprised.

I was as surprised as anyone that such a thing could happen to me. I did not see this coming. I was as unlikely and undeserving a candidate for this as anyone I could think of. Even after years of meditating I still had flaws you could drive a truck through. My daily routine was not nearly as balanced as I would have liked. Given all my responsibilities, I figured I was doing the best I could.

Yet here *it* was, and *it* was undeniable.

I can't really point to anything dramatic or flashy that had been happening either in meditation or out that suggested this was about to occur. It just seemed to be the time. It's kind of like being a homeless person one day and the next day finding out you're actually King of Norway.

Was there anything flashy about the transition itself?

No. It is a quiet, subtle experience. In fact, it is not an experience, as such, at all, but a simple realization. It is the clear and perfect recognition of what has always been the case. I am far more than just my thoughts, emotions, body, and actions. It is the "more" that had been missing, or unseen. The "more" is the totality of any identity I can ever ascribe to myself.

Believe me, I know this is no accomplishment of mine. Any kudos for this are due to Maharishi and the remarkable power of his techniques. This is not false modesty, this is the truth.

The only thing I ever did was to follow the simple (thank goodness) instructions Maharishi gave for the practice of the TM and TM-Sidhi programs. Really, that's all I ever did. That it resulted in this growth for me is as miraculous as anything I can think of. Yet it's utterly real, utterly simple, and utterly available to all. That I know for certain. If my life serves no other purpose, it is to demonstrate that if this can happen to someone like me, it can happen to anyone and everyone.

What developed from there?

In those first days and weeks it seemed so delicate. Yet much more was to come. To my increasing delight, it matured into something even grander, more all-encompassing, more totally engrossing. It was as if the floodgates had been opened and nothing and no one could close them again.

In Cosmic Consciousness, as Maharishi describes it, one experiences pure consciousness as an unchanging continuum underlying the changing states of waking, dreaming, and sleeping. What is your experience?

The underlying field of pure awareness remains unchanged whether going into or coming out of sleeping, dreaming, or waking — always unchanged, unperturbed, unaltered, with no detectable transition. It is my Self, there at all times, under all conditions, in all circumstances, fully, beautifully, totally, unalterably.

At first pure consciousness is experienced more as a backdrop to these changing states, a kind of screen against which all other things are experienced. But as it grows stronger, this abiding experience of pure awareness ultimately *eclipses* waking, dreaming, and sleeping, which comprise what we thought of as living. They become so diminished as to be hardly recognizable as states of consciousness at all. They become insignificant, irrelevant, as if they had never existed, much as getting a PhD diminishes and eclipses the experiences of prior education. Probably not a great example, but you get the point.

And what's left is so much richer and more textured and fuller and more comprehensive and wiser and more stable and more filled with beauty than what you had before that it's like you are living life for the first time — like someone has turned on the light that *is* life and it can never again be extinguished. One now owns the very essence of life.

What was sleep like for you after this change took place?

I could no longer speak of falling asleep. That phrase doesn't fit the reality. Now I *fall awake*. The difference is subtle but real. When one falls awake, one loses awareness of the body but not the wakefulness of pure awareness. Dreams come and go, but nothing disturbs the abiding pure awareness.

When one "awakens" in the morning, there is not the slightest change. It is always simply the Now moment, whether asleep or in waking state. It is just the predominant awareness of Now. Pure Now, if you will.

This is what I mean by falling awake — though in reality there is no falling, just this seamless transition from one diminutive state of consciousness to another, both of which are now totally erased by the overpowering experience of pure awareness.

So there is nothing like sleep for me anymore. Nothing. The body may be asleep, but that is all. The same pure consciousness that occupies my awareness in the depths of meditation and in activity remains fully lively at night in what I used to call sleep. But it is not sleep. It is pure wakefulness, pure awareness. There is not the slightest shift from being "awake," as we call it, to being asleep. Not the slightest ripple or bump. It is all just one thing. One thing, one endless totality, one smooth and perfect field of consciousness, one sameness.

And what is your waking experience?

"Relative life" is still there, but is eternally and completely cloaked in, saturated by, and imbued with this indescribable, attributeless softness of one's own eternal Self. When that is the ultimate reality for you, life is just softer, more filled with those most fundamental qualities of creation: beauty, love, sweetness, and wholeness, in a perfectly integrated way — in their finest, most mist-like, indescribable value. It is lovely beyond words.

What is your experience with thoughts and thinking during the day?

My mind is no longer filled with the noise of thoughts. Instead of thoughts I have what I can only describe as awareness, pure awareness. This is a very different thing — pure silence in the mind, at all times, under all conditions. What needs to be known is known. What needs to be done is done. What needs to be said is said. But these experiences are not accompanied by anything resembling what I used to know as thinking. Instead there is this silence, this awareness, this simplicity.

What I used to think of as thoughts, those perturbations of pure consciousness that bubble up as something more concrete in our minds, now seem to pass through and around this experience, but I am not "thinking." I am aware. Purely and perfectly aware, and that is all. Interesting that one can be just aware of being aware. Such a simple and perfect state.

When this happens, life consumes much less energy, because this way of existing is so much simpler, easier, more natural. The noise is gone. I go about my business in the world perfectly easily and unnoticed. I do everything I always did but in a totally different way now.

Initially, everything and everyone, including myself, is seen as if from a distance, from some perspective outside of what we formerly regarded as our normal perspective in activity. It's as if we're watching a continually unfolding play. We see even ourselves, our body and personality, as part of that play. One begins to see that one is not the body at all, not the limited personality, but something beyond that — something eternal, unchanging, unbounded, removed from the fray of what we used to consider daily life.

Maharishi has described Cosmic Consciousness as the "normal" level of human consciousness, reflecting normal functioning of the nervous system.

This is good to remember. It makes it sound quite ordinary, and in a way it is. It's kind of like driving a car you've owned for years that has lots of little problems, and then suddenly finding all the problems gone. The rough idling, the worn-out shocks, the squeaky brakes, the old tires and wiper blades and radio — everything's been fixed. All those things make quite a difference — but it's not like you're driving a new vehicle.

This is all new for you, but it is still very "normal." Then, gradually, somehow that old four-cylinder engine gets replaced with a fuel injected six that's even more fuel efficient and smoother. Now you have more passing power and can even tow a small camper. Then you find there's a new braking system that can detect a collision before you see it and apply the brakes. And then you discover a backup camera has been installed.

From the outside, your car looks pretty much the same (other than that someone managed to detail it while you were sleeping). So no one but you really notices the differences. It's not like you suddenly changed from a Yugo to a Maserati that wows all your friends. No, the changes are virtually invisible.

But there's no denying that these changes are substantial, even dramatic. Things keep improving, but so gradually that there is never any shock factor, never any overwhelming feeling of being in an entirely new, expensive luxury car. Each new step simply redefines "normal." You begin to take for granted that, yes, this is what it should always have been like. Obviously you appreciate each new change, but you don't linger on what the car was like before. You just accept the new features with gratitude and move forward.

As one moves through Cosmic Consciousness and beyond, there is more joy, more wholeness, more expansion, more knowledge, more inexpressible bliss. This is always something you feel very, very happy about — this new normal. As with the car, no one sees the difference but you. The change is internal and invisible. Maybe the most your friends and family notice is that your engine is running a bit smoother.

Tennyson, describing his experiences of transcending, says that he came to see death as "an almost laughable impossibility."

I remember my birthday five years after that day in November. I thought of it as my first "non-birthday." Never before in my life had the whole realization of timelessness, agelessness been so utterly crystal clear. Never before had it been so obvious that I have always been, that there is no end to me.

Whatever the condition of my body, it has nothing to do with my eternal nature. This is no fanciful notion. This is the absolute truth and the Truth of the Absolute. This realization is as undeniable as it is simple, as real as life itself. In the face of the eternal reality of my Self, the idea of life beginning at birth or ending at death is like a candle next to a bonfire. It is simply eclipsed.

You talked about the experience of pure consciousness growing stronger.

The experience of pure consciousness grows more and more dominant. At first it's more on the level of the mind, more interior. But then it begins moving outward, so to speak. One begins to recognize it in one's entire persona — in one's ego, one's heart, in every fiber of one's body.

The experience of the Self became ever more insistent, more dense within and around me, ever more powerful. And now, in addition to the ongoing experience of it in my own awareness, it has become apparent in all things.

When I began to enjoy glimpses of more glorified states following Cosmic Consciousness, I was certain they would be as profoundly distinct from

Cosmic Consciousness as Cosmic Consciousness was from what preceded it. I guess that is why Maharishi used these specific markers to delineate the key signposts along the way. As you pass by each of these signposts, life changes so dramatically as to be a whole new experience that eclipses what came before.

What about the refined perception that typifies God Consciousness?

Let's start with inner experience. One cannot be soaked in pure consciousness without realizing that this is the field of the divine, the field of love, the field of divine bliss, the field of divine light. This recognition grows as one gains more experience in this field.

At first pure consciousness seemed to be just a kind of benign emptiness. But gradually one comes to experience it as the essential nature of the divine. Just as one cannot separate wetness from water, one becomes increasingly unable to separate this level of awareness from God.

One begins to see in a different way. This includes a refinement and purification of all "normal" avenues of experience, with a much greater degree of heart. The result is a new and captivating experience that reveals such a fine level of existence in everything. Everything, and I mean *everything*, takes on a quality of inexpressibly moving beauty.

One wonders: How could I have missed this? When I look at a tree, or even a stone, or anything, it's so apparent now that all things are structured in so many refined layers — they are so much more than the physical thing we normally see or experience. One experiences this "so much more" as finer and finer levels of creation and ultimately as consciousness or Being itself.

And what's the culmination of this process?

Eventually the experience of pure consciousness eclipses everything — because it *is* everything. And because it is everything one soon stops trying to differentiate pure consciousness from the physical aspect of existence. As this process progresses, it leaves no room for even the concept of individual — no room for duality, no room for separateness, no room for boundaries. Everything continues to melt away in the face of this ongoing, persistent, and tenderly determined experience of wholeness.

Now pure Being, pure awareness, shines at me from all things and all people. My own Self is everywhere, in everything and everyone. The burdens and troubles and vicissitudes of life seem all but gone or, at least, drastically mitigated. In their place is an indescribable lightness and delight and sweetness.

Whether observing another person, an animal, a tree, or even, literally, concrete, one perceives the most divine level of life. Pure awareness permeates everything, all day and all night.

Elaborate on what you mean by "a much greater degree of heart."

Increased love and tenderness, toward all living things. As Maharishi told us years ago, all love is ultimately directed toward the Self. This feeling of love toward even insects, plants, a blade of grass, even a stone, is due to us perceiving, to some degree, our own unbounded Self in that object. It is all the Self, and to the degree that we "recognize" this as we meander through the relative world, we cannot help but love, love, love. It spills from us like liquid gold toward all things.

This is why even total strangers (if there is such a thing anymore) are so familiar to us and why we can feel such human warmth toward them, why we want to speak to them spontaneously, why we want to smile at them.

This growth of love is the growth of Unity. It is not a mood, it is not even glorious. It is just the growth of Unity. It is just love flowing from the Self toward the Self — consciousness appreciating itself. This must be the purpose of manifestation.

So this is another symptom of growth of enlightenment — loving all things more and more, and more purely and spontaneously. One cannot, nor should one even try, to make this happen. That, like all trying, only muddles things. Just let it flow. Or, if it isn't flowing right at this minute, OK, let that be too. Nothing to be forced.

It sounds very attractive.

Increasingly now, I experience everything and everyone I encounter as nothing other than my own Self. This is especially clear when walking in the woods. But it's also apparent in town or anywhere, really. It seems that Being is shining and glistening and even smiling at me from the surface of everything.

This is difficult to describe. It's as if pure consciousness, the Self of everything, somehow rises to the surface and makes itself apparent — though I know it has always been there and it's only that I'm now able to perceive it.

It is a truly simple experience — truly simple, beautiful, magnificent, all at once. And with this experience of becoming aware of my own Self in all things, love begins to flow, love without boundaries, without exceptions, without considerations of any sort. Love flows out toward all that I perceive and seems to flow back to me as well. This grand, blissful, soothing, infinite silence is saturated with love — love for everything and everyone. It is not flashy or overwhelming. It is quiet and profound and supremely unshakable.

This experience is utterly full of delight, joy, bliss, and love. I feel so physically insubstantial at times that it seems my feet are not touching the ground. I feel I am constantly surrounded by a dense sphere of pure consciousness cushioning me from the world as I had come to know it before. And that pure consciousness is my own Self and the Self of all things.

I know you wrote a poem about this.

Yes. I think it does a better job of capturing this experience. Here it is:

> There is only pure transparency, now.
> One perceives the infinite depths of each thing
> Until only the infinite transparent remains.
> What else is there to say about this golden silence
> In which I am perpetually engulfed?
> I cannot wrap any words around it.
> It is clear, it is without boundaries,
> Unless you consider silence a boundary.
> It seems tinged with gold, though when I look closely
> It is just pure and clear transparency.
> There is nothing but this for me.
> Each part of the relative is just a thin covering
> For It. Each part of everything is just It.
> It often leaves me speechless, wordless

And without any thoughts.
When there are thoughts it's not as if
I am the thinker, rather, I am just aware of them.
There is only awareness, and that awareness
Is infinitely and purely transparent.
I have learned again and again,
It is fruitless to try to understand this.

Beautiful....

It is increasingly difficult to think of myself as this body anymore, or as a separate entity of any kind. It's as if the edges of me gradually dissolved into the edgelessness of Self. The solute and the solvent became one inseparable thing.

What is so fascinating about it, so utterly unexpected, is that it is so very, very simple, uncomplicated, literally unremarkable. One hardly notices it happening. I would say one *doesn't* notice it until it reaches a certain point. And then one cannot deny it. Perhaps that's why many may feel no sense of progress — when in fact there are infinitudes of progress every second of our lives.

At any rate, this experience of losing one's boundaries and merging with the totality is the most delicate thing one can imagine. I cannot explain how I came to notice it. It was not what I was expecting. (Note to self: Stop expecting anything in regard to "enlightenment." The process continues to be wholly impossible to predict.)

When one experiences that there is nothing but That, nothing but Brahman, nothing but this shoreless ocean of pure awareness, pure reality, pure consciousness, pure knowledge, and this ocean contains within it the totality of both the relative and the Absolute — this is such an obvious and powerful realization, one wonders how one could have ever experienced otherwise.

It's interesting to hear about the gradualness with which this develops.

This has been a gradual unfolding for me as the daily and continual experience of pure awareness has dominated more and more and more over the past several years. And yet it goes on and on. There is simply no place in this ocean where one cannot be wet with its essential nature. No place to be not IT, no place where IT is not. Nothing one sees is separate from IT. Being, one's pure, essential nature, takes over every last element of existence. One is then forced to conclude, to realize, to see that *That* is all there is. There is nothing that is not That. There is no other. There is no duality. There is no separateness. There is only the undeniable and continual presence of wholeness. Only That, only That, only That.

And so I try to express what is frustratingly inexpressible because the truth of it, the importance of it, is so immense as to belie the simplicity of the expression. As this all-pervading experience grows, I am increasingly at a loss for how to describe it. What is there to describe? There is only one thing, and it is absolute simplicity, absolute clarity, absolute purity.

And It has drowned the other states of consciousness — waking, dreaming, sleeping, even Cosmic Consciousness — in the limitless ocean of *itself*. They have been inundated and washed away by It, just as sleeping and dreaming get washed away by the waking state. How pure and simple and effortless, how gentle and whole Life truly is, how miraculous, all encompassing, and frictionless.

It is the essence of simplicity. No effort is required to attain it. In fact, effort would be counterproductive. This is pure simplicity, pure life, pure awareness, unstained by anything from the relative. Where is it? It is here and now, the place it has always been for each of us. One wonders how it could ever have been hidden. Just a few clouds can block the sun's radiance. Just a few clouds of stress or complexity or strain block this unimaginable simple fullness. Just a few wisps of clouds.

> **What about your sense of your "relative" self? Your ego? The charming personality people experience when they're with you?**

People experience me pretty much as they always have. But for me, the "small" self simply disappeared into the vast and silent and boundless ocean of the Self. That's it. No fanfare. No banners waving. No cheering crowds. Just this effortless transition to one's true identity. Nothing that has gone before could have prepared me for the utter simplicity of this. Nothing. It is so liberating and so amazing. I have no idea what else to say.

It's so much easier than what went before. There is no false identity to maintain anymore. No fake ID to carry around. It's as if you were a secret agent all these years, always hiding who you really were. Imagine the strain of that. And then one day you retire from this strenuous profession. And you go back home and rid yourself of all the trappings of this false person and finally and utterly can just be yourself. Imagine how it would be to be free to be just yourself, or in this case, your *Self*.

This is a subtle yet very profound transition. When I began to experience my identity as That, only then did I really see that all I used to consider as "me" was gone. It is a remarkable thing. I cannot begin to describe it. All I can say is that it is hugely liberating.

What do you experience now when you meditate?

Almost as soon as I close my eyes, I find myself in a very silent, sanctified place, surrounded by light. It is utter softness, utter calmness, and a subliminal feeling of joy or extreme ease. I feel as if I am literally sitting at the feet of the Divine. I don't even know what that means, but that is the experience.

This is so difficult to describe because it is not "flashy." It is perfectly natural and normal. It is just the awareness that *I Am That*, as the Upanishads say. Just the awareness of being everything. Just the awareness that there is only one thing, and it is I, the Self. It's an experience of such utter wholeness and completeness and simplicity. It is perfection itself.

I go deeper and deeper. It is beyond peaceful, beyond serene. Then something quite extraordinary happens. The ocean disappears. I mean it just is gone, and I am in an indescribable place. I am alone with my Self in a way I have never been so clearly and entirely and fully awake to. There is nothing but That — no ocean, no me, no anything but totality. It is just impossible to describe.

I could say the individual "I" had become the Cosmic "I." But that is not quite it. Rather it's that there never was anything but the Cosmic I. The individual "I" never existed to begin with. The wave was never anything but the ocean . . . never anything but the ocean.

This sounds like an intellectual realization. It wasn't. It was just this knowingness, this simple, utterly remarkable fact. The wave was never anything but the ocean.

There is no feeling of, "Oh, I'm in the transcendent." There is just the Self, just oneness. There is no I and no transcendent. They are one thing. They are not consciously realized as one thing. They just *are* one thing.

But you still have a body. What's the experience at that level?

Each morning when I come out of meditation, I feel as if I am emerging with an entirely new physiology. I feel as if every cell in my body is clean, or more accurately, brand new. I experience an unalloyed purity in my whole being, a pristine crystal clarity, and the world and everything in it appears totally refurbished. It's almost as if I have landed on a planet I've never seen before.

My psychology also feels that way — as if it has undergone a deep, deep cleaning. I am filled with a kind of sparkling happiness that I feel must be pouring from me and infecting everything and everyone around me. I don't know if this is happening, but it feels that way.

And then the next morning, the same thing happens. It's like a snake shedding his skin. Only in this case the snake is doing it every day. Every day a whole new me emerges and it doesn't go away. To some degree it gets muted as I attend to the business of my life and living, but that feeling of utter newness persists through the day and evening.

It's as if my whole being gets saturated with this new, refined, glorified, indescribable level of my own awareness — as if this level is becoming increasingly structured in the very fabric of my whole body, my whole psychology, my entire being day after day.

This is a very beautiful thing, a beautiful and gradual unfolding — a blossoming. If Cosmic Consciousness changes everything, Unity Consciousness does so even more. But, again, this is impossible to describe. There is nothing to do but live It, be It, enjoy It. Nothing else to do.

How do you experience the past and the future now, the flow of time?

I feel I'm outside of time. That is to say, the convention we call time has ceased to exist for me. Of course, I will still say "it's 2:30," or "we're late," or phrases like that, but only for the purpose of communication. Otherwise, time has no reality for me, as it had in the past.

It's not just that I do not dwell on the past as much. Rather, the very existence of the past is eradicated almost. Even the recent past, like yesterday or a few minutes ago, retreat to a place more like what the distant past used to be: remembered but of no impact, no importance, no value. This is very refreshing. One is no longer required to carry around any elements of the past. Living in the now is just simpler and easier. It requires less energy.

The same with the future. What it may or may not contain becomes less and less consequential, something we have no control over. The present takes on magnitude, or allness, or, dare we say it, totality.

Time, as I used to conceive of it, has simply been replaced by the huge and undeniable presence of Being. It's perfectly natural and easy and simple . . . very, very simple.

Along with time, all the other conventions we hold to be true in this relative existence are disappearing as well, as the oneness of life is dawning — life truly lived in non-duality.

It's not just the wave becoming aware that it's the ocean but that the ocean is all there is — even the idea of the wave is gone. The more one is the ocean, the less one is the wave. The more one is unlocalized, the less one is localized. The more one is in the now, the less one is in the past or future. The more one is silent, the less one is caught up in thoughts and feelings and emotions.

Do you feel you're losing anything?

Just the opposite. I understand perfectly that if you're captured in the relative, material world, as virtually everyone is, what I've just described may sound undesirable, even a little frightening. After all, we still like our "things," our relative enjoyments, don't we?

All I can say is, this is not about losing anything. It's about gaining everything. As Maharishi has said, it's like moving from a hut to a palace. When you first hear about the palace, you may want to stay in your familiar little hut. But once you start to experience the palace, you never want to go back.

What about the idea of living in accord with natural law, becoming instruments of the laws of nature, a feature of growing enlightenment?

One comes to realize with increasing clarity that nature orchestrates all our actions. We may have known this intellectually before, but now one sees and experiences it as the truth. That happens as the "I," the individual entity, the wave, begins to disappear. I know of no other way to express this. The individual self begins to disappear, to be irrelevant in the face of the experience of Self, the oneness, the singularity, unity.

I have also realized that this process began in earnest the first time I meditated, some 40 years ago at the Cambridge TM center. This assimilation of wholeness, of pure unbounded consciousness — this movement away from individual and toward oneness — started the first time I transcended. And regardless of my "experiences" or lack thereof in meditation over all these years, it has progressed and progressed to this point. I am sure it was progressing as quickly and surely during those times, when all seemed "flat," as it is now.

Never in my wildest dreaming about what higher states of consciousness might be like could I have conceived of anything so profound, complete, magnificently delightful, utterly divine. And believe me, I spent many hours trying to imagine what that might be like.

What about the *support of nature* Maharishi says comes with higher states?

Ah, support of nature. Yes, this is a lovely and sweet connection one begins to notice not only in Cosmic Consciousness and beyond, but even as soon as one begins to meditate. It's as if life rises up to fulfill your needs and desires.

You don't ask life to do that, but it does. Life, or nature, or the environment, whatever you want to call it, becomes your friend, your ally. There is nothing mystical about this. It's just what happens. Everything wants to assist you. And everything *does* assist you in the most innocent, remarkable, effortless way. It's beautiful, simple, and profound.

So many times each day I notice that things just get taken care of. Sometimes it's mundane, sometimes important. Maybe it concerns someone close to me, maybe it's a health or financial issue — it just easily and sweetly gets addressed. And it's done. And then one is freer to just enjoy life. Life gets richer. And it's all just that because we are now more in the flow of nature, of cosmic life. We no longer experience ourselves as somehow outside of nature. No, we have innocently become completely identified with nature. The result is that we encounter fewer obstacles and nature seems to be assisting us at every turn.

We tend to think of support of nature in terms of big events, like getting unexpected money when we need it. But it's much more subtle. Support of nature removes the little blocks that can make day-to-day life bumpy — simply, innocently, and continually. Being in the flow of things makes everything smoother and softer. There are fewer twists and turns, fewer interruptions to the effortless flow of life. Yes, barriers come up from time to time. But the things that made the road rocky mostly get smoothed over or just eliminated.

You repeatedly say this experience is impossible to describe.

I struggle for words to convey the experience of this level of pure awareness where knower and known are one and the same thing, where wholeness and sanctity and bliss are so rich it's as if they have been distilled to their purest, most essential form. Words fail to reveal anything but a hint of it. You cannot put boundaries around the boundless, and words are boundaries as surely as stone walls.

What about terms like *infinity* and *eternity*?

I have come to realize that infinity is not a measure of distance — it is utterly devoid of even the concept of distance. Eternity is not a measure of time — it is the utter vacancy of even a concept of time.

This pure awareness that knows only itself is a beautiful mystery that one can comprehend, can experience, but never explain. And this pure awareness which is infinite silence paradoxically also hums with the infinite frequency of infinite dynamism.

One simply cannot even imagine the silence, bliss, and sanctity that is beyond any concept we have of those notions. There are no boundaries to the experience of these, no limits, no edges. They flow together in limitless waves of infinitude. They flow even beyond the concept of flowing. How incredibly beautiful and full it is, how divine beyond all concepts.

What about the word *bliss*?

Bliss is the very nature of pure consciousness, of the transcendent. Here again words always fail miserably. In trying to describe this we may say, "It was very blissful," or, "I was filled with bliss," as if that could possibly cover it. It doesn't.

As with the Absolute itself there are infinite gradations of bliss. So what to say, then, of those more refined experiences of bliss, those rarefied, exquisite, delicate, atomized experiences of bliss that seem to disassemble every atom of mind and body and spray it as some kind of divine mist into the ethers, the bliss that becomes you and you become, on some nano-particle level, the bliss that dissolves the last figment of your boundaries until there is only It? *That* is the bliss you can't talk about.

No one has made words for this, even in Sanskrit. No one has made thoughts or concepts for this. Words, by comparison, are like crude boulders that crash down the mountainside, crushing trees and dislodging other boulders on the way. Using words to describe this kind of bliss is like trying to use telephone poles to embroider with.

Ah, but the experience — it is not just divine, it is the essence of merging with the divine. The essence of blending yourself seamlessly with God.

This perspective on God differs from what is probably the common one.

Just as one comes to be aware that one's true Self is without boundaries and is, in fact, the essence of all things, one also comes to be aware that God is not separate from anything in creation or cosmic life. God is not separate from ourselves or anything. God is the totality.

Maharishi emphasizes remaining *innocent* about one's experiences — not looking for anything in particular, but simply allowing consciousness to develop through regular TM practice.

Nature seems to have a way of gently, innocently, quietly, infusing more pure consciousness when you are ready, it seems. But, trust me, there is no value I can see in looking for this to happen or having expectations of what it will be like. It *will* happen, and we cannot begin to imagine how it is going to be until it has happened. And when it does, my guess is it will be so smooth and effortless that you may not even notice at first. It is increasingly obvious to me that this is a very, very, very natural process.

What value do you see in sharing your experiences like this?

Well, for one thing, I am not trying to be a teacher. This is not my intention at all. All I can ever do is report the experiences I am having as clearly as possible in the hope of giving a perspective that others can understand. Understand what? The utter simplicity and beauty of this, the reality of it, and the form my own personal experience has taken.

No one should assume that this is definitive or in any way what their own experience "should" be like. It's highly likely that people will experience it with subtle nuances and differences that reflect their own individual nervous systems. In fact, I find this to be the case when I talk with others. Yes, there is a commonality to the experience. But we all experience it with shades and degrees of differences. For that matter, one could say the same of waking, dreaming, and sleeping.

I know what it is to go decades without feeling much in the way of growth, even though one is meditating diligently every day. I know what flatness can feel like. I know what it is to hear the exalted experiences of others when my experience seems remarkably less, light years away. I know what it is to have relinquished hope of achieving such a breakthrough. Really, I know all that.

All I can offer is that each person can break through that flat experience to experiences of wholeness that simply defy words. As I said, if I can do it, anyone can. If I am special in any way, it's that there is nothing special about me at all. What I am enjoying every day is what everyone, everywhere, without exception can enjoy on this utterly perfect path that has been so sweetly and carefully structured for us by Maharishi and Guru Dev. Maharishi has given us everything we need.

And when it finally happens, I think it may well seem to you, as it did to me, that as remarkable as it is, it has always been just a blink of an eye away. I mean this with all my heart.

And one realizes again, it has always, always been there. It has always been who I am. Always.

Notes

NOTE 1 – The perennial philosophy (pages 33 and 42)

The argument here, and throughout the book, falls into what has been called the *perennial philosophy school*, advanced by such scholars as William James, Evelyn Underhill, Joseph Maréchal, Aldous Huxley, Mircea Eliade, Rudolf Otto, W.T. Stace, Frithjof Schuon, Alan Watts, and Huston Smith. This group contends that mystical experience involves direct connection with something underlying and absolute and thus that there is a common core to all mystical experience, independent of cultural, religious, and historical traditions.

Starting in the late 1970s, certain philosophers vigorously challenged this viewpoint. Led by Steven Katz, they argued that there is no common core — that the content of mystical experience is shaped or "mediated" by one's context, by one's expectations, culture, beliefs, and language. Thus different cultural and religious traditions must give rise to different kinds of experiences. This criticism, in turn, grew out of a paradigm shift in the humanities to what is called constructivism. Drawing on Kant and other such philosophers, constructivists argue that all human experience is largely constructed or shaped by our culture, beliefs, expectations, and so forth.[1]

From the early 1980s forward, another group of scholars sharply challenged this constructivist paradigm as it applies to mystical experience, arguing that human beings do possess an "innate capacity" for such experience. Many traditions, including those as diverse as Zen Buddhism and the Catholic monastic *Cloud of Unknowing*, explicitly emphasize that all the aspects of cultural content that Professor Katz and his colleagues are concerned with must be left behind before one can gain the content-free, quality-free state they seek. In other words, in the fundamental mystical experience (the state Maharishi terms Transcendental Consciousness), there is no "content" to be shaped. One transcends the relative contents of consciousness — concepts, values, language, thought, memory, emotion — to experience consciousness in its pure form, as content-free unbounded awareness. Only afterward does one try to represent the experience verbally, in which case one inevitably uses the language of one's tradition.[2]

Experience with the Transcendental Meditation technique adds support to the perennialist claim, in that individuals from a wide variety of cultural and religious backgrounds, utilizing this simple procedure, have transcendental experiences that share common subjective characteristics — characteristics closely resembling those reported in mystical experiences from a variety of cultures and historical epochs.

The scientific research on the Transcendental Meditation technique (Chapter 9) adds further support. As these studies indicate, subjects' experiences are accompanied by a unique set of neurophysiological changes. The "physiological signature" of Transcendental Consciousness, as elicited by the Transcendental Meditation technique, is by now well-defined and predictable and is independent of expectation, culture, belief, and language. These studies thus indicate that the body as well as the mind has an "innate capacity" for transcendence.

NOTE 2 – "The Kingdom of God is within you" – Luke 17:21 (page 72)

Some later translations render the final line of this passage as "The kingdom of God is among you" or "in your midst." Ilaria Ramelli, a professor at Catholic University of the Sacred Heart, in Milan, Italy, has meticulously analyzed the ancient Syriac texts as well as the Greek grammar for this passage and other Gospel passages, and she concludes that the proper translation is "God's Kingdom is inside you."

She also notes that, in its context, only this translation makes sense. She points out that "the Pharisees are notoriously accused by Jesus precisely of giving importance only to exteriority and ostensibility, formal practices and human glory. Jesus, instead, emphasizes that God's Kingdom is interior, invisible, impossible to locate in one place or another, in that it is of a spiritual nature" — "My kingdom is not of this world," as Jesus declares (John 18:36). In the Gospel of Luke, Ramelli observes, Jesus repeatedly underscores the opposition between this world and the kingdom of God — for example, when he asks what good it is for a person to gain the whole of this world but lose himself (Luke 9:25) and when he says that to enter the kingdom one must leave everything else (Luke 18:28–29). She also shows that this interpretation is consistent with several statements Jesus makes in *The Gospel of Thomas* about the kingdom of heaven residing inside us.[3]

But suppose the correct translation actually is "The kingdom of God is among you." Then we should ask, "If it's already among us, how do we access it? How do we harness the life-transforming power Jesus ascribes to it?"

"The father's kingdom is spread out upon the earth, and people do not see it," Jesus says in *The Gospel of Thomas*. That is, the kingdom may be "among you," but people have not experienced it.

The Kingdom of God is within you — Maharishi referred many times to this passage. Here is one comment:

> That state of eternal peace and bliss is just here. The Kingdom of Heaven is within me, and "me" means the "me" of everything, not only the "me" of man but the "me" of everything. The Kingdom of Heaven is within every object of creation and in the innermost recesses of everyone's heart. It is the essential substratum of life. The "me" is the innermost life principle. This is the state of Being. To establish ourselves in That nothing is needed; already everyone is established in himself. The "I" is there, so every man is already established in himself; only his attention is outside, and what is needed is to bring the attention within himself.
>
> Once the attention is brought within, then one becomes established in that eternal peace and bliss.[4]

So Maharishi's explanation supports both translations of Luke 17:21. He also comments on the related verse, Matthew 6:33:

> Christ said: "Seek ye first the Kingdom of Heaven within and all else will be added unto thee." The word "first" is important: first thing in life, first thing during the day. "Do this first and everything will be added unto you" was spoken on the strength of some method of getting to the transcendent state of Being. Christ brought to light the forgotten system of reaching the Kingdom of Heaven within; and then, "all else will be added" — life will be joyful, happy, all desires fulfilled.[5]

NOTE 3 – On Jesus in the Gospel of John (page 367)

I am aware of the work of modern Biblical scholars, for example the Jesus Seminar, to determine the historicity of Jesus's sayings. These scholars generally identify Matthew, Mark, and Luke (the *synoptic gospels*) as more historical and John as more spiritual.

In this book I am concerned primarily with what Jesus is widely believed to have said — statements that, whatever their origin, have profoundly inspired billions of people value across two millennia and that we appreciate in a new light with the understanding of higher states of consciousness.

The issue of historicity is even more pronounced with such figures as Laozi and the Buddha, where there is little certainty about what they actually said. But this takes nothing away from the immense power of the words attributed to them and their relevance to the knowledge of enlightenment we have from Maharishi.

References

Some British spellings have been Americanized in passages reprinted in this book.

Dedication page – "Enlightenment is the supreme awakening to the true nature of life." Maharishi Mahesh Yogi, in discussion with Dr. Steven Rubin, Switzerland, 1976. Personal communication.

CHAPTER 1
Moments of Awakening

Quotations at the beginning of the chapter:
- Henry David Thoreau, Walden (New York: T.Y. Crowell, 1910), 117.
- William James, "Energies of Men" (address presented to the American Psychological Association, New York, December, 1906). First published in *Science*, N.S. 25, no. 635 (1907): 321–332.

1. William Wordsworth and S.T. Coleridge, *Lyrical Ballads 1798* (London: Duckworth, 1898), 252 (Notes: W.W. 1843).
2. William Wordsworth, *Lyrical Ballads* (London, Bristol: Biggs and Cottle, for T.N. Longman, Paternoster-Row, 1798), 203–204.
3. The short quotations from historical figures in this chapter are excerpted from longer passages that appear in Chapters 4, 5, 6, and 7. Full references may be found in the chapter notes to the passages in those chapters.
4. Thomas Merton, *New Seeds of Contemplation* (1962; reprint, New York: New Directions, 1972), 226.
5. Edward Carpenter, *The Art of Creation: Essays on the Self and Its Powers* (London: George Allen & Unwin, 1921), 65.
6. Eugene Ionesco, *Present Past Past Present*, trans. Helen R. Lane (New York: Grove Press, 1971), 157.

CHAPTER 2
Reviving an Ancient Tradition of Human Development

1. Maharishi Mahesh Yogi, "Vedic Cognition: Knowledge Is Structured in Consciousness" (videotaped lecture), February 17, 1974, Interlaken, Switzerland. Also Maharishi's Global Press Conference, November 27, 2002. Source: Institute of Science, Technology and Public Policy, Maharishi University of Management.
2. Elaine Pagels, *The Gnostic Gospels* (New York: Vintage Books, 1989), xxi.
3. Ralph Waldo Emerson, *Journal of Ralph Waldo Emerson*, eds. Edward Waldo Emerson and Waldo Emerson Forbes (New York: Houghton Mifflin, 1912), 551.
4. Henry David Thoreau, *The Writings of Henry David Thoreau: Journal, 1837–1846*, ed. Bradford Torrey, F.B. Sanborn (Boston: Houghton Mifflin, 1906), 53–54.
5. Henry David Thoreau, *A Week on the Concord and Merrimack Rivers* (Boston: Ticknor and Fields, 1868), 146.
6. Henry David Thoreau, *The Writings of Henry David Thoreau: Familiar Letters*, ed. F.B. Sanborn (Cambridge: Houghton Mifflin, Riverside Press, 1906), 6:175.
7. C.N. Alexander et al., "Transcendental Meditation, Mindfulness, and Longevity: An Experimental Study with the Elderly," *Journal of Personality and Social Psychology* 57 (1989): 950–964.
8. This chart summarizes the studies on the cumulative effect of the Transcendental Meditation tech-

nique on cognitive and personality development discussed in Chapter 9. Recent studies indicate that intelligence growth can fluctuate in adolescence, in tandem with changes in the brain as it develops; see, for example, Scott Barry Kaufman, *Beautiful Minds,* October 21, 2011. "Intelligence Is Still Not Fixed at Birth," *Psychology Today,* psychologytoday.com/blog/beautiful-minds/201110/intelligence-is-still-not-fixed-birth. Retrieved July 13, 2012.

9. This research is presented in greater detail, along with reference citations, in Chapter 9.
10. See, for example, Aldous Huxley, *The Perennial Philosophy* (London: Chatto & Windus, 1969). Also see Chapter 3, Note 3.
11. For some Aboriginal tribes, the Dreamtime is the primordial golden age when the ancestors were first created. But as Robert Lawlor writes in his book *Voices of the First Day,* "In Pintupi [the western Australian tribal language] the word for Dreamtime or Dreaming, *tjukurrtjana,* can be translated as the absolute ground of being or the fundamental universal continuum from which all differentiation arises. In Aboriginal cosmology, the universal manifesting field is consciousness, which simply externalizes or dreams the world of thoughts, forms, and matter." Robert Lawlor, *Voices of the First Day: Awakening in the Aboriginal Dreamtime* (Inner Traditions, 1991), 264.
12. Rik Veda 1.164.46. Also translated as "The one being the wise speak of in many ways."
13. Rabindranath Tagore, *Sadhana: The Realisation of Life* (New York: Macmillan,1916), 35.

QUOTATIONS ON PAGE 34:

- *Zoroaster* – *The Chaldean Oracles,* attributed to Zoroaster, quoted by Proclus in *Theologiam Platonis,* hermetic.com/texts/chaldean.html. Retrieved June 1, 2013.
- *Laozi* – Lao Tzu, *Tao Te Ching: The Definitive Edition,* trans. Jonathan Star (New York: Jeremy P. Tarcher/Putnam, 2001), 46.
- *Buddha* – *Wisdom for the Soul: Five Millennia of Prescriptions for Spiritual Healing,* ed. Larry Chang, (Washington, DC: Gnosophia Publishers, 2006), 624.
- *Confucius* – Confucius, *Analects,* in *The Ethics of Confucius,* ed. Miles Menander Dawson (New York: Cosimo, 2005), 2. Also at sacred-texts.com/cfu/eoc/eoc06.htm. Retrieved June 1, 2013.
- *Jesus Christ* – *Holy Bible, New Living Translation* (Carol Stream, Illinois: Tyndale House, 1971). Luke, 17:20–21.
- *Marcus Aurelius* – Marcus Aurelius, *The Meditations,* trans. George Long, classics.mit.edu/Antoninus/meditations.7.seven.html. Retrieved June 1, 2013.
- *Plotinus* – In R.M. Bucke, *Cosmic Consciousness,* sacred-texts.com/eso/cc/cc13.htm. Retrieved June 1, 2013.

QUOTATIONS ON PAGE 36:

- *Hermetic Writings* – *Hermetica: The Ancient Greek and Latin Writings Which Contain Religious or Philosophic Teachings Ascribed to Hermes Trismegistus,* ed. Walter Scott (Oxford, England: Clarendon Press, 1924), 4:340.
- *St. Augustine* – *De vera Religion,* ch. 39, 72. In *The Philosopher in Early Modern Europe: The Nature of a Contested Identity,* eds. C. Condren, S. Gaukroger, and I. Hunter (New York: Cambridge University Press, 2006), 191.
- *The Talmud* – H. Polano, *The Talmud: Selections* (1876), sacred-texts.com/jud/pol/pol27.htm. Retrieved June 1, 2013.
- *Sikhism* – In Merv Fowler, "Sikhism," in *World Religions: An Introduction for Students,* eds. Jeaneane Fowler et al. (Portland, Oregon: Sussex Academic Press, 1999), 334.
- *Hayashi-Razan* – In Genchi Kato, *A Study of Shinto: The Religion of the Japanese Nation* (London: Curzon Press, 1971), 182.

CHAPTER 3
The Seven States of Consciousness

1. See, for example, P.R. Pintrich, "Implications of Psychological Research on Student Learning and College Teaching for Teacher Education," in *Handbook of Research on Teacher Education*, eds. W.R. Houston, M. Haberman, and J. Sikula (New York: Macmillan, 1990), 926–857.
2. Maharishi Mahesh Yogi, *Science of Creative Intelligence Teacher Training Course*, "Lesson 23: The Seven States of Consciousness" (videotaped lecture), (Fiuggi, Italy: Maharishi International University, 1972).
3. Maharishi spent hundreds of hours in videotaped lectures and discussions describing the nature and dynamics of higher states of consciousness. He also describes higher states of consciousness in a number of books, including *Science of Being and Art of Living* (New York: Meridian, 1963 [1995]; reprint, New York: Plume/Penguin Putnam, 2001) and *Maharishi Mahesh Yogi on the Bhagavad-Gita: A Translation and Commentary, Chapters 1–6* (1967; reprint, Harmondsworth, Middlesex, England: Penguin Books, 1988). The discussions of higher states of consciousness in this book draw on these sources.
4. Eva Wong, *Cultivating Stillness: A Taoist Manual for Transforming Body and Mind* (Boston: Shambhala, 1992), 7.
5. Idries Shah, *The Sufis* (New York: Anchor Books, 1971), 344–345.

CHAPTER 4
The Fourth State — Transcendental Consciousness:
Pure Consciousness Awake to Its Own Unbounded Nature

1. Maharishi Mahesh Yogi, *Creating an Ideal Society* (Rheinweiler, Germany: Maharishi European Research University Press, 1977), 123.
2. Maharishi Mahesh Yogi, *Thirty Years Around the World: Dawn of the Age of Enlightenment 1* (The Netherlands: MVU Press, 1986), 461.
3. Maharishi Mahesh Yogi, *Vedic Knowledge For Everyone* (Holland: Maharishi Vedic University Press, 1994), 54.
4. David Hume, *A Treatise of Human Nature* (London: Oxford University Press, 1975), 253.
5. *Thirty Years Around the World*, 294. Ellipses are in the original text.
6. *Maharishi Mahesh Yogi on the Bhagavad-Gita: A Translation and Commentary, Chapters 1–6* (International SRM Publications: 1967; reprint, London: Penguin Books, 1988), 339.
7. For a thorough discussion of this topic, see, for example, Maharishi Mahesh Yogi, *Vedic Knowledge for Everyone* (Holland: Maharishi Vedic University Press, 1994), 6–30.
8. *Maharishi Mahesh Yogi on the Bhagavad-Gita*, 312.
9. Maharishi Mahesh Yogi, *Science of Being and Art of Living* (New York: Meridian, 1963 [1995]; reprint, New York: Plume/Penguin Putnam, 2001), 30–32.
10. Maharishi Mahesh Yogi, *Science of Creative Intelligence Teacher Training Course*, "Lesson 1: Experience, the Practical Basis of the Science of Creative Intelligence" (videotaped lecture), (Fiuggi, Italy: Maharishi International University, 1972).
11. *Science of Being*, 3–4.
12. For example, Maharishi Mahesh Yogi, "Inaugural Address," *Life Supported by Natural Law* (Fairfield, Iowa: Maharishi International University Press, 1988). Also see pages 95–96.
13. *Maharishi Mahesh Yogi on the Bhagavad-Gita*, 261.
14. *Science of Being*, 4.

REFERENCES

15. C.N. Alexander, "Ego Development, Personality and Behavioral Change in Inmates Practicing the Transcendental Meditation Technique or Participating in Other Programs: A Cross-Sectional and Longitudinal Study" (Cambridge: Harvard University, 1982), *Dissertation Abstracts International* 43, no. 2 (1982), 539–B. Sections of this study are reprinted in *Collected Papers* 3, 2127–2134.

16. In *Maharishi Vedic Science and Technology: Teacher Training Course* (Fairfield, Iowa: Maharishi International University Press, unpublished manuscript), ch. 7:3.

17. *Creating Heaven on Earth through Maharishi's Vedic Science and Technology: Experience of Experts in Maharishi's Vedic Science and Technology Discovered in the Eternal Record of the Bhagavad-Gita* (Maharishi University of Management, unpublished manuscript), section 2:37.

18. *Creating Heaven on Earth*, section 2:18.

19. Gackenbach, R.W. Cranson, and C.N. Alexander, "Lucid Dreaming, Witnessing Dreaming, and the Transcendental Meditation Technique: A Developmental Relationship" (paper presented at the convention of the International Association for the Study of Dreams, Ontario, Canada, 1986).

20. *Creating Heaven on Earth*, section 2:6.

21. *Invincible America Assembly: Experiences of Higher States of Consciousness of Course Participants*, vol. 2 (Fairfield, Iowa: Maharishi University of Management Press, in production).

22. *St. Bernard's Sermons on the Canticle of Canticles*, trans. a priest of Mount Melleray (Waterford: Browne and Nolan, 1920), 2:520–521.

VEDIC LITERATURE

1. *Maharishi Patanjali Yoga Sutra*, trans. Thomas Egenes (Fairfield, Iowa: 1st World Publishing, 2010), 11, 33, 37, 39.

2. *Mandukya Upanishad*, in *The Upanishads*, trans. Alistair Shearer and Peter Russell (New York: Harper Colophon Books, 1978), 18–19.

3. *Mundaka Upanishad*, in *The Upanishads*, trans. Shearer and Russell, 37–38.

LAOZI • c. 604–531 BC

1. Lao Tzu, *Tao Te Ching: The Definitive Edition*, trans. Jonathan Star (New York: Jeremy P. Tarcher/Putnam, 2001), 29.

2. Lao Tzu, 14. | 3. Lao Tzu, 50. | 4. Lao Tzu, 61.

5. *Hua Hu Ching: The Unknown Teachings of Lao Tzu*, trans. Brian Walker (San Francisco: HarperOne, 1995), 7.

THE BUDDHA • c. 563–c. 483 BC

1. *The Sutta-Nipata: A New Translation from the Pali Canon*, trans. H. Saddhatissa (New York: Routledge, 1995), 126.

2. *The Wisdom of Buddhism*, ed. Christmas Humphreys (London: Curzon Press, 1987), 127.

3. *The Buddha Speaks*, ed. Anne Bancroft (Boston: Shambhala, 2000), 92.

4. Thomas William Rhys Davids, *Early Buddhism* (London: Archibald Constable, 1908), 72–73.

5. *The Buddha Speaks*, 91. | 6. *The Buddha Speaks*, 35. | 7. *The Buddha Speaks*, 98–99.

8. *Mahayana Mahaparinirvana Sutra*, trans. Kosho Yamamoto, nirvanasutra.buddhistisksamfund.dk/ch12.html. Retrieved June 8, 2013.

PLATO • 428–348 BC

1. *The Collected Dialogues of Plato*, ed. Edith Hamilton and Huntington Cairns, Bollingen Series, no. 71 (Princeton: Princeton University Press, 1973), xiii, xv, xvi.

2. Plato, *The Dialogues of Plato*, trans. Benjamin Jowett (Oxford, England: The Clarendon Press, 1892), 222.

3. *The Collected Dialogues of Plato*, 562–563.

ZHUANGZI • 4TH CENTURY BC

1. *The Complete Works of Chuang Tzu*, trans. Burton Watson (New York: Columbia University Press, 1968), 241.
2. *Musings of a Chinese Mystic: Selections from the Philosophy of Chuang Tzu*, trans. Lionel Giles (London: John Murray, 1911), 90.

JESUS CHRIST • 7–2 BCE – 30–36 CE

1. *Holy Bible, New Living Translation* (Carol Stream, Illinois: Tyndale House, 1971) — Luke 17:20–21. All other Bible passages in this section from the *The Holy Bible, King James Version* (New York: American Bible Society, 1999).
2. Bart D. Ehrman, "Christianity Turned on Its Head: The Alternative Vision of the Gospel of Judas," in *The Gospel of Judas*, eds. Rudolphe Kasser, Marvin Meyer, and Gregor Wurst (Washington, DC: National Geographic, 2006), 78.
3. The Gnostic Society Library, The Gospel of Thomas Collection, gnosis.org/naghamm/nhl_thomas.htm. Retrieved June 13, 2013. Also Stevan Davies, "Mark's Use of the Gospel of Thomas," Neotestamentica 30, no. 2 (1996), 307–334. Available at users.misericordia.edu//davies/thomas/tomark1.htm. Retrieved June 13, 2013.
4. *The Gospel of Thomas*, in *The Gnostic Gospels of Jesus*, ed. and trans. Marvin Meyer (New York: HarperSanFrancisco, 2005), 7.
5. *The Gospel of Thomas*, 12.
6. Elaine Pagels, *Beyond Belief* (New York: Random House, 2003), 53.
7. Pagels, *Beyond Belief*, 56.
8. *The Book of Thomas*, in *The Gnostic Gospels of Jesus*, 209–210.
9. *The Gospel of Philip*, in *The Gnostic Gospels of Jesus*, 68.

MARCUS AURELIUS • 121–180

1. *The Meditations*, trans. G.M.A. Grube (Indianapolis: Hackett, 1983), 84.
2. *The Meditations*, 70.

THE HERMETIC WRITINGS • 2ND & 3RD CENTURIES

1. *Hermetica: The Ancient Greek and Latin Writings Which Contain Religious or Philosophic Teachings Ascribed to Hermes Trismegistus*, ed. Walter Scott (Oxford, England: Clarendon Press, 1924), 1:189.
2. *Hermetica*, 1:155. | 3. *Hermetica*, 1:355. | 4. *Hermetica*, 1:543. | 5. *Hermetica*, 4:340.

PLOTINUS • 205–270

1. William Ralph Inge, *The Philosophy of Plotinus* (London: Longmans, Green, 1918), 1:x.
2. Richard Maurice Bucke, *Cosmic Consciousness* (Seattle: White Crow Productions, 2011), 145–146.
3. Plotinus, *The Enneads*, trans. Stephen MacKenna (London: Faber and Faber, 1930), 63.

ST. AUGUSTINE • 354–430

1. Augustine of Hippo, *The Confessions of Saint Augustine*, trans. Albert Outler (Philadelphia: Westminster Press, 1955), 191.

SHANKARA • 700?–750?

1. Maharishi Mahesh Yogi, *Science of Being and Art of Living* (New York: Meridian, 1963 [1995]; reprint, New York: Plume/Penguin Putnam, 2001), 19.
2. Shankara, *Vivekachudamani (The Crest Jewel of Discrimination)*, trans. for this book William Sands,

PhD, Associate Professor of Maharishi Vedic Science and Sanskrit, Maharishi University of Management. (Lines 124–126, 128, and 131–136).

3. *Vivekachudamani.* (Lines 254–263).

4. *Vivekachudamani.* (Lines 408–409, 410, 412, and 426–427).

MILAREPA • 1052–1135

1. *The Hundred Thousand Songs of Milarepa,* trans. Garma C.C. Chang (New York: Harper & Row, 1970), 158.

2. *Drinking the Mountain Stream: Songs of Tibet's Beloved Saint, Milarepa,* trans. Lama Kunga, Kunga Rinpoche, and Brian Cutillo (Boston: Wisdom Publications, 1978), 46.

SUN BU-ER • 1119–1182

1. *Immortal Sisters: Secret Teachings of Taoist Women,* trans. and ed. Thomas Cleary (Berkeley, California: North Atlantic Books, 1996), 38.

2. *Immortal Sisters,* 48.

ATTAR OF NISHAPUR • 1145–1221

1. *The Persian Mystics,* trans. Margaret Smith (London: John Murray, and New York: E.P. Dutton, 1932), 97.

MUKTABAI • 13TH CENTURY

1. *The Shambhala Anthology of Women's Spiritual Poetry,* ed. Aliki Barnstone (Boston: Shambhala, 1999), 72.

2. *Shambhala Anthology,* 72.

RŪMĪ • 1207–1273

1. *The Mathnawi of Jalalu 'ddin Rūmī,* trans. Reynold A. Nicholson, "E.J.W. Gibb Memorial" Series, n.s. 4 (London: Luzac, 1926), 2:405–406.

2. *Rūmī: In the Arms of the Beloved,* trans. Jonathan Star (New York: Jeremy P. Tarcher/Penguin, 1997), 3–5.

HADEWIJCH • 1220–1260

1. Hadewijch, trans. Nynke Passi, 2011, personal communication. For an alternative, published translation, see *Women in Praise of the Sacred: 43 Centuries of Spiritual Poetry by Women,* ed. Jane Hirshfield (New York: Harper Perennial, 1995), 106.

2. *Women Mystics in Medieval Europe,* trans. Sheila Hughes (St. Paul: Paragon House, 1989), 133.

3. *Women Mystics in Medieval Europe,* 124.

ANGELA OF FOLIGNO • 1248–1309

1. *Angela of Foligno: Complete Works,* trans. Paul Lachance (Mahwah, New Jersey: Paulist Press, 1993), 82.

2. *Angela of Foligno, The Book of Visions and Instructions,* trans. a secular priest (Leamington: Art and Book, 1888), 98. I have modernized the language slightly ("seemeth" = "seems," etc).

3. *Visions and Instructions,* 77–78. | 4. *Visions and Instructions,* 77.

MEISTER ECKHART • 1260–c. 1327

1. Edmund Colledge and Bernard McGinn, *Meister Eckhart* (Mahwah, New Jersey: Paulist Press, 1981), xviii.

2. *Meister Eckhart: Sermons & Treatises,* trans. and ed. M. O'C. Walshe (Longmead, Shaftsbury, Dorset, Great Britain: Element Books, 1979), 1:144.

3. See, for example, Robert Foreman, *Meister Eckhart: Mystic as Theologian* (Longmead, Shaftsbury, Dorset, Great Britain: Element Books, 1991), 194.

4. *Sermons & Treatises*, 2:105. | 5. *Sermons & Treatises*, 1:60–61. | 6. *Sermons & Treatises*, 1:216–217. 7. *Sermons & Treatises*, 1:3. | 8. *Sermons & Treatises*, 1:74.

DANTE • 1265–1321

1. Dante Alighieri, *The Divine Comedy*, trans. H.R. Huse (New York: Rinehart, 1956), 426.
2. *Divine Comedy*, 434.
3. T.S. Eliot, *Selected Essays: 1917–1932* (New York: Harcourt, Brace and Company, 1932), 212.
4. *Divine Comedy*, 479. | 5. *Divine Comedy*, 480. | 6. *Divine Comedy*, 480. | 7. *Divine Comedy*, 481.

KABIR • 1398–1448

1. *One Hundred Poems of Kabir*, trans. Rabindranath Tagore and Evelyn Underhill (London: Macmillan, 1921), 81.

ST. TERESA OF ÁVILA • 1515–1582

1. Teresa of Ávila, *The Complete Works of St. Teresa of Jesus*, trans. Edgar Allison Peers (London, New York, and Harrisburg, Pennsylvania: Continuum International Publishing Group, 2002), 1:306–307.
2. Teresa of Ávila, 1:327.
3. William James, *Varieties of Religious Experience* (London: Longmans, Green: 1903), 408–409.

ST. JOHN OF THE CROSS • 1542–1591

1. *The Collected Works of St. John of the Cross*, trans. Kieran Kavanaugh and Otilio Rodriguez (1964; reprint, Washington, DC: ICS Publications, 1973), 494.
2. *Collected Works*, 645. | 3. *Collected Works*, 149. | 4. *Collected Works*, 195.
5. *Collected Works*, 145–146. | 6. *Collected Works*, 718–719.

THOMAS TRAHERNE • 1637–1674

1. *The Works of Thomas Traherne*, ed. Jan Ross (Woodbridge, Suffolk, UK: D.S. Brewer, 2005), 1:238.
2. Thomas Traherne, *Select Meditations*, ed. Julia Smith (Manchester, United Kingdom: Fyfield Books, 1997), 115.
3. "The Preparative," in *The Poetical Works of Thomas Traherne*, ed. Bertram Dobell (London: Bertram Dobell, 1906), 15–18. For the third line of my excerpt from this poem, Dobell has "Just bounded with the sky." I have replaced this with "Far wider than the sky," from the more recent version edited by H.M. Margoliouth: Thomas Traherne, "The Preparative," in *Poems and Thanksgivings*, vol. 2 of *Thomas Traherne: Centuries, Poems, and Thanksgivings*, ed. H.M. Margoliouth (London: Oxford University Press, 1958), 20–24.
4. Thomas Traherne, *Centuries of Meditations*, ed. Bertram Dobell (London: P.J. & A.E. Dobell, 1950), 136–137.
5. *Select Meditations*, 65–66.

For a detailed discussion of Traherne's work in light of higher states of consciousness, see James J. Balakier, "Thomas Traherne's Concept of Felicity, the 'Highest Bliss,' and the Higher States of Consciousness of Maharishi Mahesh Yogi's Vedic Science and Technology," in *Literature*, vol. 6 in the series *Consciousness-Based Education: A Foundation for Teaching and Learning in the Academic Disciplines Consciousness-Based Education and Literature*, ed. Terrance Fairchild (Fairfield, Iowa: Maharishi University of Management Press, 2012).

HAKUIN ZENJI • 1685–1769

1. *The Embossed Tea Kettle: Orate Gama and Other Works of Hakuin Zenji*, trans. R.D.M. Shaw (London: George Allen & Unwin, 1963), 98–99.
2. *Embossed Tea Kettle*, 111. | 3. *Embossed Tea Kettle*, 114. | 4. *Embossed Tea Kettle*, 117–118.

5. *Embossed Tea Kettle*, 147. | 6. *Embossed Tea Kettle*, 153.

DOV BER OF MEZERITCH • 1710–1772

1. *Your Word Is Fire*, ed. and trans. Arthur Green and Barry W. Holtz (New York: Paulist Press, 1977), 56.
2. *Your Word is Fire*, 57. | 3. *Your Word is Fire*, 59

JOHANN WOLFGANG VON GOETHE • 1749–1832

1. Goethe, from "Eins und Alles," *Select Minor Poems, translated from the German of Goethe and Schiller*, trans. John S. Dwight (Boston: Hilliard, Gray, 1839), 151.
2. Paul Carus, *Goethe* (Chicago and London: Open Court, 1915), 242.
3. *Johann Wolfgang von Goethe: Selected Poems*, ed. and trans. Christopher Middleton et al. (Princeton, NJ: Princeton University Press, 1994), 267.
4. Wilhelm Friedrich Nietzsche, *Human, All Too Human: A Book for Free Spirits*, trans. Marion Faber, Stephen Lehmann, Arthur C. Danto (Lincoln, Nebraska: Bison Books, University of Nebraska Press, 1996), 259.

RALPH WALDO EMERSON • 1803–1882

1. Ralph Waldo Emerson, "The Over-Soul," in *Ralph Waldo Emerson, Essays: First Series* (Boston: James Munroe and Company, 1884), 219.
2. Ralph Waldo Emerson, "Self-Reliance," in *Essays: First Series*, 35.

ALFRED, LORD TENNYSON • 1809–1892

1. Hallam Tennyson, *Alfred, Lord Tennyson: A Memoir by his Son* (London: Macmillan, 1897), 1:320.
2. Hallam Tennyson, 2:473.
3. "The Ancient Sage," in *Poems of Tennyson*, ed. Jerome Hamilton Buckley (Cambridge: Riverside Press, 1958), 504.
4. Hallam Tennyson, 2:90.

HENRY DAVID THOREAU • 1817–1862

1. Henry David Thoreau, *Writings*, ed. Bradford Torrey (New York: AMS Press, 1968), vol. 6, 175.
2. *The Writings of Henry David Thoreau: Journal*, eds. Bradford Torrey and F.B. Sanborn (Boston: Houghton Mifflin, 1906), 53–54.
3. Henry David Thoreau, *Summer: from the Journal of Henry D. Thoreau*, ed. H.G.O. Blake (Boston and New York: Houghton Mifflin, Riverside Press, 1884), 207–208.
4. Henry David Thoreau, *Autumn: from the Journal of Henry D. Thoreau*, ed. H.G.O. Blake (Cambridge, Massachusetts: Houghton Mifflin, Riverside Press, 1892), 435.

EMILY BRONTË • 1818–1848

1. Emily Brontë, "Julian M. and A.G. Rochelle," *The Complete Poems of Emily Jane Brontë*, ed. C.W. Hatfield (New York: Columbia University Press, 1941), 238–239.

WALT WHITMAN • 1819–1892

1. "Ralph Waldo Emerson (1803–1882) to Walt Whitman (1819–1892)," in "Revising Himself: Walt Whitman and Leaves of Grass," loc.gov/exhibits/treasures/ww0017-trans.html. Retrieved on September 1, 2012.
2. Walter Whitman, *Democratic Vistas* (New York: J.S. Redfield/Washington, DC, 1871), 41.
3. *Democratic Vistas*, 47.
4. Walt Whitman, "Passage to India," *Leaves of Grass* (Philadelphia: David McKay, 1891), 315.
5. Walter Whitman, "Song of Myself," *Leaves of Grass* (Philadelphia: David McKay, 1892), 77.

HENRI FRÉDÉRIC AMIEL • 1821–1881

1. Henri Frédéric Amiel, *Amiel's Journal: The Journal Intime of Henri-Frédéric Amiel*, trans. Mrs. Humphry Ward. gutenberg.org/files/8545/8545-h/8545-h.htm. Retrieved June 19, 2015.
2. *Amiel's Journal*. | 3. *Amiel's Journal*. | 4. *Amiel's Journal*.

EMILY DICKINSON • 1830–1886

1. Emily Dickinson, Untitled poem, "306," *The Complete Poems of Emily Dickinson*, ed. Thomas H. Johnson (Boston: Little, Brown and Company, copyrights 1890 to 1960), 144.
2. Emily Dickinson, Untitled poem, "1695," *The Complete Poems of Emily Dickinson*, 691.

EDWARD CARPENTER • 1844–1929

1. Edward Carpenter, *The Art of Creation: Essays on the Self and Its Powers*, 5th ed. (London: Allen & Unwin, 1921), 227–230.
2. *The Art of Creation*, 265.
3. Edward Carpenter, *The Drama of Love and Death: A Study of Human Evolution and Transfiguration* (New York and London: Michell Kennerly, 1912), 82–84.

BLACK ELK • 1863–1950

1. Joseph Epes Brown, *The Spiritual Legacy of the American Indian* (Bloomington, Indiana: World Wisdom, 2007), 106.
2. Joseph Epes Brown, *The Sacred Pipe: Black Elk's Account of the Seven Rites of the Oglala Sioux* (New York: Penguin Books, 1971), 5, 6, 14. Also see *The Sixth Grandfather: Black Elk's Teachings Given to John G. Neihardt*, ed. Raymond J. DeMallie (Lincoln: University of Nebraska Press, 1984), 81.
3. *The Sacred Pipe*, 138.
4. *The Sacred Pipe*, 129, 131.

RABBI ABRAHAM ISAAC KOOK • 1865–1935

1. *The Essential Kabbalah: The Heart of Jewish Mysticism*, ed. Daniel C. Matt (Edison, New Jersey: Castle Books, 1997), 124.
2. *The Essential Writings of Abraham Isaac Kook*, ed. and trans. Ben Zion Bokser (Amity, New York: Amity Books), 1988), 153.
3. *Essential Writings of Abraham Isaac Kook*, 160.

PAUL VALÉRY • 1871–1945

1. Paul Valéry, "Meditation Before Thought," in *Poems in the Rough*, trans. Hilary Corke, in *The Collected Works of Paul Valéry*, ed. Jackson Matthews, Bollingen Series, no. 45 (Princeton: Princeton University Press, 1969), 2:61–62.

MARTIN BUBER • 1878–1965

1. Martin Buber, *Between Man and Man*, trans. Ronald Gregor Smith (London, New York: Routledge, 2002), 13–14.
2. Martin Buber, "Introduction: Ecstasy and Confession," in *Ecstatic Confessions*, ed. Paul Mendes-Flohr, trans. Esther Cameron (San Francisco: Harper & Row, 1985), 2–7.

ALBERT EINSTEIN • 1879–1955

1. Jeremy Bernstein, *Einstein* (New York: Viking Press, 1973), 11.

HELEN KELLER • 1880–1968

1. Helen Keller, *My Religion* (New York: Swedenborg Foundation, 1927, reprint 1980), 35.
2. Helen Keller, *The World I Live In* (New York: Century, 1908), 132–133.

REFERENCES

MORIHEI UESHIBA • 1883–1969

1. Morihei Ueshiba, *The Art of Peace*, trans. and ed. John Stevens (Boston: Shambhala, 2002), 11.
2. Mitsugi Saotome, *Aikido and the Harmony of Nature* (Boston: Shambhala, 1993), 17. | 3. Saotome, 31.
4. *Art of Peace*, 49. | 5. *Art of Peace*, 66. | 6. *Art of Peace*, 44. | 7. *Art of Peace*, 91. | 8. *Art of Peace*, 51.
9. *Art of Peace*, 57. Also see *The Essence of Aikido: Spiritual Teachings of Morihei Ueshiba*, ed. John Stevens (New York City: Kodansha USA, 2013), 97.
10. Saotome, 31. | 11. *The Art of Peace*, 87.
12. John Stevens, "Aikido & Yoga," *Yoga Journal*, Sept.–Oct. 1988, 63.
13. John Stevens, *Abundant Peace: The Biography of Morihei Eushiba, Founder of Aikido* (Boston: Shambhala, 1987), 106.

D.H. LAWRENCE • 1885–1930

1. E.M. Forster, Letter to The Nation and Atheneum, March 29, 1930. In "D.H. Lawrence," en.wikipedia.org/wiki/D._H._Lawrence. Retrieved June 4, 2012.
2. D.H. Lawrence, *The Rainbow* (New York: Random House, Modern Library, 1943), 70–71.
3. D.H. Lawrence, "The Real Thing," in *The Cambridge Edition of the Works of D.H. Lawrence*, ed. James T. Boulton, *Late Essays and Articles* (Cambridge: Cambridge University Press, 2004), 310.

FRANKLIN MERRELL-WOLFF • 1887–1985

1. Franklin Merrell-Wolff, *The Philosophy of Consciousness Without an Object: Reflections on the Nature of Transcendental Consciousness* (New York: Julian Press, 1973), 37–48.
2. Franklin Merrell-Wolff, *Pathways through to Space* (New York: Julian Press, 1973), 4–5.

HOWARD THURMAN • 1899–1981

1. Howard Thurman, *The Inward Journey* (Richmond, Indiana: Friends United Press, 1961), 112.
2. *The Inward Journey*, 123–124. | 3. *The Inward Journey*, 130. | 4. *The Inward Journey*, 96.

DAG HAMMARSKJÖLD • 1905–1961

1. "The Dag Hammarskjöld interview with biographer Roger Lipsey," *Read the Spirit* (nd). readthespirit.com/explore/the-dag-hammarskjold-interview-with-biographer-roger-lipsey/. Retrieved May 1, 2015.
2. Dag Hammarskjöld, *Markings* (New York: Knopf, 1964), 152. | 3. *Markings*, 76. | 4. *Markings*, 166. | 5. *Markings*, 165. | 6. *Markings*, 118.
7. "'A Room of Quiet' — The Meditation Room, United Nations Headquarters," un.org/depts/dhl/dag/meditationroom.htm. Retrieved April 29, 2015.

ARTHUR KOESTLER • 1905–1983

1. Arthur Koestler, *The Invisible Writing* (New York: Macmillan, 1954), 350–353.
2. *The Invisible Writing*, 353.

EUGENE IONESCO • 1909–1994

1. Eugene Ionesco, *Present Past Past Present*, trans. Helen R. Lane (New York: Grove Press, 1971), 150–154.

THOMAS MERTON • 1915–1969

1. Thomas Merton, *New Seeds of Contemplation* (New York: New Directions, 1972), 226–228.
2. Thomas Merton, *Silence in Heaven: A Book of the Monastic Life* (London: Thames & Hudson, 1956), 24.

ANWAR EL-SADAT • 1918–1981

1. Anwar el-Sadat, *In Search of Identity* (1977; reprint, New York: Harper & Row, 1979), 73, 79, 84–87.
2. Sadat, 80–81.

CHAPTER 5
The Fifth State — Cosmic Consciousness:
Unbounded Awareness as a Permanent Reality

1. Billie Jean King with Kim Chapin, *Billie Jean* (New York: Harper & Row, 1974), 191.
2. *Billie Jean*, 197–201.
3. Maharishi Mahesh Yogi, *Science of Creative Intelligence Teacher Training Course*, "Lesson 23: The Seven States of Consciousness" (videotaped lecture), (Fiuggi, Italy: Maharishi International University, 1972).
4. *Science of Creative Intelligence Teacher Training Program, Teacher's Handbook* (Santa Barbara, California: Maharishi International University Press, 1972), "Lesson 23: The Seven States of Consciousness," 17–18.
5. Maharishi Mahesh Yogi, *Science of Being and Art of Living* (New York: Meridian, 1963 [1995]; reprint, New York: Plume/Penguin Putnam, 2001), 40.
6. *Science of Being*, 65.
7. *Maharishi Mahesh Yogi on the Bhagavad-Gita: A Translation and Commentary, Chapters 1–6* (1967; reprint, Harmondsworth, Middlesex, England: Penguin Books, 1988), 314.
8. Maharishi Mahesh Yogi, "Metabolic Rate of Cosmic Consciousness" (audiotaped lecture), June 25, 1971, Amherst, Massachusetts. Also Maharishi Mahesh Yogi, "CC Experiences" (videotaped lecture), December 6, 1971. Also see *Science of Being*, 98.
9. *Maharishi on the Bhagavad-Gita*, 313. Also *Science of Being*, 38.
10. *Maharishi on the Bhagavad-Gita*, 184.
11. *Science of Being*, 231.
12. *Maharishi on the Bhagavad-Gita*, 145.
13. *Maharishi on the Bhagavad-Gita*, 98–99, 291–292.
14. *Science of Creative Intelligence Teacher Training Program, Teacher's Handbook*, 16–17.
15. Maharishi Mahesh Yogi, "Characteristic Values of Higher States of Consciousness" (videotaped lecture), July 4, 1971, Amherst, Massachusetts. Also *Science of Being*, 245.
16. *Maharishi on the Bhagavad-Gita*, 156–157, and *Science of Being*, 89–90. Also see Vernon Katz, *Conversations with Maharishi: Maharishi Mahesh Yogi Speaks About the Full Development of Human Consciousness* (Fairfield, Iowa: Maharishi University of Management Press, 2011), 1:22–24.
17. *Maharishi on the Bhagavad-Gita*, 424.
18. For a collection of Maharishi's lectures on this topic, see Maharishi Mahesh Yogi, *Life Supported by Natural Law* (Fairfield, Iowa: Maharishi International University Press, 1988).
19. *Maharishi on the Bhagavad-Gita*, 142–143.
20. *Life Supported by Natural Law*, 97–98.
21. *Science of Being*, 74.
22. *Science of Being*, 247–248.
23. *Creating Heaven on Earth Through Maharishi's Vedic Science and Technology: Experience of Experts in Maharishi's Vedic Science and Technology Discovered in the Eternal Record of the Bhagavad-Gita* (Maharishi University of Management, unpublished manuscript), section 2:39.
24. Charles N. Alexander and Robert W. Boyer, "Seven States of Consciousness: Unfolding the Full Potential of the Cosmic Psyche in Individual Life through Maharishi Vedic Psychology," *Modern Science and Vedic Science* 2, no. 4 (Winter 1989), 344.
25. *Creating Heaven on Earth*, section 3:5.

26. Alexander and Boyer, 344.
27. From an unpublished paper by Denise Gerace and Charles Alexander.
28. From the archives of sleep researcher Lynne Mason, personal communication.
29. C.N. Alexander et al., "Transcendental Consciousness: A Fourth State of Consciousness Beyond Sleep, Dreaming, and Waking," in Jane Gackenbach, ed., *Sleep and Dreams: A Sourcebook* (New York: Garland Publishing, 1987), 295.
30. *Invincible America Assembly: Experiences of Higher States of Consciousness of Course Participants*, vol. 2 (Fairfield, Iowa: Maharishi University of Management Press, in production).
31. *Invincible America Assembly: Experiences of Higher States of Consciousness of Course Participants, 2006–2009*, vol. 1 (Fairfield, Iowa: Maharishi University of Management Press), 270.

VEDIC LITERATURE

1. *Maharishi Patanjali Yoga Sutra*, trans. Thomas Egenes (Fairfield, Iowa: 1st World Publishing, 2010), 17, 18, 79.
2. *Maharishi Mahesh Yogi on the Bhagavad-Gita: A Translation and Commentary, Chapters 1–6* (1967; reprint, Harmondsworth, Middlesex, England: Penguin Books, 1988), 342.
3. *Maharishi on the Bhagavad-Gita*, 135. | 4. *Maharishi on the Bhagavad-Gita*, 154.
5. *The Upanishads*, trans. Juan Mascaró (Harmondsworth, Middlesex, England: Penguin Books, 1965), 100.
6. Swami Venkatesananda, *The Concise Yoga Vasishta* (Albany, New York: State University of New York Press, 1984), 44.

LAOZI • 6TH CENTURY BC

1. Lao Tzu, *Tao Te Ching: The Definitive Edition*, trans. Jonathan Star (New York: Jeremy P. Tarcher/Putnam, 2001), 69.
2. *Hua Hu Ching: The Unknown Teachings of Lao Tzu*, trans. Brian Walker (San Francisco: HarperOne, 1995), 106.
3. *Wen-Tzu: Understanding the Mysteries*, trans. Thomas Cleary (Boston and London: Shambhala, 1992), 7.
4. *Wen-Tzu*, 20. | 5. *Wen-Tzu*, 81.

THE BUDDHA • 5TH CENTURY BC

1. *The Dhammapada*, in *Two Suns Rising*, trans. Jonathan Star (New York: Bantam, 1991), 62–63.
2. *The Buddha Speaks*, ed. Anne Bancroft (Boston: Shambhala, 2000), 34.
3. *The Word of the Buddha*, ed. Bhikkhu Nyanatiloka (Rangoon: International Buddhist Society, 1907), 15–16.
4. Bikkhu Nanamoli, *The Life of the Buddha: According to the Pali Canon* (Kandy, Sri Lanka: Buddhist Publication Society, 1992), 188.

ZHUANGZI • 4TH CENTURY BC

1. *The Complete Writings of Chuang Tzu*, trans. Burton Watson (New York: Columbia University Press, 1968), 144.
2. *Complete Writings of Chuang Tzu*, 133–134. | 3. *Complete Writings of Chuang Tzu*, 235.

JESUS CHRIST • 7–2 BCE – 30–36 CE

1. *The Holy Bible*, International Standard Version, isv.scripturetext.com/luke/6.htm. Retrieved April 23, 2013. The same teaching is given in Matthew 7:24–27.
2. The remaining Bible passages in this section are from the *The Holy Bible, King James Version* (New York: American Bible Society, 1999).

3. *The Gospel of Thomas*, in *The Gnostic Gospels of Jesus*, ed. and trans. Marvin Meyer (New York: HarperSanFrancisco, 2005), 15–16.
4. *The Gospel of Thomas*, in *The Gnostic Scriptures*, trans. Bentley Layton (New Haven: Anchor Bible/Yale University Press, 1995), 389.
5. *The Gospel of Thomas*, in *The Gnostic Gospels of Jesus*, 10–11.

PLOTINUS • 205–270

1. Plotinus, *The Enneads*, trans. Stephen MacKenna (London: Faber and Faber, 1956), 44–51.
2. Plotinus, 63.

ANGELA OF FOLIGNO • c. 1248–1309

1. Angela of Foligno, *The Book of Visions and Instructions*, trans. a secular priest (Leamington: Art and Book, 1888), 96.

MEISTER ECKHART • 1260–c. 1327

1. *Meister Eckhart: Sermons & Treatises*, trans. and ed. M. O'C. Walshe (Longmead, Shaftsbury, Dorset, Great Britain: Element Books, 1979), 3:120–128.

ST. TERESA OF ÁVILA • 1515–1582

1. St. Teresa of Ávila, *The Interior Castle*, trans. and ed. E. Allison Peers (London: Continuum International Publishing Group, 2002), 127.
2. "Spiritual Testimonies," in *The Collected Works of St. Teresa of Ávila*, trans. K. Cavanaugh and O. Rodrigues (Washington, DC: Institute of Carmelite Studies, ICS Publications, 1976), 1:363.

HAKUIN ZENJI • 1685–1769

1. *The Embossed Tea Kettle: Orate Gama and Other Works of Hakuin Zenji*, trans. R.D.M. Shaw (London: George Allen & Unwin, 1963), 82.
2. *Embossed Tea Kettle*, 62–63.

RALPH WALDO EMERSON • 1803–1882

1. Ralph Waldo Emerson, *Nature*, published as part of *Nature; Addresses and Lectures* (Boston and New York: Phillips, Samson and Ralph Waldo Emerson, 1849), 15.

HENRY DAVID THOREAU • 1817–1862

1. Henry David Thoreau, *Walden* (New York: T. Y. Crowell & Co., 1910), 177.
2. *Early Spring in Massachusetts and Summer: From the Journal of Henry D. Thoreau*, ed. H.G.O. Blake (Boston: Houghton Mifflin, Riverside Press, 1893), 157.
3. *Walden*, 117.

WALT WHITMAN • 1819–1892

1. Walter Whitman, "Song of Myself," *Leaves of Grass* (Philadelphia: David McKay, 1892), 31. Available at whitmanarchive.org/published/LG/1891/poems/27. Retrieved July 3, 2103.
2. Whitman, "The Mystic Trumpeter," *Leaves of Grass*, 358. Available at whitmanarchive.org/published/LG/1891/poems/268. Retrieved July 3, 2103.

LEO TOLSTOY • 1828–1910

1. Leo Tolstoy, *Anna Karenina*, trans. Constance Garnett (New York: P.F. Collier & Son, 1917), 240–242.
2. Leo Tolstoy, *War and Peace*, trans. Louise and Aylmer Maude (New York: Simon & Schuster, 1942), 468.

REFERENCES

EMILY DICKINSON • 1830–1886

1. Emily Dickinson, Untitled poem, "1684," in *The Complete Poems of Emily Dickinson*, ed. Thomas H. Johnson (Boston: Little, Brown and Company, n.d.), 687–688.
2. Dickinson, Untitled poem, "1309," in *The Complete Poems of Emily Dickinson*, 569.

JOHANNES BRAHMS • 1833–1897

1. Arthur M. Abell, *Talks with Great Composers* (New York: Philosophical Library, 1955), 5–6.
2. Abell, 9. | 3. Abell, 66.

EDWARD CARPENTER • 1844–1929

1. Edward Carpenter, *My Days and Dreams* (London: Allen & Unwin, 1921), 106–107.

ROMAIN ROLLAND • 1866–1944

1. William Thomas Starr, *Romain Rolland: One Against All* (The Hague, Paris: Mouton, 1971), 209. Passage translated from the French by Daniela Hathaway for this book.
2. Romain Rolland, *Le Cloître de la Rue d'Ulm: Journal de Romain Rolland 1886–89* (Paris: Editions Albin Michel, 1952), 87. Passage translated from the French by Daniela Hathaway.
3. Rolland, *Le Cloître de la Rue d'Ulm*, 115–116. Passage translated from the French by Daniela Hathaway.

PAUL VALÉRY • 1871–1945

1. Paul Valéry, "Lost Verses," from *Poems in the Rough*, trans. Hilary Corke, in *The Collected Works of Paul Valéry*, ed. Jackson Matthews, Bollingen Series, no. 45 (Princeton: Princeton University Press, 1969), 2:165–168.

ANTONIO MACHADO • 1875–1939

1. Antonio Machado, "Has my heart gone to sleep?" *Border of a Dream: Selected Poems of Antonio Machado*, trans. Willis Barnstone (Port Townsend, Washington: Copper Canyon Press, 2003), 89.
2. Antonio Machado, untitled poem, in *The Dream Below the Sun,* trans. Willis Barnstone (Trumansburg, New York: Crossing Press, 1981), 109.
3. Machado, untitled poem, in *The Dream Below the Sun*, 113.

MORIHEI UESHIBA • 1883–1969

1. Morihei Ueshiba, *The Art of Peace*, trans. and ed. John Stevens (Boston: Shambhala, 2002), 53.
2. *The Art of Peace*, 66. | 3. *The Art of Peace*, 44. | 4. *The Art of Peace*, 89. | 5. *The Art of Peace*, 61.
6. Jules Aib, *The Secret Science of Combat Strategy* (Bloomington, Indiana: Balboa Press, 2012), 157.
7. *Art of Peace,* 47.
8. Mitsugi Saotome, *Aikido and the Harmony of Nature* (Boston: Shambhala, 1993), 52.
9. *The Art of Peace,* 75. | 10. *The Art of Peace,* 67.

EDWIN FISCHER • 1886–1960

1. Alfred Brendel, "Edwin Fischer: Remembering My Teacher," from *Musical Thoughts and Afterthoughts* (London: Robson Books, 1976, 1998), oocities.com/Vienna/2192/essays3.html. Retrieved February 28, 2011.
2. Paul Badura-Skoda, *Interpreting Bach at the Keyboard* (Epilogue), trans. Alfred Clayton (Oxford: Clarendon Press, 1993), 525.

FRANKLIN MERRELL-WOLFF • 1887–1985

1. Franklin Merrell-Wolff, *Pathways through to Space* (New York: Julian Press, 1973), 20.
2. *Pathways through to Space*, 115.

HENRY MILLER • 1891–1980

1. Henry Miller, *Tropic of Capricorn* (1939; reprint, New York: Grove Press, Black Cat Books, 1962), 284–286.
2. Henry Miller, *The Wisdom of the Heart* (New York: New Directions, 1941), 88–89.

CHARLOTTE WOLFF • 1897–1986

1. Charlotte Wolff, *On the Way to Myself: Communications to a Friend* (London: Methuen, 1969), 35–37.

HOWARD THURMAN • 1899–1981

1. Howard Thurman, *The Inward Journey* (Richmond, Indiana: Friends United Press, 1961), 25.
2. Howard Thurman, *Meditations of the Heart* (Boston: Beacon Press, 1953), 24.
3. *The Inward Journey*, 90.

CHARLES LINDBERGH • 1902–1974

1. Charles Lindbergh, *Autobiography of Values*, ed. William Jovanovich (New York: Harcourt Brace Jovanovich, 1977), 11–12.
2. Lindbergh, 375, 383. | 3. Lindbergh, 383. | 4. Lindbergh, 398. | 5. Lindbergh, 357–358.

CLARE BOOTH LUCE • 1903–1987

1. John A. O'Brien, *The Road to Damascus: The Spiritual Pilgrimage of Fifteen Converts to Catholicism* (Garden City, New York: Doubleday, 1949), 223–24.

EUGENE IONESCO • 1909–1994

1. Eugene Ionesco, *Present Past Past Present*, trans. Helen R. Lane (New York: Grove Press, 1971), 154–157.

ROGER BANNISTER • b. 1929

1. Roger Bannister, *The Four-Minute Mile* (Guilford, Connecticut: The Lyons Press/Globe Pequot Press, 2004), 167–173. Several of the ellipses are in the original text.

RAY REINHARDT • b. 1930

1. Gwyneth Richards, "The World a Stage: A Conversation with Ray Reinhardt," in *San Franscisco Theatre Magazine*, Winter 1977: 43.

VÁCLAV HAVEL • 1936–2011

1. Václav Havel, *Letters to Olga*, trans. Paul Wilson (New York: Henry Holt, 1989), 221.
2. *Letters to Olga*, 329.
3. *Letters to Olga*, 331–332.
4. Marci Shore, "Havel: A Life,' by Michael Zantovsky," *The New York Times Sunday Book Review*, December 26, 2014, nytimes.com/2014/12/28/books/review/havel-a-life-by-michael-zantovsky.html. Retrieved April 21, 2015.
5. Václav Havel, speech made in Independence Hall, Philadelphia, July 4, 1994, constitutioncenter.org/libertymedal/recipient_1994_speech.html. Retrieved February 28, 2011.

PATSY NEAL • b. 1938

1. Patsy Neal, *Sport and Identity* (Philadelphia: Dorrance, 1972), 91.
2. *Sport and Identity*, 166–167.

PELÉ • b. 1940

1. Pelé with Robert L. Fish, *My Life and the Beautiful Game: The Autobiography of Pelé* (Garden City, New York: Doubleday: 1977), 51.

REFERENCES

ECKART TOLLE • b. 1948

1. Eckhart Tolle, *The Power of Now* (Novato, California: New World Library, 1999), 1.
2. *Power of Now*, 1–2. | 3. *Power of Now*, 2–3. | 4. *Power of Now*, 9–10. | 5. *Power of Now*, 108. | 6. *Power of Now*, 187.
7. Eckhart Tolle, *Stillness Speaks* (Novato, California: New World Library, 2003), 57.
8. *Stillness Speaks*, 23–24. | 9. *Power of Now*, 111. | 10. *Stillness Speaks*, 57–58.

CHAPTER 6
The Sixth State — God Consciousness:
Perceiving Nature's Celestial Glories

1. Rabindranath Tagore, *Letters to a Friend*, ed. C.F. Andrews (New York: Macmillan, 1929), 25–26.
2. Rabindranath Tagore, "The Fountain Awakes," trans. Hiren Mukherhjee, *Poems of Rabindranath Tagore*, ed. Humayun Kabir (West Bengal, India, UBSPD Visva-Bharati, Santiniketan, 2005), 2–3.
3. *The Gospel of Thomas*, in *The Gnostic Gospels of Jesus*, ed. and trans. Marvin Meyer (New York: HarperSanFrancisco, 2005), 25.
4. William Blake, *The Marriage of Heaven and Hell* (New York: Oxford University Press, 1975), xxi.
5. Maharishi Mahesh Yogi, *Science of Being and Art of Living* (New York: Plume/Penguin Putnam, 2001), 246.
6. Maharishi Mahesh Yogi, *Transcendental Meditation with Questions and Answers* (Meru, Holland: Maharishi Vedic University, 2011), 10.
7. Maharishi Mahesh Yogi, *Science of Creative Intelligence Teacher Training Course*, "Lesson 23: The Seven States of Consciousness" (videotaped lecture), (Fuiggi, Italy: Maharishi International University, 1972).
8. Maharishi Mahesh Yogi, "Mechanics of Perception of a Man in Brahman Consciousness and a Vedic Seer" (videotaped lecture), May 26, 1975, Zinal, Switzerland.
9. *Science of Creative Intelligence Teacher Training Program, Teacher's Handbook* (Santa Barbara, California: Maharishi International University Press, 1972), "Lesson 23: The Seven States of Consciousness," 13, 15.
10. *Science of Creative Intelligence Teacher Training Program, Teacher's Handbook*, "Lesson 23: The Seven States of Consciousness," 13. Also Vernon Katz, *Conversations with Maharishi: Maharishi Mahesh Yogi Speaks About the Full Development of Human Consciousness* (Fairfield, Iowa: Maharishi University of Management Press, 2011), 1:36.
11. *Maharishi Mahesh Yogi on the Bhagavad-Gita: A Translation and Commentary, Chapters 1–6* (London: Penguin Books, 1988), 206.
12. Maharishi Mahesh Yogi, "How Cosmic Consciousness Evolves to God Consciousness" (audiotaped lecture), August 6, 1970, Humboldt, California.
13. Maharishi, "Mechanics of Perception of a Man in Brahman Consciousness and a Vedic Seer."
14. *Conversations with Maharishi*, 1:348–349.
15. *Conversations with Maharishi*, 1:353–354.
16. Maharishi Mahesh Yogi, "Love: Expansion of the Heart, Refinement of Perception" (videotaped lecture), 1973 (no date or place available).
17. Maharishi Mahesh Yogi, "Soma: Its Effects and How It Is Produced" (videotaped lecture), November 29, 1971, Mallorca, Spain. Also Maharishi, "Love: Expansion of the Heart."
18. Maharishi, "Soma: Its Effects and How It Is Produced."
19. *Maharishi on the Bhagavad-Gita*, 315.
20. *Maharishi on the Bhagavad-Gita*, 307.

21. *Conversations with Maharishi*, 1:32.
22. Maharishi Mahesh Yogi, "Culturing the Nervous System to Maintain Pure Consciousness" (videotaped lecture), March 6, 1971, Mallorca, Spain.
23. *Maharishi on the Bhagavad-Gita*, 314–315.
24. Maharishi Mahesh Yogi, *Science of Being and Art of Living* (New York: Meridian, 1963 [1995]; reprint, New York: Plume/Penguin Putnam, 2001), 246–247.
25. *Science of Being and Art of Living*, 267–268.
26. *Science of Being and Art of Living*, 268.
27. *Science of Being and Art of Living*, 272.
28. *Science of Being and Art of Living*, 273–274.
29. *His Holiness Maharishi Mahesh Yogi: Thirty Years Around the World – Dawn of the Age of Enlightenment* (The Netherlands: MVU Press, 1986), 585–586.
30. *Conversations with Maharishi*, 1:37.
31. *Science of Being and Art of Living*, 270–271, 275–277.
32. *Science of Being and Art of Living*, 275–276.
33. *Science of Being and Art of Living*, 272.
34. Maharishi, "How Cosmic Consciousness Evolves to God Consciousness."
35. *Maharishi on the Bhagavad-Gita*, 444.
36. *Maharishi on the Bhagavad-Gita*, 444–445.
37. For a full discussion of the topic of natural law and the will of God, see Maharishi Mahesh Yogi, *Vedic Knowledge for Everyone* (Vlodrop, Holland: Maharishi Vedic University Press, 1994), 224–259.
38. *Conversations with Maharishi*, 36–37. Ellipses are in the original text.
39. C.N. Alexander and R.W. Boyer, "Seven States of Consciousness: Unfolding the Full Potential of the Cosmic Psyche in Individual Life through Maharishi Vedic Psychology," *Modern Science and Vedic Science* 2, no. 4 (Winter 1989), 358.
40. Maharishi Mahesh Yogi, *Creating an Ideal Society* (Rheinweiler, Germany: Maharishi European Research University Press, 1977), 81–82.
41. *Invincible America Assembly: Experiences of Higher States of Consciousness of Course Participants*, vol. 2 (Fairfield, Iowa: Maharishi University of Management Press, in production).

VEDIC LITERATURE

1. *Kaushitaki Upanishad*, in *The Upanishads*, trans. Juan Mascaró (Harmondsworth, Middlesex, England: Penguin Books, 1965), 106–107.
2. *Isa Upanishad*, in *The Upanishads*, 49.

JESUS CHRIST • 7–2 BCE – 30–36 CE

1. *The Gospel of Thomas*, in *The Gnostic Gospels of Jesus*, ed. and trans. Marvin Meyer (New York: HarperSanFrancisco, 2005), 25.

THE HERMETIC WRITINGS • 2ND & 3RD CENTURIES

1. *Hermetica: The Ancient Greek and Latin Writings Which Contain Religious or Philosophic Teachings Ascribed to Hermes Trismegistus*, ed. Walter Scott (Oxford, England: Clarendon Press, 1924), 1:221–223.

SOPHIA VON KLINGNAU • 13TH OR 14TH CENTURY

1. Martin Buber, *Ecstatic Confessions*, ed. Paul Mendes-Flohr, trans. Esther Cameron (San Francisco: Harper & Row, 1985), 82.

REFERENCES

KABIR • 1398–1448
1. Kabir, *Songs of Kabir*, "XLI," trans. Rabindranath Tagore (New York: Macmillan, 1915), 88.

THOMAS TRAHERNE • 1637–1674
1. Thomas Traherne, *Centuries of Meditations*, ed. Bertram Dobell (1908; reprint, London: P.J. & A.E. Dobell, 1950), 152–153.
2. *Centuries of Meditations*, 186. | 3. *Centuries of Meditations*, 19–20. | 4. *Centuries of Meditations*, 156.

JONATHAN EDWARDS • 1703–1758
1. *The Works of Jonathan Edwards* (London: Willliam Ball, 1839), 1:lv.

NAZIR • 1735–1830
1. *Indian Mystic Verse*, trans. Hari Prasad Shastri (London, Shanti Sadan, 1984), 99.

WILLIAM WORDSWORTH • 1770–1850
1. William Wordsworth, "Ode: Intimations of Immortality from Recollections of Early Childhood," bartleby.com/106/287.html. Retrieved December 4, 2016.
2. "Ode: Intimations of Immortality."
3. William Wordsworth, *The Prelude* (London: Edward Moxon, 1850), 61.
4. William Wordsworth, "The Excursion," *The Poetical Works of William Wordsworth*, ed. Thomas Hutchinson (London: Oxford University Press, 1920), 759.
5. William Wordsworth, "Lines Composed a Few Miles Above Tintern Abbey," William Wordsworth and S.T. Coleridge, *Lyrical Ballads* (London: T.N. Longman, 1798), 203–204.
6. William Wordsworth, "Author's Note," *Ode: Intimations of Immortality from Recollections of Early Childhood* (London: Lothrop, 1884), 9.

AHMAD HATIF OF ISFAHAN • b. 1784
1. Margaret Smith, *Readings from the Mystics of Islam* (London: Luzac, 1950), 132.
2. Smith, 133.

HENRY DAVID THOREAU • 1817–1862
1. Henry David Thoreau, "Inspiration," *Excursions and Poems* (Cambridge, Massachusetts, Riverside Press, 1906), 396–397.

WALT WHITMAN • 1819–1892
1. Walt Whitman, "Prayer of Columbus," *Leaves of Grass* (Philadelphia: David McKay, 1891–92), 323. Available at The Walt Whitman Archive, whitmanarchive.org/published/LG/1891/whole. Retrieved April 16, 2013.
2. Walt Whitman, "As In a Swoon," "In Whitman's Hand: Poetry Manuscripts," The Walt Whitman Archive, whitmanarchive.org/manuscripts/transcriptions/yal.00004. Retrieved July 22, 2012.
3. Richard Maurice Bucke, *Cosmic Consciousness* (Seattle: White Crow Productions, 2011), 259.
4. Walt Whitman, "Song of Myself," *Leaves of Grass*, 76. Available at the Whitman Archive website.
5. "Song of Myself," 32.
6. Walt Whitman, "Carol of Occupations," *Leaves of Grass*, 173. Also at the Whitman Archive website.

BERNARD BERENSON • 1865–1959
1. Bernard Berenson, *Aesthetics and History* (Garden City, New York: Doubleday, 1954), 79–81.

RAY STANNARD BAKER • 1870–1946

1. David Grayson [Ray Stannard Baker], *Adventures in Contentment*, in *Adventures of David Grayson* (Garden City, New York: Doubleday, Page, 1925), 8–12.
2. Grayson, *Adventures in Contentment*, 94.
3. David Grayson, "The Friendly Road," in *Adventures of David Grayson*, 86–87.

LUCY MAUD MONTGOMERY • 1874–1942

1. Lucy Maud Montgomery, *The Alpine Path: The Story of My Career* (Canada: Fitzhenry & Whiteside, 1917), 47–48.
2. Lucy Maud Montgomery, *Emily of New Moon* (1923; reprint, Toronto: Bantam Books, 1983), 6–8.
3. *Emily of New Moon*, 338.

MARY WEBB • 1881–1927

1. Mary Webb, *Precious Bane* (London: Jonathan Cape, 1933), 59–61.

EVELYN UNDERHILL • 1875–1941

1. Evelyn Underhill, *The Letters of Evelyn Underhill*, ed. Charles Williams (London: Darton, Longman and Todd, 1991), 80.
2. Evelyn Underhill, *Mysticism* (New York: Dutton, 1911), 310.

MARGARET PRESCOTT MONTAGUE • 1878–1955

1. Margaret Prescott Montague, *Twenty Minutes of Reality* (originally published anonymously, *Atlantic Monthly*, 1916; reprint, St. Paul, Minnesota: Macalester Park Publishing Company, 1974), 14–23.
2. *Twenty Minutes of Reality*, 30–31. | 3. *Twenty Minutes of Reality*, 33–34.

JOHN NEIHARDT • 1881–1973

1. John G. Neihardt, *The Divine Enchantment: A Mystical Poem* and *Poetic Values: Their Reality and Our Need of Them* (Lincoln, Nebraska: University of Nebraska Press, 1989), 71–72.

HOWARD THURMAN • 1899–1981

1. Howard Thurman, *The Inward Journey* (Richmond, Indiana: Friends United Press, 1961), 19–20.
2. *The Inward Journey*, 52. | 3. *The Inward Journey*, 54.

ROSAMOND LEHMAN • 1901–1990

1. Rosamond Lehmann, *The Swan in the Evening: Fragments of an Inner Life* (Great Britain: Virago, 2002), 114–115. All ellipses in the original.

GOPI KRISHNA • 1903–1984

1. Gopi Krishna, *Living With Kundalini: The Autobiography of Gopi Krishna* (Boston: Shambhala, 1993), 228–231.

KATHLEEN RAINE • 1908–2003

1. Kathleen Raine, *The Land Unknown* (London: Hamish Hamilton, 1975), 119–120.

EUGENE IONESCO • 1909–1994

1. Eugene Ionesco, *Present Past Past Present*, trans. Helen R. Lane (New York: Grove Press, 1971), 160–62.

JACQUETTA HAWKES • 1910–1996

1. Jacquetta Hawkes, *Man on Earth* (New York: Random House, 1955), 9–11.
2. Hawkes, 227.

IRINA STARR • 1911–2002

1. Irina Starr, *From These Waters* (Ojai, California: Pilgrim's Path, 1991), 181.
2. Irina Starr, *The Sound of Light: Experiencing the Transcendental* (Ojai, California: Pilgrim's Path), 1–11.
3. See Vernon Katz, *Conversations with Maharishi: Maharishi Mahesh Yogi Speaks About the Full Development of Human Consciousness* (Fairfield, Iowa: Maharishi University of Management Press, 2011), 1:42.

JANE GOODALL • b. 1934

1. Jane Goodall, *Reason for Hope: A Spiritual Journey* (New York: Warner, 2000), 173–175.

CHAPTER 7
The Seventh State — Unity Consciousness:
All Experience in Terms of the Unbounded Self

1. Rita Carter, *Exploring Consciousness* (Berkeley: University of California Press, 2002), 280–281.
2. Maharishi Mahesh Yogi, *Science of Creative Intelligence Teacher Training Course*, "Lesson 23: The Seven States of Consciousness," videotaped lecture (Fiuggi, Italy: Maharishi International University, 1972).
3. Maharishi Mahesh Yogi, *Science of Creative Intelligence Teacher Training Course*, "Lesson 23: The Seven States of Consciousness."
4. Vernon Katz, *Conversations with Maharishi: Maharishi Mahesh Yogi Speaks About the Full Development of Human Consciousness* (Fairfield, Iowa: Maharishi University of Management Press, 2011), 1:41.
5. *Conversations with Maharishi*, 1:41.
6. Maharishi Mahesh Yogi, *Maharishi Mahesh Yogi on the Bhagavad-Gita: A Translation and Commentary, Chapters 1–6* (1967; reprint, Harmondsworth, Middlesex, England: Penguin Books, 1988), 359.
7. Maharishi Mahesh Yogi, "Relationship with God in God Consciousness and Unity" (videotaped lecture), July 23, 1974, Livigno, Italy.
8. Maharishi, *Science of Creative Intelligence Teacher Training Course*, "Lesson 23: The Seven States of Consciousness."
9. *Science of Creative Intelligence Teacher Training Program, Teacher's Handbook* (Santa Barbara, California: Maharishi International University Press, 1972), "Lesson 23: The Seven States of Consciousness," 11, 18–19.
10. Maharishi, "Mechanics of Perception of a Man in Brahman Consciousness and a Vedic Seer" (videotaped lecture), May 26, 1975, Zinal, Switzerland.
11. Maharishi's Global Press Conferences, July 16, 2003, September 29, 2004, and December 20, 2006. Source: Institute of Science, Technology and Public Policy, Maharishi University of Management.
12. Maharishi's Global Press Conferences, December 11, 2002, April 16, 2003, May 5, 2004, and June 2, 2004.
13. Maharishi Mahesh Yogi, "The Story of Two Fullnesses" (videotaped lecture), January 16, 1973. La Antilla, Spain.
14. *Science of Creative Intelligence Teacher Training Program, Teacher's Handbook*, 15–16.
15. Maharishi Mahesh Yogi, *Vedic Knowledge For Everyone* (Holland: Maharishi Vedic University Press, 1994), 45.
16. *Creating Heaven on Earth through Maharishi's Vedic Science and Technology: Experience of Experts in Maharishi's Vedic Science and Technology Discovered in the Eternal Record of the Bhagavad-Gita* (Fairfield, Iowa: Maharishi International University Press, unpublished manuscript), section 7:9.
17. Robert Cranson, "Intelligence and the Growth of Intelligence in Maharishi's Vedic Science and

Twentieth-Century Psychology" (PhD Dissertation, Maharishi University of Management, 1989), *Dissertation Abstracts International* 50, no. 08A (1989): 2427.

18. Maharishi Mahesh Yogi, *Creating an Ideal Society* (Rheinweiler, Germany: Maharishi European Research University Press, 1977), 78.
19. *Achievements, First Quarter* (Rheinweiler, Germany: Maharishi European Research University Press, 1977), 31.
20. *Invincible America Assembly: Experiences of Higher States of Consciousness of Course Participants*, vol. 2 (Fairfield, Iowa: Maharishi University of Management Press, in production).
21. *Invincible America Assembly*. | 22. *Invincible America Assembly*.

VEDIC LITERATURE

1. Rik Veda, 7.1.1., verse trans. Maharishi Mahesh Yogi, in Maharishi Mahesh Yogi, *Maharishi's Absolute Theory of Defence* (India: Maharishi Vedic University, 1996), 360.
2. *Isa Upanishad*, in *The Upanishads*, trans. Alistair Shearer and Peter Russell (New York: Harper Colophon Books, 1978), 15.
3. *Mundaka Upanishad*, in Shearer and Russell, *The Upanishads*, 35.
4. *Chandogya Upanishad*, in *The Upanishads: Breath from the Eternal*, trans. Swami Prabhavananda and Frederick Manchester (New York: Signet Classic, 2002), 73. Original text says "such an one."
5. Maharishi Mahesh Yogi, *Maharishi Mahesh Yogi on the Bhagavad-Gita: A Translation and Commentary* (New York: Penguin, 1988), 441, 447.

LAOZI • 6TH CENTURY BC

1. *The Tao Te Ching*, trans. Stephen Mitchell (New York: Harper Perennial Modern Classics, 2006), 13.
2. *Wen-Tzu: Understanding the Mysteries*, trans. Thomas Cleary (Boston and London: Shambhala, 1992), 6.
3. Jonathan Star, *Tao Te Ching: The Definitive Edition* (New York : Jeremy P. Tarcher/Putnam, 2001), 45.

THE BUDDHA • c. 563–c. 483 BC

1. *The Buddha Speaks*, ed. Anne Bancroft (Boston: Shambhala, 2000), 116–117.
2. *The Buddha Speaks*, 29–30. | 3. *The Buddha Speaks*, 34.
4. Dwight Goddard, *A Buddhist Bible* (Boston: Beacon Press, 1994), 299. Available at sacred-texts.com/bud/bb/bb11.htm (81–82).

JESUS CHRIST • 7–2 BC–30–36 CE

1. All Bible passages in this section from the *The Holy Bible, King James Version* (New York: American Bible Society, 1999).
2. *The Gospel of Thomas*, in *The Gnostic Gospels of Jesus*, ed. and trans. Marvin Meyer (New York: HarperSanFrancisco, 2005), 12.
3. *The Gospel of Thomas*, 24. | 4. *The Gospel of Thomas*, 20. | 5. *The Gospel of Thomas*, 17.

THE GOSPEL OF TRUTH • 2ND CENTURY

1. *The Gospel of Truth*, in *The Gnostic Gospels of Jesus*, ed. and trans. Marvin Meyer (New York: HarperSanFrancisco, 2005), 95.
2. *The Gospel of Truth*, in *The Gnostic Bible*, eds. Willis Barnstone & Marvine Meyer (Boston & London: New Seeds, 2006), 249.
3. Barnstone & Meyer, 243. | 4. Barnstone & Meyer, 255. | 5. Barnstone & Meyer, 247.

PLOTINUS • 205–270

1. Rudolf Otto, *Mysticism East and West* (New York: Macmillan, 1932), 66.
2. William Ralph Inge, *The Philosophy of Plotinus* (London: Longman's Green, 1918), 2:85–86.

3. Otto, 67.

HERMETIC WRITINGS • 2ND & 3RD CENTURIES

1. *Hermetica: The Ancient Greek and Latin Writings Which Contain Religious or Philosophic Teachings Ascribed to Hermes Trismegistus*, ed. Walter Scott (Oxford, England: Clarendon Press, 1924), 1:241.

SHANKARA • 700?–750?

1. Shankara, *Vivekachudamani (The Crest Jewel of Discrimination)*, trans. William Sands, PhD, Associate Professor of Maharishi Vedic Science and Sanskrit, Maharishi University of Management. (Lines 478, 481, 484–485, 489, 491–493, 495, 502).
2. *Vivekachudamani*. (Lines 435 and 439). | 3. *Vivekachudamani*. (Lines 386–387, 389–390, 393, 398).

ATTAR OF NISHAPUR • 1145–1221

1. Margaret Smith, *Readings from the Mystics of Islam* (London: Luzac, 1950), 89–90.

RŪMĪ • 1207–1273

1. *Rūmī: In the Arms of the Beloved*, trans. Jonathan Star (New York: Tarcher/Putnam, 1997), 130.
2. *A Garden Beyond Paradise: The Mystical Poetry of Rūmī*, trans. Jonathan Star and Shahram Shiva (New York: Bantam, 1992), 53–54.
3. *Garden Beyond Paradise*, 82. | 4. *Garden Beyond Paradise*, 86.

MEISTER ECKHART • 1260–c. 1327

1. *Meister Eckhart: Sermons & Treatises*, trans. and ed. M. O'C. Walshe (Longmead, Shaftsbury, Dorset, Great Britain: Element Books, 1979), 1:84–85.
2. Rudolf Otto, *Mysticism East and West*, trans. Bertha L. Bracey and Richenda C. Payne (New York: Macmillan, 1972), 64.
3. Walshe 3:110.
4. Walshe 3:111–112.
5. *Meister Eckhart: Teacher and Preacher* (Mahwah, New Jersey: Paulist Press, 1986), 289.
6. Otto, 61.
7. *Breakthrough: Meister Eckhart's Creation Spirituality in New Translation*, trans. Matthew Fox (Garden City, New York: Doubleday, 1980), 327.

THOMAS TRAHERNE • 1637–1674

1. *The Poetical Works of Thomas Traherne*, ed. Bertram Dobell (London: Bertram Dobel, 1906), 42–47. I have updated two lines to conform with the more recent Margoliouth edition: "*truly* seem'd to dwell" – "truly" is not italicized in Dobell. "It was Indivisible, and so Pure" – Dobell has "It was so quick and pure. Thomas Traherne, "My Spirit," in *Poems and Thanksgivings*, vol. 2 of *Thomas Traherne: Centuries, Poems, and Thanksgivings*, ed. H.M. Margoliouth (London: Oxford University Press, 1958), 50, 52, 54, 56.

RALPH WALDO EMERSON • 1803–1882

1. Ralph Waldo Emerson, *The Journals and Miscellaneous Notebooks of Ralph Waldo Emerson*, 1835–1838, ed. Meton M. Sealts, Jr. (Cambridge, Massachusetts: Belknap Press, 1965), 5:336–337.

HENRI FRÉDÉRIC AMIEL • 1821–1881

1. Henri Frédéric Amiel, *Amiel's Journal: The Journal Intime of Henri-Frédéric Amiel*, trans. Mrs. Humphry Ward. gutenberg.org/files/8545/8545-h/8545-h.htm. Retrieved June 19, 2015.
2. *Amiel's Journal*. | 3. *Amiel's Journal*.

GUSTAVE FLAUBERT • 1821–1880

1. Gustave Flaubert, *The Temptation of Saint Anthony*, in E.F.N. Jephcott, *Proust and Rilke: The Literature*

of Expanded Consciousness (New York: Harper & Row, Barnes & Noble Books, 1972), 31.

WILLIAM HALE WHITE • 1831–1913

1. Mark Rutherford [William Hale White], *More Pages from a Journal* (London: Oxford University Press, 1910), 181–183.
2. White, 183.

EDWARD CARPENTER • 1844–1929

1. Edward Carpenter, *The Drama of Love and Death: A Study of Human Evolution and Transfiguration* (New York and London: Mitchell Kennerly, 1912), 79–81.
2. Richard Maurice Bucke, *Cosmic Consciousness* (New York: E.P. Dutton, 1969), 240.
3. Edward Carpenter, *The Art of Creation: Essays on the Self and Its Powers* (London: Allen and Unwin, 1927), 59–60.

BLACK ELK • 1863–1950

1. Black Elk, *The Sacred Pipe: Black Elk's Account of the Seven Rites of the Oglala Sioux*, ed. J.E. Brown (New York: MJF Books, 1989), 115.

BERNARD BERENSON • 1865–1959

1. Bernard Berenson, *Sketch for a Self-Portrait* (Bloomington: Indiana University Press, 1958), 18–19.
2. Bernard Berenson, *Aesthetics and History* (Garden City: Doubleday, 1954), 93.

ROMAIN ROLLAND • 1866–1944

1. Romain Rolland, *Jean-Christophe*, trans. Gilbert Cannan (New York: Modern Library, 1913), 252–255.
2. Jean-Bertrand Barrer, *Romaine Rolland* (Paris: Seuil, 1955), 93. Passage translated from the French by Daniela Hathaway for this book.

H.G. WELLS • 1866–1944

1. H.G. Wells, *The Bulpington of Blup* (London: Hutchinson, n.d.), 76–80.

MARY AUSTIN • 1868–1934

1. Mary Austin, *Experiences Facing Death* (Indianapolis: Bobbs-Merrill, 1931), 24–25.

MARTIN BUBER • 1878–1965

1. Martin Buber, *Daniel: Dialogues on Realization*, trans. Maurice Friedman (New York: Holt, Rinehart and Winston, 1964), 140.
2. Martin Buber, *I and Thou*, 2nd ed., trans. Ronald Gregor Smith (New York: Charles Scribner's Sons, 1958), 98.

MORIHEI UESHIBA • 1883–1969

1. John Stevens, *Abundant Peace: The Biography of Morihei Eushiba, Founder of Aikido* (Boston: Shambhala, 1987), 81.
2. Mitsugi Saotome, *Aikido and the Harmony of Nature* (Boston: Shambhala, 1993), 17.
3. Robert Frager, "The Spiritual Legacy of a Great Man, Master Morihei Ueshiba," *Yoga Journal* (March 1982), 13.

FRANKLIN MERRELL-WOLFF • 1887–1985

1. Franklin Merrell-Wolff, *The Philosophy of Consciousness Without an Object: Reflections on the Nature of Transcendental Consciousness* (New York: Julian Press, 1973), 66–73.

VLADIMIR NABOKOV • 1899–1977

1. Vladimir Nabokov, *Speak, Memory* (New York: G.P. Putnam's Sons, 1966), 139.

REFERENCES

HOWARD THURMAN • 1899–1981

1. *For the Inward Journey: The Writings of Howard Thurman*, ed. Anne Spencer Thurman (San Diego, New York, and London: Harcourt Brace Jovanovich, 1984), x.
2. Howard Thurman, *The Inward Journey* (Richmond, Indiana: Friends United Press, 1961), 51–52.

GOPI KRISHNA • 1903–1984

1. Tom Zatar Kay, "An Interview with Gopi Krishna, New York, 1983." Available at ecomall.com/greenshopping/gopinterview.htm. Retrieved June 7, 2012.
2. Gopi Krishna, *Living With Kundalini* (Boston: Shambhala, 1993), 289–292.

DAG HAMMARSKJÖLD • 1905–1961

1. Dag Hammarskjöld, *Markings* (New York: Knopf, 1964), 8. | 2. *Markings*, 83. | 3. *Markings*, 122. | 4. *Markings*, 127. | 5. *Markings*, 174. | 6. *Markings*, 165. | 7. *Markings*, 156. | 8. *Markings*, 154, 159.

KATHLEEN RAINE • 1908–2003

1. Kathleen Raine, *Farewell Happy Fields: Memories of Childhood* (London: Hamish Hamilton, 1977), 13.
2. *Farewell Happy Fields*, 14.

PEACE PILGRIM • 1908–1981

1. *Peace Pilgrim: Her Life and Work in Her Own Words, Compiled by Some of Her Friends* (Santa Fe: Ocean Tree Books, 1983), 21–22.
2. *Peace Pilgrim*, 128–129.

MARGIAD EVANS • 1909–1958

1. Margiad Evans, *Autobiography* (Oxford: Basil Blackwell, 1943), 94–96.

IRINA STARR • 1911–2002

1. Irina Starr, *The Sound of Light: Experiencing the Transcendental* (Ojai, California: Pilgrim's Path, 1991), 34–41.

BERNADETTE ROBERTS • b. 1931

1. Bernadette Roberts, *The Experience of No-Self* (Albany, New York: State University of New York Press, 1993), 32.
2. Roberts, 87. | 3. Roberts, 81.

CAROL BURNETT • b. 1934

1. Carol Burnett, *One More Time* (New York: Random House, 1986), 9.

DAVID YEADON • b. 1942

1. David Yeadon, *The Back of Beyond* (New York: Harper Collins, 1991), 442.

CHAPTER 8
A Technique for Transcending — Systematically Cultivating Higher States of Consciousness

1. Fred Travis and Jonathan Shear, "Focused Attention, Open Monitoring and Automatic Self-Transcending: Categories to Organize Meditations from Vedic, Buddhist and Chinese Traditions," *Consciousness and Cognition* 19 (2010): 1110–1118. (Chart by Craig Pearson)
2. See Craig Pearson, *The Complete Book of Yogic Flying* (Fairfield, Iowa: Maharishi University of Management Press, 2008).

3. Maharishi Mahesh Yogi, *Thirty Years Around the World: Dawn of the Age of Enlightenment* (The Netherlands: MVU Press, 1986), 496.

4. Maharishi Mahesh Yogi, *Maharishi Mahesh Yogi on the Bhagavad-Gita* (New York: Penguin, 1988), 9.

For more information about the Transcendental Meditation technique, see tm.org.

CHAPTER 9
Meditation in the Laboratory

BRAINWAVE (EEG COHERENCE) DURING TM PRACTICE

1. P. Levine, "The Coherence Spectral Array (COSPAR) and Its Application to the Study of Spatial Ordering in the EEG," *Proceedings of the San Diego Biomedical Symposium* 15 (1976): 237–247.

   M.C. Dillbeck and E.C. Bronson, "Short-Term Longitudinal Effects of the Transcendental Meditation Technique on EEG Power and Coherence," *International Journal of Neuroscience* 14 (1981): 147–151.

   D.W. Orme-Johnson and C.T. Haynes, "EEG Phase Coherence, Pure Consciousness, Creativity, and TM-Sidhi Experiences," *International Journal of Neuroscience* 13 (1981): 211–217.

   K. Badawi, R.K. Wallace, D.W. Orme-Johnson, and A.M. Rouzeré, "Electrophysiologic Characteristics of Respiratory Suspension Periods Occurring During the Practice of the Transcendental Meditation Program," *Psychosomatic Medicine* 46, no. 3 (1984): 267–276.

   F.T. Travis and R.K. Wallace, "EEG and Autonomic Patterns During Eyes-Closed Rest and Transcendental Meditation Practice: The Basis for a Neural Model of TM Practice," *Consciousness and Cognition* 8 (1999): 302–318.

   F.T. Travis and C. Pearson, "Pure Consciousness: Distinct Phenomenological and Physiological Correlates of 'Consciousness Itself,'" *International Journal of Neuroscience* 100 (2000): 77–89.

   F. Travis, "Autonomic and EEG Patterns Distinguish Different Experiences During Practice of the Transcendental Meditation Technique," *International Journal of Psychophysiology* 42 (2001): 1–9.

   R. Hebert et al., "Enhanced EEG Alpha Time-Domain Phase Synchrony During Transcendental Meditation: Implications for Cortical Integration Theory," *Signal Processing* 85 (2005): 2213–2232.

   F.T. Travis and A. Arenander, "Cross-Sectional and Longitudinal Study of Effects of Transcendental Meditation Practice on Interhemispheric Frontal Asymmetry and Frontal Coherence," *International Journal of Neuroscience* 116 (2006): 1519–1538.

   F. Travis et al., "Self-Referential Awareness: Coherence, Power, and Eloreta Patterns During Eyes-Closed Rest, Transcendental Meditation and TM-Sidhi Practice," *Journal of Cognitive Processing* 11, no. 1 (2010): 21–30.

   F. Travis et al., "Effects of Transcendental Meditation Practice on Brain Functioning and Stress Reactivity in College Students," *International Journal of Psychophysiology* 71 (2009): 170–176.

2. M. Ludwig, "Brain Activation and Cortical Thickness in Experienced Meditators" (PhD dissertation, California School of Professional Psychology, San Diego, California, 2011).

INCREASED FRONTAL ALPHA COHERENCE

3. R.K. Wallace, "The Physiological Effects of Transcendental Meditation: A Proposed Fourth Major State of Consciousness" (PhD dissertation, Department of Physiology, School of Medicine, University of California at Los Angeles, Los Angeles, California, 1970).

   R.K. Wallace et al., "A Wakeful Hypometabolic Physiologic State," *American Journal of Physiology* 221 (1971): 795–799.

   R.K. Wallace et al., "The Physiology of Meditation," *Scientific American* 226 (1972): 84–90.

   F. Travis et al., "A Self-Referential Default Brain State: Patterns of Coherence, Power, and Eloreta

Sources During Eyes-Closed Rest and Transcendental Meditation Practice," *Cognitive Processing* 11 (2010): 21–30.

INCREASED BLOOD FLOW TO THE BRAIN

4. R. Jevning et al., "Alterations in Blood Flow During Transcendental Meditation," *Psychophysiology* 13 (1976): 168.

R. Jevning et al., "Redistribution of Blood Flow in Acute Hypometabolic Behavior," *American Journal of Physiology* 235, no. 1 (1978): R89–R92.

R. Jevning and A.F. Wilson, "Behavioral Increase of Cerebral Blood Flow" (Abstract), *The Physiologist* 21(1978): 60.

INCREASED BRAIN TRANSMISSION SPEED

5. A. Wandhöfer and K.H. Plattig, "Stimulus–Linked DC–Shift and Auditory Evoked Potentials in Transcendental Meditation (TM)," *Pflueger's Archiv* 343 (1973): R79.

G. Kobal et al., "EEG Power Spectra and Auditory Evoked Potentials in Transcendental Meditation (TM)," *Pflueger's Archiv* 359 (1975): R96.

A. Wandhöfer et al., "Shortening of Latencies of Human Auditory Evoked Brain Potentials During the Transcendental Meditation Technique," *Zeitschrift EEG–EMG* 7 (1976): 99–103.

J.P. Banquet and N. LeSevre, "Event-Related Potentials in Altered States of Consciousness," *Motivation, Motor and Sensory Processes of the Brain, Progress in Brain Research* 54 (1980): 447–453.

T.M. McEvoy, L.R. Frumkin, and S.W. Harkins, "Effects of Meditation on Brainstem Auditory Evoked Potentials," *International Journal of Neuroscience* 10 (1980): 165–170.

R. Cranson, P. Goddard, and D. Orme-Johnson, "P300 Under Conditions of Temporal Uncertainty and Filter Attenuation: Reduced Latency in Long-Term Practitioners of TM," paper presented at the 30th Annual Meeting of the Society for Psychophysiological Research, October 17–21, 1990. (Abstract in Supplement to Psychophysiology 27 (1990): 4A.

P.H. Goddard, "Transcendental Meditation as an Intervention in the Aging of Neurocognitive Function: Reduced Age-Related Declines Of P300 Latencies in Elderly Practitioners" (PhD dissertation, Maharishi University of Management, 1992), *Dissertation Abstracts International* 53, no. 06B (1992): 3189.

F. Travis and S. Miskov, "P300 Latency and Amplitude During Eyes-Closed Rest and Transcendental Meditation Practice," *Psychophysiology* 31 (1994): S67 (Abstract).

BRAIN RESERVES AWAKENED

6. N.N. Lyubimov, "Electrophysiological Characteristics of Mobilization of Hidden Brain Reserves," *Human Physiology* 25 (1999): 171–180.

INCREASED PRODUCTION OF SEROTONIN

7. M. Bujatti and P. Riederer, "Serotonin, Noradrenaline, Dopamine Metabolites in Transcendental Meditation Technique," *Journal of Neural Transmission* 39 (1976): 257–267.

K.G. Walton, and D. Levitsky, "A Neuroendocrine Mechanism for the Reduction of Drug Use and Addictions by Transcendental Meditation," *Alcoholism Treatment Quarterly* 11 (1994): 89–117.

K.G. Walton et. al, "Stress Reduction and Preventing Hypertension: Preliminary Support for a Psychoneuroendocrine Mechanism," *Journal of Alternative and Complementary Medicine* 1 (1995): 263–283.

K.G. Walton and D.K. Levitsky, "Effects of the Transcendental Meditation Program on Neuroendocrine Abnormalities Associated with Aggression and Crime," in *Transcendental Meditation in Criminal Rehabilitation and Crime Prevention,* eds. C.N. Alexander, K.G. Walton, D.W. Orme-Johnson, R.S. Goodman, and N.J. Pallone (Binghamton, New York: Haworth Press, 2003), 67–87.

RESTFUL ALERTNESS

8. R.K. Wallace, "The Physiological Effects of Transcendental Meditation: A Proposed Fourth Major State of Consciousness" (PhD dissertation, Department of Physiology, School of Medicine, University of California at Los Angeles, Los Angeles, California, 1970).

R.K. Wallace et al., "A Wakeful Hypometabolic Physiologic State," *American Journal of Physiology* 221 (1971): 795–799.

R.K. Wallace et al., "The Physiology of Meditation," *Scientific American* 226 (1972): 84–90.

R. Jevning, R.K. Wallace, and M. Beidebach, "The Physiology of Meditation: A Review. A Wakeful Hypometabolic Integrated Response," *Neuroscience and Biobehavioral Reviews* 16 (1992): 415–424.

REDUCED BREATH RATE / BREATH SUSPENSION

9. R.K. Wallace, "Physiological Effects of Transcendental Meditation," *Science* 167 (1970): 1751–1754.

J. Allison, "Respiratory Changes During Transcendental Meditation," *Lancet* 295, no. 7651 (1970): 833.

R.K. Wallace et al., "The Physiology of Meditation," *Scientific American* 226 (1972): 84–90.

J.T. Farrow and J.R. Hebert, "Breath Suspension During the Transcendental Meditation Technique," *Psychosomatic Medicine* 44 (1982): 133–153.

P. Gallois, "Neurophysiological and Respiratory Changes During the Practice of Relaxation Techniques," *L'encéphale [The Brain]* 10 (1984): 139–144.

K. Badawi et al., "Electrophysiologic Characteristics of Respiratory Suspension Periods Occurring During the Practice of the Transcendental Meditation Program," *Psychosomatic Medicine* 46, no. 3 (1984): 267–276.

F.T. Travis and R.K. Wallace, "Autonomic Patterns During Respiratory Suspensions: Possible Markers of Transcendental Consciousness," *Psychophysiology* 34 (1997): 39–46.

MORE RELAXED AUTONOMIC NERVOUS SYSTEM

10. D.W. Orme-Johnson, "Autonomic Stability and Transcendental Meditation," *Psychosomatic Medicine* 35 (1973): 341–349.

J.T. Farrow and J.R. Hebert, "Breath Suspension During the Transcendental Meditation Technique," *Psychosomatic Medicine* 44 (1982): 133–153.

M.C. Dillbeck and D.W. Orme-Johnson, "Physiological Differences Between Transcendental Meditation and Rest," *American Psychologist* 42 (1987): 879–881.

F. Travis, "Autonomic and EEG Patterns Distinguish Different Experiences During Practice of the Transcendental Meditation Technique," *International Journal of Psychophysiology* 42 (2001): 1–9.

RELAXATION OF MUSCLES

11. T. Kemmerling, "Electromyographic Evidence of Deep Muscular Relaxation," *Psychopathometrie* 4 (1978): 437–438.

R. Jevning, A.F. Wilson, and J.P. O'Halloran, "Muscle and Skin Blood Flow and Metabolism During States of Decreased Activation," *Physiology and Behavior* 29, no. 2 (1982): 343–348.

R. Jevning et al., "Forearm Blood Flow and Metabolism During Stylized and Unstylized States of Decreased Activation," *American Journal of Physiology* 245, no. 1 (1983): R110–R116.

A.F. Wilson, R. Jevning, and S. Guich, "Marked Reduction of Forearm Carbon Dioxide Production During States of Decreased Metabolism," *Physiology and Behavior* 41 (1987): 347–352.

PROFOUND OVERALL RELAXATION

12. M.C. Dillbeck and D.W. Orme-Johnson, "Physiological Differences Between Transcendental Meditation and Rest," *American Psychologist* 42 (1987): 879–881.

REFERENCES

REDUCED CORTISOL (STRESS HORMONE)

13. R. Jevning, A.F. Wilson, and J.M. Davidson, "Adrenocortical Activity During Meditation," *Hormones and Behavior* 10, no. 1 (1978): 54–60.

    R. Jevning, A.F. Wilson, and W.R. Smith, "The Transcendental Meditation Technique, Adrenocortical Activity, and Implications for Stress," *Experientia* 34 (1978): 618–619.

    S. Subrahmanyam and K. Porkodi, "Neurohumoral Correlates of Transcendental Meditation," *Journal of Biomedicine* 1 (1980): 73–88.

    A.J.W. Bevan, "Endocrine Changes in Transcendental Meditation," *Clinical and Experimental Pharmacology and Physiology* 7 (1980): 75–76.

    K.G. Walton et al., "Psychosocial Stress and Cardiovascular Disease 2: Effectiveness of the Transcendental Meditation Technique in Treatment and Prevention," *Behavioral Medicine* 28, no. 3 (2002): 106–123.

REDUCED LACTATE (METABOLIC WASTE BYPRODUCT)

14. R.K. Wallace, H. Benson, and A.F. Wilson, "A Wakeful Hypometabolic Physiologic State," *American Journal of Physiology* 221 (1971): 795–799.

    R.K. Wallace and H. Benson, "The Physiology of Meditation," *Scientific American* 226 (1972): 84–90.

    R. Jevning, H.C. Pirkle, and A.F. Wilson, "Behavioral Alteration of Plasma Phenylalanine Concentration," *Physiology and Behavior* 19 (1977): 611–614.

    R. Jevning, A.F. Wilson, R. Smith, and M.E. Morton, "Redistribution of Blood Flow in Acute Hypometabolic Behavior," *American Journal of Physiology* 235, no. 1 (1978): R89–R92.

    R. Jevning, A.F. Wilson, J.P. O'Halloran, and R.N. Walsh, "Forearm Blood Flow and Metabolism During Stylized and Unstylized States of Decreased Activation," *American Journal of Physiology* 245 (Regulatory, Integrative, and Comparative Physiology 14), (1983): R110–R116.

    M.C. Dillbeck and D.W. Orme-Johnson, "Physiological Differences Between Transcendental Meditation and Rest," *American Psychologist* 42 (1987): 879–881.

RED BLOOD CELL METABOLISM

15. R. Jevning and A.F. Wilson, "Altered Red Cell Metabolism in TM," *Psychophysiology* 14 (1977): 94.

    R. Jevning et al., "Metabolic Control in a State of Decreased Activation: Modulation of Red Cell Metabolism," *American Journal of Physiology* 245 (1983): C457–C461.

INCREASED BRAINWAVE COHERENCE OUTSIDE OF MEDITATION

16. M.C. Dillbeck and E.C. Bronson, "Short-Term Longitudinal Effects of the Transcendental Meditation Technique on EEG Power and Coherence," *International Journal of Neuroscience* 14 (1981): 147–151.

    F.T. Travis, "Eyes Open and TM EEG Patterns After One and After Eight Years of TM Practice," *Psychophysiology* 28, no. 3a (1991): S58.

    F.T. Travis, J. Tecce, A. Arenander, and R.K. Wallace, "Patterns of EEG Coherence, Power, and Contingent Negative Variation Characterize the Integration of Transcendental and Waking States," *Biological Psychology* 61 (2002): 293–319.

    F.T. Travis, A. Arenander, and D. DuBois, "Psychological and Physiological Characteristics of a Proposed Object-Referral/Self-Referral Continuum of Self-Awareness," *Consciousness and Cognition* 13:2 (2004): 401–420.

INCREASED BRAINWAVE COHERENCE OUTSIDE OF MEDITATION

17. F.T. Travis, "Comparison of CNV Amplitude and P300 Latency and Amplitude in Subjects Practicing the Transcendental Meditation Technique for Less than 1 Year or More than 8 Years," *Psychophysiology* 33 (1996): S83.

    L.I. Mason et al., "Electrophysiological Correlates of Higher States of Consciousness During Sleep in

Long-Term Practitioners of the Transcendental Meditation Program," *Sleep* 20, no. 2 (1997): 102–110.

C.N. Alexander, S.M. Druker, and E.J. Langer, "Introduction: Major Issues in the Exploration of Adult Growth," in *Higher Stages of Human Development: Perspectives on Adult Growth*, eds. C.C. Alexander and E.J. Langer (New York: Oxford University Press, 1990), 3–32.

D.W. Orme-Johnson, G. Clements, C.T. Haynes, and K. Badawi, "Higher States of Consciousness: EEG Coherence, Creativity, and Experiences of the Sidhis," Centre for the Study of Higher States of Consciousness, Maharishi European Research University, Switzerland, 1977. *Collected Papers* 1: 705–712.

INCREASED BRAINWAVE COHERENCE OUTSIDE OF MEDITATION

18. F.T. Travis and A. Arenander, "Cross-Sectional and Longitudinal Study of Effects of Transcendental Meditation Practice on Interhemispheric Frontal Asymmetry and Frontal Coherence," *International Journal of Neuroscience* 116 (2006): 1519–1538.

INCREASED POWER OF ATTENTION (CNV)

19. F.T. Travis, "Comparison of CNV Amplitude and P300 Latency and Amplitude in Subjects Practicing the Transcendental Meditation Technique for Less than 1 Year or More than 8 Years," *Psychophysiology* 33 (1996): S83.

F.T. Travis, "CNV Rebound and Distraction Effects Before and After a TM Session," *Psychophysiology* 34 (1996): S89.

F.T. Travis, J.J. Tecce, and J. Guttman, "Cortical Plasticity, Contingent Negative Variation, and Transcendent Experiences During Practice of the Transcendental Meditation Technique," *Biological Psychology* 55 (2000): 41–55.

F.T. Travis, J. Tecce, A. Arenander, and R.K. Wallace, "Patterns of EEG Coherence, Power, and Contingent Negative Variation Characterize the Integration of Transcendental and Waking States," *Biological Psychology* 61 (2002): 293–319.

INCREASED BRAIN FLEXIBILITY

20. J.E. Bennett and J. Trinder, "Hemispheric Laterality and Cognitive Style Associated with Transcendental Meditation," *Psychophysiology* 14 (1977): 293–296.

UNIQUE BRAINWAVES DURING WITNESSING SLEEP

21. L.I. Mason et al., "Electrophysiological Correlates of Higher States of Consciousness During Sleep in Long-Term Practitioners of the Transcendental Meditation Program," *Sleep* 20, no. 2 (1997): 102–110.

HIGHER EEG COHERENCE IN WORLD-CLASS PERFORMERS

22. F.T. Travis et al., "Patterns of EEG Coherence, Power, and Contingent Negative Variation Characterize the Integration of Transcendental and Waking States," *Biological Psychology* 61 (2002): 293–319.

H.S. Harung, "Illustrations of Peak Experiences During Optimal Performance in World-Class Performers: Integrating Eastern and Western Insights," *Journal of Human Values* 18, no. 1 (April 2012): 33–52.

H.S. Harung et al., "High Levels of Brain Integration in World-Class Norwegian Athletes: Towards a Brain Measure of Performance Capacity in Sports," *Scandinavian Journal of Exercise and Sport* 1 (2011): 32–41.

F. Travis et al., "Effects of Transcendental Meditation Practice on Brain Functioning and Stress Reactivity in College Students," *International Journal of Psychophysiology* 71 (2009): 170–176.

H.S. Harung and F. Travis, "Higher Mind-Brain Development in Successful Leaders: Testing a Unified Theory of Performance," *Cognitive Processing* 13 (2012): 171–181.

REFERENCES

INCREASED INTELLIGENCE

23. K.R. Pelletier, "Influence of Transcendental Meditation Upon Autokinetic Perception," *Perceptual and Motor Skills* 39 (1974): 1031–1034.

    A. Tjoa, "Meditation, Neuroticism, and Intelligence: A Follow-up," *Gedrag: Tijdschrift voor Psychologie [Behavior: Journal of Psychology]* 3 (1975): 167–182.

    H.E. Shecter, "The Transcendental Meditation Program in the Classroom: A Psychological Evaluation" (PhD dissertation, Graduate Department of Psychology, York University, North York, Ontario, Canada), *Dissertation Abstracts International* 38, 7–B (1978): 3372B.

    A.P. Aron, D.W. Orme-Johnson, and P. Brubaker, "The Transcendental Meditation Program in the College Curriculum: A Four-Year Longitudinal Study of Effects on Cognitive and Affective Functioning," *College Student Journal* 15 (1981): 140–146.

    A. Jedrczak, M. Beresford, and G. Clements, "The TM-Sidhi Program, Pure Consciousness, Creativity and Intelligence," *The Journal of Creative Behavior* 19, no. 4 (1985): 270–275.

    A. Jedrczak, M. Toomey, and G. Clements, "The TM-Sidhi Programme, Age, and Brief Test of Perceptual-Motor Speed and Nonverbal Intelligence," *Journal of Clinical Psychology* 42 (1986): 161–164.

    M.C. Dillbeck et al., "Longitudinal Effects of the Transcendental Meditation and TM-Sidhi Program on Cognitive Ability and Cognitive Style," *Perceptual and Motor Skills* 62 (1986): 731–738.

    S.I. Nidich and R.J. Nidich, "Holistic Student Development at Maharishi School of the Age of Enlightenment: Theory and Research," *Modern Science and Vedic Science* 1 (1987): 433–468.

    R.W. Cranson et al., "Transcendental Meditation and Improved Performance on Intelligence-Related Measures: A Longitudinal Study," *Personality and Individual Differences* 12 (1991): 1105–1116.

    So Kam-Tim and D.W. Orme-Johnson, "Three Randomized Experiments on the Holistic Longitudinal Effects of the Transcendental Meditation Technique on Cognition," *Intelligence* 29, no. 5 (2001): 1–22.

INCREASED MORAL REASONING ABILITY

24. S.I. Nidich and D.W. Orme-Johnson, "Kohlberg's Stage Seven, Natural Law, and the Transcendental Meditation and TM-Sidhi Program," *Proceedings of the International Symposium of Moral Education* (Fribourg, Switzerland), Sept. 3, 1982.

    S.I. Nidich et al., "Kohlbergian Cosmic Perspective Responses, EEG Coherence, and the Transcendental Meditation Program," *Journal of Moral Education* 12 (1983): 166–173.

    H.M. Chandler, C.N. Alexander, D.P. Heaton, and J. Grant, "The Transcendental Meditation Program and Postconventional Self-Development: A 10-Year Longitudinal Study," *Journal of Social Behavior and Personality* 17, no. 1 (Spring 2005): 93–121.

INCREASED FIELD INDEPENDENCE

25. K.R. Pelletier, "Influence of Transcendental Meditation Upon Autokinetic Perception," *Perceptual and Motor Skills* 39 (1974): 1031–1034.

    K.R. Pelletier, "The Effects of the Transcendental Meditation Program on Perceptual Style: Increased Field Independence," *Collected Papers* 1, 337–345.

    A. Jedrczak and G. Clements, "The TM-Sidhi Program and Field Independence," *Perceptual and Motor Skills* 59 (1984): 999–1000.

    M.C. Dillbeck et al., "Longitudinal Effects of the Transcendental Meditation and TM-Sidhi Program on Cognitive Ability and Cognitive Style," *Perceptual and Motor Skills* 62 (1986): 731–738.

    So Kam-Tim and D.W. Orme-Johnson, "Three Randomized Experiments on the Holistic Longitudinal Effects of the Transcendental Meditation Technique on Cognition," *Intelligence* 29, no. 5 (2001): 1–22.

IMPROVED MENTAL CAPACITIES

26. M.C. Dillbeck and S. Araas-Vesely, "Participation in the Transcendental Meditation Program and Frontal EEG Coherence During Concept Learning," *International Journal of Neuroscience* 29 (1986): 45–55.

    D.P. Heaton and D.W. Orme-Johnson, "The Transcendental Meditation Program and Academic Achievement," *Collected Papers* 1: 396–399.

    P. Kember, "The Transcendental Meditation Technique and Postgraduate Academic Performance," *British Journal of Educational Psychology* 55 (1985): 164–166.

    C.N. Alexander et al., "Transcendental Meditation, Mindfulness, and Longevity: An Experimental Study With the Elderly," *Journal of Personality and Social Psychology* 57 (1989): 950–964.

GREATER RELAXATION OUTSIDE OF MEDITATION

27. M.C. Dillbeck and D.W. Orme-Johnson, "Physiological Differences Between Transcendental Meditation and Rest," *American Psychologist* 42 (1987): 879–881.

    C.N. Alexander et al., "Effects of the Transcendental Meditation Program on Stress Reduction, Health, and Employee Development: A Prospective Study in Two Occupational Settings," *Anxiety, Stress and Coping: An International Journal* 6 (1993): 245–262.

    C.N. Alexander et al., "The Effects of Transcendental Meditation Compared to Other Methods of Relaxation in Reducing Risk Factors, Morbidity, and Mortality," *Homeostasis* 35 (1994): 243–264.

    K.G. Walton et al., "Stress Reduction and Preventing Hypertension: Preliminary Support for a Psychoneuroendocrine Mechanism," *Journal of Alternative and Complementary Medicine* 1, no. 3 (1995): 263–283.

    V.A. Barnes and D.W. Orme-Johnson, "Prevention and Treatment of Cardiovascular Disease in Adolescents and Adults through the Transcendental Meditation Program: A Research Review Update," *Current Hypertension Reviews* 8, no. 3 (2012): 1–16.

MORE APPROPRIATE RESPONSE TO STRESS

28. D.W. Orme-Johnson, "Autonomic Stability and Transcendental Meditation," *Psychosomatic Medicine* 35 (1973): 341–349.

    J.S. Brooks and T. Scarano, "Transcendental Meditation in the Treatment of Post-Vietnam Adjustment," *Journal of Counseling and Development* 64 (1985): 212–215.

    C.N. Alexander et al., "Transcendental Meditation, Mindfulness, and Longevity: An Experimental Study With the Elderly," *Journal of Personality and Social Psychology* 57 (1989): 950–964.

    V. Barnes, R. Schneider, C. Alexander, and F. Staggers, "Stress, Stress Reduction and Hypertension in African Americans: An Updated Review," *Journal of National Medical Association* 89, no. 7 (1997): 464–476.

    C.R. MacLean et al., "Effects of the Transcendental Meditation Program on Adaptive Mechanisms: Changes in Hormone Levels and Responses to Stress after Four Months of Practice," *Psychoneuroendocrinology* 22, no. 4 (1997): 277–295.

    V.A. Barnes et al., "Acute Effects of Transcendental Meditation on Hemodynamic Functioning in Middle Aged Adults," *Psychosomatic Medicine* 61 (1999): 525–531.

    V.A. Barnes, F.A. Treiber, and H. Davis, "Impact of Transcendental Meditation on Cardiovascular Function at Rest and During Acute Stress in Adolescents with High Normal Blood Pressure," *Journal of Psychosomatic Research* 51, no. 4 (2001): 597–605.

FASTER REACTION TIME

29. S. Appelle and L.E. Oswald, "Simple Reaction Time as a Function of Alertness and Prior Mental Activity," *Perceptual and Motor Skills* 38 (1974): 1263–1268.

    W.R. Holt, J.L. Caruso, and J.B. Riley, "Transcendental Meditation vs. Pseudo–Meditation on Visual

Choice Reaction Time," *Perceptual and Motor Skills* 46 (1978): 726.

R.W. Cranson et al., "Transcendental Meditation and Improved Performance on Intelligence-Related Measures: A Longitudinal Study," *Personality and Individual Differences* 12 (1991): 1105–1116.

FASTER MOTOR REFLEXES AND MOTOR NEURONS

30. D. Warschal, "Effects of the Transcendental Meditation Technique on Normal and Jendrassik Reflex Time," *Perceptual and Motor Skills* 50 (1980): 1103–1106.

FASTER H-REFLEX TIME

31. C.T. Haynes et al., "The *Psychophysiology* of Advanced Participants in the Transcendental Meditation Program: Correlations of EEG Coherence, Creativity, H–Reflex Recovery, and Experiences of Transcendental Consciousness," *Collected Papers* 1: 208–212.

M.C. Dillbeck, D.W. Orme-Johnson, and R.K. Wallace, "Frontal EEG Coherence, H–Reflex Recovery, Concept Learning, and the TM-Sidhi Program," *International Journal of Neuroscience* 15 (1981): 151–157.

R.K. Wallace et al., "Modification of the Paired H-Reflex through the Transcendental Meditation and TM-Sidhi Program," *Experimental Neurology* 79 (1983): 77–86.

J.-R. Chenard, "A Controlled Study of the Influence of Transcendental Meditation on a Specific Value of the H-Reflex (Hoffman Reflex) Recruitment Curve and the Surface EMG," *Collected Papers* 3: 1660–1665.

P. J. Mills and R.K. Wallace, "The Effect of the Transcendental Meditation and TM-Sidhi Program on the Paired Hoffman Reflex," *Collected Papers* 3: 1752–1755.

IMPROVED PERCEPTUAL ABILITIES

32. K.R. Pelletier, "Influence of Transcendental Meditation Upon Autokinetic Perception," *Perceptual and Motor Skills* 39 (1974): 1031–1034.

R.K. Wallace, M.C. Dillbeck, E. Jacobe, and B. Harrington, "The Effects of the Transcendental Meditation and TM-Sidhi Program on the Aging Process," *International Journal of Neuroscience* 16 (1982): 53–58.

So Kam-Tim and D.W. Orme-Johnson, "Three Randomized Experiments on the Holistic Longitudinal Effects of the Transcendental Meditation Technique on Cognition," *Intelligence* 29, no. 5 (2001): 1–22.

IMPROVED ATHLETIC ABILITY

33. M.K. Reddy, A.J.L. Bai, and V.R. Rao, "The Effects of the Transcendental Meditation Program on Athletic Performance" (A.P. Sports Council, Lal Bahadar Stadium, and Nilouffer Hospital Hyderabad, Andhra Pradesh, India, 1974), *Collected Papers* 1, 346–358.

M.K. Reddy, "The Role of the Transcendental Meditation Program in the Promotion of Athletic Excellence: Long- and Short-Term Effects and Their Relation to Activation Theory" (Master's thesis, Centre for the Study of Higher States of Consciousness, Maharishi European Research University, Switzerland, 1976), *Collected Papers* 2: 947–948.

REDUCED HIGH BLOOD PRESSURE

34. R.K. Wallace et al., "Systolic Blood Pressure and Long-Term Practice of the Transcendental Meditation and TM-Sidhi Program: Effects of TM on Systolic Blood Pressure," *Psychosomatic Medicine* 45 (1983): 41–46.

R.H. Schneider et al., "A Randomized Controlled Trial of Stress Reduction for Hypertension in Older African Americans," *Hypertension* 26 (1995): 820–827.

R.H. Schneider, F. Staggers, C.N. Alexander, W. Sheppard, M. Rainforth, K. Kondwani, S. Smith, and C. King, "A Randomized Controlled Trial of Stress Reduction for Hypertension in Older African Americans," *Hypertension* 26 (1995): 820–827.

C.N. Alexander et al., "A Trial of Stress Reducation for Hypertension in Older African Americans (Part II): Gender and Risk Subgroup Analysis," *Hypertension* 28, no. 2 (1996): 228–237.

R. Herron et al., "Cost-Effective Hypertension Management: Comparison of Drug Therapies with an Alternative Program," *American Journal of Managed Care* 2, no. 4 (1996): 427–437.

V.A. Barnes et al., "Acute Effects of Transcendental Meditation on Hemodynamic Functioning in Middle Aged Adults," *Psychosomatic Medicine* 61 (1999): 525–531.

V.A. Barnes, F.A. Treiber, H. Davis, "Impact of Transcendental Meditation on Cardiovascular Function at Rest and During Acute Stress in Adolescents with High Normal Blood Pressure," *Journal of Psychosomatic Research* 51 (2001): 597–605.

V.A. Barnes et al., "Impact of Transcendental Meditation on Mortality in Older African Americans with Hypertension — Eight-Year Follow-up," *Journal of Social Behavior and Personality* 17, no. 1 (Spring 2005): 201–216.

M.V. Rainforth et al., "Stress Reduction Programs in Patients with Elevated Blood Pressure: A Systematic Review and Meta-Analysis," *Current Hypertension Reports* 9, no. 6 (2007): 520–528.

J.W. Anderson, C. Liu, and R.J. Kryscio, "Blood Pressure Response to Transcendental Meditation: A Meta-Analysis, *American Journal of Hypertension* 21 (2008): 310–316.

IMPROVEMENT IN OTHER RISK FACTORS FOR HEART DISEASE

35. M.J. Cooper and M.M. Aygen, "Effect of Transcendental Meditation on Serum Cholesterol and Blood Pressure," *Harefuah* [Journal of the Israel Medical Association] 95, no. 1 (1978): 1–2.

J.J. Cooper and M.M. Aygen, "Transcendental Meditation in the Management of Hypercholesterolemia," *Journal of Human Stress* 5, no.4 (1979): 24–27.

S. Subrahmanyam and K. Porkodi, "Neurohumoral Correlates of Transcendental Meditation," *Journal of Biomedicine* 1 (1980): 73–88.

C.N. Alexander et al., "The Effects of Transcendental Meditation Compared to Other Methods of Relaxation in Reducing Risk Factors, Morbidity, and Mortality," *Homeostasis*, no. 35 (1994): 243–264.

C.N. Alexander, P. Robinson, and M. Rainforth, "Treating and Preventing Alcohol, Nicotine and Drug Abuse Through Transcendental Meditation: A Review and Statistical Meta-Analysis," *Alcohol Treatment Quarterly* 11 (1994): 13–87.

K.G. Walton et al., "Stress Reduction and Preventing Hypertension: Preliminary Support for a Psychoneuroendocrine Mechanism," *Journal of Alternative and Complementary Medicine* 1, no. 3 (1995): 263–283.

D.L. DeArmond, "Effects of the Transcendental Meditation Program on Psychological, Physiological, Behavioral, and Organizational Consequences of Stress in Managers and Executives" (PhD dissertation, Maharishi University of Management, 1996), *Dissertations Abstracts International* 57, no. 06B (1996): 4068.

A. Castillo–Richmond et al., "Effects of Stress Reduction and Carotid Atherosclerosis in Hypertensive African Americans," *Stroke* 31 (2000): 568–573.

M. Paul-Labrador et al., "Effects of a Randomized Controlled Trial of Transcendental Meditation on Components of the Metabolic Syndrome in Subjects with Coronary Heart Disease," *Archives of Internal Medicine* 166, no. 11 (2006): 1218–1224.

V.A. Barnes and D.W. Orme-Johnson, "Prevention and Treatment of Cardiovascular Disease in Adolescents and Adults through the Transcendental Meditation Program: A Research Review Update," *Current Hypertension Reviews* 8, no. 3 (2012): 1–16.

REDUCTION IN FREE RADICALS

36. R.H. Schneider et al., "Lower Lipid Peroxide Levels in Practitioners of the Transcendental Meditation Program," *Psychosomatic Medicine* 60 (Jan–Feb 1998): 38–41.

E.P. Van Wijk, H. Koch, S. Bosman, and R. Van Wijk, "Anatomical Characterization of Human

REFERENCES

Ultraweak Photon Emission in Practitioners of Transcendental Meditation and Control Subjects," *Journal of Alternative and Complementary Medicine* 12, no. 1 (2006): 31–38.

E.P. Van Wijk, R. Ludtke, and R. Van Wijk, "Differential Effects of Relaxation Techniques on Ultraweak Photon Emission," *Journal of Alternative and Complementary Medicine* 14, no. 3 (2008): 241–250.

That the Transcendental Meditation technique reduces free radicals is also indicated by the reductions in the disorders associated with free radical activity, from heart disease to aging.

REDUCTION IN DAMAGE TO THE HEART

37. J.W. Zamarra et al., "Usefulness of the Transcendental Meditation Program in the Treatment of Patients with Coronary Artery Disease," *American Journal of Cardiology* 77, no. 10 (1996): 867–870.

A. Castillo-Richmond et al., "Effects of Stress Reduction and Carotid Atherosclerosis in Hypertensive African Americans," *Stroke* 31 (2000): 568–573.

R.H. Schneider et al., "Effects of the Transcendental Meditation Technique and Health Education on Left Ventricular Hypertrophy in Older African Americans," presented at the International Society for Hypertension in Blacks, June 13–16, 2004, Detroit, Michigan. Abstract published in *Ethnicity and Disease* 14, no. 4 (Fall 2004).

K. Kondwani et al., "Left Ventricular Mass Regression with the Transcendental Meditation Technique and a Health Education Program in Hypertensive African Americans," *Journal of Social Behavior and Personality* 17, no. 1 (Spring 2005): 181–200.

R. Jayadevappa et al., "Effectiveness of Transcendental Meditation on Functional Capacity and Quality of Life of African Americans with Congestive Heart Failure: A Randomized Control Study," *Ethnicity and Disease* 17 (2007): 72–77.

V.A. Barnes, G.K. Kapuku, and F.A. Treiber, "Impact of Transcendental Meditation on Left Ventricular Mass in African American Adolescents," *Evidence-Based Complementary and Alternative Medicine* 2012, article ID 923153, doi: 10.1155/2012/923153, ncbi.nlm.nih.gov/pubmed/22675392

REVERSAL OF AGING

38. R.K. Wallace et al., "The Effects of the Transcendental Meditation and TM-Sidhi Program on the Aging Process," *International Journal of Neuroscience* 16 (1982): 53–58.

EXTENDED LIFESPAN AND QUALITY OF LIFE FOR THE ELDERLY

39. C.N. Alexander et al., "Transcendental Meditation, Mindfulness, and Longevity: An Experimental Study With the Elderly," *Journal of Personality and Social Psychology* 57 (1989): 950–964.

C.N. Alexander et al., "A Randomized Controlled Trial of Stress Reduction on Cardiovascular and All-Cause Mortality in the Elderly: Results of 8- and 15-Year Follow-Ups," *Circulation* 93, no. 3 (1996): 19.

EXTENDED LIFESPAN FOR PEOPLE WITH HYPERTENSION

40. R.H. Schneider et al., "Long-Term Effects of Stress Reduction on Mortality in Persons >55 Years of Age With Systemic Hypertension," *American Journal of Cardiology* 95 (2005): 1060–1064.

REDUCED RISK OF MORTALITY, HEART ATTACK, AND STROKE

41. R. Schneider et al., "Stress Reduction in the Secondary Prevention of Cardiovascular Disease: Randomized, Controlled Trial of Transcendental Meditation and Health Education in Blacks," *Circulation: Cardiovascular Quality and Outcomes* 5, no. 6 (2012): 750–758.

SELF-ESTEEM

42. W.P. van den Berg and B. Mulder, "Psychological Research on the Effects of the Transcendental Meditation Technique on a Number of Personality Variables," *Gedrag: Tijdschrift voor Psychologie [Behavior: Journal for Psychology]* 4 (1976): 206–218.

M.S. Nystul and M. Garde, "Comparison of Self-Concepts of Transcendental Meditators and Nonmeditators," *Psychological Reports* 41 (1977): 303–306.

H.E. Shecter, "The Transcendental Meditation Program in the Classroom: A Psychological Evaluation" (PhD dissertation, Graduate Department of Psychology, York University, North York, Ontario, Canada), *Dissertation Abstracts International* 38, 7–B (1978): 3372B.

M.J. Turnbull and H. Norris, "Effects of Transcendental Meditation on Self-Identity Indices and Personality," *British Journal of Psychology* 73 (1982): 57–68.

INCREASED SELF-ACTUALIZATION

43. W. Seeman, S. Nidich, and T. Banta, "Influence of Transcendental Meditation on a Measure of Self-Actualization," *Journal of Counseling Psychology* 19 (1972): 184–187.

S. Nidich, W. Seeman, and T. Dreskin, "Influence of Transcendental Meditation: A Replication," *Journal of Counseling Psychology* 20 (1973): 565–566.

L.A. Hjelle, "Transcendental Meditation and Psychological Health," *Perceptual and Motor Skills* 39 (1974): 623–628.

P. Gelderloos et al., "Transcendence and Psychological Health: Studies With Long-Term Participants of the TM and TM-Sidhi Program," *Journal of Psychology* 124, no. 2 (1990): 177–197.

C.N. Alexander, M.V. Rainforth, and P. Gelderloos, "Transcendental Meditation, Self Actualization, and Psychological Health: A Conceptual Overview and Statistical Meta-Analysis," *Journal of Social Behavior and Personality* 6 (1991): 189–247.

INCREASED EGO DEVELOPMENT

44. H.M. Chandler, C.N. Alexander, D.P. Heaton, and J. Grant, "The Transcendental Meditation Program and Postconventional Self-Development: A 10–Year Longitudinal Study," *Journal of Social Behavior and Personality* 17, no. 1 (Spring 2005): 93–121.

INCREASED EGO DEVELOPMENT AMONG PRISONERS

45. C.N. Alexander, K.G. Walton, and R.S. Goodman, "Walpole Study of the Transcendental Meditation Program in Maximum Security Prisoners I: Cross-Sectional Differences in Development and Psychopathology," *Journal of Offender Rehabilitation* 36 (2003): 97–126.

C.N. Alexander and D.W. Orme-Johnson, "Walpole Study of the Transcendental Meditation Program in Maximum Security Prisoners II: Longitudinal Study of Development and Psychopathology," *Journal of Offender Rehabilitation* 36 (2003): 127–160.

Transcendental Meditation in Criminal Rehabilitation and Crime Prevention, eds. C.N. Alexander, K.G. Walton, D.W. Orme-Johnson, R.S. Goodman, and N.J. Pallone (Binghamton, New York: Haworth Press, 2003).

REDUCED ANXIETY

46. L.A. Hjelle, "Transcendental Meditation and Psychological Health," *Perceptual and Motor Skills* 39 (1974): 623–628.

T. Candelent and G. Candelent, "Teaching Transcendental Meditation in a Psychiatric Setting," *Hospital & Community Psychiatry* 26, no. 3 (1975): 156–159.

P.C. Ferguson and J.C. Gowan, "Psychological Findings on Transcendental Meditation," *Journal of Humanistic Psychology* 16, no. 3 (1976): 51–60.

M.C. Dillbeck, "The Effect of the Transcendental Meditation Technique on Anxiety Level," *Journal of Clinical Psychology* 33, no. 4 (1977): 1076–1078.

D.P. Kanellakos, "Transcendental Consciousness: Expanded Awareness as a Means of Preventing and Eliminating the Effects of Stress," in C.D. Speilberger and I.G. Sarason, eds., *Stress and Anxiety* 5 (Washington, DC: Hemisphere Publishing, 1978): 261–315.

J.S. Brooks and T. Scarano, "Transcendental Meditation in the Treatment of Post-Vietnam Adjustment," Journal of Counseling and Development 64 (1985): 212–215.

K. Eppley, A. Abrams, and J. Shear, "The Effects of Meditation and Relaxation Techniques on Trait Anxiety, a Meta-Analysis," *Journal of Clinical Psychology* 45, no. 6 (1989): 957–974.

D.H. Sheppard, F. Staggers, and L. John, "The Effects of a Stress Management Program in a High Security Government Agency," *Anxiety, Stress and Coping* 10, no. 4 (1997): 341–350.

So Kam-Tim and D.W. Orme-Johnson, "Three Randomized Experiments on the Holistic Longitudinal Effects of the Transcendental Meditation Technique on Cognition," *Intelligence* 29, no. 5 (2001): 1–22.

INTERPERSONAL RELATIONSHIPS

47. D.R. Frew, "Transcendental Meditation and Productivity," *Academy of Management Journal* 17 (1974): 362–368.

S.V. Marcus, "The Influence of the Transcendental Meditation Program on the Marital Dyad" (PhD dissertation, California School of Professional Psychology, 1977), *Dissertation Abstracts International* 38 (1977): 3895–B.

E.N. Aron and A. Aron, "Transcendental Meditation Program and Marital Adjustment," *Psychological Reports* 51 (1982): 887–890.

BRAINWAVE COHERENCE CORRELATED WITH INTELLIGENCE, ETC.

48. C.T. Haynes et al., "The *Psychophysiology* of Advanced Participants in the Transcendental Meditation Program: Correlations of EEG Coherence, Creativity, H–Reflex Recovery, and Experiences of Transcendental Consciousness," *Collected Papers* 1: 208–212.

D.W. Orme-Johnson and C.T. Haynes, "EEG Phase Coherence, Pure Consciousness, Creativity, and TM-Sidhi Experiences," *International Journal of Neuroscience* 13 (1981): 211–217.

M.C. Dillbeck, D.W. Orme-Johnson, and R.K. Wallace, "Frontal EEG Coherence, H–Reflex Recovery, Concept Learning, and the TM-Sidhi Program," *International Journal of Neuroscience* 15 (1981): 151–157.

D.W. Orme-Johnson et al., "Improved Functional Organization of the Brain through the Maharishi Technology of the Unified Field as Indicated by Changes in EEG Coherence and Its Cognitive Correlates: A Proposed Model of Higher States of Consciousness," presented at the American Psychological Society Annual Convention, Los Angeles, California (September 1981) and the 15th Annual Winter Conference on Brain Research, Steamboat Springs, Colorado (January 1982), *Collected Papers* 4: 2245–2266.

F.T. Travis et al., "Patterns of EEG Coherence, Power, and Contingent Negative Variation Characterize the Integration of Transcendental and Waking States," *Biological Psychology* 61 (2002): 293–319.

F.T. Travis, A. Arenander, and D. DuBois, "Psychological and Physiological Characteristics of a Proposed Object-Referral/Self-Referral Continuum of Self-Awareness," *Consciousness and Cognition* 13, no. 2 (2004): 401–420.

F.T. Travis and A. Arenander, "Cross-Sectional and Longitudinal Study of Effects of Transcendental Meditation Practice on Interhemispheric Frontal Asymmetry and Frontal Coherence," *International Journal of Neuroscience* 116 (2006): 1519–1538.

MODERN MEDICINE AS THE FOURTH LEADING CAUSE OF DEATH

49. M. Angell, "The American Health Care System Revisited: A New Series," *The New England Journal of Medicine* 340, no. 1 (January 7, 1999): 70–76.

B. Starfield, "Is US Health Really the Best in the World?" *JAMA [Journal of the American Medical Association]* 284, no. 4 (2000): 483–485.

G. Null, C. Dean, M. Feldman, D. Rasio, and C. Dean, *Death by Medicine* (Edinburg, Virginia: Axios Press, 2011).

DECREASED INCIDENCE OF DISEASE

50. D.W. Orme-Johnson, "Medical Care Utilization and the Transcendental Meditation Program," *Psychosomatic Medicine* 49 (1987): 493–507.

D.W. Orme-Johnson and R.E. Herron, "An Innovative Approach to Reducing Medical Care Utilization and Expenditures," *The American Journal of Managed Care* 3, no. 1 (1997): 135–144.

R.E. Herron and S.L. Hillis, "The Impact of the Transcendental Meditation Program on Government Payments to Physicians in Quebec: An Update," *American Journal of Health Promotion* 14, no. 5 (2000): 284–291.

R.E. Herron and K.L. Cavanaugh, "Can the Transcendental Meditation Program Reduce the Medical Expenditures of Older People? A Longitudinal Cost-Reduction Study in Canada," *Journal of Social Behavior and Personality* 17, no. 1 (Spring 2005): 415–442.

R.E. Herron, "Changes in Physician Costs Among High-Cost Transcendental Meditation Practitioners Compared With High-Cost Nonpractitioners Over 5 Years," *American Journal of Health Promotion*, no. 26 (2011): 56–60.

REDUCED HEALTH CARE COSTS

51. D.W. Orme-Johnson, "Medical Care Utilization and the Transcendental Meditation Program," *Psychosomatic Medicine* 49 (1987): 493–507.

D.W. Orme-Johnson and R.E. Herron, "An Innovative Approach to Reducing Medical Care Utilization and Expenditures," *American Journal of Managed Care* 3, no. 1 (1997): 135–144.

REDUCED HEALTH CARE COSTS IN CANADA

52. R.E. Herron et al., "The Impact of the Transcendental Meditation Program on Government Payments to Physicians in Quebec," *American Journal of Health Promotion* 14, no. 5 (1996): 208–216.

R.E. Herron and S.L. Hillis, "The Impact of the Transcendental Meditation Program on Government Payments to Physicians in Quebec: An Update," *American Journal of Health Promotion* 14, no. 5 (2000): 284–291.

R.E. Herron and K.L. Cavanaugh, "Can the Transcendental Meditation Program Reduce the Medical Expenditures of Older People? A Longitudinal Cost-Reduction Study in Canada," *Journal of Social Behavior and Personality* 17, no. 1 (2005): 415–442.

BENEFITS FOR EDUCATION

53. S.J. Grosswald et al., "Use of the Transcendental Meditation Technique to Reduce Symptoms of Attention Deficit Hyperactivity Disorder (ADHD) by Reducing Stress and Anxiety: An Exploratory Study," *Current Issues in Education* 10, no. 2 (2008).

F. Travis, S. Grosswald, and W. Stixrud, "ADHD, Brain Functioning, and Transcendental Meditation Practice," *Mind & Brain, The Journal of Psychiatry* 2, no. 1 (2011): 73–81.

54. David Lynch Foundation, davidlynchfoundation.org

BENEFITS FOR MANAGEMENT

55. D.R. Frew, "Transcendental Meditation and Productivity," *Academy of Management Journal* 17 (1974): 362–368.

K.E. Friend, "Effects of the Transcendental Meditation Program on Work Attitudes and Behavior," *Collected Papers* 1, 630–638.

C.N. Alexander et al., "Effects of the Transcendental Meditation Program on Stress Reduction, Health, and Employee Development: A Prospective Study in Two Occupational Settings," *Anxiety, Stress and Coping: An International Journal* 6 (1993): 245–262.

B. Gustavsson, H.S. Harung, "Organizational Learning Based on Transforming Collective Consciousness," *The Learning Organization: An International Journal* 1, no. 1 (1994): 33–40.

H.S. Harung, D.P. Heaton, and C.N. Alexander, "A Unified Theory of Leadership: Experiences of Higher States of Consciousness in World-Class Leaders," *Leadership & Organization Development Journal* 16 (1995): 44–59.

J. Schmidt-Wilk, C.N. Alexander, and G.C. Swanson, "Developing Consciousness in Organizations: The Transcendental Meditation Program in Business," *Journal of Business and Psychology* 10, no. 4 (1996): 429–444.

D.H. Sheppard, F. Staggers, and L. John, "The Effects of a Stress Management Program in a High Security Government Agency," *Anxiety, Stress and Coping* 10, no. 4 (1997): 341–350.

H.S. Harung, "Improved Time Management through Human Development: Achieving Most with Least Expenditure of Time," *Journal of Managerial Psychology* 13, nos. 5/6 (1998): 406–428.

D. Heaton, H.S. Harung, "Vedic Management: Enlightening Human Resources for Holistic Success," *Chinmaya Management Review* 3 (1999): 75–84.

J. Schmidt-Wilk, "Consciousness-Based Management Development: Case Studies of International Top Management Teams," *Journal of Transnational Management Development* 5, no. 3 (2000): 61–85.

D. Heaton and H.S. Harung, "Awakening Creative Intelligence and Peak Performance: Reviving an Asian Tradition," chapter in *Human Intelligence Deployment in Asian Business*, eds. J Kidd et al. (London: Macmillan; and New York: St. Martin's Press, 2001).

J. Schmidt-Wilk, "TQM and the Transcendental Meditation Program in a Swedish Top Management Team," *The TQM Magazine* 15, no. 4 (2003): 219–229.

D. Heaton, J. Schmidt-Wilk, and F.T. Travis, "Constructs, Methods, and Measures for Researching Spirituality in Organizations," *Journal of Organizational Change Management* 17, no. 1 (2004): 62–82.

J.R. Broome, D. Orme-Johnson, and J. Schmidt-Wilk, "Worksite Stress Reduction through the Transcendental Meditation Program," *Journal of Social Behavior and Personality* 17, no. 1 (2005): 235–276.

H. Harung, F. Travis, W. Blank, and D. Heaton, "Higher Development, Brain Integration, and Excellence in Leadership," *Management Decision* 47, no. 6 (2009): 872–894.

For books on this topic, see G. Swanson and R. Oates, *Enlightened Management* (Fairfield, Iowa: MIU Press, 1989), J. Marcus, *Success From Within* (Fairfield, Iowa: MIU Press, 1991), and H. Harung, *Invincible Leadership* (Fairfield, Iowa: Maharishi University of Management Press, 1999).

BENEFITS FOR SUBSTANCE ABUSE

56. R.K. Wallace et al., "Decreased Drug Abuse with Transcendental Meditation: A Study of 1,862 Subjects," in *Drug Abuse: Proceedings of the International Conference*, ed. CJD Zarafonetis (Philadelphia: Lea and Febiger, 1972), 369–376.

J.B. Marcus, "Transcendental Meditation: A New Method of Reducing Drug Abuse," *Drug Forum* 3, no. 2 (1974): 113–136.

G. Ljunggren, "The Influence of Transcendental Meditation on Neuroticism, Use of Drugs and Insomnia," *Lakartidningen* 74, no. 4 (1977): 4212–4214.

R. Monahan, "Secondary Prevention of Drug Dependency through the Transcendental Meditation Program in Metropolitan Philadelphia," *International Journal of the Addictions* 12, no. 6 (1977): 729–754.

A. Aron and E.N. Aron, "The Pattern of Reduction of Drug and Alcohol Use Among Transcendental Meditation Participants," *Bulletin of the Society of Psychologists in Addictive Behaviors* 2, no. 1 (1983): 28–33.

G. Clements, L. Krenner, and W. Mölk, "The Use of the Transcendental Meditation Program in the Prevention of Drug Abuse and in the Treatment of Drug-Addicted Persons," *Bulletin on Narcotics* 40, no. 1 (1988): 51–56.

P. Gelderloos et al., "Effectiveness of the Transcendental Meditation Program in Preventing and Treating Substance Misuse: A Review," *International Journal of the Addictions* 26 (1991): 293–325. This article reviews 24 different studies on the Transcendental Meditation program and substance abuse.

D.W. Orme-Johnson, "Transcendental Meditation as an Epidemiological Approach to Drug and Alcohol Abuse: Theory, Research, and Financial Impact Evaluation," *Alcoholism Treatment Quarterly* 11, nos. 1–2 (1994): 119–168.

H.M. Sharma, M.C. Dillbeck, and S.L. Dillbeck, "Implementation of the Transcendental Meditation Program and Maharishi Ayur-Veda to Prevent Alcohol and Drug Abuse among Juveniles at Risk," *Alcoholism Treatment Quarterly* 11, nos. 3–4 (1994): 429–457.

S. Taub, S.S. Steiner, E. Weingarten, and K.G. Walton, "Effectiveness of Broad Spectrum Approaches to Relapse Prevention in Severe Alcoholism: A Long-Term, Randomized, Controlled Trial of Transcendental Meditation, EMG Biofeedback, and Electronic Neurotherapy," *Alcoholism Treatment Quarterly* 11 (1994): 1–2.

C.N. Alexander, P. Robinson, and M. Rainforth, "Treating and Preventing Alcohol, Nicotine and Drug Abuse Through Transcendental Meditation: A Review and Statistical Meta-Analysis," *Alcohol Treatment Quarterly* 11 (1994): 13–87.

F. Staggers Jr., C.N. Alexander, and K.G. Walton, "Importance of Reducing Stress and Strengthening the Host in Drug Detoxification: The Potential Offered by Transcendental Meditation," *Alcoholism Treatment Quarterly* 11, nos. 3–4 (1994): 297–331.

K.G. Walton and D. Levitsky, "A Neuroendocrine Mechanism for the Reduction of Drug Use and Addictions by Transcendental Meditation," *Alcoholism Treatment Quarterly* 11, nos. 1–2 (1994): 89–117.

For a book on this topic, with papers by many researchers, see *Self Recovery: Treating Addictions Using Transcendental Meditation and Maharishi Ayur-Veda*, eds. D.F. O'Connell and C.N. Alexander (New York: Haworth Press, 1994).

BENEFITS FOR PRISON REHABILITATION

57. A.I. Abrams and L.M. Siegel, "The Transcendental Meditation Program and Rehabilitation at Folsom State Prison: A Cross-Validation Study," *Criminal Justice and Behavior* 5 (1978): 3–20.

D.W. Orme-Johnson, "Prison Rehabilitation and Crime Prevention through the Transcendental Meditation and TM-Sidhi Program," in *Holistic Approaches to Offender Rehabilitation*, ed. L.J. Hippchen (Springfield, Illinois: Charles C. Thomas, 1981), 346–383 (Chapter 15).

C.N. Alexander, "Ego Development, Personality and Behavioral Change in Inmates Practicing the Transcendental Meditation Technique or Participating in Other Programs: A Cross-Sectional and Longitudinal Study" (PhD dissertation, Harvard University, 1982), *Dissertation Abstracts International* 43:2 (1982), 539–B.

C.R. Bleick and A.I. Abrams, "The Transcendental Meditation Program and Criminal Recidivism in California," *Journal of Criminal Justice* 15 (1987): 211–230.

M.C. Dillbeck and A.I. Abrams, "The Application of the Transcendental Meditation Program to Corrections," *International Journal of Comparative and Applied Criminal Justice* 11, no. 1 (1987): 111–132.

F. Anklesaria and S.T. Lary, "A New Approach To Offender Rehabilitation: Maharishi's Integrated System of Rehabilitation," *Journal of Correctional Education* 43, no. 1 (1992): 6–13.

C.N. Alexander, K.G. Walton, and R.S. Goodman, "Walpole Study of the Transcendental Meditation Program in Maximum Security Prisoners I: Cross-Sectional Differences in Development and Psychopathology," *Journal of Offender Rehabilitation* 36 (2003): 97–126.

C.N. Alexander and D.W. Orme-Johnson, "Walpole Study of the Transcendental Meditation Program in Maximum Security Prisoners II: Longitudinal Study of Development and Psychopathology," *Journal of Offender Rehabilitation* 36 (2003): 127–160.

C.N. Alexander et al., "Walpole Study of the Transcendental Meditation Program in Maximum Security Prisoners III: Reduced Recidivism," *Journal of Offender Rehabilitation* 36 (2003): 161–180.

M.A. Hawkins, "Effectiveness of the Transcendental Meditation Program in Criminal Rehabilitation and Substance Abuse Recovery: A Review of the Research," *Journal of Offender Rehabilitation* 36 (2003): 47–66.

M.A. Hawkins et al., "Consciousness-Based Approach to Rehabilitation on Inmates in the Netherlands Antilles: I. Psychosocial and Cognitive Changes," *Journal of Offender Rehabilitation* 36 (2003): 205–228.

F.K. Anklesaria and M.S. King, "The Transcendental Meditation Program in the Senegalese Penitentiary System," *Journal of Offender Rehabilitation* 36 (2003): 303–318.

M.A. Hawkins, D.W. Orme-Johnson, and C.F. Durchholz, "Fulfilling the Rehabilitative Ideal through the Transcendental Meditation and TM-Sidhi Programs: Primary, Secondary, and Tertiary Prevention," *Journal of Social Behavior and Personality* 17, no. 1 (2005): 443–488.

For a collection of articles on the effectiveness of the Transcendental Meditation program in treating and preventing criminal behavior, see C.N. Alexander et al., *The Transcendental Meditation Program in Criminal Rehabilitation and Crime Prevention* (New York: Haworth Press, 2003). Also published in *Journal of Offender Rehabilitation* 36, nos. 1–4 (2003).

BENEFITS FOR POST-TRAUMATIC STRESS DISORDER

58. J.Z. Rosenthal et al., "Effects of Transcendental Meditation in Veterans of Operation Enduring Freedom and Operation Iraqi Freedom With Posttraumatic Stress Disorder: A Pilot Study," *Military Medicine* 176, no. 6 (2011): 626–630.

J.S. Brooks and T.Scarano, "Transcendental Meditation in the Treatment of Post-Vietnam Adjustment," *Journal of Counseling and Development* 64, no. 3 (1986): 212–215.

B. Rees et al., "Reduction in Posttraumatic Stress Symptoms in Congolese Refugees Practicing Transcendental Meditation," *Journal of Traumatic Stress* 26, no. 2 (2013) 295–298.

MEDITATION TECHNIQUES COMPARED / META-ANALYSES

59. There is now a considerable body of research comparing different systems of meditation and other meditation, relaxation, and self-development techniques. For a complete list of these studies and a summary of results of each one, see tm.org/research-meta-analyses.

P.C. Ferguson, "An Integrative Meta-Analysis of Psychological Studies Investigating the Treatment Outcomes of Meditation Techniques" (PhD dissertation, University of Colorado, 1980), *Dissertation Abstracts International* 42, no. 4A (1980): 1547.

M.C. Dillbeck and D.W. Orme-Johnson, "Physiological Differences Between Transcendental Meditation and Rest," *American Psychologist* 42, no. 9 (1987): 879–881.

K. Eppley, A. Abrams, and J. Shear, "The Effects of Meditation and Relaxation Techniques on Trait Anxiety, a Meta-Analysis," *Journal of Clinical Psychology* 45, no. 6 (1989): 957–974.

C.N. Alexander, M.V. Rainforth, and P. Gelderloos, "Transcendental Meditation, Self-Actualization, and Psychological Health: A Conceptual Overview and Statistical Meta-Analysis," *Journal of Social Behavior and Personality* 6 (1991): 189–247.

C.N. Alexander, P. Robinson, and M.V. Rainforth, "Treating and Preventing Alcohol, Nicotine, and Drug Abuse Through Transcendental Meditation: A Review and Statistical Meta-Analysis," *Alcoholism Treatment Quarterly* 11 (1994): 13–87.

D.W. Orme-Johnson and K.G. Walton, "All Approaches to Preventing or Reversing Effects of Stress Are Not the Same," *American Journal of Health Promotion* 12, no. 5 (1998): 297–299. Review article.

M.V. Rainforth et al., "Stress Reduction Programs in Patients with Elevated Blood Pressure: A Systematic Review and Meta-analysis," *Current Hypertension Reports* 9, no. 6 (2007): 520–528.

J.W. Anderson, C. Liu, and R.J. Kryscio, "Blood Pressure Response to Transcendental Meditation: A Meta-Analysis, *American Journal of Hypertension* 21 (2008): 310–316.

60. R.D. Brook et al., "Beyond Medications and Diet: Alternative Approaches to Lowering Blood Pressure. A Scientific Statement from the American Heart Association," *Hypertension* 61 (2013): 1360-1383.

REDUCED CRIME RATE WHEN 1% OF A POPULATION PRACTICES THE TM TECHNIQUE

61. C.L. Borland and G.S. Landrith III, "Improved Quality of City Life through the Transcendental Meditation Program: Decreased Crime Rate," *Collected Papers* 1: 639–648.

    M.C. Dillbeck, G. Landrith III, and D.W. Orme-Johnson, "The Transcendental Meditation Program and Crime Rate Change in a Sample of Forty-Eight Cities," *Journal of Crime and Justice* 4 (1981): 25–45.

    M.C. Dillbeck, C.B. Banus, C. Polanzi, and G.S. Landrith III, "Test of a Field Model of Consciousness and Social Change: The Transcendental Meditation and TM-Sidhi Program and Decreased Urban Crime," *The Journal of Mind and Behavior* 9, no. 4 (1988): 457–486.

    G.D. Hatchard, A.J. Deans, K.L. Cavanaugh, and D.W. Orme-Johnson, "The Maharishi Effect: A Model for Social Improvement. Time Series Analysis of a Phase Transition to Reduced Crime in Merseyside Metropolitan Area," *Psychology, Crime, and Law* 2, no. 4 (1996): 165–174.

    D.W. Orme-Johnson, "Preventing Crime through the Maharishi Effect," *Journal of Offender Rehabilitation* 36 (2003): 257–281.

REDUCED WARFARE IN THE LEBANESE CIVIL WAR

62. D.W. Orme-Johnson et al., "International Peace Project in the Middle East: The Effects of the Maharishi Technology of the Unified Field," *Journal of Conflict Resolution* 32, no. 4 (1988): 776–812.

    D.W. Orme-Johnson, C.N. Alexander, and J.L. Davies, "The Effects of the Maharishi Technology of the Unified Field: Reply to a Methodological Critique," *Journal of Conflict Resolution* 34 (1990): 756–768.

REDUCED WARFARE IN THE LEBANESE CIVIL WAR – REPLICATIONS

63. J.L. Davies, "Alleviating Political Violence Through Enhancing Coherence in Collective Consciousness: Impact Assessment Analysis of the Lebanon War" (PhD dissertation, Maharishi University of Management, 1988), *Dissertation Abstracts International* 49, no. 8 (1988): 2381A.

    J. Davies and C.N. Alexander, "Alleviating Political Violence through Reducing Collective Tension: Impact Assessment Analyses of the Lebanon War," *Journal of Social Behavior and Personality* 17, no. 1 (Spring 2005): 285–338.

REDUCED INTERNATIONAL TERRORISM

64. D.W. Orme-Johnson et al., "Effects of Large Assemblies of Participants in the Transcendental Meditation and TM-Sidhi Program on Reducing International Conflict and Terrorism," *Journal of Offender Rehabilitation* 36, nos. 1–4 (2003): 283–302.

REDUCED VIOLENT CRIME IN WASHINGTON, DC

65. R.S. Goodman, "The Maharishi Effect and Government: Effects of a National Demonstration Project and a Permanent Group of Transcendental Meditation and TM-Sidhi Program Practitioners on Success, Public Approval, and Coherence in the Clinton, Reagan, and Bush Presidencies" (PhD dissertation, Maharishi University of Management, 1997), UMI # 9735103, UMI Dissertation Abstracts 58–06A (1997): 2385.

    J.S. Hagelin et al., "Effects of Group Practice of the Transcendental Meditation Program on Preventing Violent Crime in Washington, DC: Results of the National Demonstration Project, June–July, 1993," *Social Indicators Research* 47, no. 2 (1999): 153–201.

    R.S. Goodman, "Transforming Political Institutions through Individual and Collective Consciousness: The Maharishi Effect in Government," *Proceedings of the 1997 Annual Meeting of the American Political Science Association*, Washington, DC, August 28–31, 1997.

REFERENCES

CHAPTER 10
Is Pure Consciousness the Unified Field?

1. The excerpts in this paragraph are taken from passages quoted earlier in the book.
2. D.J. Chalmers, "Facing Up to the Problem of Consciousness," *Journal of Consciousness Studies* 2, no. 3 (1995): 200–219.
3. Edward Harrison, *Masks of the Universe* (New York: Macmillan, 1985), 234.
4. Albert Einstein, *Ideas and Opinions* (New York: Crown, 1954), 299.
5. In P.C.W. Davies, *The Mind of God* (New York: Simon & Schuster, 1992), 151.
6. Eugene Wigner, "The Unreasonable Effectiveness of Mathematics in the Natural Sciences," in *Communications in Pure and Applied Mathematics* 13, no. 1 (February 1960) (New York: John Wiley & Sons, 1960). Available at dartmouth.edu/~matc/MathDrama/reading/Wigner.html. Retrieved August 28, 2012.
7. Morris Kline, *Mathematics and the Search for Knowledge* (New York: Oxford University Press, 1985), 216.
8. Denis Brian, *The Voice Of Genius: Conversations with Nobel Scientists and Other Luminaries* (New York: Basic Books, 2000), 127.
9. Hamilton Priday, *Seizing the Essence* (Bloomington, Indiana: XLibris, 2007), 37.
10. George Greenstein, *The Symbiotic Universe: Life and Mind in the Cosmos* (New York: William Morrow, 1988), 223.
11. Brandon Carter, *The Anthropic Principle: The Conditions for the Existence of Mankind in the Universe* (New York: Cambridge University Press, 1993).
12. Freeman Dyson, *Disturbing the Universe* (New York: Basic Books, 1979), 251.
13. Greenstein, *Symbiotic Universe*, 238.
14. D.B. Klein, *The Conception of Consciousness: A Survey* (Lincoln, Nebraska: University of Nebraska Press, 1984), front matter.
15. Eugene P. Wigner, "The Place of Consciousness in Modern Physics," in *Consciousness and Reality*, eds. C. Musès and A.M. Young (New York: Outerbridge & Lazard, 1972), 133–134.
16. James Jeans, *The Mysterious Universe* (Cambridge: Cambridge University Press, 1930), 158.
17. A.P. Sanoff, "Mankind's Place in the Cosmos: A Conversation with Freeman Dyson," *U.S. News and World Report*, April 18, 1988, 72.
18. Sir Arthur Eddington, *The Nature of the Physical World* (New York: Macmillan, 1929), 276.
19. David Bohm, *Wholeness and the Implicate Order* (London: Routledge & Kegan Paul, 1980), 62.
20. David Bohm and Basil J. Hiley, *The Undivided Universe: An Ontological Interpretation of Quantum Theory* (Abingdon, Oxon: Routledge, 1993), 323.
21. David Bohm and Francis Peat, *Science, Order, and Creativity* (London: Routledge, 2000), 2010–2012.
22. Renée Weber, *Dialogues with Scientists and Sages* (New York: Arkana, 1990), 101.
23. "The Super-Implicate Order," in *The Essential David Bohm*, ed. Lee Nichol (London: Routledge, 2002), 139–157.
24. Amit Goswami, *The Self-Aware Universe* (New York: Tarcher/Putnam, 1993), 10.
25. Goswami, 11.
26. The arguments and quotations from John Hagelin in this section are drawn from Dr. Hagelin's videotaped course, *Foundations of Physics and Consciousness: Discovery of the Unified Field and Its Practical Applications for Perfection in Life*. See elearning.mum.edu/physics-online-course.php. Also see John S. Hagelin, "Is Consciousness the Unified Field? A Field Theorist's Perspective," *Modern Science and Vedic Science* 1, no. 1 (1987): 29–87. mum.edu/pdf_msvs/v01/hagelin.pdf. Retrieved June 8, 2012.

27. A.S. Eddington, *The Nature of the Physical World* (New York: Macmillan, 1929), 282.
28. See, for example, Maharishi Mahesh Yogi, *Life Supported by Natural Law* (Fairfield, Iowa: Maharishi International University Press, 1988), 34.
29. Robert Browning, "Paracelcus," *The Complete Poetic and Dramatic Works of Robert Browning* (Cambridge: Houghton, Mifflin, The Riverside Press, 1895), 18.

CHAPTER 11
The Future of the World Is Bright

1. Lao Tzu, *Tao Te Ching: The Definitive Edition*, trans. Jonathan Star (New York: Jeremy P. Tarcher/Putnam, 2001), 52.
2. Ralph Waldo Emerson, *Nature; Addresses and Lectures* (Boston and New York: Phillips, Samson & Co. and Ralph Waldo Emerson, 1849), 77.
3. Vernon Katz, *Conversations with Maharishi: Maharishi Mahesh Yogi Speaks About the Full Development of Consciousness* (Fairfield, Iowa: Maharishi University of Management Press, 2011), 1:55.
4. Maharishi Mahesh Yogi, *Thirty Years Around the World: Dawn of the Age of Enlightenment* (The Netherlands: MVU Press, 1986), 284–285.
5. In "Maharishi Establishes the Brahmanand Saraswati Trust," January 11, 2008. press-conference.globalgoodnews.com/archive/january/08.01.11.html. Retrieved February 6, 2013.

NOTES

1. See, for example, *Mysticism and Philosophical Analysis*, ed. Steven T. Katz (New York: Oxford University Press, 1978), and *Mysticism and Religious Traditions*, ed. Steven T. Katz (New York: Oxford University Press, 1983).
2. See, for example, *The Problem of Pure Consciousness: Mysticism and Philosophy*, ed. Robert K.C. Forman (New York: Oxford University Press, 1997), and *The Innate Capacity: Mysticism, Psychology, and Philosophy*, ed. Robert K.C. Forman (New York: Oxford University Press, 1998). For a summary article, see Jonathan Shear, "On Mystical Experiences as Empirical Support for the Perennial Philosophy," *Journal of the American Academy of Religion* 62, no. 2 (1994).
3. Ilaria Ramelli, "Luke 17:21: 'The Kingdom of God Is Inside You' — The Ancient Syriac Versions in Support of the Correct Translation," *Hugoye: Journal of Syriac Studies* 12, no. 2 (2009): 259–286. The quoted passage is on page 374. syrcom.cua.edu/Hugoye/Vol12No2/HV12N2Ramelli.pdf
4. Maharishi Mahesh Yogi, *Transcendental Meditation with Questions and Answers* (Meru, Holland: Maharishi Vedic University, 2011), 94.
5. *Transcendental Meditation with Questions and Answers*, 55.

Acknowledgments

Copyright acknowledgments

We have made every effort to secure permission to reproduce material protected by copyright. We would be pleased to make good any omissions brought to our attention in future printings of this book.

- *Farid ud-Din Attar* – From "The Triumph of the Soul," in Margaret Smith, trans., *The Persian Mystics* (1932). By permission of John Murrays Company, United Kingdom.
- *Farid ud-Din Attar* – From *Readings from the Mystics of Islam*, by Margaret Smith (1950, 1972). By permission of Pir Press Inc.
- *Mary Austin* – From *Experiences Facing Death*. Reprinted with permission of Macmillan Publishing Company. Copyright 1931 by Bobbs-Merrill.
- *Bernard Berenson* – Reprinted from *Aesthetics and History in the Visual Arts* by permission of Pantheon Books, a division of Random House, Inc. Copyright 1948 by Pantheon Books, Inc.
- *Black Elk* – From *The Sacred Pipe: Black Elk's Account of the Seven Rites of the Oglala Sioux*, ed. J.E. Brownbook (New York: MJF Books, 1989). Reprinted by permission of University of Oklahoma Press.
- *Johannes Brahms* – From *Talks With Great Composers*, by Arthur M. Abell. © 1955 by Philosophical Library, New York.
- *Emily Brontë* – "Julian M. and A.G. Rochelle," from *The Complete Poems of Emily Jane Brontë*, ed. C.W. Hatfield. Copyright © 1941 Columbia University Press. Reprinted with permission of the publisher.
- *Martin Buber* – From *Ecstatic Confessions*, ed. Paul Mendes-Flohr, trans. Esther Cameron (1925). By permission of the Estate of Martin Buber, The Balkin Agency, Amherst, Massachusetts.
- *Martin Buber* – From *Between Man and Man*, trans. Ronald Gregor Smith (2002). By permission of Routledge (Cengage Learning EMEA, Ltd.), UK.
- *Buddha* – From *The Dhammapada, Two Suns Rising*, trans. © Jonathan Star (New York: Bantam, 1991). Reprinted by permission of Jonathan Star.
- *Buddha* – From *The Buddha Speaks*, by Anne Bancroft, © 2000. Reprinted by arrangement with Shambhala Publications, Inc., Boston, MA. www.shambhala.com.

- *Carol Burnett* – From *One More Time*, by Carol Burnett (New York: Random House, 1986). Reprinted by permission of Random House

- *Rita Carter* – From *Exploring Consciousness*, © 2003 by Rita Carter. Reprinted by permission of University of California Press.

- *Dante Alighieri* – *The Divine Comedy*, trans. H.R. Huse (New York: Rinehart, 1956). Reprinted by permission of the Howard Russell Huse Trust.

- *Emily Dickinson* – Reprinted by permission of the publishers and the Trustees of Amherst College from *The Poems of Emily Dickinson*, Thomas H. Johnson, ed., Cambridge, Massachusetts: The Belknap Press of Harvard University Press. Copyright © 1951, 1955, 1979, 1983 by the President and Fellows of Harvard College.

- *Ralph Waldo Emerson* – Reprinted by permission of the publisher from *The Journals and Miscellaneous Notebooks of Ralph Waldo Emerson: Volume V - 1835-1838*, edited by Merton M. Sealts, Jr., pp. 336–337, Cambridge, Massachusetts: The Belknap Press of Harvard University Press, Copyright © 1965 by the President and Fellows of Harvard College.

- *Margiad Evans* – From *Autobiography* (1943). By permission of Oneworld Classics, London.

- *Edwin Fischer* – From *Interpreting Bach at the Keyboard* ("Epilogue"), by Paul Badura-Skoda, trans. Alfred Clayton (1993). By permission of Oxford University Press.

- *Gospel of Truth* – From *The Gnostic Gospels of Jesus*, by Marvin W. Meyer. © 2005 by Marvin W. Meyer. Reprinted by permission of HarperCollins Publishers.

- *Gustave Flaubert* – From "The Temptation of Saint Anthony," in *The Literature of Expanded Consciousness*, by E.F.N. Jephcott, published by Chatto & Windus. Reprinted by permission of the Random House Group, Ltd.

- *Jane Goodall* – From *Reason For Hope*, by Jane Goodall with Phillip Berman, Copyright © 1999 by Soko Publications, Ltd., and Phillip Berman. By permission of Grand Central Publishing.

- *Hadewijch* – In *Women Mystics in Medieval Europe* (St. Paul, Minnesota: Paragon House, 1989), poem translated from the French by Sheila Hughes for Paragon House and reprinted by permission.

- *Ahmad Hatif* – From *Readings from the Mystics of Islam*, by Margaret Smith (1950, 1972). By permission of Pir Press, Inc.

ACKNOWLEDGMENTS

- *Vaclav Havel* – Speech made in Independence Hall, Philadelphia, July 4, 1994. (constitutioncenter.org/libertymedal/recipient_1994_speech.html). Used with permission of the National Constitution Center.

- *Vaclav Havel* – From *Letters to Olga*, by Vaclav Havel, trans. Paul Wilson, translation copyright © 1984 by Rowahlt Taschenbuch Verlag. Translation copyright © 1988 by Paul Wilson. Copyright © 1983 by Vaclav Havel. Used by permission of Alfred A. Knopf, a division of Random House.

- *Jacquetta Hawkes* – The excerpt by Jacquetta Hawkes from *Man on Earth*, © 1955 Jacquetta Hawkes, is reproduced by permission of PFD (pfd.co.uk) on behalf of the Estate of Jacquetta Hawkes.

- *Hermetic Writings* – From *Hermetics: The Ancient Greek and Latin Writings Which Contain Religious or Philosophic Teachings* (Vol. 1 OCLC 162969520), ed. Walter Scott (1924). By permission of Oxford University Press.

- *Eugene Ionesco* – From *Present Past Past Present*, © Mercure de France (1968). Reproduced by permission of Mercure de France, Paris.

- *Jesus* – From *The Gnostic Gospels of Jesus*, by Marvin W. Meyer. © 2005 by Marvin W. Meyer. Reprinted by permission of HarperCollins Publishers.

- *Jesus* – From the Holy Bible. Scripture quotations from The Authorized (King James) Version. Rights in the Authorized Version in the United Kingdom are vested in the Crown. Reproduced by permission of the Crown's patentee, Cambridge University Press. From Holy Bible, New Living Translation, copyright © 1996, 2004, 2007 by Tyndale House Foundation. Used by permission of Tyndale House Publishers, Inc., Carol Stream, Illinois 60188. All rights reserved.

- *St. John of the Cross* – From *The Collected Works of St. John of the Cross*, trans. Kieran Kavanaugh and Otilio Rodriguez, Copyright © 1979 Washington Province of Discalced Carmelite Friars, Inc. ICS Publications, 2131 Lincoln Road, NE, Washington, D.C. 20002 USA.

- *Helen Keller* – From *My Religion*, The Swedenborg Foundation, 1927, reprint 1980. By permission of the Swedenborg Foundation.

- *Billie Jean King* – From *Billie Jean*, by Billie Jean King, © 1982. Reprinted by permission of HarperCollins Publishers.

- *Arthur Koestler* – From *The Invisible Writing*, copyright © 1954 by Arthur Koestler. Reproduced by permission of PFD (pfd.co.uk) on behalf of the Estate of Arthur Koestler.

- *Gopi Krishna* – Gopi Krishna, *Living With Kundalini: The Autobiography of Gopi Krishna*. Reprinted by permission of The Kundalini Research Foundation, Ltd.
- *Gopi Krishna* – "An Interview with Gopi Krishna," New York, October, 1983. Reprinted by permission of The Kundalini Research Foundation, Ltd., and Tom Zatar Kay.
- *Laozi* – From *Tao Te Ching: The Definitive Edition*, New York: Jeremy P. Tarcher/Putnam, 2001, © Jonathan Star. Reprinted by permission of Jonathan Star.
- *Laozi* – From the *Hua Hu Ching: The Unknown Teachings of Lao Tzu*, by Brian Walker. © 1992 by Brian Browne Walker. Reprinted by permission of HarperCollins Publishers.
- *Laozi* – From *Wen-Tzu: Understanding the Mysteries*, trans. Thomas Cleary, © 1992. Reprinted by arrangement with Shambhala Publications, Inc., Boston, MA. www.shambhala.com.
- *D.H. Lawrence* – *The Rainbow*, first edition: London, Methuen & Co. 1915. Reproduced by permission of Random House.
- *Charles Lindbergh* – From *Autobiography of Values*, by Charles Lindbergh, copyright © 1978 by Harcourt, Inc., and Anne Morrow Lindbergh. Reproduced by permission of Houghton Mifflin Harcourt, Publishing Company. All rights reserved.
- *Clare Boothe Luce* – From *The Road to Damascus: The Spiritual Pilgrimage of Fifteen Converts to Catholicism*, by John A. O'Brien. © 1949 by John A. O'Brien. Used by permission of Doubleday, a division of Random House, Inc.
- *Antonio Machado* – Poems reprinted by permission of Willis Barnstone, translator.
- *Franklin Merrell-Wolff* – From *Pathways through to Space*, Julian Press, New York, 1973. From *Philosophy of Consciousness Without an Object*, Julian Press, New York, 1973. By permission of Doroethy Leonard.
- *Thomas Merton* – From *New Seeds of Contemplation*. © 1961 by The Abbey of Gethsemane, Inc. Reprinted by permission of New Directions Publishing Corp.
- *Milarepa* – From *Drinking the Mountain Stream*, trans. Lama Kunga and Brian Cutillo, © 1978. Reprinted by arrangement with Wisdom Publications, Inc., Boston, Massachusetts. wisdompubs.org.
- *Henry Miller* – From *Wisdom of the Heart*, © 1960, reprinted by permission of New Directions Publishing Corp. From *Tropic of Capricorn*, © 1961 by Grove Press, Inc., used by permission of Grove/Atlantic, Inc. Any third party use of this material, outside of this publication, is prohibited.

ACKNOWLEDGMENTS

- *Lucy Maud Montgomery* – The excerpts from *Emily of New Moon* and *The Alpine Path: The Story of My Career*, by L.M. Montgomery are reproduced with the permission of Heirs of L.M. Montgomery, Inc. L.M. Montgomery is a trademark of Heirs of L.M. Montgomery, Inc.

- *Muktabai* – From *The Shambhala Anthology of Women's Spiritual Poetry*, ed. Aliki Barnstone, 1999. Reproduced with the permission of the editor, Aliki Barnstone, and the translator, Willis Barnstone.

- *Akbarabadi Nazir* – From *Indian Mystic Verse*, trans. H.P. Shastri, Shanti Sadan, London, 1984. By permission of Shanti Sadan.

- *Patsy Neal* – From *Sport and Identity* © 1972. By permission of Patsy Neal, Morristown, Tennessee. All rights reserved by the author.

- *Peace Pilgrim* – From *Peace Pilgrim: Her Life and Work in Her Own Words, Compiled by Some of Her Friends*, © 1982 by Friends of Peace Pilgrim. Reprinted by permission of Ocean Tree Books, P.O. Box 1295, Santa Fe, New Mexico 87504, peacepilgrim.org.

- *Pelé* – *My Life and the Beautiful Game: The Autobiography of Pelé*, with Robert L. Fish, © 1977.

- *Plato* – From Edith Hamilton, *The Collected Dialogues, including the Letters*, © 1961 Princeton University Press, 1989 renewed. Reprinted by permission of Princeton University Press.

- *Kathleen Raine* – Excerpts from *The Collected Poems of Kathleen Raine, The Land Unknown*, and *Farewell Happy Fields: Memories of Childhood*. Reproduced by permission of the Literary Estate of Kathleen Raine, © 2010.

- *Ray Reinhardt* – From "The World a Stage: A Conversation with Ray Reinhardt," by Gwyneth Richards, in *San Francisco Theatre Magazine*, Winter 1977. By permission of Ray Reinhardt and Gwyneth Richards.

- *Bernadette Roberts* – From *The Experience of No-Self*, by Bernadette Roberts, Albany, New York: State University of New York Press, 1993). Reprinted with permission of State University of New York Press.

- *Romain Rolland* – From a letter from Romain Rolland to Mme Cruppi, September 19, 1912, in William Thomas Starr, *Romain Rolland: One Against All* (1971). By permission of the publisher, Walter de Gruyter. Passage translated for this book by Daniela Hathaway.

- *Rūmī* – Maharishi University of Management Press, which has reproduced the works in this book, acknowledges the material derived from *The Mathnawī of*

Jalāl Al-Dīn Rūmī as edited, translated into English, and commented upon by R.A. Nicholson. This work is published by the Trustees of the E.J.W. Gibb Memorial Trust, who have granted their consent.

- *Rūmī* – *Rūmī, In the Arms of the Beloved*, trans. © Jonathan Star (New York: Jeremy P. Tarcher/Penguin, 1997). Reprinted by permission of Jonathan Star.

- *Anwar Sadat* – From *In Search of Identity: An Autobiography*, by Anwar el Sadat. © 1977, 1978 by the village of Mit Abu el Kom. English language translation © 1978 by Harper & Row Publishers, Inc. Reprinted by permission of HarperCollins Publishers.

- *Shabistari* – From *Readings from the Mystics of Islam*, Margaret Smith (1950, 1972). By permission of Pir Press, Inc.

- *Sun Bu-er* – From *Immortal Sisters: Secret Teachings of Taoist Women*, translated and edited by Thomas Cleary, published by North Atlantic books, © 1996 by Thomas Cleary. Reprinted by permission of the publisher.

- *Rabindranath Tagore* – "The Fountain Awakes," trans. Hiren Mukherjee, *Poems of Rabindranath Tagore*, ed. Humayun Kabir, © 2005 Visva-Bharati. Reprinted by permission of Visva-Bharati, Santiniketan, West Bengal, India, and UBSPD.

- *St. Teresa of Ávila* – From *The Complete Works of St. Teresa of Jesus*, trans. E. Allison Peers, published by Sheed & Ward Ltd., London.

- *Morihei Ueshiba* – From *The Art of Peace: Teachings of the Founder of Aikido*, by Morihei Ueshiba, translated by John Stevens, © 2002 by John Stevens. And from *Abundant Peace: The Biography of Morihei Ueshiba, Founder of Aikido*, by John Stevens, © 1987. Both reprinted by arrangement with Shambhala Publications, Inc., Boston, MA. www.shambhala.com.

- *Evelyn Underhill* – From *The Letters of Evelyn Underhill*, ed. Charles Williams (1991). By permission of Darton, Longman and Todd, London.

- *Upanishads* – From *The Upanishads*, trans. © Alistair Shearer and Peter Russell (New York: Harper Colophon Books, 1978). Reprinted by permission of Alistair Shearer and Peter Russell.

- *Paul Valéry* – From *Poems in the Rough*, trans. Hilary Corke, *The Collected Works of Paul Valéry*, Vol. 2, © 1969, 1997 renewed by Princeton University Press. Reprinted by permission of Princeton University Press.

- *H.G. Wells* – From *The Bulpington of Blup*, reprinted by permission of A.P. Watt, Ltd., on behalf of The Literary Executors of the Estate of H.G. Wells.

- *David Yeadon* – From *The Back of Beyond*, © 1991 by David Yeadon. Reprinted by permission of the author.

ACKNOWLEDGMENTS

- *Hakuin Zenji* – From *The Embossed Tea Kettle: Orate Gama and Other Works of Hakuin Zenji*, trans. R.D.M. Shaw (1963). Published by George Allen & Unwin, London.

- *Zhuangzi* (Chuang Tzu) – From *The Complete Works of Chuang Tzu*, trans. Burton Watson, © 1968 Columbia University Press. Reprinted with permission of the publisher.

Photo and illustration acknowledgments

Many images are taken from Wikipedia, where source information is available.

- *Attar of Nishapur* – Photograph by Richard Jeffrey Newman, translator of classical Persian poetry, courtesy of Professor Newman.

- *St. Augustine* – Icon of Saint Augustine, written by Father Richard Cannuli, O.S.A., Villanova University. Used with permission.

- *Sir Roger Bannister* – Photograph copyright and courtesy of Charles Warner.

- *Bernard Berenson* – Biblioteca Berenson, Villa I Tatti – The Harvard University Center for Italian Renaissance Studies, courtesy of the President and Fellows of Harvard College.

- *The Buddha* – Photograph by Michel Wal | Head of the Buddha from Hadda, Central Asia | Gandhara art, Victoria and Albert Museum, London.

- *Rita Carter* – Photograph courtesy of Rita Carter.

- *Margiad Evans* – From the second series of Literary Postcards produced by Academi and The Rhys Davies Trust | Photograph by Peter North, National Library of Wales.

- *Edwin Fischer* – Drawing by Fritz Tennigkeit | Photo by Peter Michael Haas.

- *Jane Goodall* – Photograph by Jeekc | Hong Kong University, October 24, 2007.

- *Hadewijch* – Photograph from poetseers.org.

- *Václav Havel* – Photograph by Ondřej Sláma | Václav Havel during his speech at the Freedom and Its Adversaries Conference, Prague, November 14, 2009.

- *Jacquetta Hawkes* – Photograph by Walter Bird, courtesy of Dr. Nicolas Hawkes.

- *Hermetic Writings* – Illustration created for this book by Lynne Marshall.

- *Jesus Christ* – Detail from Deesis mosaic, Hagia Sophia, Istanbul | Photograph by Edal Anton Lefterov.

- *Billie Jean King* – Photograph courtesy of Russ Adams | Thanks to Michael Tette.

- *Arthur Koestler* – Photograph by Hans Chaim Pinn, German-born Israeli photographer (1916–1978).
- *Gopi Krishna* – Photograph courtesy of the Kundalini Research Foundation, Ltd., Gene Kieffer, President.
- *D.H. Lawrence* – Rendered by Elinor Wolfe.
- *Clare Boothe Luce* – Photograph by Carl Van Vechten.
- *Franklin Merrell-Wolff* – Photograph courtesy of Doroethy Leonard, Merrell-Wolff's granddaughter.
- *Thomas Merton* – Photograph by Sibylle Akers | Used with permission of the Merton Legacy Trust and the Thomas Merton Center at Bellarmine University.
- *Henry Miller* – Photograph courtesy of The Bancroft Library, University of California, Berkeley.
- *Margaret Prescott Montague* – West Virginia and Regional History Center, West Virginia University Libraries
- *Lucy Maud Montgomery* – Photograph courtesy of the L.M. Montgomery Trust and the University of Guelph Library | Library and Archives Canada.
- *Vladimiar Nabokov* – Vladimir Nabokov Archive, Berg Collection, New York Public Library | Courtesy of Professor Brian Boyd, Department of English, The University of Aukland, New Zealand.
- *Patsy Neal* – Photograph courtesy of Patsy Neal.
- *Peace Pilgrim* – Peace Pilgrim in Hawaii, 1980 | Photograph by James B. Burton | Courtesy of Friends of Peace Pilgrim.
- *St. Teresa of Ávila* – Photo of portrait by Peter Paul Rubens, 1615 | Kunsthistorisches Museum, Vienna, Austria.
- *Kathleen Raine* – Photograph by Pamela Chandler | Copyright holder, Diana Willson.
- *Ray Reinhardt* – Photograph courtesy of Gwynneth Richards and Ray Reinhardt.
- *Shankara* – Courtesy of Frances Knight, from her painting of the Holy Tradition of Vedic Masters.
- *Howard Thurman* – Used with permission of Friends United Meeting.
- *Eckhart Tolle* – Photograph by Kyle Hoobin.
- *Thomas Traherne* – Photo of St. Mary's Church, Credenhill, by Julian P. Guffogg.
- *Paul Valéry* – Used by permission of Gerhard Richter | © Gerhard Richter 2011 | from "48 portraits 1971-72," oil on canvas | Museum Ludwig, Köln, Germany.

ACKNOWLEDGMENTS

Personal acknowledgments

This book has been possible only with the help of a large number of people, to whom I express my deep gratitude. First and foremost I thank my wife, Melissa, who assisted in every facet of this project over many years. This book would not have been written and published but for her extraordinary support.

I also thank Susan Runkle and Alison Wasielewski for their immense help and support.

Kenneth Chandler, Geoffrey Wells, and Robert Oates offered valuable suggestions during the formative stages. Rogers Badgett provided early support and suggestions. Denise Gerace, Chris Jones, Sanford Nidich, Randi Nidich, and Evelyn Toft reviewed part of an early draft of this as members of my dissertation committee. Sam Boothby, Gerry Geer, and Jane Aikens provided an important review of the final manuscript.

Thank you to David Orme-Johnson for his careful review of Chapter 9, the scientific research on the Transcendental Meditation and TM-Sidhi programs as well as the references to that chapter, and to Rhoda Orme-Johnson, for her proofreading and suggestions.

I thank Dr. Steven Rubin for the book's title and his encouragement and support over many years. Thank you to Shepley Hansen for the cover design. Thanks to my brother Erich Pearson for his help with many of the photographs and to my son Soren Pearson for technical support across the lifespan of multiple computers. Thanks to Lynne Marshall, Elinor Wolfe, and Becky Pearson for their help with graphical elements. Thank you to Jeffrey and Rona Abramson for their inspiration and support. Thanks to John Raatz for his thoughts on this second edition and help with promotion.

Many other people gave support in various ways, including James Balakier, Bonnie Barnett, Ron Barnett, Harry Bright, Sue Brown, Fran Clark, Michael Collier, Neil Dickie, Larry Domash, Tom Egenes, Peter Freund, Daniela Hathaway, William Hathaway, Nicolas Hawkes, Jim Karpen, Dara Llewellyn, Burton Milward, Bob Notestine, Donal O Laoghaire, Mario Orsatti, Sally Rosenfeld, Bob Roth, Bill Sands, David Scharf, Craig Shaw, Fred Travis, Rick Weller, Sue Weller, Ken West, Mary Zeilbeck, and more. Thank you to the interlibrary loan staff in the Maharishi University of Management Library, who helped procure the many books I required.

Many people, as they became aware of my research, contributed accounts of higher states of consciousness they had noted in their reading, which went into the pool from which this selection was drawn. My thanks to all of you.

I thank Dr. Bevan Morris, President of Maharishi University of Management, for his steadfast leadership, support, and encouragement. Thanks also to Dr. John Hagelin.

Finally, my deepest gratitude goes to Maharishi. Every significant idea in this book is his. The technologies of consciousness that he has brought to light are enabling ever-increasing numbers of people to enjoy these magnificent experiences, to rise in enlightenment and create a brighter world for all. One hopes only to do his knowledge justice.

Please share your own discoveries

The glimpses of higher states of consciousness included in this book represent only some of what I have collected and only a small fraction of the treasure hidden in the world's literature.

If you know of any passages such as the ones in this book — glimpses of higher states of consciousness, whether described in prose or poetry, fiction or nonfiction — please send them to me.

If possible, please scan or photocopy the book's title page and relevant pages and email them to me. Or please send as complete a reference as possible (book title, author, and page numbers), or a link if it's online.

e-mail: higherstates@mum.edu

Or mail to:

Box 757

Maharishi University of Management

Fairfield, Iowa 52557

For more information

Further reading

■ Maharishi Mahesh Yogi, *Science of Being and Art of Living* — Maharishi explores the understanding of pure Being, pure consciousness, as the basis of life and how higher states of consciousness develop through regular experience of this field with the Transcendental Meditation technique. He discusses the applications of this knowledge for every area of life.

■ *Maharishi Mahesh Yogi on the Bhagavad-Gita: A New Translation and Commentary, Chapters 1–6* — Maharishi calls the Bhagavad-Gita the essence of Vedic literature and a complete guide to practical life. In his commentary, he describes higher states of consciousness in detail.

■ Vernon Katz, *Conversations with Maharishi: Maharishi Mahesh Yogi Speaks About the Full Development of Human Consciousness* — English writer Vernon Katz worked closely with Maharishi in the early years and records his conversations about higher states of consciousness. A second volume is in production.

■ *Invincible America Assembly: Experiences of Higher States of Consciousness of Course Participants*, 2006–2009 — Advanced experiences recorded by people involved in extended group practice of the Transcendental Meditation and TM-Sidhi programs, including Yogic Flying, in Fairfield, Iowa, at Maharishi University of Management.

■ Harald S. Harung and Fred Travis, *Excellence through Mind-Brain Development: The Secrets of World-Class Performers* — Presents the research on world-class performance and integrated brain functioning (pages 451–452) and the implications for leadership.

These books are available through Maharishi University of Management Press, mumpress.com.

Other websites

■ *tm.org* — Information about the Transcendental Meditation program.

■ *mum.edu* — The website of Maharishi University of Management.

Index

Boldface indicates major entry

Aborigines (Australia), 35
Absolute, 35, 37, 48, 282, 283, 284, 287, 350, 503, 507, 514. *Also see* pure consciousness, Being, unified field.
Ahmad Hatif of Isfahan, **300**
American Heart Association, 465
Amiel, Henri Frédéric, **134, 393**
Anaximander, 35
Angela of Foligno, 25, **98, 210**, 491
Anthropic principle, 476
Aristotle, 35, 66
Attar of Nishapur, **89, 379**
Augustine, St., 30, **80**
Austin, Mary, **406**

Baker, Ray Stannard, **311**
Bannister, Sir Roger, **257**
Being, 35 (Aristotle)
   defined, 48
   Maharishi on, 45, 48, 82, 283, 284, 286, 287, 351
   personal experience of, 194, 195, 287, 358, 359
   referred to in historical accounts, 63 (The Buddha), 78–79 (Plotinus), 100–102 (Meister Eckhart), 105 (Kabir), 116 (Traherne), 123 (Goethe), 127 (Tennyson), 138 (Carpenter), 125, 210, 218, 390 (Emerson), 135 (Amiel), 143 (Kook), 149 (Einstein), 170, 255, 337 (Ionesco), 173–174 (Merton), 175 (Sadat), 197 (Upanishads), 230 (Rolland), 252 (Hammerskjöld), 262 (Havel), 270–272 (Tolle), 304 (Wordsworth), 340 (Hawkes), 372 (Plotinus), 384 (Meister Eckhart), 386 (Traherne), 398 (Carpenter), 403 (Rolland), 404 (Wells), 411 (Merrell-Wolff), 418 (Raine), 425 (Starr)
Berenson, Bernard, **310, 400**
Bernard of Clairvaux, St., 35, 54
Bhagavad-Gita, 27, 81, 196, 197, 362, 367, 384
Black Elk (Hehaka Sapa), **140, 399**
Blake, William, 26, 276, 334
Bodhi, 42
Bohm, David, 480–481
Brahmananda Saraswati (Guru Dev), 29, 438–439
Brahman Consciousness, 355–356
Brahms, Johannes, **226**, 473
brain
   coherent functioning through Transcendental Meditation, 30–33, 50, 190, 442–444, 448–449, 460–461, 464, 466, 488, 493
   coherent functioning through the TM-Sidhi program, 438
   other changes through Transcendental Meditation, 444–445, 446, 450, 456, 457, 493
   coherent functioning correlated with other positive values, 460–461

functioning different with different meditation techniques, 37, 433–434, 465
states of consciousness, functioning in different, 40–41
neuroplasticity, 433
ability to experience the unified field, 487–488
consciousness and, 474, 482
sleep, typical functioning during, 40
sleep, unique functioning during, among TM meditators, 450
dreaming and, 40
athletic performance and, 451–452
Brontë, Emily, **130**
Browning, Robert, 489
Buber, Martin, **146, 408**
Buddha, 34, 42, 43, **63**, 118, **201**, 213, **364**, 415, 519
Buddhism, 26, 34, 35, 42, 43, 64, 65, 86, 201, 365, 434, 516
Burnett, Carol, **429**

Carpenter, Edward, 23, 24, 55, **138, 228, 396**
Carter, Brandon, 476
Carter, Rita, 23, **347**
Catholicism, 96, 106, 109, 172, 427, 516, 517
Chalmers, David John, 473
Cloud of Unknowing, 320, 516
Confucius, Confucianism, 34, 36
consciousness
    fourth major state of, 30, 446
    pure consciousness, 29–30, 42, 44–45. *Also see* Transcendental Consciousness.

pure consciousness identical with unified field, 48–49, 472–489
knowledge, unique for each state, 39
physiological functioning, unique for each state of, 39
Transcendental Consciousness, 29–30, 32–33, 41, 44–177
Cosmic Consciousness, 32, 41, 42–43, 178–272
God Consciousness, 41, 43, 273–346
Unity Consciousness, 41, 43, 347–431
Brahman Consciousness, 355–356
Vedic rishis' experience of, 25–26
seven states of, 38–43
waking, dreaming, and sleeping, 40
Cosmic Consciousness, 32, 41, 42–43, 178–272
    compared with typical waking consciousness, 190
    scientific research on, 448–461
creativity
    enhanced through Transcendental Meditation, 31, 442, 452, 460
    referred to in historical accounts, 226–227 (Brahms), 271 (Tolle), 331 (Lehmann)
    pure consciousness as an infinite reservoir of, 48
    supported by sleep, 40

Dante Alighieri, **102**
Daoism, 34, 35, 42, 60, 61, 62, 69, 88, 198, 199, 363, 364, 472, 492. *Also see* Laozi, Sun-Buer, Zhuangzi, Tao Te Ching.
Delphi, Temple of Apollo at, 34
Devekut, 42

Dickinson, Emily, **136, 225**
Dov Ber of Mezeritch, **120**
dreaming, 39, 40, 56, 181, 183, 186, 190, 203
   witnessing dreams, 280, 353, 358, 500, 508, 515
   experiences of witnessing, TM participants, 193, 194
   experiences of witnessing, suggested in historical accounts, 82–83 (Shankara), 233–234 (Machado)
Dreamtime, 35, 521
Dyson, Freeman, 476, 480

Eckhart, Meister, 99, 164, 194, 202, **211**, 252, **383**
Eddington, Sir Arthur Stanley, 480, 486, 487
Edwards, Jonathan, **299**
EEG. *See* brain.
Ein sof, 35
Einstein, Albert, **149**, 229, 273, 474, 475, 477, 478, 480, 482
Eliade, Mircea, 516
Emerson, Ralph Waldo, 23, 24, 26, 27, 35, **124**, 128, 131, **218**, 242, **390**, 472, 492
Evans, Margiad, **422**

Fischer, Edwin, **237**
Flaubert, Gustave, **393**
freedom
   Cosmic Consciousness as a state of, 185, 190–191
   in Buddhism, 64
   Maharishi on, 185
   referred to in historical accounts, 58–59 (Vedic literature), 61 (Laozi), 64 (Buddha), 78–79 (Plotinus) 84–85 (Shankara), 87 (Milarepa), 93 (Rūmī), 106 (Kabir), 112 (St. John of the Cross), 116 (Traherne), 130 (Brontë), 132 (Whitman), 142–143 (Kook), 147 (Buber), 149–151 (Einstein), 152 (Keller), 154 (Ueshiba), 159–161 (Merrell-Wolff), 165 (Hammarskjöld), 173–174 (Merton), 176 (Sadat), 196–197 (Vedic literature), 200–202 (Buddha), 222 (Whitman), 211–213 (Meister Eckhart), 252–253 (Hammarskjöld), 255 (Ueshiba), 270–271 (Tolle), 296 (Traherne), 364 (Buddha)

Gandhi, Mahatma, 162, 223, 229, 261
Gautama Buddha. *See* Buddha.
God. *Also see* God Consciousness.
   experience of, in Maharishi's understanding, 273–290
   experience of, referred to in historical accounts, 68 (Plato), 72 (Jesus), 77 (Hermetic Writings), 80 (Plotinus), 94–95 (Rūmī), 98 (Angela of Foligno), 100–102 (Meister Eckhart), 107–108 (St. Teresa of Avila), 109–110 and 113 (St. John of the Cross), 115 (Traherne), 118 (Zenji), 120–121 (Dov Ber of Mezeritch), 125 (Emerson), 134 (Amiel), 157 (Lawrence), 163 (Thurman), 166 (Hammarskjöld),

174 (Merton), 177 (Sadat), 253 (Hammarskjöld), 265 (Neal), 272 (Tolle), 275 (Tagore), 290 (Vedic literature), 292 (Hermetic Writings), 293–294 (Sophia von Klingnau), 295 (Kabir), 296–298 (Traherne), 299–300 (Edwards), 301 (Ahmad Hatif of Isfahan), 305 (Wordsworth), 307 (Thoreau), 308–309 (Whitman), 314 (Baker), 323 (Montague), 344 (Starr), 367 (Jesus), 379 (Attar of Nishapur), 380 (Rūmī), 384–385 (Meister Eckhart), 388–389 (Traherne), 390–391 (Emerson), 392–393 (Amiel), 391 (Carpenter), 414 (Carpenter), 425–426 (Starr), 428 (Roberts)
   kingdom of (kingdom of heaven), 34, 35, 71–73, 148, 206–207, 223, 276, 285, 291, 341, 367–369, 386, 415, 496, 517–518
   will of, equivalent to natural law, 206, 215, 286
God Consciousness, 39, 41, 42, 43, 191, 224, 270, 272, 273–346, 349, 350, 351, 352, 353, 354, 365, 367, 391, 394, 405, 421, 426, 441, 498, 504
Goethe, Johann Wolfgang, **122**, 227
Goodall, Jane, **345**
Gopi Krishna, **332, 414**
Gospel of Thomas, 72–74, 206, 207, 276, 291, 368–369, 370, 518
Gospel of Truth, **370**
Goswami, Amit, 482
Greenstein, George, 476

Guru Dev (Brahmananda Saraswati), 29, 438–439

Hadewijch, **96**
Hagelin, John, 483–489
Hakuin Zenji, **117, 216**
Hammarskjöld, Dag, **164, 251**
Harrison, Edward, 474
Hasidism, 120, 146
Havel, Vaclav, 22, **260**
Hawkes, Jacquetta, **338**, 491
Hayashi–Razan, 36
health
   economic, 466
   enhanced through Transcendental Meditation, 5–8, 31, 32, 441, 454, 457, 461–465, 493
   health care costs reduced through TM practice, 461–462
   psychological health enhanced through Transcendental Meditation, 457–459
   referred to in historical accounts, 129 (Thoreau), 222 (Whitman), 243 (Miller)
   sleeping and dreaming and, 40
Hegel, Georg Wilhelm Friedrich, 26, 35
Heisenberg, Werner, 175
Hermetic writings, 36, **76, 292, 373**
Human development, unfreezing of, 31, 452, 459
Hume, David, 46
Hunhu/Ubuntu, 35
Huxley, Aldous, 244, 516

---

intelligence
   body's inner, 280, 454, 457

brain functioning and, 442, 460
characteristic common to both pure consciousness and the unified field, 49, 479, 483, 486, 487
enhanced through Transcendental Meditation, 31, 181, 188, 190, 450, 452, 462, 466, 493
lack of in the world, 471, 492
mathematics and, 475
Maharishi on, 282, 284
nature's, 49, 73, 285, 480, 488
pure consciousness as infinite reservoir of, 48, 50, 150, 182, 188, 189, 199, 213, 227, 353, 354, 493
referred to in historical accounts, 115–116 (Traherne), 126 (Emerson), 197 (Vedic literature), 210 (Plotinus), 271 (Tolle), 366 (Buddha), 407 (Austin)
Tao as field of, 69
Wakan-Tanka as field of, 141
Ionesco, Eugene, 22, 23, 24, 55, **170, 254, 337**, 432
IQ, 31, 452, 460. *Also see* intelligence.
Islam, 43, 71, 89, 92, 105

James, William, 19, 27, 516
Jeans, James, 475, 479
Jesus Christ, 34, **71, 205,** 276, **291, 367,** 370, 384, 472, 517–519
John of the Cross, St., 106, **109**
Jung, Carl, 35

Kabir, **105, 295,** 320
Kant, Immanuel, 245, 408, 516
Katz, Steven, 516
Keller, Helen, **151**

Kensho, 42, 43
King, Billie Jean, **178**
Kingdom of God, kingdom of heaven, 34, 35, 71–73, 148, 206–207, 223, 276, 285, 291, 341, 367–369, 386, 415, 496, 517–518
Klingnau, Sophia von, **293**
Know thyself, 34, 36, 352
Koestler, Arthur, 22, **167,** 433
Kook, Rabbi Abraham Isaac, **142**

laws of nature. *See* natural law.
Laozi, 22, 34, 55, **60,** 69, **198, 363,** 472, 492, 519
Lawrence, D.H., **156**
Lehmann, Rosamond, **330**
Lindbergh, Charles, **248**
Luce, Clare Booth, **250**

Machado, Antonio, **233**
Maharishi Mahesh Yogi, 28–33, 37, 38–39, 43, 494–496
Maharishi Effect, 466–471, 485–486, 493–494
Marcus Aurelius, 34, **75**
Maréchal, Joseph, 516
Maslow, Abraham, 458
Maugham, Somerset, 28
Maxwell, James Clerk, 477
meditation techniques, compared, 433–435, 465–466
Meister Eckhart, **99,** 164, 194, 202, **211,** 252, **383**
Merrell-Wolff, Franklin, 24, 55, **158, 238, 410,** 432, 440, 473
Merton, Thomas, 22, 23, **172,** 440
Milarepa, **86**

INDEX

Miller, Henry, **242**, 440
Milton, John, 227
mindfulness meditation, 433–434, 456, 466
moksha, 42
Montague, Margaret Prescott, **322**
Montgomery, Lucy Maud, **315**, 432–434
moral development
    brain functioning and, 442, 460
    enhanced through Transcendental Meditation, 31, 452–453, 458, 459, 462, 464
    in peak performers, 451–452
    referred to in historical accounts, 123 (Goethe), 132 (Whitman), 134–135 (Amiel)
    self-actualization and, 457
Muktabai, **90**
mysticism, mystical experience, 26, 33, 43, 121, 159, 168, 252, 260, 346, 401, 402, 425
    debate over common core of, 516–517
    Einstein and, 150
    Gopi Krishna on, 415–416
    Jewish, 121, 146
    Maharishi on, 286
    Sufi, 415
    Kathleen Raine on, 419
    Evelyn Underhill on, 320–321

Nabokov, Vladimir, **412**
Nag Hammadi library, 72–74, 370. *Also see* Gospel of Thomas.
National Institutes of Health, 32, 455
natural law. *Also see* unified field.
    pure consciousness and the unified field, 48–49, 50, 188, 472–489
    equivalent to will of God, 206, 215, 286
    equivalent to reverberations within pure consciousness, 484–485
    life out of accord with, 492–493
    life supported by, 188–189
    life in accord with, suggested in historical accounts, 198–199 (Laozi), 201 (Buddha), 203 (Zhuangzi), 205–206 (Jesus), 211–213 (Meister Eckhart), 215 (St. Teresa of Ávila), 246 (Howard Thurman)
    mastery of, 353–354, 487–488
Nazir, **302**
Neal, Patsy, **263**, 491
Neihardt, John, 40, **326**
Neoplatonism, 34
Nirvana, 42, 63, 64, 122, 415

Otto, Rudolf, 516

Patanjali, Yoga Sutras, 56, 196
peace, inner
    Black Elk on, 399
    in Buddhism, 64
    experiences during TM practice, 51, 53, 194, 509, 289, 359
    referred to in historical accounts, 56 and 59 (Vedic literature), 60 and 62 (Laozi), 64–65 (Buddha), 77 (Hermetic Writings), 85 (Shankara), 98–99 (Angela of Foligno), 107 (St. Teresa of Avila), 109 and 112 (St. John of the Cross), 118 (Zenji), 122–123 (Goethe), 125 (Emerson), 129 (Thoreau), 130 (Brontë), 131–133

(Whitman), 143–144 (Kook), 155 (Ueshiba), 159 (Merrell-Wolff), 166–167 (Hammarskjöld), 168–169 (Koestler), 171 (Ionesco), 173 (Merton), 176 (Sadat), 180 (King), 196–197 (Vedic literature), 200–202 (Buddha), 215 (St. Teresa of Avila), (216 (Zenji), 228 (Carpenter), 230 (Rolland), 231 (Valéry), 235–236 (Ueshiba), 252 (Hammarskjöld), 263 (Neal), 267 (Pelé), 269–271 (Tolle), 296–298 (Traherne), 299 (Edwards), 309 (Whitman), 377 (Shankara), 392 (Amiel), 394 (Flaubert), 399 (Black Elk), 421 (Peace Pilgrim)
   Laozi on, 492
   Maharishi on, 187, 518
peace, world
   as Maharishi's goal, 494–496
   Black Elk on, 399
   created through group practice of the Transcendental Meditation and TM-Sidhi programs, 466–471
   Laozi on, 492
Peace Pilgrim, **420**
Pelé, **266**
perennial philosophy, primordial tradition, 33–37, 473, 489, 516–517
Planck, Max, 479
Plato, 23, 28, 35, 55, **66**, 76, 213, 245
Plotinus, 34, 35, 55, 76, **78, 208, 372**
post–traumatic stress disorder (PTSD), effects of Transcendental Meditation on, 459, 464–465
prana (breath), 82
   refined in Cosmic Consciousness, 279

primordial sounds, 484
pure consciousness. *See* consciousness, Transcendental Consciousness.

Raine, Kathleen, **334, 418**, 432
Ramana Maharishi, 28
Reinhardt, Ray, **259**
Rik Veda, 35, 360, 484–485
Rishis, Vedic, 25–26, 484–485
Roberts, Bernadette, **427**
Rolland, Romain, **229**, 273, **402**, 473
Rūmī, 89, **92, 380**, 490

Sadat, Anwar El, **175**
samadhi, 30, 56, 85, 86, 87
satori, 42, 43
Schiller, Friedrich, 227
Schuon, Frithjof, 516
self–actualization, 457–458, 459, 462, 465
Self–knowledge, 46
Shankara, **81**, 158, **375**
Shao Yung, 36
Shintoism, 36
Sikhism (Adi Granth), 26, 36
sleep, 40
   in Cosmic Consciousness, 181, 183, 185–187, 239, 500
   in God Consciousness, 279
   experiences of witnessing, TM participants, 193–194, 500
   scientific research on experiences of witnessing, among TM participants, 450
   experiences of witnessing, suggested in historical accounts, 197 (Vedic literature), 209 (Plotinus), 220

(Thoreau), 232 (Valéry), 233 (Machado), 240 (Merrell-Wolff)
Smith, Huston, 516
soma (product of optimal digestion), 280
Stace, W.T., 516
suchness, 365–366
Sufism, 43, 89, 135, 158, 300, 415
Sun Bu-er, **88**, 472
superstring theory, 35, 477–478, 483, 485

Tagore, Rabindranath, 35, 158, 162, 229, **273**, 276, 280, 320, 327
Talmud, 36
Tao Te Ching, 34, 60–62, 198, 363, 472, 492
Tennyson, Alfred, Lord, 22, 24, 55, **126**, 227, 491, 503
Teresa of Ávila, St., **106**, 109, **214**, 440
Thoreau, Henry David, 19, 22, 27, 28, 54, **128, 219**, 242, **307**
Thurman, Howard, **162, 246, 328, 413**, 491
Tolle, Eckhart, **268**
Tolstoy, Leo, **223**, 229
Traherne, Thomas, **114, 296**, 304, **386**, 400, 491
Transcendental Consciousness, 29–30, 32–33, 41, 44–169
  compared with waking consciousness, 50
  compared with Unity Consciousness, 355
  scientific research on, 442–448
Transcendental Meditation technique 28–33, 37, 38–39, 47, 432–439
  defined by Maharishi, 45
  experiences of Transcendental Consciousness through, 51–53
  experiences of growing Cosmic Consciousness through, 191–195
  experiences of growing God Consciousness through, 287–289
  experiences of growing Unity Consciousness through, 356–359
  scientific research on, 30, 440–471
  compared with other techniques, 433–435, 465–466
TM-Sidhi program,
  defined, 437–438
  scientific research on, 451–452, 462, 467–471, 485, 493, 497, 498, 499. *Also see* Maharishi Effect.

Ueshiba, Morihei, **153, 234, 409**
Unbounded awareness 33–34
Underhill, Evelyn, **320**, 516
unified field, 35, 41, 49, 50, 188, 190, 283, 288, 354
  Einstein's quest, 149–151, 478
  identical with pure consciousness, 48–49, 50, 188, 472–489
  identify with pure consciousness, suggested in historical experiences, 62 (Laozi), 69–70 (Zhuangzi), 74 (Jesus), 88 (Sun Bu-er), 124–126 (Emerson), 129 (Thoreau), 227 (Brahms), 229–230 (Rolland), 244–245 (Wolff), 369 (Jesus)
Unity Consciousness, 41, 43, 347–431
  growth to, compared with the process of transcending, 354
  compared with Transcendental Consciousness, 355

Upanishads, 76, 81, 362, 383, 394, 429, 509
  quotations from, 57–59, 197, 290, 360–362

Valéry, Paul, **144, 231**
Vedic literature, 25–28, 30, 35, **56**, 81, **196, 290, 360**, 375, 438, 484–485, 495. *Also see* Bhagavad-Gita, Rik Veda, Upanishads.
  correspondence with structure of unified field, 484–485
  influence on Emerson and Thoreau, 26–28, 124, 128
  origin of, 25–26
Vedic rishis, 25–26, 484–485
Vivekananda, Swami, 28

Wakan-Tanka, 141, 399
waking consciousness, 40
  compared with Transcendental Consciousness, 50
  compared with Cosmic Consciousness, 190
Watts, Alan, 516
Webb, Mary, 318
Wells, H.G., 273, **403**, 491
Wheeler, John, 475–476
White, William Hale, 368, **395**
Whitman, Walt, 23, 55, **131, 221**, 242, **308**, 491
Wigner, Eugene, 475, 479
will of God. *See* God, will of.
witnessing (feature of Cosmic Consciousness), 280–281, 353–354, 448, 451. *Also see* sleep.
  defined, 185–187

experiences of TM participants, 192, 193, 195
scientific research on, among TM participants, 450
suggested in historical accounts, 60 (Laozi), 82–83 (Shankara), 197 (Vedic literature), 204 (Zhuangzi), 216 (Hakuin), 218 (Emerson), 219–220 (Thoreau), 221–222 (Whitman), 233 (Machado), 237–238 (Fischer), 241 (Merrell-Wolff), 254–257 (Ionesco), 258–259 (Bannister), 259–260 (Reinhardt), 274-275 (Tagore), 411 (Merrell-Wolff)
Wolff, Charlotte, **244**
Wordsworth, William, **19**, 26, 28, 30, 55, 126, 227, **303**, 440
world peace. *See* peace, world.

Yeadon, David, **430**
Yoga, 42, 56, 196, 362, 434
Yoga Sutras, 56, 196, 437
Yoga Vasishta, 197
Yogananda, Paramahansa, 28
Yogic Flying. *See* TM-Sidhi program.

Zen Buddhism, 42, 43, 117, 172, 434, 516. *Also see* Buddhism.
Zenji, Hakuin, **117, 216**
Zhuangzi, 23, **69, 203**, 472, 490
Zoroaster, 34

About the author

CRAIG PEARSON is Vice-President of Academic Affairs at Maharishi University of Management in Fairfield, Iowa, and a leader in Consciousness-Based education. He has spoken around the United States on this unique approach to education as well as on Maharishi's programs to create world peace.

He has held a number of positions at Maharishi University of Management, including Dean of Faculty, Dean of the College of Arts and Sciences, Dean of Students, Director of Freshman Composition, and Director of Maharishi University of Management Press.

Dr. Pearson holds a PhD in Maharishi Vedic Science from Maharishi University of Management. He is the author of *The Complete Book of Yogic Flying*. He is also the coauthor, with Brad Moses, of *Peace on Earth*, a collection of songs about enlightenment and world peace (available on iTunes). He lives on the Maharishi University of Management campus with his wife Melissa and son Soren.

He can be reached at higherstates@mum.edu.

The Supreme Awakening

Over the past century, a number of books, each a landmark work, each still read today, have endeavored to understand the sublime, exalted experiences reported by people through history: R.M. Bucke's *Cosmic Consciousness* (1901), William James's *Varieties of Religious Experience* (1902), Evelyn Underhill's *Mysticism* (1911), Aldous Huxley's *The Perennial Philosophy* (1945), Marghanita Laski's *Ecstasy* (1961), and others.

These books have inspired millions of readers by calling attention to these experiences and showing that there is far more to human potential than we ordinarily experience.

The Supreme Awakening extends the scope of these books. Drawing on the work of Maharishi Mahesh Yogi, *The Supreme Awakening* explains the origins of these experiences and provides a systematic way of categorizing them.

Most important, it describes a practical method — the simple, effortless technique of Transcendental Meditation — that anyone can use to cultivate these remarkable experiences and enjoy the unparalleled benefits for themselves.

"An inspirational resource for years to come."

— Alan D. Hodder, PhD,
   Professor of Comparative Religion,
   Hampshire College

CPSIA information can be obtained
at www.ICGtesting.com
Printed in the USA
BVHW040008221218
535589BV00020B/5/P